THE
INSIDERS' GUIDE
TO
Bermuda

THE INSIDERS' GUIDE TO

Bermuda

by
Liz Jones
and
James Ziral

Insiders' Publishing Inc.

Co-published and marketed by:
The Royal Gazette Ltd.
2 Par-La-Ville Road
Hamilton, Bermuda
(441) 295-5881

Published by:
Insiders' Publishing Inc.
105 Budleigh St.
P.O. Box 2057
Manteo, NC 27954
(919) 473-6100
www.insiders.com

Sales and Marketing:
Falcon Publishing Co. Inc.
P.O. Box 1718
Helena, MT 59624
(800) 582-2665
www.falconguide.com

•

First EDITION
1st printing

•

Copyright ©1998
by The Royal Gazette Ltd.

•

Printed in the United States
of America

•

Publications from The Insiders' Guide®
series are available at special discounts
for bulk purchases for sales promotions,
premiums or fundraisings. Special
editions, including personalized covers,
can be created in large quantities for
special needs. For more information,
please write to Insiders' Publishing Inc.,
P.O. Box 2057, Manteo, NC 27954 or
call (919) 473-6100 x 241.

ISBN 1-57380-040-6

The Royal Gazette Ltd.

General Manager
Keith Jensen

Project Manager
delMonte Davis

Account Executives
Lori Eddy
Sharon West

Advertising Production
Hope Robbins
June Ming

Insiders' Publishing Inc.

Publisher/Editor-in-Chief
Beth P. Storie

President/General Manager
Michael McOwen

Creative Services Director
Giles MacMillan

Director of New Product
Development
David Haynes

Managing Editor
Dave McCarter

Project Editor
Dave McCarter

Project Artist
Stephanie Wills

Cover Photos:
GIS/Porter-Novelli

Preface

Bermuda easily attracts pretty words. Like fragrant scents yielded by delicate evening blossoms, they float effortlessly from the tongue, spilling into imagery. Paradise. Eden. These are two of the more common descriptions, used so frequently they almost embarrass us. This is the land that unabashedly seduced Mark Twain with its "lovely vistas of blue water that went curving in and out, disappearing through jungle walls of brilliant foliage."

Yet there is more here than a beautiful face enhanced by spring colors and winter subtleties. Our smile is genuine, and our people are some of the most friendly this side of the pearly gates. Yes, we've been called Heaven, too, despite our eccentricities, the very natures of which make it difficult to quite define ourselves. It is a sweet mystery. Maybe that's why Twain loved us so much. That and the fact he found us "tidy, the right country for a jaded man to loaf in."

Ah, but we're not just for loafing. There's business and there's play, and often the twain do meet. Some of our guests tote golf clubs across the ocean to our shores, and in chasing low scores and business deals find themselves overlooking those "lovely vistas of blue water" that stretch on languid days like clear glass toward a peaceful horizon. Others often find their ball "disappearing through jungle walls of brilliant foliage." But all remains well. A sense of quiet contentment soothes.

No matter the words or the imagery, the best way to get to know us is to visit. We won't meet you on arrival with garlands of flowers. But as you travel our winding roads and country lanes, loaf on pristine beaches, dive on ancient wrecks or climb to the top of our tallest lighthouse and thrill as your vision takes wings over our landscape, you'll always find a welcome in our smiles, in our laughter, in our open arms of friendship. Once you visit, you'll find us irresistible and will long to return. We'd like that. And so will you.

About the Authors

Liz Jones

In 1970, Liz Jones was studying literature at the University of East Anglia, England. In a bar one evening, she met Mike, who explained he was from Bermuda. She did not have the slightest idea where Bermuda was. Being more interested in the Romantic Poets than in the intricacies of geography, she decided not to pursue the topic. Three years later, Liz married Mike and met Bermuda, where she has lived happily ever since. In 1977, Liz felt the family name was in serious danger of dying out. Douglas Dewar Jones duly arrived. The other three important people in her life are all called William: William Shakespeare, William Blake and William Butler Yeats.

Having grown up in English villages and the Scottish Highlands, Liz has always had the good fortune to live in beautiful surroundings. Bermuda is, of course, stunningly beautiful, but there is more to it than that. Teaching English language and literature at Bermuda's Berkeley Institute and at the Bermuda College gave Liz the opportunity to enjoy the island's great asset — the diversity of its people. Compiling an anthology of oral history for Bermuda's Ministry of Community, Culture & Information gave her additional exposure to senior citizens whose memories of Bermuda stretched back to the early 1900s. Liz is also passionate about creative writing. In the past, she conducted creative writing workshops for the Bermuda College, but these days she would rather practice than preach. As a member of Bermuda Writers' Collective, she enjoyed contributing a story to *An Isle So Long Unknown*, an anthology of Bermudian short stories.

Currently, Liz is enjoying the freedom of freelance writing for a variety of Bermudian and British publications including *Bermuda Magazine* and the *Guardian Weekly*. She also has fun writing a lighthearted "That's Life" column for the *Mid-Ocean News*. One day, she hopes, she might create a decent novel. Where will it be set? In Bermuda. Of course.

James Ziral

James Ziral was 15 when he sold his first article to the *Bermuda Sun*, a local newspaper. Seventeen years later he would become an investigative reporter and columnist at the same paper. Although writing always sat on his shoulder and thumped him between the shoulder blades, he ignored it in pursuit of making what he thought was *real* money. But in 1977 he realized that working for a real estate agency, an insurance company and a radio and television station were not career choices that truly satisfied him. In a moment of complete clarity, James wrapped up his business in Bermuda and boarded a plane to New York where he lived and worked for six years before returning to his island home.

Despite having graduated years earlier from the local Cable & Wireless Training School, and having studied business in New York, James remained intimate with the manual typewriter, finally committing to writing for the newspaper where he had sold his first story — it had something to do with Christmas, he recalls.

As an investigative journalist and columnist, he learned much about Bermuda behind the scenes. However, a travel bug that had been with him since his teens bit down hard — in 1985 he resigned from the *Sun* and flew off to London, where he lived for four years. It was, he admits, just another step in learning more about the world through being there. Travel to the Bahamas, Martinique, Canada and a number of American cities helped broaden that experience, as did living in Michigan for a while.

Returning to Bermuda in 1989, James continued to write for publications both here and abroad, among them *Civil War Times Illustrated*, *Destination Bermuda* and *Bermuda Cruise*; he eventually became an associate editor for *The Bermudian* magazine until leaving in 1994. It was during this period that he authored the text for *Emeralds On A Silver Zone*, a coffee-table book on early color photography in Bermuda. In 1992 he was voted the island's Journalist of the Year.

After a subsequent stint as editor of the *Bermuda Times,* James became fascinated with television; he soon produced and directed the television news magazine *64 West*, his own concept that took its title from Bermuda's longitudinal position. Also during this time James accepted an invitation to become a member of the Bermuda Arts Council and wrote ad copy for local and international company brochures and annual reports.

Since 1995, after recovering from a stroke, James has been a full-time freelance writer, writing regularly for the *Mid-Ocean News*, *Bermuda*, *The Bermudian*, *Caribbean Week*, *American Visions* and other publications. In 1997 he wrote, produced and directed a half-hour television documentary on tourism for the Ministry of Community and Cultural Affairs. It was his second television project for that ministry.

Restless, curious, and hard to satisfy, when James is not at the computer keyboard, he collects rare books, Haitian paintings, ancient maps, Bermuda cedar sculpture, African sculpture and 18th- and 19th-century original lithographs of botanicals. The house he shares with wife, Helen, has been described as a museum and art gallery.

"Bermuda is one of the most complex little places on the planet," James says, "and treat with caution anyone who tells you they really understand it."

With the Compliments
of the
Minister of Tourism
Hamilton, Bermuda   Tel. 292-0023

It is clear that there are many destinations where people can go to unwind, become reacquainted or rejuvenated. Bermuda introduced resort tourism to the world, and today we offer an exceptionally varied and rich experience in a total island resort. We are delighted that so many visitors choose Bermuda time after time. Whether it's your first visit or your twenty-first, you will see that we are devoted to making Bermuda everything you want it to be.

That you are reading this first edition of *The Insiders' Guide®* to *Bermuda* is exciting to all of us. We hope it will help you find exactly the right place to stay, choose your preferred activities and select places for dining and fun.

If you are thinking of Bermuda for a quick escape for two, a much-needed holiday for the family, a small gathering of associates or friends for sports or business or a major event, we think you have made the right choice, and we hope to see you very soon!

This guide will assist you in your decision-making before you arrive and after, whether you are a return visitor or a first-timer.

Come, enjoy . . . and please visit us again!

With warmest regards,

The Hon. David Dodwell, JP, MP
Minister of Tourism

True story: It was approaching midnight, and the 1996 Fall Conference of the New England Association of Circulation Executives (newspaper executives) was unofficially being brought to a close. When asked about any interesting new developments or projects, an executive from Hyannis, Massachusetts, described an enormously successful and exciting visitors guidebook that his newspaper had recently published. The explanation sounded too fantastic to be real, especially to this circulation executive from tourism-driven Bermuda. Besides, given the hour, maybe, just maybe, my friend had had one or two of New England's version of a Bermuda Dark 'N' Stormy (a rum and ginger beer concoction).

But that late-night tale was 100 percent true. My friend, Don Waterman, circulation director at *The Cape Cod Times*, soon made all the introductions to his, and now our, co-publishers in Manteo, North Carolina. And the rest, as they say, is history. Thanks Don, you are much appreciated for all of the assistance, support, experience and wisdom you so willingly share with your colleagues in the business. In this case, you have shared something that will make a positive contribution to an enterprise very important to all of us in Bermuda — tourism, our bread and butter.

Thanks go to Mr. Keith Jensen, for giving this opportunity his critical review and blessing. Thanks also to Gary Ritchie (I think) for suggesting that I tackle this project.

Between that chance discussion with Don and the release of this guide, there has been a great deal of effort on the part of many. Along the way, often at critical times, just about everyone in The Royal Gazette building helped. Thanks go to Mr. David White, David Pethen, Bill Zuill, Carol Parker-Trott, Adrian Robson, Libby Francis, Deborah Charles, Brin Jones, Nicole Williams, Bob Amesse, John Burchall, Henry Adderley, Tim Hodgson, Becky Zuill, Hope Robbins (when she's around, there's always hope), Steve Dunkerley, Joseph Simmons, Sabrina Trott, Regina Woods, James Rego, Ramon Doars and Melinda O'Connor. Special thanks go to June Ming.

I am indebted to Pat Phillip-Bassett, Terry Greenslade, Al Seymour, Jennifer Johnson at The Bermuda Department of Tourism and their colleagues at Porter-Novelli in New York. Thanks also to Jenny Hollis, Tony Martin and Ormond Hodgson, Rick Hawke, Tom Crolius and Linda Harmon. And thanks also to the patient lady at Federal Express. It's not 3 o'clock yet, is it?

And now to Beth and Michael and their associates at Insiders' Publishing Inc.: Thanks very much for what you do so well. Let's do it all again, sometime soon — including Ocean Boulevard!

Thank you Sharon West for taking on the marketing challenges presented by this project and for laboring on, at times under difficult circumstances. And for Sharon (and myself), many thanks to our colleagues and all the businesses, organizations and individuals that supported this project through advertising, providing information and encouragement. Thanks also to Lori Eddy for her timely and efficient assistance and to Pauletta Furbert for her efforts.

Nearly last, but certainly not least, a thousand thanks go to Liz Jones and James Ziral for taking so much care in and enjoyment from your craft. You caused me to laugh out loud about this and that, and to stop and realize there were things about Bermuda I never knew. Thank you for dedication beyond — far beyond — what was required. Only you (apart from Dave McCarter) know the true dimensions of this beast, but I am most appreciative for the many, many hours you spent pursuing and detailing the thousands and thousands of items for this book. I have enjoyed every minute of work with you and have learned many facts and gained new insights about our island home. I am your greatest fan.

I have almost certainly overlooked a name or two but for all of you who were so kind and generous with your time and support, I am grateful.

Finally, thanks Marty, for your patience and for listening when I was thinking out loud about "insiders."

For the readers, we hope this book will help guide you to a memorable experience in our home, Bermuda.

delMonte Davis
Circulation Manager

The Royal Gazette

Acknowledgments

Liz Jones

As Molière said, often "Books and marriage go ill together." My greatest thanks, then, go to Mike, who definitely proved Molière wrong. I want to thank him for dealing with bouts of penicillin appearing on our walls, for cooking eggs when they were urgently required, for keeping me in socks and for generally being entirely understanding about my nine-month retreat from normal living. Thanks also go to our son, Doug, for providing me with useful bits of information on all sorts of topics, including watering holes and watery excursions.

Where writing for Insiders' Guides® is concerned, ignorance is most certainly not bliss. I must therefore thank a number of people who helped to fill gaps in my knowledge. Millard Beach has to be one of the most tactful people in Bermuda since he didn't laugh once when I got confused about what constitutes a golf hole and what does not. The same cannot be said of Claire Rushe or of Brian and Kim Webb, who did laugh. (But they also helped to improve my golf vocabulary.) Brian and Kim's help on international business and Bermuda's real estate scene was also much appreciated, as was the assistance of Wayne Jackson. George Rushe's help on a whole range of Bermuda topics was invaluable, as is his book, *Your Bermuda*. And Nathalie and Philip Rushe's help on insurance and soccer was immensely helpful too.

I must also thank Adrian Robson and Dexter Smith for help with Bermuda's sports world. Thanks also go to Derek and Sally Singleton for their tennis information and to Randy Benjamin and Richard Tucker for more help with cricket and sports. Juliet Jackson and William and Joyce Zuill added to my knowledge of Bermuda's wedding traditions while Wayne Augustus helped me identify trees. Thanks also to William H. Cook for helping me with parks information and to John Barnes for info on flora and fauna. I'd also like to thank Anne-Marie Gosling for accompanying me on a park exploration and showing me that there are 13 Ways of Looking at a Grain of Sand as well as at a Blackbird.

Thanks to Jeremy Hindle I was able to understand the principles of weather prediction so important to the insurance business. Ronald Lightbourne, Bermuda's Renaissance man, helped me enormously with music, nightlife, history and cricket. Ianthe Wade gave up time to show and supply me with information about Summerhaven, and Peter Frith explained with great patience and clarity the hotels' different rate systems. Thanks also go to Charles Barclay and Emma Mitchell for their massive funds of information and useful contacts, to Terri Greenslade for answering a myriad of questions and to Pam Shailer, Nelda Simons and Lyn Brady. A special thank you must go to my young friend and neighbor, Sarah Fletcher, who made all sorts of useful suggestions about sports and recreations.

I am very grateful to Pauletta Furbert, who contributed four chapters — Worship, Media, Getting Here, Around and Home and Kidstuff — and who has been extremely supportive throughout. On her behalf, I'd like to thank Mike Osborne, Dan Simmons, Bill Nearon and George Morton for their help with transportation and Mary Winchell, Anne Kermode, Louise Jackson, Paula Durham, Al Seymour, Cathy Gosling and Janice Hollis for all their valuable time. A thank you, too, goes to Nicole Williams for information about worship.

Many thanks go to delMonte Davis, who kept me calm and well supplied with ideas, and to Dave McCarter, whose meticulous editing has helped enormously. Last, but by no means least, I want to thank my co-author, James Ziral. It's not that we met very often; for obvious reasons, we were far too busy. However, our regular telephone communication kept my brain alive and my spirits cheered.

James Ziral

This has been both an intense and an interesting ride. During the journey several people provided information and assistance. But thanks must first go to Helen, my wife, who provided the encouragement, love and support needed when the sheer volume of work and tight deadlines threatened to send me to the funny farm with a glazed and strange expression.

And thanks must go to those persons who went the extra mile with no self-interest involved. Many of them actually wish to remain in the background without their names mentioned in print. So to everyone who showed me new ways of appreciating this tiny little corner of the world, I say thanks with all my heart.

I also want to extend my appreciation and gratitude to Kelly Phillips at the Special Services Division of the Bermuda Monetary Authority and Vernee Fullerton at the Bermuda Maritime Museum. Special thanks go to those cedar sculptors who taught me much about their medium, among them Chesley Trott, the dean of cedar carvers, and Roy Boyer, both of whom have helped in this project without realizing it. Thanks also to Dennis Eldridge, the computer guy who came to the rescue of Liz and me when seemingly perverse technology tried its best to be uncooperative. Thanks also to Nancy Acton, Tom Butterfield and Louise Jackson.

I cannot ignore delMonte Davis, who as always was a complete gentleman throughout the project, and most definitely I must say thanks to Dave, my patient and understanding editor who provided timely encouragement and suggestions.

She doesn't read English, but I must thank Girlie, my calico cat, who seemed to know when her affection was needed and found a home on my lap as I labored at the keyboard.

And last but not least there is Liz, my co-author, who knows what it is like to be in the trenches. Thanks Liz, your support was invaluable.

U.S.$ CHECKS ACCEPTED

IN BERMUDA AT THESE LOCATIONS:

2001 Cuts
2002 JR's
2003 TAT 2
27th Century Boutique
A One Stores
A & J Games
A F Smith Trading
All Wrapped Up
Alomas Bed & Bath
Arnold's Family Market
Arnold's Supermarket
Arretta's Place
Aston & Gunn
Auto Express
Back on the Rack
Bda College Bookstore
Bda Glass Blowing
Bda Railway Museum
Bda. Golf Academy
Bda.Country Cabinets
Bda.Taxi Services Ltd.
The Beach
Bermuda College
Bermuda Perfumery
Bermuda Rentals
Black Horse Tavern
Boaz Island Shell
Bouchee
British American Ins. Co.
Burrows Lightbourne Ltd.
C Mart Ltd.
CW Ltd.
Canada Villa Guest House
Captains Lounge
Car World
Carole Holding FS Ltd
Carousel Liquors
Cellular Centre
Chancery Wine Bar
Changes Beauty Salon
China Black's Boutique
Churchills
Cob Web
Cock and Feather
Colosseum'Ltd.
Cotton Ginny
Cotton Ginny Plus
Cracker Box
Davison's of Bermuda

Demco Ltd.
Dismont Robinson
Docksider
Dockyard Marina
Dollar Savers
Donald Smith Travel
Dowlings
Dr. Burton Butterfield
Dub City
Elbow Beach Hotel
Empire Grocery
English Sports Shop
Enterprise Grocery
Enzo Organic Nail Spa
Essence
Everich Jewellry
Eves Cycle
Flanagans
Flatts Gift Shop
Fleetwood Co.
Flybridge Tackle
Footstop Shoe Store
Four Star Pizza
Frangipani
Freddies Pub
Friths Liquor
G & M Beauty Salon
Galleria Ltd.
Gloria's Fash/Fabrics
Gosling Brothers Ltd.
Grants Ladies Boutique
Hair Studio
Halfway House Rest.
Harmony Club
Hartleys Underwater Ad.
Hayward's Grocery
Hayward's Liquors
Henry the 8th
Henry's Pantry
Hodge Podge
Home Paint Supply Co.
Horshoe Bay Beach House
House of Flowers
Ice Queen, Hamilton
Ice Queen, Paget
Island Health & Beauty
Island Pet Supply
J & R Associates
Jeans Plus

Jiffy Photo
Junius Burrows Ltd.
Just Kickin It
K.E.M.H.
Karl's Guys and Dolls
Kit N Caboodle
Kitchen Korner
Knick Knack
La Corte II
Lines Food and Liquor
The Little Theatre
Lobster Pot Restaurant
The London Shop
M & M International
M.R. Onions
The MarketPlace Stores
Marks & Spencer
Marriott's Castle Harbour
Matthew's Sales Agency
TheMatchbox
Maxi Mart
Maynes Furniture Co.
Meyer Industries Ltd.
Meyer Freight and
Shipping
Meyer Travel
Mick's Mens Ware
Mikado's
Noah's Ark
North Rock Brewing
Palmetto Hotel
Peniston Brown
Personality Footworks
Personalized Jewellry
Pier 6
Pinks Deli
Pirates Port
Plus Woman Boutique
Port O Call
Price Busters Ltd.
Quickie Lickie
Riddell's Bay Esso
Robinson's Marina Ltd.
Roomers
Roosters Restaurant
Rowe Spurling Paint Co.
SAL
Secrets
Shannon's Boutique

Shapers
Shoe Centre
Shopping Center
SI Tech (Radio Shack)
Smuggler's Reef
Somerset Country Squire
Sonesta Beach Resort
The Source
Speciality-Inn Restaurant
Sports 2000
Sports 'R' Us. Ltd.
The Sports Source
St George Parasail
St.Georges Liquor
Staples Ltd.
Sticca & Associates
Telecom
Terceira's North Shore
Tolaram Ltd.
Tourist Trap, The
Toys and Stuff
Triple R Paint Co.
Twins Variety
U.S. Air
Van Buren Ltd.
Vera P Card
Wadson's
Warwick Gas Station
Washington Lane Shoe
Waters Edge Marine Ltd.
Wharf Tavern
Wheels Ltd.
White & Sons Ltd
White Horse Tavern
White Sands Hotel
Wilson Associates
Yankee Store
York Street Mens Shop
Your Supermarket
Zig Zag

This symbol represents your protection against, check fraud—provided by The Bermuda Financial Network Ltd.

SAFE MEMBER

Table of Contents

Directory of Maps

Bermuda (East)

Bermuda (West)

City of Hamilton

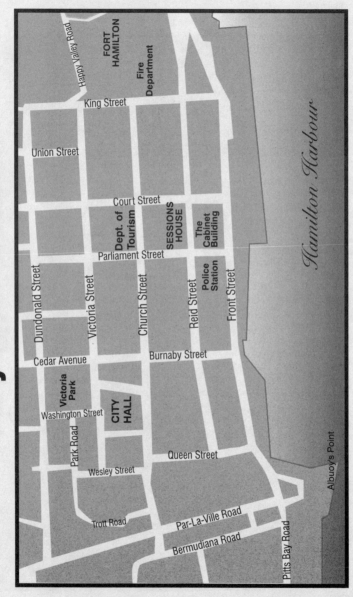

Hamilton Harbour

FORT HAMILTON

Happy Valley Road

Fire Department

King Street

Union Street

Court Street

Dept. of Tourism

SESSIONS HOUSE

The Cabinet Building

Parliament Street

Dundonald Street

Victoria Street

Church Street

Reid Street

Police Station

Front Street

Cedar Avenue

Burnaby Street

Victoria Park

CITY HALL

Washington Street

Park Road

Queen Street

Wesley Street

Trott Road

Par-La-Ville Road

Bermudiana Road

Pitts Bay Road

Albuoy's Point

Town of St. George

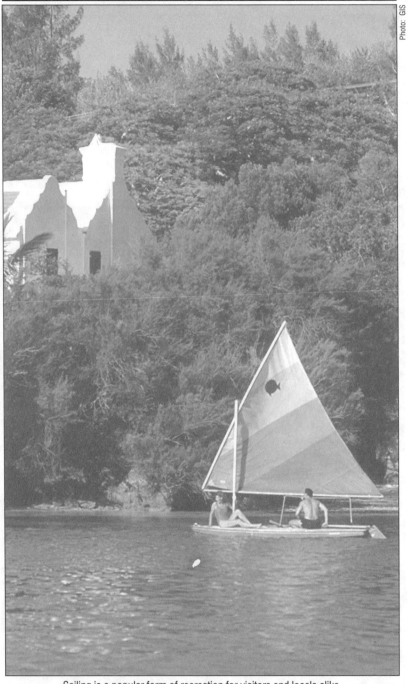

Photo: GIS

Sailing is a popular form of recreation for visitors and locals alike.

How to Use This Book

Emily Dickinson once wrote, "There is no Frigate like a Book/To take us Lands away." The book you hold in your hands is designed take you to Bermuda and let you sail easily through a myriad of facts and details about our small but complex island. We'll tell you where to stay, eat and shop, of course. And we'll tell you about our beaches, parks, recreations, attractions and a multitude of other features.

But perhaps most important of all, we'll identify and try to explain our idiosyncrasies that may at first puzzle those of an American mindset. Strangely enough, our American visitors tend to think that Bermuda is like a small version of England, while our British visitors think that the island is a minuscule America. We know better, on both accounts. Bermuda is, quite simply, Bermuda. It's unique. Our History, Let's Explain Bermuda and Area Overview chapters will give you an insight as to what makes us different. Read our History chapter, for instance, and you'll understand why we add an extra layer to the meaning of "onion." Let's Explain Bermuda will give you the long and short of it regarding our famous Bermuda shorts.

Organization is key for any travel guide. How have we organized this book? Well, chapter titles should tell you where to dip for the specific information you want. In terms of style and format, our chapters fall into two categories: those that are written in a narrative voice, and those that contain individual listings of businesses, events, beaches, services or what have you. All our chapters, of course, begin with introductions that will alert you as to what to expect.

With the chapters that use individual listings, we have maintained a consistent geographical order. Bear in mind that Bermuda does not have states or provinces or even counties (although counties do count where cricket's concerned; see our Spectator Sports chapter for an explanation). Instead our island is divided into nine parishes (see our Area Overviews chapter for more on the origin of our parishes), and it is their names we use as major headings.

When you arrive at Kindley Airport, you will have landed in St. George's Parish, at the eastern end of Bermuda. It's only logical then that in every chapter with listings, we start with St. George's and then take you parish by parish east to west — Hamilton Parish, Smiths Parish, Devonshire Parish, Pembroke Parish (where the City of Hamilton is located), Paget Parish, Warwick Parish, Southampton Parish and, lastly, Sandys Parish, where Somerset Village and the Royal Naval Dockyard are situated. Listings in each parish are generally placed thereafter in alphabetical order. However, there are some exceptions. For example, in our Beaches chapter we use a geographical rather than alphabetical order for those beaches that are part of our South Shore Park. And in our Attractions, Restaurants and Shopping chapters, listings for the Town of St. George are grouped together, as are those for the City of Hamilton.

Most listing headers include a street number address. However, we confess that finding street numbers to go with names has often been a challenge. Another of our Bermudian idiosyncrasies is that we're not too keen on street numbers, preferring instead to identify buildings by their color and their relationship with each other, as in: "You know, the pink building with white trim, next to the church." If there's no street number in a header, well, there was none to be found. The good thing is that most anyone you might ask for assistance likely wouldn't know the location you're looking for by number anyway.

Interspersed at the bottom of various pages throughout the chapters, you'll find several Insiders' tips, offering advice or nifty pieces of information. In addition, some chapters have Close-ups — feature stories that offer in-depth information on a number of topics including Bermudian coinage, wedding traditions and the infamous Bermuda Triangle. In every chapter that includes phone numbers we remind you that our international telephone area code is 441, important to know only if you're telephoning a destination outside Bermuda. Inside Bermuda you won't have to dial it.

If you're the sort of reader who has to start at page one and keep going until the end,

you'll probably notice we frequently make use of cross-references. Let's give you some examples. Without a doubt, you'll find historical information in our History chapter, but you'll also find nuggets of it in others, such as the Resort Hotels or Area Overviews chapters. We both love our history. Should you be interested in flowers and animals, you'll naturally head for the Flora and Fauna chapter, but there is valuable information on these topics in other chapters as well. How could we describe our parks, for instance, without pointing out some trees, or birds, flowers and weeds? And how could we take you snorkeling or diving in our Watersports chapter without showing you fish and marine life? So watch out for those cross-references. The index should prove extremely valuable as well.

You may be surprised that for such a small island we have produced such a fat book. When we started on this project, even we underestimated just exactly how much Bermuda has to offer. Bermuda *is* small and yet . . . and

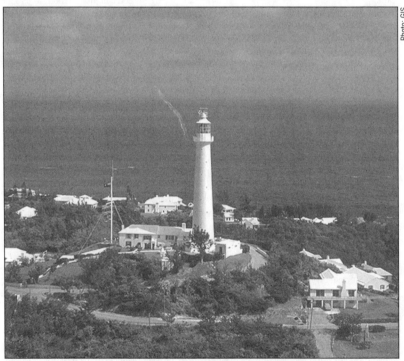

Photo: GIS

Gibb's Hill Lighthouse is one of Bermuda's most famous landmarks.

yet. . . . We could agree with Mark Twain, who once reputedly said: "Bermuda is the largest small place in the world."

Lastly, we in the Insiders' Publishing family value feedback from our readers. After all, you're the only ones who can tell us if we are giving you what you need. To that end, if you spot an error or an omission that you feel should be brought to our attention (remem-ber, virtually all Insiders' Guides® are updated annually), we encourage you to contact us. Visit us online at www.insiders.com, or write to us at:

The Insiders' Guide® to Bermuda
c/o Insiders' Publishing Inc.
P.O. Box 2057
Manteo, NC 27954

In this chapter we've provided some Insiders' tips and tidbits that will prove helpful in understanding what makes Bermuda and Bermudians tick.

Let's Explain Bermuda

Can thousands of our repeat visitors be on to something? We think so and apparently so do they, or they wouldn't return to Bermuda time after time, agreeing that our unique characteristics put us pretty close to a sunlit fairy tale. But our allure is not simply one of picture-postcard vistas and colorful snapshots for the photo album. . . . It is a state of mind, a sense of history, a moped-ride through a mid-ocean Arcadia transformed over the last 20 years into a modern and sophisticated Shangri-La.

We have some of the friendliest people you'll ever meet, no income tax, a low unemployment rate, comparatively little crime, a superior education system, excellent and up-to-date healthcare and a stable government, all nestled within a pollution-free environment.

Millions have visited Bermuda through the years, yet many still don't quite know where we are. This is not new. In the 16th century some maps put us off the Florida coast; in this century some folk put us off the west coast of Africa and, if one gentleman at a cricket game in London is to be believed, we're really a British stronghold in the Pacific!

In this chapter we've provided some Insiders' tips and tidbits that will prove helpful in understanding what makes Bermuda and Bermudians tick. For example, we often refer to our corner of paradise as the "Rock," and a trip to the United States is a "jump across the pond."

Now there's no hard and fast pattern to our explaining a land where many of us grew up riding Shank's Mare (traveling on foot) or rumbling through the countryside as passengers on the old Rattle and Shake (train) before it finally rattled off into oblivion. This, after all, is a place where no sidewalk shoeshine men exist, and when it rains during bright sunshine we know the devil is abusing his wife.

Our portrait will not only introduce some useful guidelines expanded upon at greater length elsewhere in the book, but as we clue you in on a few governmental rules and special gems, we also include a few quirks, tales, habits and customs so you'll know us better when we meet. This, we believe, could be the beginning of a beautiful friendship.

Wedded To the Sea

While we appear on any map as a dot in the Atlantic Ocean, our land mass is really a cluster of 180 small islands, islets and rocks, all situated a two-hour flight and 673 miles southeast of New York City or 564 miles dues east of Cape Hatteras on North Carolina's Outer Banks. And we're not a part of the Caribbean, though many of our forebears came from various Caribbean islands, and their cultural influence is a part of our rich heritage.

If you're a paranormal scientist or supermarket tabloid fan, you'll be interested in knowing we are at the northern apex of the infamous Bermuda Triangle (the other vertices generally considered to be San Juan, Puerto Rico and Miami). For more on this three-sided, mid-'70s brand of phenomenon, see the Close-up in our Watersports chapter.

The Triangle and other Sargasso Sea anomalies notwithstanding, most local fishermen simply won't go to sea on Good Friday. "Those who have gone out," says an experienced fisherman who has been pulling a living from Bermuda's waters for almost a half-century, "simply don't come back." Superstition? Perhaps. But most of these chaps would rather do something else, even engage in marble competitions, on Good Friday, or fly wood-framed, colored tissue-paper kites, a tradition with an elusive beginning.

But for those of us who own pleasure craft and don't fly kites or "nick" marbles — and you'll find every bay and cove dotted with our boats — almost any day is a good day to go to sea, and it is highly unlikely you'll find a sail or motor-cruise charter captain who'll refuse to take you a-cruising. If he does refuse, he probably was once a fisherman.

FYI

Unless otherwise noted, the area code for all phone numbers listed in this guide is 441.

Tied To the Land

Bermuda is 21.6 square miles of parks, beaches, farms, private estates and open spaces zealously watched by environmental groups. We have more forts and churches per square mile than any other place — cannon and canon juxtaposed, both rimmed by aqueous borders.

We're passionate campers who, during the summer and on holidays like Cup Match (see our Annual Events chapter), take to the beaches and designated camping areas like mature turtles staking out a patch of ground during breeding season. Some of us, for a week or two, even travel to work and back from tents pitched less than 100 yards from sand and surf.

Our population, hovering around 60,000, is comprised of 58.6 percent black and 36.4 percent white citizens. Ethnically, we're a soup bowl of British, West Indian, Portuguese, Philippine, American, African, Canadian, European and Asian seasonings.

Bermuda's climate is the envy of most areas, with temperatures heating up in April, then leveling off to the high 80s or low 90s until the end of September. High humidity is a frequent feature of the local climate and can make for some bad hair days. Many folks believe it can be just as bad when the wind is from the south. But you're in paradise, so who cares about hair? When bitter winter winds bite elsewhere, we enjoy temperatures that generally remain in the mid-60s. Occasionally, but not too often, the mercury will fall into the 50s, particularly during the first three months of the year. This gives us the best of both worlds — superb in the summer and splendid during the winter.

A few years ago, and probably only about a handful of people believe it really happened, it was rumored that there were a few snow flurries at our airport. And in March 1784, the Bermuda Gazette reported that snow had fallen overnight. But don't bother to pack your skis, they'd really be quite useless.

While arrival protocol is not quite as simple as grabbing your bag and hailing a cab, immigration and customs officials have made getting into Bermuda relatively painless. All visitors who arrive by air will need to present a valid passport, return airline ticket and completed Bermuda Immigration Visitor Arrival Card. There are other requirements depending on where you're coming from, how long you plan to stay and when you are leaving. See our Getting Here, Around and Home chapter for the complete rundown.

Leave the Driving to Us

You won't find Avis trying harder and Hertz offering discounts in Bermuda. Car rental services simply are not allowed. But fear not, we wouldn't invite you without ensuring you'll be able to get around quickly and easily. And we offer a very popular mode of visitor transportation for the more daring — mopeds. You'll find a number of moped rental firms that will deliver the bikes to your guest house or hotel door if desired. Well, not exactly your hotel door, but you get the point.

INSIDERS' TIP

Songwriter Hubert "Hubie" Smith, who wrote "Bermuda Is Another World," is the only Bermudian to have had a private, 10-minute audience with England's Queen Elizabeth.

However, never forget that here we drive on the *left*, and our speed limit is only 20 mph. Sure, you'll see locals whizzing past faster than that on occasion, but we advise that you be very careful and observant on local roads. For those accustomed to straight, several-laned freeways, our narrow, winding roads can be a challenge.

If you decide to forgo zipping smartly along on a rented moped (helmets are compulsory, by the way), our taxi services are excellent, with our cab drivers generally considered our frontline ambassadors. You cannot be gouged — all rates are fixed and fares are shown on taxi meters.

An efficient bus system also makes it easy to get around; you can't miss their pink and blue profiles. The bus-stop poles are color-coordinated as well: Pink on top means the bus is inbound, headed for the City of Hamilton; blue on top means the bus is heading away from the city. Keep in mind that bus travel will be a great deal less stressful, and ultimately cheaper, if you purchase transportation passes obtained at the central bus terminal in Hamilton and at hotels, guest houses, post offices and the visitors service bureaus. Bus operators are not supposed to accept paper money and are not allowed to make change. But don't be bashful about asking fellow passengers if they can change a couple of notes.

Bermuda Shorts (Or, Parade of Knees)

Before we go any further, we have to tell you: Bermuda is essentially a conservative country . . . with flamboyant ironies. Our ad campaign invites you to "Let Yourself Go," but don't go too far and shed everything on our beaches. Nudity is a no-no. We deal with specific dress requirements and expectations in several different chapters, but be aware that you might need to upgrade your usual loafing wardrobe to feel at home on Bermuda's streets. Men should never go shirtless, and short-shorts, tank tops and scanty cover-ups should be replaced by more genteel leisure threads.

And then there are our Bermuda shorts, those colorful Irish linen or tropical worsted wear items that are standard attire for an army of local businessmen. Hanging a couple of inches above the knee, the shorts originated in India around the turn of the century. Baggy British Army khaki trousers were chopped off below the knees and eventually incorporated into accepted military wear.

Our men have developed a sartorial rule that insists they be worn with blazer, tie and knee socks. Whatever color the blazer, do not attract the fashion police by wearing similar colored shorts. Egad! And the color of your knee socks should match either blazer or shorts.

Now we mentioned fashion police somewhat tongue-in-cheek, but in the 1950s, when shorts began inching indiscreetly upwards, our actual police politely ticketed wearers with a "green card" as an admonition against wearing them higher than two inches above the knee. It was all very proper, complete with the application of a six-inch ruler to ascertain the number of inches of offense. Today no tickets will be issued, this style of business attire having entered the establishment with no apologies for exposed knees.

Oh, lest we forget: Although accepted as our national dress, parliamentarians, judges and lawyers are forbidden to wear Bermuda shorts within our House of Assembly and courts of law. The conservatives have had the last word on that.

But having made that admission, our judges can be (and have in the past been) much less conservative in other areas, and we must tell you one of our favorite stories. In the 1930s the case of a man charged with stealing a turkey was made difficult by defense and prosecution witnesses who appeared so obviously to be lying that the judge dismissed the case in disgust and confiscated the turkey for his own Christmas dinner.

The Price of Paradise

You'll quickly notice that Bermuda is not a cheap thrill. Depending on what other destinations you compare us with, you will probably find things more expensive here. But be mindful that everything we supply in our restaurants, shops and grocery stores has to be imported, and because we have no income tax, our customs duties and the subsequent increased business overhead impact pricing.

Visiting us during winter can be a bonus, as you'll find various discount packages available for travel, dining and accommodations. Some hotels and cottage colonies offer discounts for honeymooners and families with children, often providing a variety of meal plans.

As for lodging, Bermuda can fill the bill, regardless of your 'druthers. There are all-inclusive resort hotels where many folks find they can have a fine vacation without ever leaving the property (but get out and see us if you want a really great vacation); old-fashioned guest houses and cottage colonies showcasing traditional architecture; housekeeping cottages (which could be considered Bermuda's version of America's efficiencies) where families on a tight budget can save a few dollars by cooking in; and small, traditional hotels and motels. Take a spin through our five chapters of accommodations offerings, and you'll get a sense of the variety.

---

www.insiders.com

See this and many other **Insiders' Guide®** destinations online — in their entirety.

Visit us today!

What's In A Name?

A rose by any other name . . . Bermuda has a thing going with names — first names, nicknames, names of boats, names of homes, names of roads, names of cars, names of you-name-it.

With first names, changes began within the past 20 or so years, particularly in the black community. Susan and John and Peter and the like have been replaced by Malika, Tioniea, Jelani and the like. Many first names are also creative mergers of fathers' and mothers' first names, and African names are often borrowed unchanged or borrowed and modified.

Nicknames provide a source of fascination. In fact, for men, to not have a nickname is more uncommon than having one. You'll find all sorts — Big Lunch, Gatepost, Peapost, Old Hell, Eager Toes, Greedy Guts — and there are those that, well, hover so close to the risque knuckle that we dare not mention them here.

It's not odd to name your boat. In fact, everybody does it all over the world. But we also name our homes (see our Arts and Culture chapter) and our cars. If you look carefully at the rear of many of our cars — and we admit that its not as common today as it was a decade ago — you'll see monikers like "Woman of Substance," "High on the Hog," "Bad Man" and "The Good Twin."

Just imagine Big Lunch leaving a house

called Spoon Fed and climbing behind the wheel of a car dubbed High on the Hog. Bermuda is, as the calypso song says, "Another World."

Greetings and Grapevine

So now that you've learned about a few of our peculiarities, you'll find Bermudians to be some of the most amiable folks you're likely to encounter. However, there is a caveat. If you want to make friends and curb some stony looks, please follow the niceties. Some of us do get a little nonplussed and downright resentful at visitors who barge right up to us without so much as an "excuse me" or "good morning" preamble before asking a question.

One of our friendliest Insiders, Johnny Barnes, may very likely be more forgiving. He has become Bermuda's literal poster-man of good wishes and blessings and can be found between 5 and 10 AM at the Crow Lane entrance to the City of Hamilton. Standing on his chosen patch of grass on the roundabout every day except Sunday, rain or shine, he waves, blows kisses and greets pedestrians and motorists alike, his "I love you" rising over the hum of traffic.

But don't err in thinking Johnny is a six-pack shy of a full case. A local television interview with him a few years back revealed a smart, likeable and deeply religious man who genuinely cares about his fellow persons. A former train and bus mechanic, he has claimed his spot at the Crow Lane spot for 15 years and has even been interviewed for German television. Now that's some distance for a good reputation to travel.

And speaking of traveling, news moves pretty quickly via the local grapevine. It used to be joked that if something happened in St. George's in the morning it would reach Somerset before lunch, and that was in the days of the horse and buggy. Today news travels even faster, the grapevine now aided by, among other things, cellular phones. But just as it was in the old days, the truth tends to get somewhat massaged during its journey, and the story arrives a little worse for wear.

One of the Safest Places in the World

We pride ourselves on living in one of the safest places in the world, yet there is no room for complacency. We are finding it necessary to take continuing bites out of crimes driven mostly by an illegal drug scourge. As anywhere else, caution and good sense will take you a long way and prevent any sort of bad experience.

When going about the island, keep all personal belongings in a safe place, and never

Now you can set up your new Bermuda address *before* arriving in Bermuda, either by phone or fax!

We provide Private Mailbox Rentals and extensive worldwide mail forwarding srvices!

- Private Mailbox Rentals
- Int'l mail forwarding service
- Banking Referrals
- Fax Service
- Answering Services
- Couriers - FedEx, UPS, DHL, Airborne Express

- Secretarial services
- Photocopies
- Mailing Lists
- Packing and shipping
- Int'l freight forwarding
- Messenger services

Mailboxes Par-la-Ville Road, Hamilton
Mailboxes Church Street, Hamilton
Mailboxes Middle Road, Warwick
Mailboxes South Road, Smiths

leave anything unlocked, be it your moped, hotel room or guest cottage. When dining out in the evening or checking out the nightlife, it's always a good idea to ask a friend to join you.

Also be aware that handbag snatching has become an irritating problem, and when renting a moped be careful of riding with camera and bags resting unsecured and exposed in a basket; another rider can simply come alongside, reach into the basket and speed off with your property.

Although we emphasize that you are safer in Bermuda than just about anywhere, we do caution that when swimming or snorkeling at any of our beaches, do not leave your camera and other valuables unattended on your beach blanket as you dip into our delightful emerald waters.

FYI

Unless otherwise noted, the area code for all phone numbers listed in this guide is 441.

A Tale of Warmth, Nourishment and Luck

In Flatts Village in Hamilton Parish is a delightful 18th-century home known as Wistowe. At one time a roadhouse, theater and bakery, it was bought early this century by Professor Reginald Fessenden, a Canadian-born inventor and radio pioneer. The property was known for its row of coconut trees, reputed at the time to be among the tallest in Bermuda.

Professor Fessenden, who many years before had been headmaster of local Whitney Institute, then a private school, believed the trees should have been yielding a more plentiful crop of coconuts. Employing a West Indian fellow who was a self-styled "coconut tree doctor," Fessenden watched as the man climbed to the tops of each tree and applied a generous serving of salt to the young fruit. Surprising to everyone except the "doctor," a bountiful crop resulted.

Later, when planting a new row of coconut palms, Fessenden followed an old Bermudian custom of placing in the holes a lump of charcoal for warmth, a pound of ship biscuit for nourishment and a horseshoe for luck!

Bucks and Banks

Unless your luck is soaring, it is unlikely you'll find any examples of Hog Money, Bermuda's first coinage dated 1616 to 1624 (see the Close-up on Hog Money in our History chapter). Find one of these ancient coins, and the Bermuda Monetary Authority will beat a path to your door.

However, our coinage and notes are still distinctive. Visitors are quick to notice our $2 bill, and tourists often comment on the variety of colors of our paper money. Our coins are also thumbnail historical, environmental and cultural sketches — with the hog on the cent, angelfish on the five-cent, longtail on the quarter and the Bermuda Fitted Dinghy (see the Close-up in our Yachting chapter) on the dollar.

Although our money looks different, it is worth the same as the U.S. dollar, which is readily accepted here. In fact, you can request that the shops you buy goods from give you change in American currency; if they can at the time, most will be quite happy to do so. But remember that shops don't purposely keep American dollars on hand. We suggest that you exchange any Bermudian money for your own currency before leaving the island, unless you want to keep a few coins and bills for keepsakes.

It is unlikely that you will need their services, but if so our three banks — the Bank of Bermuda Limited, the Bank of N.T. Butterfield and Son Limited and the Bermuda Commercial Bank Limited (which primarily handles pri-

---

INSIDERS' TIP

The Bird Cage is a famous Bermuda landmark at the junction of Queen and Front streets. A favorite of photographers and visitors, it is sometimes manned by constables directing traffic. Built in 1962, it is named for "Dickie" Bird, the Corporation of Hamilton's engineer who designed it.

The Majesty and Mystery of the Gombeys

The pulsing cadence of the drum reaches out and grabs you as it rushes out of the hinterland to run unfettered through the streets. And from around the bend, appearing as suddenly as midday apparitions, come the Gombeys, leaping flashes of color and pulse-pounding agility, with their peacock-feathered headdresses waving in counterpoint to the drumbeat, always the drumbeat . . . its passionate and staccato tempo igniting some secret place deep in the soul.

Then the drum changes voice, its command subtle, and the Wild Indian (bow and arrow at the side), the Trapper and chiefs and warriors obey, slipping easily into the "snake dance." Shrieks from the Captain's

Close-up

whistle pierce the air, punctuating the throb of the drum, and he high-steps and turns and bends and sunlight bounces from 100 or more bits of broken mirror sewn into his cape.

Shuffling behind the masked dancers are the drummers, faces exposed, nimble fingers rapping drumsticks against the tight face of the snare drums, the deep-throated kettle drum joining in thumping chorus. Bringing up the rear of the Gombey "crowd" are men, women and children, hips rocking and swaying, shoes clapping on the hard street, responding to the language, the symbolism, the artistry of a dance cultivated from native soil, nurtured through slavery and celebrated in freedom.

Yet most visitors rarely see them.

The Gombeys appear at many Bermudian festivals throughout the year.

No one is certain when the Gombeys first appeared. We do know they were active around the end of the 18th century and into the 19th century, their name derived from the African *gumba*, a word for drum. Had some inhabitants had their way, the dance would have been outlawed.

"The savage and nonsensical exhibition of the *Gomba*, practiced here by the idle, should be done away with, as a thing not suited to a civilized community, and highly dangerous to passengers on horses or in carriages," complained a letter writer to the *Bermuda Gazette* in 1837.

The appearance of the Gombeys on Boxing Day — a local holiday celebrated the day after Christmas — was one of the season's anticipated highlights. It was then, as now, a pastiche of dancers leaping, doing splits and pirouettes. Men and women daubed their faces red and yellow,

— continued on next page

their scarlet dress enhanced by ribbons and flowers. As they danced and sang from house to house, they were accompanied by the hypnotic tempo of the drum, its distinctive beat confirmed in 1970 at a UNESCO Cultural and Conservation Conference as entirely unique.

There have been several influences on the development of the Gombey tradition over the past hundred or more years, chief among them some Native American adaptations. Tomahawks, bow and arrow and feathers are readily evident. The "Wild Indian" is an obvious borrowing, and the dance ritual itself, while essentially African, has much in common with some aspects of Indian tribal dancing.

But perhaps the most significant factor lies in its family traditions. Each of the five or six separate troupes or crowds is generally composed of males (and recently one or two females) from one family who maintain and pass on traditional dance techniques from generation to generation. This makes the survival of the Gombey both a family and cultural tradition.

Apart from a few holidays and an annual competition when they appear in their vibrant costumes that are sewn by female family members, they will take to the streets without costume at odd times through the year, attract eager crowds and then disperse quickly.

They are, for many, Bermuda's most powerful cultural tradition.

---

vate corporate accounts) — are more than capable of handling any requirements. You will find bank reception staff most helpful.

Run out of cash? All you need is your Visa, MasterCard or any bank card connected to the Cirrus or Plus systems. Between them the banks have 13 branch offices and 40 Easylink and BankCardPlus ATM machines at various points throughout the island, a few just outside or inside some supermarkets and pharmacies. You can withdraw up to your credit limit through the Cirrus network or up to $500 a day through the Plus system.

The Bank of Bermuda, 6 Front Street, Hamilton, 295-4000, and the Bank of N.T. Butterfield and Son Limited, 65 Front Street, Hamilton, 295-1111, both offer assistance with travelers' checks and wire transfers.

By the People and for the People

A British dependent territory, Bermuda has a parliamentary system dating from August 1, 1620, when the first colonial parliament was held in St. George's. Queen Elizabeth II is the head of all governmental power, and a governor — always a British civil servant appointed for a minimum of three years — represents her in Bermuda, aided by a deputy who is also appointed in London.

The Bermuda constitution gives the governor responsibility for Bermuda's defense, police and internal and external security. However, he generally takes his cues from the premier and elected government before exercising these powers. Our parliament, or House of Assembly, consists of 40 representatives elected from 40 constituencies or electoral districts within our nine parishes. Three parties vie for government's reins during a general election — the United Bermuda Party (UBP), the Progressive Labour Party (PLP) and the National Liberal Party (NLP).

The winning party's leader, confirmed by the governor as premier, then chooses a cabinet comprised of ministers, each of whom is responsible for a particular portfolio or ministry. However, with 12 ministries, some ministers may hold more than one portfolio.

Our bicameral system includes an 11-member senate, with five senators selected by the governor, premier and leader of the opposition party. But the senate has no legislative powers and serves as a debating and moderating influence. Both the senate and cabinet meet at the Cabinet Building on Front Street, where the premier's office is also found.

Most visitors won't likely need the services of a particular ministry, but there are a few instances that require contact. These include obtaining a marriage license, extending your stay, taking up residence and obtaining a work permit or driver's license.

If you are pierced by Cupid's irrepressible arrow and plan on "jumping the broom" or tying the knot while here, you will need to contact the Registrar General (see our chapter on Weddings). The Department of Immigration, 30 Parliament Street, Hamilton, 297-7941, can assist with issues relating to length of stay or obtaining a work permit, and the Department of Transport Control's Examination Centre, 11 North Street, Hamilton, 292-2255, can help regarding a driving license.

Phone and Post

Public pay phones are conveniently located throughout the island. A local call costs 20 cents — if you don't have two dimes you can use a quarter, but don't expect a nickel in return. Cash calling cards can be purchased at the Bermuda Telephone Company (Telco), 30 Victoria Street, Hamilton, 292-5272, or at any of its satellite offices in St. George's and Sandys parishes. Telco also has a card dispenser at the Clocktower at the Royal Navy Dockyard.

TeleBermuda International Ltd., Mintflower Place, 8 Par-la-Ville Road, Hamilton, 296-9000, is Bermuda's newest licensed long distance carrier, providing a full range of telephone, fax and data services. In order to take advantage of TeleBermuda rates, which are generally cheaper, visitors can obtain prepaid calling cards directly from them. Call 292-SAVE for commercial locations carrying the cards.

Should you need cellular service during your visit, call 292-6032 to arrange advanced registration with Telco Mobility prior to arrival. Once here, you can acquire service by dialing the same number. Billing can be credited to your American Express, Visa or MasterCard. For the yacht skipper wanting to use a cell phone, call 292-6032 when within 50 miles of the island. Cellular visitor rates are currently as follows: service activation charge, $10; daily access charge, $5; peak minute charge (7 AM to 7 PM), 60¢ per minute; off-peak charges (7 PM to 7 AM), 35¢ per minute.

Mail in Bermuda is delivered quickly and efficiently. We've moved quite a long way since the 18th century, when the blowing of a horn by a letter carrier, a slave on horseback, announced that post was near. The General Post Office, 56 Church Street, Hamilton, 297-7893, is open from 8 AM to 5 PM weekdays and until noon on Saturdays. There is one sub-post office in each parish, and you can find addresses and phone numbers in the blue pages of the telephone directory.

At 11 Queen Street, Hamilton, you'll find the Perot Post office (no, there's no relation to Ross; the pronunciation is "Pea-Rut"). This post office, also a part of the government-run system, was used in 1848 by William B. Perot, who owned the building and was the postmaster at Hamilton. During the years before the mid-19th century, some postmasters in the United States, on their own authority, issued "postmaster stamps." Perot, aware of this, imitated the experiment, and in so doing created what is now known as the Perot Stamp, of which only about a dozen specimens remain. There are two varieties, one blue-black, the other red, and both are among the more valuable stamps in the philatelic world.

You will notice as you travel about the island that we have bright-red pillar letter boxes at various locations. Secure from theft, mail is collected from them daily.

Incidentally, if your visit lasts through December, and you want to mail a letter from Bermuda to arrive before Christmas in the United States, your correspondence should be sent on or before the established deadline of 9:30 AM on December 12.

INSIDERS' TIP

If it rains during a funeral it means the person being buried has led a good Christian life.

An aerial view showcases the splendid beauty of Horseshoe Bay.

Water, Water, Use It With Care

There are times when rain pours out of the clouds with a vengeance, slashing straight down onto our roofs as though bent on piercing it. That is the kind of rain we like — "tank rain."

We are always mindful however, that no matter our aquifer resources (see our Area Overview chapter for more on Bermuda's approach to its water supply), we must not waste water. In 1949 and into 1950, a drought so devastated the island that tens of thousands of gallons had to be imported from overseas. Henry Gross, a dowser from the United States (that's someone skilled in locating underground water sources, by the way), was eventually brought in under the auspices of a leading politician to locate underground water supplies. Gross was successful in St. George's, dowsing a subterra-

nean spring that yielded what was described as "the freshest water ever produced out of the ground in Bermuda."

We've had a couple of lean years since, but nothing quite so bad. We generally do not fill the tub to the brim when at home, but joyfully and shamelessly indulge ourselves when we travel. When you visit the Rock, be clean, but be water-conscious when taking a shower or luxuriating in that bubble bath.

Bermuda's Work Force

Our latest 1996 employment survey showed our economic engine is maintained by a labor force of 34,633 persons. When analyzed, the working population is 78 percent Bermudian and 22 percent non-Bermudian. Factor in gender, and women make up 48 percent of workers.

Leading employers continue to be government and the hotel industry, closely followed by the retail sector. Although far less labor-intensive, Bermuda's collection of international companies, represented by more than 7,000 registered corporations, accounts for an average of 2,420 positions held by Bermudians. These businesses engage in varied enterprises, including insurance and reinsurance, investment holdings, commercial trading, shipping and chemical trade.

We must point out that of these thousands of corporations registered here and known locally as "exempt" companies, less than 300 have an actual physical presence. (See our International Business chapter for more details.)

Keep Bermuda Beautiful

We try to keep our face clean and well-scrubbed by placing public trash receptacles throughout the City of Hamilton and the outlying parishes. Keep Bermuda Beautiful, 295-5142, is a volunteer organization that relies on contributions from individuals, small businesses and corporations to promote a national "Keep Bermuda Beautiful" message.

A government recycling program begun five years ago has received tremendous support. Since 1993 we have recycled 3,743 tons of glass, with 271 tons of aluminum and 846 tons of steel recyclables shipped to America for reprocessing. During that period we have disposed of 35,000 pounds of household batteries, 48,663 lead acid batteries, 154,000 fluorescent tubes and 231,000 gallons of used motor oil. Most of our recyclable materials go to New Jersey and Pennsylvania.

Our Rock Watcher program is directed at individuals and groups, encouraging responsibility for keeping a particular area clean. Every May, hundreds of Bermudians engage in islandwide neighborhood tidying, and every two years scuba divers and snorkelers slip beneath the surface to haul up stuff carelessly dumped in Neptune's locker.

It Takes a Whole Island

But our concern is not only about refuse and recyclables, oceans and open spaces; we're also a place where people really do reach out to help other people, both at home and abroad. We have always responded when disasters strike areas overseas, such as in the mid-'90s, when Eleuthera in the Bahamas suffered severe hurricane damage. Through the past several decades, in the face of various crises, we have made financial contributions, donated clothing and blankets, sent troops from our Bermuda Regiment to help in rebuilding efforts and, in some cases, provided all three services simultaneously. BELCO, our utility company, has also sent out personnel and equipment during emergencies.

The element of caring extends into every facet of our community life. It's a force that helps link our multicultural society. We have approximately 182 registered charities, excluding church- and government-operated organizations. There are Rotarians and Lions' clubs, banks and businesses, and health and community organizations staffed and supported almost entirely by volunteers (among them our "Pink Ladies"; see our Healthcare chapter), all of which get into the act. Add to that mix the Salvation Army and a host of other individuals and groups that support and promote existing programs and help structure new ones. On many Fridays and Saturdays throughout the year, you will find men and women stationed outside several of our supermarkets, banks and malls to collect charitable donations from passersby to support any number of worthy causes.

Since 1991 the Centre on Philanthropy, 7 Par-la-Ville Road, Hamilton, 292-5320, has been one of the key players in Bermuda's charitable community. It offers support, information and assistance to charitable concerns through educational workshops, publications, a lending library, an inquiry service, develop-

Photo: GIS

The *Dreamward* negotiates the Cut, a narrow passage into Tiger Bay.

ment of a directory of registered charities and much more. It is integral in bringing together donors, charities and the public. If while visiting Bermuda you want to locate a branch of a charity you're involved with or interested in, the Centre will be happy to assist you.

Healthcare

We're proud of a lot of things here in Bermuda, and tops on the list is our healthcare system. Visitors who have had the misfortune of needing emergency medical care offer high praise for the facilities, staff and treatment at King Edward VII Memorial Hospital, 7 Point Finger Road, Paget, 236-2345. To reach the hospital emergency room directly, call 239-2009. And, same as in America, dial 911 for immediate ambulance, fire department or police response.

In emergency situations, a patient not needing admittance to the hospital must pay for treatment at the time it is received. Payment for outpatient care can be made with cash, check or credit card. No overseas medical insurance is accepted for outpatient treatment. However, should medical treatment require admittance to the hospital, Blue Cross and Blue Shield insurance is accepted. (For much more information, see our Healthcare chapter.)

When You Leave Us

If you are departing by air, check in at Bermuda International Airport at least an hour or more before your scheduled departure. The Bermuda immigration form and other documentation received at the time of your arrival should be attached to your ticket. All passengers pay a departure tax of $20, which is included in airline fares.

Logistical details regarding departure can be found in the Getting Here, Around and

Home chapter. Check to see what the limitations are for taking various plants or foods off the island. Certainly the U.S. Department of Agriculture representative may want to know what you have in your possession. You are not allowed to carry indigenous flowers or greenery or sea life (such as sea cucumbers, urchins and brain coral). Soil and seedlings are a major no-no as well. But you can take items such as flowers bought from a florist, seashells that don't have any critters growing inside them, frozen seafood, Portuguese sausage in plastic store wrapping or cassava pie, if it's filled with no other meat but poultry.

Should you return home with one of these pies — a big part of most Bermudian Christmas dinners along with turkey — then you will be carrying across the pond a genuine taste of Bermuda, an echo of a unique experience and a personal invitation to return.

Early survival on a group of tiny islands almost 700 miles from the nearest land and with no freshwater rivers or streams was difficult but possible.

History

Prologue

Coughed from the belly of the Atlantic 100 millennia ago, this fishhook-shaped coral archipelago perched at the summit of an extinct submarine volcano was once avoided like the plague. Believed discovered in 1503 by Spaniard Juan Bermudez, a mariner from Palos, Spain, the islands were haunted by demons, or so the stories went.

This superstition had a simple enough origin. The trills of hundreds of thousands of birds, floating on the wind to the ears of passing 16th-century seafarers, were oddly interpreted as the cries of devils. Appearing early in the century on many manuscripts and printed maps as *Las Bermudas*, this land was quickly dubbed *Ya de Demonios* by Spanish mariners. Despite its unalluring reputation, some historians believe it was used occasionally as a base by a small number of French privateers familiar with safe passages through treacherous reefs that brought grief to sailors on hundreds of ancient vessels.

French explorer Samuel de Champlain, returning from the West Indies in 1600, described this "Isle of Devils" as a place where, "It almost always rains, and thunder is so frequent that it seems as if heaven and earth must come together. The sea is very tempestuous about the said island and the waves as high as mountains." Nine years later heaven and earth did come together violently, conspiring in a scenario that led to near death and subsequent habitation.

Shipwreck and Settlement

In 1609, as England stretched her hand across the Atlantic to grasp at North America, Jamestown, founded two years earlier on the banks of the James River in Virginia, was slip-ping into oblivion. Backed by a syndicate of influential London merchants operating as the Virginia Company, the young settlement was decimated by disease, starvation and Indian attacks.

During trade development with the lands bordering the Eastern Mediterranean Sea and the East Indies, company stakeholders had gained considerable experience in supporting far-flung commercial enterprises. Moving quickly to save their Virginian investment, in June 1609 they dispatched Admiral Sir George Somers from Plymouth, England, in command of a fleet of nine ships. The mission was to rescue settlers who were many weeks and an ocean away.

All went well until the fleet neared the dreaded Bermudas. They were within seven or eight days of making Cape Henry on the Virginia coast when they sailed head first into disaster. "A dreadful storme and hideous began to blow from out the Northeast, swelling and roaring as it were by fits and at length did beate all the light from Heaven; which, like an hell of darkenesse turned blacke upon us," wrote Silvanus Jourdan and William Strachey, passengers on board Somers' 300-ton flagship *Sea Venture*.

The ship was battered for a day and a half by hurricane winds and pounding seas that broke open the seams of its hull. "Windes and seas were as mad as fury and rage could make them," Jourdan and Strachey wrote. As water rushed in, the passengers and crew threw weapons and chests overboard to lighten the load. And just as it seemed that even their prayers had failed, the ship was edged between reefs at the eastern end of Las Bermudas and wrecked within sight and striking distance of shore.

Fortuitously there was no loss of life as the exhausted settlers struggled ashore. Somers promptly claimed the land for England, and Bermuda's opening chapter of permanent settlement had begun, not with a placid landfall, but with a preface of howling winds, angry seas and personal possessions being hurled into a summer maelstrom.

The 150 men and women found a chain of islands heavily forested with cedars and palmettos and populated with birds and wild hogs. But while the tiny isles proved more hospitable than the lands of seafarers' superstitious tales, Jamestown was not forgotten. The settlers there were still expecting the cavalry. In little more than nine months, two new ships, the *Deliverance* and *Patience*, were built from local cedars and salvaged *Sea Venture* timbers.

www.insiders.com

See this and many other **Insiders' Guide®** destinations online — in their entirety.

Visit us today!

However, even as the new vessels took shape during those months of sojourn, this island that would inspire Shakespeare to pen *The Tempest* was the setting for one murder, an execution, five deaths from natural causes, a marriage, two births and three mutinies. When the Admiral and the ships finally departed a land that had proved challenging but essentially tranquil, they left two men behind. One of them, Christopher Carter, was Bermuda's first permanent inhabitant, remaining here until he died.

News of the shipwreck intrigued the Virginia Company. In 1612 a subsidiary known as the Bermuda Company was formed with the direct intent of colonization. That same year the first wave of 60 white settlers, led by company-appointed Governor Richard Moore, left England for Bermuda. On July 11 they arrived in St. George's Harbour, anticipating carving a prosperous life from an isolated wilderness.

Early Years

Survival on a group of tiny islands almost 600 miles from the nearest land and with no freshwater rivers or streams was difficult but possible. Water was caught in wooden barrels, "cabbens" were erected using cedar and palmetto thatching, and within a decade several small fishing boats had been built.

In 1616 the first black man and first Indian were brought from the West Indies to dive for pearls. The company had grandiose dreams of realizing profits from cargoes of pearls, rare spices, whale oil and ambergris, but few profits materialized. Investors were disappointed, but men continued to arrive and explore many of the smaller islands. Women, however, remained scarce.

The arrival in 1621 of "certaine younge maydes" from England created excitement. It was an arrangement with a price attached. Those single men who could scrape together 100 pounds of tobacco secured themselves wives. By the latter part of the century, several communities sprang up around Flatts, Crow Lane, Riddell's Bay and Mangrove Bay. Each of these pocket-sized settlements boasted a small inlet that served as a haven for privateers and smugglers. In these sheltered bays cargo was unloaded far from the prying eyes of inspectors based in St. George's, Bermuda's political center, commercial hub and first capital.

Tobacco, whaling, cedar and salt were critical to the infant economy. Cedar forests were cleared for the cultivation of potatoes, cabbages, onions and tobacco, which emerged as a principal commodity grown only for export to England. As early as 1626, triers and tasters were sent to out to ensure that the quality of tobacco was acceptable; quantities judged unfit were burned, sometimes at the grower's doorstep. By 1687 Bermuda and Virginia shared a monopoly on the tobacco trade. But the quality of the Bermuda variety was poor, with local tobacco farmers battling worms, ants and wireweed. With tobacco production banned at home, the British government was not hesitant in taxing that grown in the colonies. Bermuda's farmers refused to pay, insisting that to do so would destroy an industry already in decline, a decline so rapid, in fact, that by 1712 Bermuda was importing rather than exporting tobacco.

An agricultural-based economy never appealed to Bermudians. From the beginning they regarded the ocean as the ultimate road to prosperity and whenever possible pursued lucrative opportunities through a trading triangle between Bermuda, the West Indies and the continental colonies.

Much of the work, whether on land or ocean, during those early years was carried out by indentured white servants and black slaves. Ultimately indentured workers were completely replaced by slaves. Although slavery here never descended to the brutal levels common elsewhere in the New World, local slaves struggled against the wretched institution — three major rebellions were planned and thwarted, and the ringleaders were executed.

Yet the Bermudian dichotomy always saw a handful of free blacks in the community who overcame various restrictions to pursue occupations as teachers, butchers, planters, blacksmiths and even landlords. Many were released from indentured servitude to become free men in the early years of the island's development, and others were granted freedom through stipulations in slaveholder wills.

The Wood of Prosperity

As owners and slaves strengthened their ties to the sea, reliance on cedar was crucial. The richly scented wood evolved from a mere commodity into the sinew and synonym for economic and cultural prosperity.

The importance of *juniperus bermudiana* prompted one naturalist to write that "in olden times the native squires of Bermuda calculated their wealth by the numbers and growth of the cedars on their estates, and tradition has it that the fair 'Mudian damsel who possessed a right and title to a thousand goodly cedars was in a certain way of possessing a husband, should she feel so inclined."

A superb asset for squires and damsels, cedar was used to build homes and make furniture, farm implements, window frames, rolling pins, cradles, altars, coffins and even fish pots. But its most significant contribution was to the success of the shipbuilding industry. Maritime activities encouraged the estab-

lishment of several shipyards that were kept busy throughout the 18th century. As many as 30 sloops were built annually, several of them destined for New York merchants.

And as Bermuda-built vessels achieved a reputation for durability and speed, it was inevitable that shipbuilders would not only receive contracts from clients engaged in legitimate commerce, but also from merchants with eyes on a different prize.

Privateering

As early as the 16th century, piracy and privateering had flourished in the Caribbean. Following Bermuda's settlement, a few local merchants and officials became closely acquainted with privateering captains who occasionally brought their brigs into St. George's harbor to stock up on supplies.

The hazardous, yet frequently rewarding, forays against ships bound north from the Caribbean to catch the prevailing westerlies for the voyage home to Spain or France was too tempting to resist for Bermudians with a thirst for adventure and profit. Several merchants outfitted their own privateers and hired white captains, slave crews and black pilots to voyage in search of plunder. As a result of countless successful engagements, the fortunes of many prominent families were founded on profits from such raids.

In 1684, when the British government took over the charter of the Bermuda Company, the island's sailors of fortune had established a reputation where they "were feared by merchantmen more than those of any other nation." Between 1685 and the middle of the 18th century, hundreds of local seamen turned to this endeavor with gusto. Some became highly successful. One of them, Nathaniel North, retired to become a rajah in Madagascar.

During the American Revolution a score of swift, copper-keeled sloops were operated as privateers, and in one month alone, September 1782, captured 20 ships. But the island became even more directly involved. A trade embargo declared by the Continental Congress against Britain and her colonies put Bermuda in a tenuous position. Squeezed by the hostilities, well-established and viable trade contacts along the eastern United States were in danger of perishing. Inability to obtain food and other essentials put the islanders so near starvation that many considered deserting the country.

A small delegation journeyed to Philadelphia to plead for Bermuda's exclusion from the embargo. Appeals fell on stony ground. Dominant in the salt trade, the islanders offered to supply as much as the states wanted. The response was quick. There was no pressing need for salt, they were informed, but if by some good fortune arms or gunpowder were somehow substituted. . . .

The delegation returned home. On August 14, 1775, one of the largest gunpowder storehouses in St. George's was raided, virtually under the nose of the governor. A hundred barrels of powder were rolled down to Tobacco Bay and rowed out to two American ships anchored just offshore. When dawn broke over the town, the gunpowder was on its way to George Washington's men, who put it to good use in driving the British out of Boston. The unwritten deal of gunpowder for provisions was honored. The embargo on Bermuda was lifted.

The Salt Trade

The salt offered the Americans by the delegation came from a thriving undertaking established a century earlier. With Turks Island in the Caribbean claimed as a Bermudian possession, salt was raked from the cays (pronounced "keys") during the winter and stored in Bermuda. In spring, supplies were taken to Virginia, Maryland, Pennsylvania, New York and Newfoundland to be traded for corn, flour, beef, salt fish and other necessities. Prior to opening the trading season, bushels of cabbages and onions were taken to the West Indies in exchange for rum, molasses and cotton.

In 1710, wanting to hone in on this enterprise, the Spanish attacked and captured the salt ponds. This audacious seizure of the salt

piles did not go unchallenged. A retaliatory expedition under Capt. Lewis Middleton routed the Spaniards and restored possession of a profitable business.

The Dockyard

Early in the 1800s British naval power in the North Atlantic was consolidated by the construction of the Royal Naval Dockyard (often simply called the Yard) at Bermuda's most western end. With two bases already established at Antigua and Halifax, the Yard provided a valuable third prong. The construction of storehouses, repair slips, timber yards, foundries, fuel tanks, engineering shops, boat sheds, living quarters for men and officers and, later, a school and hospital, generated the largest military defense utilization of money, manpower and materials in 19th-century Bermuda.

The strategic value of this mid-Atlantic naval post was immediately evident during the War of 1812, when Rear Admiral Sir George Cockburn sailed from here in the summer of 1813 to harass the Delaware and Chesapeake bays. The following year Admiral Sir Alexander Cochrane set out with a task force to help in the attack on Washington.

At the beginning of the war, the Yard was still relatively embryonic, with the work carried out by slaves, free blacks and craftsmen from England. Little known is that during this war large numbers of American slaves, including entire families fleeing bondage, sought help from British sea captains. There men and women were taken away on British ships, and many of them were brought to Bermuda.

Restricted to the Dockyard confines, the men were employed in direct construction while the women and children were put to work picking oakum, a fiber often treated with tar and used chiefly for caulking seams in wooden ships. While the majority of local and American blacks were unskilled laborers, an 1823 Dockyard Table of Wages does show that quite a few blacks were employed as shipwrights, caulkers, masons, blacksmiths, sawyers and sailmakers.

On a number of occasions, captured American merchant and war vessels were brought into Bermuda with onboard slaves who voluntarily offered their services as labor-

Hog Money Discovery at Castle Island

In summer 1994, employees from the Bermuda Monetary Authority led by Dr. Edward Harris, director of the Bermuda Maritime Museum, and Professor Norman Barka from the College of William and Mary in Williamsburg, Virginia, headed up two volunteer teams in an archaeological dig on Castle Island.

This 3½-acre island near the entrance of Castle Harbour, barren except for a few stunted cedars and tricky to get on to, is the site of the ruins of King's Castle, once the main fortification of 17th-century Bermuda.

The focus of the excavations was a defensive ditch cut between 1612 and 1620. Appearing to have been used as a trash dump following its initial construction, the ditch yielded substantial amounts of bird, fish and animal bones. After sifting through the soil and detritus of almost 400 years, the diggers were elated on discovering 13 pieces of "Hogge Money" (usually referred to as Hog money). These ancient, rare coins are believed to be among the earliest such coinage in the British colonies.

Excavations undertaken a year earlier by the William and Mary team had unearthed a sixpence and a twelvepence. The sixpence, a remarkably fine specimen, showed surprisingly little wear from either handling or contact with other coins. The twelvepence, however, typical of many pieces of this type, was considerably debased.

Numismatist E. Rodovan Bell, writing a half-century ago on Hog money, speculated that the coins were probably first minted in London. Presumably struck in a short period of time and perhaps by more than one mint, the quantity produced is unknown, as are the designer and engraver. It appears that the number of coins minted was never large and there was the problem, noted by historian Henry Wilkinson, that, "Coin had always been scarce and the little there had been had nearly all gone to passing ships for aqua vitae (whisky, brandy or other strong liquor)."

The earliest reference to a coinage for Bermuda is found in the commission granted

— continued on next page

Photo: The Royal Gazette

Eighteen Hog money coins have been unearthed at King's Castle on Castle Island.

Photo: The Royal Gazette

11311

This Hog money sixpence (circa 1616) features a wild boar.

by the Virginia Company to Governor Moore in 1612. After stipulating the amount of wages for skilled and common laborers, the company promised to "speedily" send out a special coin for the purpose.

It is believed the first minted coins were sent to the island in February 1616 with a proscription that their use be restricted to Bermuda. The denominations are generally supposed to have been in the values of twelvepence, sixpence, threepence and twopence. Of similar design, they varied in size and weight and were made of a mixed metal termed "brasse." The ship design on one side probably represents the *Sea Venture*, with the obverse showing a wild boar.

There is some speculation as to the origin of the term Hog money, but most believe it derived from the abundance of wild pigs found on Bermuda in the early days of habitation. Although there have been suggestions purporting the existence of a fourpence and one-penny denomination, neither has ever been found. The most common is the shilling or twelvepence, the rarest the threepence.

In 1996 four more coins were found at Castle Island. As far as is currently known, these 19 coins are the only pieces of Hog money found in an archaeological context. With all the coins authenticated by the Bermuda Monetary Authority, they comprise the Castle Island Collection, on display at the authority's headquarters on Burnaby Hill in Hamilton.

---

ers and craftsmen. They became known as the "King's Blacks." Eight years or so after the end of the war, most of these refugees were sent to Trinidad.

The arrival in 1824 of the *Antelope* marked an escalation of manpower and opened an entirely new chapter in the Yard's construction. On ship were 300 convicts from England. From then until 1863, housed on filthy prison ships called "convict hulks," thousands of prisoners were put to forcible labor, a development that ironically coincided with the slowly dying institution of slavery. Historian Roger Willock, in writing about that era, stated that "perhaps the most pleasant thing that can be said of, or written about, the convict establishment at Bermuda was that it was brought to a close in 1863."

Emancipation

Ten years after the first shipload of English convicts arrived in these waters, slavery was

abolished in the British colonies. But the months leading up to August 1, 1834, the Day of Emancipation, were filled with contradictions, greed and great sadness.

During that summer, the Emancipation Proclamation appearing in the local newspaper shared space with advertised slave auctions. And as slaves anticipated release from bondage, many slave owners noticed that impending abolition in the colonies had driven up prices of slaves sold in the United States. Although the British government had set aside 20 million pounds for distribution to its colonies as compensation for freed slaves, local owners transported their slaves out of Bermuda destined for American auction blocks, sometimes in dozen lots of "various shapes and sizes."

This continued up to the day before emancipation. During those final hours slaves were being marched to the Devonshire Dock and Flatts Inlet where, wrote author Nellie E. Musson, "rowboats carried them to the slave ships. Those who refused to walk were put in chains and carried away."

When August 1 did arrive, celebrations were joyous but muted as families attended various church services to pray for friends and family members transported from the island and sold overseas.

The Century Closes

It is said the first genuine tourist to Bermuda was the Rev. Michael Wigglesworth, who arrived in 1663 from Malden, Massachusetts, after a long and unpleasant voyage. Be that as it may, Bermuda did not begin to get a glimpse of its tourism possibilities until 1852, when a 36-room hotel was built in Hamilton.

Located in Pembroke Parish, Hamilton had replaced the Town of St. George as the island's capital in 1815 over the strenuous and bitter objections of that town's citizens. Centrally located with an excellent harbor, Hamilton was a logical choice. However, when the American Civil War broke out in 1861, Hamilton may have been the capital, but St. George hosted all the action.

When the Union-imposed blockade on Southern ports made direct shipments from abroad impossible, it was no surprise that Bermuda would once again become involved in matters affecting its closest neighbor. Strong family and commercial ties between prominent Bermudians and their counterparts in Virginia and other Southern states guaranteed the island would become one of the focal points of trade between Europe and the Confederacy. From headquarters in the old Globe Hotel on King's Square in St. George's, the Confederacy's chief political agent negotiated with shipping suppliers and agents, arranged payment for goods and secured the shipment of food, arms and ammunition destined for the South.

Blockade runners — shrewd seamen who could slip through the sea lanes past Union ships — crowded the alleys and byways of the small town. Money flowed freely. The town's merchants pocketed more gold and silver in one year than they had in any 10 previously. The economic bonanza lasted until its decline was sealed in January 1865, when Fort Fisher in North Carolina fell to a combined Union land and sea assault. The fort's 12-pounder Whitworths had protected blockade runners as they ran along the coast of the Carolinas and into the entrance of Cape Fear River. The news dismayed merchants in Bermuda, who were left holding surplus goods when the dust finally cleared. Within a year St. George's ancient alleys were once again tranquil and sedate.

Ten miles away, Hamilton seemed to have ignored the intrigue that marked activities at the East End. The city's business leaders were more concerned with promoting Bermuda as a welcoming place to visit for a restoration to good health. In 1874 the Bermuda government and the Quebec Steamship Company signed a contract establishing regular steamship service between New York and Bermuda. It was the beginning of a concerted thrust to develop tourism. When Princess Louise, daughter of Queen Victoria, visited the island in the winter of 1883, the owners of the Pembroke Hotel renamed it The Princess in her honor (see our Resort Hotels chapter).

But whether royalty or commoner, few visitors were as entranced as Mark Twain, who described Bermuda as "an earth-bound heaven." Twain's heaven, while starting to market itself overseas, still depended on an economy bolstered by agricultural exports to the United States and Canada. Steamship services subsidized by the government carried potatoes, arrowroot and onions to those markets.

This development and expansion of the agricultural trade had necessitated the importation of additional laborers several years earlier. In 1849, Bermuda had invited Portuguese agricultural workers from Madeira to come to the island on contract. The invitation was quickly accepted, the first dozen men and their families arriving in November on the ship *Golden Rule*. Throughout the rest of the century the Portuguese population grew, with the overwhelming majority continuing to be engaged in farming. Onions were the staple produce.

In fact, so critical was the onion that Twain observed during one of his visits, "The onion is the pride and joy of Bermuda. In her conversation, her pulpit, her literature, it is her most eloquent figure. In Bermuda metaphor, it stands for perfection."

In other words, an Englishman might be a Limey, but a Bermudian was an Onion and remains one to this day.

The 20th Century

As the doors to a new century flew open, Bermuda's economy pivoted on tourism development and maintenance of the agricultural trade. With export a major economic player, bringing visitors to these shores did not get into full swing until 1912, when a syndicate of merchants backed an advertising promotion in Atlantic City, New Jersey, that included an exhibit of live Bermuda fish. A year later this was followed up with a display at the Grand Central Palace in New York.

Tourism slowly began to achieve greater importance as Bermuda became increasingly popular as a winter resort. Yet, while spoken of as a place of legendary beauty and serenity, many simply did not know where it was. Its location was variously sited off the coast of Africa, Florida or in the West Indies. During a conversation between two elderly gentlemen watching a cricket match in London, one was heard to remark, "Bermuda is our stronghold in the Pacific!"

Early in the 1930s, a writer for the Bermuda Trade Development Board (the precursor of today's Department of Tourism) penned a vivid portrait that tried to capture every color of the rainbow. "The road to yesterday will take you far from the chill bleak cities of here and now," he wrote. "It will lead you to a gleaming group of coral isles, riotous with tropical colour, set in an azure sea, warmed by a golden sun that will flood your veins with youth. It is a soft road, paved with cushions of green, spume-flecked velvet, bordered with white flowers of healthy salt-spray."

On June 12, 1937, Darrell's Island Marine Airport, in the Great Sound, was opened, and the first commercial flight, a seaplane, touched down six days later. Jaded Americans tired of noise and nasty winters could now have their veins flooded with youth faster than voyaging here by sea. As tourism ascended, agriculture faced decline. Throughout the 1930s it was hit by American protective tariffs. By the 1940s domestic sales were more profitable. And as mid-century dawned, agricultural exports virtually died. Bermuda's economy now turned exclusively on tourism.

The '30s also brought the rumblings of social and political change. Blacks were becoming increasingly restless about discrimination and prejudice, and women began a long fight for voting rights. Despite being taxed equally with men, they were denied the vote. In 1923 the Bermuda Woman Suffrage Society had been founded, but after several years of trying and failing to be taken seriously, the society drew up a document and sent it to the Secretary of State for Colonies in London.

The 1929 petition, spearheaded by Mrs. Gladys Missick Morrell and a core of other determined women, requested that a Royal Commission examine the subject of women's suffrage. The petition was returned to local governing politicians for them to handle. They refused to budge. One stated reason was that women were "unduly dominated by clergy" and giving them the vote would lead to a "Priest-ridden Bermuda." Indignant, Mrs. Morrell traveled to London in 1931 for a face-to-face confrontation with Lord Passing, the Secretary of State, but her efforts were fruitless.

The suffrage struggle, initially an effort by white upper-class women, changed complexion as it entered the 1940s. Black women, hitherto written out of the scenario, were courted by Mrs. Morrell when she addressed a forum at a black club. By 1944, with the support of black women, the fight prevailed. The House of Assembly passed the voting measure by a 20 to 13 margin. That same year the first woman to cast her vote was Edna Williams Tucker, a black landowner. Mrs. Morrell saw out the end of 1944 and the beginning of 1945 as Bermuda's first elected vestrywoman. And in the 1948 general election, two women were elected to the House.

INSIDERS' TIP

The Hon. Premier Pamela Gordon is the first woman to hold the office of premier of Bermuda.

Photo: GIS

The Ducking Stool — punishment 17th-century style — is
the site of colorful re-enactments.

Railroad, Automobiles and Turtles in the Net

For many years the debate on the introduction of the motor car had been lobbed back and forth around the community. Bermudians in general were aghast at the thought of such contraptions spluttering and wheezing along peaceful country lanes, and a law prohibiting its importation brought sighs, perhaps even neighs, of relief. Horse power had served the island faithfully for centuries, but transportation could not remain forever dependent on dobbin (or, work horses). The decision to establish a railway was believed a suitable compromise as well as a deterrent to the automobile. Property was purchased by the Bermuda Railway Company, a syndicate of private investors, and bridges were erected, trestles raised along coastlines, tunnels cut and tracks laid from Somerset to St. George's.

When the first train ran on October 31, 1931, its presence was generally welcomed. But some visitors were appalled. The editor of *Harper's Bazaar* castigated it as "an iron serpent in the Garden of Eden." Although the railway proved a boon for those living at opposite ends of the island — scores of folk had never ventured out of Somerset or St. George's until the railway — the Garden of Eden was soon rid of its iron serpent. Costly to run, it was a financial disaster. In 1946 the government surprisingly purchased this losing enterprise, even as new legislation allowed the import of the motor car. By 1948 the train had become a snake needing only to be put out of its misery. A deal with British Guyana resulted in the sale of the train and its tracks to that country.

However, even as Bermuda continued to debate the relative merits of horse, road and rail throughout the life of the railway, a sea-related incident occurred five years after the train's introduction. Bermuda's waters were known for claiming vessels run aground on outlying reefs. In the 19th century, wreckers would row out to plunder these helpless "turtles in the net." In 1936 the Spanish ship *Cristobal Colon* joined the roster of turtles. Despite their best efforts, local authorities were unable to prevent the ship from being boarded and looted. For several months afterward, scores of homes were searched and the stolen goods were retrieved. One man, accused of having a radio taken from the wreck, protested indignantly, "Why would I steal a Spanish radio? I can't speak Spanish!"

American Bases

World War II brought in the American military. Britain appealed for help from the United States in the first year of the war, and in 1941 a House of Commons announcement by Sir Winston Churchill offered the Americans air base facilities on Bermuda for 99 years. It was a land-for-ships trade, with Britain receiving 50 U.S. destroyers.

On March 27, 1941, President Roosevelt and Prime Minister Churchill signed the Land Lease Agreement. As a result of this agreement, St. David's, a 500-acre island at the eastern end, was divided, with 250 acres taken over by the American military. Construction began quickly as a massive landfill project got under way with soil dredged from nearby Castle Harbour. When completed in 1943, homes and even graveyards had been buried forever.

During these war years, the island also hosted more than 100 British censors. The British government requisitioned the Princess and Bermudiana hotels, closed at the outbreak of war. The Princess became the focal point, where all mail between Europe and the United States was opened and the contents studied for microdots and coded messages. A few spies were indeed unmasked during this imperial censorship.

With the construction of the Kindley Air Force Base and the building of the Naval Air Station in Southampton completed by war's end, the economy was energized by the spending power of American personnel. Another distinct advantage was that the Kindley base was constructed in tandem with the Bermuda Civil Air Terminal, located at the base's west end.

In January 1946, Pan American airways began regularly scheduled flights from La Guardia in New York City to Kindley Field. Darrell's Island, which for nine years had been the entry point for visitors arriving by seaplane, was closed down.

Parties, Protest and Confrontation

Postwar resurrection of a stalled tourist trade gathered momentum in the '50s, but in this vital effort color prejudice dictated that the thrust be divided along black and white lines. While the white-controlled Bermuda Trade Development Board embarked on major promotions, black-owned hotels, guest houses, restaurants and clubs formed their own organizations to promote penetration of the black American market. These efforts were effective, and black tourist dollars directly benefited the local black community. Equally successful were the separate white promotions. Bermuda cashed in, but race problems lurked in the wings.

In 1959 NASA established a tracking station on Coopers Island, part of the East End base. The station participated in tracking the orbital flights of John Glenn and Walter Schirra and provided a crucial communications link when Apollo 11 made the first manned lunar landing in July 1969.

The same summer of the lunar landing and "one giant step for mankind," racial tensions that had been simmering finally bubbled to the surface. A peaceful boycott against segregated seating in cinemas continued until the color bar was dropped. White-owned hotels abandoned discrimination in their restaurants and nightclubs. The black community became more active in challenging racial frictions in the workplace. In 1963 the Progressive Labour Party (PLP) was founded to promote interests of the predominantly black working class. The following year the predominantly white United Bermuda Party (UBP), headed by Henry Tucker (later Sir Henry), was formed, and Bermudian politics entered an entirely new arena.

In 1966 a Bermuda Constitutional Conference attended by representatives from both parties was held in London. At the beginning of 1967, a new Parliamentary Election Act became law, granting "one man, one vote" to every British subject older than 21 and resident in Bermuda for three or more years. That summer a new Bermuda Boundaries Commission approved the division of the nine parishes into 40 voting constituencies.

On February 6, 1970, the Bermuda pound was scrapped and the island went decimal, welcoming dollars and cents. In August 1971 a dollar crisis that temporarily closed foreign exchanges saw Bermuda's banks refusing to accept U.S. currency and traveler's checks. The local government, in the interests of preserving a smooth-running tourist trade, then pegged the local currency to the American dollar.

The '70s were dominated by strikes and dissention, and by the decade's close, a police commissioner had been killed, a governor and his aide assassinated and their two killers executed. The violence and retribution that had claimed the lives of victims and perpetrators came as startling by-products of a violent element in the thrust for civil rights. But while the decade was marked by volatility, the island rejoiced in 1979 when Miss Bermuda, Gina Swainson, was crowned Miss World in London.

Toward the 21st Century

When Bermudians awoke on January 1, 1983, they found that whatever benefits they had received from carrying a British passport had been unceremoniously eliminated. As a result of a new British nationality law, they had become British Dependent Territory Citizens, and the old passport was invalid. Prior to this development, the original Bermudian passport allowed an almost automatic option of living and working in England without much of a problem. The new passport nullified that.

While tourism, once the island's unquestioned mainstay, vacillated, the construction industry found the 1980s an unequalled golden egg. By 1990 Hamilton literally doubled its commercial office space in the past decade, while home building also recorded significant gains.

It was a period of unbridled expansion. The resident population increased, employment grew 34 percent, and more cars cluttered the roads. The domestic economy was buoyant. Bermuda was ranked fourth in the world in per capita income and was loving it. The economic surge did not last, however. Development reached a plateau and tapered off as the country entered the '90s. Jobs in the construction trades declined. Bermuda began to experience the pains of unemployment in a way it never had before. And tourism, which had always led the economic charge, was trembling with a bad cold.

Concern over the state of the economy and the environment took center stage along with the issue of independence. The idea had bounced back and forth since the late '70s, when it was the subject of a 1978 Royal Commission. It emerged again as an issue in the mid-1990s, brought to the political front-burner by Bermuda's premier, Sir John Swan, the second black UBP leader. The majority of his party was set firmly against Bermuda's severing ties with Britain. The country was bitterly divided.

On August 16, 1995, an Independence Referendum, which failed to gain support from the PLP (who advised their members to abstain), was shot down in flames by voters. Only 58 percent of the electorate went to the polls, among them 18-year-olds who voted for the first time as a result of 1990 legislation. Faced with the defeat of his initiative, Premier Swan resigned.

Although the original Land Lease Agreement called for both military bases to revert to Bermudian ownership on March 27, 2040, on September 1, 1995, the Bermuda government took possession of the base properties after they ceased operations and were returned by the United States. With some 10 percent of Bermuda's total land mass returned, the government has embarked on a 20-year redevelopment plan involving both areas.

In March 1997, as the UBP regrouped, Pamela Gordon, daughter of legendary black Labor leader Dr. E.F. Gordon — a thorn in the side of the white establishment of the '40s and '50s — was voted premier. She is the first woman to hold the position. The previous year, Jennifer Smith was elected as the new leader of the PLP.

As the island winds toward the 21st century, it faces several critical issues, among them drug-related crime, the environment, educational restructuring (see our chapter on Education) and stalled tourism. They are Bermuda's most pressing challenges.

Yet Bermuda has always faced challenges and emerged stronger and revitalized. It is in the national genes it seems — a grit that turns adversity into an enviable prosperity.

From the sky, Bermuda's mainland appears as seven islands joined by bridges tiny enough to thread the eye of a needle, dotted by jellybean-colored houses.

Area Overviews

Viewed from several thousand feet, on the glide path into its airport, Bermuda appears a flat green carpet dropped in a pale blue puddle. It's mainland, seven islands joined by bridges tiny enough to thread the eye of a needle, is dotted by jellybean-colored houses topped by white roofs. They hug the landscape like candies in an emerald jar.

Outlying barrier reefs, burnished black and deep brown by wind and waves, are reminders that beneath a sea warmed by the gulf stream lie the bones of hundreds of once-proud ships. In this silent aquatic world, these skeletons have become home to sea fans, delicate sea anemones and purple sponges. Magnets for divers hopeful of retrieving some overlooked memento from another age, some of the vessels have indeed yielded genuine treasures.

Bermuda's physical beauty is undeniable, making it one of the most expensive pieces of beachfront in the world. But the island is more than just a pretty face. Scratch the surface, and just beneath the "tranquil and contenting" skin is a country that within 20 years has evolved from an almost mythical sleepy hollow into a dynamic international business hub.

The effect of this growth is reflected to varying degrees in all of the island's nine parishes, each named after a prominent shareholder in the Bermuda Company. The only exception is St. George's Parish, which was named after England's patron saint. Our parishes, originally called "tribes," were surveyed and divided by English mapmaker Richard Norwood, who began traversing the island in 1615 and finished the following year. However, the designation "tribe roads" (and not "parish roads) remains.

With the exception of St. George's, Hamilton and Smiths, every parish has them. Running north to south, they are public rights of way, and several are tiny, quiet lanes opening onto major arteries like South Road and Middle Road. Others are little more than footpaths.

In 1913 a Tribe Road Commission was appointed to look into these off-roads that often meander through the most unlikely places, some sliding past homes nestled behind stone walls deep in the heart of rural Bermuda. Their origin is not quite clear, though in 1620 the first government created specific pathways to deter persons from trespassing through corn patches and tobacco fields. Interestingly, the locations of these roads were never recorded on any map, and the commission identified 31 such roads remaining out of an estimated 46. Today most serve as shortcuts to somewhere else.

East End

The Town of St. George, on the cusp of a new makeover, is redefining its economic and physical terrain. Here, street names like Blockade Alley and Petticoat Lane have a quaint but often lurid history. Cultural tourism has become the password in an impetus by St. Georgians to preserve, develop and promote a lingering Old World ambiance.

A $20 million-plus, five-year project begun in the town in 1997 is motoring through the green light. Area plans include construction of a waterfront boardwalk beginning near the Ordnance Island cruise ship terminal, to run west along the harbor's edge and end at Penno's

Wharf. This is one of the principal features of a scheme that includes perking up the streets with the installation of antique-style lamps.

The planting of additional trees is directed toward an image-softening of King's Square, an ancient venue for floggings, executions and disciplining of gossiping women. The overall facelift has an additional goal: The St. George's Foundation, overseeing the project, ultimately seeks recognition of the town as a United Nations International Heritage Site.

www.insiders.com

See this and many other
Insiders' Guide® destinations
online — in their entirety.

Visit us today!

This small community, an enclave with minimal population growth since 1960, has taken some enervating economic body blows over the past decade or so, precipitated in 1987 by the temporary closure of the area's largest hotel (it was originally the St. George's Hotel, then a Holiday Inn, then a Club Med) following a particularly nasty hurricane. Temporary has ultimately become permanent. Atop a hill overlooking Fort St. Catherine, the once-popular landmark now begs conversion to something other than a vacant multimillion-dollar pink elephant.

But the town, once a mecca attracting adventurers and poets, clerics and pirates, has never lost its personality. Neither have its people. Many former St. Georgians have moved back to the area, buying and restoring old homes. Reserved but friendly, the people are fiercely loyal to their patch of turf. However, it takes time for "outsiders" to grow on them. As one old St. Georgian said recently to a "newcomer" who has been living there for more than 15 years, "You better say nice things about St. George's because the ink on your passport is not yet dry."

Just as loyal about their community are the residents of St. David's, a part of St. George's Parish lying just across the harbor south of the town. A short bus ride away, this area could be the poster community for quiet contemplation. Many of its original inhabitants claim Native American ancestry, their Pequot forebears renowned as intrepid whalers and superb boat builders. It is also from here that shark hash, turtle soup and fish chowder meandered across the island, establishing reputations for seducing the palate.

While the St. David's neighborhood has retained much of its traditional flavor, other neighborhoods throughout the island have not, with two main factors contributing to a seemingly unavoidable, certainly sobering impact.

The increased migration of people from parish to parish over the past 20 years has seen new local and non-local faces reshaping neighborhoods and ultimately parish characters. Once considerably more distinct, with easily definable personalities, most parishes have succumbed to cookie-cutter profiles.

Although reflecting diversity through expanded populations, several have lost the intimacy once common within neighborhoods where everyone knew everyone else. Among them, Southampton has recorded the largest influx of people at 26 percent since 1980. And while housing developments in Warwick, Devonshire, Hamilton and Smiths parishes have stimulated the economy, they have also redefined much of those parishes' ambient characteristics. Yet, some subtleties do remain.

As we travel through the parishes during the summer months, we find temporary stands where snowballs — crushed and flavored ices — are sold to thirsty motorists and curious visitors. This is the local cousin to the sidewalk lemonade stand, and Bermudians are just wild about the simple sweet treat.

Fishermen selling the day's catch in island neighborhoods and at roadside locations are as indelible a part of local life as are the longtails, Bermuda's unofficial harbingers of spring (see our Flora and Fauna chapter). Returning from their sea journey, the longtails

---

INSIDERS' TIP

Courtesy is very important to Bermudians. We mind our p's and q's, and we also like our "Good mornings," "Good afternoons" and "Good evenings."

can be seen cavorting around shorelines between March and October, soaring on air currents, sweeping in graceful aerial courtships.

And while courtship between these satin-white, open-ocean birds leads to them laying eggs in crevices and holes in rugged sea cliffs, Bermuda's own courtship of international businesses continues to attract more and more Fortune 500 companies to the island's economic nest. Their presence has made Bermuda the world's leading domicile for the insurance and reinsurance industries (see our International Business chapter).

City of Hamilton

Hamilton, Bermuda's capital, is the nucleus for this emergence onto the global theater, firmly putting the lie to the island's motto: *Quo Fata Ferunt* or, "whither the fates carry us," an adaptation from Virgil's *Aenid* . . . (and so we set sail, though none could say where fate may take or settle us). Bermuda has indeed hoisted sails, but its fate is manipulated not by chance but by determined political and economic policies.

The city's skyline has stretched higher as Hamilton itself continues to inch outward, absorbing every potential chunk of commercial and industrial real estate. The wrecker's ball has claimed many old buildings — to the consternation of preservationists — that were architectural remnants from an era when horse, buggy and bicycle left their tracks in the dust of narrow roadways.

Commensurate with this brisk growth and development has been a marked population exodus from within the city boundaries, hastened by increased commercial use of existing and new buildings. An efficient public transportation system has also aided expansion. But transportation has bred its own array of issues. If there is a leading vote-getter in the environmental grab bag of Bermudian dichotomies, it is found in the number of motor vehicles whose wheels daily hit the island's 1,346 named roads.

Photo: GIS

This aerial view features the revitalized Royal Naval Dockyard area.

When cars were introduced for private use in 1946, the prediction was that they would never exceed 1,000. It was a wishful peek into the future and deserves a blue-ribbon prize for optimism. The leap from horse power to horsepower has resulted in the current number of motorized vehicles (including auxiliary cycles, private cars and other commercial vehicles) exploding to 49,000, slightly less than half of which jostle into Hamilton each morning and limp out every evening.

Yet, while Hamilton is by turns both brash and coy, with the surrounding countryside stepping daintily to the cadence of economic progress, golden arches have been rejected and neon glitz spurned. And you won't find billboards cluttering our highways. This may seem surprising, for this colony has embraced North American habits with a passion. But it does attempt to hold on to its homegrown traditions — like "lunch wagons."

Similar to big converted vans, and with a dedicated clientele, only three of these mobile dispensers of fast food survive. Each proprietor is confined to operating his business from set locations within the city limits. Businessmen in Bermuda shorts rub elbows with construction workers in overalls, and secretaries and government workers line up to be served homemade hamburgers and beef pies. These wagons are, in cultural ethos, reminiscent of the heyday of the North American diner.

But even as Bermuda celebrates a high standard of living fueled largely by the American visitor, it is plowing through the middle, or more accurately, the muddle of coming to grips with changed and changing population and business dynamics. Significant numbers of the workforce have been caught flat-footed and unprepared for the 21st-century workplace. Global corporate giants, almost 9,000 of which are registered here to take advantage of tax breaks (see our International Business chapter), have generated a rapid social and financial metamorphosis that has yanked the island, in some instances kicking and screaming, toward the next millennium.

The construction industry, which toppled from '80s boom to a pronounced early '90s bust, gathered a second wind in 1997 with some $70 million spent in the first three-quarters on private and public sector expansion and renovation.

Although the business of Bermuda has always been business (former finance minister and premier Dr. David Saul dubbed the island "Bermuda Inc."), other issues, including those related to protection of the environment, have merged into the day-to-day lives of citizens.

West End

Whatever the vagaries of the weather — and local weather can at times be remarkably capricious — there are no signs of the island experiencing an economic drought. Even as Hamilton and St. George's repaint the signposts to prosperity, the West End municipalities have not been couch potatoes. On the contrary, Somerset Village, through which buses en route to the Royal Naval Dockyard must travel, has asserted itself. Still, its neighbor, the Dockyard, heads the list of places in which to kick back and relax.

There is big sky and open spaces at the "Yard," a place from which men once set to sea to do battle. An hour away from Hamilton by bus or a 30-minute ferry ride past sheltered bays and inlets (some rides are longer, depending on the stops along the way), this westernmost area has been sculpted from its original architectural shell.

Rising from the ashes of neglect more than 10 years ago like a mid-Atlantic phoenix, the Dockyard has been transformed from a tarnished Victorian eyesore into a charming wa-

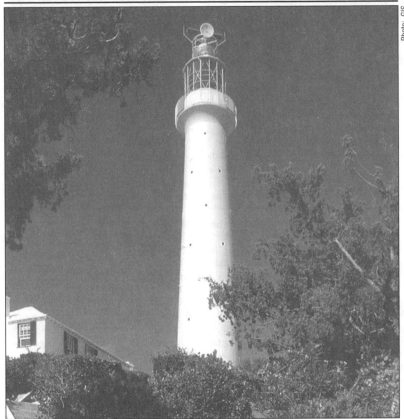

Photo: GIS

Visitors are invited to climb to the top of Gibb's Hill Lighthouse for the commanding, 360-degree view it affords of the island.

terfront village. More than 50 businesses are located within the solid, thick-walled, renovated buildings that are a legacy of British sea power in the Atlantic. Dilapidated storehouses, foundries, power plants and timber yards have been replaced by restaurants, a Maritime Museum (see Attractions), an Arts Centre, a movie theater and a score of other amenities.

Environment

The pecking away at open spaces and green belts on the island has alarmed environmentalists. During the past 15 years farmers have taken some serious hits. The long-term future of their industry is inextricably linked to the extent of the protection of Bermuda's arable land. Between 1981 and 1991 the distribution of farmlands — and their sizes — throughout the nine parishes declined.

While there are more than 1,500 individual fields, only two exceed 5 acres, and the overwhelming majority are a half-acre or less. Although the Department of Agriculture, Fisheries and Parks plays a critical role in promoting the farming industry, housing developments have taken an irreversible toll. Subdivision has fragmented many neighboring fields and ruptured the integrity of several farm units. This situation is aptly illustrated by one of Bermuda's major farmers having to cultivate 25 acres broken up over seven parishes.

If there is a leading environmental beacon, it is not found in tracts of farmland, but on

Nonsuch Island, a 14.5-acre preserve of native and endemic plant and animal species. Sited southeast of Castle Harbour, and privately owned until purchased by government in the late 19th century, it is frequently referred to as a living museum.

On this patch of ground, Dr. David Wingate, the chief conservation officer, has carved a vivid recreation of "Las Bermudas," prior to man cutting a swath through pristine forests. A virtual Eden has been forged, with land and sea birds, native crabs and the Bermuda skink (related to the lizard) living among cedars and other tree species.

Wingate, who lives on Nonsuch, has also played the key role in saving Bermuda's oldest bird species, the cahow (pronounced KA-how) from extinction. Believed to have gone the way of the Dodo before the turn of the century, the cahow's ultimate survival is a story of a man who has dedicated himself to saving it, and of a creature that has refused to die.

However, with just over a few dozen nesting pairs — a far cry from its estimated population approaching one million when the island was discovered — the cahow, roughly the size of a pigeon but with a larger wingspan, has been seen by few. It spends most of its life floating low over ocean waves, coming ashore only to breed. (See our Flora and Fauna chapter for much more on the birds and animals of Bermuda.)

Cave Systems

Among the unique and attractive aspects of the local environment are the natural caves. The eastern end of Harrington Sound, a virtually landlocked body of water bordered by Hamilton and Smiths parishes, is where the concentration of caves is highest. Formed thousands of years ago when the island perched much higher above sea level, today many of these caves are underwater. Created by acidic rainwater filtering through soft limestone, several of them interconnect below ground to form extensive and far-reaching systems. Crystal Cave, said to have been discovered by two boys looking for their lost cricket ball, is the best known (see our Attractions chapter), drawing thousands annually to its cool and quiet beauty.

But Bermuda's caves have an added ecological importance. Several species of shrimp unique to the island live in the marine caves, and endemic Bermuda cave ferns have been discovered just within and close to above-water entrances.

Sadly, many cave systems have been compromised or destroyed by careless disposal of garbage and the encroachments of stone quarrying and housing construction. Toward the end of 1997, battle lines were drawn when environmentalists challenged the proposal of a private company seeking to build a $65 million housing development above a Hamilton Parish cave system that contained 11 endangered species of microscopic shrimp-like creatures.

Studies commissioned by each side proved contradictory. However, what generally emerged was that chlorine from pools and pesticides from gardens could threaten the delicate ecology of the cave system if allowed to permeate the soil and seep through natural fissures above the cave.

Water Resources

Few things are as critical to Bermuda as its water supplies. The island does not have the luxury of streams, rivers or freshwater lakes. We rely instead on water caught via roofs and on underground "lens" — caves of water lying deep below ground.

The full potential of the four major supply areas — St. George's, Somerset, Southampton and the Central Lens, which covers nearly 1,700 acres and sprawls under much of Pembroke, Devonshire and Smiths parishes — has only been tapped within the last couple of decades. Monitored by the hydrogeology section of the Department of Works and Engineering, their total capacity is in the billions of gallons.

INSIDERS' TIP

The average tides in Bermuda rise and fall between three and four feet.

Approximately 30 percent of the island's annual rainfall permeates the ground to replenish these lens, from which an average of 1.5 million gallons are extracted daily. The water is treated and chlorinated to health department standards, purchased by homeowners and delivered by private water truckers when tanks under houses run dry, a common occurrence during summers when rainfall is below normal, precipitating near drought-like conditions.

Race and Immigration

Sustaining an upward economic curve has required the immigration via work permits of non-Bermudians into the local workplace. The physical presence of hundreds of international corporations, and particularly those in the brokerage, chemical and insurance fields, has resulted in growing numbers of professional guest workers moving here with their families for varying periods of time. And in the service sectors of tourism, foreign workers are filling gaps. The most recent census of population and housing reveals that non-Bermudians comprise 19.1 percent of a total population of 58,460. These numbers have sparked some local feelings of resentment toward the foreign-born worker.

This side of the socioeconomic coin is generally kept fairly well hidden, and relationships for the most part are conducive to good business. However, while there are enclaves of social, racial and financial separatism, any echoes of Marx vanished in the Bermuda Triangle long ago, and racial violence is nonexistent.

An insight into our society may be gleaned through a perusal of the *Royal Gazette's* letters to the editor, through not only their content, but the large percentage written by persons lobbing ideas, opinion and biases from behind the net of the pseudonym. To use a real name seems almost a badge of courage. However, bear in mind that Bermudians traditionally don't believe in airing spoiled linen in public, especially to guests. As perfect hosts, we prefer to kick these things around in our own backyard. Taking up the cudgels against racism is a case in point.

Five years ago, in bringing the subject to the social front burner, *RG Magazine* conducted a series of monitored interviews of blacks and whites drawn from almost every financial and social strata. The results indicated that many, perhaps most, black and white respondents recognized the lingering problem, and expressed disgust with prevailing racial divisions.

These and other challenges notwithstanding, Bermuda is facing the better of times, has largely sidestepped the worst and is gradually learning to cope with onrushing social and technological change. Future shock may be here, but it is losing some of its sting under bright blue skies.

On the upside of all of this is the fact that most Bermudian residents, whether local or foreign, are devoted to fostering a society that is more than a mere parody of tranquility and friendliness. At the end of the day, there is a reputation to uphold, and nobody does it better.

You can't rent a car while visiting Bermuda, but just like Bermuda sunshine, taxi service is plentiful.

Getting Here, Around and Home

You can travel to Bermuda by major airline. You can fly here in a corporate jet. You can come by cruise ship or in your own private yacht, sailing across oceans deep. One thing is certain: No matter what mode of transportation you choose to reach our friendly shores, you should be prepared to let yourself go and experience a way of life touched by the gracious hospitality of Bermudians.

Centuries ago referred to as the "Isle of Devils," our tiny 21-mile-long island has evolved into a cosmopolitan region attracting both tourists and corporate clientele from around the globe. Bermuda is a delightful mix of Old World cultures, where the pace may be a wee bit slower than you are accustomed to. Some sound Insiders' advice is to relax, take a deep breath and enjoy our less-stressful approach to living. Whether you're strolling along Front Street or putting together a multimillion-dollar business transaction, when in Bermuda, do as the Bermudians do. Regardless of how laid-back we may appear, you'll learn to appreciate that things do get done quite effectively and in a timely fashion.

Getting Here By Air

No matter the distance you have to travel by air to reach Bermuda, you'll be pleasantly surprised upon arrival. Starting when you are asked to fasten your seat belts, you sense an air of excitement filling the cabin. Watches are reset to reflect the change to Bermuda time. Looking out a window of the plane just before you land, you'll see a panoramic view of a breathtaking scene that's straight off a postcard: crystal-clear aquamarine waters lapping over shadowed coral reefs; lush, tropical green land scattered with a kaleidoscope of colored houses accented with mint-white slated roof tops sparkling in the reflection of the sun's rays.

According to figures released from the Bermuda Department of Tourism, during 1996, 391,450 visitors arrived in Bermuda via airplane from North America, Canada, the United Kingdom and Europe. Of that figure, 294,065 visited during the peak season of April through October. Part of Bermuda's appeal as a prime vacation destination is its proximity to the east coast of the United States — it's easily accessible by airplane.

Bermuda's first airport was the sea itself. On January 7, 1931, a young married couple flew a biplane from the United States and landed in the harbor at Albouys Point in Hamilton. Bermuda has had several airports connected to the naval fleets stationed here. Darrell's Island Marine Airport, in the Great Sound, formally opened on June 12, 1937. A Cavalier flying boat of Imperial Airways (now

British Airways) made the first commercial flight from Bermuda a few days before on June 6, 1937. Twelve passengers made the six-hour journey to Port Washington, New York.

During World War II, Darrell's Island became a vital mid-Atlantic refueling point for military aircraft, but the construction of U.S. bases here diminished its importance, and the final seaplane service was in 1946. Bermuda's civilian air terminal — at the western end of what was then the U.S. base at St George's — developed toward the end of World War II. The expansion of the airport has continued to this day.

In 1995 the United States government closed McKinley Naval Air Base. With the closure, the air traffic control services that had served the island for 50 years departed as well. Bermuda assumed total responsibility for the whole operation of the newly named Bermuda International Airport. Changing from a military to a civilian air facility has involved some major alterations and upgrades to international civil aviation standards.

FYI

Unless otherwise noted, the area code for all phone numbers listed in this guide is 441.

Bermuda International Airport

2 Kindley Field Rd., St. George's Parish
• 293-2470

On June 1, 1995, USAirways Flight 599 was the first flight to land here with the airport under the island's control. Since that flight it has been business as usual for Bermuda's only airport, with Canadian-based Serco Aviation Service providing infrastructure maintenance and running ground operations: namely, air traffic control; meteorological services; crash, fire and rescue services; and ground electronics systems.

The Bermuda International Airport continues to undergo major physical renovations to help better accommodate visitors arriving on and leaving the island. With the 1996 completion of a refurbishing project and those proposed for the next several years, an excess of $17 million will have been spent on upgrading the airport facilities. These architectural changes are immediately noticeable because they are both aesthetically pleasing and functional. The airport will soon provide for those in transit a new, duty-free shopping mall (expected in 1998) and a food court for refreshments.

Commercial Flights

There are eight commercial airlines offering transportation to Bermuda. All except British Airways, which operates on a three-day schedule, provide service seven days a week. During peak season from March to November most of the airlines increase the number of flights per day. It is best to verify flight information with your travel agent or wholesaler or call the airline services directly before arranging your visit here.

The following commercial airlines fly to Bermuda.

From the U.S.

American Airlines, (800) 433-7300, offers daily nonstop service from New York City (JFK) and Boston. The number of flights increases during peak season. Continental Airlines, (800) 231-0856, has nonstop service from Newark, New Jersey. This flight is also subject to change without notice. Delta Airlines, (800) 221-1212, flies nonstop from Boston and Atlanta. USAirways, (800) 622-1015, offers nonstop flights from Baltimore/Washington, Charlotte, Philadelphia and New York (LaGuardia).

Outside the U.S.

Air Canada, (800) 776-3000, offers nonstop service from Toronto and Halifax, with connecting services throughout Canada and Europe. The flights from Halifax are seasonal. Continental Airlines and United Airlines are Air Canada's U.S. partners. From the U.K., British Airways, (800) 354-8722, has nonstop service from London (Gatwick) on Tuesdays,

Thursdays and Saturdays. For individuals traveling from Europe, British Airways provides connecting flights. Contact your travel agent or call the airline directly.

Private and Leased Air Craft

The Bermuda International Airport functions as an exempt company base for private aircraft owned by Bermuda-based international businesses and traveling executives and as a landing point for those individuals who fly their own planes.

From April through October, 25 to 30 (sometimes it's as high as 60) private aircraft normally fly here within any given five-day period. December, January and February are the slowest months for this area of the airport.

It is a requirement of the Bermuda government that all private and leased aircraft exercising commercial traffic rights arrange to be ground-handled by an approved agency. There are two authorized independent handling agencies in Bermuda that reserve the right to accept or reject any request for service. They are **Bermuda Aviation Service Ltd.**, P.O. Box HM 719, Hamilton HM CX, 293-2500; VHF frequency: 131.6 MHz, and **Mid-Atlantic Aviation Ltd.**, Suite 43, P.O. Box 11 GE CX, Bermuda Air Terminal, 293-4622; VHF frequency: 131.65 MHz

These agencies act as island-based representatives for the crew and passengers aboard private or leased aircraft. The agency handles all customs and immigration procedures, assuring that documentation is in order; aircraft-related requirements and services; tolling; coordination in provision of hangar services; and transportation for crew and passengers.

An Executive Aircraft Handling Facility is due to open at the airport in the near future. It will serve as a lounge and communication center for business executives, private aircraft passengers and crew.

Immigration Procedures

After leaving your airline you will enter the new arrivals/departures walkway and the recently refurbished Immigrations Hall. Once inside, you'll see lines for Bermuda residents and for visitors, who may again be divided as U.S. residents and residents of other foreign countries. Once in line, an immigrations officer will verify your documentation for entry into Bermuda as quickly as possible.

While still aboard the plane, flight attendants should have provided an opportunity for you to complete your Bermuda Immigration Visitor Arrival Card. You can't enter Bermuda without completing this card. Immigration officers will request it, along with additional valid ID. You will be asked to verify whether this is your first visit and where you will be staying while on the island. As in most countries, the immigration area is a no-nonsense place where detailed procedures are carried out in processing forms. If you do not have the forms completed or do not have the proper identification, you will be asked to leave the Immigrations Air Arrival Facility, and an officer will assist you into an office to help expedite your processing.

Once you've received your valid stamp to enter Bermuda, you will be able to pick up your luggage in the baggage area. Depending on when you visit, you may find this area under repair as well. Work on the Customs Hall and traffic flow/ parking areas of the airport is due to be finished sometime in 1998.

Coming and Going

To enter Bermuda you must present the following documents to the Immigration Office.

All Arriving Passengers (visitors)
- Valid passport
- Return airline ticket
- Completed Bermuda Immigration Visitor Arrival Card.

U.S. Citizens (visitors)
- Return airline ticket
- Completed Bermuda Immigration Visitor Arrival Card
- One of the following:
—Valid passport
—U.S. birth certificate and photo ID
—U.S. Naturalization Certificate and photo ID
—Voter registration card and photo ID

U.S. Residents (visitors)
- Valid passport
- Return airline ticket
- Completed Bermuda Immigration Visitor Arrival Card

Returning Bermuda Residents
- Valid passport
- Completed Bermuda Immigration Residents Arrival Card
- Entry or Re-entry permit (where applicable)

Arrive by Air, Leave by Ship
- Proof of citizenship
- Cruise ship ticket
- Completed Bermuda Immigration Visitor Arrival Card

Public Transport
BERMUDA

Buses...

A great way to see
Bermuda
and all its attractions

Customs

Inside the baggage hall, Skycap Porter Service workers can assist with your luggage and guide you to the Customs Hall. You can also trust these knowledgeable folks to help you find the correct line in customs to help expedite your clearance. Once a customs officer has examined your baggage (the extent of this check will vary from officer to officer; your luggage contents may not be checked at all, but be prepared to have your things looked through), the same Skycap will meet you on the other side of the line, reload your luggage and walk you into the arrival area and the sunny skies of Bermuda.

Her Majesty's Customs Regulations

Visitors to Bermuda may bring their own personal clothing and valuables with them duty-free (no tax). This includes such items as sports equipment, cameras, hair dryers, a portable TV or radio, small computer, travel iron, etc., provided these items accompany the visitor when departing the island. Liquor, wine and tobacco are also duty-free, but strict quantity measures are enforced. Only 1 quart of wine or other spirits, 200 cigarettes, 1 pound of tobacco and 50 cigars are allowed. A reasonable amount of beer may be brought in for personal consumption, but a duty must be paid — about 30¢ per can or bottle.

Visitors may bring in gifts with no more than a total value of $30. As long as the gift is not intended for resale, it is duty-free. Anything worth more than $30 is subject to customs duty. Some foods are dutiable between the rate of 5 percent and 22.25 percent of value.

There is no quarantine facility in Bermuda; hence customs will not allow you to import plants, fruits, vegetables or pets without an import permit from the Department of Agriculture and Fisheries, 169 South Shore Road, Paget Parish, 236-4201. All plants, fruits and vegetables will be held for inspection as their importation is strictly regulated. Animals arriving without proper documentation will be refused entry and returned to the port of origin. Each animal must be accompanied by a general health certificate issued by a licensed veterinarian within 10 days of its arrival in Bermuda. Pets that come in and leave with visitors are duty-free.

All prescription medications must be declared to the customs officer, and the quantity should be sufficient only for the duration of your stay. Note that the government of Bermuda is very concerned about illegal drugs and the negative impression of the island drugs can cause. Laws in Bermuda pertaining to the importation of drugs are designed to protect the local people and the visitor. We strongly suggest that visitors do not attempt to import any illegal drugs (or anything that may appear strange or not easily identifiable as legal, for that matter), as such action will only cause embarrassment at the airport and might ruin your stay with a visit to a Bermudian jail.

The same strict penalties apply to firearms. You cannot import any firearm or ammunition into Bermuda without a license granted by the Commissioner of Police. Normally such licensing would be granted only to visiting rifle club members attending a meet in Bermuda. Spear guns and a variety of dangerous weapons (handguns, rifles, etc.) are treated as firearms, but antique weapons made more than a century ago can be imported as long as the importer can prove the item is antique. For yacht captains, Verey pistols or signal guns are classified as firearms.

Although examination of your luggage by customs is most often necessary, follow the established guidelines, and it will be a mere formality carried out pleasantly and quickly.

Leaving the Airport

So, now that you've touched down, your documentation is in order and you've cleared customs, what's next? Well, unless someone is picking you up, you'll need transportation from the airport to where you are staying.

As you leave the customs clearance hall at the airport, you'll find the arrival hall is directly outside. Don't expect to see any signs advertising Hertz or Avis, because there are no "drive yourself" cars for rent in Bermuda. We realize that may be difficult to accept, but don't fret. Take our word: Transportation is readily available, and getting around our island by using alternate modes of transportation can be a charming and fun approach to finding the many hidden treasures tucked away here in paradise.

Taxi Service

OK, so you can't rent a car while visiting Bermuda. Just like Bermuda sunshine, taxi service is plentiful. No matter what time your plane arrives, Bermuda's taxi services are readily available to serve you directly from the airport's new Taxi Holding Facility (something you won't find at many metropolitan airports) adjacent to the arrival hall.

Some Insiders maintain taxi drivers are Bermuda's best ambassadors. Proud of their heritage, they're brimming with information about the history and geographical layout of the island. Most taxi drivers are ready tour guides and enjoy conversing with the passengers — sharing facts and folklore about their homeland.

Hailing a taxi is one of the easiest ways to get around our island. From the airport, expect to ride four to six persons in a group, depending on the amount of luggage you have. It costs about 25¢ for each piece of luggage carried in the boot (trunk) or on the roof of a cab.

All taxi services, independent or incorporated, must meet the professional standards set and controlled by the Bermuda Transport Control Department, the sole authority for the issue of licenses to operate and drive a taxi.

Some of the frequently used taxi operators in Bermuda include:

Bermuda Taxi Radio Cabs Ltd., Trott Road, Hamilton, 295-4141.

B.I.U. Taxi Co-op Transportation, 40 Union Street, Hamilton, 292- 4476.

Bermuda Taxi Operators Company Ltd., P.O. Box HM 1433, Hamilton HM FX, 292-4175.

Bermuda Taxi Services Ltd., P.O. Box HM 2252, Hamilton HM JX, 295-8294.

Trott Travel Ltd., P. O. Box HM 721, Hamilton HM CX, 295-0041.

In Bermuda, taxi rates are metered, and the tariffs are fixed by law. These fares are for the taxi only and not the individual passengers, which means there are per-rider charges. Taxi fares are also set to reflect Bermuda currency; in other words, don't expect to find stateside prices. You may hire a taxi by the hour, day or mile by hailing them on the street, at the taxi stand at the larger hotels or by telephone. All taxis are equipped with two-way radios and meters.

There are no reduced fares for children. However, two children younger than 12 count as one passenger. Note that when hiring a taxi, you'll receive the first five minutes free. Once you're seated in the taxi, the meter is set at $3.12 for one to four passengers and $3.90 for five to six passengers. There are five rates of fare (including surcharge rates) that apply to both four- and six-seated taxis. The following rates were effective as of January 1997 and are subject to change.

Rate 1: per mile from 6 AM to midnight for one to four passengers is $4.80 for the first mile. Each additional mile is $1.68.

Rate 3: per mile from 6 AM to midnight for five to six passengers is $6 for the first mile. Each additional mile is $2.10.

Surcharge rates add additional charges at various times. Surcharges apply to Rate 1 at 25 percent of the regular fare from midnight to 6 AM for one to four passengers, and all day Sunday and on public holidays for one to four passengers.

Surcharge rates (**Rate 4**) apply on Rate 1 at 50 percent from midnight to 6 AM for five or six passengers, and all day on Sunday and public holidays for five or six passengers.

Taking a sightseeing tour by taxi is a comfortable way to observe some of the more remote locations on the island. Tour rates are set by the hour starting at $30 (**Rate 2**) for one to four passengers and $42 (**Rate 5**) for five to six passengers.

Should you have any concerns regarding taxi service, contact the Bermuda Transport Control Department on weekdays between the

---

INSIDERS' TIP

Illicit drugs and firearms are strictly prohibited in Bermuda. Importation of these items can lead to imprisonment and heavy fines.

hours of 8:30 AM and 4:45 PM at 292-1271. When filing a complaint, you must be able to supply the taxi license number, date, time and journey.

Airport Coaches

When planning transportation from the airport, you can also hire one of two different airport coach services. The limousine-bus services seat 20 to 26 passengers, with one company also offering six-seater vans. These air-conditioned vehicles travel between the airport and the hotels. Bookings must be made in advance — either by a travel agent or by directly contacting the companies: **Bee-Line Transportation (Bda) Ltd.**, P.O. Box HM 2270, Hamilton HM JX, 293-0303, and **Bermuda Hosts Ltd.**, P.O. Box CR 46, Hamilton Parish CR BX, 293-1334.

You will be charged individually when riding an airport coach. The zone you are bound for determines the rate, with prices increasing the farther you travel away from the airport. You can arrange to ride one way or purchase a round-trip fare to return to the airport when leaving the island. Rates include baggage but do not include payments such as gratuities for the driver.

Getting Here By Water

Cruise Ships

Cruising to Bermuda aboard a luxury ocean liner is a popular mode of transportation enjoyed by singles, couples, families and business executives. From April through December as many as 180,000 visitors travel to Bermuda by cruise ship, with close to 35,000 of them traveling during July, a peak month for cruises.

Cruise liners destined for our island in the sun depart from Baltimore, Boston, Florida, Philadelphia and New York City and travel about 36 to 48 hours before entering Bermuda waters. For some visitors, cruise ships are ideal because they are an economical, all inclusive means of travel providing most everything you could possibly need on vacation. Similar to a resort hotel, most cruise liners have suites, boutiques, a swimming pool, a spa and workout area, a beauty salon, dining rooms, nightclubs, a movie theater, a chapel and more.

If you are planning on taking a cruise to Bermuda, there are as many packages available to suit your budget as there are ways to enjoy yourself once your ship berths in either Hamilton, St. George's or Dockyard. Note that some of the cruise ships that come to Bermuda are too large to berth at any of our docks. For these liners, a specially arranged ferry run by Bermuda's Marine and Ports Department accommodates the ships anchored in Bermuda waters. The ferry is scheduled to run from Somerset to Dockyard on Tuesday, Wednesday and Thursday evenings to carry cruise passengers to port for shore excursions, shopping and other Bermuda encounters, then to take them back to the ship.

Bermuda on Cruise Control

Five cruise ships service Bermuda regularly, and five additional ships visit on occasion. We suggest you contact a travel agent to arrange traveling by cruise ship to Bermuda.

• *Dreamward* of the Norwegian Cruise Line carries 1,242 passengers and 513 crew members. It arrives in Hamilton on Monday and departs on Thursday from April through November.

• *Royal Majesty* of Majesty Cruise Lines carries 1,056 passengers and 518 crew members. She arrives in St. George's on Tuesday and departs on Friday from April through November.

• *Horizon* of Celebrity Cruises carries 1,374 passengers and 693 crew members. This ship arrives in the West End on Tuesday and departs Friday from April through October.

• *Zenith*, also of Celebrity Cruises, carries 1,374 passengers and 693 crew members. She arrives in Hamilton on Monday and departs on Tuesday from April through October.

• *Song of America* of the Royal Caribbean Cruise Line carries 1,402 passengers along with 500 crew members arrives in Hamilton

on Tuesday and departs on Friday from April to November.

Other cruise liners that visit Bermuda on occasion are include **Crystal Harmony** of Crystal Cruises; **QE2** and **Royal Viking Sun** of Cunard's Cruises; **Costa Victoria** of Costa Cruise Lines; and **Maasdam** of the Holland America Lines.

The same travel documentation is needed when traveling aboard a cruise ship as when traveling by air into Bermuda (see the Coming and Going section earlier in this chapter). Visas are not required of passengers from the United States and most other countries. Exceptions are nationals from the following places:

Albania, Algeria, Armenia, Azerbaijan, Belarus, Bosnia-Hercegovina, Bulgaria, China, Croatia, Cuba, the former Czechoslovakia, Georgia, Haiti, Iran, Iraq, Jordan, Kampuchea (Cambodia), Kazakhstan, Kirgizstan, Lebanon, Libya, Macedonia, Mongolia, Morocco, Nigeria, North Korea, Romania, Russian Federation, Slovakia, Slovenia, the former Soviet Union, Sri Lanka, Syria, Tajikstan, Tunisia, Turkmenistan Ukraine, Uzbekistan, Vietnam (North and South) and Yugoslavia (Federal Republic of Serbia).

All cruise ship passengers pay a $60 tax, collected in advance by the shipping line. Presently, children younger than 2 are exempt from the tax.

Types of Cruises

Traveling aboard a cruise ship can be a creative, adventurous way for corporations to approach business and training sessions. Many travel agencies are developing unique packages that arrange for on-ship conventions, seminars, business meetings and other ventures. These specialty cruises are growing in popularity, allowing business to be done during the day and leaving the evening open for fun. It is also a great way to combine business with pleasure.

Various theme cruises are also on the rise not only for singles, seniors and families, but also for church groups, clubs and other organizations that enjoy traveling by cruise ship. If you're enjoying a special event or occasion when taking your cruise, inform your travel agent beforehand if you want to have a celebration. Also, to better enjoy your cruise, remember to make your dining arrangements (time of meals and whether you desire a smoking or smoke-free area) with your travel agent.

Cruising to Bermuda is also a great opportunity for pampering yourself at the ship's spa, gym or hair salon. Book these appointments early, because spaces fill up rapidly. This will save you the hassle of scheduling appointments while in port and give you more time to enjoy the island.

Sailing to Bermuda

Navigating full sail on crystal clear, quiescent waters beneath Bermuda's blue skies is the realization of many a captain's fantasy. Even to watch the ships from afar, this picturesque scene conjures images of grandeur. It is still common for skippers to enjoy the pleasure of sailing from the east coast to Bermuda, which is some 640 nautical miles from Norfolk, Virginia, and 687 nautical miles from Boston.

Although various types of small craft have successfully completed passage to Bermuda, it is suggested that a boat be at least 30 feet long to avoid excessive risk and discomfort. However, a well-equipped vessel of 35 feet with a seasoned crew of at least four or five should be satisfactory for a normal ocean passage.

Bermuda is not in a trade wind zone, and the northeasterly flow of weather systems over the Eastern Seaboard of the United States continues over the island. According to the Bermuda Department of Tourism, private yachts sailing to Bermuda during the summer months will find a high-pressure cell between the Azores and Bermuda that usually produces a wind speed averaging 15 knots. Referred to as a Bermuda-Azores High, it is the predominant meteorological factor for sailors. The Gulf Stream also has an effect on our weather. Its northward flow between the United States and Bermuda warms the island's waters and stabilizes the climate.

If you are considering piloting a ship to Bermuda, note that there is much more weather information in our Flora and Fauna chapter, including a Close-up on hurricanes. Our Yachting and Marinas chapter provides comprehensive information on sailing to and from Bermuda.

Getting Around Bermuda

When tourists first started coming to Bermuda more than a century ago, bicycles and horse-drawn carriages were popular ways to see the island. Many years later in October 1931, the Bermuda Railroad Company opened for business, presenting another means of transportation for locals and visitors. Operating 17 years, the Bermuda Railway (locally known as the old Rattle and Shake; see our Let's Explain Bermuda chapter for more) transported 14 million passengers over millions of miles.

Interestingly, it was World War II that began the demise of the railroad, as it brought with it increased use by the military forces that flooded the island. Faced with a million-pound repair bill after the war, the government decided to sell the railway. The old train route is accessible, consisting of 21 miles of the most enchanting scenery on the island. The Bermuda Railway Trail, a hiking path, is a delightful option to consider to view a different aspect of the island. (See our Recreations chapter for much more on the Railway Trail.)

Although the old railway is no longer a viable means of mobility (there is, however, a short tour available in a scaled-down replica of a Baldwin locomotive; see subsequent listing), you can still enjoy a good walk, a healthy bicycle trek or the age-old pleasure of a horse-drawn buggy ride around the island. Visitors and Insiders enjoy carriage rides, and seeing a passing buggy on the road always causes a stir of excitement. There is a carriage depot

INSIDERS' TIP

Should you lose an item while traveling on the bus, call the Bermuda Public Transportation Board, 292-3851, and they will gladly help you locate anything you've lost.

on Front Street in Hamilton close to the No. 1 shed, about a half-block away from the corner of Queen Street, directly across from Trimingham's Department Store.

Moped and scooter rentals are also popular. Riding with the wind at your back can be exciting, and a motorized cycle gives you the freedom to come and go as you desire. There are more than 25 cycle liveries on the island, renting motor bikes, pedal bikes and equipment. Rates for cycle rentals are competitive, and they generally are on a sliding scale that makes each day of use cheaper as you keep the bikes longer. (For complete information on cycle liveries, see our Recreations chapter.)

No matter which way you decide to tour the island — whether by bike, bus, ferry, moped, taxi or on foot — it is easy and safe once you understand a few basic rules of the road you must follow when getting around the rock.

Road Rules, Bermuda Style

1. It is imperative to understand that Bermudians drive on the left side of the road. This is the most significant difference North American visitors will discover. This will affect you not only when you ride a bike or moped (be careful at spots where you may instinctively want to veer to your right), but also when crossing streets. The island's major roadways are easy to remember — North Shore Road, Middle Road and South Road.

2. Generally speaking, no one is in a hurry. You will notice there are no expressways in Bermuda, and traffic moves slowly, particularly on our long, narrow roadways. The islandwide speed limit is 35 kilometers per hour (about 21 mph). In the town of St. George's the speed limit is reduced to 25 kph, and it is even lower — 24 kph, or 15 mph — in the City of Hamilton and other congested areas. Note that our winding roads are very slippery when wet.

3. With no expressways, there are few

FYI

Unless otherwise noted, the area code for all phone numbers listed in this guide is 441.

traditional intersections. Traffic circles are called roundabouts. Vehicles already on a roundabout have the right of way over vehicles attempting to enter. The rule is to always give way to traffic already on the roundabout, coming from the right. Once you are on the roundabout, you have the right of way. Never stop on a roundabout or at road intersections to study maps or wait for friends to catch up. Always pull off the roadway where it is safe.

4. It is illegal to ride a motorized cycle without wearing a safety helmet. This rule of the road can not be overemphasized. If an accident should occur, your helmet is the only thing protecting you from banging your head against our hard Bermuda limestone walls. When you rent your motor bike, the cycle livery will go over the rules of the road and provide a lesson in the proper technique for riding your bike. A motor bike is simple to manage, but do not attempt to ride one until you are completely familiar with the controls. It is best to practice in a safe area before riding in traffic.

5. When riding a motorized cycle, wear the proper clothing. Bathing suits or abbreviated clothing is not permissible attire unless you wear some kind of beaching cover-up. Do not attempt to maneuver your vehicle in flip-flops, clogs, sandals or with bare feet; it is against the law.

6. Any pedestrian has the right of way on a crosswalk. In Bermuda, if any pedestrian has walked on the crosswalk or looks as if they may step onto a crosswalk, you must stop. Also do not jaywalk — use the pedestrian crossings where they are available. Slow down at Zebra (striped) crosswalks and Pelican crosswalks, which are found in the City of Hamilton at junctions with traffic lights. At these intersections, buttons allow pedestrians to stop the flow of traffic.

7. Walk facing the traffic. This is safer because of our narrow roads. Also when walking early mornings and at dusk wear light-colored or reflective garments and carry a flashlight if possible. This will help motorists to see you more clearly. Never walk two abreast on the road.

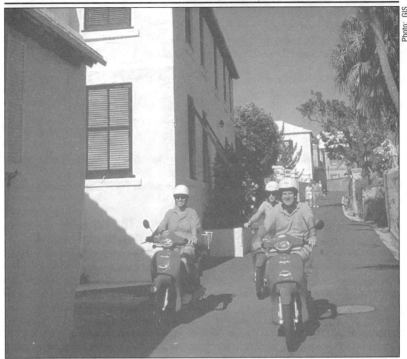

Photo: GIS

Mopeds are a fun way to investigate the nooks and crannies of the Town of St. George.

Riding the Buses

Taking a trip on a pink and blue bus in Bermuda is guaranteed to be one of the most pleasant public transportation adventures you'll ever experience.

Bermuda's first buses were horse-drawn carriages, but the islandwide system has undergone years of metamorphosis. In 1995 the Bermuda Public Transportation Board celebrated its 50th anniversary of operating regularly scheduled buses to some of the most popular sections of the island. Starting with only six used yellow buses purchased from Newark, New Jersey, in 1946, Bermuda's only public transportation company has grown to its present capacity — 106 buses providing transportation across the island.

Riding the bus is elementary. As a matter of fact, you will notice the youngest Bermudian school children use the public transportation system daily without getting lost. The same goes for our visitors. You can't get lost riding the bus in Bermuda. Buses travel along our major roadways from the East to the West End and along the North Shore, Middle Road and South Shore.

Bus stops along the main thoroughfares are designated with poles painted pink and blue. Poles painted pink on top indicate service inbound to the City of Hamilton. Poles painted blue on top indicate service outbound from Hamilton.

Bus schedules are available islandwide. As you leave the arrival hall at the airport, you'll find bus schedules among the number of brochures and maps conveniently displayed. You may also pick up bus schedules at the Visitors Service Bureau (Front Street, Hamilton, between Point Pleasant and Heyl's Corner), at the hostess desk at your hotel, guest house or resort, or at the central bus terminal on Washington Street, just off Church Street, a few steps east of City Hall in Hamilton.

The bus schedule includes a table of the most frequently visited attractions on the island and displays the number of the routes serving each destination. The schedule also provides a map showing the 14 bus route zones (each about 2 miles in length) and the location of the main attractions within each zone.

Bus Fares

When riding the bus, you are required to have a day or weekly pass or the exact change in coins or tokens. No paper currency is accepted on the bus, but the Bermuda $1 coin is accepted. When you board, drop your fare in the fare box or show the driver your bus pass. Bus drivers are not permitted to provide change, but if you don't have the right amount, other passengers can sometimes help you out.

Bus tokens are sold at the main post office and branches, the central bus terminal in Hamilton, PTB headquarters on Palmetto Road in Devonshire and at hotels.

One-, three- and seven-day transportation passes may be obtained at the Visitors Service Bureau, the central terminal in Hamilton, PTB headquarters and many hotels and guest houses. Valid passes are good for unlimited trips through all zones on buses and ferries. The days of validity are printed on the front of the passes. A passenger may choose their traveling days by having the suitable days and month on the card punched.

Bus tickets are also sold in books of 15. However, tickets may only be used on the buses. These tickets are sold at the central terminal in Hamilton and many of the branch post offices. Children younger than 5 currently ride free, as do Bermuda seniors who are 65 or older.

Adult Bus Fares

Cash fares: $2.50 for 3 zone and $4 for 14 zone

Tokens: $2.25 for 3 zone and $3.75 for 14 zone

Tickets (15 per book): $15 for 3 zone and $24 for 14 zone

1-Day Transportation Pass (All zones): $10

3-Day Transportation Pass (All zones): $21

7-day Transportation Pass (All zones): $34

Monthly Pass (All zones): $40

3-Month Pass (All zones): $105

Student-Child Bus Fares (Ages 5 through 16)

Cash fares (All zones): $1

Tickets (15 per booklet, all zones): $6

Visitor 3-Day Transportation Pass: $10.00

Visitor 7-Day Transportation Pass: $15.00

Term Pass (for student usage; all zones): $38.00

The Wheels Go Round and Round

Now you are ready to begin your bus journey. Before boarding, wait a moment to see if anyone is coming off the bus. In Bermuda, the driver will not allow you to enter before he checks for and allows those passengers departing to get off the bus.

Remember that between 7:30 and 9 AM and 3:30 to 5:30 PM, the buses are crowded with school children and individuals traveling to work. You may want to consider avoiding these rush hours, or you may see it as an excellent occasion to mingle with the locals.

When boarding the bus, drop your token or ticket in the fare box or show your pass. If you need a transfer, you must request it when you first board. Transfers are free where appropriate, but you cannot get off the bus in Hamilton, shop and expect to reboard a bus to your next destination using the same transfer. Transfers are punched when the next bus leaves the terminal and must be used when departing one bus and connecting to another to continue your trip.

It is customary to say hello to the other passengers as you board the bus. Everyone greets each other with a robust "good day" when climbing on board. When departing, remember to thank the driver for his service.

The public buses in Bermuda are not accessible by wheelchair. There are no buses with the necessary hydraulic lifts or storage space. However, persons with limited mobility may be able to enter with some help. Also, remember that buses don't run after midnight on most routes. Should you need transportation after the witching hour, you'll need to call or hail a taxi (see previous listings in this chapter). If you have any doubt as to where you are going, just ask the bus driver to announce your stop and he or she will gladly do so.

Taking the Ferries

On a clear day you can see forever as you ride the waves around Bermuda's nooks and crannies. Using the government-owned and operated ferry system is a terrific way to traverse close to 15 miles of exceptionally beautiful and protected waterways around the bays and islands of Bermuda.

Beginning in 1902, Walter Ingham ferried passengers in his rowboat back and forth on the Hamilton Harbour. Retiring in 1952, it is said that Ingham rowed the equivalent of eight times around the world. Nowadays, the ferries are diesel-powered and provide an economical way to travel. Try the route from St. George's to Dockyard during the peak season of April through

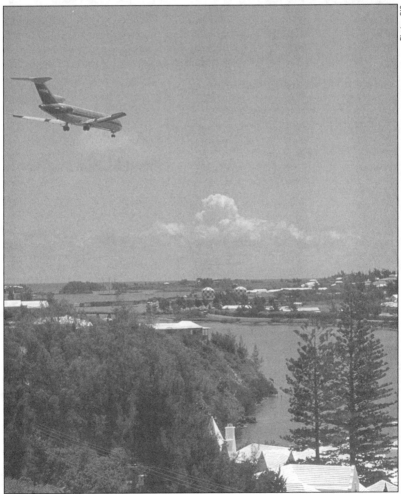

Photo: GIS

Another jet descends to the Bermuda International Airport.

October. The main ferry terminal is next to the Visitors Service Bureau on Front Street in the City of Hamilton between Point Pleasant Road and Heyl's Corner. At the terminal, you can get set up for ferry service with stops in Paget, Warwick and Somerset. There is also service to several residential islands.

The timetable for the ferries is included in the bus schedule and may be obtained at the same locations. You can take the ferry using the same one-, three- or seven-day passes used to ride the buses. The monthly and term pass rates apply here as well. Ferry tokens may be obtained at the ferry terminal before boarding.

Optional Methods of Transportation

In addition to the previously mentioned modes of transportation, there are other ways to get around our island.

Mini Buses

There are two mini-shuttle bus companies servicing the East and West ends of the island.

St. George's Mini-Bus
St. George Square, Town of St. George
• **297-8492**

This service is conveniently located next to City Hall. These blue buses (which carry up to 22 passengers) travel to the outlying beaches, the Town of St. George, St. George's Parish and St. David's.

St. George's service operates seven days a week from May through September. Buses are available Monday through Friday from 7 AM until 11 PM, Saturday from 8:30 AM to 11 PM and Sunday from 9 AM to 6 PM. During the winter season, buses are scheduled to operate Monday through Friday from 7 AM until

8 PM, Saturday from 8:30 AM to 8 PM and Sunday from 9 AM to 6 PM. Fares vary between $2 and $5 per person traveling one way. For information on reduced rates for seniors, children and frequent riders, contact the office.

West End Mini-Bus
Hook and Ladder Ln., Somerset Village
• **234-2344**

West End provides shuttle service for the entire area between Somerset Bridge and the Royal Naval Dockyard. There are two buses that carry 14 passengers each. Buses run Monday through Saturday from 8:30 AM to 5 PM and on Sunday from 8:30 AM to 1 PM, from April to November. From December to March, buses are available from 8:30 AM to 5 PM on Wednesday and Friday and from 8:30 AM to 1 PM on Monday, Tuesday, Thursday, Saturday and Sunday. The highest fare is $3 one-way; Senior citizens living in Bermuda pay $1. Call ahead to arrange advance bookings.

Getting Back Home

Your vacation has come to an end, and you're ready to return home. You'll be happy to find that departing Bermuda is a simple procedure.

All airline passengers should check in at the Bermuda International Airport at least an hour or more before a scheduled departure. When arranging transportation to the airport, allow for considerable travel time based on where you are staying.

The Bermuda immigration form and other documentation received at the time of your arrival should be attached to your ticket. All passengers traveling to the United States pay a departure tax of $20, which is included in your fare. You're exempt of this tax if you are flying directly to your destination; children 2 or younger are also exempt.

INSIDERS' TIP

For parents with babies and toddlers, there are diaper-changing stations at the airport — one in the departing lounge on the main floor and another upstairs near the area where the food court will be found.

Clearing U.S. Customs

Pre-clearance of U.S. customs is available in Bermuda for all scheduled flights. It's a simple procedure that saves time. All passengers departing to the United States must fill out a written declaration form before clearing customs in Bermuda.

Once you've checked in at the airline reservation counter, you will enter into the U.S. Customs Terminal. While waiting in line to see a customs officer, a representative from the U.S. Department of Agriculture will question you regarding the types of souvenirs you have, particularly plants and foods. This is usually a formality, as inspectors are looking for insects, pests or anything that may carry infectious germs into the States. It is important to remember that you can not take back any indigenous flowers or greenery (such as hibiscus, pine and Bermuda cedar) or sea life (such as sea cucumbers, urchins, brain coral and soil). You may leave with such items as flowers bought from a florist, sea shells that don't have anything growing inside them, frozen seafood, cassava pies filled with poultry (but not beef or pork) and Portuguese sausage in plastic store wrapping. A list of fruits allowed into the United States may be obtained from the United States Department of Agriculture's International Services offices in Bermuda, 293-2752.

U.S. residents who have been out of their country for 48 hours or more may take back (once every 30 days) articles valued up to a total of $400. Anyone entering Canada must now make written declarations regardless of whether they have something to declare or not. If you have been absent from Canada for 24 hours or more, you can claim exemption on $50 worth of goods (not including alcohol or tobacco); if you have been out of the country 48 hours, the exemption limit is $200 worth of goods, and it rises to $500 if you have been away for seven days. Citizens from the United Kingdom are allowed up to £136.

A duty-free shop is expected to open in spring 1998 at the airport. Located upstairs, the shop will allow passengers to find last-minute gifts before departing Bermuda. A new food court is also scheduled to open, providing a variety of dishes to satisfy hungry appetites before boarding flights.

When you arrive, you will immediately notice a plethora of trees, foliage and flowers on our road and hillsides. This chapter will help you identify a sampling of them.

Flora and Fauna

"Wherefore my opinion sincerely of this Iland is that it is in truth the richest, healthfullest, and pleasing land — and meerley natural as euer man sat foote upon."
—Sylvester Jourdain, 1610

Jourdain surely knew what he was talking about since he was one of the crew who survived the wreck of the *Sea Venture* in the hurricane of July 1609. (See our History chapter for more details.)

Once the passengers and crew had reached the safety of Bermuda and the winds had dropped, it must have been a case of "summertime, and the living is easy." The island then was covered with cedars and palmettos. Birds, particularly the cahow, were abundant and so tame they were just asking to be eaten. And the fish were certainly jumping. As for meat lovers, well, they could depend on the wild hogs left by an earlier visitor for a feast of roast pork. A "meerely natural" paradise indeed. However, humanity being what it is, the island did not stay "natural" for long.

When the first settlers looked at the cedars, they immediately thought "ships." In fact, the first thing Sir George Somers, admiral of the *Sea Venture*, did was build the *Patience* entirely out of cedar. And when the settlers looked at the landscape, they thought, "What can we plant?" In a short period of time, they planted wheat, beans, "cowcumbers" and other seeds they had brought with them from England. Naturally, they also had an eye on profit. As Jourdain put it, "they have made a greate deale of Tobacco and if some would come that have skill in making it it would be very commodious both to the Merchant and to the maker of it." And so they started the trend for introducing new plants to Bermuda.

Biologists will tell you Bermuda's flora and fauna consist of what is endemic — that is, unique to Bermuda — and what is not. It is noteworthy that just 17 endemic plants, including our Bermuda cedar, exist today in contrast to the other species that number more than 3,000. It is more difficult to assess how many animals are endemic. Apparently, there are dozens of unnamed small moths and even smaller insects that may be endemic. However, one bird species and one lizard species are definitely individual to Bermuda. When we mention specific plants and animals, we will tell you if they are endemic. If we don't mention their status, so to speak, you may take it they are not unique to our island but have been introduced, either by natural phenomena or by humankind.

Until fairly recently, Bermuda's environment was primarily rural. Agriculture took an upturn in the 19th century with the coming of the New York steamers, and Bermudians became well-known for their export of agricultural produce to the New York markets. They exported tomatoes, celery, potatoes and arrowroot but were particularly famous for their Bermuda onions and beautiful Bermuda Easter lilies. Indeed, so famous was the Bermuda onion, the colony became known as "The Onion Patch," with the result that true Bermudians still refer to themselves as "Onions." Visitors in those days would have seen large areas of arable land — large, that is, considering the island is only about 21 square miles. In addition, many Bermudians had access to fairly spacious pieces of land where they planted vegetables, herbs and fruits for personal consumption.

After World War II, the picture changed with the growth of our two main industries, tourism and international business. Instead of "plant," "build" became the key word. Tourists needed hotels, and exempt companies (see our International Business chapter) needed office space. Moreover, the growing population and increase of foreign workers meant a need for more houses and apartments. Building was especially intense during the '70s, and since that time Bermuda has become more and more urban. As a result, concern about dwindling natural space has led to some legislation for the protection of land and species (see our Parks and Conservation and Fishing chapters for details) and the careful landscaping of new buildings.

While Bermuda is more urban, it definitely still feels rural. Gardens may be smaller and patios may be larger, but we do want to plant, as our gardening centers will testify. When you arrive, you will immediately notice a plethora of trees, foliage and flowers on the roads and hillsides. This chapter will help you identify a sampling of them. It will also alert you to other living things in the sky, the sea and the land, although not necessarily in that order. Much of our flora and fauna is contained in parks and nature reserves, so look in the Parks and Conservation chapter for additional information, particularly for information about exotic trees and plants.

Climate

Because climatic conditions shape the environment, we will start by explaining our weather. Bermuda is situated near 32 degrees north latitude, 65 degrees west longitude. Our location means we are more subtropical than tropical, but our proximity to the Gulf Stream guarantees a White Christmas is most definitely a dream. Hail we have occasionally, but absolutely no snow.

However, we do have seasons: winter,

spring and summer. During the first three months of the year, our temperatures can drop below 60 degrees Fahrenheit, but they tend to stay in the mid-60s. While visitors appear comfortable in shorts and tops, we wrap up in woollies and scarves. Our blood is thin, you see. Besides, we get to enjoy a change of wardrobe.

Spring can lead to clothing confusion. Mornings tend to be chilly and call for sweaters, but by the middle of the day we eagerly shed them. Sometimes spring is not necessarily much warmer than winter, but it is always marked by the coming of the longtails, the blooming of our freesias and lilies and the appearance of abundant fruit on the loquat trees.

Temperatures start to heat up in April, and in July, August and September they can reach the high 80s or low 90s. High humidity is a feature of our climate and often affects our energy levels. It may explain why we walk so slowly. Sea breezes and a dip in the ocean can help reduce lethargy. Humidity also creates mildew problems, so we have to be particularly careful about how we store our food and our clothes. Bread, for example, belongs in the refrigerator — otherwise it rapidly grows penicillin — and a closet heater helps to protect our wardrobe, particularly our shoes.

"Hey," you might say, "What about the fall? Don't you have autumn?" Well, yes and no. At precisely the time people in more northerly climates are harvesting, we are planting. In late September and October we grow vegetables and flowers that will arrive in time for Christmas. In November we plant our bulbs. Nonetheless, we do have our fair share of autumnal colors, but sometimes they appear in April rather than the traditional fall months, as you will discover when we subsequently discuss hedges and trees. And we don't experience that autumnal chill in the air in September and October. So for us, these months count as an extension of summertime.

As for rainfall, it is usually spread over the year. At least that is what we hope. When it rains, often we are split between sympathy for our visitors — who, after all, have come for sun — and relief that our water tanks are being replenished. Our water supply, you see, depends on how much rain we can catch from our roofs. True, we can buy water, but who needs the expense? In addition, we value the lush greenness of our surroundings. A prolonged period without rain means brown grass.

Because we have such a small land mass, you would think that rains must of necessity cover the whole island. It isn't necessarily so. It's perfectly possible for St. George's to be drowned out in a deluge, while the western end of the island remains dry as a bone. In fact, sometimes you can walk on one side of the road in clear sunshine and watch rain fall on the other side. This phenomenal localization of rainfall may explain why we often have amazing rainbows.

Insiders distinguish between rain and "good tank rain." A drizzle may relieve plants but is not much use to our catchments. Actually, it rarely drizzles in Bermuda. Usually the rain comes in torrents. Torrential rain is good tank rain, provided it falls straight down. The horizontal rain that comes with high winds is no good at all.

"Winds?" you might ask. Yes, we have them. Winter winds are common, and in the summer hurricanes sometimes happen. The optimistic side to winds is that they make for spectacular seascapes. (See this chapter's Close-up on Hurricanes for more information.)

Trees, Plants and Flowers

Hedging Our Bets

Face it, we in Bermuda love to hedge, and we love to stonewall. When you explore, whether by bike, bus or on foot, you will see most of our roads are lined with foliage and flowers. Hedges rise up behind limestone walls of varying heights. If you like uniform hedges,

fair enough, you will see them. Many consist entirely of oleander, which flowers continuously most of the year but thrives on brilliant sunshine. It has thin, pointed leaves and clusters of flowers that are most commonly pink. However, there are hedges of white and red oleander dotted around the island.

The other common hedge is hibiscus that flowers in a variety of colors — pink, red, white, peach and yellow. Sizes vary, but some flowers are 4 or 5 inches in diameter. The flowers have long, protruding pistils: Brush against them, and you will be dusted with bright yellow pollen. Hibiscus flowers for much of the year.

Another hedging plant is pittosporum of the Victoria box variety. With its dense, dark green leaves and small but fragrant white flowers, it is popular because it can survive well in windy, exposed areas. "Match me if you can," a copper-colored hedge, gives us a touch of autumn year round. Its name sounds like a tease, doesn't it? If you have children to distract, ask them to find two identical leaves on this plant. They won't be able to manage it. The plant's variegated leaves range in color from green to copper to pink. To this day, Bermudians use them to make poultices.

Many of our hedges, however, are more mixed than uniform. The pale blue flowers of the plumbago, a plant that can be hedge or vine, tumble with the orange of the honeysuckle and the pinks and purples of the bougainvillea. Incidentally, the vibrant colors of bougainvillea are thanks to its "bracts" — modified leaves — not to its flowers, which are tiny and white. This plant can also be trained as a vine.

Vines are very common in Bermuda, and it would be impossible to mention all of them. Watch out for the bright yellow trumpet flowers of the allamanda vines that scramble down walls. Blue cascades of morning glory are common, although gardeners aren't too keen on them. If allowed, morning glory takes over. Should you explore in the evening during the summer months, you might be lucky enough to see the night-blooming cereus, which has exquisite, white flowers that come out one hour after sunset and smell of vanilla ice cream. By morning, the flowers are shriveled.

Hedges also incorporate a huge variety of grasses and ferns. These have a more subtle beauty and perhaps can best be appreciated first thing in the morning, when drops of dew touched with sunlight hang from the feathered grasses. And asparagus fern, so useful for wedding decorations, looks even spikier and greener in the early morning light. Wildflowers are also part of the melange. In springtime, look for the little purple Bermudiana flower (endemic) and for riotous tumblings of nasturtium flowers which, from a practical point of view, are excellent in a salad.

Trees and Shrubs

Trees and shrubs, of course, can be classified in many ways: deciduous and evergreen, tropical and subtropical, small and large and so on. We have decided to classify them into two very practical categories — those you can eat from and those you cannot. We must mention here that some of the plants mentioned above, such as hibiscus and oleander, can also be grown as trees. Where hedges and trees are concerned, we have to confess we sometimes beat around the bush.

Incredible Edibles

Come late February and March, many children disappear into the loquat trees that are then weighed down with their yellow to orange, pear-shaped fruits. Introduced from China, this small tree can be found throughout the island. The fruit makes for delicious jams, chutneys and pie fillings. Some of us also like to soak the loquats, together with rock candy, in rum or gin so that six months later we can enjoy a tot of loquat liqueur after dinner.

The Surinam cherry tree is another favorite. Twice a year, it produces clusters of red, ridged fruits that have a distinctively tart tang and can be cooked to make jam and jellies. Sometimes the taste of the fruit varies in sweetness from tree to tree. By the way, we often use the cherry tree as hedging, because it is hardy and easy to grow. And while we're talking jams and jellies, we must mention the guava, a tree that grows up to 30 feet and produces round yellow fruits. Guava jelly goes excellently with roast lamb.

Citrus trees have a long history here. They are not endemic but go back to 1616, when seeds were sent to Gov. Daniel Tucker. In that century, rents were sometimes paid in fruit. Our oranges, to quote Andrew Marvell, are like "golden lamps in a green night." In addition, we have lemons, limes and grapefruit. They mostly grow in private orchards that you may glimpse as you ride or walk by. You will also be able to see small plantations of banana trees that were also introduced here in 1616. Their sweet, almost nutty flavor is quite different than that of the ones we occasionally import. And when dried, their tattered leaves come in very useful for making our traditional banana-leafed dolls. Historically, the leaves were also used for stuffing mattresses and as a remedy for burns.

Paw-paw trees, originally from Colombia, are extremely popular in Bermuda. They appear in pairs (male and female) and have succulent trunks. Their fingerlike leaves have seven lobes, and their oval fruits serve as both savory and dessert. When green, the fruits are tasty in a stew and are an effective meat tenderizer. When yellow, they can contribute to a fruit salad. The paw-paw has medicinal properties — according to our senior citizens, its juice helps to reduce high blood pressure. Another local fruit-vegetable is the avocado pear. Salad is just not salad without the nutty taste of the avocado. One problem with the avocado pear tree has to do with its complex

INSIDERS' TIP

Bermuda has a unique collection of old established roses. The Bermuda Rose Society has published a book called *Roses in Bermuda* that includes a guide to roses you can see in the public gardens, parks and hotel grounds of the island. You can buy it at any of Bermuda's bookstores.

Photo: GIS

The Bermuda longtail has become a national symbol of sorts.

cross-fertilizing system. Apparently, the tree changes gender once a day — difficult for us and for it. Growing an avocado tree is easy. Getting it to bear fruit is a trickier matter.

One more fruit must be mentioned, although it does not grow on trees. Locust and wild honey are extraordinary vines with large leaves that have slits and holes in them. It's as if someone has attacked them with a pair of scissors to create interesting patterns. A white flower spath encloses the fruit, which is scaled. Imagine a furry version of the pineapple, and you will have some idea of the taste.

Look But Don't Cook

No book on Bermuda could be complete without mention of our beloved, endemic cedar tree, the *Juniperus Bermudiana* no less. In a way, we are incorrect to put it in the "inedible" category, since once upon a time Bermudians fed themselves and their animals on cedar berries. The berries were also fermented to make a cough syrup. But these days, those practices have died out. The Bermuda cedar has had a rather bumpy ride of it throughout history. When the first settlers arrived, cedars were plentiful, but so many were felled to make boats, houses and furniture that in the 1600s the Bermuda Company tried to enforce orders against cutting them down.

In the 18th century, the landscape was once again filled with cedars, though they were still highly prized. One John Crevecoeur wrote in 1784: "A girl's fortune is counted by the number of cedars — that of my hostess has been two thousand, seven hundred." Disaster struck in the mid-1940s when a blight caused by an insect destroyed approximately 80 percent of the trees. No longer could we go out and cut a cedar for our Christmas tree. Since then, thanks to the Department of Agriculture, Fisheries and Parks' reforestation program, cedars have made a comeback, although they do not dominate the landscape to the extent they did in 1609. Watch out for them behind hedges and on our hillsides.

Why do we love our cedars so much? Well, the older trees (some did survive the blight) have a dusty but evergreen appearance. They add a biblical effect to our landscape and gardens. And the wood appeals to at least two of our senses: It has a pink, warm glow and smells delicious. Sachets of cedar shavings put in closets and chests give a fragrant smell

When the Wind Blows . . .

"It's an ill wind that blows nobody any good," the saying goes. While it is true that a hurricane in 1609 fortuitously started Bermuda's first settlement, most of us would rather do without hurricanes altogether. However, whether we like it or not, we do have a hurricane season. Officially, it starts June 1 and ends November 30, but the following old Bermudian doggerel, found in Terry Tucker's *Beware the Hurricane!*, is often apposite:

June. Too soon.
July. Stand by!
August. One must.
September. Remember?
October. All over!

How do we distinguish between a hurricane and a tropical storm? Well, when we experience sustained winds of 73 miles per hour and greater, we know for sure we're having a hurricane. These nasty gyratory tempests are divided into five categories, each one nastier than the last.

Category 1 has winds of 73 to 95 mph; Category 2, 96 to 110; Category 3, 111 to 130; Category 4, 131 to 155; and Category 5 . . . We won't even think about Category 5. Winds stronger than 156 mph are just too horrendous to contemplate.

Of course, weather satellites are extremely useful in that they do give us some warning, and we do have a hurricane watch system. However, there are oldtimers who feel their own methods of hurricane prediction are far more reliable than those of meteorologists. St. David islanders, in particular, swear by shark oil. After hanging a shark's liver in the sun so that the oil can drip, they pour about a cup of the liquid into a clear glass bottle, which they then cork and hang outside in a shady place. Clear oil means sunny skies. Churned, cloudy oil means trouble is coming.

Bermudians have other predictors too. "Listen to the South Shore roaring!" is one piece of advice. When a storm starts 500 or 600 miles to our south, our waters react long before we experience a breath of wind. Tides rise higher than usual, and huge swells pound onto the rocks and beaches. The longer the interval between the swells, the more severe the storm will be.

Silk spiders warn us as well. If they weave their webs close to the ground then, the argument goes, they know we're in for trouble and therefore so do we. A leaden atmosphere is another sign. Sometimes the air is so heavy with humidity that we have to fight lethargy in order to prepare for the brewing storm.

A day or so before the storm arrives, our birds fall ominously silent. They know there's nothing to sing about. Preparing for a hurricane is tedious but essential. This is the time when some of us wish we had not bought so many planters or so many items of outdoor furniture that we must now put away. Others fret over their boats. And "battening down" becomes our stock phrase as we close our shutters or hammer boards over the windows of our houses and shops.

Candles become vital articles of equipment, as are batteries for radios and lamps. As for fresh water, we store it in as many containers as possible. The bathtub is the most capacious one. And all the while, we tend to think uncharitable thoughts: "The hurricane can hit anywhere else it likes, but please let it not come to Bermuda."

Sometimes we're extremely lucky, and the hurricane, changing its mind at the last moment, bypasses Bermuda altogether. Other times it plays cat and mouse, teasing us with gale force winds, loving us and then mercifully leaving us without directly hitting us.

— continued on next page

Photo: The Royal Gazette

Bermuda has seen its share of hurricanes.

In August 1995, Hurricane Felix indulged in such a flirtation. It caused enough havoc to cause a one-day postponement of our Independence referendum. Once the island voted against saying goodbye to dependency, Felix had the nerve to return, as if showing disapproval of our decision.

Because of our tiny land mass, we tend not to suffer direct hits that often. Nevertheless, Hurricane Emily of 1987 taught us never to be smug. She came literally out of the blue one morning in September. Short, sharp and vicious, she destroyed one-third of our trees, blocked many of our roads and left us without electricity for weeks after she had gone. Lack of light and running water made us feel utterly powerless (pun intended). And many of us realized that although suffragettes Susan Anthony in the United States, Emily Pankhurst in Britain and Gladys Morrell in Bermuda had a lot to do with women's liberation, the most powerful factor was electricity.

Ten percent of our roofs went sky high, although no houses were totally destroyed and no people were killed. The sturdiness of our architecture stood us in good stead. Though Emily was a very ill wind indeed, some good did come out of it. The community came together in a way it had not for years. Those who regained electricity gave new meaning to "shower parties" by opening up their houses to people desperate for flowing water, and people rallied to help those whose houses were badly damaged. Still, Hurricane Emily is not an experience we'd like to repeat.

to our clothes. It smells even better when it is burning, but these days using cedar for firewood seems sacrilegious. Incidentally, Spanish moss loves cedars too. Very often you will see masses of its long, silver-gray threads growing and hanging from cedar branches.

Many of our hillsides, once dominated by the cedars, are now covered with casuarinas, deliberately planted in the '50s and '60s to reforest the island. Casuarinas, also known as Australian pines, are evergreens and have small fruits grouped in woody, cone-like structures. These cones are useful for making Christmas decorations. Because these trees are resilient to wind and salt, may gardeners like to grow and cut them as hedges.

Yikes! Fronds and Spikes

Palmetto is also endemic, and, like the cedar, was once the source of food and drink.

Both people and animals fed on the black berries. Some people made an alcoholic drink called "bibby" out of the liquid drawn from the trunk. No doubt the drink was ample compensation for the lack of British ale. The crown was eaten instead of cabbage.

Palmettos, with curved, green fronds whose leaf blades are touched with yellow, had other practical uses as well. Its leaves were used to thatch houses and to plait baskets, ropes, bonnets and hats for export. Today craft makers use the leaves to create dolls or Christmas ornaments. You will see palmettos of varying sizes all over the island. Often they intermingle with our hedges or stand alone on hillsides. In gardens they can give shade to other plants that find the sun too fierce.

Numerous palms of other kinds lend our island a tropical look. Some are aristocratic, to say the least. We have the Cuban royal, the queen and the princess palms, together with the more plebeian spindle, date and coconut trees. The coconuts, by the way, are not too good to eat.

Watch out for our spiky plants. Their sharp edges give spunk to the landscape, but a close encounter with Spanish bayonet, for example, can be very painful. Its leaves are so sharp, you could use them as fencing foils. Century plants, a variety of aloes and cacti all add a tropical touch.

Spice and All That's Nice

Mexican pepper trees are abundant, and their small red berries come in very handy at Christmas for decorations. The allspice tree is feathery — scrunch a leaf in your hand, and you will smell the spice. Its tiny white flowers are exquisitely fragrant.

The pride of India tree is also prevalent. Although deciduous, it offers shade in the summer. Don't eat its yellow berries, though — They are poisonous. Remember we promised you autumnal visual effects? The fiddlewood splashes the island with the reds and oranges associated with the fall. But unlike the maple tree, for example, it drops its leaves twice a year: once when it "should" and once in springtime. Similarly, the bay grape tree, which has round, shiny leaves and withstands wind and salt spray well, also has the eccentric habit of turning red in April.

Bermudian Gardens

Very often our hedges, walls and trees screen gardens, both public and private. Public gardens will be discussed in our Parks and Conservation and Attractions chapters. Remember that public landscaping in Bermuda is a priority. Roundabouts, for example, are not just for vehicles. Very often, their centers are covered with flowers. And restaurant owners or managers take just as much pride in their gardens as they do in their menus.

Where private gardens are concerned, don't be afraid to be discreetly pokey (Bermudian for inquisitive). If you can look over or though a hedge, by all means do so. In spring you will see banks of creamy white freesias, subtly streaked with purple and gold. But we also like more vividly colored freesias as well. Pinks, purples, yellows, reds — we like them all. Other popular bulbs are paper whites (which we plant in November in time for Christmas), the dramatically striped amaryllis and lilies, including, of course, our Easter lily.

Come October, we flock to the garden centers to buy our annuals. Impatiens (sometimes known as "busy lizzies"), petunias, pansies and snapdragons give a medley of color to our gardens, patios and pots from Christmas through early summer. Geraniums are popular too and in the past were also grown as hedges. In July, August and September, begonias and periwinkles take a more prominent place because they can cope with fierce sun.

Of course, private gardens vary according to the owners' tastes. Some are formal and carefully manicured while others have more

---

INSIDERS' TIP

Please be kind to our endemic plants. Picking the flowers will prevent the plants from reseeding. If you're into botany, bring your guidebook with you to the plant itself.

of a wilderness effect. Ambitious gardeners often go for the exotic. The bird of paradise plant is a favorite. Named for its appearance, it has stiff, bright orange flowers and blue stamens. (See the cover for a beautiful example of this flower.) Bottlebrush is another favorite, and, yes, its vibrant, scarlet flowers do resemble a baby's bottlebrush.

Exotic trees include the gigantic Indian rubber tree, the equally huge Indian laurel and the banyan tree. These will be described more fully in our Parks and Conservation and Attractions chapters. However, we must mention the tall, graceful jacaranda, which has lilac-colored flowers, and the frangipani tree, which comes with either white or pink, fragrant flowers. Deciduous, the budding of the frangipani marks the coming of spring. Also deciduous is the glorious royal poinciana tree that graces so many gardens. The poinciana starts to bud in April, then for some weeks the leaves bunch at the end of the branches. By June, the tree looks like a massive leafy parasol, and by the end of the month, it is covered with fiery red blossoms. Come July and August, it offers respite against the blazing sun. Sit under the poinciana, gaze up into the intricate design of its lacy leaves and you may understand the infinite geometry of fractals.

Arable Fields

Agreed we are no longer the farming community we once were, but we still have acres of land devoted to the planting of vegetables and flowers. These areas are mostly tended by people of Portuguese descent. Look out for plots of reddish-brown earth planted with Bermuda onions, potatoes, cabbages, carrots and broccoli, to name just a few of our vegetables. At Easter you will see our beautiful Bermuda lilies (a selection of which, by the way, we annually send to Her Majesty, Queen Elizabeth) and other flowers, such as chrysanthemums and snapdragons. These flowers, along with the vegetables mentioned, are sold in our stores and in stands along the roadsides.

Birds, Fish and Other Animals

In Bermuda, animals can be bright and beautiful, but they are definitely small rather than great. We don't have deer or foxes or elk, for example. True, whales sometimes visit us (see our Attractions and History chapters), and true, some exotic larger animals can be seen at our Aquarium (see our Attractions and Kidstuff chapters). But the largest wild animals you will see on the island are feral cats, chickens and rabbits. Even these are not wild in the true sense of the word. They originated from abandoned pets or animals kept for domestic use. Much as we like to visit the bigger wild animals when we travel to larger countries, we're on the whole happy not to have them here. Given the size of our island, our vegetation could not support them. As for the rabbits, we are keeping an eye on them. They may be cute, but they can over populate. Where our gardens are concerned, too many a bunny isn't funny.

Fine, Feathered Friends

When Bermuda was a peaceful, rural community, our birds were probably much happier. Horse-drawn traffic, once our chief means of transportation, was far less threatening to them than the motorized kind, introduced in 1946. And the reduction of open spaces, together with the destruction of trees, has led to a decline in some of our species. Domestic and feral cats don't help either.

Nevertheless, we are still lucky in that on average, some 200 species seen in Bermuda are recorded each year. Many of our migrating birds come from North America, but some-

INSIDERS' TIP

When you go for a walk, do yourself a favor and leave your Walkman behind. That way you won't miss the busy call of the "chick of the village" or the melodious song of the redbird. Be sure to appreciate Bermuda's sweet sounds.

times gulls and ducks can arrive from the Old World, from the West Indies, from Greenland and from South America. We have 22 nesting species, and it is a small sampling from this category that we will describe in this chapter. (See our Recreations, Beaches, and Parks and Conservation chapters for more information about woodland, sea, pond and marshland birds.)

The Bermuda petrel, or cahow, was the bird that the first settlers saw in such vast numbers. Within 20 years they managed to eat most of them. So cahows were almost — but not quite — wiped out. Some 300 years later, in 1951, the cahow was miraculously rediscovered. You will find a description of its rediscovery, its breeding habits and numbers in the Parks and Conservation chapter, but we mention it here because it is Bermuda's most famous endemic bird.

White-tailed Tropic Bird or Longtail

Though longtails are here for just eight months of the year, we have claimed them as our own. Almost a Bermudian emblem, they decorate our pottery, glass and jewelry. Sometimes these pelagic birds can be seen in late February, but the majority arrive in March, bringing with them the promise of spring.

Be sure to take a walk on the South Shore cliffs for a Bermuda longtail experience. Gaze across the sea and up into sky. At first, the sky may seem empty, but eventually you will be able to just make out a flash of white separate from the whiteness of the waves breaking on the reef. The flash will rise into the air and then swoop towards the cliff, the black markings on its wings and sleek tail clearly identifiable now. Seconds later, its mate will follow and together they will tilt and swerve along the coast in aerial dance. Sometimes the birds will veer towards each other; sometimes they diverge so that once again it can be difficult to distinguish them from the spray. But back they will come, plunging and soaring — their curved wings hammering the air, their twin tail feathers bending gracefully into the breeze. The gilded version of the longtail, so popular in Bermuda as a pendant or brooch, seems a mockery when we witness the elegant vibrancy of the true longtails' flying courtship.

Eastern Bluebird

The male bird's back feathers are as blue as its name. Its chest is a warm, pinkish brown. Once plentiful, our lovely bluebirds suffered from the introduction of the house sparrow and the kiskadee. However, the Department of Agriculture, Fisheries and Parks and the Audubon Society have encouraged the setup of special nesting boxes, and as a result, in recent years more of these birds have been mating. Whether bluebirds enjoy watching golf is uncertain, but they certainly haunt our golf courses. Look out for them there (see our Golf chapter). You might be interested to know that ornithologists are debating the possibility that our bluebirds may be a subspecies endemic to Bermuda.

Great Kiskadee

You will see this flamboyant bird all over the island. It is predominantly bright yellow with some brown and rufous (that's tinged with red) feathers. You will hear it as it literally calls "kiskadee." Some Insiders claim it is calling in French — asking the question, "Qu'est-ce-qu'il dit?" (Translation: "What is he saying?") Our visitors love this bird, but we are more cautious in our affection for it. It is rough and rude, you see, and it terrorizes the bluebirds. Introduced in 1951 to control our lizards, it must have changed its mind about its meal preferences. We still have plenty of lizards.

Northern Cardinal or Redbird

We love our cardinals, especially the male ones, which are definitely very red. In the morning they like to perch on trees or telephone wires and serenade you. Their song is pure and true, in contrast to their comically pompous appearance. They also like to show off their own importance by puffing out their chests.

Chick-of-the-Village

This yellow, white and black bird is also called a white-eyed vireo. It sings merry notes and is partial to fruits and berries. Always known to be native to Bermuda, it's now thought to be possibly an endemic subspecies. You also will see migrant white-eyed vireos whose plumage is similar but brighter and whose songs and calls are more nervous than our own chick-of-the-village.

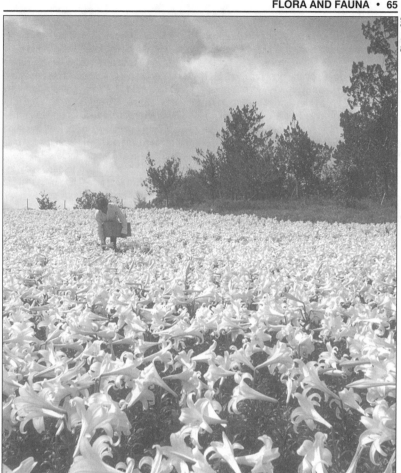

Photo: GIS

Easter lilies grown in Bermuda are presented annually to
Queen Elizabeth II of England on her birthday.

Fish Are Jumpin'

Surrounded as we are by ocean and reefs, we obviously have fish. And it's not just two little fishes and a mama fish too. We have a wonderful variety of species, ranging from the massive marlin to the diminutive sergeant major. Since scuba diving and snorkeling are the best means of observing our fish, we will give you more detailed information in our Watersports and Beaches chapters. The former is also where to look if you are more interested in catching than observing — in Watersports, we cover all aspects of fishing and our fish conservation laws. In our Attractions chapter we will alert you to the aquarium where visitors may see many species. Here, we want to introduce you to just a few of our more ornamental fish and some of their behavior and habits that can only be described as, well, fishy.

Parrotfish

These are perhaps our favorite. They come in all colors, the most common being blue-green. Parrotfish are not shy at all, and often they swim so close to shore that you can see them from your window or the water's edge. What you probably won't notice is that the male parrotfish is apt to change sex. Let us explain this extraordinary phenomenon. You see, parrotfish swim in groups with one dominant female. When that female dies, the next most dominant male in the group changes sex and takes over. Apparently the sex change takes about two weeks to complete.

Angelfish

Angelfish are multicolored but predominantly blue with yellow markings. They are very pretty, and, where mating is concerned, they do behave like angels. They mate for life. When one dies, the other pines until it dies. Who says that monogamy is against nature?

Four-eyed Butterfly Fish

This tiny fish is most commonly pale yellow. However, it doesn't really have four eyes. It just pretends to have them. A conspicuous black spot that resembles an eye is positioned on each side of its tail, but its real eyes are cunningly concealed by two black stripes, each running from the fish's nape to its gill cover. Result? Predators get tricked because they can't see eye to eye.

Sergeant-Major

Like human sergeant majors, this tiny fish can be aggressive. It is usually yellow but changes to a dark blue or olive gray when in captivity or when attacked. It always has distinctive, black stripes as befits its rank.

Frogs and Other Fauna

Tree Frogs

In the summer months, come evening and nighttime, you may well be reminded of Caliban's lines in Shakespeare's *The Tempest*: "Be not afear'd. The isle is full of noises/ Sounds and sweet airs, that give delight and hurt not." Our diminutive tree frogs, hiding in trees and shrubbery, love to sing in the dark. Their favorite tune ought to be "Singing in the Rain," because it is after rainfall that they are particularly loud. But "sing" perhaps is not accurate. "Whistle" is better.

Don't let anyone tell you they produce their sound by rubbing their back legs together. That simply isn't true. The sound very definitely comes from their little throats. Tree frogs are easy to hear but hard to see. They are greenish brown with protruding eyes that are large in proportion to their body size.

Giant Toads

These are much more visible. You will often find a giant toad sitting in contemplative silence next to a puddle. Female toads are brown and black; males are brown and yellow. Both types have very wise expressions although where traffic is concerned, they are, unfortunately, not wise at all. They particularly like to sit in the middle of roads after a rain shower.

Deliberately brought to Bermuda in 1885 from what was then British Guyana, the toads were and still are useful consumers of cockroaches and other pests. However, dogs must watch out. Biting toads is not a good idea because they have poison glands that secrete a deadly mucous. If your dog is silly enough to attack a toad, wash its mouth out immediately with vinegar and take it to a vet for an antidote.

Lizards

All over Bermuda you will see lizards scuttling on walls, trees and hedges. They are cold-blooded creatures and descendants of the large vertebrate class of reptiles that dominated the earth 70 to 200 million years ago. Of course, the largest reptiles were the dinosaurs that so mysteriously died out. Indeed, our lizards have the look of miniature dinosaurs — that is their chief charm.

INSIDERS' TIP

Every year the Garden Club of Bermuda arranges visits for locals to private houses and gardens especially noted for their beauty. If you come to Bermuda in April, you too can enjoy this privilege. Call the Visitors Service Bureau at 295-1480.

We actually have one endemic lizard, known as the Bermuda rock lizard, or skink. It is 6 to 7 inches long and when young has black, tan and white stripes and a brilliant blue tail. Unfortunately, it is only abundant in protected areas (see our Parks and Conservation chapter), but if you are lucky, you might see some in the quieter areas of Castle Harbour, North Shore and Somerset.

Our other lizards are of the anolis family. While it is true that they change color, it is not true that they are chameleons. Introduced to us from the West Indies at the beginning of the century, they have settled down nicely. The Jamaican anolis is the most common. It changes its brownish black color to bright or gray green, and the male has a throat pouch that flashes orange to attract the ladies. The Warwick lizard is larger and is distinguishable by its lime green color and the yellow rings around its eyes. Sometimes lizards like to live in our houses. Don't be too horrified. They don't make a mess, and they do eat our flies. Hence, lounge lizards can be useful.

Butterflies, Bugs, Creepy-Crawlers and Pests

Let us start with the good news. We have beautiful butterflies. We have the Gulf fritillary, which has orange and black markings and silver underneath its wings. We have the cloudless sulfur, which, as you might guess, is bright yellow. But above all, we have the Monarch butterfly. It is large with glorious white and tortoiseshell markings. For some years we were worried it might disappear from Bermuda, and for that reason, during the '80s and early '90s, the Department of Agriculture, Fisheries and Parks annually offered free milkweed seeds to grow in our gardens. Monarchs dine on milkweed. As of now, our schools have taken over the project, planting milkweed in student gardens. So far, the numbers seem to be increasing.

We also have silk spiders. If you are frightened of spiders, at least appreciate their large, intricate webs that are so exquisite in the dew of the early morning.

Now for the bad news. We have cockroaches. And though the toads are doing their best, they are just not eating enough of these hideous insects. Our roaches are large — some can be more than 2 inches long. What's worse is that sometimes they are indecent enough to fly. However, do not mistake our hard-back beetles for cockroaches. Beetles do not deserve to be swatted or sprayed. They can be distinguished by their black, shiny backs and the clicking noise they make with their wings. Frequently, the beetles land on their backs, their legs waving helplessly in the air. When that happens, be kind to them, please, and turn them the right way up.

Other less than pleasant bugs include horseflies, mosquitoes that bite but don't spread disease, and termites that are very partial to munching our wooden furniture. Perhaps the worst news of all is that we have rats, which are often attracted to banana plantations. At night they can be seen running down cable lines. Yuck. What more can we say? Cats and Bermuda's pest control companies help to make them keep their distance. Besides, Bermuda cannot be perfect. And at least we have absolutely no snakes.

Rooms tend to be heavily booked in the summer season, so we advise you to reserve at least 30 days in advance.

Resort Hotels

For two-and-a-half centuries, Bermudians were too busy earning their living at sea or on land to worry much about providing luxury accommodations for visitors. Tourism had modest beginnings in 1850 when trickles of visitors were brave enough to come here in small sailing boats from the United States and Canada.

Past and Present

In 1851 the Corporation of Hamilton decided it might be a good idea to open a hotel to suit these visitors' needs. After much procrastination, disagreement and delay, the Hamilton Hotel opened in 1863. Unfortunately, the United States was suffering its Civil War at the time. Since tourism and war do not usually go hand in hand, business for the Hamilton Hotel during the 1860s was not too good. However, by the early 1870s the picture changed as steamships regularly visited Bermuda from New York. For many years the Hamilton Hotel prospered, and tourism grew to the extent that in 1884 another hotel was built in the city of Hamilton. (See The Princess listing in this chapter.)

In those days, incidentally, our high season was during the winter months to suit the many North Americans who wanted to escape the rigor of their climate. But according to William Zuill in his *Bermuda Journey*, in 1910 the Bermuda-Atlantic Steamship Company enticed visitors to come in the summer by offering them a round trip on the *Oceana* for just $10. Unfortunately, many of the passengers did not realize how distant Bermuda was, so when they arrived, they had no money for lodging. Locals saw a great deal of them sleeping out in Victoria Park and in other open spaces in Hamilton. Bermuda's first hippies, perhaps?

World War I put a temporary stop to Bermuda's tourism, but after 1918 the island took the hospitality industry even more seriously. Many Bermudians still remember the London-based Furness Withy and Company shipping line. Its ships, *Monarch of Bermuda* and *Queen of Bermuda*, were regular visitors to Hamilton. The growth of our luxury hotels was largely financed by that company during the '20s and '30s.

Once again tourism came to a halt at the outbreak of World War II, but some of the hotels were put to use. Bermuda became the base for Imperial Censorship, and the censors worked from the Princess Hotel and from the Bermudiana (now a derelict building on Bermudiana Road in Hamilton). After 1945, tourism again became vitally important, and, indeed, at present it is our key industry, matched only by international business.

Today, Bermuda has a huge range of accommodations, but in this chapter we will concentrate on our larger, more luxurious hotels. (See our Cottage Colonies and Timesharing chapter for a different luxury option and the Small Hotels chapter for less expensive lodging choices.) Bermuda has six resort hotels, each in a prime location and offering an extensive range of activities, entertainment and amenities. It would be a mistake, however, to view them as being identical. In our individual listings we explain the features and ambiance particular to each. First, we will discuss the policies and qualities they have in common.

Staff and Seasonality

Ask any of the resort managers what they are most proud of, and they will inevitably mention their staff. The word "resort" can connote impersonality, but in Bermuda hospitality staff are generally truly hospitable, so that even the larger resorts have more of a personal, family atmosphere.

Whereas in the past our peak season was in the winter, now it is most definitely summer. Typically the summer season begins April 1 and ends at the end of October, while the winter season begins November 1 and finishes at the end of March. However, season dates do vary from hotel to hotel, so we will specify any variations in each listing. Some hotels, for example, have a third, shoulder season, which we will also specify when applicable. Seasonality affects availability of rooms, prices and services offered. We will explain these effects when we discuss each topic.

FYI

Unless otherwise noted, the area code for all phone numbers listed in this guide is 441.

Reservations and Cancellations

Make reservations either by calling the hotel directly or by calling a travel agency. All the resort hotels require a two-night room deposit. Some stipulate a first and last night deposit. When this requirement applies, we will tell you so in the listings. In all cases, you may use major credit cards or pay with cash, traveler's checks or, in some cases, personal checks. Generally speaking, cancellations within 14 days prior to arrival result in loss of deposit.

Rooms tend to be heavily booked in the summer season, so we advise you to reserve at least 30 days in advance. Nevertheless, last-minute cancellations can make last-minute bookings possible. So if you are a spur-of-the-moment person, do give the hotel of your choice a call. Check-in and check-out times differ, so look for information about these in the listings.

Location, Amenities and Other Policies

Whether your hotel is in Hamilton Parish, Paget, Pembroke or Southampton — wherever it is — you are certain to have easy access to both sea and beach. Some of the resorts perch on hills, allowing stunning views of our island's most scenic ocean vistas; others almost hug the water so that you can reach the sea within two minutes of leaving your room. When beaches are not actually on the property, you will usually be able to take shuttles or golf carts to them. All the beaches are equipped with chairs, loungers and umbrellas. Changing and shower facilities are often right on the beach, as are food and beverage facilities. If not, they are within easy reach. However, there are no lifeguards.

If you want to explore our reefs and marine life, tour directors will help you make arrangements for snorkeling and scuba diving, fishing and trips in glass-bottom excursion boats. They will arrange other excursions too, such as a guided tour around St. George's or the botanical gardens (see our Attractions chapter for more details). If you want to explore Bermuda by moped or bicycle, you will find that cycle liveries are often on or near the hotel grounds. You'd rather have pool than sea? Then you'll be relieved that every resort has at least one swimming pool. Many have outdoor Jacuzzis as well. Be aware, though, that beach and pool facilities are sometimes reduced and beach bars and cafes generally close in the winter season.

For many tourists, Bermuda would be unimaginable without its golf and tennis. Some of the hotels have their own golf courses while others have arrangements with neighboring courses, some of which are world-famous (see our Golf chapter). All but one of the resorts have tennis courts you can enjoy free of charge or for a reasonable fee.

Perhaps you would rather exercise inside than out. Exercise rooms and fitness centers,

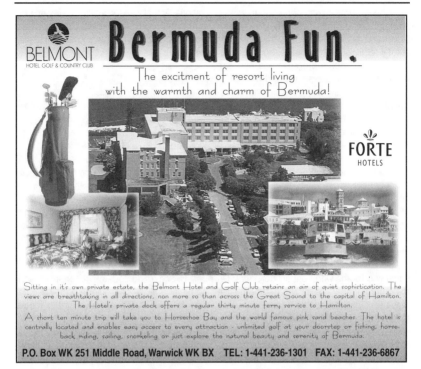

equipped with weights, treadmills and other fitness machines, are available in several of the resorts. So are spas and hair and beauty salons where you will be pampered with massages, facials and hairstyling.

Kids are very welcome at our luxury hotels and, in some cases, special kids' programs supervised by staff are available. We will alert you to these in the resort listings and in our Kidstuff chapter. In all cases, hotel staff can arrange babysitting for additional cost.

Not all our resorts are suitable for guests who are confined to wheelchairs. We give an assessment of room and beach accessibility for wheelchairs in each listing.

On the whole, the resorts have relaxed smoking policies. However, some do offer completely smokefree rooms. If the leftover smell of smoke bothers you, be sure to specifically request a nonsmoking room. Similarly if you wish to smoke, state that preference. Generally smoking is allowed in lobbies, lounges and designated areas in the restaurants and dining rooms. When there are exceptions, we will tell you.

Pets, including dogs, are only allowed at one of the resorts, and this is explained in the writeup.

Eating, Drinking, Being Merry

"There is no love sincerer than the love of food." Well, that's what George Bernard Shaw said anyway. If food is your love, our resorts will not disappoint you. Many have several restaurants or dining rooms that specialize in all sorts of cuisine. In our listings, we will briefly mention the restaurants available, but they will be described more fully in the Restaurants chapter. Some have dine-around plans, which we will also explain in the listings. In the summer months, you will certainly be able to dine under the stars and by the sea. Bermudians love their evenings outdoors, so our hotels make full use of outside terraces for starry, starry night experiences.

Where rooms are concerned, our resorts' managers and staffs generally pride themselves on high standards. They therefore constantly refurbish and upgrade rooms and facilities. Most rooms are spacious and can easily accommodate a king bed as well as other bedroom and living area furniture. Frequently, the furniture includes pullout sofas that can sleep one or two extra persons. However, decoration and furnishings vary in style from resort to resort. Some are more classical and formal; others are more "island" and informal. But most are freshly painted and in excellent condition. Many have private balconies or patios. Amenities differ, but all rooms come with hair dryers in the bathroom and ironing boards, irons and safes. By the way, televisions (satellite or cable) are in every room.

So you have a large family? You can reserve two rooms with connecting doors. On the other hand, a one- or two-bedroom suite may be for you. Most of the resorts offer suites that have separate living rooms as well as bedrooms. The larger suites also appeal to business travelers who may wish to entertain associates and guests. Some suites come with wet bars, refrigerators and small kitchen areas.

Recently, resorts have begun catering to the business traveler as well as the tourist. Many offer conference rooms, lecture rooms and all kinds of audiovisual equipment. However, we must stress that managers are well aware that visitors who are here for fun and relaxation do not want to feel they are in a fast-paced working environment. For that reason, very often business travelers check in and out in a different area of the hotel. And business packages tend to be offered during the winter season.

Room Rates

Room prices are typically based on water view, or on proximity to water, rather than on size. What does "water view" mean? Well, it can mean an uninterrupted view of the ocean, harbors or bays. It can also mean a partial view of water, interrupted by roofs or buildings. If a water view is important to you, be sure to be specific when you make your reservations. Actually, resort staffs are very up front about the room views available. They want you to be happy with what you see out of your window.

Pricing Key

The daily rates listed in the key below are based on room only for double occupancy during the peak season. They do not include the 7.25 percent Bermuda government hotel occupancy tax, the resort levy, gratuities or additional charges for meal plans, telephone calls or other expenses. They are also based on the rooms visitors would most typically reserve. As we have explained, many of our resorts have a variety of suites, but they are not included in the price ranges we quote. Call the hotel for information about suite prices.

Bear in mind, too, that resort levies and gratuity policies can differ, so they will be stated in each listing. Rates during winter can be dramatically lower. Often the hotels offer special packages. Sometimes there is no extra room charge for children younger than 17. We will explain each resort's policy about charges for children in the individual listings.

$	Less than $225
$$	$226 to $260
$$$	$261 to $320
$$$$	$321 and higher

Meal Plans

Most resorts will ask you whether you want EP, BP or MAP. Baffled? Don't worry, we can explain. EP means European Plan, which offers room only and includes no meals. BP means Bermuda Plan and offers room and full breakfast. MAP means Modified American Plan and offers room, breakfast and dinner.

Our pricing key is based on the European Plan. Generally, the MAP plan costs approximately $50 per person per day, plus a fixed $13.90 gratuity that covers all meals and service. The BP plan costs about $16 per person a day plus $8.96 gratuity. Stay EP and you will pay a $6.40 gratuity. Room service is offered 7 AM to 11 PM.

Bermuda's Resorts

And now for the listings, which we present east to west, parish by parish, subset by subset and, thereafter, in alphabetical order.

Hamilton Parish

Grotto Bay Beach Hotel and Tennis Club

$ • 11 Blue Hole Hill, Bailey's Bay • 293-8333, (800) 582-3190

In the lower price range, this resort will suit you if you want leisure, relaxation and comfort in an intimate, island atmosphere. Managers mingle with the guests and solicitously ask if you're observing the 30/30 sun factor rule.

When you leave the airport and cross the Causeway, you will immediately see the white roofs of Grotto Bay on your right. Overlooking Ferry Reach, it has 11 lodges, many named after our parishes, with 18 rooms per lodge. A word here about the landscape: The property spreads over 21 beautifully landscaped acres that gently slope down to the water and the private beach. As you walk down, you will see on your left two natural grottoes. Descending a short broad flight of steps cut out of solid rock, you can enter Prospero's Cave, named after the central character in Shakespeare's *The Tempest*. Stalactites both fat and thin hang from the roof, and a deep lake fills part of the cave. Apparently many years ago, a carriage driver told a visitor: "Oh, that's where Mr. Shakespeare took shelter in a storm." A bust of the Bard is set in the rock near the entrance. If you've ever wanted the mystical, but cold, experience of swimming in an underground lake, you can do so in the second grotto, Cathedral Cave. In any case, now you know how Grotto Bay got its name. Palm trees, bay grapes and cedars surround the hotel, and

the pathways have rustic, wooden fences. A moon gate facing the ocean adds a romantic touch.

Guests can absolutely depend on enjoying a room with a water view and having their own private balcony or patio. Lodges can be two or three stories high. The more expensive rooms are directly on the water, whereas the less expensive ones on the hill overlook it. All of the rooms have bathrooms with full baths, showers and hair dryers. They also have telephones, refrigerators, coffee makers, clock radios and televisions. They are tiled throughout and painted in soft Bermuda colors. Island-related pictures and photographs decorate the walls. King beds covered with floral spreads fit comfortably in the rooms as do tables and chairs. Up to two extra adults sharing the room can stay, but not eat, for free. Grotto Bay welcomes children. Younger than 16, they stay free in their parents' room, and younger than 12, they can eat free if their parents are on the MAP plan. Cribs and babysitters are on hand for an extra charge. From June to Labor Day, trained counselors organize daily excursions to local attractions, games and swimming activities for children older than 4, but never on a Sunday. A special room offers video games. Ground-level rooms are wheelchair-accessible as are many of the facilities. Be aware, though, that there is no room service. Incidentally, check-in time is 3 PM; checkout is noon. The resort levy is $3 per person per day.

Grotto Bay's MAP is a good value at $48 per person per day, plus a $12.80 gratuity. It includes full breakfast and a five-course dinner. BP costs $15 a day plus $6.40 gratuity. Both meals are served in the Hibiscus dining room (smoking permitted in designated areas), which you will find in the main building. Spacious and decorated in Bermuda pinks and greens, the dining room evokes the island's tranquil but bright

INSIDERS' TIP

Marriott's Castle Harbour was named, of course, after the harbor. But that body of water probably acquired its name when Governor Moor in 1912 built a fort on an island he subsequently named Castle Island. The ruined fort is still there.

atmosphere. You can also enjoy that British tradition, afternoon tea, for no extra charge. In summer, you will delight in eating around the outdoor pool. During the day, you may relax in loungers, dip in the pool when you are hot and order lunch from the pool bar when you are hungry. If you start to feel lazy, indulge in a little self-torture in the exercise room. The Jacuzzi will help you recover from it afterwards. At night, you will enjoy Bermuda Island barbecue theme nights, swizzle parties and live entertainment featuring steel bands and island shows. Have you ever harbored a secret dream to be a famous singer? Then karaoke is on hand especially for you.

Watersports are easy with the Blue Hole Water Sports and Diving Shop right next door (see our Watersports chapter). The sunken barge in the water across from the beach marks a spot for excellent snorkeling as does the private deep-water dock. Anyone for tennis? For $8 an hour, you can play at any of four all-weather courts. Two courts are lit: If you fancy a midnight game, no problem. It will cost you an additional $4. Staff is happy to arrange golf for you, and if you feel adventurous enough to try riding a moped, you can go to the cycle livery that's right on the property.

Marriott's Castle Harbour Resort
$$$ • 2 Paynters Rd. • 293-2040

The chief feature at Marriott's Castle Harbour is its offer of traditional elegance with all the comfort of modern amenities. When you first approach the resort, you may well think, "Surprise, surprise! It really is a castle." The main building, built in 1931 by the Furness Withy Line, appropriately has stone walls that have been left unpainted to emphasize the castle effect. Multi-storied, it rises up from the surrounding golf course and semi-tropical gardens and overlooks the Harrington Sound on one side and Castle Harbour (naturally) on the other.

Additional wings have rooms with superb water views. The more expensive rooms, remember, are the ones that definitely directly overlook the ocean and offer private balconies. All rooms have telephones with data ports, clock radios and color TVs with remote control. Many also have shoe polishers, safes and minibars that are stocked on request. Walls are tastefully decorated in restful, pastel shades. Floral bedspreads complement the dark wood of the tables and chairs. Spacious, these rooms can accommodate a king bed or two oversized doubles. They also offer good closet space. The bathrooms, all with full bath and shower, are roomy and equipped with hair dryers.

Marriott's Castle Harbour also has a good selection of one- and two-bedroom suites that come with garden, pool or water views. These suites are ideal for larger families. In addition, there are suites for visitors here on business. Indeed, with 10,000 square feet of business space, the hotel can cater to groups of 10 to 900 people. There is a business center, together with the huge Harbour Ballroom that divides into five sections and the Conference Center that divides into three.

Do not make the mistake of thinking, however, that Marriott's Castle Harbour does not welcome families and children. For starters, children younger than 18 (yes, 18!) can stay free if they are in the same room as their parents. (Actually, there's no additional charge for any extra guest in the room.) Second, children younger than 13 enjoy for free the same meal plan as their parents. Kids older than 13 get the plan for half price. Staff organize activities for kids during summer (see our Kidstuff chapter), and babysitters will always look after your children should you want an evening alone. Cribs and pullout sofas are on hand. This hotel welcomes guests in wheelchairs. Many rooms are wheelchair-accessible as are most of the facilities.

Marriott's MAP plan is an excellent value. For just $52 per person (plus gratuity), you can eat a full breakfast and a five- course dinner at a choice of restaurants. You can dine more formally in the elegant Windsor Restaurant or in Mikado's, Bermuda's only Japanese restaurant. These restaurants, by the way, are completely smokefree. (See Restaurants for details on menus and ambiance.) Other, less-formal eating venues include the View Restaurant, also smokefree, the Pub and several pool and beach snack bars. The BP plan is available for $16 a day plus gratuity. Be aware that during the winter season (No-

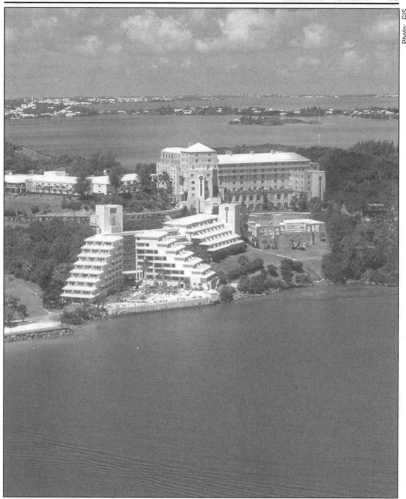

Photo: GIS

Some Bermuda resorts provide a range of activities without leaving the property.

vember to the end of March) some of the restaurants may close and entertainment will be reduced.

The Bayview Lounge — you will find it in the main building — has the sumptuous elegance of the 1930s. Every afternoon, staff there serves a complimentary English tea. Don't worry about calories. Remember that the prestigious American writer Henry James once described afternoon tea as "an innocent pastime." Sink into the comfortable armchairs, admire the wooden paneling and stone fire-

place and then enjoy sandwiches and cake and tea. Monday evenings, managers meet guests during complimentary swizzle parties. And in the summer season, the Bayview offers live music every night. Steel drum bands, trios and the sounds of the 1970s and '80s characterize the entertainment (see our Nightlife chapter) You want to dance? Go for it. It's allowed. Enjoy, too, Blossoms, a lounge where you can sip cocktails in a Japanese atmosphere.

If you can't help thinking about calories,

you can burn them off in a variety of ways. You can, for example, swim. Where? You have a choice of three freshwater swimming pools: two heated and one not. You can enjoy the Castle Harbour watersports beach or the hotel's very own South Shore Beach, a stroll away from your room. The hotel has a private dock, and staff is happy to make arrangements for deep-sea fishing, boat rides or watersports. Golfers will be in their seventh heaven. Castle Harbour golf course is on the edge of the property, and guests receive preferred tee times. On Mondays, Wednesdays and Fridays, guests can also play at the Mid-Ocean Club course next to Castle Harbour's course (see our Golf chapter). As for tennis players, they can use any of the six all-weather courts.

FYI

Unless otherwise noted, the area code for all phone numbers listed in this guide is 441.

Not enough exercise? Then the health club is for you. A session on the treadmill will help, and there's nothing like a sauna to help you lose a few pounds. Use of exercise equipment is free. You can also enjoy beauty treatments at the beauty salon (see our Attractions chapter). Other services include laundry, valet and room service. A doctor is on call, and porters will greet you and help with luggage and golf clubs. Check-in is 3 PM and check-out at noon. The resort levy is $3.75 per person per day.

Pembroke Parish

The Princess
$$$ • 76 Pitts Bay Rd., Hamilton
• 295-3000

Once upon a time, a very long time ago, there was a princess. She was the daughter of a queen called Victoria, and her name was Princess Louise, Marchioness of Lorne. Her husband was the Governor General of Canada, so, naturally, she went to live there. Now Louise wasn't just any old princess — she was an artist as well. In 1883 she decided she needed a break from the bleak Canadian winter, and she came to Bermuda. Princess Louise drew lots of pictures while she was here, but she also explored the island and met lots of Bermudians. She had

such a good time she recommended it as a vacation spot to all of her friends.

When Harley Trott built the first privately financed hotel in Bermuda, he thought of Princess Louise. And so in 1885, The Princess came to town. The first wooden building is gone, but The Princess that now stands is built on the original site.

Today, The Princess treats you like royalty from the moment you meet the door persons at the front entrance. It's a question of *noblesse oblige*. The lobby gives you an immediate impression of Colonial warmth and graciousness with its carpets and dark, Queen Anne-style furniture. Lush plants hang from the staircase railings, and a waterfall, together with more plants, gently cascades down one of the walls. On this level you will find the Colony Pub, with its distinctive canopy of cedar shutters, and a shopping arcade that includes gift and clothing stores. There is also a beauty salon and exercise facility, complete with intimidating machines that you can use for free.

The cheaper guest rooms have a garden view, others look out onto Pitts Bay Inlet, and the more expensive ones offer a view of Hamilton Harbour and the Great Sound beyond. Not all the rooms come with balconies, but if you procure one you can sit on your private balcony and enjoy watching ships and boats cruise past. All rooms have king beds or two doubles. A pullout sofa allows for children or an extra guest. The traditional ambiance of the lobby continues in the bedrooms. Discreet regency wallpaper and Bermuda-related art decorate many of the walls and, again, the furniture is dark and elegant. Bathrooms have full baths and showers, and many rooms, but not all, come with hair dryers, ironing boards, data port telephones and minibars. All have safes, telephones, TVs and clock-radios. Two rooms are equipped for guests in wheelchairs.

The Princess also offers a variety of suites for families and business travelers. The hotel's city location makes it ideal for travelers wanting to do business or attend conferences in

Hamilton. The Princess itself has all kinds of meeting space including the Princess Room, a huge banqueting room that is easily divided into three separate soundproof rooms. The Adam Lounge is another particularly stately space within the hotel and is ideal for social functions. Call for more details of business facilities.

As for meal plans, BP for adults is $15 per person per day, plus $8.65 gratuity. The Princess does have MAP but calls it DAP, short for Dine Around Plan. This package allows guests to use an ID card for dining at the Southampton Princess (see subsequent listing), a sister hotel acquired in the '70s. There is a choice of three restaurants at The Princess in Hamilton, all with designated smoking areas. Harley's offers continental cuisine, while the Colony Pub Steakhouse serves beef (but of course) and other delights. Every princess has to have a tiara, right? Hence, the graceful Tiara Room, which offers a formal, elegant atmosphere and à la carte fare. Be aware that some restaurants may close in winter.

Although The Princess tends to appeal to older guests, children are welcome. Those younger than 12 can stay in their parents' room free, but they are charged for food and pay $28 for MAP. Kids older than 12 and younger than 16 pay full price for meals but only a $6.40 gratuity.

Room service is available. Complimentary afternoon tea, so fitting in this royal atmosphere, is served twice a week in the Colony Pub. Monday nights, the managers will be available at the complimentary swizzle parties on the outdoor terraces, where you can gaze peacefully at the water and ponder on Dinah Washington's "Harbor Lights." The landscaping has a Japanese touch. A small garden with water and tiny bridges exemplifies a Princess tradition of featuring water to unusual effect.

As for entertainment, there is the Gazebo, a cocktail theater where the Jabulani Repertory Company performs British farces and murder mysteries Monday through Thursday.

A variety of excellent musicians and singers perform at the Colony Pub Steakhouse (see our Nightlife chapter). On Tuesday, you can ballroom dance.

Overlooking the harbor are two outdoor swimming pools — one small with salt water; the other large with heated fresh water. Fishing and watersports happen right off the hotel's private, deep-water dock on the harbor. There is a putting green as well. You want beach, tennis and golf? This is where a sister can be so useful. A ferry ride across the sound will take you to the other Princess hotel, and from there you can take the shuttle to the South Shore private beach and enjoy all the facilities (see our subsequent listing for Southampton Princess). Guests at The Princess in Hamilton have full privileges at the Southampton Princess golf course and can use any of the 11 all-weather tennis courts, three of which are lighted.

Back to children. Babysitters are available, but kids' activities are not. However, at no charge youngsters can join in kids' programs offered at the Southampton sister hotel (see our Kidstuff chapter). Check-in time at The Princess is 2 PM; check-out is noon. The resort levy is $3 per person per day.

Paget Parish

Elbow Beach Bermuda
$$$$ • 60 South Rd. • 236-3535, (800) 223-7434

It's difficult to imagine this hotel having any other name since the long, sandy strand of Elbow Beach is directly next to it. But once it was called the Elba Beach Hotel. All we can say is had Napoleon Bonaparte stayed here, instead of on Elba Island, he would never have bothered to escape.

Built in 1908, the hotel has been through various stages of expansion. Always a long building, echoing the length of the beach, it now has separate suites and lanais. When you walk through the recently added front porch, supported by four imposing pillars, you might think you are in the marbled hall of a prince instead of a hotel lobby. The floor is marble — a rich, forest green. Real Italian marble is a feature you will also notice in the Elbow Beach bathrooms.

Most rooms offer a view of the beach, the ocean and the South Shore reef. Some are decorated with elegant, pale green wallpaper (astounding for Bermuda, since humidity and wallpaper don't get along). You have a choice of a king bed or two twin beds. Pull-out sofas allow for extra people who, by the way, pay meal plan, gratuity and levy prices only. All rooms have a balcony or patio, safes, umbrellas, bedroom slippers and terry robes. Closets are spacious, and the bathrooms, as we have mentioned, have marble floor and tile, full baths and showers, hair dryers and scales. (You are not required to step on the scales . . . Who wants to face reality when on vacation?)

Separate from the main building, which is on top of a hill, there are rooms near the pool and terrace and others in the sloping gardens that lead to the beach. Some rooms offer both garden and ocean views. In addition to standard rooms, Elbow Beach Bermuda offers a variety of charming suites — ideal for larger families and business travelers. There are 10,000 square feet of meeting space and a number of rooms that are ideal for business functions and conventions.

While the hotel does have some wheelchair-accessible rooms, we do not recommend Elbow Beach for guests with severe walking impairments. The terraced landscaping and the steps leading down to the beach make access to the ocean difficult.

As for meal plans, adults pay $15 per day plus $10.41 gratuity for BP; $50 plus $13.80 gratuity for MAP. EP gratuity is $6.70. Children are welcome and stay free in their parents' rooms. (Cribs and high chairs are also free.) Kids younger than 2 eat free. Those 2 to 12 can have BP for $7.50 a day or MAP for $25; those 13 to 18 have BP for $15 a day or MAP for $35. Between May and October, the hotel offers plenty of kids' activities. Children go on treasure hunts, beachcombing sessions and all sorts of excursions (see our Kidstuff chapter). Babysitters are on hand.

While the children are doing their own thing, you can enjoy golf, tennis or watersports. Staff can book tee times at most Bermuda courses and will make your watersports arrangements. You can play for reasonable cost at any of the hotel's tennis courts — two are lighted for night play. There is swimming in the sea (beach facilities available) or the pool, which is complete with Jacuzzi. The health club with whirlpool may appeal to you as well as the beauty salon. The lobby shops come in handy if you don't want to make a trip into town.

Elbow Beach Bermuda has an interesting choice of restaurants, all with designated smoking areas. Gracious, formal Ondine's serves a daily buffet breakfast and excellent five-course dinners. On Sunday, an excellent brunch is served, and Saturday nights feature Chinese cuisine. Spazzizi's, by the swimming pool, serves seafood and steak in a more casual atmosphere for lunch and dinner. Whatever you do, make sure you dine at Cafe Lido. It's right on the beach, so whether you dine inside or out, you will see stars and ocean glinting in the night light, discreetly provided by cunningly placed spotlights.

Spazzizi's Pub offers live entertainment. However, if you want some quiet with your evening drink, try the Library Bar, extensively stocked with leather-bound books. If you're interested in German, economics or ecclesiastics, this is the place for you. Where else would you find a copy of *Theologia Fundamentalis*? If such topics don't interest you, go for the cigars and aperitifs. Entertainment and restaurant choices are reduced in the winter season. Room service, laundry and valet service are available. Check-in is 3 PM, and check-out is at 11 AM. The resort levy is $4.50 a day.

Warwick Parish

Belmont Hotel and Golf Club
$ • 97 Middle Rd. • 236-1301

Driving into Belmont, you could be forgiven for thinking the hotel's main view is of the golf course. Naturally, an 18-hole, par 70, championship course does take up a lot of space. However, once you enter the hotel, you realize your mistake. Built atop a hill, the hotel has a marvelous view of Hamilton Harbour and the Great Sound.

Originally, Belmont was a privately owned manor. In 1834 a pastor lived there. While his church was being renovated, he used the lower floors of his home for services. Because there wasn't enough space for all his congregation, people living west of the church came one Sunday, and people living east came the next. In 1907 the hospitality was extended, and Belmont became a real hotel. During World War II, Belmont was home to members of the Royal Air Force and Ferry Command that ferried lend-lease bombers from the United States to Britain.

Today's Belmont is a very good bargain for those who want a sporting or family holiday. Kids younger than 17 stay and eat free under the MAP plan if they share their parents' room. Given that MAP costs $53 per person, that's a real savings. Rooms are not the height of luxury, but they are very comfortable, with space for king or two queen beds and full bathrooms. Rooms have Queen Anne-style furniture and cheerful floral curtains and spreads. Many have picture windows looking onto the Harbour, so be sure to request one if it's important to you. The third floor is completely smokefree. Guests in wheelchairs can request rooms specially equipped for them.

You can play golf all day with absolutely no greens fees. Golf carts are mandatory, though, and cost $40 for 18 holes, $20 for nine. Guests also have complete access to the golf club's facilities and bar. Enjoy yourself on the tennis courts during the day, and again, you pay nothing. There's a small fee to play tennis at night.

A lagoon-shaped swimming pool will help you cool down when you're through playing, and so will a drink at the pool bar. If a swim in the ocean is more to your taste, take a free shuttle to the island's best South Shore beach, Horseshoe Bay (see our Beaches chapter). Belmont is ideal if you want easy access to Hamilton. Take a ferry ride across the Harbour, and you're there in 5 minutes.

You'll have breakfast and dinner in the Tree Frogs Restaurant. (No frog legs for starters and no whistling, we promise!) Decorated in island style, the dining room has a relaxed atmosphere. Smoking is allowed in designated areas. Belmont staff serves complimentary afternoon tea every day in the lounge. Take a minute between tea and cake to enjoy the view and appreciate the brownish-pink glow of the room's Bermuda cedar paneling.

Throughout the summer season, Tree Frogs and the Harbour Bar host entertainment six or seven nights a week. If you're into jazz, don't miss Hubie's Jazz Band — they are always at Belmont on Sunday (see our Nightlife chapter). A complimentary rum swizzle party is held each week.

Primarily a tourist hotel, Belmont does have conference and banquet facilities. Call for details. Check-in is at 3 PM, and check-out is at noon. The resort levy is included in the MAP gratuity, which is $15 per person per day.

Southampton Parish

Sonesta Beach Hotel and Spa
**$$$ • 5 South Rd. and Sonesta Dr.
• 238-8122**

Of all the resorts in Bermuda, Sonesta is the only one to be bang on the beach. And so its slogan: "Best on the Beach in Bermuda." Sonesta actually has three beaches, all on the South Shore. Sinky Bay is sheltered and quiet. You *will* sink — into loungers under palmetto-thatched umbrellas. Boat Bay is ideal for families, and Cross Bay is the ocean beach. Cross Bay is usually good-tempered, but if you like surf, you'll get it here. It is also the hotel's center for activities and entertainment.

The hotel has one bay wing and a six-story

INSIDERS' TIP

If you want internal access to the room next to you, be sure to ask for connecting rooms, not adjoining rooms.

main building that curves gently around the promontory on which it was built. The less expensive rooms have a view of the hillside and roof or of the roof and pool. If a view of the South Shore or Boat Bay is important to you, be sure to ask for it. All rooms have private balconies or lanais. They are decorated island style with subdued color schemes of pink, turquoise or cream accented with floral curtains and bedspreads. Unusual abstract paintings decorate the walls throughout the hotel. Rooms have one king or two queen beds. Each room has a clock-radio, minibar, safe, ironing board and iron and phone with data port. Bathrooms have full baths, showers and hair dryers.

The hotel also offers a variety of split-level suites ideal for business travelers and larger families. Some are equipped with wet bars, sinks, refrigerators and ice makers. Sonesta does cater to many business and conference guests, but if you don't want to feel as if you are in a working environment, fear not: Groups and conventions check in separately and have their own floor. Ramps allow easy access to the beach for guests in wheelchairs. All the rooms in the bay wing are wheelchair-accessible and have baths with rails, and the main building has one room that is completely equipped.

BP for adults is $15 per person per day, plus gratuity, while MAP runs $55 per person. Room service is available from 7 AM to midnight. Kids younger than 16 stay free in their parents' room. They can sleep in a connecting room with a 30 percent discount on the second-room price. Children get for free the same meal plan as their parents.

You can enjoy full or continental breakfast on your balcony, or you can let La Sirena entice you into her dining room for breakfast served buffet style. By the way, she doesn't like smoking — it isn't allowed in La Sirena. The Cafe, which serves light lunches and pastries, is also smokefree. You have more choice of restaurants in the evening. The Sea Grape outdoor restaurant lets you dine and stargaze at the same time; Lilians offers Italian cuisine; and the Boat Bay Club, a restaurant and lounge that overlooks the ocean, is another attractive alternative.

Local music groups entertain in the Boat Bay Club, with jazz, reggae and contemporary music every night of the summer season. The Palm Court Club is a sports bar with TV, billiards and other games. The Honeymoon Point, a terrace carved out of a rock, overlooks the ocean and a Sonesta-made waterfall. Ideal for weddings, it is also a venue for the cocktail party held every week to celebrate repeat visitors, honeymooners and other VIPs.

Sonesta has a full range of activities that include scuba diving, snorkeling, boating, mountain biking, bingo and dice games. Two climate-controlled pools — one outdoor, one inside — are close by, complete with changing facilities, loungers and chairs. A croquet lawn and putting green offer ball-hitting variations. Tennis is $8 an hour on any of the six Laycold courts, two of which are lighted. Want to improve your game? Book a place in the free tennis clinics given three mornings a week. Since the hotel is just 10 minutes away from four courses (including the one on the property), golf is no problem. The Sonesta tour director can arrange tee times for Riddells Bay, Southampton Princess, Port Royal and Belmont (see our Golf chapter). The "Just Us Kids" program offers games, parties, excursions, bike rides and other fun things for children (see our Kidstuff chapter). Babysitting is available for additional charge.

One of those options might be useful if you want to luxuriate in the comfort of the spa after a workout in the exercise room. There is a Jacuzzi, sauna and shower, and masseuses and beauty therapists are on hand to give a variety of relaxing treatments. Ten of Bermuda's major shops are housed in the Sonesta's main building (see our Shopping chapter).

Check-in is at 3 PM, and check-out is 11 AM. However, a number of courtesy rooms with showers and lockers are available for early arrivals. They come in handy, too, if you want that last dip before leaving for the airport. The resort levy is $3.50 per person per day. Sonesta is the only resort hotel in Bermuda that accepts pets. Call for more details.

Southampton Princess
$$$$ • 101 South Rd. • 238-8000

This resort is the younger sister of The

Luxurious accommodations are sprinkled along Bermuda's coasts.

Princess in Hamilton. Younger she may be, but little she is not. Built nine stories high atop a large hill, this hotel is as familiar a local landmark as the Gibbs Hill Lighthouse nearby. The Southampton Princess looks down on 100 acres of landscaped grounds, including an 18-hole, par 3 golf course, and out over the South Shore on one side and the Great Sound on the other.

Typically, first-time visitors prefer the South Shore option, while repeat visitors often go for the Great Sound view, so they can watch ships that pass in the night. Some rooms actually have views of both. Since the rooms on the higher floors offer the more

spectacular waterscapes, they are the more expensive options. With the less expensive rooms, water views can be partially obstructed by the roof of the restaurant. Given that proviso, be assured that all rooms have water views and private balconies. If you hate cigarette smoke, ask for a room on one of the two smokefree floors. Six rooms are specially equipped for guests in wheelchairs.

Many of the rooms are decorated in aquamarine shades that are accented by floral spreads and curtains. They offer one king or two double beds. Cribs are available for children. The TV is in the armoire, and your terry robe is in the closet, with the ironing board and iron. Clock-radios, telephones with data ports, refreshment centers, safes and hair dryers are in every room. Refrigerators are no additional charge. Bathrooms are spacious, with a separate sink and vanity area.

The Southampton Princess has a large variety of luxurious suites, duplexes and Newport Club rooms (on a special concierge floor). The hotel has extensive space and facilities for visitors on business. It has the largest ballroom in Bermuda and boasts a state-of-the-art multimedia amphitheater.

For adults, the DAP (as the two Princess hotels prefer to call it) costs $50 a day, plus $13.90 gratuity. Again, the Dine Around Plan gives guests a choice of six restaurants at Southampton, plus the three eateries at The Princess in Hamilton (see previous listing). It's free for children younger than 16 if they share their parents' room. During the summer season (mid-April through mid-November), kids can also eat in some of the restaurants for free. However, they will be charged a $10.15 daily gratuity. During the winter season, children enjoy DAP for $28 or BP for $12.

Hotel restaurants include Wickets Brasserie, Windows on the Sound (yes, it does overlook the water) and the Newport Room. Fitted with mahogany and teak, the Newport Room will give you the illusion that you are dining aboard a luxurious yacht. Another option is to take the hotel trolley from the front entrance and visit the Waterlot Inn, which also overlooks the Great Sound. Originally built more than 300 years ago, this restaurant was rebuilt after a fire in 1975 and will tempt you with Mediterranean and traditional island dishes, all presented with silver service.

If you'd rather eat on the beach, take the trolley to the Whaler Inn, perched above the surf of the South Shore, where you can feast on exquisite seafood and enjoy the waters. If you're a meat lover, try barbecue beef ribs and chops at the Rib Room in the Golf Club House, a 4-minute stroll from the indoor pool. All restaurants have large nonsmoking areas. Room service is available from 6 AM to 1 PM for an extra charge.

For a casual drink or cocktails before dinner, the lobby lounge is ideal. It offers light evening entertainment. The Neptune Club has live entertainment and dancing, and Jimmy Keyes, famous for his comic impressions, performs there. On Mondays, the managers will greet you at a swizzle party.

Activities abound at the Southampton Princess. Let's start with the kids. A complimentary, Tiny Tot sitting service caters to children 2 to 4 three mornings a week (9 AM to 2 PM). Children and teens can enjoy free activity programs from mid-June to September. These will allow them play all sorts of games, swim, go on excursions and enjoy many other activities. Perhaps most exciting of all, children can shake hands and swim with dolphins! (See Kidstuff for details of these programs.)

For adults, there is golf on the hotel's executive course. Play all day for $50, cart included. In addition, the tour director will be happy to make arrangements for you to play other island courses. There is croquet, and the Southampton Princess boasts 11 tennis courts, three of which are lighted. Rates for tennis are $12 an hour for daytime play, $15 at night. Two swimming pools — one indoors, one out — will let you improve your stroke, but if the sea calls, you can take a trolley to Princess Beach on the South Shore. There is a cabana that serves everything from a piña colada to a hamburger. The Beach Club and Nautilus Dive Shop are good stops to arrange scuba diving and snorkeling for a close encounter with the fish (see our Watersports chapter). The hotel's Secret Garden has beauty therapists and hair-care professionals and offers massages, facials and all kinds of treatments. There is a gym and sauna.

For more information about Bermuda, you might like to attend lectures. As for shopping, the hotel has a large selection of Hamilton branch shops. When you explore the hotel and the grounds, you will notice a variety of graceful bronze figures. These are the work of Desmond Fountain, whose gallery is also in the hotel (see our Arts and Culture chapter). Other artists and experts in crafts display and sell their work in the hotel.

The Southampton Princess has three seasons. Summer season starts in mid-April, the "shoulder season" runs from about September 7 to November 15 and the winter season is from mid-November to mid-April. In winter, some of the restaurants close. Entertainment is reduced but so are room rates. Check-in is 2:30 PM, and check-out is at noon. The resort levy is $3 per person per day.

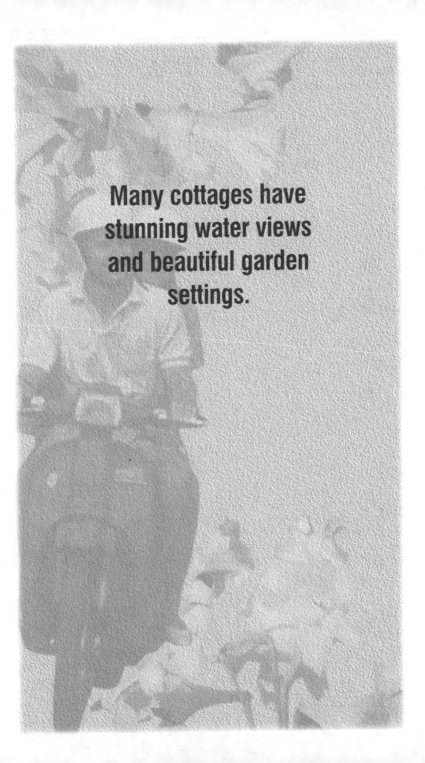

Many cottages have stunning water views and beautiful garden settings.

Cottage Colonies

Gaston Bachelard, a French philosopher, once wrote that "the house allows one to dream in peace." That is exactly what Bermuda's cottage colonies allow you to do. Smaller, more intimate and definitely more Bermudian than the larger hotels, they offer a haven from the stresses of 20th-century living. If your idea of bliss is the peace that "comes dropping slow," then the cottage colony experience may well be for you. Be assured, though, that you won't miss out on 20th-century luxury.

What exactly is a cottage colony? As you might expect, it is a collection of cottages separate from a main building that often houses front desk, restaurants, bars and lounge areas. However, the word "cottage" needs explanation. It originally meant a very small, detached house, and indeed some of our older colonies do have old cottages that fit this description. But the newer buildings could be better described as cottages with anywhere from two to five units. Rooms can be offered as individual units for double occupancy rates, or they can be offered as suites. In some cases, then, you could have a cottage to yourself for suite rates. If you opt for an individual room, rest assured you will have a private balcony or terrace and a private bathroom.

The cottage colonies generally have some features of the traditional Bermudian house — a buttery, for example, and a white ridged roof — and they all offer comfort, graciousness and privacy. Some of the suites have separate living rooms. Bear in mind that the living and dining area is always spacious, and bathrooms, without exception, are roomy and luxurious.

Many cottages have stunning water views and beautiful garden settings. You can sit on your private terrace or balcony and savor the fragrance of the flowers and the blues, greens and pinks that are Bermuda's true colors. Above all, you will feel that you are in the house of your dreams and not in a hotel at all. In fact, the tranquility they offer makes them ideal for honeymooners, so be sure to ask for information on honeymoon packages. There's just one problem. We have seven cottage colonies. Which one will you choose? Just as dream houses vary in detail and ambiance, so do these properties. The individual listings describe these variances, but first we concentrate on the policies and features the properties share. Having said that, we must point out that some of the premises are wheelchair-accessible, and some are not. In the listings we will tell you which ones are suitable for guests in wheelchairs.

Even by Bermudian standards, the staff at most of the cottage colonies are remarkable for their friendliness and helpfulness. Many have worked at one colony more than 25 years and feel a personal loyalty to their managers and guests. Take the time to talk to them. They will certainly give you information and insights that will enrich your experience in Bermuda. But please, remember the social niceties of civilized life. "Good mornings" are important, as are "please" and "thank you."

Kids, Pets, Smoking

If you want plenty of add-on entertainment and activities for children, then the cottage colony option may not be for you. The emphasis is generally on peace and tranquility. If, on the other hand, you want casual time with your family for talking and walking, sailing and swimming, then that is what you will have. Some cottage colonies are more family-oriented than others. For that reason, we will tell you in each listing whether the colony welcomes children.

On the whole, cottage colonies have a relaxed smoking policy. Without exception, you may smoke in your rooms, in the bars and in the lounges. In some dining rooms you can smoke in designated areas, while in others you cannot smoke at all. In the individual listings, we'll specify smoking policies where dining rooms are concerned.

We're afraid that dogs, cats and other animals must stay at home. No pets are allowed in any of the cottage colonies.

FYI

Unless otherwise noted, the area code for all phone numbers listed in this guide is 441.

Seasonality, Reservations and Cancellation Policies

Cottage colonies are very popular, particularly in the summer season. There is also a high repeat visitor rate, so be sure to book as early as possible. We will give you the necessary lead time in each listing, since they range anywhere from 30 days to six months. Generally speaking, the colonies require a first and last night deposit, usually refundable if you cancel up to 21 days before your reservation date. Be aware that some do not accept credit cards; we will specify which ones in the listings. In all cases, you can pay by personal check, travelers' checks or by money order. Guests, by the way, usually reserve through a travel agent, or they call direct.

Typically, the summer season starts in April and ends October to November. We will again be specific in each listing, as season dates can vary from property to property. Do verify these dates because they can make an enormous difference in cost. A few properties close to refurbish for a short period in the winter. In all cases during the winter season, entertainment is reduced and beach facilities, such as beach clubs, close. Check for special packages (for golfers, for example) that are often offered during the winter season.

Rates of Rooms

Here we must confess that we have found it difficult to create a completely consistent pricing code. Nearly all the cottage colonies base their daily rates on MAP *for two*. MAP, you may recall from the Resort Hotels chapter, means Modified American Plan, and it offers room, breakfast and dinner. However, two of the listings in this chapter do not include MAP in the code that we quote. As it happens, both of these have been allocated one dollar sign. We explain what the rate covers in those individual listings. You may take it, then, that all cottage colonies showing two to four dollar signs include MAP in the daily rates.

Pricing Key

The daily rates listed in the pricing key are based on the rooms visitors would most typically reserve during the peak season. They do not include the 7.25 percent Bermuda hotel occupancy tax, gratuities or additional charges for telephone calls or other expenses. Bear in mind that gratuity policies can differ, so they will be stated in each listing. Rates are always subject to change.

$	$325 to $350
$$	$351 to $376
$$$	$377 to $400
$$$$	$400 or more

Cottage Listings

We now go to our listings, presented east to west, parish by parish, subset by subset and thereafter in alphabetical order.

St. George's Parish

St. George's Club
$ • Rose Hill • 297-1200

St. George's Club is Bermuda's newest cottage colony, built in 1982. In 1997, the property was completely refurbished, and 10 new luxury cottages were added to bring the total

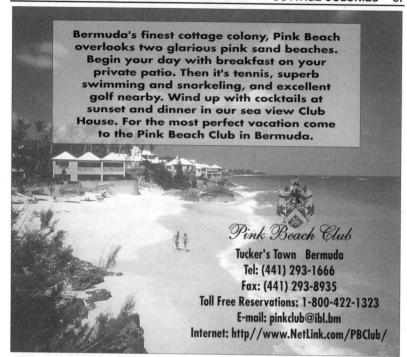

number of cottages to 71. An affiliate of Resort Condominiums International, St. George's Club is also Bermuda's first and premier time-sharing resort.

As explained in the introduction, the price code for St. George's Club does not include an MAP plan or any food plan. Thus, the code given refers to the price per night for a one-bedroom cottage that can house up to four guests with no meals included. As you will see, two-bedroom cottages are also available for about $200 a night extra. These can house up to six guests.

The clubhouse and cottages sit prettily on top of Rose Hill and overlook the old town of St. George's and St. George's Harbour on the one side and St. George's Golf Course on the other. In fact, proximity to Bermuda's old capital is what draws guests to visit again and again. Modern the property may be, but history surrounds it. A short walk down steps in the grounds takes you to the town's many historic attractions.

Cottages are mostly double-storied, containing two bedrooms, two bathrooms, a kitchen and a living/dining room. (The second bedroom can be converted into a private studio if you want the one-bedroom option.) Stairs with attractive cedar railings lead up to the large master bedroom decorated in pastel shades and equipped with a double closet. A cedar chest adds a traditional Bermudian touch. Here you will also find a luxurious sunken tub. Sink in bubbles and watch palm trees outside your window sway in the breeze. You will find a separate shower in the bathroom and a double sink.

The living/dining area has a dining table, a pull-out sofa, comfortable chairs and a coffee table. There's also a television — the VCR you can rent. If you feel up to doing a little cooking, the kitchen will please you. It is equipped with microwave, electric stove, fridge, dishwasher, toaster, blender and coffee maker, together with all the china and glasses you might need. A convenience store on the property supplies the basics for breakfast and snacks. Each cottage has a washer and dryer, and there's also an ironing board.

All cottages have private balconies or terraces with garden views. Sit out and enjoy your breakfast to the music of Bermuda's sounds. Listen carefully and you will hear the church bells of St. George's and children's laughter in the town's recreational park below. There's no room service, by the way, but there is maid service twice a week. Feel like some action? Three swimming pools (one heated) will let you cool off. Three tennis courts on the property (two lighted for night play) offer a little more strenuous activity. Tennis, incidentally, is free. Golf? But of course — the St. George's Golf Course surrounds you (see our Golf chapter). The cottage colony itself has a putting green and a croquet lawn.

www.insiders.com
See this and many other **Insiders' Guide®** destinations online — in their entirety.
Visit us today!

If the ocean calls you, no problem. St. George's Club has its own private beach club that overlooks a beach shaped like a heel. Its name? Achilles Bay, naturally. But don't worry, it is neither sulky nor dangerous, unlike the ancient Greek hero it's named after. Achilles Bay offers some of the best snorkeling on the island, and a concession there will make arrangements for scuba diving. It will also make arrangements for sailing in a Sunfish or boating in a canoe. For evening romance, take a sunset cruise. As for the beach club, it has a sun deck where you can enjoy lunch, snacks and cocktails from 11:30 AM to 10 PM. To reach it (and the golf clubhouse), you can take a shuttle that in high season runs every half-hour.

You will find two restaurants in the clubhouse: the Margaret Rose Restaurant for more formal dining and the Bar and Bistro. We must tell you here that on Sunday, Bermudians love Margaret Rose dearly for her sumptuous brunches. She does not require jacket and tie, but she definitely doesn't like smoke. On Mondays and Fridays there is live island music.

Kids are very welcome here. Cribs and high chairs are always on hand, and babysitters are $10 an hour. St. George's is not, however, a good option for guests in wheelchairs. The hilly setting makes wheelchair access difficult.

We mentioned timesharing, and it is big here. Every year 70 percent of the cottages are sold as timesharing units. Timesharing guests can buy anywhere from one week to 11 weeks of annual holiday. On average, they tend to buy two. Because Bermuda is an extremely popular vacation destination, timeshares booked at this resort have very strong trading power.

Remember that if you do book timesharing at St. George's Club, you will reserve a particular cottage at a particular time or times of year. For more details on timesharing rates and conditions, call the hotel direct.

St. George's Club is unusual in that it has two shoulder seasons (March 1 through March 29 and November 8 through January 2). High season is March 31 through November 8. Check these dates with the hotel, as they are subject to change. For the summer season, book at least six months in advance to be sure of a cottage, although last-minute cancellations can make spur-of-the-moment reservations possible. You can use major credit cards to pay your first and last night deposit, which you lose should you cancel within 21 days of your arrival date. Check-in is at 4 PM, checkout at 10 AM, and courtesy rooms are available for early arrivals or late departures. In addition to the cottage rate, a $6.40 per person daily fee is charged for housekeeping.

Hamilton Parish

Pink Beach Club and Cottages
$$ • 116 South Rd. • 293-1666

You can guess how this cottage colony got its name, can't you? Yes, it does have its own private beach — two, actually. And yes, the beaches are pink, thanks to the trillions of minuscule pink shells and skeletons that make up the sands of our South Shore.

Originally, Pink Beach's 16.5 acres were used for farming. Come the Depression in the '30s, an American family bought the land and built their own house on it. After World War II was over, Bermudian Harold Gibbons decided a cottage colony would be a good idea for people who wanted to travel again. He acquired the land and personally supervised the completion of the Club House and nine cottages. W.A. "Toppy" Cowen, general manager of Pink Beach until last year, had some wonderful stories to tell about Mr. Gibbons. Indeed, he has recorded some of them in newsletters that he distributed to guests. Apparently Harold was a stickler for etiquette and for the work ethic. Even Gary Cooper, the film star, came under his watchful eye. When Cooper arrived late for dinner one evening, he received a strong reprimand for "upsetting the dining room." Staff today are convinced that Mr. Gibbons' ghost prowls the premises at night and that he is still enforcing the very high standards he always expected.

Since Mr. Gibbons' time, more cottage units and suites have been added, but they all retain the white ridged roofs of the traditional Bermudian cottage. You will also see buttery towers and long chimneys. The outer walls of the buildings are all painted pink — but naturally.

The Club House is the focal part of the property. In it you will find the main dining room, where breakfast and dinner are served, and a small, very comfortable lounge, complete with fireplace. Both have fantastic views of the South Shore reef. You will also find the bar, more familiarly known as Leon's Bar because Leon presides over it. Have a quiet drink here before dinner, and be sure to admire the Bermuda cedar bar structure. If you want a game of skittles or cards, find the games room

that is also in the Club House. Walk out of the bar to find the pool area, which was recently expanded and tiled. Ideal for outdoor dining, barbecues and management swizzle parties, it is also the venue for top local entertainment. Most nights in the summer season, Calypso and steel bands and pianists will serenade you. You want to "dance with the dancers and drink with the drinkers"? Feel free. There's plenty of floor space. During the day you can dip in the pool, then relax under an umbrella.

The cottage units and suites dot the landscape. All the ones within the price range we have quoted have close views of the ocean and reef. In fact, some are so close that you can actually see parrotfish from your patio or balcony. Early morning or evening you may see silver fish jumping right out of the water.

All the rooms are spacious, even if they have a combined living room and bedroom. They can accommodate a king-size bed or two doubles, and they are comfortably furnished with table and chairs, sofa, desk and plenty of drawer and closet space. Some have cathedral, beamed ceilings, others the Bermudian tray ceilings. Many have sliding doors that open onto the patio or balcony. All come with clock-radio, telephone, safe and trouser press. Bermudian art decorates the walls. Note well, however, that television is only available if you specifically request it. The idea, you see, is that for a little space you enjoy quiet contemplation and gentle conversation without the

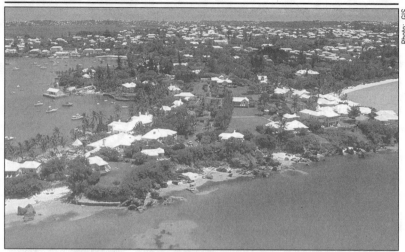

Photo: GIS

This aerial shot offers a view of a section of Sandys Parish.

rude interruption of the screen box. Bathrooms are spacious and often have double sinks.

Instead of watching television, you can rent snorkeling equipment and introduce yourself to the fish. If you are a strong swimmer, you can swim out to the reef and enjoy the glories of the marine world. Feel like exploring the island? Rent a motorized bike from Wheels, right on the property. Or you can have a gentle game of tennis on one of the two courts. A tennis pro is on hand to help you improve your serve. As for golf, Pink Beach is right next door to Bermuda's famous Mid Ocean Club course. Mondays, Wednesdays and Fridays you can play on this exclusive club's lay-out. You can also play at Castle Harbour, another prestigious golf club nearby (see Golf chapter for details). The staff will be happy to make arrangements for you.

You might be wondering about children. They are very welcome, but they do stay at additional cost. Call direct for details of room rates. No activities are available specifically for children, but if you want to share leisure and activity time with your kids, Pink Beach is ideal.

Book at least 30 days in advance to be sure of a reservation. Public holidays are booked up particularly quickly. You may use major credit cards to pay the first and last night deposit. Cancel within 21 days of your

arrival date, and you will lose your deposit. Gratuity is 10 percent of your room rate. Check-in is at 2 PM, check-out at noon. Courtesy rooms will let you have that extra swim if you want to arrive early or leave late.

Devonshire Parish

Ariel Sands Beach Club
$$$ • 34 South Rd. • 236-1010, (800) 468-6610

Ever since the Dill family converted this property into a cottage colony in 1954, Ariel Sands has had a distinctly theatrical flavor. This is hardly surprising, given that acting runs in the Dills' genes. When Matthew Dill starred in *The Tempest*, his grandmother decided to name the property after Shakespeare's sprite, Ariel, who is associated with magic, spirit and art. Besides, she thought the rock in the South Shore bay looked like him. In 1976, J. Seward Johnson sculpted Ariel out of 500 pounds of stainless steel. There he stands on that same rock as if poised for flight.

In 1995 the beach club underwent extensive expansion, and a new character appeared on the scene: Caliban's Seaside Restaurant and Bar, which offers even more spirit than Ariel. More exciting developments happened in 1997, when actor Michael Douglas (son of actress Diana Dill Darrid and Kirk Douglas) led a $5 million dollar renovation of the property. In addition to completely refurbishing the cottages and the bar, Douglas also added The Ariel Sands Fitness Centre & Spa and Ariel's Seaside Conference Centre. (Call the hotel for information about business and conference facilities.)

Ariel Sands makes full use of its hillside ocean setting. As soon as you arrive, you will notice the lush foliage of the landscaping and the tropical touch of the palm trees against the sky. You will also notice the traditional white ridged roofs so loved by Bermudians. Front desk and lobby are in the one-story main building, as are the lounge and bar. The lobby sports a blue, yellow and white tent-like ceiling, which gives a light but exotic effect. A huge double fireplace, which can burn logs on both sides, divides the bar from the lounge. In the bar, the Bermuda cedar bar structure, canopy and mantle contrast strikingly with charcoal-gray painted walls. Photographs hanging in the bar allow you to become acquainted with Michael Douglas. The lounge, overlooking the pool and ocean, has white-paneled French doors that lead you into Caliban's. It also has comfortable chairs where you can curl up with a good book or chat with friends. A baby grand piano adds elegance and, in the evening, relaxing music.

Cottage units and suite names continue the Shakespearean theme. You could, for example, stay in Miranda's Cabana or in Prospero's Deluxe. It is difficult to describe a "typical" room or suite since, like most cottage colonies, Ariel deliberately adds individual touches to enhance the home-away-from-home effect. However, whether they have a separate living room or not, rooms are all spacious with plenty of vanity and living space. They tend to have Bermudian tray ceilings, and they are tiled throughout. Some have indoor shutters; others have natural fiber curtains. Walls are in vibrant yellows, greens, pinks and blues. All units are fully equipped with cable television, refrigerator, coffee maker, iron, umbrella and safe. Bathrooms are tiled and come with hair dryers. Private patios give you your own little garden space. All rooms have views of the South Shore, but the nearer to Ariel's beach, the higher the price. Actually, it's impossible for you to be more than 100 yards from the beach. We should add that there are four rooms for guests who use wheelchairs. Please book these well in advance.

Mornings, you can stroll down to Caliban's for your breakfast, or you can have it delivered to your cottage by one of the staff. (Staff at Ariel Sands are so friendly, by the way, that it is not unusual for them to pick up repeat visitors from the airport in their own cars on their own time.) Caliban's has an inside dining room, but it extends out to a wooden terraced deck — ideal for alfresco dining under the stars and for the outdoor bar (see our Restaurants chapter). If you want to catch a glimpse of Bermuda's politicians and civil servants, have lunch here. It's their favorite escape from the pressing problems of the day. The restaurant has a relaxed smoking policy — for now there is no nonsmoking section. During the summer season, a steel band plays outside four nights a week. Other nights you can listen to the piano or guitar. Ariel has a dine-around plan, incidentally, meaning you can use your MAP to dine at other restaurants that are members of the Bermuda Collection dine-around plan.

Relaxation is the name of the game at Ariel; even so, activities await you. You can swim in the heated freshwater pool or in one of two unusual, ocean-fed pools. Then there's the sea itself, of course. Snorkeling equipment available for rent will allow you to frolic with Ariel and also with the fishes. Or you can just relax under the palmetto umbrellas that dot the beach. Tennis is easy — you can play free of charge right on the property. A putting green will let you practice your golf before playing at any of Bermuda's famous golf courses (see our Golf chapter). The staff will happily make those arrangements for you. Mondays, Wednesdays and Fridays, you can play at the famous Mid Ocean Club. The new private spa offers a full gym with equipment for self-torture (open 24 hours a day), two massage rooms, a Jacuzzi and facilities for hydrotherapy (open until 7 PM). Feet, face and hands may all be looked after by expert therapists.

Children are accepted at Ariel. Having said that, there are a few restrictions. For example, because the spa is close by the freshwater pool, young children are not allowed to swim in it. The relaxed elegance of this cottage colony is perhaps more suitable for the adult visitors who want a carefree experience.

Book at least 60 days in advance to be sure of a reservation. Public holidays are particularly booked up quickly. You may use major credit cards to pay the first and last day deposit. Cancel within 21 days of your arrival date, and you will lose your deposit. Gratuity is 10 percent of your room rate. Check-in is at 2 PM, check-out at noon.

Paget Parish

Horizons and Cottages
$$$$, no credit cards • 33 South Rd. • 236-0048

On top of a hill, this cottage colony certainly does have horizons. Gazing across pool and tropical gardens, you can let your eyes concentrate on the blue of the Atlantic. Some days, however, you might ask yourself, "Now exactly where does the sky end and the ocean begin?"

Horizons' history goes back to 1710, when one of its owners, a Capt. Lewis Middleton, went off to the Turks Islands to squabble with the French and Spanish over a few salt beds. Nearly 200 years after that, an Alfred Blackburn Smith fell in love with it, expanded and renovated it and opened it as a guest house in 1928. If he were alive today, no doubt he would

FYI

Unless otherwise noted, the area code for all phone numbers listed in this guide is 441.

be gratified to know that Horizons is currently a member of Relais et Chateau. Membership depends on maintaining the five C's: calm, comfort, charm, cuisine and courtesy. Horizons achieves these qualities by blending the best of the old with the luxury of the new.

The historic atmosphere of the property is very apparent, especially in the main building, where the architecture is distinctively Bermudian. For starters, there's the white ridged roof, which is charmingly bumpy in places, and the white painted chimneys. White keystone corners and "in and outs" edge the sides of pink outer walls. Dark green shutters emphasize the traditional look.

Walk into the drawing room, and you feel all the charm of an 18th-century country house. Alcoves and archways divide it so that you can enjoy a variety of seating areas. Armchairs and sofas are comfortable, while the dark wooden floors and occasional tables suggest the antique. The deep tray ceiling, cedar beams and cedar chest remind you that you are in Bermuda. Every afternoon you can enjoy tea in this enchanting room.

Books are an important feature at Horizons. In addition to the bookcases in the lounge, a well-stocked library will ensure that you're never short of a good read. While you're there, admire the dark oak Welsh hutch and the corner cabinet's display of beautiful china plates.

The pub, in the oldest part of the building, uses some of the original beams. Again, alcoves are a feature, dividing the room into different sections and giving the effect of nooks and crannies. Here you can have a drink before dinner or a game of skittles. If you are a golfer, you may well become a member of the Hole in One Club — a plaque displays all the names of players who have achieved this extraordinary feat. Bear in mind, though, that if you do get a hole in one, you are morally bound to buy everyone a drink! More on golf later.

Dining at Horizons means dressing up for the occasion, so jacket and tie are mandatory most nights. When you see the gracious formality of the dining room, you'll understand why informal wear would be unthinkable. How-

Photo: GIS

From atop Rose Hill you can see the ancient Town of St. George, its harbor and the ocean beyond.

ever, Friday nights are casual nights, when you can enjoy a barbecue on the terrace that overlooks the South Shore. Mondays, Thursdays, Fridays and Saturdays, enjoy live entertainment that ranges from the melodious notes of the classical guitar to the traditional island music of the Bermuda Strollers. Dancing is definitely encouraged. Horizons, by the way, has a dine-around plan that enables guests to use their MAP for meals at any of her three sister hotels: Coral Beach Beach and Tennis Club (a prestigious private club), Newstead in Paget and Waterloo House in Hamilton (see our Small Hotels chapter).

Horizons 13 cottages, spread over 25 acres of beautifully landscaped gardens, offer 48 accommodations. For every five rooms there is a common room that, like the main drawing room, offers guests an opportunity to make friends with each other in comfortable, elegant surroundings. All rooms have private patios that allow guests peaceful contemplation of oleander, bamboo, palmetto and palm and sometimes of the ocean beyond. Again, it is difficult to describe a typical room, as Horizons prides itself on avoiding the boring and uniform. The rooms are decorated in a variety of colors, though fabrics for curtains and furnishings tend to be European. All the rooms have spacious living areas with comfortable

chairs and sofas. Antique desks and chests add a traditional touch, and many units have working fireplaces — so cheering in the winter months. The private bathrooms are also spacious, as are the vanity areas, some of which sport charming kidney-shaped dressing tables that date to the 1930s. All are stocked with hair dryers and tissue boxes. Clock-radios and ice boxes are also provided. Television and VCR, by the way, are available if you request them. Room service is special at Horizons because this is the one cottage colony where a maid will follow the old Bermudian practice of preparing your breakfast in the kitchen area of the cottage. Yes, each cottage has a kitchen but worry not. Only staff are allowed to cook there. The main building also has guest rooms, two of which are wheelchair-accessible and specially equipped with racks.

The swimming pool, together with the mashie nine-hole golf course and three tennis courts on the grounds, will prevent you from becoming lazy. Both golf and tennis cost $4 a day. If you want more recreational facilities and access to the sea, you will enjoy them across the road at Coral Beach and Tennis Club, which has a stunning beach with coral sands (comfortable loungers and towels are provided), plus excellent tennis and squash and an 18-hole putting green. You can also use the health club. On weekdays, Horizons' guests pay $6 a day for use of Coral Beach's facilities; on weekends, they pay $12 a day.

Children are very welcome. No kids' programs are available, but if you crave that precious, quality time with your family so difficult to find in these hectic times, you will have it at Horizons. Babysitting is available.

Book as early as possible, particularly for dates between March 15 and January 3 (high season). Be aware that Horizon's does not accept any credit cards. A deposit for two nights is required. You can pay with personal or travelers' checks, cash or money order. If you cancel within 21 days of your arrival date, you will have a year in which to book another holiday at the property, otherwise you lose your deposit. Check-in time is flexible. Check-out is at noon. Horizons has a 10 percent service charge per room.

Warwick Parish

Fourways Inn
$ • 1 Middle Rd. • 236-6517,
(800) 962-7654

Before we describe Fourways, we must remind you that the price code does not include MAP. However, it does include your room and continental breakfast for two. An MAP plan is available at $42.50 per person, providing you take it for at least three nights.

There are actually four ways to reach this inn. It stands at a four-way junction near Amen Corner that marks the boundary between Paget and Warwick parishes. In fact, it has stood there ever since the early 1700s, when a certain John Harvey decided he wanted a Bermudian house made of coral limestone and native cedar. John, by the way, was a member of the Canadian Harvey family, famous for Harvey's Bristol sherry. In 1727 the house was duly built, and he sailed to Bermuda from Newfoundland to live in it. It's location was very important to him because it meant that his friends could easily reach him by horse and carriage. Apparently, they enjoyed his lavish parties so much, they ended up staying the night — no doubt they suffered from an excess of sherry and fine wine.

The house remained a private, albeit hospitable, residence until the 1950s when it became a guest house. Bermudian owner, Mr. Moss, advertised it as "Old England in a New World setting with an English Tap Room." Come the mid-1970s, a W. Sommer, together with a group of Bermudian entrepreneurs, bought it and converted it into one of the island's top restaurants. When Bermudians think of Fourways, they invariably think of Christmas dinner. The Old World charm of the dining room, which features stone walls and cedar, makes it an ideal setting for a Dickensian Christmas extravaganza. A favorite dining choice for locals, Fourways also caters to business travelers. Smaller dining areas off the main dining room and a banquet room are very suitable for business meetings and conventions. Smoking is allowed. In the summer months, dinner is served on the Palm Garden terrace. Every night, you can relax to the classical pianist's romantic music (see our Restaurants chapter for menu options). The Peg Leg Lounge and Bar also have a quaint atmosphere. The bar's old Bermuda fireplace and exposed beams in the ceiling remind us of the inn's history. To add to the atmosphere, the bar has a great selection of cigars. Lunch, high teas and cocktails are served in the lounge, where in the evening you can hear live guitar music.

Fourways is also famous locally for its pastry shop on the property. Many a dieter has been successfully tempted with fresh-baked croissants or almond danishes. You can depend on your breakfast including baked goodies straight from the oven. It's delivered to your room every morning, together with *The Royal Gazette*.

Which brings us to accommodation. Five separate cottages were added to the property in 1986. Double-storied, they surround a small freshwater pool in the middle of a palm and oleander garden. Deluxe rooms with private bathrooms are on the top stories; one bedroom suites with private terraces are on the ground level. The price code covers the price of both. Rooms come with king-size bed, pull-out sofa, chairs and desk. Arrangements of cut flowers grace the table. All have double closets containing a safe, ironing board and iron, slippers and a bathrobe. Cable TV, telephone and clock-radio are all supplied. Bathrooms are spacious with marble double sinks. Hair dryers are also on hand. In addition, a small kitchenette area gives you a burner, fridge and sink. There's a coffee maker, together with a kettle and a toaster oven. The suites offer a microwave oven as well.

Fourways does not have its own beach. However, guests can obtain passes that allow them access to the private facilities on Elbow Beach (see our Beaches and Resort Hotels chapters). The staff is happy to make arrangements for golf at Port Royal, Belmont and Riddles Bay golf courses, and tennis at Elbow Beach and Belmont. If you are interested in watersports, they will arrange those too. You may want to rent bikes (staff will help you out there as well), but bear in mind that a bus stop is just around the corner, and a ferry stop is about five minutes away.

Kids are welcome here. Those younger than age 11 stay with their parents for free. This is where the pull-out sofa comes in useful. Children older than 11 are charged $40. We should tell you here that in the dining room, younger children are encouraged to come at 6:30 PM. Fourways is probably not a good option for guests in wheelchairs. Access is not impossible, but it is difficult.

High season is April 1 to October 31. Low season is November 1 to March 31. You may pay your two night deposit with major credit cards. Cancel within 21 days of your scheduled arrival, and you lose your deposit. There's a 10 percent service charge per room, plus a 15 percent per person gratuity if you opt for MAP. Check-in is at 2:30 PM; check-out is 11:30 AM.

Sandys Parish

Lantana
$$$ • 53 Wellway Reserve, Somerset Bridge, Somerset Village • 234-0141, (800) 468-3733

Lantana involucrata is the Latin name given to the common sage bush, a fragrant shrub that is extremely prevalent in Bermuda. This property is therefore well-named, with its 22 acres of beautiful gardens that cascade down from the Main Club house to the edge of the Great Sound. Peter Leseur, the only owner of a cottage colony who is also manager, shares with his wife a deep love of gardening. As soon as you drive into the property (situated, by the way, next to Somerset Bridge, the smallest drawbridge over the Atlantic), you will notice the flower beds of petunias, begonias and impatiens, glorious vines and the rich variety of trees such as bay grape, palm and the beautiful jacaranda. If you stay here, be sure to explore the grounds thoroughly. We can promise you a rose garden planted by Mrs. Leseur and also the small Palmetto Point farm, which is filled with Bermuda onions, potatoes, parsley and thyme to supply the kitchen with fresh homegrown vegetables and herbs.

Gardening is, of course, an art form, but the Leseurs enjoy art in more forms than one. Throughout the grounds you will see bronze sculptures collected from around the world. In fact, Lantana has been appropriately described as "a museum without walls." As you approach La Plage waterside restaurant, you may notice an extremely bronzed young lady who sits peacefully and brazenly naked on a garden bench, reading an equally bronzed paper. She is one of the many creations of Bermuda's own sculptor, Desmond Fountain, and she is a favorite with local visitors who like to sit next to her for a few minutes.

Lantana has 61 units in all. Many of the rooms are right on the water, and all have private balconies or terraces that will allow you contemplative appreciation of the gardens and the fish who will swim in to greet you. Here you can sit and enjoy a continental breakfast. From the outside, the cottages are distinctively Bermudian in appearance with their pink walls and white ridged roofs and shutters. Inside, though, they are more Mediterranean in design with lots of terra cotta tile, bright print curtains and spreads and light rattan furniture. The overall effect is cool, light and airy. Bathrooms are spacious, and there are large vanity areas. All rooms come with honor bar, coffee maker, fridge, telephone with data port, clock-radio and safe. They also come with irons, hair dryers, umbrellas and Barnard bathrobes. Individually controlled air conditioning units allow you to choose your own room temperature. Television is available upon request.

FYI

Unless otherwise noted, the area code for all phone numbers listed in this guide is 441.

The Main Club house sits on top of a hill overlooking the Great Sound and, like the cottages, is Bermudian in exterior appearance and Mediterranean in interior design. The Leseurs' love of flowers, plants and art is again evident. If by any extraordinary chance you tire of the water view, then you can let your eyes rest on the flower arrangements and lush hanging baskets. Here you can enjoy a cocktail or after-dinner drink in the Carousel Bar, the Main Lounge or on the Marine terrace. And here in the dining room, surrounded by paintings and sculptures, you can wine and dine and appreciate a perfect blend of fine and culinary art .

Children, by the way, are welcome at Lantana, but children younger than 3 — while they stay free — are not allowed in the dining room. Babysitters are always available. Smoking is not allowed in the dining room either, but everywhere else you may smoke if you wish. Three nights a week you can dance to live Calypso, and managers will meet you at their complimentary swizzle party on Monday night. Every afternoon, the staff serves complimentary afternoon tea at 4 PM.

For a more informal eating experience try La Plage, which, as its name implies, is right at the water's edge and also close to the swimming pool. Trees rooted into the outside terrace offer shade from the glare of the sun. La Plage is an absolute favorite of locals, who typically come on Sundays to partake of fish chowder and codfish cakes.

A whole host of activities await you at Lantana. You can practice on the putting green or indulge in a vicious game of croquet on one of two lawns. You can play tennis for free on the all-weather tennis courts. Golf is your game? No problem. You can play at Port Royal or at Riddell's Bay (see our Golf chapter), both of which are close by. If the prestigious Mid Ocean Club appeals, you can play there Mondays, Wednesdays and Fridays. Lantana's private beach means you can swim with the fishes. More interested in catching them? Deep-sea fishing is available. In fact, Windjammer Watersports is right on the property and offers every water-related sport imaginable other than scuba diving. But that's no problem either — staff will make scuba arrangements for you at Blue Water Watersports and Robinson's Marina in Somerset (see our Watersports chapter). And if you want a trip to town or to Dockyard, you can easily pick up the government ferry from the stop close by.

Book with a two-night deposit at least nine weeks ahead of your vacation. High season is April 16 through November 15. Lantana accepts major credit cards, and the 21-day cancellation rule applies. Check-in is at 2 PM, check-out at noon. In the summer a daily 10 percent room service gratuity is charged. Because of its terraced grounds, Lantana is not a good option for visitors in wheelchairs.

Cambridge Beaches
$$$$, no credit cards • 30 King's Point Rd. • 234-0331, (800) 468-7300

You could be forgiven for thinking this cottage colony got its name from beaches called "Cambridge." True, it actually has five private beaches, but none of them has ever been called Cambridge. (More on the beaches later.) No, the name goes back more than 200 years, when a house called Cambridge was built close to the entrance of this property. You can still see it, though now it is called Torwood. During the late 1920s, Hugh Gray and his wife fixed it up as a guest accommodation for tourists visiting in the then-popular winter season. In the meantime, the Gilbert family ran "The Beaches" as a guest cottage. Mr. Gray eventually bought the property from the Gilberts to expand his business, and so the marriage of names. That cottage is now Cambridge Beaches' Main House. Over the years Mr. Gray gradually bought out other private homes. "So what?" you might ask. Well, many of them are more than 150 years old. One, Pegem, was built by a seafaring entrepreneur more than 350 years ago. You can still see the original cedar beams in the ceilings.

And so Cambridge Beaches is the oldest cottage colony still in existence. Many of its cottages have a history behind them, and so does its location on the small peninsula off Somerset Island. Mangrove Bay, which it overlooks on one side, was a favorite anchorage for Bermudian smugglers, who would unload their merchandise there to escape the watchful eye of officers at the St. George's Custom's House. And families in Somerset, you may be interested to know, disobeyed the Bermuda government by supporting the rebels during the American Revolution (see our History chapter).

Today, Cambridge Beaches is the ultimate experience for those who seek romance. Michael Winfield, the colony managing director, put it this way: "For many, relaxation is a

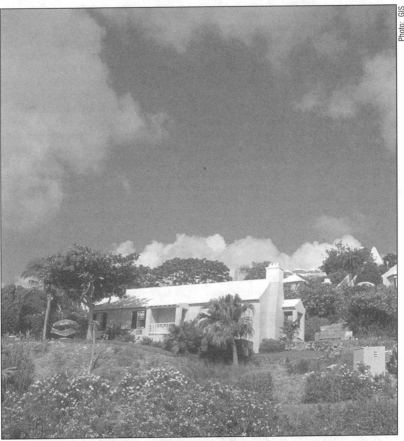

Photo: GIS

Cottage colonies make for a uniquely Bermudain vacation experience.

forgotten art. We want our guests to rediscover it. . . . We offer a sophisticated but romantic environment in which guests can do nothing and do it well." What does "doing nothing" entail? Well, you can enjoy the 25 acres of beautifully landscaped grounds. You can swim in the outdoor pool or at any of the five aforementioned beaches that include Long Bay, Turtle Cove, Point Beach and numerous coves. You can take a boat to the three islands off King's Point; if you fancy a picnic, staff will prepare you a lunch basket. A marina on the property offers sailing, kayaking, motor boats and fishing and snorkeling equipment. You can even go out for a cocktail or an after-dinner moonlight sail. You can play tennis on any of the three all-weather outdoor courts (free during the day, $2.50 per half-hour on a lit court), enjoy croquet on the lawn or practice on the putting green. Cambridge Beaches has membership at all of Bermuda's golf courses, including the Mid-Ocean Club, so games are easily arranged. Port Royal Golf Course is just 10 minutes away (see our Golf chapter).

If by any chance the elements are unkind to you, the new spa will definitely cheer you up. A European health and beauty operation, it has six treatment rooms, sauna, steam, hair and beauty facilities. An all-weather facility, the lower level houses the Ocean Spa with its six treatment rooms, sauna, steam, hair and beauty facility. In addition to the therapists on hand to pamper you with a myriad of treatments, there are counselors who can advise you on healthier lifestyles. Meanwhile, you needn't go hungry. After contorting yourself in the exercise rooms, you can always get refreshment at the cafe. The upper level, the Seven Seas Solarium, has an indoor swimming pool under a retractable glass ceiling, and exercise pool, a whirlpool and gym.

In fact, it would be entirely possible to stay on the property for the whole of your vacation. There's even a shop for that special gift you need to send to Uncle George or Auntie Agatha. However, if you feel like a more extensive shopping and/or sightseeing excursion, you can always take the complimentary ferry shuttle to Hamilton.

So what about the cottages? There are 38 in all and 81 units. As we mentioned, many are old, but several have been built much more recently. They are all traditional in design and modern in luxury. Of course they have the Bermudian white ridged roofs and shutters. Inside, fireplaces and antique furniture give them the country elegance of an 18th-century English house. Walls are pale; upholstery is fresh and bright. In most you will find an antique desk where you can practice the equally 18th-century art of writing letters. Bathrooms are magnificently marble and contain whirlpool tubs and bidets, double sinks and plenty of vanity space. Terry robes are on hand.

All rooms have safes, toasters and umbrellas; many have fridges and irons. And all have private terraces, where you can enjoy your full breakfast and views of coconut palms curving around the water's edge. Most rooms, incidentally, have a water view, but a few do not. If a water view is important, make sure you ask for one. Television? Only if you request it. The charge for television and VCR in your room is $5 a day.

Now to the Main House, which again evokes 18th-century elegance. Two fireplaces and a cathedral ceiling in the tea room area add to that effect. Feel like a leisurely read? Well-stocked bookcases will help you out. Here

INSIDERS' TIP

Before refrigerators cooled Bermuda down, butteries were once used as storage buildings for perishable food. The thickness of their walls and the slits on all sides of the building helped to chill drinks and food such as milk and, of course, butter. These days butteries are still popular, particularly in the cottage colonies, but they tend to be used as bathrooms. How do you recognize a buttery? It's often separate from the main building and has a distinctive white roof that is like a rounded pyramid or a vanilla ice cream cone with ridges.

you will take morning coffee or complimentary afternoon tea at 4 PM. The Main House also contains the Port of Call Bar, where you can have lunch. In the evening enjoy a predinner drink and then, on formal nights, proceed to the candlelit Tamarisk dining room for exquisite food prepared by award-winning chef Jean-Claude Garzia. You'll need to dress up for those occasions — jacket and tie are mandatory for men. Smoking is allowed in the dining rooms in designated areas. On alternate nights you can let down your hair by dining less formally out on Mangrove Bay Terrace. Gaze at the waters, the moon and the stars, and when the mood takes you, dance to the music played live every night. Also in the Main House, take the time to check out a plaque inscribed with the names of repeat visitors. The list is impressive. You might like to know that when we visited, one guest was enjoying his 71st stay. That speaks for itself. Many of Cambridge Beaches' repeat visitors originally came as honeymooners.

Kids are welcome, but those younger than 5 must be accompanied by a professional nanny or nurse. The idea, you see, is that you are meant to enjoy emotion recollected in tranquility. Colicky babies have a way of interfering with tranquility. Check with the reservations staff for rates for kids. Generally speaking, an additional guest pays $120 a day MAP. Cambridge Beaches is a good cottage colony choice for guests with wheelchairs. Some rooms and the spa and dining room are definitely wheelchair-accessible. A variety of rooms also make it a good choice for business travelers. Call the cottage colony direct for details and rates of conventions.

Visitors typically reserve by calling the cottage colony direct. Book as early as possible. For the summer season (April 16 through November 15), we advise a six-month lead-in. Cambridge Beaches has a shoulder season between March 1 and April 15, and winter season is November 16 to February 28. Be aware that the colony does not accept any credit cards. First and last night deposit is required to reserve a room. Cancel within 28 days of your arrival date, and you lose your deposit. Check-in is at 2 PM; check-out is at noon. Changing rooms around the pool and at the spa will allow you that last precious post-checkout swim before you take off for the airport. In addition to the $12.80 per person per day gratuity, there's a 4 percent energy charge.

Room rates in the low season can be considerably cheaper. Check the hotels for special packages they may offer during the winter.

Small Hotels

Diversity is the name of the game in Bermuda, and this is certainly true of our small hotels. When tourism began to take off in the 1920s and '30s (see the introduction to our Resort Hotels chapter), our small hotels developed. Some, especially the ones closer to Hamilton, were originally gracious private homes converted and sometimes structurally extended into tourist accommodations.

After World War II, tourism again saw an upsurge, but during this time, summer became more the high season than winter, and visitors became increasingly interested in our beaches and water-related activities. Then, during the late '40s and the '50s, some custom-built hotels with close access to beaches were built. It would be a mistake, therefore, to see our hotels as being identical. They differ in location, ambiance and the facilities they offer. In this chapter, we describe the differences as well as the characteristics they share.

Rates of Rooms and Meal Plans

We have to confess that creating a consistent pricing key for our small hotels was just about impossible. Why? Because of the meal plans they may or may not offer. Let us remind you of the terms EP, BP and MAP that we introduced in our Resort Hotels chapter. EP means European Plan, which offers room only. BP means Bermuda Plan and offers room and full or continental breakfast. MAP means Modified American Plan and offers room, breakfast and dinner.

The daily rates listed in the pricing key below are based on double occupancy during peak season. They do not include the 7.25 percent per room hotel occupancy tax, gratuities or telephone calls or other expenses. Rates we use also are based on the rooms visitors would most typically reserve. So far, so good.

The majority of hotels, but not all of them, have quoted a BP rate. One has EP only, while offering BP and MAP for additional charge. Another offers only MAP, and yet another has an inclusive policy whereby the rate covers all meals, all drinks, all recreational activities and all gratuities. Gratuity policies also differ; some hotels charge no gratuity at all. Please read the individual listings very carefully to see exactly what the rates cover.

Pricing Key

Be aware that fewer dollar signs do not necessarily mean a lower standard of accommodation. For one thing, all hotels are licensed by the Bermuda government's Department of Tourism. To retain that license, they have to pass strict annual inspections by tourism, health and fire inspectors. A lower dollar sign doesn't necessarily mean fewer facilities or less personal service either.

Likewise, a higher dollar-sign code need not necessarily mean your stay at the hotel will be significantly more expensive since that rate may cover more than breakfast or breakfast and dinner. You see it can be confusing. It's best that you read our descriptions closely, and bear in mind that rates can be subject to change.

$	$150 to $206
$$	$207 to $258
$$$	$259 to $335
$$$$	$336 and higher

Seasonality, Reservation and Cancellation Policies

Typically, the summer season starts in April and ends October to November. However, some hotels charge high-season rates during Christmas and New Year holidays as well. We will be specific in each listing, as season dates can vary from property to property. Some hotels, for example, have a third "shoulder" season that we will specify when applicable. In any case, do verify these dates because they can make an enormous difference in cost.

Room rates in the low season can be considerably cheaper. Check the hotels for special packages they may offer during the winter season. For example, package rates are sometimes offered for golfing guests. A few hotels close to refurbish for a short period in the winter. In all cases, during the winter season entertainment is reduced and beach facilities, such as beach bars, close.

Visitors reserve usually by calling the hotel directly. Nearly all hotels require a two-night room deposit. Some stipulate a first- and last-night deposit. This means that if you cut short your holiday, you still lose the cost of the last night. When this requirement applies, we will tell you so in the listings. All properties listed accept major credit cards; alternatively, you may pay with cash, travelers' checks or, in some cases, personal checks. Generally speaking, guest cancellations within 14 to 21 days of arrival result in loss of deposit. How long should you book in advance? Most hotels are heavily booked during American public holidays — book as soon as possible for those. But we must tell you that while some hotels tend to be heavily booked in July and August, others are busier in May and June or September through November. Check the individual listings for recommended length of advance notice. Remember that last-minute cancellations can make last-minute bookings possible. If you are a spur-of-the-moment person, give the hotel of your choice a call. Check-in and check-out times differ, so look for those in the listings.

Policies on Kids and Other Issues

All but one of the properties listed accept children. But only two offer programs specifically for them. Room and meal rates for kids

> # FYI
>
> Unless otherwise noted, the area code for all phone numbers listed in this guide is 441.

and extra persons in the rooms can vary enormously so do look closely at the individual listings for those costs. We will let you know which hotels are more family-oriented than others. Babysitting, by the way, can always be arranged.

Some hotels are wheelchair-accessible and have appropriately fitted bathrooms. When this is the case, we will tell you. The remaining hotels do not have facilities suitable for guests completely confined to wheelchairs. If you use a walker, however, some of the properties could work for you. Call the hotel directly to discuss details about steps, bathrooms and access so that you can be assured the accommodations will suit your needs.

Nearly all the hotels have a relaxed smoking policy. Some do not allow smoking in the dining rooms; we'll tell you when that is the case. All allow smoking in guest rooms. Some hotels accept pets on request, particularly small dogs that are participating in dog shows on the island. If we don't mention pets, assume they are not accepted. When they are, we'll tell you.

Location and Amenities

Basically, you have the choice between staying in a hotel very close to Hamilton or in one that has access to a private beach. Bear in mind that many of our small hotels have gorgeous private beaches on the South Shore that often allow easy access to the reefs. For kids, these can be ideal. Generally speaking, all hotels are a short distance from either a bus or ferry stop.

All the hotels we list have at least one lounge area. Most, but not all, have licensed bars and dining rooms. And every guest room has a private bathroom. Some hotels have a small number of suites or cottages suitable for larger families or groups. We'll mention them, but you should call the hotel directly for those rates. Every hotel has an outdoor swimming pool. Some also have facilities more often associated with resorts, such as tennis courts and fitness rooms. Where they do, we'll tell you in the individual listings. We cannot emphasize enough that all hotels have staff who will make your arrangements for golf, tennis, watersports, cycle rentals and any other activities or excursions you can think of. That you may take for granted. Hotel staff and management pride themselves on friendliness and personal service. That's why many of the hotels enjoy a high repeat visitor rate.

And now for the listings, which, as usual, we will present east to west, parish by parish, subset by subset and thereafter in alphabetical order.

Smiths Parish

Palmetto Hotel and Cottages
$ • 1 Harrington Sound Rd., Flatts Inlet • 293-2323

Built more than 100 years ago and once a family mansion, Palmetto looks over Flatts Inlet on one side and the calm waters of Harrington Sound on the other. Inside the main building you'll find a reception area; the Ha'penny Pub, where you can have lunch and a drink; and the Inlet Restaurant, which actually overlooks the sound. If you opt for the MAP (it costs $32 per person per day), then you will enjoy your three-course dinner here. You'll also find the lounge at Inlet Restaurant, and every afternoon you can indulge in complimentary tea. If you are musically inclined, try out the piano. Outside dining is on the front terrace, and from there you can see the Inlet. Smoking, by the way, is allowed everywhere on the property.

Guest rooms are in the main building and separate cottage units. Some rooms are very large and have two double beds; others have king-size or two twin beds. Rooms have closets, chairs and a dresser. All come with private balconies or patios, where you can have your complimentary continental breakfast or, for approximately $10, a full breakfast. While many rooms have gorgeous views of the water, an ocean view is not guaranteed. Be sure to request one if a water vista is important to you.

Rooms are equipped with telephones; ironing boards and irons are available on request. Coffee makers and clock-radios are in each room. There are no safes, so do leave your valuables in the front-office safe. Cottage units offer free cable TV. In rooms that are less expensive than the price range we quote, you can rent a television for $5 a day. Room service is available for lunch and dinner; a $3 service charge is added to the cost of the meal. Most bathrooms have showers and tubs, but six have showers only.

Kids are welcome. Younger than 2, they stay for free; younger than 12, the charge is $19 a day. Cribs are available for no extra charge. A small, artificial beach lets you swim in Harrington Sound. You can also swim in the saltwater pool. Loungers and towels are on hand.

Palmetto is just one minute's walk away from the Bermuda Aquarium (see our Kidstuff chapter) and from a bus route that will take you to Hamilton and to St. George's. Book at least two weeks ahead of your visit, especially in the high season between April 1 and October 31. A one-night deposit is required, which you will lose if you cancel within 14 days of your holiday. For BP, there's an $8.86 daily charge per person; for MAP it's $12.80 per person. Check-in is at 3 PM, check-out at noon.

Pembroke Parish

Rosedon
$$ • 61 Pitts Bay Rd. • 295-1640, (800) 367-0040

Rosedon was built in 1906 as a luxurious private home. In the years before electric light, Rosedon was famous because it was the only house in Bermuda to be lit by gas instead of by kerosene lamps. It became a guest house in the 1930s and then, after the war years, evolved into a small hotel.

As soon as you walk into the front entrance, complete with pillars and a gracious veranda, you will notice its elegant proportions and the archways and high ceilings so characteristic of its period. A separate office on the right is for friendly front-desk reception. On your left are two comfortable lounges, one of which has an honor bar and a VCR for nightly movies. You sign a voucher for each drink you take, and the price is added to your final bill.

Complimentary afternoon tea is also served in this room. There's no smoking here, please. Everywhere else, it's OK.

There is no formal dining room at Rosedon, but some meals are offered. The price we quote includes a full breakfast, which is served in your room, by the pool or on the verandas. For an extra charge, you can order a light à la carte lunch. You can order soup, salad and sandwiches for $10 a person in the evenings.

In addition to rooms in the main building, 38 double rooms have been added in the garden area. All but three have access to balconies that guests share. "The idea behind this design," says Ms. Muriel Richardson, manager, "was that guests could talk to each other." Before we talk about rooms, a quick word about the garden. Filled with huge shade trees, poinciana, palmetto and frangipani, and with lush subtropical and tropical plants, it offers a hidden haven from the busy city that's just minutes away. The large outdoor, freshwater swimming pool and terrace is probably its focal point. You can relax in loungers there and after dark appreciate the lights that illuminate the garden. In the winter, the pool is heated.

All rooms in the price range we quote are air-conditioned and have ceiling fans. They are carpeted and painted in pastel shades. Rooms in the main house have the more traditional Queen Anne-style furniture while those around the pool have light, tropical furnishings. They all have spacious living areas and come equipped with telephones with dataports, clock-radios, mini fridges, safes, irons and ironing boards and hairdryers. Beds are either kings, doubles or twins.

Children are welcome. Younger than 18, they pay $20 per person for the BP plan. Having said that, Ms. Richardson confides that couples typically tend to come alone. The hotel's location makes it ideal for visitors coming on business who prefer the homey atmosphere of a smaller, less formal hotel. They also appreciate the fax service and the daily complimentary copy of *The Royal Gazette*. Many of the staff members have worked at Rosedon for more than 20 years, and, to quote

www.insiders.com

See this and many other **Insiders' Guide®** destinations online — in their entirety.

Visit us today!

Ms. Richardson, "They have acquired the art of making our guests happy."

Pay an extra $4 a day and you can use the Elbow Beach tennis and beach facilities (see our Resort Hotels chapter); you'll receive free taxi transportation. Ms. Richardson recommends that you book for summer season (April 1 until November 30 at Rosedon) at least two months ahead of time. A two-night deposit is required, and it is not refunded if you cancel within 14 days of your arrival. Service charge is 10 percent of your room rate. Check-in is flexible; check-out is at noon.

Royal Palms Hotel
$ • 24 Rosemont Ave. • 292-1854, (800) 678-0783

Until 1946, in the days before motorized traffic, Rosemont Avenue was a select part of Bermuda, containing gracious residences of manorial proportions. The avenue's proximity to Hamilton made for easy horse and carriage travel. Many of those residences are still there, including Royal Palms, which was built in 1903 as a private home. Between the world wars the owners started to take in guests, and eventually the property was converted into a hotel. Its location is still ideal for visitors who want easy access to the city and the tranquillity of a rural setting. And you can still hear the clip-clop of the horses and carriages that now take tourists around the neighborhood.

Richard Smith, who owns and manages the hotel with his sister, Susan Weare, takes pride in caring for the stunning gardens at Royal Palms. As well as palms, you'll see frangipani, a glorious poinciana, bananas (which you will have for breakfast in season) and superb purple bougainvillea. What might not interest you (but definitely interests us) is that the garden has an apple tree that actually bears fruit. Since apple trees need frost, which we never have, this is a remarkable gardening feat.

Outdoor terraces allow you to enjoy the gardens. See-through blinds and awnings mean you can stay outside even in cold or windy weather. An outdoor swimming pool will refresh you after your trip to town.

The price we quote in our key includes room and a generous breakfast that you can eat in a dining room with a fireplace (useful in winter) or outside on the terrace. You will have toast, fresh pastries and scones, fresh fruit and, if you wish, eggs. Susan and Richard will help you with the intricacies of eating boiled eggs in egg cups, typically used by the British (see the Insiders' Tip in our Guest Houses chapter). The two like to meet their guests in the mornings to discuss what recreational arrangements need to be made. Incidentally, Richard is a member of the Mid Ocean Golf Club. That means you can play there any day of the week, provided tee times are available.

Can you dine at this hotel? Absolutely. Ascot's Restaurant is within the hotel but is owned by Claudio Vigilante and Edmund Smith, who also run the lounge bar (open from noon to 3 PM and 6:30 PM to 1 AM). Your MAP rate costs an additional $36 per person per day and can be used as a dinner supplement for the à la carte menu offerings. We should tell you that Ascot's is a restaurant much loved by locals, particularly on special occasions (see our Restaurants chapter). Female guests needn't bother wearing fancy hats. Dining is the name of the game here, not horse racing, although the atmosphere is country British. Smoking is not encouraged in the dining room but is OK everywhere else. Room service, by the way, is available.

Rooms are all spacious, with living areas that are individually painted in pastel colors and furnished with bright fabrics. They are all light, thanks to large windows that sometimes have charming window seats, and they are all air-conditioned. Bed setups offer kings or two doubles, and all rooms come with ceiling fans, clock-radios, coffee makers, irons, telephones with dataports and cable television. Hairdryers and refrigerators are available on request. Bathrooms come with tubs and showers, and many have Corian (marble-like) vanity areas with sinks. For a higher price than the one in the code, mini-suites overlooking the pool are available with a kitchen area equipped with fridge, microwave and toaster-oven. Call the hotel for those rates and for those of a one-bedroom cottage with living room and kitchen. When you see the overall standard of accommodation, it will come as no surprise that in 1997 Susan and Richard won the Department of Tourism Buttery Award, for achieving a consistently high standard of accommodation during a four-year period.

Kids are welcome. Those younger than 3 stay free; for those between 3 and 16, the charge is $25 a day per child. Pets, such as small dogs, are allowed on request.

Royal Palm's summer season runs from April 1 to November 15. For the busy months of May and June, book about two months ahead, although last-minute cancellations can make last-minute vacancies possible. A two-day deposit is required, and a 14-day cancellation policy applies. A 10 percent service charge is added to your room rate. Check-in is flexible; check-out is at noon.

Waterloo House

$$$$ • 100 Pitts Bay Rd. • 295-4480, (800) 468-4100

This hotel may have the name of a famous European battlefield, but when you meet your Waterloo here, you enter a haven just minutes away from the City of Hamilton. As soon as you walk through the road entrance, you can see the beautifully terraced grounds that lead right down to Hamilton Harbour.

Waterloo House is a sister hotel to Horizons and Cottages (see our Cottage Colonies chapter) and The Newstead Hotel (see listing in this chapter). Like Horizons, it is currently a member of Relais et Chateaux. Membership depends on maintaining the five C's: cuisine, calm, comfort, charm and courtesy.

Let us begin, then, with the dining room, where all these qualities are evident manifested. Ragged-glazed, the walls are the color of crushed raspberries. The effect is stunning and contrasts strikingly with the cedar fireplace and the elegant, dark wood of antique dressers and cabinets. You will see on one of the walls a portrait of the Duke of Wellington, in whose honor the dining room is named. You can use your MAP ($36 per person per day) to dine in the Wellington Restaurant, where you will enjoy the exquisite creations of Steve Blumenthal, the award-winning executive chef (see our Restaurants chapter for details). Dining is formal, so jacket and tie are mandatory. Smoking's OK here (except for cigars), as it is everywhere in the hotel.

While we're talking about food, we must tell you that in the summer months, dining also is offered outside on the Poinciana Terrace that overlooks Hamilton Harbour. Jacket is still required but no tie. Lunch is served there, much to the delight of locals who want an hour's respite from the city. In the unlikely event you want to try another restaurant, remember that you can use your MAP to dine at the sister properties, Horizons Cottages, The Newstead Hotel and Coral Beach and Tennis Club.

The main building has many other rooms where you can relax in aesthetically pleasant surroundings. There's the Long Room Bar, which is indeed long, and which, again, has an unusual wall finish. Walls are washed with yellow and have a clear gloss stripe that you only notice when the light falls on it. The bar is open from 11 AM to 1 AM. Want catch up on international news? You'll find complimentary international newspapers in the drawing room, in addition to the free *Royal Gazette* and the *New York Fax Times* each guest receives every morning. In the afternoons, you'll have complimentary tea. You won't find a television, though. Watching television in a drawing room is just not done. The sun lounge is light and airy with pastel washed walls, hanging baskets and light wicker furniture. Fancy a game of skittles or backgammon? A well-equipped game room is also in the main building, with an honor bar just outside it.

All the rooms in the price range we quote have harbor views. Rooms with garden views are less expensive. All rooms have private balconies or terraces where you may have your breakfast (full or continental) delivered in the mornings for no extra charge. (If you want company, breakfast is also served in the Wellington Restaurant. Breakfast is included in the rate we quote.) Each room is individually decorated with all the tastefulness we have come to anticipate from Horizons Property Ltd. Seating areas are spacious. Beds are king-sized, or there are two twins. All rooms are air-conditioned and have ceiling fans. They come with clock-radio, cable TV, dataport telephone, safe, umbrella, trouser press and hairdryer. Fridges, irons and ironing boards are available on request. Naturally, all rooms have private bathrooms with tubs and showers. In fact, many of the bathrooms have Jacuzzi baths.

Kids are welcome at Waterloo House. If they are 12 or younger and stay in their parents' rooms, the charge is $45 per person for BP and an additional $18 for MAP. If they are older than 12, the charge is $90 and the full MAP rate. Kids sleep on pull-out sofas or extra beds. In addition, Waterloo House has a variety of delightful suites that are suitable for larger families. Call the hotel for those rates. Pets are accepted on request.

The grounds at Waterloo House are charming. All over the property you'll find shady nooks with garden or water views and plenty of veranda space. Split-level terraces are filled with flowers. The freshwater outdoor swimming pool will also keep you cool. If you want further recreation, remember that you can use all of the tennis and beach facilities at Coral Beach for no charge. Golf is easily arranged, and you can play Horizon's nine-hole mashie course (see our Golf and Cottage Colonies chapters for details). A private launch will take you across the harbor to Newstead. Want to picnic at one of the islands in the harbor? No problem. The launch will take you there. On some enchanted evenings, it will take you for a Hamilton Harbour cocktail cruise as well. In the summer season at Waterloo, entertainment is offered every night and four lunch times a week. A three-piece band may well get you dancing. In addition, Calypso and soft piano music will relax you in the evening as you dine.

High season at Waterloo House runs from April 1 to November 30, then from December 20 until January 1. Low season is January 1 until March 31. Interestingly, the hotel can be busier in the winter months than in summer.

For July and August, you may safely book a week or two in advance. For September to November, book three to four months ahead. You reserve with a two-night deposit that you will lose if you cancel within 21 days of your scheduled arrival. The service charge is 10 percent of your room rate. Check-in is at 2 PM, check-out at noon.

Paget Parish

Harmony Club
$$$$ • 109 South Rd. • 236-3500

The first thing we must tell you is that Harmony Club is Bermuda's first and only all-inclusive hotel. The rate for two in high season is $525. Don't be shocked. That rate includes a lot more than room and breakfast for two. In fact, it includes just about everything — even the government's 7.25 percent tax and all gratuities. From the moment you reach Bermuda, you'll scarcely need to open your wallet.

First, you will be met at the airport and taken to the hotel for free. Once at Harmony, you will discover that the only time you'll deal with money is when you pay your final bill. The rates include the following for two: room, breakfast, lunch, dinner (with house red or white wine) and an open bar serving complimentary soft drinks and alcoholic beverages from 11 AM to 11 PM. There is also free use of beach facilities at Elbow Beach Bermuda, free greens fees at Belmont Hotel and Golf Club (you must pay for the mandatory cart) and free tennis on Harmony's two courts (see our Resort Hotels chapter for more on Elbow Beach and Belmont).

Anything else? After you pay the $12 non-refundable insurance waiver required by the cycle shop, you get free use of a two-seat motor scooter for the duration of your stay. You also get free cover charges for admission to The Club and The Oasis, two nightclubs in Hamilton (see our Nightlife chapter). Drinks at the clubs you must pay for. And you can eat (but not drink) for free at restaurants under the Little Venice Dine Around Plan.

As William Griffiths, general manager, pointed out, "This inclusive policy means that the staff have more time to spend on the guests to create a friendly atmosphere. The bartender, for example, doesn't have to concentrate on dealing with cash." You'll find the barkeep in the Tavern Bar, where lunches are served daily in addition to evening cocktails and hot hors d'oeuvres. Mornings, you'll find a full buffet breakfast in the Casuarina Restaurant, freshly decorated in green and white with hanging baskets of plants creating a garden effect. In the evenings, you'll dine there too (no smoking allowed at Casuarina, but it's OK everywhere else). On Thursday and Sunday nights, a jacket is required. Other nights, smart casual dress is fine but no jeans, please . . . and no sneakers or T-shirts.

Six nights a week in summer you can dance the night away in the spacious Bay Grape Lounge to live pop, Calypso, reggae or jazz. Once a week in the summer, a poolside barbecue allows you to eat outside. You'll see the pool once you walk through the moongate in the beautiful garden grounds. In addition, a Jacuzzi, sauna and three tennis courts are available. If you fancy an evening of games or television, try out the Games Room, once known as the Gombey Lounge. Incidentally, in the 1940s and '50s, Nat King Cole and Eartha Kitt sang here. So if you start humming, "Chestnuts roasting round an open fire," or "I'm just an old-fashioned girl," you'll know why — you'll be picking up on the vibes. If you want an old-fashioned millionaire, dream on. But then again, in Bermuda, you never know.

The rooms are bright and cheerful, mostly in cabanas with garden and pool views. All but nine of the 68 rooms come with balconies. They are all furnished with king or twin beds and come with telephone, radio, satellite television and tea- and coffee-making facilities. All rooms have bathrooms equipped with tubs and showers, hairdryers and bathrobes. Harmony does not allow extra guests in rooms, and all guests must be older than 18 years of age. So if you're looking for a respite from the children, this could be the place for you.

The architecture of the main house, Paget Manor, is interesting. Painted coral pink with a white ridged roof, its walls feature "in and outs" — white, decorative brickwork edgings. Some windows have around their arches similar brick work known as "eyebrows."

Harmony Club's summer season runs from May 1 to October 31. Winter season starts December 21 and ends February 28. Two shoulder seasons run from March 1 to April 30 and November 1 to November 30. The hotel closes for refurbishing from December 1 to December 20. Rates vary during the shoulder seasons, so call the hotel directly for those rates and winter rates. For May and October (both very busy months) reserve at least six weeks in advance. Otherwise, a four-week lead-in on your reservation is recommended. A two-night deposit is required, which you will lose if you cancel within 14 days of your scheduled holiday. Check-in is at 2 PM, check-out at noon.

Stonington Beach Hotel
$$$$ • 8 College Dr. (off South Rd.) • 236-5416

This hotel is unique to the island in the sense that it is owned and operated by the Bermuda College. Built in 1980, it was the first building to go up on the Stonington Bermuda College campus. Although the hotel is run by fully qualified staff, you may well meet student chefs, waiters, front-desk receptionists and others studying for associate degrees in hotel management. Under supervision, they work for a stipend during the holiday months as part of their training.

Stonington Beach Hotel overlooks the South Shore, and its private beach is (but of course) called Stonington. Located at the eastern end of Elbow Beach, the beach is small with pinkish sand. After a severe storm, it tends

Window boxes and planters burst with blooms, keeping every corner
of Bermuda's homes colorful and pretty.

to shrink for a few weeks; it also shrinks in the winter months. However, this part of the ocean is a prime spot for snorkeling since the pot-boilers are close enough to shore that at low tide you can wade out to them. On the beach, you will find a small bar for drinks and lunch. You may also rent a mask and snorkel for $5 per half-day, $8 for a full day. Flippers cost $10 a day. You might also like to rent an underwater camera for $20 a day. Use of umbrellas, loungers and beach chairs is complimentary. Two tennis courts and an outdoor freshwater pool (heated in winter) offer additional recreation.

Upon entering the main building, you will immediately find yourself in the lobby lounge, where complimentary tea is served every afternoon at 4 PM. Here, too, you will find the Overplus Bar open weekdays and Saturdays from 11 AM until 1 AM and from noon until 1 AM on Sundays. The Norwood dining room is also in this building, where you may enjoy the full or continental breakfast (your preference) that is included in the rate we quote. In the evening, The Norwood offers dinner. The MAP rate, by the way, costs an additional $30 per person. There is no smoking in the dining room and no casual dress either. A jacket is required except on the weekly barbecue night, held on the terrace by the freshwater pool. For an extra charge

plus a 15 percent gratuity, you may also have lunch on the terrace. While you dine, you will appreciate the music of either a pianist or saxophonist. On Saturday nights, a small band will encourage you to dance. Incidentally, Stonington is a member of The Bermuda Collection, so you can use your MAP to dine at other restaurants that are also members.

Rooms in unit blocks all have close views of the South Shore, and all have terraces with outdoor furniture. If you can't face socializing first thing in the morning, you may have your breakfast delivered to these rooms for a $2 per person room-service charge. They are air-conditioned and come with ceiling fans, clock-radio, telephone with dataport, cable television, safes and mini fridges. Irons and ironing boards, hairdryers and umbrellas are also on hand. Rooms are uniformly decorated in pale beige and furnished with drapes and spreads of blue and yellow design. Seating areas have small tables, armchairs and a pull-out sofa. Bathrooms are marble and come with tubs and showers. One bathroom, incidentally, is spacious and fitted with railings designed for guests in wheelchairs. Bathrobes are available upon request. You may smoke in your rooms and everywhere else in the hotel except the dining room.

Kids are welcome. For ages 3 through 12,

the charge is $52 per person per day for BP, and those older than 12 are charged $62 for BP. For rates for children younger than 3 and for MAP rates for children, call the hotel directly. An extra adult staying in the same room pays $82 a day for BP and an additional charge of $30 per person for MAP. Pets are permitted upon request. One honeymoon apartment is available. Overlooking the ocean, it has a kitchen with a refrigerator and microwave and a separate living room. Call the hotel for those rates. One other cottage is also available.

Stonington has three seasons. For the summer season (May 1 until October 31), book at least three months ahead. For American public holidays, book six months in advance. Winter season is November 1 until April 15, and the shoulder season is April 16 to April 30. Reserve with a two-night deposit, which you will lose if you cancel within five days of your expected arrival. Be aware that other than the 7.25 percent government tax and the 15 percent gratuity on lunch and extra drinks, there is no other service charge added to the room rate. Check-in is at 3 PM, check-out at noon.

The Newstead Hotel
$$$ • 27 Harbour Rd. • 236-6060, (800) 468-4111

Newstead is a sister hotel of Horizons and Cottages (see our Cottage Colony chapter). Built in the 19th century as a private house, it still has the ambiance of a Colonial manor house with beautifully landscaped gardens displaying the vibrant splendor of purple bougainvillea vines. It became a hotel in about 1923, and guests then no doubt appreciated the tranquil view of Hamilton Harbour, just as they do today. During the late '60s and early '70s, the owners created two landscaped outdoor terraces on the harbor side so that guests could dine out and enjoy the sunset and night views.

Smoking is OK in the rooms and in designated areas in the dining room and lounge. Dress for dinner is formal except for Tuesday nights, when casual dress is encouraged. Lately the lounge has been repainted to stunning effect. Walls are a deep green, glazed over with a dark blue. The resulting green is

reminiscent of a cave lagoon. Throughout the hotel, antique and Oriental pieces contribute to the overall tastefulness of the decor.

All the rooms in our price range come with harbor views and balconies or terraces. They all have clock-radios, safes, telephones, cable television and coffee makers. Refrigerators are available on request, as are irons and ironing boards. Each room is individually decorated and furnished — one might have carpet while another has wooden flooring — but you can depend on the exquisite taste so characteristic of all Horizons' properties. Bathrooms are spacious and come with tubs and showers. They are also equipped with hairdryers. Separate vanity areas have an additional sink.

FYI

Unless otherwise noted, the area code for all phone numbers listed in this guide is 441.

Kids are welcome. Indeed, Newstead encourages them to take part in the Department of Tourism's Partaking Camp Bermuda for children (see our Kidstuff chapter). Cribs are free. Children younger than 13 pay $50 per person per day for an additional bed in their parents' rooms. Older than 13, they pay $75, which brings us to an explanation of the rate we quote. It's BP, but you can have MAP for an additional $35 dollars per person per day. You can use your MAP here or at the sister properties: Horizons Cottages (see our Cottage Colonies chapter), Coral Beach and Tennis Club and Waterloo House (see previous listing in this chapter). Waterloo House is just a ferry ride away.

For entertainment and recreation there is live music (a mixture of Calypso and jazz) every night except Thursday. Friday evenings, you can take a cocktail cruise around Hamilton Harbour and listen to the Calypso music of Stan Seymour. Outside, a freshwater swimming pool (heated in winter) will let you cool down in summer. Complimentary afternoon tea is served daily in the dining room. Tuesday evenings and Saturday mornings, you can join a water aerobics class for $11.50 a session. Tennis is $3.50 an hour on one of the two courts on the property. In addition, for $6 a day during the week or $12 a day on weekends, you can use all beach, tennis and fitness facilities at the Coral Beach and Tennis Club (see the Horizons and Cottages listing in our Cottage Colonies chapter).

Newstead's high seasons run from May 1 to November 30 and from December 15 to January 4. Low seasons are December 1 to December 14 and January 5 to March 15. March 16 to April 30 is the shoulder season. Call the hotel for winter and shoulder season rates. A two-night deposit is required, which you lose if you cancel within 21 days of your expected arrival. For a vacation here in May or October, book as early as possible. For other months, Newstead recommends booking a month in advance. A 10 percent service charge is added to your room rate. Check-in is at 2 PM, check-out at noon. Courtesy rooms, which come in useful should you want to stay a bit past check-out time, are available for no extra charge.

White Sands and Cottages

$$ • 55 White Sands Rd. • 236-2023, (800) 548-0547

This hotel has the advantage of close access to one of Bermuda's more secluded beaches, Grape Bay, and of being very close to Hamilton. For this reason, White Sands concentrates on affordable, relaxing accommodations rather than on a range of activities and entertainment. After all, stay here, and you are just a 10-minute drive away from the city's nightclubs and attractions.

Having said that, the hotel does have two licensed bars and a dining room, called The Captain's Table. Except on designated casual nights, a jacket is required for dining. The price we quote includes a full American breakfast — sometimes kippers and Bermudian codfish cakes are offered to add variety. But for an extra $44 added to the room rate, (i.e., for two people, not per person) you can also have MAP. There is no smoking in the dining room, by the way, but you can indulge everywhere else.

The hotel also has a freshwater swimming pool with a partially covered terrace where lunch is served. You will find one of the bars there, open from noon until 6:30 PM. The other, The Sandbar Pub, is in the main building and is open from 6:30 PM until 1 AM. Thursdays and Sundays, there is live music to entertain you, and on Mondays, a managers' party will introduce you to the rum swizzle. A comfortable lounge with an area that overlooks the South Shore will make you feel at home rather than in a hotel lobby. That's why it's actually referred to as the living room. Here, you may enjoy complimentary afternoon tea.

Rooms are in the main house and in a terrace wing. All air-conditioned, they come with telephone, clock-radio, cable television, safe, mini refrigerator and coffee maker. Hairdryers, irons and ironing boards are available on request. Beds will be either one king or two doubles. Some of the rooms in the price range we quote have balconies with garden or South Shore ocean views. If an ocean view is important to you, tell the manager when you reserve. All have bathrooms with tubs and showers. Room service is available for breakfast and dinner and costs $3 a person.

Kids are welcome. Those younger than 6 stay free; ages 6 to 12 are charged $34 for BP and $45 for MAP. Cribs and rollaway beds are available. White Sands also has one two-bedroom and two three-bedroom cottages, all of which overlook the ocean. They can accommodate up to six persons each, have living rooms and kitchens and are ideal for families. Call the hotel for these rates — they can sometimes work out to be lower than the rate we quote. Guests in wheelchairs should call the hotel for details of access. Some rooms may be suitable. Pets are permitted on request.

Summer season is April 1 to November 15. For public holidays and the last two weeks of May and June, book as soon as possible. The rest of the season, you're advised to book four to six weeks in advance. A first- and last-night deposit is required, which you lose if you cancel within 21 days of your scheduled arrival. Check-in is at 2 PM, check-out at noon.

INSIDERS' TIP

If no safes are available in your rooms, leave valuables such as your passport, money and jewelry with the staff at the front desk. They will have either a safe or safety-deposit boxes available.

Warwick Parish

Mermaid Beach Club
**$$ • 30 South Rd. • 236-5031,
(800) 441-7087**

"I have heard the mermaids singing each to each." So said T.S. Eliot's J. Alfred Prufrock. We can't promise that you'll hear them singing here, but we can tell you that just as mermaids have to swim, so will you when you see this hotel's private South Shore beach. In fact, owner and manager Brian Alcon will probably swim with you. He swims approximately 2 miles a day and will tell (or show) you where the best snorkeling areas are on the reef. Parrotfish and angelfish, manta rays, octopi, crabs, lobsters and barracudas — he's seen them all around the part of the reef you can reach from Mermaid Beach. He's even seen an occasional moray eel. Snorkeling gear can be rented for a small charge. If you swim in the morning and return at noon, you'll be able to quench your thirst at the beach bar — it stays open from noon until 6 PM. Relax in a lounger, enjoy the shade of an umbrella and contemplate your next swim in the ocean or in the outdoor freshwater swimming pool. Or think about tennis — one court's available for a small charge.

The rate we quote here is for room only. A BP rate is unavailable, but for an additional $45 a person, you can have MAP. Dining in the hotel is at The Jolly Lobster, a popular restaurant with locals, especially during the Bermuda lobster season (September through March). In the summer you can dine out on the terrace. In addition, there's The Old Ship Pub and lounge area where you can still enjoy the ocean view along with a rum swizzle or a something-and-tonic. If you must, you can watch cable television here as well. Smoking, by the way, is allowed everywhere on the property. Entertainment? On Fridays and Saturdays a disc jockey is on hand to get people dancing, and on Sundays a magician practices the art of illusion. On Mondays you can swizzle your way through a complimentary party.

Rooms in the price range we quote all have seating areas and one double or two twin beds. They are all air-conditioned and come with refrigerator, clock-radio and telephone. You can request a television for a weekly charge of $25. All rooms have grass terraces or patios with good views of the ocean. For an extra $10 a day, you can get a kitchen equipped with refrigerator, electric cooker, china and utensils and microwave. The fee includes maid's service.

Kids are very welcome. Cribs, high chairs and rollaways are available on request. Children 12 and younger stay and eat free if parents take the MAP. Extra guests (kids included) older than 12 stay for $25 a day. However, extra guests are only allowed in suites. Call the hotel for suite rates. Be aware, too, that Mermaid offers family, golf and honeymoon packages; again, call for those rates. Incidentally, this is one of the few hotels that will take dogs on request, especially those taking their chances in local dog shows.

Mermaid recommends that you reserve at least two months in advance for the summer season. A first- and last-night deposit is required, and a 21-day cancellation policy applies. For EP a $7 per person per day gratuity is added to the final bill. Gratuity per person for MAP is $14 a day. In addition, there's a 3 percent per person per day energy surcharge. Check-in is at 2 PM, check-out at 11 AM. Courtesy rooms are available, should these times prove inconvenient.

Southampton Parish

Pompano Beach Club
$$$ • 36 Pompano Beach Rd. • 234-0222

Named after the many pompano fish that love to swim off the South Shore, this hotel opened in 1955 as Bermuda's first fishing club. Visitors used to go fishing on the club's deep-

---

INSIDERS' TIP

Many of our hotels have beautiful grounds and gardens. Take the time to explore them — they can be an excellent introduction to Bermuda's rich flora.

Photo: GIS

Bermuda's hotels and other accommodations are some of the finest to be found worldwide.

sea boat, bring their spoils back and have them cooked for dinner the same day.

While that doesn't happen anymore, we should tell you that Pompano's location still makes it an ideal resort for water-related activities. In fact, it has been described as Bermuda's best underwater beach. It faces a sand bar, you see, and the South Shore reef line. Dig in the sand bar with your feet, and you just might find a sand dollar shell. The sand bar means that at low tide you can wade out in waist-high water and become intimately acquainted with the reef's potboilers (see our Beaches chapter for an explanation of boilers) and the pompanos and other fish that hang out there.

If you don't fancy a watery walk, you can hire one of the many boats from the hotel's own watersports shop. Take a paddle boat, windsurfer or raft for $12 an hour. We particularly recommend a Sun Cat ($35 for one hour, $25 for a half-hour), which is like a motorized

chaise lounge for two. The reef may well tempt you into snorkeling for a closer look at the fish. You can rent a mask and snorkel for $7 a day. The hotel might not cook your catch anymore, but it will encourage you to go fishing. Light tackle and bait are complimentary. Yes, Pompano does have a small, private, sandy beach that until recently tended to come and go according to the tides. However, a larger beach has been created by dredging up sand from the sand bar. In addition, there's a freshwater swimming pool with plenty of poolside space and loungers for relaxing. Staff will serve you drinks, lunch and snacks there for additional charge. Two outdoor Jacuzzis will also help you relax.

While we're on the subject of activities, we must tell you this hotel is right next door to the No. 8 hole of Port Royal Golf Course. Of course, staff will happily book your tee times for you (see our Golf chapter). They will also provide a complimentary shuttle service, but it will be for your golf clubs only — Bermudian law prohibits these shuttles from carrying people. But golfers can easily walk to the first tee, which is about 500 yards away from No. 8. You can also play tennis free of charge on the hotel's clay tennis court or on the courts at Port Royal. Fitness rooms on the property give you complimentary access to a treadmill, Nordic Track, two exercise bikes, weights and a stair machine. Feel like exploring Bermuda? Hire a moped or a scooter from the on-site rental center.

And now to the accommodations. The clubhouse, otherwise known as the main building, houses reception, the Cedar Room for dining (no smoking allowed here), delightful lounge areas and the Foc'sle Bar (smoking allowed but no cigars or pipes). All offer spectacular views of the ocean. Because Pompano is situated on a southwest peninsula, all offer terrific views of sunsets as well. Breakfast and a five-course dinner are served in the dining room (see our Restaurants chapter). During the summer months, weekly barbecues and swizzle parties are held by the pool, and you can depend on live music every night. A five-piece band plays every Friday; four nights a week, there's live piano music; Saturday, there's a steel-drum duo; and Wednesday, it's live Calypso guitar music. In winter, live entertainment depends on occupancy. Pompano Beach Club, by the way, is a member of the Bermuda Collection (see our Cottage Colonies chapter for more details of this dine-around plan), which means you can use your MAP to dine at any of the other five restaurant members. The rate we quote includes breakfast. MAP costs $20 a person — excellent value.

Rooms are in double-storied pink buildings that are clustered on a hillside. With spacious living areas, they come with rattan furnishings, king-size bed, telephone, safe, clock-radio, refrigerator and cable television. Clothes are crumpled? Then the iron and ironing board will come in handy. Bathrooms have a shower and tub, hairdryer and bathrobe. All rooms have private patios or balconies, and all overlook the ocean. If you don't feel like being sociable first thing in the morning, have your continental breakfast there. Be aware, though — other than breakfast delivery, there is no room service. You can, incidentally, smoke in your rooms.

Kids are very welcome here. There are no organized activities, but the swimming and the sand bar are ideal for them. Babysitters can be arranged for an additional charge. Children younger than 4 are charged $30 per night MAP; younger than 12, they pay $50 MAP and older than 12, the charge is $70. Rollaway beds and cribs are complimentary.

Guests typically book by calling Pompano directly. For high-season reservations, book at least three weeks in advance. You should know that for summer season and public holidays, the hotel sometimes requires a minimum stay of four nights. Because of local functions, the restaurant is closed to hotel guests from December 6 to Christmas Day. That date may change, so check with the hotel if you want to stay in December. Pompano's summer season is May 1 to November 14. Winter season is from November 15 to March 31. The shoulder season is during the month of April. A first- and last-night deposit is required, and it is non-refundable if you cancel within 21 days of your scheduled arrival. Gratuity is 10 percent of your room rate, and a 15 percent gratuity is added to extra drinks, snacks and lunch bills. Check-in is at 2 PM, check-out at noon. However, arrangements can always be made for guests who want to arrive earlier or leave later.

The Reefs
$$$$ • 56 South Rd. • 238-0222, (800) 742-2008

This hotel certainly lives up to its name. It stands on a cliff overlooking the South Shore reef line and its own private beach, Christian

Bay. The clubhouse was originally built in the 1600s. At one point (no one knows when) it was a farmhouse belonging to a man with the illustrious name of Marmaduke Dando. In 1946, the clubhouse was extended and became the main building of a hotel. It still retains some of the original structure and, with its chimneys and white ridged roof, is traditionally Bermudian in appearance.

Inside, you will find friendly reception staff, an elegant, comfortable lounge and bar and a large dining room that stretches across the width of the building. On the south side, it overlooks the terrace and ocean; on the north side, it has a glass house or conservatory extension. Dining here is fairly formal. Except for Mondays and Thursdays, jackets are required in the evening. No smoking is allowed in the dining room, but it's fine in the lounge and bar. While we're talking about dining, we should tell you there are other eating options at The Reefs. You can dine on the terrace in front of the clubhouse or at Coconuts, a delightful restaurant on a covered deck right on the beach. Coconuts is a favorite with locals, who often take a break from work and come for lunch. In addition, you can use your MAP to dine at any of the restaurants that are members of the Bermuda Collection (see our Cottage Colony chapter). In summer, you are guaranteed entertainment every night. A three-piece band will get you dancing in the dining room or on the terrace. Thursdays and Sundays you can join the party on the beach and dance to live soca music.

Rooms are in double-storied buildings, and each has a balcony or patio overlooking the water and coastline. Staff will deliver full or continental breakfast to your room. If you want an ocean view that is completely unobstructed, be sure to ask for one. All rooms have king beds or two double beds, and all have spacious sitting areas with a pull-out loveseat, dresser and comfortable wicker chairs. Walls are moonstone in color; curtains and bedspreads are bright. Rooms come with safes, telephones, ironing boards and irons, umbrel-

las, refrigerators and clock-radios. They do not, however, come with televisions. You can get a VCR on request. When you arrive, you'll find two little bottles of black rum, two ginger beers and an instructional leaflet on how to make your own dark and stormy. Alternatively, you can stick to Perrier. A separate vanity area with a sink leads into the bathroom, where there is a shower, tub and an additional sink. Hairdryers are supplied.

Kids are welcome at The Reefs. If they stay in their parents' rooms and are younger than 5, they pay $30 a day MAP; those younger than 16 are charged $58; those 16 and older pay $78. In addition to the rooms we have described, there are some separate one-, two- and three-bedroom cottages. Call the hotel for those rates. Apart from breakfast, there is no other room service.

The beach means excellent swimming and snorkeling. Masks, flippers and snorkels you can borrow for free. Beach chairs and towels are also on hand. If you'd rather swim in fresh water, the heated swimming pool will be for you. And if you're into serious keep-fit routines, try out the exercise bikes, weights and exercise station in the fitness room. There's a jogging machine, but why jog on a machine when you can jog on a beach? You can play tennis free on the hotel's courts across South Road, directly opposite the property. A cycle livery is also there. Staff will happily help you with golf and watersports arrangements.

For summer season months, book at least six months ahead. A first- and last-night deposit is required, and the 21-day cancellation policy applies. Summer season starts the last week of April and ends November 7. Winter season goes from December 1 to March 31. There are two shoulder seasons: the first three weeks of April and the last three weeks of November. The price code denotes the MAP rate for two people. If you want breakfast only, deduct $20 per person from your bill. Gratuity is 10 percent of your room rate, and a 15 percent gratuity is added for extra drinks, snacks and lunch bills. Check-in is at 3 PM, check-out

INSIDERS' TIP

If a view of the ocean, harbor or bay is important to you, check when you reserve to ensure that one is available.

at noon. Changing rooms are available for late departures and early arrivals.

Sandys Parish

Willowbank
$$ • 126 Somerset Rd. • 234-1616, (800) 752-8493

We must tell you immediately that Willowbank is an entirely nonprofit organization. How can this be? Well, in 1960 it was created by a group of Christian trustees who wanted a hotel where people, to quote their motto, "in a hurried and anxious world might find rest, recreation and renewed purpose." Willowbank is, therefore, a nondenominational Christian charitable trust, which under British law cannot allow personal financial profit. Terri Allison, manager, explains it this way: "Profits go back into Willowbank's ministry and are used to maintain and refurbish the property. They are also used to help local charities."

Does religion play a part in your stay at Willowbank? The answer to that question is that it can if you want it to. Morning devotions and a 30-minute "Serendipity" Bible study happen every day in private rooms, but they are optional. "There's absolutely no proselytizing," said Terri, "and no campaigns either. But you know, tranquillity can lead to spiritual reflection. That's true for non-believers as well. Staff are here to talk and to listen, if that's what our guests want." She also made the point that "the personal touch" can be a buzz phrase. "At Willowbank we really do care. It's not just words to us. For example, Mrs. Morag Whitehead, our guest relations director, is a wonderful listener and helps people in all sorts of ways."

Before we describe Willowbank, know that the price we quote offers MAP. No other plan is offered. You'll be pleased to note that other than the 7.25 percent government tax, there are no extra gratuities or room-service charges. As for children, they are more than welcome. If they stay in their parents' rooms and are younger than 2, they stay for free; those younger than 12 are charged $21 per person per day for meals; and those younger than 17 pay $37 per person per day. An extra adult costs $70 a day. Some suites with adjoining rooms for older children are available; call the hotel for those rates.

Willowbank is the one small hotel that has a special program for children. The Willow Kids program operates during July and August for children ages 4 through 12 and offers a variety of activities such as tie-dyeing, fishing and sand-castle building. Children also go swimming and on excursions to places such as the Bermuda Aquarium (see our Kidstuff and Attractions chapter). In the evenings, supervisors are available to look after children who have finished their meals so that parents can enjoy dinner without interruption. Other than charges incurred for bus tickets, drinks or lunches, these supervised activities are free.

Perhaps the main source of recreation and tranquillity here is the beauty of Willowbank's two beaches. One is on Ely's Harbour; the other is on the South Shore, with easy access to the reefs that are close to the beach. Snorkeling is excellent here. (The hotel sells snorkeling equipment but does not rent it.) After breakfast and dinner, guests like to go on a walking tour to the dock and feed the fish with bread. Parrotfish, pompanos, angelfish, sergeant-majors — you'll see them all. Early in the mornings, you'll even see green turtles. Birds like Willowbank too. Look out for longtails, bluebirds and yellow-crested night herons. A freshwater outdoor pool (heated in winter), two tennis courts, mallet pool and a ping-pong table offer additional fun.

In the main manor house, which is more than 200 years old, you will find the Loaves and Fishes Dining Room. A full breakfast is served every day except Sunday, when breakfast is continental. Dinner is served in the evenings. Meals are served at one sitting, family style. Guests are seated at round tables and, therefore, are encouraged to talk to one another. An ancient ship's bell announces when food is ready. A Christian grace, by the way, is said at the beginning of every meal. A jacket and tie are required every evening except Tuesday, Thursday and Sunday (except in the hotter months of July and August). No smoking is allowed. In fact, you cannot smoke in any public area of the hotel, including at the beaches and pool. You can smoke in your room. There is no licensed bar, and no liquor is served in the dining room. However, you may consume your own liquor in your room. Lunch is available at very reasonable prices in the coffee shop for no extra gratuity.

The main house also houses two delightfully furnished lounges with open beams, tray ceilings and fireplaces, private meeting rooms and a library, where complimentary tea is served every afternoon. In addition, there's a video library. Verandas and patios allow outdoor relaxation.

There's an unusual mixture of entertainment five nights a week in the summer. Along with Calypso music, you will have the opportunity to listen to school and local gospel choirs. Sometimes movies are shown. Entertainment is suitable for the whole family and lasts from about 8:30 to 9:30 PM.

Rooms are in unit blocks spread throughout the grounds. All the rooms in the price range we quote have beautiful ocean views and balconies or terraces. They are also air-conditioned and have ceiling fans. Rooms come with small water heaters for making hot drinks — coffee, tea, etc., are provided. Hairdryers, irons and ironing boards are also provided. There are no televisions in the rooms nor are there telephones. If you absolutely have to watch TV, there's one with local channels in the lounge. A panic alert button in each room will connect you with the office staff in case of an emergency. Some rooms are very wheelchair-accessible and equipped with rails in the bathrooms; call the hotel directly for details. Pets are accepted on request.

For the summer season (April 1 through November 15), book your room about two months in advance. A first- and last-night deposit is required, and the 21-day cancellation policy applies. Check-in is at 2 PM, check-out at noon.

So what do you prefer? The ambiance of a cottage, townhouse or mansion? All are available in our guest houses.

Guest Houses

Only the very rich can afford to vacation in Bermuda, right? Wrong. True, we have a wide variety of hotels and cottage colonies for those guests who want luxury. But we also have choices that offer more affordable, comfortable accommodations. See our Housekeeping Apartments and Cottages chapter for one option. The guest house experience is the other.

So what can you expect from a guest house? In our listings we'll describe the features and atmosphere of each because, believe us, they do vary. Why? Because they so often reflect the personalities of the owners who typically live on or near the property and are responsible for running the business. Guest houses can also meet different needs. If you want easy access to shops and restaurants, choose one that is within walking distance of St. George's or Hamilton. If you want quiet and scenic views, opt for one well out of town. All, by the way, are close to bus and/or ferry stops.

So what do you prefer? The ambiance of a cottage, townhouse or mansion? All are available, so look carefully at our descriptions before making your choice. Whatever you choose, though, you will find a relaxed, informal atmosphere that allows easy social mingling with other guests. That's where the breakfast rooms and guest lounges come in. They are often common areas where guests can exchange sightseeing ideas and experiences. Spontaneous parties and singalongs sometimes happen. None of the listed guest houses has a licensed bar, but in all cases you may bring your own beer or liquor to your room or lounge. Some proprietors like to treat you to a complimentary rum swizzle or glass of wine. Smoking policies vary in common areas, but all guest houses except one allow you to smoke in your own rooms. Proprietors are, without exception, happy to help with arrangements for golf, tennis and other activities or to give helpful advice.

All guest houses offer full maid service, so your rooms will be tidied and your beds will be made. Children are welcome in nearly all the guest houses. Where they are not, we will tell you, and we give you rates for kids. Some guest houses take pets on request; some do not. We will specify the pet policies in the listings.

Facilities and Meals

Before we go to our listings, we should tell you that with one exception these accommodations do not have facilities suitable for guests completely confined to wheelchairs. (See our Close-up on Summerhaven in this chapter for an alternative.) If you use a walker, however, some of the listings could work for you. Call the guest house directly to discuss details about steps and access so that you can be assured the accommodation will suit your needs.

Typically, the room rate includes either a full breakfast or a generous continental one. When there's an exception, we'll tell you. Generally no other meal plan is offered. However, in most cases guests have access to a refrigerator, ice maker and coffeepot or kettle. In some cases they also have access to a kitchen or kitchenette. If kitchen facilities are important to you, check out our Housekeeping Apartments and Cottages chapter for more options. But if you'd rather eat out, ask the proprietor for information on affordable restaurants and, of course, explore our Restaurants chapter.

Most rooms come with private bathrooms. Where they do not, we will tell you. Some bathrooms may have showers only. Again we will stipulate in each of the listings whether tubs are included or not. Hairdryers and ironing boards in every case are made available upon request.

Seasonality, Reservations and Cancellation Policy

Some guest houses have two seasons: summer and winter. Typically, the summer season runs from the beginning of April to the end of October, but dates can vary. We will be specific in the listings. Often, though not always, rates can be lower in the winter season. Other guest houses close for two months in the winter. Again, we will tell you if that is the policy.

Because of the personal atmosphere of these guest houses, the owners often have a loyal following of guests. Repeat business is very characteristic, and many visitors reserve for next year's vacation when they check out. Having said that, it is always worth calling on the spur of the moment since last-minute cancellations can happen. We will provide the suggested advance notice needed for reservations.

Generally speaking, proprietors require a two-night deposit, usually refundable if you cancel up to 14 or 21 days before your reservation date. Be aware that some do not accept credit cards; we will specify this policy in the listings. In addition, some will accept personal checks for deposits only. Travelers' checks, cash or money orders are often preferred. Guests, by the way, usually reserve by calling direct.

Rates

With one exception, the rates provided include room and breakfast. We want to emphasize that a lower dollar-sign code for the price of a guest house does not necessarily mean a lower standard of accommodation. For one thing, all properties taking six or more guests are licensed by the Bermuda government's Department of Tourism. To retain that license, they have to pass strict annual inspections by tourism, health and fire inspectors. Winners of the government's annual Cedar Tree Award are recognized for achieving very high standards in these areas.

Pricing Key

The daily rates listed in the pricing key are based on the rooms visitors would most typically reserve during the summer season. Rates do not include the 7.25 percent per room Bermuda government hotel occupancy tax, gratuities or additional charges for telephone calls. Bear in mind that gratuity policies can differ, so they will be stated in each listing. Rates are always subject to change.

$	$70 to $90
$$	$91 to $115
$$$	$116 to $125
$$$$	$126 and higher

Guest House Listings

The accommodations included are listed in order from east to west, parish by parish, subset by subset and thereafter in alphabetical order.

St. George's Parish

Aunt Nea's Inn at Hillcrest
$$$ • 1 Nea's Alley, Old Maid's Ln., Town of St. George • 297-1630

Before we describe this inn, you might like to be introduced to Nea. The alley where she lived may be off Old Maid's Lane, but there was nothing old-maidish about her at all. She was married to a William Tucker and had children by him. When Irish poet Thomas Moore arrived in 1803, she succumbed to his charms, much to the distress of her husband. It was probably just as well that Moore stayed in Bermuda just four months. Anyway, poor Nea died in 1817, at the young age of 31.

This gracious two-story house (probably built somewhere between 1750 and 1760, with additions in the 19th century) is steeped in history. The original owner was one Richard Pruden, a shipper and possibly a sea captain. He wasn't as prudent as his name suggests — he was probably involved in privateering.

Situated on a hill, the guest house has an upper and a lower veranda that both overlook St. George's Harbour. When it is busy, owner and manager Delaey Robinson likes to crack

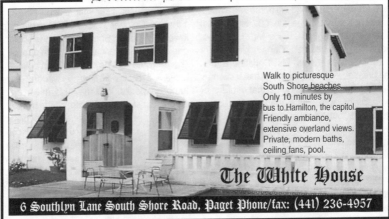

Bermuda Bed and Breakfast

Walk to picturesque South Shore beaches. Only 10 minutes by bus to Hamilton, the capitol. Friendly ambiance, extensive overland views. Private, modern baths, ceiling fans, pool.

The White House

6 Southlyn Lane South Shore Road, Paget Phone/fax: (441) 236-4957

open a couple of complimentary bottles of wine and invite his guests to sit on the top veranda and exchange stories. Delaey has been involved in research covering all aspects of Bermuda. If the history of St. George's intrigues you, Delaey will most likely be able to tell you stories that will intrigue you still more, including the one about Nea.

All but two of the 10 rooms have bathrooms with tubs, showers and sinks. The remaining two have showers only. For an additional $10 per day, you can have one of the five bedrooms equipped with a Jacuzzi bath. The guest rooms all feature unusual four-poster beds. Some are handmade out of wrought iron while others are wooden with cotton canopies. In addition, there are sleigh beds that look like — well, let's say Santa Claus would find them comfortable, and so will you.

You'll enjoy the old paneling and staircase at Nea's and the interesting mixture of furniture styles, which includes the antique and the Oriental. Each room has a special name with ornaments or artwork that relate to it. You'll find a tree frog sculpture, for example, in the Tree Frog room. Rooms come with air conditioning, sets of drawers (often handpainted), a desk or vanity, rails for towels, clock-radios, bathrobes, shower caps and toiletries. No television, though. If you must, you can watch it in the downstairs lounge. One suite with a bedroom, upper lounge and bathroom is also available for $180.

The room price covers a continental breakfast (freshly baked goodies along with cereal, fruit and juice, coffee or tea), which you enjoy in the coffee nook off the downstairs lounge. During the day, tea and coffee (iced or hot) are always available for no extra charge. And you may use the refrigerator. You may not, by the way, smoke in any room in the building. However, you can smoke outside on the verandas.

Kids are welcome, particularly older ones. Younger than 12, they stay for much lower rates. Call directly for information about accommodating the kids. A 10 percent service charge is added to the room rate. Check-in is at 1 PM, check-out at 11 AM.

Aunt Nea's Inn is within easy reach of St. George's historic attractions, but it is also within reach of Tobacco Bay, St. Catherine's Beach and Achilles Beach. Book your room by calling the hotel directly. A two-night deposit is required, and you'll lose it if you cancel within 14 days of your arrival date. For public holidays, book at least two months ahead. Otherwise, reservations should be made one month in advance. Major credit cards are accepted.

Pembroke Parish

Canada Villa
$$ • 123 St. John's Rd. • 292-0419
This traditional Bermudian home has long

been the property of the Barritts, a family well-known for their contribution to island politics. Howard Barrit converted the home into a guest house some time in the late '60s. However, it was built in the 1920s by a Mr. J.C. Vallis. Apparently, he included "Canada" in many of his properties' names. Ms. Christine Barritt, the present proprietor, suggests that Vallis may have had a special feeling for that country, or perhaps his wife was Canadian. No one is quite sure, but as coincidence would have it, Barritt herself is half Canadian.

This guest house is the least expensive one that is close to Hamilton. A 10-minute walk will take you to the city's shops and restaurants. On the second floor of the house, you'll find the guest lounge. Light and airy, it's furnished with rattan furniture. You can watch cable television in this area, or sit out on the veranda and appreciate (in June and July anyway) the scarlet blossoms of the royal poinciana and the coronation tree. But the indoor focal point for guests is probably the kitchen. Continental breakfast is served there from 8 AM until noon (Christine knows that some guests like to sleep in when they're on holiday). By the way, you may not smoke in the kitchen or the halls, but you may smoke in the lounge or in your rooms. After breakfast is finished, you may use the kitchen for cooking your own meals until 8 PM. It's fully equipped with china, cutlery, pots, stove, dishwasher and microwave.

There are five guest rooms altogether. Two of these are for two adults, each with a private bathroom containing shower and tub. (The rate for these is covered in our pricing code.) For about $20 less, two others share a bathroom with a shower only. For a higher rate (about $18 more), you can have a triple room (three beds), ideal for families. Rooms have one king or two twin beds. All rooms have ceiling fans, air conditioning and clock-radios. Kids are welcome. If they are younger than 3, they stay for free. Children ages 3 to 12 pay half the room rate.

After a day's shopping, you will appreciate the outdoor freshwater swimming pool, which is good for swimming laps. Lounge chairs will help you relax. Should you want to hit one of the beaches, Christine will supply you with beach mats and snorkeling equipment.

Canada Villa's summer season runs April 1 through October 31. Call Christine direct for lower winter rates. She recommends booking one month in advance. A two-night deposit is required, and a 14-day cancellation policy applies. A $15 service charge is added to returned deposits. You may use major credit cards, but if you pay with cash, travelers' checks or personal check, you will receive a 5 percent discount on your final bill. That means your room service charge will be 5 percent instead of 10 percent. Check-in is at 1 PM, check-out at noon.

FYI

Unless otherwise noted, the area code for all phone numbers listed in this guide is 441.

Edgehill Manor Guest House
$$$$, no credit cards • 36 Rosemont Ave. • 295-7124

Yes, Edgehill does have manorial proportions. Built more than 100 years ago, it was once a private mansion. The present owner, Bridget Marshall, runs it as a guest house, together with manager Maria Myers and assistant manager Cora Torres. One of them will make sure that on the afternoon of your arrival you receive complimentary English tea. (For the remainder of your stay, afternoon tea is available on request for $3 a person.) The room rate used in our code covers continental breakfast, which is served in the dining room that's charmingly decorated with floral wallpaper — an amazing feat when you consider the humidity of Bermuda's climate. It contrasts nicely with the dark wood of the doors. Guests often use this room for playing games such as Monopoly or cards.

Guest rooms, located upstairs and downstairs, are as airy and spacious as you would expect to find in a manor house. All nine double rooms have extra beds or pull-out sofas for extra guests. Kids are welcome — those younger than 2 stay free; between ages 2 and 15, there is a $15 charge. An extra adult costs $20. All rooms covered by our pricing code have balconies or terraces with garden views. One on the lower level has its own private entrance. All these rooms have air conditioning and come with a ceiling fan, cable television and a clock-radio. Two have private telephones. (A pay telephone is available down-

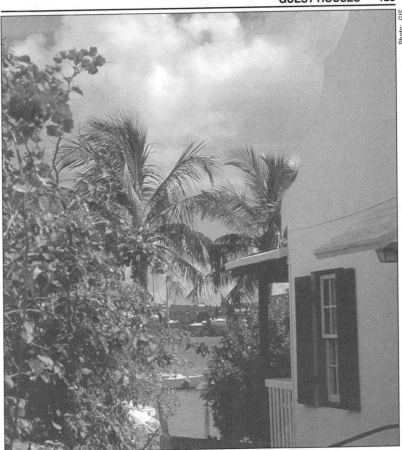

Photo: GIS

Traditional Bermudian architecture is elegantly simple.

stairs for guests without phones.) All rooms have private bathrooms with showers, and all but one have tubs.

Smoking is allowed everywhere, but Maria says smokers tend to go outside. Edgehill is ideally situated for easy access to Hamilton's shops and restaurants. But even though Hamilton is just a seven-minute walk away, the guest house has the secluded atmosphere of Bermuda's countryside. An outdoor freshwater swimming pool by the side of the house will let you cool down after a busy day's shopping.

Summer season runs from April 15 through November 15. Book at least two weeks in ad-

vance. A two-night deposit is required within 10 days of making a reservation. You can pay your deposit with a personal check, but you should pay your final bill with travelers' checks, money orders or cash. A 10 percent service charge is added to your bill. Check-in and check-out times are at noon.

Fordham Hall
$$ · 53 Pitts Bay Rd. · 295-1551, (800) 537-4163

Built in 1850, this guest house has the high ceilings and spaciousness of a comfortable 19th-century townhouse. In fact, in 1920 the Prince of Wales felt so comfortable that he apparently had lunch here. (That Prince of Wales, incidentally, became Edward VIII in 1936, abdicated in the same year and subsequently became the Duke of Windsor.) A 10-minute walk from Hamilton, Fordham Hall is ideal if you want easy access to the city's shops and restaurants.

The guest lounge is huge. With walls painted moonstone (off-white) and woodwork turquoise, it has a lovely bay window complete with a curved window seat. Chairs are comfortable, and there are plenty of books plus cable television. There is no smoking in the lounge or in the breakfast room, which gives you access to a fridge, ice maker, microwave and tea and coffee all day. Here you will enjoy continental breakfast as well as a clear view of Hamilton Harbour. You also may notice some hooks in the walls. While Admiralty House was being built in 1850 (see our Beaches chapter), British admirals used to sleep in hammocks in this room, hence the hooks.

The 12 guest rooms include one extremely large bedroom with a pull-out couch for an additional guest. Kids, by the way, are welcome. As Adelheid Johnson put it, "I could never say no to anyone." Call her directly for rates. All rooms have either queen or double beds, private bathrooms (just one has no tub — only a shower) and air conditioning. They come with television, clock-radio and coffee maker. Some have a good view of the harbour.

For summer season and public holidays, try to book at least one month ahead. A two-night deposit (credit cards acceptable) is required, and a 14-day cancellation policy applies. Service charge is 10 percent per room. Check-in is flexible; check-out is 11 AM.

Hi-Roy Guest House
$$, no credit cards • 22 Princess Estate Rd. • 292-0808

Why Hi-Roy? Everard Jones, owner and manager, will be happy to explain to you the reason for the name. He says, "'Hi' is for my wife, Hyacinth. When she was alive, she used to run the guest house. We ran it together. And people would call her Hi. For some rea-

son, many people would call me Elroy instead of Everard. That's where the 'Roy' comes from."

So now you know. But what does he like to be called these days? Jonesy, and that's how we'll address him from now on. He has four loves: Bermuda, people, cooking and music. Jonesy makes no bones about it: "We live in the most beautiful place on this planet." By the end of their first stay, he has most of his guests convinced — that's why they tend to come back over and over again. When they arrive, he treats them to a complimentary rum swizzle or a dark and stormy; then he shows them the view.

Hi-Roy is on a hill overlooking the North Shore. Sit outside in the lawn seating areas or on the guest balcony, and you can watch the cruise ships gliding into Bermuda. You also can watch them while you're in the enclosed glass sun porch dining room, eating Jonesy's home-baked rolls for breakfast. Breakfast, by the way, is different every day. Sometimes you will be treated to salmon cooked with Bermuda onions and Bermuda tomatoes that he grows in his garden. "People get tired of eggs," he says. Breakfast is included in the price-code rate, but Hi-Roy is the only guest house in Bermuda that offers an MAP plan. If you've read the Resort Hotels chapter, you know that MAP means Modified American Plan and offers room, breakfast and dinner for one price. Jonesy's MAP costs $140 for two, and there is a different dinner every evening. Typically, the meal will include potatoes and two other fresh vegetables, often culled from his garden, and meat or Bermuda fish. Dessert could be homemade apple, lemon, blackberry or peach pie. Jonesy makes sure he finds out guests' special likes and dislikes where food is concerned. He also provides a complimentary glass of wine with dinner.

In addition to the sun porch, there's another dining room with a large table where guests like to play cards. There's a lounge with cable TV, a large curved sofa and comfortable chairs. Off the dining room, there's a "family bar" that guests can stock with their own alcohol. As well as being a teller of Bermuda stories, Jonesy is a serious jazz pundit.

---

www.insiders.com

See this and many other **Insiders' Guide®** destinations online — in their entirety.

Visit us today!

In fact, from time to time he has his own jazz program on local radio. The extremely good news is that he has a music room full of tapes and CDs. If you like jazz, he will invite you to listen to music here. Chances are you'll hear John Coltrane or Miles Davis — his favorites. And if you like boxing or basketball, you can watch them on the 60-inch TV in this room.

All five guest rooms have two twin beds or one double. They all have garden views and come with bathrooms (one has a tub — the others have showers only). They also have clock-radios, cable television, ceiling fans and air conditioning. Children are welcome. There's one "family room" that actually consists of two rooms with an adjoining door. Kids younger than 2 stay for free; those 12 and younger stay for $28. Smoking is allowed outside and in the rooms but nowhere else.

The rates for Hi-Roy are the same year round. Mid-November to mid-December, the guest house closes for refurbishing, but it is always open in time for Christmas. A two-night deposit is required, which you may pay with a personal check. However, you must pay your total bill with travelers' checks, cash or money order. Check-in is flexible. Check-out is at noon.

Oxford House

$$$$ • **20 Woodbourne Ave., Hamilton** • **295-0503, (800) 548-7758**

Winner of the Bermuda government's Cedar Tree merit award in 1996 and 1997, Mrs. Ann Smith prides herself on maintaining the high standards required by health, fire and tourism inspectors.

Built in 1938, Oxford House was apparently the first custom-designed guest house in Bermuda. Walk through the front entrance and you are in a lounge area that has comfortable chairs and round tables where you can enjoy continental breakfast, served buffet-style. It includes eggs that are boiled in a pan on the table. We mention this because you will be introduced to the curious British habit of eating an egg in a special egg cup. You will also be introduced to Staffordshire fine china. Ann makes sure your tea is served in thin china cups — it makes all the difference to the taste.

A curving staircase takes you up to another charming seating area and to the bedrooms. The rate in our pricing code refers to a double room. However, rooms for three and four are available at approximately $40 extra per person. Children are welcome, and they stay for free if they are younger than 3. Cribs are supplied. Each room is individually furnished with bright English print drapes and bedspreads. English antique desks and chests add to the British ambiance. Beds are king-, queen- and twin-size — whichever you request. All rooms are air-conditioned and come with cable television, direct-dial phones, radios and tea and coffee makers. Each room also has a private bathroom supplied with soaps, tissues and face cloths. Hairdryers and irons are available on request. Freshly cut flowers greet you when you arrive, and honeymooners receive a free bottle of wine. Ann has a relaxed smoking policy throughout the guest house, but she says that so few people smoke these days, it's not really an issue.

Oxford is also popular because it is just a three-minute walk from Hamilton's shops and restaurants. It's the one guest house that is within the city's boundaries. The summer season starts March 16 and ends November 30. Book your

INSIDERS' TIP

If you choose a boiled egg for breakfast, you may well be presented with a special egg cup, used particularly by the British. Here's how to eat a boiled egg British style. Do *not* shell it first. Place the egg, pointed side up, in the cup. Holding the cup with one hand, take a teaspoon in the other and give the top of the egg a smart tap. You should then be able to easily slice off the top, which now resembles a small cap. Use your teaspoon to scoop and eat the white from the cap. Sprinkle salt and pepper on top of the yolk left in the shell in the cup. Scoop and eat again until you are left with an empty shell.

room at least two months in advance. A two-night deposit is required, which you lose if you cancel within 14 days of your arrival date. A 10 percent service charge is added to your bill. Major credit cards are accepted. Check-in is at noon, check-out at 11:30 AM.

Paget Parish

Little Pomander Guest House
$$ • 16 Pomander Rd. • 236-7635

Little Pomander is a delightful house situated on a picturesque country road, one side of which overlooks Hamilton Harbour. Patricia Harvey, owner and manager, says that it was built about 360 years ago. "It may have been one of the first houses to have been built this end of the island," she says. Its location means that you can enjoy seclusion while being just a five-minute drive away from Hamilton's restaurants and shops.

Walk through the entrance, and you'll find to your left a charming guest lounge with sofas and chairs. An archway divides it from the dining room where you will enjoy continental breakfast. You have access to the refrigerator here but not to the kitchen. Since all bedrooms are supplied with microwaves and refrigerators, this does not present a problem. While we're talking about rooms, we should mention that they all have private bathrooms with showers and tubs. They also come with telephones, cable television and a clock-radio. Some feature old fireplaces that, for now, are ornamental. "My dream," says Patricia, "is to get them working again."

Vinia is in charge of room service, and thanks to her the rooms are spotless and bright. Her ready sense of humor and welcoming manner will set your mood for the day. One of the rooms has an extra-large bathroom and is suitable for guests in wheelchairs. Another room can easily accommodate four people since it has two pull-out sofas and a king bed. Kids are welcome. Younger than 2, they stay for free; younger than 12, they stay for $15. An extra adult pays $30. Two of the five rooms have a view of the Harbour. You may smoke anywhere on the property.

For at least one evening of your stay, make sure you sit out on the front lawn. Take in the harbor view and watch the sunset that bathes the water and boats with a pink glow. If you're a tennis fan, for just $10 you may join the Pomander Gate Tennis Club on the other side of the road. Membership lasts the duration of your stay. Once you've paid your membership, for $5 an hour you can play on one of their two courts.

Patricia recommends that you book a month in advance. A two-night deposit is required, which you will lose if you cancel within 21 days of your arrival. A 10 percent service charge is added to your bill. Her summer season starts April 1 and ends October 31. Credit cards are accepted. Check-in and check-out times are flexible.

Loughlands Guest House
$$$, no credit cards • 79 South Rd. • 236-1253

Mrs. Mary Pickles, owner and manager of this guest house, will tell you about one Mr. Lough (pronounced "Luff"). He was president of the Savings Bank in Staten Island, and he decided he wanted a private home in Bermuda. In 1920, he had this beautiful mansion built in the middle of 9 acres of grounds. Double-storied and stately, it has often been dubbed "The White House."

Walk into the gracious entrance hall, and you'll see a curving staircase that leads to the bedrooms. Look to the wall above the stairs, and you'll be confronted with a forbidding portrait of Queen Victoria. "We took it down for a while," Mrs. Pickles says, "but the guests wanted her back." She certainly does not cramp their style — an easy, relaxed atmosphere pervades the guest house. Perhaps it is Queen Victoria who influenced the style of the lounge, which you will find to the left of the staircase. Large, it has plenty of velvet chairs and a fireplace. Oriental and lladro figurines would have appeased Victoria's passion for ornamentation, and the books her passion for novels. We're not sure what she would have thought of the television, but she would definitely have approved of the no-smoking rule here. To the right of the stairs is the dining room (again, no smoking) where continental breakfast is served every morning. Off the main hall is a big refrigerator and ice maker, specifically for guests.

Meeting the Challenged

You may notice that opposite John Smith's Bay (see our Beaches chapter), next to Winterhaven Nature Reserve, there's a driveway off the South Road with the sign "Summerhaven" posted. Summerhaven is a first-class residence, specifically designed for the physically challenged.

As we explained in the introduction to this chapter, none of our guest houses have appropriate access and facilities for visitors in wheelchairs. But Summerhaven keeps aside one of its 14 self-contained studio apartments especially for guests from Bermuda and from abroad. That means it is possible for tourists in wheelchairs to vacation in Bermuda at an affordable cost.

Before we go on to describe the residence and facilities, you may like to know the story of Summerhaven. It's an inspiring one that illustrates how philanthropy, determination and courage can triumph over indifference and apathy. According to Mrs. Ianthia Wade, the present administrator, the story started in 1977 when Sir Peter Ramsbotham, together with his wife, arrived in Bermuda to take up his position as governor. Their daughter had been paralyzed in a diving accident, so Lady Ramsbotham took particular interest in the needs of the physically challenged. She quickly discovered that care and facilities for them at the time were woefully inadequate — those who were unable to live at home were forced to stay in the extended-care unit at King Edward VII Hospital. That meant that young people were spending most of their time with the elderly, and that brought about the idea for a specially designed residence to allow a home setting and as much independence as possible for the physically challenged.

Lady Ramsbotham met with Sir Richard Gorham, a Bermudian well-known for his philanthropic interests, and he subsequently took charge of fund-raising. Individual donors, such as impresario Robert Stigwood, and exempt companies generously contributed. So did the Bermuda government, which agreed to a 99-year lease of land

— continued on next page

Photo: Liz Jones

Summerhaven is a great housing option for visitors with physical disabilities.

for the project and a grant that provided and still provides 85 percent of the running costs.

The next character to arrive on the scene, Margaret Carter, herself confined to a wheelchair, had founded and was president of the Bermuda Physically Handicapped Association. She was a woman of indomitable courage and fierce determination. Although she was financially independent and able to live in her own home, she was extremely sensitive to the needs of others less fortunate. Her suggestions and advice, together with those of the current president of the BPHA, Willard Fox, helped to ensure that Summerhaven was ergonomically designed. In 1983 the residence officially opened.

Enter the house and you will find yourself in a spacious hall that leads to a large, gracious lounge decorated in pastel shades. A fireplace, comfortable furniture and cut flower arrangements and plants help give it a pleasant atmosphere. Fittingly, a portrait of Lady Ramsbotham hangs on the wall. The front of the lounge has easy access to an outdoor patio, overlooking the ocean. In addition, there's a kitchen and a dining room where supper is served five nights a week. No smoking is allowed in the dining area, but guests may smoke everywhere else. There are no alcohol restrictions either — residents can buy their own liquor at local stores.

Summerhaven residents live within the house in studio apartments — large living/bedrooms that are equipped with cooking facilities and decorated and furnished according to the individual taste of the occupants. Private telephones are available. Rooms come with large, well-designed bathrooms. Each studio has a patio overlooking the South Shore.

Summerhaven has a bus for residents, conveniently designed with a hydraulic lift and high windows that allow passengers a clear view. Tourists can make arrangements to have a Bermuda tour in this bus. In addition, the BPHA has a bus and a van (usually driven by volunteers) that are available for residents. As was noted, John Smith's Bay is a short distance away. The grounds of Summerhaven are ramped to the roadside and so is the entrance of the beach. Access to John Smith's is easy, and you can borrow a space buggy — a special beach chair that does not sink into the sand — that will let you reach the water. The lifeguard will let you borrow the chair for free. If no lifeguard is there, you can call the Department of Agriculture, Fisheries and Parks at 236-4201. They will deliver a buggy to the beach.

Summerhaven is at 133 South Road in Smiths Parish. Should you be interested in vacationing at Summerhaven, make reservations by calling directly, 293-2099, at least two months ahead of time. Priority, you see, is given to local guests. Be aware that you must be accompanied by an attendant so that staff at Summerhaven can feel assured your particular needs will be met. Although attendants are on hand for residents, there are not enough to assist extra persons. The rate for both guest and attendant is $100 total, and it includes supper. Reserve with a one-night deposit. No credit cards or personal checks are accepted, so pay with travelers checks or cash.

All 25 rooms are air-conditioned and come with private bathrooms, most of which have tubs (four have showers only). Beds are twin, double or queen. Rooms are equipped with coffee and tea makers and radios. There are no room telephones, but there is a pay phone. For $5 a day, you can have television in your room, where you are allowed to smoke. Kids are welcome, and cribs cost $5 a day. Call directly for details of room and breakfast rates for children. Mrs. Pickles will also accept dogs on request.

Loughlands has a tennis court where you can play for free, and an outdoor, freshwater, unheated swimming pool. Lounge chairs at poolside are good for relaxing, and this property is within easy access of the South Shore beaches (see our Beaches chapter). It also is close to a bus route that can take you to Hamilton or all the way to Dockyard in Sandys Parish.

As is often the case with guest houses, Loughlands has a high repeat-visitor rate. For summer season (April 1 through November 15), book at least three months ahead of time — preferably six months. Credit cards are not accepted here. Travelers' checks, cash or personal checks are fine. A two-night deposit is required, and a 14-day cancellation policy applies. You can check in whenever you arrive. Check-out is at 11 AM.

Que Sera
$, no credit cards • 28 Astwood Rd.
• 236-1998

This little guest house has a garden setting on a quiet road that is opposite the King Edward VII Memorial Hospital. In fact, Mrs. Harriet Grimes started the business because hospital staff asked her to give accommodation either to convalescing patients or to patients' relatives who wanted to visit the ward.

The rate in our pricing code covers the cost of an apartment for two people. It can actually accommodate four people, so double the rate for an additional couple. The apartment has two bedrooms, each with a sitting area, private bathroom and a kitchen equipped with fridge and deep freeze, kettle, coffee maker, toaster and electric stove. For $20 less per person, she also has two double rooms within the main house that share a bathroom. They have refrigerators, coffeepots and tea kettles. All rooms have cable television, telephones, irons and clock-radios, and all bathrooms have tubs and showers. Hairdryers are available on request. Guests have use of an inviting lounge that has a large bay window with a window seat. Smoking is allowed throughout the property.

The rate does not include breakfast. However, guests without access to a kitchen can walk over to the hospital coffee shop, a popular local meeting and eating spot, and enjoy breakfast for reasonable prices . Kids are welcome (check with Harriet for rates — they tend to be flexible), and they will no doubt enjoy the freshwater swimming pool at the back of the property. You can sit in lounge chairs around the pool and enjoy the fragrance of the oleander bushes and frangipanis in the garden. Pets are permitted on request.

The summer season starts at the beginning of March and runs until the end of December. January and February are generally put aside for refurbishing. If you want to stay in the winter months, call directly for room availability and rates. "Book," Harriet says, "as soon as you know." Two nights' deposit is required, which you lose if you cancel within 14 days of your arrival. Que Sera accepts personal checks and cash. Service charge per room is a mere 5 percent. Check-in and checkout times are flexible.

Salt Kettle Guest House and Cottages
$$, no credit cards • 10 Salt Kettle Rd.
• 236-0407

As soon as they reach the arrival hall of the airport, guests of this establishment will see a local taxi driver, Mr. Harris, waiting for them with a Salt Kettle placard in his hand. Salt Kettle owner and manager Hazel Lowe likes to make sure that you are met at the airport. That is just one of the many personal touches that make this guest house so popular. When you arrive at Salt Kettle, Hazel will immediately take you into her inviting kitchen (large table, plants and family photographs everywhere and a gorgeous view of the harbour) and sit you down with an orange juice or coffee. Then she will explain how to travel 'round the island (the ferry is a three-minute walk away from the property), where to swim and where to eat at reasonable prices. Within 10 minutes you will feel as if you've known Salt Kettle and Hazel all your life.

So what about the accommodations? The price we quote in our code covers a cottage for two with a spacious living area, bathroom and a kitchen that is fully equipped with stove, coffee maker, kettle, toaster, blender and refrigerator. In addition, there's a cottage for four (five if you use the pull-out sofa in the living room) and an apartment for two with a separate living room and kitchen. For a lower rate, there are two double rooms with bathrooms in the main house. Guests in these rooms may use a courtesy kitchen that runs parallel to Hazel's. Call Salt Kettle directly for details of those rates.

All rooms are individually furnished and decorated, and with their floral curtains and bedspreads, pictures and cut flower arrangements, they have the charm of an English cottage. A word here about beds. As a former nurse, Hazel knows the importance of a comfortable bed, especially for people who have back problems. Every bed, therefore, has an orthopedic mattress. You can have a king or two twins, depending on your preference. Sheets are fresh and pretty. All rooms have air conditioning and ceiling fans, and two have fireplaces. Some bathrooms have tubs; some do not. If a bath is important, be sure to say so. There are no room telephones, but you can use a pay call box in the main house. Smoking in the rooms is allowed.

FYI

Unless otherwise noted, the area code for all phone numbers listed in this guide is 441.

All cottages have a view of the harbour. And speaking of views, the property actually has two water views — the front of the guest house looks over picturesque Salt Kettle Bay. (The name "Salt Kettle," incidentally, goes back to the days when many Bermudians were involved with the salt trade — see our History chapter for details.) The grounds reflect Hazel's love of gardening. Throughout you will find vibrant vines (she loves the yellow allamanda most of all), trees and, on her front porch, pots and hanging baskets filled with annuals. There is also plenty of patio and terrace space with comfortable chairs, a hammock and outdoor tables. Fancy cooking a barbecue? Hibachis are on hand.

The rate includes a full breakfast, which is served on a huge antique cedar table at the end of the guest lounge. Beyond that is the enclosed sun porch with small tables and chairs. You can enjoy your breakfast there while gazing at the harbour. The lounge is spacious (you may smoke in it, but not on the porch) with a Bermudian tray ceiling, fireplace and comfortable chairs. Plenty of games and books are on hand. If you have to, you can watch cable television there (just one cottage has its own television). As Hazel explained, the lounge is very important because it gives guests the opportunity to mingle and share their experiences of the day. Every morning, Hazel will greet you here to go over any arrangements you want her to make. You can, for example, join the private Pomander Tennis Club for a $10 fee, then play there for $5 an hour. Hazel loves to host children. Those younger than 1 stay free (a high chair and Victorian crib are available) and those younger than 12 are charged $35 per person.

Reserve by calling Hazel directly. Her summer season starts March 2 and lasts until December 1. Typically, first-time guests will immediately make reservations on departure for their next vacation at Salt Kettle — 95 percent of the visitors are repeat guests, so the earlier you book, the better. Hazel suggests reserving three months in advance. Of course, last minute cancellations make vacancies possible. A deposit of $200 may be paid with travelers checks, personal checks or cash. There's a 21-day cancellation policy. In addition to your BP rate, there's a 10 percent service charge. Check-in and check-out times are flexible.

The White House
$$, no credit cards • 6 Southlyn Ln. • 236-4957

First, we must tell you that this listing is, strictly speaking, a bed and breakfast inn rather

INSIDERS' TIP

Our water supply depends on how much rain we can catch from our roofs. Particularly in the summer months, we try to conserve water. It's not that we run out — if there's a drought, we can buy it. Take showers and baths, by all means, but do be considerate about water. You can help by making sure that you do not leave taps or toilet flushes running. If you notice that a tap drips, be sure to tell your host. A dripping tap can cost more than a drop in the bucket.

than a licensed guest house accommodation. Second, it is for adults and not children. Madame Odette Rémond, together with her husband, Monsieur André, owns and runs The White House because she enjoys making her guests feel comfortable and welcome. For this reason, she prefers to have no more than five guests at one time. "If I were to have more," she said, "I would have too little time to enjoy them."

With the official approval of the Visitors' Service Bureau, there are three guest rooms, a guest lounge and dining room. The house is just as elegant as its name promises. The lounge features graceful archways and a fireplace that most definitely is used for log fires during the winter. Do take notice of the magnificent Swiss wall clock — 200 years old, its face is set in the middle of a bas-relief of deer carved out of wood. Odette's taste in antique tables and chests accentuates the pleasing proportions of the rooms. The rate includes continental breakfast, which is served in the dining room. Tea and coffee are available all day.

The guest rooms are upstairs. All light and airy with fresh floral curtains and bedspreads, they come with either one double or two twin beds, clock-radio and ceiling fan. They are not air-conditioned, but the thick Bermuda stone walls keep the whole house pleasantly cool. All rooms have private bathrooms with showers. Upstairs you will also find a handy ice maker. There is a freshwater pool outside. Stone walls surround it, giving you privacy.

The White House is ideal if you want an adult, relaxed, informal vacation. As Odette explained, flexibility is what she is about. That's why you can smoke if you wish. It's a three-minute walk to a bus stop, where you can catch a ride to Hamilton or to Dockyard in Sandys Parish. The Paraquet Restaurant is a short distance away and so is a grocery store.

A two-night deposit is required, and a 14-day cancellation policy applies. You may pay your deposit with a personal check, but the final bill must be handled with travelers checks, a money order or cash. There is no additional service charge or gratuity. Check-in and check-out times are flexible.

Southampton Parish

The Greenes' Guest House

$$, no credit cards • 71 Middle Rd.
• 238-0834

Yes, this one is run by the Greene family: Jane and Walter, David and Lisa. Actually, Lisa helps out when she is not studying for her postgraduate degree in psychology. Jane says, "Our aim is to make our guests happy." That's why she often makes gingerbreads, loaves and cookies as extra treats for her visitors. Complimentary alcoholic drinks also are offered from time to time.

The guest house stands by the side of Middle Road, which means it is within easy reach of a bus route that can take you to Hamilton or to Dockyard in Sandys Parish. It is also within reach of Port Royal Golf Course (see our Golf chapter). However, once you walk through the reception area into the guest kitchen, dining and lounge areas, you will forget about the road. Look out the windows, and you'll see the waters of the Great Sound stretching out before you.

Mornings, you have a full breakfast with eggs, pancakes, etc., in a dining area with attractive blue tablecloths and white Wedgwood china. The dining area, by the way, is the only place where you can't smoke. Once breakfast is done you have full access to the kitchen, which is equipped with all the facilities you could possibly need. Coffee makers, stove, microwave, toasters, refrigerator, china, glasses, cutlery — they are all there. Downstairs, there's another large lounge. A dart board, chess boards and radios help to keep guests happy. They have been known to dance inside and also around the pool area. The pool is ideal for children. Half salt water, half fresh, it has a shallow end for nonswimmers. Walk through a moongate covered with bougainvillea, and you'll find a large field that offers plenty of space for ball games. Kids, obviously, are welcome. Call Jane directly for rates.

Three of the six bedrooms have water views; the other three look over the garden. All have private bathrooms with tubs and showers. Painted beige with blue floral drapes and bedspreads, the rooms are comfortable and equipped with an iron, a small fridge, tea and

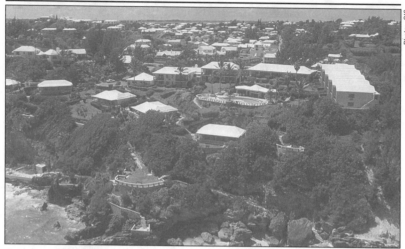

Surf Side Beach Club overlooks spectacular South Shore.

coffee maker and cable television. Honeymooners receive a complimentary bottle of wine on arrival. In addition, there's a two-bedroom, two-bath apartment, complete with living and dining room and kitchen. This apartment looks directly over the Great Sound. If two guests stay there, the rate is covered in the price code; double the rate for four.

Summer season starts April 1 and ends at the end of October. Call Jane directly for winter rates. Required deposit is two nights, payable by personal check. The total bill must be paid in cash, by money order or by travelers checks. A 10 percent service charge is added to your bill, and a 21-day cancellation policy applies. Check-in and check-out times are flexible.

Royal Heights Guest House
$$$ • 4 Crown Hill • 238-0043

This three-story guest house certainly has reached royal heights. Situated atop a rocky hill, it commands panoramic views of the Great Sound and the Little Sound. It also has reached lofty heights as a lodging option: In 1996 and '97, Royal Heights won the Department of Tourism Award for achieving a consistently high standard of accommodation over a four-year period.

Most owners of guest houses overlooking the ocean are convinced that their view is the best. Mrs. Jean Richardson, who, together with her husband, Russell, is owner and manager here, *knows* hers is the best. "It's both active and hypnotic," she says. "It's pure Bermuda. Islets, water, boats, roof tops — everything works together." As soon as you walk into the dining area and the guest lounges on the second floor, you will have to agree. Look to your left and you will see the curve of the coastline that stretches to Dockyard. Look to your right and you will see Hamilton Harbour.

You will take continental breakfast in the dining room in the morning. No doubt Jean's generous servings of muffins, pastries, cheese and fresh fruit will distract you for a while from the view. The lounge is spacious, with an oval ceiling and recessed lighting. Outdoor balconies surround it. A television? "No," says Jean very firmly. "A lounge is for chatting." It's also for the occasional impromptu rum swizzle party (complimentary, of course) and for playing the games and reading the books that are available. The other focal point for guests is around the outdoor, saltwater swimming pool. There you can relax on lounge chairs under umbrellas and still enjoy the view.

But do the rooms come with water views? Two of the six rooms do not — they overlook greenery and Gibb's Hill Lighthouse; the others do. All have balconies, and all have separate entrances. Some guest rooms are on the first level and overlook the pool; others are on the third level. All rooms have private bathrooms, most of which have tubs and showers. A few rooms have showers only, so ask for a tub if you want one. If you have to watch television, you'll find one in your room (with cable) along with a clock-radio, coffee maker and refrigerator. There are no in-room telephones, but you'll find one in the lounge. Some rooms come with microwaves as well. All are painted moonstone and have floral curtains and spreads. Extra beds or pull-out sofas are available for additional guests. Extra persons are charged $65. One suite has an adjoining room and is ideal for families — call Jean for the suite rates. Kids are welcome at $50 per person, but Jean says that on the whole her guests are romantic couples. Honeymooners, by the way, receive a complimentary bottle of wine, and seven-night honeymoon specials are available. Call for details. Smoking's fine in your room and the lounge, and Jean will take pets on request.

Royal Heights has just one season: April 1 to November 31. December to March, Jean closes the house. "When you know, let me know," she says of reservations — two months' notice is recommended. There is a two-night deposit required, and you will lose it if you cancel within 21 days of your arrival. Major credit cards are accepted. There's a $10 service charge on returned deposits, and a 10 percent service charge is added to your bill.

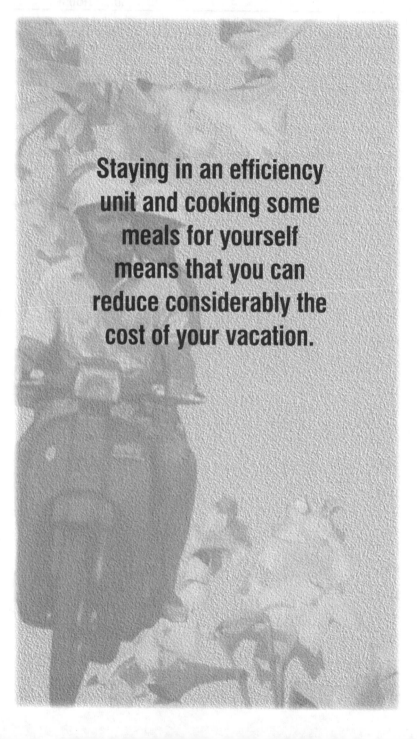

Staying in an efficiency unit and cooking some meals for yourself means that you can reduce considerably the cost of your vacation.

Housekeeping Cottages & Apartments

So what do we mean by "housekeeping cottages and apartments?" As our Department of Tourism defines them, they are the Bermudian equivalent of "efficiency units." Typically, they offer cooking facilities in a kitchen or kitchenette as well as one or more bedrooms, a bathroom and, in some cases, a living room.

Cooking some meals for yourself means that you can reduce considerably the cost of your vacation, as eating out two or three times a day can get very expensive here. This option is also ideal for families who prefer to do their own thing rather than being restricted by hotel meal programs. Cribs, pull-out sofas or extra beds are available for children, and proprietors can usually arrange babysitting. We'll state lodging rates for children in the individual listings, as they can vary enormously.

Since Bermuda has such a large selection of these types of units, we have chosen just a sampling for this chapter. All but one of those listed are licensed by the government's Department of Tourism. To retain the license, owners of these properties have to pass strict annual inspections by tourism, health and fire inspectors. Some accommodations consist of self-contained cottages or of units within cottages, some consist of upper and/or lower apartments in one- or two-story complexes, and others occasionally are in a main house that is occupied by the owner and/or manager. Whereas guest houses typically have lounge and dining areas, housekeeping accommodations often do not. However, they generally do have common outdoor areas where you can meet other visitors and perhaps arrange a barbecue together. We'll be very specific about communal areas in our listings.

Facilities and Meals

Some of these properties are suitable for guests in wheelchairs, particularly those visitors who are able to use walkers for a short period of time. However, we suggest you call the proprietor to discuss details of access and bathrooms.

Generally speaking, this category of accommodation offers an EP plan only — that is, room with no meals available at all. Nevertheless, there are exceptions to the rule. A few offer breakfast, and one offers dinner as well. When this is the case, we'll tell you and state the additional costs.

Part of the Department of Tourism's licensing criteria demands that proprietors supply their guests with dishes, pots and pans, cutlery and glassware, so you may assume that these are available, as well as barbecue equipment. Kitchen facilities do vary — some cook-

---

INSIDERS' TIP

On Wednesdays, some of Bermuda's supermarkets have a 5 percent reduction on the price of goods (other than liquor and cigarettes). Check grocery store ads in *The Royal Gazette* for details.

ing stoves, for example, have top burners only, while others have ovens. Again we'll be specific about this in our listings. Most rooms come with private bathrooms. Where they do not, we will tell you. Some bathrooms may have showers only. Again, we will stipulate in each of the listings whether tubs are included or not.

All the properties have maid service. You may assume that maids will clean and tidy your rooms and make your beds either every day or every other day. However, the policy about washing dishes can vary. Some maids will wash breakfast dishes, some will wash all dishes and others will wash none at all.

You will find that owners and managers are very friendly and willing to advise you on transportation, recreation arrangements, grocery stores and affordable restaurants. Often they will help by driving you to a grocery store, particularly at the start of your stay.

Seasonality, Reservations and Cancellation Policy

Some housekeeping apartments have two seasons (summer and winter), and some have an additional, slower, shoulder season. Typically, the summer season runs from the beginning of April to the end of October, but dates can vary. We will specify them in the listings. Often, though not always, rates are lower in the winter. Other accommodations close from two to three months in the winter. Again, we will tell you if that is the policy.

Because of the personal atmosphere of these properties, owners frequently have a loyal following of guests. Repeat business is very characteristic, and, indeed, many visitors reserve next year's vacation while they are checking out. Having said that, it is still worth calling on the spur of the moment since last-minute cancellations can happen. We will also give you the lead-in reservation times suggested to us. Generally speaking, proprietors require a two-night advance deposit, usually refundable if you cancel more than 14 or 21 days before your reservation

date. If credit cards are not accepted, we will tell you in the headings for the listings. Guests, by the way, usually reserve by calling direct.

Pricing Key

The daily rates listed in the pricing key are based on the rooms two adults would most typically reserve during the summer season. They do not include the 7.25 percent per room hotel occupancy tax, gratuities or additional charges for telephone calls. Bear in mind that gratuity policies can differ, so they will be stated in each listing. Rates are always subject to change.

$	$ 90 to $110
$$	$111 to $136
$$$	$137 to $182
$$$$	$183 and higher

Property Listings

As usual, our listings are presented east to west, parish by parish, subset by subset and thereafter in alphabetical order.

St. George's Parish

Taylor House
$ • Aunt Peggy's Ln., Town of St. George • 297-1161

The Town of St. George, with its winding streets and narrow alleyways, has retained its 17th- and 18th-century charm, as you already know if you've read our Attractions and Area Overview chapters. Taylor House, thought to have been built originally in 1690, epitomizes that charm. In fact, it is protected by the St. George's Preservation Authority, and the owners, the Rowe family, received a National Trust Restoration Award for renovations carried out in the late '70s and early '80s.

The house is on Aunt Peggy's Lane, which runs between Silk Alley and Old Maid's Lane. It's also closely bounded by Queen Street and Taylor's Alley. Who was Aunt Peggy? According to G. Daniel Blagg in his *Bermuda Atlas and Gazetteer*, Aunt Peggy was said to have been born a slave

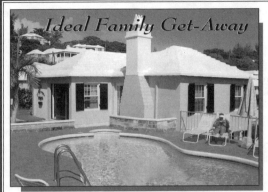
but eventually had her own house that was featured on turn-of-the-century Bermuda postcards. Apparently she lived to an old age and would sit by an open window so that she could chat with visitors and tell stories of what life was like in the old days. Present owner Mark Rowe is not sure about the origin of the name "Taylor." Early in St. George's history, there was a postmaster called Taylor, but whether he owned or lived in the house is uncertain.

The outside of the house has white walls and pink trim. Mark, who lives at the east end of the property, has converted the west end into a self-contained guest apartment. Its charm is immediately apparent when you walk through the stable front door into the living room. The ceiling is wooden and painted white, while an inset alcove adds to the room's character. The living room, with white walls and pale green woodwork, is charmingly furnished with carpet, a sofa and two comfortable armchairs. Feel like reading? The bookcase will supply you with plenty of material.

A word about the windows: They're of 17th-century design and therefore have no counterweights. You can prop them up half open with the sticks provided or open them fully by using the "fish tails" that are screwed on the inside of the window frames. Rotate the fish tail toward you and rest the bottom corner of the sash in the notch. In case you think you're really going back in time, rest assured there's one anachronistic item in this room: the cable television.

A wooden staircase in the living room takes you up to the bedroom, where you'll find a queen-size bed plus one single bed. (However, Mark generally rents the apartment to no more than two guests.) You'll find two side tables, a chest of drawers and a roomy closet. If you're security-conscious, place your valuables in a lockable cupboard. If you like to watch TV in bed, a second television with cable will let you do so. A clock-radio, hairdryer and cordless telephone are on hand. The bedroom has air conditioning.

What about cooking and dining? Go back down to the living room, and on your left you'll see steps that lead down to the kitchen. Double chimneys at one end (they once served as baking ovens) and a single fireplace at the other will once again remind you of the house's age. The fireplace doesn't work because the chimney is blocked, but we're glad it remains since it adds to the charm. . . . So does the dresser where you'll find plates. A little door leads to the water tank where once upon a time you would have dipped water with a bucket. You'll be glad to know that as much as Mark values the historic appearance of his house, he does believe in modern amenities: These days water runs from a tap. The kitchen is equipped with a full electric stove, microwave, coffee maker, fridge and freezer. There's also an ironing board. You can dine here at a small dining table that has two chairs. On this level you'll also find the bathroom with tub and shower.

Smoking is not permitted in the house, but you can smoke outdoors in the private garden. There you'll find poinsettia, prickly pear, lantana and, when in season, bananas that you're welcome to eat. A table, chairs and umbrella mean you can eat alfresco or simply relax. On Sundays you'll hear the bells of St. Peter's.

Taylor House is ideally located for easy access to golf and beaches, as well as to the restaurants and attractions of the town. Tobacco Bay and Achilles Bay are 15- to 20-minute walks away, while St. George's Golf Club is just a 10-minute walk (see our Beaches and Golf chapters). If you want to explore the rest of the island, you're within reach of a bus route to Hamilton. A grocery store is a five-minute walk away on York Street; if you don't feel like walking, the store offers free delivery.

At any time of the year, Mark's rates are extremely reasonable. They include water, electricity and laundering of linen. For an extra fee, maid service is available once a week. We suggest you call him directly to discuss rates, as they depend on the length of your stay. The daily rate is lower if you stay a minimum of one week. It's also lower in the winter season, which runs from November 1 to April 31. Call Mark to discuss deposits; they, too, depend on the length of your booked stay. A 21-day cancellation policy applies. Check-in and check-out are flexible.

Hamilton Parish

Clear View Suites and Villas

$$$ • Sandy Ln., Crawl Hill • 293-0484, (800) 468-9600

Come to Clear View and you'll be tempted not to bother visiting other parts of the island. The view of the North Shore is staggering — even on hazy days you can see forever. Sit out on your private patio or terrace and gaze on nothing but the blues and greens of the ocean. Walk down to the sea and you'll find a small cove, ideal for children, inexperienced swimmers and snorkelers. On the grounds you will also find two swimming pools and a tennis court.

Rooms in the price range we quote all have this view. Some are studios with living areas; others have a separate living room. They all have clock-radios, cable television and private telephones, and they are all air-conditioned. Kitchenettes are supplied with a fridge, electric stove and oven, microwave on request, coffee maker and kettle. Private bathrooms have tubs and showers. Children are welcome at Clear View. If they are younger than 2, the charge is $12 per child per night; between 2 and 12, they pay $24. Extra adults staying in the rooms cost $40. You can, by the way, smoke in your rooms. Mrs. Paynter, owner and manager of the property, says that some of the rooms are accessible to wheelchairs. Call her directly to check that these rooms are suitable for your needs.

Unlike the operators at most of the housekeeping cottages and apartments, Mrs. Paynter offers eating plans. If you want BP (again, that stands for Bermuda Plan), you pay an additional $12 per person per night for full or continental breakfast, which you may have in your room or in the dining room. MAP (short for Modified American Plan), offering breakfast and dinner, costs $37 a person. Wine and beer are served. You will enjoy dinner in the elegant Landfall Restaurant. A conference room that has more of a lounge than business atmosphere is available for meetings.

Clear View is ideally located for access to both St. George or Hamilton. A bus route is a few minutes' walk away and will take you to either town. Rent a moped and you can reach Shelly Bay Beach in just two minutes (see our Beaches chapter). A grocery that delivers is nearby. If you're interested in art, you'll find the Clear View's Art Gallery interesting. It features the work of Otto Trott, Mrs. Paynter's son-in-law. He is happy to offer art workshops and individual lessons.

Mrs. Paynter recommends that you book as soon as you know you want to come to the island. She has a very high repeat visitor rate.

FYI

Unless otherwise noted, the area code for all phone numbers listed in this guide is 441.

Incidentally, her rates are the same year round. "There's no such thing as winter in Bermuda," she says firmly. You'll pay two nights' deposit to reserve, and you will lose it if you cancel within 14 days of your scheduled arrival. Although there is maid service every day, Mrs. Paynter does not have a mandatory service charge. She says that tipping is at the guests' discretion. Check-in is flexible, check-out at 11 AM.

Angel's Grotto
$$$ • 83 Harrington Sound Rd. • 293-1986

The cottage units in the price range we quote all have water views of Harrington Sound. Guests share access to balconies and a patio, where they can enjoy the water view over breakfast. Can you swim in the sound? Absolutely. A private dock is handy for swimming, fishing and snorkeling. Daisy Hart, owner and manager, will advise you where to hire snorkeling equipment. If you prefer a beach, then John Smith's Bay is just a short walk away. Daisy will also direct you to a convenience store that's a three-minute walk away; another larger store will deliver groceries. The property is right next to a bus route to St. George or Hamilton.

Accommodations here are extremely spacious and well-maintained. Indeed, in 1996 and 1997 Angel's Grotto won the Department of Tourism's Hibiscus Award for excellent maintenance. The units include a double bedroom, a large living/dining area, a fully equipped kitchen and a private bathroom with a tub and shower. You'll have a queen-size bed or two twins. Rooms are all air-conditioned and come with clock-radio, cable television and private telephones. Hairdryers and ironing equipment are available on request. Kitchens have a full-size gas stove with oven, plus a fridge, microwave, coffee maker and toaster oven. Smoking is fine everywhere on the property.

In addition to the accommodations we describe, Daisy has an apartment that can take up to eight people; call for rates. Kids younger than 13 pay $15 dollars a night. Extra adults are $30 a night. Daisy recommends that you book about three months ahead for July and August. Her summer season, incidentally, starts April 1 and runs through November 16. A two-night deposit is required, and you will lose it if you cancel within 21 days of your expected arrival. For service, add 10 percent of your room rate to the final bill. Maids clean guest rooms every day but will wash up only breakfast dishes. Check-in is at 1 PM, checkout at 11 AM.

Pembroke Parish

Robin's Nest
$, no credit cards • 10 Vale Close • 292-4347

First we must tell you that the rate we quote

does not change according to season. Summer or winter, Robin's Nest is extremely reasonable considering you will have an apartment consisting of a bedroom, a living room with an adjacent area for extra beds, a kitchen and a bathroom. Three of the four apartments have air conditioning and ceiling fans. Bedrooms have queen, king or two twin beds, clock-radios and private telephones for local calls. (You may not smoke in your bedroom, but you may everywhere else.) Bathrooms all have tubs as well as showers, and hairdryers are available on request.

Kitchens are fully equipped, most of them with an electric stove (one has gas), fridge with large freezer, coffee maker, iron and ironing board and microwave (on request). Open the fridge when you arrive, and you'll see that owners and managers Milt and Renée Robinson have left you a few complimentary drinks. Living rooms are spacious and come with wicker furniture and cable television. Each unit has a private outdoor seating area with table and chairs in a garden setting. Hibachis are available if you feel like a barbecue. A freshwater swimming pool in a separate garden area will cool you down after a trip to town. Robin's Nest is near a bus route that will take you to Hamilton. It's also close to a grocery store on the North Shore and to Clarence Cove Beach (see our Beaches chapter).

Kids are welcome at Robin's Nest. The charge if they are younger than 12 is $10 per person per night. Those older than 12 pay the extra adult rate of $30 per person per night. Three apartments, by the way, can accommodate two couples each. For four people, double the rate we quote. One apartment could be suitable for guests who use wheelchairs but can walk a little. Call Renée to make sure it suits your needs.

Renée recommends that you book about two months ahead, as she has a high repeat visitor rate. Cancel within two weeks of your expected visit, and you lose your two-night deposit. Add a service charge of 10 percent of your room rate to your final bill. Maid service, by the way, happens every other day,

and the housekeepers will wash breakfast dishes. Check-in is flexible; check out is at noon.

Rosemont Guest Apartments
$$ • 41 Rosemont Ave. • 292-1055, (800) 367-0040

If you're looking for easy access to Hamilton, an apartment at this property may well be for you. Before the days of motorized travel, Rosemont Avenue was a highly elite residential area, mostly because horses and carriages could easily get from there to the city. A five-minute walk will take you to town. Sisters Karen and Lorri Cooper, Rosemont's owners and managers, want you to enjoy the atmosphere of the traditional Bermudian family. They will be happy to make various recreational arrangements for you and to advise you on reasonable restaurants.

Air-conditioned rooms have seating areas and come with king or two twin beds, cable television, telephone with dataport and iron and ironing board. They are cheerfully decorated with white walls, floral curtains and blue bedspreads. Bathrooms have showers, tubs and hairdryers. In most cases, kitchens are separate and equipped with electric stove and oven, coffee maker, kettle, toaster and a small fridge with freezer. Need a microwave? You can use the one in the office. Maids visit daily and will wash dishes.

All rooms have private balconies overlooking the garden or the pool. In the garden you will see poinciana, citrus and banana trees. Naturally, Karen and Lorri will let you enjoy the fresh fruit when it's in season. The outdoor, unheated pool will cool you down after a shopping spree in Hamilton.

Kids are absolutely welcome. If they stay in their parents' rooms and are younger than 13, the charge is $20 a day. If they are 13 or older, they pay $25. The children sleep in cribs or on rollaway beds, or you may ask for adjoining rooms. We must tell you that this property has facilities for guests in wheelchairs. Bathrooms are specially equipped with railings and bench seats, and the garden is

TAYLOR HOUSE
—— circa 1690 ——

GUEST ACCOMMODATION

Charming, fully furnished town house in historic St. George's Town. Includes living room, bathroom, well equipped kitchen/dining room and upstairs bedroom. Ideally located: within walking distance of shops, restaurants, waterfront, golf course, beaches, museums and bus-stop.

Telephone: **441-297-1161**   Aunt Peggy's Lane, St. Georges.   GE05

---

wheelchair accessible. The only drawback is that Rosemont is on top of a hill. We suggest you call the guest house for advice. Also, no smoking is allowed in the rooms or the lounge area.

For the summer season (April 1 until November 30), book at least one month ahead. A two-night deposit is required, which you will lose if you cancel within 14 days of your scheduled holiday. There is a service charge of $6 per person per day ($3 per extra person). Check-in is at 3 PM, check-out at noon.

Paget Parish

Barnsdale Guest Apartments
$$ • 2 Barnes Valley, off Middle Rd.
• 236-0164

This property is run by sisters Jane and Jennifer Conyers. When you arrive, one of the sisters will take at least half an hour to introduce you to Barnsdale and to Bermuda's attractions.

Accommodations are studio apartments with an open-plan bed/sitting room, kitchenette and separate bathroom. Rooms are air-conditioned (with units that heat the rooms in winter) and have ceiling fans. They come with clock-radio, cable television, telephone, hairdryer and iron and ironing board. Beds are mostly queen-size, though two apartments have kings or two twins. Pull-out sofas in the

seating area can also sleep two persons. Kids are welcome, and they stay free if they are younger than 4. If one parent and a child older 4 come to stay, that counts as double-occupancy. Every extra person older than 4, in fact, costs $25 a night. Some rooms could be suitable for guests in wheelchairs; call Jane or Jennifer to discuss whether they are suitable for your needs. Smoking, by the way, is allowed everywhere.

Rooms are painted white, and windows have valency curtains and venetian blinds that create a light and airy effect. Floors are mostly tiled. No studio, however, is decorated exactly the same. Some bathrooms have tubs; two out of the five studios do not. If you want a tub, be sure to ask for one. Kitchenettes have two-burner stove tops, large toasters, apartment fridges and, on request, microwaves. A few studios have full kitchens with ovens. Tell Jane or Jennifer if you want one. Need coffee first thing in the morning? The stove percolator will provide it. Meals are taken in a seating area with table and chairs in the kitchenette, or you can eat in the garden-view seating areas around the outdoor freshwater pool.

Barnsdale is centrally located. It's on a bus route that will take you to Hamilton or Sandys, and it's a 10-minute walk to a ferry stop. A five-minute walk will take to the Modern Mart grocery store. More importantly, a five-minute walk will take to Elbow Beach (see our Beaches chapter). If you're feeling adventurous, you can rent a moped from a cycle livery just down the road.

Summer season runs from April 1 until October 31. Be aware that if two or more guests stay in one studio for a week during the summer season, they get their seventh night free. During the winter season, visitors on extended stays get the fifth night free. A two-night deposit is required, which you will lose if you cancel within 21 days of your expected arrival. Add 10 percent of the room rate to the final bill for maid service. Maids come every day, but they do not wash dishes. Check-in is at 2 PM; check-out is 11 AM. However, Barnsdale allows a 5:30 PM check-out for guests departing on the British Airways flight to London.

Elbow Beach (see our Beaches chapter). Work permitting, Celia will give you a ride in her car to Hamilton, particularly if it is raining. Children are welcome at Dawkins Manor. If they are ages 4 through 12, the charge is $25 a night. If they are younger than 4 and need a crib, the charge is $15 a night; otherwise, the very young ones stay for free.

Book for the off-season as soon as you know you're coming. For summer season (March 15 to November 30) Celia recommends booking three months in advance with a two-night deposit that you will lose if you cancel within 21 days of your arrival date. Add 10 percent of your room rate to your final bill for maid service. Maids come every day and are willing to wash dishes. Check-in is at 1 PM, check-out at 11 AM.

Dawkins Manor
$$$ • 29 St. Michael's Rd. • 236-7419

Dawkins Manor has two categories of accommodations. For the lower end of the price code we quote, you can stay in a spacious bed/sitting room with a separate bathroom that has a tub and shower. The room comes with air conditioning, king bed, coffee table and chairs, telephone, clock-radio, cable television, iron and ironing board. There's no kitchen, but you will have a refrigerator, hot pot for making drinks and some dishes and cutlery, so homemade breakfast and snacks are possible. Some rooms may be suitable for guests in wheelchairs. Call Celia Dawkins, owner and manager, to check for details.

At the higher end of the rate range, you can get a suite consisting of a bedroom, separate kitchen with a sitting/dining area and a private bathroom with tub and shower. Again, the bed is a king. The kitchen is equipped with an electric stove and oven, microwave, coffee maker and toaster. A private patio overlooks the freshwater pool in a garden setting.

A guest lounge has cable television, a supply of books and, of course, plenty of comfortable chairs and sofas. A coin-operated laundry makes washing clothes easy. The property is centrally located. A two-minute walk will get you to the Modern Mart grocery store, and a five-minute one will get you to

Grape Bay Cottages
$$$$ • Grape Bay Dr. (off Middle Rd.)
• 236-1194

If your idea of bliss is to live in splendid isolation in a detached cottage right on the sea, then think about Grape Bay Cottages. There are two of them, each with a living/dining room, kitchen, two bedrooms, a private bathroom (with shower and tub) and a shady veranda overlooking the ocean. The first thing you will hear in the morning is the hushed song of the sea calling you to hurry up and have that pre-breakfast swim. Grape Bay is one of Bermuda's more secluded beaches, so you won't find yourself inadvertently sunbathing cheek to cheek with a perfect stranger. It can, however, have an undertow during windy weather. (Check the Beaches chapter for information about currents on the South Shore beaches.)

The cottages are spacious enough to comfortably accommodate two families of up to six adults. The rate for each cottage is $300 a night and covers up to four people. Extra adults cost $35 per person per night. Of course, kids are welcome. If they are younger than 2, they stay free; younger than 12, the charge is $20 per night. Rooms are air-conditioned, have ceiling fans and come with a telephone and clock-radio. If you want local television, you'll have to watch it in the living room. Irons and ironing boards are available.

Kitchens are fully equipped with a four-burner electric stove and oven, big refrigerator, toaster, coffee maker and microwave. Incidentally, because Grape Bay Cottages is about a 15-minute walk away from a grocery store, owners Steve and Diana Martin will be happy to buy groceries for you in time for your arrival. Phone or fax them with details of what you would like. You'll reimburse them for the groceries, of course, but you won't be charged extra for the service. They can also advise you on public transportation and will recommend hiring a moped for easier access to Hamilton and Bermuda's attractions.

What about maid service? You'll probably meet Gwen Saltus, who has been looking after the cottages for 28 years. As she says, "I've watched guests' children grow up and get married. Now they're back with their own kids." Gwen will tidy up every day except Sunday. However, she doesn't wash dishes, other than a few breakfast ones she might find in the morning. Smoking, by the way, is fine.

Because these cottages are popular in winter and summer, Steve and Diana recommend that you book at least six months in advance. Summer season starts March 2 and extends to November 16. When you make your reservation, you'll be asked for a credit card number, which is held until your two-night deposit is received. You lose your deposit if you cancel within 21 days of your expected arrival date. Add 10 percent of the cottage rate for the service charge. Check-in is flexible; check-out is at 11 AM.

Greenbank and Cottages
$$ • Salt Kettle Rd. • 236-3615

A word about Salt Kettle before we describe this property. A peninsula protruding out into Hamilton Harbour, Salt Kettle was one of the first settlements on the harbor side. Its name goes back to the days when Bermudians involved with the salt trade made salt pans. Today it is a very quiet, picturesque part of

Bermuda and an ideal location for a restful holiday.

Greenbank is a beautiful 200-year-old house. There you will find the office and a large guest lounge with tray ceilings, charmingly furnished in English country style. Guest singalongs sometimes happen 'round the piano here. Plenty of comfortable chairs and sofas will help you relax. If you must, you can watch television there. For a lower rate than the one we quote in the price code, guests can stay in one of the two double rooms with private bathrooms in the main house. These rooms have refrigerators and coffee pots, but they do not have full kitchen facilities. For that reason, lower rates include continental breakfast. Accommodations in the range covered by the price code all have kitchens. With those units, breakfast is not included.

The accommodations represented in our price code consist of cottages with a bedroom/sitting room, a bathroom and kitchen. You'll have a king, queen or two twin beds, and living areas have a table and dining chairs plus two other comfortable chairs. All cottages have telephones and clock-radios; umbrellas, ironing boards and irons are available on request. Some bathrooms have tubs as well as showers; some do not. Be sure to request a tub if you want one. Kitchens are equipped with gas or electric stoves with ovens, plus a toaster, refrigerator and coffee maker. Loungers, chairs and tables on your patio will let you enjoy the view. Smoking is allowed throughout.

If a cruise in a yacht or motor cruiser appeals, you can take advantage of Salt Kettle Yacht Charters, which is right on the property (see our Yachting and Marinas and Watersports chapters). Or you can swim off Greenbank's private dock. Greenbank is not near a bus route, but it's just a minute's walk away from Salt Kettle ferry stop. When you take a ferry to Hamilton, you might like to consider that in 1867 Salt Kettle was the first place on the island to operate a steam ferry.

Kids are definitely welcome, and cribs are available. Call Greenbank for childrens' rates. An extra adult pays $25 a night. Note that, for very reasonable prices, Greenbank has waterside and garden apartments that can accommodate four people. Call directly for those rates. Also note that some apartments have large bathrooms that allow access for guests in wheelchairs. Again, call to ensure that they are suitable for your needs.

You should book as soon as you know you're coming to Bermuda; a two-night deposit is required, and you will lose it if you cancel within 21 days of your scheduled arrival. Add 10 percent of the room rate to your bill for maid service. Maids come every day. Check-in is at 1 PM, check-out at 11 AM.

SkyTop Cottages
$$ • 65 South Rd. • 236-7984

SkyTop's is in an ideal location if you want reasonably priced accommodations offering easy access to both beach and city. Here, you're a five-minute walk away from Elbow Beach (see our Beaches chapter) and a 10-minute drive from the City of Hamilton. If you don't feel like cooking, you'll be within walking distance of a variety of restaurants. Owners John and Andrea Flood are happy to make recommendations. If you are in the mood to cook, the Modern Mart is five minutes away. On rainy days, John or Andrea will drive you there, and if you want groceries waiting for you on your arrival, they will arrange it. The Floods' aim is to make your vacation as relaxing and carefree as possible. If you are interested in golf, tennis, diving or snorkeling, they'll fix up the bookings for you.

So what are the accommodations like? As befits its name, SkyTop is on a hill and has a view of the South Shore. John and Andrea take obvious pride in their property's 2-acre garden setting. Frangipani and palmetto trees grace the lawns, and the bougainvillea, together with hibiscus, add splashes of color. In winter John and Andrea are happy to let you

INSIDERS' TIP

Be aware that hotel-owned or controlled private beaches have no lifeguards. Check the Beaches chapter for guidelines on safe swimming.

Like Bermuda itself, *SkyTop* is small, gracious and wonderfully welcoming.

**P.O. Box PG 227,
Paget, PG BX,
Bermuda
Tel: (441) 236-7984
Fax: (441) 232-0446
email: skytop
@bermuda.com**

eat citrus from the garden. Throughout the year, Bermuda bananas grow here too. A large field allows space for a football or Frisbee game. Should you feel like a game of that genteel but vicious pastime — croquet — hoops and mallets can be supplied. Want a stroll in leafy shade? The Railway Trail runs on the edge of the grounds (see our Recreations chapter).

There are 11 units altogether. All have patios, and all but one (a bedroom unit) have kitchens. Each kitchen has a four-burner stove with oven, plus a microwave, refrigerator with freezer compartment, toaster, coffee maker and ironing board. Barbecue facilities are available on request. You can eat inside — dining areas are comfortable with a dining table, dining chairs and armchairs — or you can dine Bermuda-style out on the patio. Bedrooms are air-conditioned and decorated in pale pastel shades with floral drapes. Closets are spacious. There is either a king bed or two twins, and a pullout or foldaway couch is on hand for an extra guest. (Kids, by the way, are welcome. Cribs can be supplied. If children are 12 or younger, the charge is $10 a day in summer. Those older than 12 pay $25.)

Four of the units have full bathrooms; the others have showers only. If you're a bubble bath enthusiast, make sure you ask for a bathroom with tub. Hairdryers are available on request. All units, incidentally, have cable television, and board games are on hand for extra amusement.

John and Andrea consider high season March 16 to November 15. The rest of the year counts as winter. During low season, they offer lower rates. Stay a week, and you get one night of the seven free. Call directly for winter rates. When you book, you'll pay a two-night deposit (first and last night) that you lose if you cancel within 21 days of your arrival. There's a 10 percent charge for daily maid service, and maids only wash up breakfast dishes. Check-in is at 2 PM, check-out at 11 AM.

Warwick Parish

Astwood Cove Apartment Resort
$$, no credit cards • 49 South Rd.
• 236-0984

While most of these apartments are modern, the homestead actually dates back to about 1710. It belongs to Nicky and Gabrielle Lewin, and they also operate the business. The apartments are on the opposite side of the road from Astwood Cove Park, so some have a partial view of the ocean, which is visible over treetops.

Originally, both apartment resort and park were part of a dairy farm. In 1915, a whaler named Antonio Marshall lived there. He was the man who, together with his crew, took out a whaling boat in raging seas to rescue British SS *Pollockshields*. His son, Joseph Marshall, remembers how worried his mother was that her husband would drown. Everyone survived except the captain of the ship, who died trying to save some kittens on board (see Elbow Beach in our Beaches chapter).

Rooms in the price range we quote have bedroom/sitting areas, kitchenettes and bathrooms with showers only. Rooms come with private telephone (local calls are free), air conditioning and ceiling fans, and they have private balconies or terraces. Beds, either two twins or one king, are all posturpedic. Children are very welcome. They sleep in cribs or in hideaway beds. If they are younger than 4, the charge is $20 per child per night; younger than 15, they pay $30. (Babysitting can be arranged.) Extra adults pay $35.

Kitchenettes are supplied with electric stove and oven, microwave, toaster, electric can opener, refrigerator, coffee maker and kettle. A coin-operated laundry is on the property — there you will also find an iron and ironing board. Maids come every day and will wash breakfast dishes. If you can't face wash-

---

INSIDERS' TIP

Electricity is very expensive in Bermuda. You can help keep costs down by making sure you close doors and windows when the air conditioner is running.

ing up after supper, you are welcome to make financial arrangements with the maids for additional help. Smoking's allowed everywhere, by the way.

A large freshwater pool will help you to relax. Barbecues are easy at Astwood: You'll find barbecue stations outside, and a communal patio and pavilion allow you to meet other guests. Citrus, loquat and banana trees can often mean fresh fruit for breakfast, especially during winter when oranges and grapefruit ripen.

The Lewins have a high repeat visitor rate. They recommend that you book about six weeks ahead of time for the summer season (April 1 until November 15). You'll secure your room with a two-night deposit that you will lose if you cancel within 21 days of your arrival. Add a 10 percent room service charge to the price quoted in our key. Travelers' and personal checks are fine. Check-in is flexible; check-out is at noon.

Clairfont Apartments
**$ • 6 Warwickshire Rd., off South Rd.
• 238-0149**

Mrs. Marilyn Simmons offers extremely reasonably priced accommodation with easy access to both city and beach. Directly opposite Warwick Long Bay, Clairfont is a five-minute walk from Jobson's Cove, an excellent beach for children (see our Beaches chapter), and a three-minute walk from a bus stop.

For the price we quote in our code, you'll stay in a very spacious, air-conditioned studio. There is a separate full kitchen and a bathroom with both a tub and shower. You'll have two twin beds or one king. Each studio is attractively furnished with a pine dining table and chairs, plus a pull-out sofa. Telephone, clock-radio, iron and ironing board and television (with local reception) are on hand. If you want cable TV, it's available on request for $2 a day. The kitchen comes with electric stove and oven, refrigerator/freezer, toaster and coffee maker. All apartments have patios or balconies with outdoor table and chairs.

For a slightly higher rate, you can have an apartment with a separate living room — ideal for families. That should tell you kids are very welcome. Those younger than 3 stay for $10 a night; it's $15 for those younger than 12. Extra adults are $20 per person. Both kids and adults will enjoy the freshwater swimming pool, and children can have fun at the Warwick Long Bay children's playground. Smoking is fine in the apartments.

In 1997 Marilyn received the Department of Tourism's Buttery Award for exceeding their high standard of maintenance. Stay at Clairfont and you'll see why. You'll also meet Betty Hall, who has worked there for 23 years. Many adults remember Betty from their stays in the '70s, back when they were students enjoying a Bermuda College Week vacation at Clairfont. They still come back to visit her.

As a rule, you should reserve about three months ahead of time at Clairfont, although last-minute cancellations are always possible. Rates are the same year round. Check-in is flexible; check-out is at 11 AM.

Marley Beach Cottages
$$$$, no credit cards • South Rd.
• 236-1143

Have you ever seen the movie *The Deep*? The opening shot was taken at Marley Beach. Part of *Chapter 2* was also filmed here. So stay at Marley Beach, and you should feel like a star. The names of some of the accommodations will encourage you to feel that you're in heaven as well. The most expensive suite is called Heaven. Others are called Half Way to Heaven and A Bit of Heaven. Igon Jenson, manager, assures us that at Marley there's no such thing as The Other Place.

For the price we quote in our code you may well stay in Next to Heaven, a family suite consisting of a master bedroom, sitting room, kitchen and bathroom. Kids are welcome, but they are mostly treated as adults where cost is concerned. If they are younger than 2, there is a crib charge of $12 a night; older than 2, they pay the same rate as an extra adult: $35 a night.

Kitchens are equipped with electric stoves for the most part (one is gas), plus microwaves, fridges, coffee makers and toasters. Bathrooms have tubs and showers. Bedrooms are all air-conditioned and have ceiling fans. They come with one king or two twin beds, local television, telephone, clock-radio and an iron and ironing board. Sitting rooms are furnished with wicker furniture and have two extra single beds made up as daybeds for extra guests.

Each suite has an adjoining studio that can be rented separately or together with the suite. Suite and studio together are an ideal setup for a family of six. Call Marley directly for studio rates. All apartments and studios have private terraces overlooking the ocean. Hibachis are available, and a heated (in winter) freshwater pool with whirlpool offers an alternative to ocean swimming.

Marley Beach is very close to a bus route that will take you to Hamilton or to Sandys. The bus will also take you to the Modern Mart grocery store in Paget. Hayward's grocery store will deliver groceries. As for pets? "We love dogs," says Igon, but there is a fumigation charge of $35. Fleas can be problematic in Bermuda.

Igon recommends that for summer season, due to Marley's high repeat visitor rate, you book about five months in advance. Summer season goes from April 15 to October 31, winter season is from January 3 to March 14 and shoulder seasons are November 1 to January 2 and March 15 to April 14. Maids come every day but do not wash dishes unless you make special financial arrangements with them. Credit card numbers are used only to guarantee the necessary two-night deposit, which you will lose if you cancel within 21 days of your arrival. Check-in is flexible; check-out is at 10.30 AM.

Vienna Guest Apartments
$ • 63 Cedar Hill • 236-3300

Will you get to hear tales from Vienna Woods? There's a distinct possibility, as Vienna's owner and manager, Leopold Küchler, was originally from Austria and is our Austrian consul. He is actually fluent in

FYI

Unless otherwise noted, the area code for all phone numbers listed in this guide is 441.

English, French and Spanish as well as German. Guests from Europe really appreciate his proficiency in languages. Stay at Vienna and you may well have a cosmopolitan experience.

You'll probably meet Leo, as he likes to be called, the moment you're in the arrival hall at the airport. He'll pick you up, drive you to Vienna (so to speak) and show you your apartment. You'll see a fully equipped, separate kitchen with electric cooker, microwave, toaster and coffee maker. Open the refrigerator, and you'll find that Leo has stocked it up with complimentary wine, beer and soft drinks. There is no objection here to smoking, by the way. Accommodations consist of the kitchen, living/dining room, double bedroom and private bathroom (with tub and shower). All are air-conditioned and have ceiling fans, telephone, clock-radio and local television. Bedrooms have queen beds plus an extra twin to accommodate a child staying in the room. Children younger than 4 stay for free. Those younger than 12 pay $20 a night. Cribs are on hand for no extra charge.

All rooms have private terraces and views of either the Great Sound or Forest Hill. One suite used often by honeymooners was once the quarters of a dairy maid who worked for a farm called Longford. Its walls are charmingly "bumpy" because they are made of old Bermuda stone, and a small old alcove with red brick edging reminds us of the candlelight era. That's where the maid would rest her candles. While we're talking about maids — they will

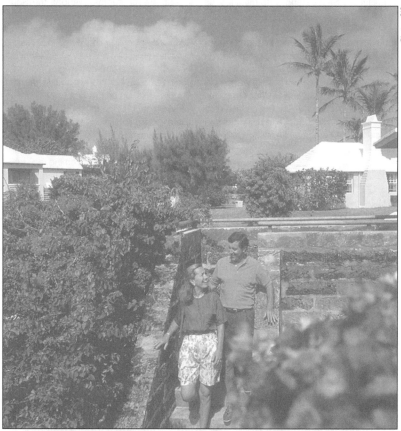

Photo: GIS

A couple roams the grounds at one of Bermuda's cottage colonies.

clean your rooms every day, but they don't do dishes. There's a coin-operated laundry on the premises.

There are two communal areas. One is around the unheated freshwater pool, where you can use the barbecue facilities, and the other is in the guest lounge that has a television and comfortable chairs and sofas. On Bermudian public holidays, Leo likes to organize barbecue parties. He'll always be readily available to advise you on transportation, recreations and activities. He'll also rent you pedal bikes (with helmets) for $7 a day. If you want to snorkel, he has mask, snorkel and flippers available for $5 a day. As for shopping, Lindos grocery store is close by. When he's available, Leo will drive you there. Vienna is a two-minute walk away from a bus route into Hamilton or Sandys and a 15-minute walk away from a ferry stop.

Vienna has a high repeat visitor rate. For the summer season (April 1 through November 15), you should book at least two months ahead of time. You secure your room with two nights' deposit, which you'll lose if you cancel within 21 days of your arrival. Check-in is flexible; check-out is at 11 AM. But chances are that you won't say goodbye to Leo when you check out. He'll probably be taking you to the airport.

Southampton Parish

Chance It Cottage Holiday Retreat
$$ • 43 Granaway Hgts. • 238-0372, 238-1579

Owner and manager Sheila Carey gave her cottages this name because, as she put it, "I took a chance when I started my own business." That was many years ago. Since then, many visitors have taken the chance to return year after year. Most address her as "Miss C," so that's what we'll call her from now on.

Cottages in the price range we quote are studios with bedroom/sitting areas, kitchenette and separate bathroom. You'll

have one king or two twin beds. Most bathrooms have showers only, but if a tub is important to you, be sure to request a studio with one available. Sitting areas have a table, sofa and chairs. Kitchenettes are equipped with an electric stove with oven, apartment-size fridge, coffee maker and microwave (on request) and an iron and ironing board. Rooms are air-conditioned (with reverse heating in the winter) and come with ceiling fans, telephone and intercom system. So what can you see from your room? Actually, the names Miss C has given to each of them will give you a clue. There's Whale Watch, and, yes, you may just spot one in the ocean during the spring whale migration season. You can guess what you'll see from Sunset, can't you? How about from Moonrise? All studios overlook the South Shore and have ocean views.

Prospective honeymooners should call Chance It for details of honeymoon packages. Newlyweds receive a variety of perks, including a free horse-and-buggy ride along the South Shore. In fact, many a couple has actually been married on this property — right under the moongate on the grounds. Let's face it, taking the marital plunge is certainly a question of chancing it.

Kids are welcome, but Miss C would like you to call her directly concerning their rates. She also has an apartment that can hold four people. (Call her for those rates too.) One lower studio could be suitable for guests in wheelchairs if they are able to walk a little. Again, call Miss C to make sure what you get suits your needs.

There are several communal areas at Chance It. If you're into keeping fit, you can try the weightlifting, cycling and treadmill machines in the fitness room. Or simply have fun with table tennis or darts. A small putting green and shuffleboard may well distract you. Cool down afterwards in the saltwater pool spa that has whirlpool pressure. Then relax under an umbrella in one of the five sitting areas outside that overlook the ocean. You're welcome

---

INSIDERS' TIP

Try not to leave dirty dishes overnight. They attract cockroaches, ants and other creepy-crawlies.

to use the barbecue facility on hand on the terrace. If you want to relax indoors, you can head to the library/den where you'll find cable television and a supply of books and games. On the walls are pictures that guests have painted. By the way, you can't smoke in the den, but you may everywhere else. To talk about matters more mundane, a coin-operated laundry is available.

If you're into diving, Miss C will make arrangements at Blue Water Divers (See Water Sports chapter) and transport your diving equipment there for free. You're into golf instead? Then at no charge she will transport your clubs to Riddell's Bay, Southampton Princess and Port Royal golf courses (see our Golf chapter).

On your first day, Miss C will drive you to a grocery store if you request it. If you choose to travel the island by bus, very often she'll drive you to the bus stop at the bottom of the hill. Chance It has an arrangement with two restaurants, Henry VIII and the Somerset Country Squire, whereby you receive about a 15 to 20 percent discount on your bill.

Miss C's summer season rates go into effect later than usual for Bermuda. Summer runs from May 1 until November 30. For April through July, book two months ahead. If you would like to request a taxi to meet you at the airport, mention it when you make your reservation. A two-night advance deposit and 21-day cancellation policy apply. Add 10 percent of your room rate to your bill for maid service. Housekeepers, incidentally, come every day and will do your dishes. Check-in is flexible; check-out is at noon. A courtesy area means you can have that last swim before leaving.

Munro Beach Cottages
$$$ • 2 Port Royal Golf Course Rd. • 234-1175

These cottages, all overlooking the South Shore, have the advantage of facing southwest. So what? So in the evenings you'll be able to sit out on your terrace and watch the sun envelop the ocean in a swath of pink. Swimming and snorkeling are ideal at Munro. The property has its own beach, Whitney Bay, which is for guests only. The sandbar in this part of the ocean means that at low tide you can wade out to the reef and say hi to the fish. Relax on the beach in loungers. There's no need for umbrellas — the coconut palm trees will give you plenty of shade. If you like golf and tennis along with your beach activities, you'll be pleased to know that this property is surrounded by the Port Royal Golf Course (see our Golf chapter). Dawn Sharp, owner and manager at Munro, will be happy to make golf and tennis arrangements there for you.

All accommodations have separate kitchens equipped with gas stove, oven/broiler, microwave, fridge and coffee maker. Hibachis are on hand for barbecues. Bedroom/sitting rooms overlook the ocean. All air-conditioned, they have ceiling fans, telephones, clock-radios and local television. You'll have one king or two twin beds; let Dawn know in advance which you prefer. Bathrooms have tubs and showers. Kids are welcome, but there are no reduced rates for them. Extra persons staying in the rooms pay $25 per person per night and sleep on pull-out couches. Cribs are available. You may, by the way, smoke in your rooms.

Grocery shopping is easy here. For a $5 service charge and a minimum order of $30, the Maximart grocery store will deliver groceries every day except Sundays and public holidays.

Dawn has three seasons. High season is from April 15 until November 14; shoulder season is from November 15 to January 14; and January 15 to April 14 is winter season. Book as soon as possible for summer. A two-night deposit is required, which you will lose if you cancel within 21 days of your arrival. Check-in is at 2 PM, check-out at noon.

Whale Bay Inn
$$, no credit cards • 34 Whaling Hill, Whale Bay Rd. • 238-0469

This one overlooks Port Royal Golf Course and, of course, Whale Bay Beach. Will you see whales? You will in April, if you're lucky. They'll be migrating northward to their summer feeding grounds. In any case this beach, just a few minutes walk away, is ideal for families, and you'll certainly encounter fish when you swim there.

Whale Bay Inn has five apartments, each

with a private bathroom (with shower and tub), separate bedroom and kitchen/dining/living room area. Bedrooms have one double and one single bed and come with cable television, telephone and clock-radio. Kids are welcome. If they are younger than 12, the charge is $20 a night; those younger than 1 stay free. Extra persons older than 12 pay $40 a night. The kitchen is equipped with a two-burner electric stove, large refrigerator, microwave, toaster and coffee maker. All apartments have private patios overlooking the South Shore and the 14th hole of the golf course (see our Golf chapter). Hibachis are on hand for barbecues. Owner/manager Philippa Metschnabel says that while there are no communal areas, spontaneous parties sometimes happen. She has no objection to smoking, by the way. Note that Whale Bay Inn is a 20-minute walk from the Maximart grocery store (remember, they deliver) and minutes away from ferry and bus stops.

Philippa recommends that you book a month in advance. A first- and second-night deposit is required, and a 21-day cancellation policy applies. Her summer season runs from April 1 until November 15.

Sandys Parish

Garden House
$-$$$, no credit cards • 4 Middle Rd, Somerset Bridge • 234-1435

When you arrive at Garden House, chances are you'll find owner/manager Rosanne Galloway wearing an extremely picturesque straw hat and driving her mini mowing tractor around the spacious lawns of her garden. On very hot days, she likes to wear her bikini and an elegant string of pearls. Of course, as soon as she sees you, she'll stop cutting the grass and personally introduce you to your apartment and Bermuda's attractions. She will also drive you to a grocery store if you need some provisions. It's very important to Rosanne that you feel Garden House is more like home than a tourist accommodation. That's why you'll find fresh flower arrangements in your room when you arrive.

You have a choice of three cottages on the Garden House property: a studio, a one-bedroom cottage with separate living room and kitchen, and a two-bedroom cottage with a huge, 37-foot living room that leads to a separate kitchen. Private bathrooms come with each cottage. Beds tend to be single kings or two twins, but in the larger cottage you'll find a lovely Bermudian antique four-poster double bed. Bedrooms have fresh print curtains and sheets and are furnished with dressing tables. They have a private telephone and clock-radio. Bathrooms have a tub and shower and a spacious cupboard faced with a full-length mirror. You may have a hairdryer on request.

The kitchen is divided from the living room by a counter-top that has bar chairs. The open-plan style gives a light and airy effect. Kitchens come with a freestanding gas stove, refrigerator/freezer, microwave, coffee maker, kettle and toaster. They also have a washing machine, iron and ironing board. Living rooms are furnished in British country house style with Bermudian touches of cedar. A generous supply of books and games is on hand, and cottages have VCRs. You may not, by the way, smoke anywhere inside the cottages, but you may smoke outside.

All cottages have patios where you can sit in a true Bermudian garden setting or barbecue on a hibachi. You can also enjoy the saltwater swimming pool. Although you cannot see the sea from the cottages, Rosanne's garden does extend down to Ely's Harbour, where she has a private dock for deep-water swimming.

Children younger than 12 stay free. If they are older than 12, the charge is $15 a night per person. Babysitting can be arranged. Rosanne recommends that you book as soon as you know you're going to visit the island. Garden House requires a $50 deposit, which you lose if you cancel within 14 days of your scheduled arrival. The prices denoted in our code are in effect from June 15 to September 15, and they apply because all cottages are air-conditioned during those months. Note that rates vary according to the size of the unit and the season; we strongly recommend you call Rosanne directly to discuss them. Be aware that Garden House is closed December through February. Service charge is 9 percent of your room rate. Maids come every day and will wash breakfast dishes. Check-in is flexible; check-out is at 11 AM. A courtesy room will let you have that last swim.

Here in Bermuda you can choose from French, Mexican, Italian, Indian, Continental, Thai, English, Irish and, of course, local Bermudian cuisine.

Restaurants

*"All human history attests
That happiness for man - the hungry sinner -
Since Eve ate apples, much depends on dinner."*

— Lord Byron

It might be argued that Byron certainly knew a little something about sinning and equally as much about fine food and wine. With our tourism mandarins inviting you to visit and "let yourself go," you'll find once you're here your dining options cover a wide range. Thus, letting yourself go — from a dining perspective — includes choosing from an exciting array of dishes, among them Bermudian, French, Mexican, Italian, Indian, Continental, Thai, English and Irish pub-style cuisines. There are even a couple of lunch wagons for burgers and soft drinks — one of them is in the City Hall parking lot.

To aid you in selecting from the more than 100 restaurants, inns, pubs and taverns on our 21 square miles of landscaped oceanfront, we have listed almost half of the possible choices. We include menu information to give you an indication of how each can satisfy your palate's desires.

However, there are a few things to keep in mind. Most of Bermuda's restaurants automatically add a 15 percent gratuity and will add the total on your charge card slip. If you're in doubt about the issue, ask. The majority of establishments accept "smart casual" dress for dinner. This description does not normally require a jacket, but some establishments prefer that men wear one. Also, while most of our restaurants are open for dinner every night including Sunday, public holidays can be another matter. Call ahead to be sure.

For those physically challenged and using a wheelchair, many of our restaurants are not readily accessible. However, you'll find restaurant staff willing to provide any assistance needed. During the summer months, when the temperature reaches into the high 80s, you can depend, except in a very few instances, on air conditioning and/or alfresco dining.

We're generally relaxed in Bermuda, and dining is a pleasure. As Virginia Woolf said, "One cannot think well, love well, sleep well, if one has not dined well." We want you to do them all well while you are here.

Price Code

The dollar-sign price code will aid you in gauging the cost of dinner entrees for two minus appetizers, beverages, dessert or gratuities. The majority of restaurants accept major credit cards and (of course) cash, but it's rare to find one that will take a personal check.

$	Less than $40
$$	$41 to $80
$$$	$81 to $100
$$$$	More than $100

St. George's Parish

Town of St. George

Bouchee
**$$ • 36 Water St., Town of St. George
• 297-2951**

Word has it that this is one of the island's best restaurants. As waterfront bistros go, it is certainly one of the most delightful. Dine indoors or outside on the waterside terrace. The menu is intriguing. Among the taste-bud seducers is the pink peppercorn-crusted beef tenderloin with rosemary bordeaux sauce. One of our favorites is the cayenne seasoned chicken and shrimp brochettes served with jalapeño mashed potatoes. But you'll discover your own. The chef welcomes any special requests. Also note that the menu is subject to change. Dress is smart casual.

Carriage House
$$$ • Water St., next to Carriage Museum, Town of St. George • 297-1270, 297-1730

Once a warehouse for the Royal Engineers, the Carriage House's vaulted 18th-century brick-walled dining room, gazing out onto St. George's Harbour, creates a unique ambiance. During the evening flickering candlelight enhances the grotto-like atmosphere. The dinner menu, a blend of continental, English and local dishes, includes prime rib served from the trolley and rack of English spring lamb carved at your table. The Bermuda Triangle, a combination of filet mignon, shrimp and chicken breast, is a favorite. Pasta specialties include linguine with julienne of chicken and green peppers flamed in cognac with shiitake mushrooms and spring onion cream sauce. The Sunday brunch is a smorgasbord of great choices. Dress is smart casual.

Freddie's Pub on the Square
$$ • King's Sq., Town of St. George • 297-1717

This pub is in a restored 18th-century building, its balcony overlooking King's Square, the town's hub. From this second-story perch, you can observe all the Square's comings and goings and even eavesdrop as a tour guide describes to visitors the ancient punishments doled out on the stocks and pillory almost directly below. From time to time, there is live music on the pub's ground floor, and a big-screen television should appeal to sports fans. English pub fare dominates, with fish & chips and Shepherd's pie the general favorites. Upstairs, dinner is served under the Bermuda cedar-beamed roof erected in the 1700s. The dinner menu is big on seafood, with tuna, grouper and snapper dishes featured along with the catch of the day. Reservations generally are not necessary. Dress is casual.

White Horse Tavern
$$ • King's Sq., Town of St. George • 297-1838

Many visitors find this a great place to take a break from their ambles through the old town. It has a waterside porch so close to the water that if you drop a morsel over the railing, you might attract curious fish. In the 19th century, the Tavern was the home of John Davenport, who amassed a fortune in gold and silver coins that he stored in his cellar in kegs. When he died and the stash was counted, his wealth amounted to hundreds of thousands of dollars. Today the Tavern is much more sedate, its dinner menu a cosmopolitan blend that includes duck liver paté with lychee and port sauce, chicken Tikka kebab and tenderloin steak. Fish and chips is a staple. Dress is casual.

FYI

Unless otherwise noted, the area code for all phone numbers listed in this guide is 441.

St. David's

Blackhorse Tavern
$ • 101 St. David's Rd., St. David's • 293-9742

Informal and friendly, the Blackhorse experience is like dining at home with friends. This is one of the places locals go to get away from the rest of Bermuda. St. David's islanders are renowned for their affinity for the sea, in the 18th and 19th century establishing reputations as superb fishermen and whalers. Dine inside or eat outside on the grass (at a table, of course) under a big umbrella and blanket of stars. Listen to the gentle lapping of the water as you dig into conch stew, stuffed lobster or any choice of fresh seafood. No reservations are required, and dress is casual.

Dennis' Hideaway
$-$$, no credit cards • Cashew City Rd., St. David's • 297-0044

Former U.S. President Jimmy Carter has eaten here, and we've been told he absolutely loved this place. So saddle up your moped and head east for a happening you'll be telling your friends about for years to come. Genuinely charming and undeniably quaint, the Hideaway wins the gold medal for unique. It's the only restaurant in Bermuda where the owner — in this case Dennis Lamb, who also is the manager and chef — suggests you bring your own liquor, wine or soft drinks. Bring your own cake or pie too if you want. This hideaway is about marvelous seafood served without frills and fancies. It's a kick-your-shoes-off (literally, if that makes you comfortable) and let-your-hair-down experience.

Other notables have dined here, some so secretly that they don't want their identities revealed — and Dennis won't tell. From the exterior, the Hideaway is not much to look at; inside it is homey and clean. "Putty and paint only makes a ship what she ain't," says Lamb, "so don't be bothered by what she looks like." Always call ahead to let him know when you want to come and how many will be in your party.

Oh yes, it might be helpful if you didn't eat much at least a month before parking your feet under a Hideaway table, especially if you want to tuck into his "fish dinner with the works." Take a deep breath and loosen your belt; you'll be here awhile. What you get is eight to 10 courses. Dennis starts you off with shark hash on toast, followed by conch fritters, mussel stew, fish chowder, fish, conch steak, shark steak and shrimp and scallops. Dress any way you like, but you must make reservations.

Hamilton Parish

Swizzle Inn
$ • 3 Blue Hole Hill, Bailey's Bay
• 293-9300

Swizzle Inn, named for the famous — perhaps infamous — Bermuda rum swizzle, has been catering to visitors and locals alike who relish its relaxed atmosphere and eclectic menu. You might begin with the escargot a la chinois, tender snails stuffed in mushroom caps and baked in a Chinese black bean, with garlic and ginger butter, and follow with the 16-ounce rib-eye, a hearty steak, simply grilled and served with sauteed mushrooms, potato, fresh steamed vegetables and salad.

The upstairs dining room has been converted into a nonsmoking environment. For the youngsters, a special menu is available upon request. You can eat and tap your feet to live music May through September. The inn is open daily, including Sunday, and reservations are only necessary for five persons or more. However, the restaurant is closed on Christmas Day, Boxing Day (in Bermuda, Boxing Day is the day after Christmas Day and is a holiday) and a couple of other holidays; call ahead to be sure. Dress is casual.

Tom Moore's Tavern
$$ • Walsingham Ln. • 293-8020

With elegant dining rooms, limestone

walls, wood beams and fireplaces, this former 17th-century private residence owes its name to the poet Tom Moore who arrived in Bermuda in 1804 to take up the position of Registrar of the Court of the Vice Admiralty. He became a frequent guest at Walsingham House, then owned by Samuel Trott. This house, which has changed hands several times over the years, is now Tom Moore's Tavern, and the dining is superb. The cuisine is continental and includes duck, veal, fish, boneless quail in puff pastry and Bermuda lobster in-season (September through March). The tavern is closed mid-January to the end of February. Jacket-and-tie is the preferred dress.

www.insiders.com

See this and many other **Insiders' Guide®** destinations online — in their entirety.

Visit us today!

Halfway House
$ • 8 North Shore Rd., Flatts Village • 295-5212, 295-4608

Flatts Village has always had an aura of tranquility. And there seems to have always been a restaurant at Halfway House's location. Cozy and clean, it has become a favorite for locals. One visit will tell you why. The food is Bermudian, excellent, and the prices superb. This is the place you always dream about finding when you travel — one that is friendly with homestyle meals cooked fresh daily. Errol Burgess, the owner and manager, welcomes you to visit the kitchen and watch the food being prepared; just ask. The varied menu encompasses specialties like lobster (in-season), T-bone steaks, filet mignon and fresh local fish. All soups, including the renowned fish chowder — some have even called it the best on the island — are homemade. "We don't use anything out of a can," says Errol. The experience is charming and delightful; savor it with wine or beer. By the way, the burgers are also homemade, with seasoning worked in before they hit the grill; no store-bought patties here, thank you.

Stop in for breakfast, lunch or dinner. Dress is casual.

Devonshire Parish

Caliban's
$$ • Ariel Sands Beach Club, South Shore Rd. • 236-1010

This Beach Club has borrowed a couple of characters from Shakespeare's *Tempest*, hence the names Ariel and Caliban. At the restaurant, you can dine alfresco by the sea, hold hands across the table under a full moon, and have breakfast on the beach in the morning. Evenings here are magical as you dance under the stars to music provided by local entertainers.

The a la carte menu is international, and the food is expertly and elegantly prepared. The roast pork tenderloin stuffed with pecans and apples set on a Calvados sauce is one of the favored selections. Finish with a dessert of hot chocolate fondant set on a butterscotch sauce and served with vanilla ice cream. Dress is smart casual.

Pembroke Parish

City of Hamilton

Ascot's
$$ • 24 Rosemount Ave., Hamilton • 295-9644

Escape the city for tranquil surroundings mere minutes away. *USA Today* has called Ascot's a "place not to be missed." This elegant 19th-century former home, nestled in an idyllic setting, now houses an award-winning restaurant that captures the ambiance of

---

INSIDERS' TIP

On some of the menus you will see lobster (in season). In season locally refers to Bermuda lobster — and very tasty our lobsters are too — that is available September through March.

a fine English country inn. Dine indoors or outside in a secluded and quiet garden setting where bougainvilleas and other flowers entertain the eyes. The dining emphasis is on provincial European cuisine and fresh local fish. Try the vegetarian mushroom Diane, chargrilled Portobello mushrooms with spinach and Taleggio cheese, all resting on a bed of grilled vegetables drizzled with rosemary infused olive oil and accompanied by grilled polenta. A non-vegetarian favorite is fresh Bermuda wahoo gravlax — home-cured, then served with a red onion and roasted tomato balsamic confit garnished with an array of salad greens drizzled with a lemongrass-infused vinegar. Stop by for the Sunday carvery where you'll find offerings such as chicken Royal Palms — chicken stuffed with sun-dried tomatoes, black olives and camborzola cheese on a bed of roasted pepper oregano cream sauce. Dress is smart casual.

The Bombay Bicycle Club
$$ • 75 Reid St. E., between Court and King Sts., Hamilton • 292-0048

Ah, for a taste of India, this is a secret visitors rarely ferret out. But if you want a genuine bite of New Delhi, this is it. Enter just right of Rego furniture store's main entrance and take the elevator to the third floor. Once here, you'll find it one of the most delightful restaurants in the city. Nicely decorated, the restaurant's ambiance is relaxing and its waiters friendly. Most times the music is authentic Indian. The lunch buffet is reasonably priced and good. The dinner menu offers enough choices that, if unfamiliar with Indian dishes, you'll probably want to spend a while perusing it before deciding. Waiters are always willing to provide advice if you want a bit more information on some offerings. The favorites include Roganjosh, a popular lamb curry, and Murg Saagwala, chicken breast and spinach in a mild curry sauce. Choose Naan bread or Parantha as an accompaniment. Dress is smart casual, and reservations generally are not required.

Café Acoreana
$ • 21 Church St., opposite the bus terminal, Hamilton • 296-0402

For a morning snack or lunch while waiting for the bus, or if you just feel like relaxing in a bright, airy and clean cafe, here you'll find a variety of fresh pastries guaranteed to break down any resistance. Indulge now, diet later. Pastry favorites include malacadas, Portuguese doughnuts that seem to disappear as quickly as they appear, and custard tarts, which vanish just as rapidly. Sandwiches include ham, turkey, tuna and egg. There is also peito de gallina (chicken breast) and Bolos de arroz, a plain but delicious muffin. Add some cakes and puddings, and your sweet tooth will e-mail a letter of appreciation. Dress is casual.

Chancery Wine Bar
$$ • Chancery Ln., Hamilton • 295-5058

Tucked away in a lane connecting Front and Reid streets (turn near the British Airways office on Front Street), this gem has a legal theme. Enter through a trellised courtyard and find three dining areas. The low vaulted ceiling is a reminder that this was once a wine cellar. And speaking of wine, you can choose from a list said to include the island's largest selection of award-winning choices. In fact, this restaurant won the 1995 Bermuda Gold Award for Overall Excellence in Food, Drink and Entertainment. A classical guitarist is on hand Thursdays and Sundays for diners' enjoyment. The menu changes monthly and is always imaginative. An example of the type of fare you'll find is the steamed salmon steak with a light horseradish-infused cream sauce, citrus basil pesto, black spaetzle and shaped vegetables. There is also a selection of fine European cheeses. A special dinner/movie package includes the price of dinner and a movie ticket. Reservations are necessary. Dress is smart casual.

Chopsticks
$ • 88 Reid St. E., Hamilton • 292-0791

Whether you've mastered Oriental chopsticks or prefer an Occidental fork, the regional Chinese and Thai dishes taste equally intriguing. The decor is flavored with rice paper fans hanging from the ceiling and large open fans and attractive Oriental-flavored paintings on the walls — nothing elaborate, but it works splendidly. The tables are well-spaced, and service is quick and friendly. The lunch menu includes a wealth of main courses, and the dinner menu features a wide range of regional dishes, among them Thai chicken with sweet basil, and Evil Jungle Prince, a vegetarian alternative. Beef Szechuan is popular. For dessert you can choose, among other things, a slice of Snicker's bar pie. Uh huh. Visit in February and join in the celebration of the Chinese New Year; the multi-course banquet is magical. Dress is smart casual. Reservations not generally necessary.

Colony Pub Steakhouse
$$ • Princess Hotel, Pitts Bay Rd., Hamilton • 295-3000

Walk through the main hotel doors, keep straight ahead, turn left and step into a cozy dining room accented by a cedar-paneled bar. You're in a steakhouse where the aged Angus beef steaks are like Texas — *big*. The shrimp and lamb chops are pretty generous too. Even the salmon are Goliath-size. You know what kind of appetite to bring to the table, and we're not kidding. During the day the pub features a good-value buffet lunch, and during the evening . . . well, we're back to those big steaks and shrimp and chops. Chef Peter Evans absolutely thrives on preparing the succulent oversized meat entrees and other dishes. Dress is smart casual.

Flanagan's Irish Pub & Restaurant
$ • Emporium Bldg., 69 Front St., Hamilton • 295-8299

For a taste of Ireland in the Atlantic, Flanagan's serves up Irish fare for lunch or dinner. Dine on the balcony overlooking Front Street and Hamilton Harbour beyond, or eat inside in an atmosphere that captures the essence of the shamrock.

This pub won the prize for Bermuda's Best Fish Chowder in 1995 and 1996. One of the menu favorites is the 8-ounce Gaelic Sirloin, a choice certified Angus strip steak, grilled or charbroiled, topped with sauteed mushrooms, served with an Irish whisky sauce and accompanied with your choice of potatoes, pasta or rice. Flanagan's is a great place for those who relish Murphy's stout or Gallagher's Irish Ale. Dress is casual, and reservations are not needed.

The Harbourfront
$$$ • 21 Front St. W., Hamilton • 295-4207

On the second floor and accessed through the cool, tunnellike entrance just off Front Street, opposite the Visitor's Service Bureau, this restaurant is a popular spot. Relax on its covered upstairs porch and absorb island life as it unfolds under balmy skies and languid breezes. From here, as you sip a cappuccino and contemplate a ferry ride to Dockyard, you get a sense of the dichotomy of Bermuda — the hectic hustle in the street below juxtaposed with sailboats gliding sedately in placid Hamilton Harbour.

The sushi bar has tasty sashimi, nigiri,

norimaki and temaki with sake and Saporo beer. If sushi is not your pleasure, dip into a pasta specialty, or perhaps duck Curaçao — tender breasts of duck, sliced and napped with an orange Curaçao-and-cumin–scented sauce, garnished with glazed red cabbage. The service is friendly and efficient. Jackets are preferred for dinner.

The Hog Penny Restaurant and Pub
$$ • 5 Burnaby Hill, Hamilton • 292-2534

For more than 30 years, this restaurant has been a local favorite. Visitors love it too. The name (see our History chapter) is derived from the Hog money issued in 1615 to provide coinage for early settlers. This is the pub where you can raise a toast in a pewter jug, shimmy up to the dark wood bar or sit at one of the tables and drink in the authentic British ambiance. Order classics like bangers and mash (traditional plump beef sausages served with fresh mashed potatoes, fresh vegetables and onion gravy), fish and chips, or go for the day's dinner special. Among the house specialties is the chicken and shrimp brochette — plump juicy shrimp and tender morsels of chicken together on a skewer with bell peppers and onions, marinated in lemon and lime juice, then broiled and served over rice with an orange and ginger sauce. Finish with a dessert of banana fritters — bananas coated in a light batter, fried and tossed in cinnamon sugar and flamed at your table with Bermuda

Black Seal Rum. Entertainment, often a guitar-strumming singer, is usually on hand. Dress is casual.

The Hungry Bear
$ • Chancery Ln., Hamilton • 292-2353

This bear is a honey, and it sure has some great coffees. Step off the lane and into a cool, neat atmosphere where flavored herbal teas, sandwiches, Italian pastries and chocolates, cinnamon and almond biscotti, pizzas and a few salads are available for a relaxing mid-morning snack or lunch. Seven different coffees are offered daily to go with the fresh pastries. The owner and manager emphasizes that The Hungry Bear serves real cappuccino, not pretenders to the throne. Although it's only open during the day, it's worth keeping in mind as a good place to take a breather from shopping. Note: You'll find some maps and visitor information here. Dress is casual.

La Trattoria
$$ • 22 Washington Ln., Hamilton • 295-1877

Relaxed, informal and in the heart of Hamilton, this is a great place for casual dining. The atmosphere is warm, accented by a wood-beamed ceiling from which a couple of plants hang. Copper utensils are displayed along a far wall. Add red and white checkered tablecloths and the picture is complete. This is home away from home. Pastas, pizza and regional Italian specialties compete to tempt a hungry palate. Fresh fillet of fish simmered in tomato sauce with garlic, white wine, olives, oregano and parsley, or sirloin steak served in a sauce of onions, fresh mushrooms and Barolo wine are two of the many choices. The convenient location (it's hard to stroll around Hamilton without noticing it) makes it ideal for lunch and a favored dinner destination. Dress is smart casual.

Le Figaro
$ • 63 Reid St., Hamilton • 296-4991

If you've never been to France, this will be your first trip. From the meals prepared by a chef who hails from Bordeaux, France, to the music that accompanies your dinner, this intimate little bistro is the real thing. One of the newest on the restaurant circuit, it has quickly become a hit. If you want a special wine, you need only to accompany the waiter across the entry way to Bacchus, the restaurant's wine shop, and select your own. Yes, the wine list is extensive. Two dinner favorites: coq au vin, rustic chicken marinated in Beaujolais and onions, braised in a rich red wine sauce and served with mashed potatoes; and steak frites, a hearty rib-eye steak, perfectly grilled and served with Maitre d' Hotel butter and home-made pommes frites. Top it off with the favorite dessert — chocolate crème brûlée. Reservations are necessary. Dress is smart casual.

Little Venice
$$ • 32 Bermudiana Rd., Hamilton • 295-3503

This restaurant has been around for sev-

eral decades, and many regard it as one of the best of Italian-food choices. It is certainly a hit with the business lunch crowd. A convivial atmosphere is augmented by fun-loving waiters. Although the tables may seem rather close together, there is a sense of privacy.

Classic Italian cuisine is showcased in an array of tempting dinner choices. The scampi alla Mediterranea — jumbo shrimp sauteed with white wine and garlic and served with a caponata-like concoction of eggplant, fresh tomatoes and zucchini (flavored with basil vinaigrette) — is one of several "lighter fare" dishes. And for dessert, crostata di frutta — crispy sugar pastry filled with vanilla cream, topped with mixed berries, finished with apricot glaze and served with mango coulis — is positively sinful. Dress is smart casual, and reservations are necessary. One of the pluses here is that, after spoiling yourself at dinner, you can burn off a few calories by taking advantage of free admission to The Club (see our Nightlife chapter) upstairs for music and dancing.

The Lobster Pot
$$ • 6 Bermudiana Rd., Hamilton • 292-6898

Live Maine lobsters are available year round; Bermuda spiny lobsters, only in-season. But this restaurant is not simply for lovers of either the local or imported crustacean; some fish, chicken and meat dishes also are served. Appetizers include curried Bermuda fish rolled in thin crepe glazed with Hollandaise sauce and mango chutney. The coconut shrimp — gulf shrimp rolled in coconut, fried

> ### FYI
>
> Unless otherwise noted, the area code for all phone numbers listed in this guide is 441.

INSIDERS' TIP

From November through March, a money-saving "dine-around" program is in effect. It allows visitors to choose from more than 30 restaurants where specially priced dinner menus are available in addition to regular offerings. To find out current participating eateries, pick up a program booklet either at your hotel or at the Bermuda Department of Tourism. Note, however, that drinks and gratuities are not included in dine-around menu prices. Because menu details and offerings may be subject to change, call ahead to avoid being disappointed.

golden brown and served with sweet Oriental sauce — is a tasty alternative. Dinner entrees include Creole shrimp pasta — shrimp sauteed with spicy sausage, fresh Mozzarella, roasted peppers and basil served over angel hair pasta. The atmosphere is somewhat like being on board a comfortable wooden sailing vessel. Dress is casual.

Monte Carlo
$$ • 9 Victoria St., Hamilton • 295-5453

Behind City Hall, this attractive restaurant, complete with murals, serves up Mediterranean cuisine amid a cozy French ambiance. Appetizers such as mushroom terrine — assorted shiitake, oyster and cremini mushrooms served with a walnut sauce — enchant the palate. Entrees are equally delightful and include Veal Monaco: rolls of veal with parma ham and Provolone cheese served with roasted garlic and tomato sauce. Monte Carlo's tagliolini St. Tropez (angel hair pasta with roasted peppers, black olives and sundried tomatoes) is another favorite. Dress is smart casual.

M.R. Onions
$$ • 11 Par-la-Ville Rd., Hamilton • 292-5012

Take a family-style approach to dining, season it with a singles-type bar where folks simply love to have a good time, add healthy portions of Internet and e-mail services so that it is Bermuda's first cyber cafe, give it a name that reminds you of the onion's importance in the island's early agricultural history, and you serve up a restaurant with upbeat character and personality that makes it downright popular. The menu crosses all culinary boundaries, from vegetarian and pasta, chicken and ribs, beef and roasted meats to fish, seafood and surf-and-turf combinations. Two favorites are the barbecued chicken and ribs, and the Menage a Trois, an adventurous pan-fried rockfish, Cajun mahi mahi and grilled wahoo served with lemon butter sauce. With a dinner selection so dubbed, it is almost predictable that this restaurant would win the Best of Bermuda Award for the Most Decadent Dessert, the Double Fudgie Wudgie — a rich chocolate brownie topped with vanilla ice cream and layered with hot chocolate sauce. Dress is smart casual.

The Porch
$ • 93 Front St., Hamilton • 292-4737

Its terrace looks out over Front Street, the harbor beyond and cruise ships docked wharfside. A big plus here: the vegetarian and fat free dishes added to the regular menu. Pub fare includes the Plougman's Lunch — pork pie, cheddar and Swiss cheese wedges, a tomato, pickled onion, Branston pickle and stick bread. The dinner menu takes you on a whirlwind journey, from boneless breast of duckling grilled with a citrus-rum sauce to Rendang Daging, a dried fried beef curry in coconut milk with onions, garlic and chiles. Pasta specials include capellini tossed with sun-dried tomatoes, peppers, onions and Parma ham in a creamy tomato sauce. Your intimate dining pleasure is accented by nightly entertainment featuring jazz or blues. Dress is smart casual.

Port O' Call
$$ • 87 Front St., Hamilton • 295-5373

For landlubbers craving a dapper, nautical theme, check out this Port on Front Street. It's a smart restaurant that caters to the Hamilton business and political crowd. Local seafood, continental and American dishes, augmented by a comprehensive wine list, make this an oft-chosen spot. Management is always happy to welcome you on board and cater to your lunch or dinner desires. Seafood choices include escargots "Fritz style," named after owner Fritz Reiter. Surf-and-turf selec-

tions include yellowfin tuna steak, broiled and served with a ginger teriyaki sauce; grouper Normandie, pan-fried or broiled and finished with a white wine sauce with mussels, shrimp and mushrooms; and roast rack of lamb, seared with herbs and Dijon mustard and served with a rosemary garlic jus. Dress is smart casual.

Portofino
$-$$ • Bermudiana Rd., Hamilton • 292-2375

This popular restaurant has a relaxed atmosphere that captivates locals and visitors alike. It's specialty is Italian cuisine for lunch or dinner; call ahead if you want to place a take-out order. Apart from pasta dishes like Ravioli Bolognese (ravioli stuffed with Ricotta cheese simmered in a Bolognese sauce with a touch of cream), there are specials such as Scaloppine Parmigiana — escallop of veal,

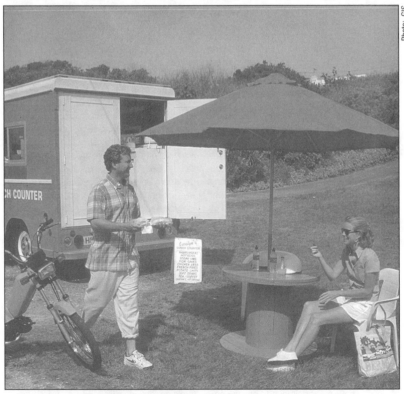

Photo: GIS

A couple takes a snack break at a South Shore lunch wagon.

BERMUDA'S FIRST BREWPUB

North Rock BREWING Cº

LUNCH
11:30 - 3 PM

DINNER
6-10 PM

HAND CRAFTED ALES

JNCT. SOUTH ROAD & COLLECTOR'S HILL
TELEPHONE 236-6633

sauteed in butter and topped with Mozzarella cheese and tomato sauce. Seafood fanciers will enjoy the Calamari Fra Diavola, calamari sauteed in a spicy tomato sauce served over linguine. Dress is casual, and reservations are advised.

Red Carpet
$$ • Armoury Bldg., 37 Reid St., Hamilton • 292-6195

You may bump into some of Bermuda's who's who here. In the Armoury Building opposite the Bank of Butterfield, this is their popular lunch spot. Red is the dominant color of the dining room. The ambiance at dinner is intimate, and if you have any special requests, put them to the maitre d'. The folks here will try, within reason, to accommodate your particular wishes. Appetizers include mussels Red Carpet (mussels simmered in Chablis, garlic, herb sauce and laced with cream) and Scottish smoked salmon garnished with onions, capers and horseradish. Entrees include rockfish Mangrove Bay, served with bananas and almonds; and Seafood Kettle St. David's, a

combination of lobster, clams, mussels, shrimp and fish stewed in Chablis, sherry peppers, Gosling's black rum and tomatoes. Top off a romantic evening with Coup Red Carpet; try it and be wonderfully surprised. Dress is smart casual.

Rock Island Coffee
$ • 48 Reid St., Hamilton • 296-2347

This is a diminutive roasting house; laidback and trendy are the key attributes. You won't find dinner here, but you will find a selection of lovely coffees, caffe latte, cappuccino and nice teas. Muffins and biscotti are available. Inside are a couple of local paintings hanging on the walls; outside, near the entrance as you step off the pavement, are tables where you can kick back if you wish. Dress, as you would expect, is casual.

Rosa's Cantina
$ • 121 Front St., 2nd Floor, Hamilton • 295-1912

Put on your 10-gallon hat or sombrero and saunter down to Bermuda's only Southwestern/Tex-Mex restaurant. The decor captures a spicy southwestern flavor, and so do many of the food choices. Thus it is appropriate that they have a broad selection of beer as well as wine, which you imbibe either by the bottle or glass to soothe your spice-tinged palate. Lunch or dinner can be had for a reasonable price, and portions are substantial. The menu includes selections ranging from Iguana eggs (cream cheese-stuffed deep-fried jalapeños) and fajitas, to chimichangas and quesadillas. The crowd here tends to be young, and it is a great place for family and kids (if they can't handle the spicy dishes, there are also burgers and pizza). Dress is casual.

Seasons In The Sun
$ • 27 Queen St., 3rd floor of Bermudiana Arcade, Hamilton • 295-9587

Although only open until 3 PM daily (closed Sundays), this is the place for imaginatively and deliciously prepared natural vegetarian food. No refined products are used, and most dishes are dairy free. Vegetables are either locally grown and/or organic. Fresh-baked desserts and breads are made with organic flours and natural sweeteners when possible. The menu is rich with a range of selections, from falafel with lemon tahini sauce to an Athens salad — spinach tossed with cucumbers, carrots, tomatoes, black olives, mushrooms, Feta cheese and a cider vinaigrette dressing. Other choices are equally interesting. Gratuities are not included in bill. Dress is casual.

Tuscany
$ • Bermuda House Lane, 95 Front St., Hamilton • 292-4507

The allure of the Tuscan countryside is reflected in this restaurant's murals, and it is easy to imagine that you are dining at an elegant restaurant in the heart of Florence. Bermuda beam-and-slate ceilings fit in well as do the handsome frescoes. A pleasant balcony for dining alfresco adds to its atmosphere. The strictly Italian menu enchants with offerings such as petto di pollo alla Dante, boneless chicken breast sauteed with sherry and tomato and topped with eggplant and Mozzarella. Dress is smart casual.

Other Parish Areas

Green Lantern
$ • 9 Serpentine Rd. • 295-6995

Outside city limits, just a couple of minutes from the center of Hamilton, locals go to this clean, tidy and friendly restaurant to find home-cooked meals without the fanfare. Green Lantern has been catering to Bermudians for many decades. Menu items include curried chicken served over white rice with the vegetable of the day. Fish & chips is also quite popular. Finish off with dessert — perhaps chocolate cake topped with fudge icing. The atmosphere is casual and relaxed. Reservations are not necessary. Dress is casual.

La Coquille
$$ • Crow Ln. • 292-6122

Located at the Bermuda Underwater Exploration Institute and situated overlooking the gentle waters of Hamilton Harbour, this fine restaurant allows you to arrive by boat if you wish. Tie up at the dock and dine on the waterfront terrace, or step inside and enjoy the local seafood dishes and French cuisine in air-conditioned comfort.

Appetizers include pan-sauteed duck liver foie gras with caramelized pears, port wine reduction and miniature brioche. Among the superb entrees are grilled semi-boneless quail and wild boar sausage, porcine mushrooms, risotto pancakes and roasted pearl onions. Another favorite is the seared rack of lamb with sun-dried tomato crust, roasted garlic whipped potatoes, sauteed baby artichokes and rosemary jus. Reservations are suggested, and dress is smart casual.

INSIDERS' TIP

There are more than 100 restaurants, cafes and pubs in Bermuda.

Monty's
$ • 75 Pitt's Bay Rd. • 295-5759

Bright, cheerful and only a few minutes walk west along Front Street, this restaurant has in a short time become a local favorite. Here you'll find a Bermuda-styled menu with imaginatively prepared food at reasonable prices. It is delightful for families. One of their signature dishes is Caribbean chicken, grilled chicken breast with a tasty papaya and mango topping, served with rice or baked potato and vegetable of the day. Another is Monty's Fish, grilled Bermuda fish topped with a flavorful champagne sauce and served with rice and vegetable. Their Friday night special is Beef Wellington. Contemporary light music accompanies your dining. Dress is casual. Reservations not required.

Primavera Ristorante
$$ • 69 Pitts Bay Rd. • 295-2167

Near the center of the city and just a minute or so from the Hamilton Princess Hotel, this Italian establishment offers what it calls the ultimate in Italian cuisine. The eye-catching entrance, book-ended by palms and with an aged barrel at the fore, lets you know that the Italian flavor begins even before you walk through the door. The selection of traditional dishes is wide-ranging. Choose from chicken specialties such as chicken alla Lariana (French-cut chicken breast stuffed with fresh vegetables and served with a raspberry and

hazelnut sauce) and fish specialties such as zuppa di pesce alla Livornese (clams, mussels, jumbo shrimp, fish fillets, fresh tomato, wine and garlic sauce). Another favorite is saltimbocca alla Romana, veal escallop with a sage, prosciutto and Marsala sauce. Dress is smart casual.

Paget Parish

Crow Lane Bakery
$ • 35 Crow Ln. • 292-2220

We cannot fail to mention this little bakery at the entrance to the city, in the pink building where Hamilton's merchants and bigwigs gathered in the late 18th century to plan the transfer of capital status from the Town of St. George to Hamilton. This is a definite favorite spot for locals looking for superb pastries, cakes and breads for take-out. It's a great little place for picking up those sinful temptations you know you shouldn't eat but can't resist. So give your taste buds a treat. After all, you're on holiday!

Fourways Inn
$$$$ • 1 Middle Rd. • 236-6517

At Amen Corner (so called because it's near the site of the Cobb's Hill Methodist Church built by slaves in the early 19th century) this restaurant has a sterling reputation. Built in 1727 of coral stone and cedar, this former private home was converted to a guest house and restaurant in the 20th century. The original kitchen, notable for its large-stepped fireplace, is now the Peg Leg Bar, a quiet spot for meeting friends and acquaintances before or after dinner. Love them or not, Fourways' chefs have garnered high acclaim for their innovative and varied menu. Internationally favored for fine cuisine, the old-world decor charms and enchants. Seafood delights include pan-seared fillet of rockfish with a Louisiana crayfish sauce and fresh dill, and Atlantic salmon wrapped in rice paper, layered with leaf spinach and mushrooms and enhanced with black grape sauce. Add a bottle of great wine from the extensive list, and you have the ingredients to concoct a romantic evening. Gentlemen are asked to wear a jacket and tie. Reservations are necessary.

Café Lido
$$ • Elbow Beach Hotel, 60 South Shore Rd. • 236-9884

For dining by the sea, this on-the-beach restaurant has few peers. Enjoy lunch either alfresco or indoors in the glass-ceilinged dining room. Imagine dining beneath a full moon, its rays bouncing off the ocean. Ah, the romance of it all. Better still, don't just imagine — experience it. The menu is seasonal, but the typical fare includes roasted free-range Amish chicken with rosemary giblet sauce, mashed potatoes with roasted garlic and Mascarpone cheese, and swordfish Cartoccio, wrapped in parchment and served with baby clams, yellow and red tomatoes, white wine, garlic and fresh basil. A jacket is necessary for dinner.

The Paraquet
$ • South Shore Rd. • 236-5842

This restaurant attracts a very mixed clientele, and families find it one of the more relaxed places to bring children. The cooking is homestyle, and the dining room is modest and straightforward. Fish & chips is big here. Waitresses are friendly, and prices are reasonable. Should you want a magazine or newspaper, a newsstand is just to your left as you enter. Take-out service is also available for those on the run. Dress is casual.

FYI

Unless otherwise noted, the area code for all phone numbers listed in this guide is 441.

Warwick Parish

Paw Paws
$-$$ • 87 South Shore Rd. • 236-7459

Paw Paws offers a welcome respite when riding your moped along South Shore Road. You'll find it about a mile west of Elbow Beach Hotel. While you can relax inside, one of the lovely features is the outdoor terrace dining. The menu has some interesting choices. A favorite here is broiled lobster on the half-shell served with a baked potato and fresh vegetables. Dress is casual.

Jolly Lobster
$$ • Mermaid Beach Club, South Shore Rd. • 236-5031

On the scenic South Shore route, in what has been called a "Jolly Roger" setting, this restaurant is all about seafood, except for the rack of lamb, sirloin steak and chicken Rollotini, chicken stuffed with asparagus, goat cheese and Parma ham and served with baby vegetables and rosemary potatoes. The Seafood Potpourri — scallops, salmon, wahoo and fried lobster-shrimp wonton served with couscous and baby vegetables in a basil-tomato sauce — is a seafood lover's favorite. Of course, Bermuda lobster and whole Maine lobster are the headliners. Dress is smart casual.

INSIDERS' TIP

As early as 1616 the cassava plant was brought from the West Indies, and today cassava pie has become a favorite Bermudian dish. In fact, Christmas to us wouldn't be the same without it. Depending on who is preparing it, the pie can be made with a chicken, pork or beef filling.

Monte Carlo

The cuisine of the South of France is aptly and poetically called "Cuisine of the Sun." A dinner at Monte Carlo is like an evening in Provence. The art of the Monegaque, and for that matter, all of southern French cooking, has benefitted from its proximity to the sea, to Italy and to the French with their intimate love of gastronomy. It's a combination that offers some of the most memorable of dishes, such as complimentary Rosemary Foccaccia with tapenade; Marinated Tuna served with capers sauce; Tagliolini St. Tropez (angel hair pasta with roast peppers, black olives and sun-dried tomatoes), or Bouillibaisse, Marseillaise, a feast of fish and shellfish prepared in the style of the South of France. Complete your meal with a selection from the dessert trolley.

9 Victoria Street, Hamilton. Reservations 295-5453

Tree Frogs

$ • Belmont Hotel, Golf & Country Club, Middle Rd. • 236-1301

Named after Bermuda's ubiquitous tiny tree frogs, this restaurant's delightful dining room and a la carte menu includes local dishes as well as provocative international cuisine. The atmosphere and food make this a pleasant and friendly place to dine. Lovely views of Hamilton Harbour and live entertainment in the Harbour Sights Bar add to your enjoyment. Dinner choices include pan-fried mahi mahi and clams with black bean and chilli sauce, and grilled filet of beef with rucola salad, sauteed new potatoes and truffle vinaigrette. Dress is smart casual.

Southampton Parish

Waterlot Inn

$$ • Middle Rd. • 238-0510

This lovingly restored dockside inn, once a 17th-century waterside private home, re-tains a captivating old-world charm. The food is enchanting, as is the piano music floating through the dining room. French and continental cuisine served in candlelit elegance guarantee a memorable experience. The wine list is impressive. Once you've dined here, you'll understand why this restaurant is so highly acclaimed. Dinner selections include roasted whole Maine lobster atop porcino mushroom risotto, garnished with fresh roasted corn and served with an asparagus sauce. There is also Châteaubriand (for two), a seared center-cut filet mignon (U.S. beef) served with sauteed Mediterranean vegetables and potatoes au gratin with Gorgonzola. Top your choice off with strawberries Romanoff (for two), flamed with Grand Marnier and brandy, enhanced by cracked green peppercorns and served over vanilla ice cream. A jacket and tie are required here. Reservations are necessary. The restaurant closes in winter (usually January and February), but call ahead to confirm.

Henry VIII

$$ • near entrance to Sonesta Beach Hotel, South Shore Rd. • 238-1977

Named after the King of England who initiated the English Reformation — and who also is well known for having two of his wives beheaded — this restaurant and pub has hosted many joyful ceremonies, parties, banquets and romantic dinners. If you lose your head here, it will be over the atmosphere and food. The four dining rooms are accentuated by rich oak paneling of which Henry himself likely would have approved. The fare is sumptuous — it also would have had old Henry raising his pewter mug in endless toasts. The wine cellar is formidable, and you can guzzle any one of a selection of English ales in the Oak Room Pub.

Specialty Night is something to be experienced! A Medieval Feast (ahem, fit for a King) is laid on, and you are a welcome guest for the feasting and festing. Apart from the Specialty Night, the dinner menu includes a delightful duck à l'orange — Royal Aylesbury duckling, flamed crisp with Grand Marnier and orange sauce — and Châteaubriand for two — a double filet steak, broiled complete with a generous variety of garden vegetables, potatoes and mushrooms and accompanied by béarnaise sauce.

Among the wide range of choices are low fat, low sodium, low calorie selections cooked in natural vegetable oil. A favorite from this lighter side of Henry's is the curried vegetable strudel, a creative and delicious offering of carrots, potatoes, cauliflower, onions and cilantro in a curry sauce, all wrapped in phyllo pastry with shredded coconut. However you slice it, Henry's is a great choice. Jackets are required for dinner.

Lighthouse Tearoom

$, no credit cards • Gibb's Hill Lighthouse, 68 St. Anne's Rd. • 238-8679

This beacon is one of the oldest iron lighthouses still in existence. Those who climb the winding 185 steps to the top are treated to a view of Bermuda as a canvas of tranquil bays, lush hills and pastel houses. At the base is a lace-curtained tea room where you can enjoy a full English breakfast or lunch and take in a splendid view of the Great Sound. The menu includes smoked salmon, pork pies, salads and sandwiches. And there's the tea, tea cakes, scones, Bermuda honey and Devon double cream. The cozy atmosphere is delightful, and after eating, you can visit the adjacent little shop to purchase jams and preserves, cups and mugs. However, cash is necessary in both the tea room and the shop. Dress is casual.

Mrs. Tea's Victorian Tearoom

$ • 25 Middle Rd. (opposite Port Royal Golf Course) • 234-1374

The key word here is Victorian. From its dainty cups and plates to the pictures on the wall, the tearoom oozes Victorian niceties without pompous conservatism. In a 17th-century Bermuda National Trust property just off the Railway Trail in Somerset, Mrs. Tea's offers traditional English tea — pastries, scones, biscuits and an assortment of delicious teas. (Remember: In British vernacular, "tea" refers as much to the event as the drink.) Casual dress is acceptable.

Sandys Parish

La Plage Waterside Bar and Grill

$-$$ • Lantana Colony Club, 53 Railway Tr., Somerset Village • 234-0141

If you belong to an exclusive country club, you'll feel at home here. And if you don't belong to one, you can simply enjoy the atmosphere and pretend. This is one of the few places where you can arrive by boat, tie up and have lunch. Art aficionados will be thrilled by the beautifully landscaped grounds enhanced by sculptures. Paintings and art objects decorate the main house. Uninterrupted views of the Great Sound only accentuate the unique ambiance. Dinner is served only Wednesdays and Fridays June through September. The lunch menu includes jasmine tea-smoked shrimp and Mediterranean Vegetable Terrine — both selections part of the "Light and Healthy Cuisine." Dress is casual for lunch. A jacket is required for the main dining room.

Freeport Seafood Restaurant and Bar

$ • 1 Freeport Rd., Royal Naval Dockyard • 234-1692

Immediately inside the entrance to the historic former Royal Naval Dockyard, this restaurant emphasizes seafood, both local and imported. A casual and relaxed atmosphere makes dining a pleasure. Lobster and even seafood pizza are on the menu, and there are daily specials. Dress is casual.

Beethoven's Restaurant and Bar

$ • Clocktower Centre, Royal Naval Dockyard • 234-5009

Two Swiss chefs own and operate this cozy restaurant, which has an easy, intimate atmosphere. The cuisine is sophisticated, delicious and well-presented. There are also fondue and Raclette nights. Dress is casual.

While much of our nightlife (particularly the club scene) is centered in Hamilton, there are nightspots scattered all over the island.

Nightlife

Perhaps you agree with Dr. Samuel Johnson that "whoever thinks of going to bed before twelve o'clock is a scoundrel." If you're of a like mind, this chapter will give you some fun options that are available in Bermuda at night.

Let's begin with what *not* to expect. Though they are the subject of debate right now, we offer absolutely no casinos. There are business people who think casinos would appeal to a younger market and inject new vigor into our tourist-oriented entertainment environment. Others are convinced casinos would go against the conservative tone of our island. Given the strong influence of religion in Bermuda, it's unlikely that casinos will come anytime soon. Don't expect the lure of huge billboards and neon lighting either. We have strict laws prohibiting large advertising signs from dominating the landscape.

Our nightlife revolves mostly around restaurants, bars and some nightclubs. You might also agree with Rupert Brooke that "cities, like cats, will reveal themselves at night." The only trouble is we've got just the one city — Hamilton. While it's true that much of our nightlife (particularly the club scene) is in the capital, there are nightspots scattered all over the island, many of them in hotels. Check out our Resort Hotels, Small Hotels and Cottage Colony chapters for detailed information on evening entertainment at various accommodations. For more on dining and menu options at nightspots that are also eateries, see our Restaurants chapter.

What's more, Bermuda offers nightlife on the water. We include a section on evening and night cruises available in the summer season. We finish up the chapter with a section on movie theaters.

What to Wear

There was a time when gentlemen would not be welcome in restaurants or nightclubs without jacket and tie. During the last five years or so, we've loosened up a bit to get in tune with our North American visitors, so few places insist on tie torture for men. Jackets are still required in the more upscale restaurants and bars, particularly those operating in hotels, but in most places smart/casual dress is now the norm. Of course, being quite conservative, "smart/casual" needs definition. To be safe, avoid wearing sneakers or jeans. Some establishments will allow them, but others won't. If you're unsure about a club's dress policies, give them a call before you go out.

Drinking and Driving, Safety

Be aware that we have breathalyzer testing here, same as in the States. If your blood-alcohol content is .08 or higher, you are over the legal drinking limit to operate a vehicle, and you could be prosecuted for drunken driving. Should you be convicted, you pay a $450 fine and will not be allowed to drive in Bermuda for one year.

We'd prefer you not drive after even moderate drinking. Remember, we drive on the left side of the road here. Most likely you're used to driving on the right. Even one alcoholic drink can cause reduced concentration and a sudden fit of right/left confusion. We don't want you careening 'round a roundabout in the wrong direction. If you want to drink, we advise that you take a taxi or choose a designated driver. Around Christmas and on New Year's Eve, bars will very often give free soft drinks to designated drivers.

We are proud of our relatively safe environment here. However, you should not be completely complacent when hitting the clubs. It's important to take the normal precautions dictated by common sense. Keep your handbags zipped or fastened, and avoid walking alone late at night.

Cover Charges and Happy Hours

Where nightclubs charge entrance fees, we'll tell you. If a listing makes no mention of prices, you can assume there is no cover charge. Alcoholic drinks can cost anywhere from $3.75 to $5.75 a glass. Many bars and nightclubs offer reduced prices during a happy hour. An hour, of course, usually consists of 60 minutes, but where happiness is concerned, time in Bermuda becomes elastic. A happy hour can be up to three hours. We'll be as specific as possible since policy differs from establishment to establishment and night to night. All prices we quote are subject to change.

FYI

Unless otherwise noted, the area code for all phone numbers listed in this guide is 441.

Bars and Nightclubs

As usual, our listings start in St. George's Parish and move from east to west.

St. George's Parish

The Wharf Tavern
14 Water St., Town of St. George
• 297-1515

This bar and restaurant is appropriately named because it sits right on St. George's Harbour. About 120 years old, the building originally had residential accommodations upstairs and warehousing downstairs. When Somers Wharf was developed for tourism about 20 years ago, the tavern came into being.

Dawn Bealing, manager of the bar, says, "Come to the Wharf Tavern, and you'll meet our local comedians." She means you'll get to hear all the discussions on local issues and politics and the other stories the regulars love to tell. You can sit at the inside bar or, on warm nights, outside on the patio overlooking the harbor. Happy hour is 4 to 6 PM every night; you'll get $1 off drinks. Normal prices range from $3 to $4.50. If you're a beer connoisseur, then you'll appreciate the fact that this is the only pub in St. George where you can buy Ramrod Smooth British beer. Other draft beers are Fosters and Bass. From April through October, guitarists play live music and often involve customers in singalongs. The dress here is casual. The Wharf Tavern is open year round (except Christmas Day) from 10 AM to 1 AM Monday through Saturday and noon to 1 AM on Sundays.

Hamilton Parish

Swizzle Inn
3 Blue Hole Hill, Bailey's Bay
• 293-9300

The Swizzle is the inn where you either celebrate your arrival in Bermuda or drink to your departure. It's just a five-minute drive from the airport, you see. For cigarette smokers coming from Hamilton, it's the last place they can indulge before arriving at the smoke-free departure lounge and bar.

You'll find the walls of the bar downstairs covered with business cards and stickers. Guests from America, Canada, Australia, Europe and Asia left these souvenirs as proof that they visited Bermuda. The Swizzle also caters to local regulars who have been coming for years. Tourists and locals often meet in the bar, chat over a game of pool or sit outside on one of the two patios. Happy hour, offering $1 off drink prices, runs Monday through Friday from 5 to 7 PM. As you might expect, this inn is famous for its rum swizzles as well its dark and stormies (a delicious but potent Bermudian drink consisting of black rum and ginger beer). Normal drink prices are about $4.75. During the summer you can enjoy live blues, jazz, calypso and rock music on Thursday, Friday and Saturday. The bar is open from 11 AM to 1 AM in the high season. From November through April, it closes every Monday and at 10 PM nightly.

Smiths Parish

North Rock Brewing Company
10 South Rd. • 236-6633

Yes, it is a brewing company, but it's also a restaurant and bar. As soon as you walk in, you'll see copper tanks containing the beers

North Rock has (since 1997) been fast becoming famous for. Brewing is done through the early hours of the morning, but at some points during the day you'll experience a waft of barley and hops.

Home-brewed beers on tap include Old Colony Bitter, Somers Amber Ale (Sir George Somers would surely have approved of it; see our History chapter), Whale of a Week and North Rock Porter. A 22-ounce glass is $4.50. These beers, by the way, are for North Rock's supply only — they are not sold to other pubs. Happy hour runs from 5 to 7 PM Monday through Friday and gives you a reduction of roughly 75¢ on all drinks. You can dine in the restaurant, relax on the patio or sit in the bar and imbibe the friendly atmosphere as well as the beer. North Rock is open from 11 AM to 1 AM year round, except for Christmas week, New Year's Eve and New Year's Day. It is completely wheelchair-accessible with a specially equipped bathroom.

Pembroke Parish

Chancery Wine Bar and Restaurant
2 Chancery Ln., Hamilton • 295-5058

The Wine Bar is a great venue for quiet conversation over an excellent glass of wine. That's why many businesspeople like to take a break here after work. Guido Estosito, in charge of the bar, will tell you about the featured wine of the week. It could be from France,

Italy, South Africa, New Zealand or California. You can buy a bottle of any of the wines, or you can choose to have just a glass. Prices obviously depend on the vintage you choose. Ask for a beer or a glass of house wine, and you'll pay about $3.50. The bar is open daily year round. Monday through Friday hours are noon to 1 AM; on Saturdays and Sundays, it's open from 6 PM to 1 AM. In the summer months we like to sit out on the patio European style and enjoy watching passersby go up and down the narrow alley that is Chancery Lane. Dress is smart/casual. Yes, there is a happy hour. It's from 5 to 7 PM Monday through Friday and offers about $1 off drinks.

The Club
32 Bermudiana Rd., Hamilton • 295-9627

This club is above the Little Venice Restaurant (see our Restaurants chapter). Open 9 PM to 3 AM, it offers a bar, music and a relaxing, cozy atmosphere. Occasionally there's live music, but on the whole it's DJ Ken Steede who'll get you dancing to rap, reggae, disco and soca (a Caribbean hybrid of calypso and American soul, served up with a heavy beat). The clientele tend to be in their 30s. The dress code is smart/casual; sneakers and cutoff jeans are not acceptable. Fridays and Saturdays are definitely the busy nights — that's when you'll meet lots of locals. Drinks cost $5, but there's no cover charge. Most of the year The Club closes only on Sunday, but in January it sometimes closes on Monday and Tuesday as well.

Coconut Rock
Williams House, 20 Reid St., Hamilton
• 292-1043

Coconut Rock has a restaurant and two bars. The main bar is open year round except Christmas and Boxing Day (that's December 26, by the way) from 11 AM to 1 AM. Happy hour runs from 5 to 7 PM, reducing drinks from $4 to $2.75. Up to about 10:30 PM, regulars like to meet for drinks, conversation and easy listening music, and they often watch videotapes of Top 40 acts in America and the U.K. After that, the Rock gets noisier, as people like to dance to European music.

Friday nights are particularly lively, and the increased party traffic leads management to open the second bar, the Bourbon Lounge, where you can listen to background jazz. Every other Sunday it's the venue for Flow Sundays, an evening featuring music and poetry. From 7 PM, DJ Beatnik plays all kinds of music: hip hop, Latin and jazz old and new. At 9 PM one featured poet and one musician give a performance. Open house starts at 10 PM: Twelve to 15 five-minute spots are given to musicians and poets in the audience. Emcee André Simons explains that this event offers an opportunity for free speech on any topic. "It's completely uncensored," says André. It also allows poets and musicians of all races and cultural backgrounds to meet and exchange ideas. Very often all performers are Bermudian, but artists from abroad are very welcome. Don't forget your sitar! Call 296-3054 or 293-1014 if you're interested in participating.

The Colony Pub
The Princess, 76 Pitts Bay Rd., Hamilton
• 295-3000

Come to the Colony Pub during the summer months, and you'll get live entertainment every night but Sunday. From 10 PM to 1 AM on Tuesdays and Fridays, you'll hear LeYoni Junos; the same hours on Thursdays and Saturdays, you'll hear Gita Blakeney. Both of these jazz and blues singers are famous in Bermuda

for their superb voices and versatile repertoires. They are accompanied by Vic Lazer, jazz pianist. On Wednesdays, Vic joins the Jazztet for a night of . . . well, yes, jazz par excellence. If assistant maître d' Dean Hayward has his way, you'll be dancing. According to Duval Minors, the club manager, he's known as "Lean Dean, the Dancing Machine."

Drinks run from $4.90 to $5. 75, depending on whether you have a beer or a highball. The atmosphere is upbeat and, as Duval puts it, "down-to-earth Bermuda." Dress is casual. Open year round, the bar operates from 11 AM to 1 AM.

Flanagan's
Emporium Bldg., 69 Front St., Hamilton
• 295-8299

This pub and restaurant is run by an Irishman — Thomas Gallagher. As he puts it, "Céad Mile Fáilte." That's Irish for "A Hundred Thousand Welcomes." On the second floor of the Emporium Building, Flanagan's is a favorite for people who like to dance as well as talk over drinks. During the summer, live music is played every night in one of the two bars. Usually about three bands play (one band per night) and offer rock, reggae, dance, soca and party music. In winter (November through March), entertainment drops to three nights a week.

Happy hour is every day from 5 to 7 PM — you get $1 off drinks that normally cost about $4.25. People of all ages like to visit, but around the holidays you'll see many students catching up on local news they missed while away. Sports fans will appreciate the sports bar, where they can watch live English, Scottish and other European soccer games on a 40-inch TV. Eight other 27-inch screens are available. Worried about missing your favorite baseball, basketball and NFL games? Don't be; they are shown here every night during the season. If you're into boxing, you can watch pay-per-view matches for a fee of $3 or $4. The sports bar also offers a variety of games including table soccer (that's Foosball to Americans), interactive golf and touch-screen games. Flanagan's is open year round (except for Christmas Day) from 10 AM to 1 AM.

The Hog Penny Restaurant and Pub

5 Burnaby Hill, Hamilton • 292-2534

The Hog Penny, named after our old hog money currency, is a tourist favorite. According to manager Andy Shirt, tourists come back year after year for the fun, friendly atmosphere that is reminiscent of a British pub. During summer, guitarists play soft rock music every night; for December, January and February, entertainment is cut down to weekends only. Happy hour runs from 5 to 7 PM Monday through Friday, offering $1 off each libation. Normal prices for drinks run at about $4.25. Dress is smart/casual. Check the Restaurants chapter for dinner and lunch menus.

Hubie's Bar

Angle St., Hamilton • 293-9287

Hubie's is open Monday through Saturday from 10 AM to 10 PM, but *the* night to come is Friday. Between 7 and 10 PM that evening, it seems all of Bermuda comes together to hear local band Jaz play, yes, jazz. The bar is packed with people of all races, cultures and ages; by 7:30 PM, it's standing room only. OK, the place closes early; for some of us who are not night owls, that's an advantage. We don't have to wait until late for the live music to start. The rest of the week, you can come for a drink ($2.75 each) and play music on the jukebox. Hubie's does not accept credit cards.

Oasis Nite Life and Rockroom

Emporium Bldg., 69 Front St., Hamilton • 292-4978

Located on the third floor of the Emporium Building, which you reach by using a very snazzy, glass-enclosed elevator, Oasis offers both live and DJ-spun music. The Kennel Boys, a Bermudian four-piece band, play modern and classic rock in the Rockroom on Wednes-days, Fridays and Saturdays during the summer season. In winter, they only leave the kennel to perform on Fridays and Saturdays. They start at midnight and keep the room rocking until closing time — 3 AM. From 9 PM to midnight, the Rockroom has various other live music offerings.

DJs spin tracks in the main nightclub, which is equipped with mirrors and state-of-the-art lighting. What kind of music? As general manager Mark Osborne puts it, "Whatever's up to date. Music's got a life of about two weeks these days." You'll get a chance to hear music that's popular in Europe as well as the U.S. The cover charge during the summer season is $10 during the week, $15 on Fridays and Saturdays, and it gets you into both areas of the club. There's no charge at all on Sundays. During winter there's no cover charge during the week (although this policy is subject to change). Happy hour is 9 to 10 PM on Friday and means about a $2 reduction on drinks that are normally $5 to $5.50.

Odyssey Night Club

Brunswick Bldg. (second floor), 119 Front St., Hamilton • 296-4390

Tracey Tucker, Odyssey owner and manager, is proud of his state-of-the-art nightclub. It has two bars — one for watching live coverage of sports (including baseball) on two 150-inch monitors; the other for music and dancing. The second bar has a large, 35-square-foot dance floor. Sectioned videos on the walls are an important feature. Dance and you'll be able to watch yourself on video. Cover charges vary from night to night, so call to be sure of what to expect. At present, there's no charge at all on Sundays. Mondays, you pay a $20 cover with no additional charges for drinks other than liquors. Karaoke night is Tuesday; Caribbean night is Wednesday — there's a $5 cover for both. A DJ will get you dancing to

---

INSIDERS' TIP

May to October is high season for our hotels. It's also high season for our summer night skies. Appreciate our smog-free atmosphere and take the time to stargaze. During summer months you can easily see the Milky Way and Scorpio. Stare at the same spot for five minutes, and we bet you'll see a shooting star.

soca, reggae, Latin and calypso music. Thursdays are strictly for clientele older than 30 (no cover charge). On Fridays and Saturdays, the cover charge is $10. Open year round (except possibly January), the Odyssey Night Club is open from 9 PM to 3 AM.

Robin Hood Pub and Restaurant
25 Richmond Rd. • 295-3314

Robin Hood has a variety of entertainment options, so chances are good that most nights you'll find lots of merry men and merry women here. During the high season (April through October), a DJ plays the latest reggae on Monday nights. Year round on Tuesdays from 8 to 10:30 PM, you can take part in quizzes on sports, general knowledge and live trivia. Wednesday nights during summer vacation, you get students (very merry ones indeed) participating in boat races. The winner of the race is the one who drinks a pint of ale in the fastest time. The prize? A bottle of champagne — just what they need. All contestants get drinks on the house. Fridays and Saturdays are jukebox nights for lovers of rock and reggae. Occasionally, local folk and jazz entertainers will play.

OK, Robin Hood has no archery, but in the sports bar you can watch live coverage of various American and British league contests. Owners Shep and Chopper pride themselves on having Bermuda's premier sports bar. Happy hour is from 4 to 8 PM Monday through Friday and from 5 to 7 PM on Saturdays and Sundays. It'll save you 75¢ on drinks that normally cost about $4. Dress is smart/casual. Robin Hood is open from 11 AM to 1 AM Monday through Saturday and noon to 1 AM on Sundays,

The Spinning Wheel
33 Court St., Hamilton • 292-7799

Named after an old song of the same name (it was The Fifth Dimension, if you can't think back that far), The Spinning Wheel has been a favorite for locals since 1970. Manager and part-owner Gladwyn Ming says "locals make up 95 percent of our business at the moment, but we welcome tourists." Atypically, more live entertainment is offered here during winter than during summer. Visit in winter, and you'll get to hear well-known local entertainers such as Ronald Lightbourne play jazz and calypso. You

can relax in the outdoor pool area or the cocktail lounge, where plenty of dark and stormies are on hand, and you can dance in the disco area. Happy hour is 5 to 7 PM Monday through Friday; drinks that normally range from $4 to $5 per glass are about $1 off. The Spinning Wheel, by the way, takes no credit cards. The bar is open from noon to 3 AM year round. Dress is casual in the summer. "In the winter," Ming says, "people like to dress up."

Sandys Parish

Club 21
16 Freeport Rd., Royal Naval Dockyard • 234-2721

If you're into jazz, then make a point of coming here on Thursday night (April through October) to hear the band Tempo. Other nights you can dance to calypso, soca and contemporary music. Or relax in the lounge area, where the music's not so loud that it squelches conversation. Cover charge is $5, and drinks are $3.75 each. Dress is smart/casual, but sneakers are OK. Club 21 is open 9 PM to 3 AM during summer and closes on Mondays. During winter, it opens on Friday, Saturday and Sunday only, with Tempo playing on Saturday. The club does not accept credit cards.

Freeport Seafood Restaurant and Bar
1 Freeport Rd., Royal Naval Dockyard • 234-1692

As soon as you enter Dockyard, you'll see this restaurant and bar on your left. It's famous for a drink it offers. Beer? Wine? No and no. It's the one place on the island where you can buy fresh mango juice. It's $3.50 for a 12-ounce glass. People who are seriously addicted to mangos after sampling them in the Caribbean islands feel that this elixir is cheap at that price.

Of course, alcoholic beverages are available too, ranging from $3.75 to $4.50 for a Fosters draft. There's no happy hour as such, but, as Valiero Ausenda told us, "That's because every hour here is a happy one." Valiero, by the way, describes himself as "owner, manager, dishwasher and busboy." He still has time to talk with his guests. Freeport is ideal for relaxing conversation since the background music

Photo: GIS

This is truly a dining room with a view.

is soft. You can sit inside or out in a garden patio area at the back. Dress is smart/casual.

The Frog and Onion
The Cooperage, 23 Freeport Rd., Royal Naval Dockyard • 234-2900

By now you're probably aware that we have whistling tree frogs, and that "onion" is our substitute name for a Bermudian. And so, The Frog and Onion. The pub and restaurant's interior is evocative of the history of this former naval building. You'll see exposed stone walls and the old forge that now operates as a fireplace in the dining room. Old bottles, barrels, flasks and compasses currently act as decoration but were once utilitarian.

Opposite the Neptune Cinema, The Frog and Onion is ideal if you want a meal and a movie. Customers are both tourists and locals. A DJ offers a selection of popular music from the '60s to the '90s on Tuesdays and Thursdays. Wednesday night is jazz night,

thanks to Doc Simons' Jazz Band, and sometimes thanks to the cruise ship crew who join Doc every other week in a jam session. Saturdays you'll hear the pianist; Fridays it's guitar music. English draft beers, such as Watneys, Flowers, Newcastle Brown and Guinness, are on tap for about $4.75 a pint. A separate game room offers pool and a variety of arcade games. The Frog and Onion is open 11:30 AM to 1 AM on Monday through Saturday and noon to 1 AM on Sundays. It's open year round but closes on Mondays from December through February. Dress is casual.

Nightlife Afloat

Oscar Wilde once wrote: "Nobody of any real culture, for instance, ever talks nowadays about the beauty of sunsets. Sunsets are quite old-fashioned. . . . To admire them is a distinct sign of provincialism of temperament. Upon the other hand they go on." They certainly do go on. And we have to confess to being both old-fashioned and provincial in temperament, because Bermudians do admire our sunsets. Taking an evening cruise is a perfect way to experience the splendor. And after the spectacle is over? Then you can look at the stars and the lights of Hamilton Harbour and know that, yes, the night does have "a thousand eyes." Here we give you some of the cruises available at sunset and after.

Pembroke Parish

Bermuda Island Cruises
96 Pitts Bay Rd. • 292-8652

Actually BIC offers other cruises during the day (see our Watersports chapter). What they offer at night is a trip in the Great Sound to Hawkins Island, where you disembark to join the Pirates' Party. That means food, drink, and entertainment. A large barbecue is on hand for chicken and steak, or you can have fish cooked in lemon-butter sauce. You'll also get a variety of salads, rolls and (afterwards) your just desserts — chocolate mousse and cake. Sea Dog the pirate and his wife will meet you and later will organize buck-off and wench-off limbo dancing competitions. Sounds sexist? Pirates were never known for being politically correct. Tony Brannon's Island Fever calypso band plays the whole night long.

You can reserve tickets ($69 per person) by calling direct. You can board the boat at Albuoy's Point in Hamilton (arrive at 6:45 PM to board at 7 PM) or at Darrell's Wharf in Paget (arrive at 7:05 PM to board as soon as possible). You'll be back at Darrell's at about 10:25 PM and Albuoy's at 10:30 PM. You can buy T-shirts and CDs for about $15 each from a small gift shop on Hawkins. In addition, you'll receive a complimentary coupon for free entry to Oasis nightclub (see previous listing). The pirates hold their parties on Tuesdays, Wednesdays, Fridays and Saturdays from May 1 to October 31.

Bermuda Water Sports
1 Fairyland Ln. • 236-1500

Bermuda Water Sports offers two-hour sightseeing cocktail cruises through Hamilton Harbour and the Great Sound. The sunset views are magnificent! For more details, see the list-ing in the Snorkeling and Sightseeing Motor Cruises section of our Watersports chapter.

Looking Glass Cruises
5 Point Pleasant Rd., Hamilton • 292-1717

This company gives you a choice of two night cruises. First, there's the Romantic Nights of Life cruise that runs Mondays, Wednesdays and Fridays from May 1 through October. The *Looking Glass* departs Hamilton's ferry terminal at 10 PM (OK, no sunset but plenty of stars) and takes you across Hamilton Harbour, so you can check out the lights. From there you'll cross the Great Sound and go over to the *Vixen* wreck and Sea Gardens off Dockyard. Floodlights will allow you to see the fish through the glass bottom of the boat. Angels are better seen at night, you will agree. The trip lasts about 2¼ hours, and the $35 per person tickets include beer, wine and sodas.

Alternatively, on summer season Tuesdays and Thursdays you can take the *Looking Glass* Dinner Cruise. You'll leave the ferry terminal at 6 PM, just in time to watch the sun go down on your way to Dockyard. Once there, you'll disembark and enjoy a four-course meal at Beethoven's, a Swiss restaurant (see our Restaurants chapter). After that it's cruising time again. You'll go to the *Vixen* and look down to see creatures of the deep. On your return you'll lift your eyes to the heavens and listen to an informative talk about the stars. Tickets cost $55 each for adults and $27.50 for children 12 and younger. This includes meals but not alcoholic drinks or restaurant gratuities. Reserve for either cruise by calling the number listed.

A Cultural Option

Jabulani Repertory Company
The Princess, 76 Pitts Bay Rd., Hamilton • 295-3000

Jabulani (a Swahili word that means "place for rejoicing") is Bermuda's only professional live theater group. Performances take place at 9 PM in the Gazebo Lounge at The Princess resort hotel from November through April. Tickets are $25 for the show, $56 for the show and dinner.

FYI

Unless otherwise noted, the area code for all phone numbers listed in this guide is 441.

Movie Theaters

Worried that a vacation in Bermuda means you'll miss the latest hot movie in the States? Don't be. Very often, films open here on the same day they do in the U.S. In addition, films are sometimes offered that might not be huge box-office successes in America but that appeal to those who appreciate the British sense of humor. *A Fish Called Wanda* swims to mind.

Typically a movie runs from Thursday to Thursday. However, some movies run longer due to popular demand. Check *The Royal Gazette* for movie information and specific starting times. By the way, smoking's prohibited in all our theaters.

St. George's Parish

New Somers Playhouse
Duke of York St., Town of St. George • 297-2821

It's actually not so new. The building goes back to just after emancipation (1834), when it was headquarters for one of the local lodges, otherwise known as "friendly societies." It then became a movie theater, which was closed down until 1993, when St. Georgians could finally again watch a movie without having to tool into Hamilton.

The Playhouse is spacious and takes us back to the era when movie theaters were palatial rather than compact. Apart from the occasional Saturday matinee for children (cost $5), there are two showings a night, Monday through Friday. This theater is known for showing quality British films, such as *Much Ado About Nothing* and *Secrets and Lies*, that are not often shown elsewhere on the island. Tickets cost $7 each.

Pembroke Parish

Liberty Theatre
49 Union Sq., Hamilton • 292-7296

Owned by the Bermuda Industrial Union (BIU), you'll find this theater off Victoria Street, between Court and King Streets. Monday through Saturday it shows a matinee at 2:30 PM ($4 a ticket) and offers three evening showings at $7 a ticket. On Sunday there's a matinee at 2:30 PM and only one evening show at 7:30 PM.

On the whole, movies shown are ones that are popular in America, but occasionally manager Nelda Simons likes to pick quality movies from Europe and the Caribbean. You can pick up advance tickets from the Liberty on weekdays from 11:30 AM to 5:30 PM.

Little Theatre
30 Queen St., Hamilton • 292-2135

During school holidays this small, intimate theater offers two matinee shows (at 2:15 and 4:30 PM) for $5 a ticket on Fridays, Saturdays and Sundays. Usually, R-rated movies are not shown in the afternoon. In addition, films for nursery kids are sometimes shown at 10 AM. Check *The Royal Gazette* to see if and when they're offered and for information about matinees during the rest of the year. There are two evening shows at $7 a ticket. You can book advance tickets by calling directly and using your credit card number. Check www.Bermudamall.com for previews of movies that are playing.

Sandys Parish

Neptune Cinema
The Cooperage, 4 Freeport Rd., Royal Naval Dockyard • 234-2923

Although this one is owned by Neptune Cinema Ltd., it's operated by the Liberty Theatre management (see previous listing). We mention this because should you miss a movie in Hamilton, you can see it here instead. Occasionally the Neptune opens new films, but, on the whole, it's a "move over house."

We love this cinema, as it means we can have a break from the city. It's also unusual in that the stone of its walls is left exposed, creating a castle effect. It's perfect, then, for watching Gothic horror movies. The Frog and Onion, located opposite, comes in very useful for a meal or a drink before or after the show (see previous listing in this chapter). There are two shows nightly, along with a 2:30 PM matinee on Sunday (and occasionally on Saturday). Pick up advance tickets from the Liberty Theatre between 11:30 AM and 5:30 PM, Monday through Friday.

Shopping

Sixty years ago, visitors shopping in Bermuda (and this generally meant in the City of Hamilton) discovered English, Canadian and European goods priced well below the going rates in the United States. Today, savings on crystal, china, some jewelry, cashmere and lambswool still can range between 30 and 40 percent over typical prices in America.

You may find a dichotomy between incredible bargains and steep prices that startle. It often depends on season, the item itself and the shop. But you will notice that we are rather laid-back; high-pressure sales tactics are absent. One guidebook published about a half-century ago pointed out that local merchants "do not tolerate sharp practices." Nothing has changed; you need not fear getting ripped off. On the other side of the coin, keep in mind that unlike some other destinations, you won't be able to strike deals with salespeople in Bermuda. Unless on sale, an item is sold as priced.

Duty-free purchases, allowed each resident of the United States who has been away from home for 48 hours or longer, apply to goods valued up to $400. These items must be declared on departure, and you will be taxed 10 percent on the first $1,000 worth of goods over the $400 limit. You are also allowed 100 cigars — no, don't even think Cuban . . . you can smoke them here, but you can't take them into the States — 200 cigarettes and one liter of booze. Remember to save your receipts for customs officials if you are near or over the duty-free limit. Antiques (defined as an item more than 100 years old) are also duty-free. For more information we suggest contacting a Visitors Service Bureau. Contact numbers are provided at the end of this chapter. Some regulations are also discussed in our Getting Here, Around and Home chapter.

You will notice that with some of our listings, street numbers are absent. Locals do not get hung up on identifying locations by street number. It is not something we worry about, taxi drivers don't request them, and in 99 percent of cases the name of the shop and the name of the street is sufficient. Frankly, many store employees don't know the street number of the shop they're working in! And just as frequently it may not even be visible. However this won't present a problem, as you will see when you start getting around.

And two other, very important things: The U.S. dollar is on par with the Bermuda dollar, and browsing through our shops in scanty attire or bathing suits is very much frowned upon.

St. George's Parish

Town of St. George

There are two key shopping streets in this ancient town — York Street and Water Street. King's Square is the town's hub, around which you'll find the Bank of Butterfield to the north and the Town Hall to the east. Public restrooms, also east, are just a skip from the Visitors Service Bureau on the square's southern side. The Carole Holding Art Studio, the Bank of Bermuda, Paradise Gift Shop and the Confederate Museum sit along the west arm.

While the square was the site of 17th-century floggings and executions, today it is the center for various events like the Peppercorn Ceremony (see our Annual Events chapter). In front of the sidewalk facing the Bank of Butterfield are cedar "stock and pillory" and whipping-post replicas — like the Ducking Stool that stands on nearby Ordnance Island — that re-create those used for those ancient punishments and humiliation. Most visitors get a kick out of photographing each other with their head and feet in the stocks, when they are not ambling through the shops of St.

George's, most of which open at 9 AM and close at 5 PM.

Somers Wharf & Branch Stores
Water St., Town of St. George

This group of shops and restaurant includes branches of the island's "name" shops — A.S. Coopers, Trimingham's, Davison's of Bermuda, the English Sports Shop and the Crown Colony Shop, all of which have clothing selections for men and women. This group of shops has its main stores in the city of Hamilton (see subsequent listings). An English pub-style restaurant, the Wharf Tavern is right on the waterside.

Book Cellar
Water St., Town of St. George • 297-0448

Just under the Tucker House Museum (see our Arts and Culture chapter), this small and quaint bookstore carries both new and secondhand books.

Vera P. Card
Water St., Town of St. George • 297-1718

Across from the Carriage Museum (see our Attractions chapter), this business has its main store at 11 Front Street in Hamilton and other branch stores at Marriott's Castle Harbour Resort and Sonesta Beach Hotel (see our Resort Hotels chapter). The jewelry is sold at duty-free prices, and Vera P. Card is the exclusive local distributor of Majorica pearl jewelry. They are so confident of their low prices that if your purchase is examined by a licensed appraiser at another Majorica retailer elsewhere within 90 days of buying it, and the fair retail value is appraised lower, the Vera P. Card store will either offer a full refund or pay the difference.

Guerlain
Water St., Town of St. George • 297-1525

Exquisite ladies' and men's fragrances, including Gucci and Chanel, Fendi and Drakkar, give this store an international scent. Here too, lower-than-U.S. prices make for a sniffer's bargain.

Taylors
30 Water St., Town of St. George
• 297-1626

Hear those bagpipes in your mind's ear? Well, if you can't play the pipes, you can dress the part. Kilts, skirts and other tartans for men, women and children will conjure up those high-pitched notes. Select a cashmere, Shetland, lambswool or mohair sweater for the feel and flavor of Scotland. There are savings of up to 50 percent over knitwear prices in the United States.

FYI

Unless otherwise noted, the area code for all phone numbers listed in this guide is 441.

Frangipani
Water St., Town of St. George • 297-1357

Across from the post office (which used to be a jail), Frangipani, named after an island flower (see our Flora and Fauna chapter), has batiks, silks, casualwear, cotton sweaters and costume jewelry. It is a riot of color and fun fashions.

Bermuda Gombey Trader
13 York St., Town of St. George
• 297-0399

Here you'll find the Gombey rag doll, handcrafted straw hats, bags and baskets, and even some jams and marmalades along with other gift items. You'll also find a branch in the Clocktower at the Royal Naval Dockyard in Sandy's Parish.

X-Pressions
26 York St., Town of St. George
• 297-1173

Island pottery made in Bermuda is the focus of this intimate little shop found near St. Peter's Church, the oldest Anglican church in continuous use in the Western Hemisphere.

Robertson's Drug Store
York St., Town of St. George • 297-1828

One of the oldest stores in St. George, Robertson's is a veritable pirate's chest of odds, ends, bits and pieces, large and small. Although prescriptions can be filled here, you'll find toiletries, books, magazines, jewelry, local and foreign newspapers, sunglasses and a myriad of everyday items.

Havana Leaf & Bean and Caffe Latte
8 York St., Town of St. George
• 296-1188

Take a break from your walking tour, ascend the steps opposite the Water Street entrance to Somers Wharf, and to your right is Havana Leaf & Bean and Caffe Latte. You can enjoy a gourmet cup of java, munch a tasty pastry and, if you wish, light up a genuine stogie from Cuba. This is a little spot of respite with a few outdoor tables and chairs, and it's just a few feet away an adjacent flight of steps will take you to the main bus stop.

Hamilton Parish

Flatts Village

The origin of the name is uncertain, but this tiny village was one of the island's earliest settlements because of its fine little harbor. Flatts Bridge, spanning the entrance to Harrington Sound, is believed to have been the first built in Bermuda. Quite often, in hoping to avoid the "searchers" in St. George's (comparable to today's customs officers), ships during the 17th century put into this picturesque harbor where various goods and contraband, including slaves, could be off-loaded without discovery. Smuggling was not uncommon.

Today there is a Shell gas station that services boats and motor vehicles, a cycle livery, pizza place, liquor store and the Halfway House (see our Restaurants chapter) at Flatts. We have listed a few of the more interesting shops.

ABC Ice Cream Manufacturing Plant
12 North Shore Rd., Flatts • 292-0093

Their claim is to be the "Home of the Double Dip" and to provide Bermuda's best quality ice cream.

Link to Link Jewelry and Metal Studio
20 North Shore Rd., Flatts • 293-4401

The range here is not as extensive as some other places, but you will find interesting pieces created by Bermudian silversmith and gold-smith Shane Robinson. He specializes in homemade jewelry, and you'll find pendants, earrings and charms. If you have in mind a special design, Shane will be more than happy to create it and ship your order to you.

Flatts Gift Shop
13 North Shore Rd., Flatts • 292-0360

Menswear, along with some sports gear and souvenirs make up the bulk of items here.

Smiths Parish

Collector's Hill Apothecary
South Rd. • 236-8664

About a half-mile east of Ariel Sands Club and Cottages (see our Cottage Colonies chapter), Collector's Hill fills prescriptions and offers a diverse range of items from colognes and gift items to cigarettes, books and magazines.

Devonshire Parish

Bermuda Florist
South Rd. • 236-2333

The location less than a quarter-mile west of Ariel Sands Club and Cottages makes this florist convenient for guests seeking bouquets for that special anniversary or birthday occasion.

Pembroke Parish

City of Hamilton

Take all the superlatives and cliches, combine them, and you have Hamilton, an eclectic shopping experience. A city since 1897 and Bermuda's capital since 1815, it is the business heart of the island. Within little more than a square mile, hundreds of shops, restaurants, banks, supermarkets and international insurance and reinsurance companies abound, cheek-by-jowl. Clean and well-run, Hamilton has always prided itself on being able to offer a taste of the world through its many and diverse stores.

Late Night Shopping Festival

Make a note on your calendar that every Wednesday, May through October, there is a late-night shopping festival from 6 to 10 PM, sponsored by the Bank of Butterfield, the Bermuda Department of Tourism and the Bank of Bermuda. Hosted by the Bermuda Chamber of Commerce, this is an occasion when Front Street is closed to vehicular traffic, and many of the City's main shops remain open later than usual. You will meet a variety of artists exhibiting their creations (craft items, paintings, etc.), all set up on Front Street itself between Parliament and Queen streets. A few temporary food stalls are set up, and a band is usually on hand to keep your feet tapping as you eat, walk and explore.

www.insiders.com

See this and many other **Insiders' Guide®** destinations online — in their entirety.

Visit us today!

City Malls and Shopping Centers

Washington Mall
Reid St., Hamilton • 295-4186

Entering the Washington Mall from Reid Street, you will first encounter Herrington Fine Jewellers, and just opposite is the Body Shop, where you can obtain natural hair and skin products. Go through the glass doors and you will find Kodak Express, where you can have your film developed and enlargements made rather quickly. If a little famished from your shopping adventure, pop into The Deli, just opposite, where pastries, sandwiches and salads are the order of the day. Nearby Telecom is a personal communications center selling various cellular phones to help you reach out and touch someone on your ambles. Magazines, many available nowhere else on the island, are at Washington Mall Magazines, along with a selection of books. Just across the way is the Mall Photographic Studio.

Beyond these two stores, you can take the stairs to the upper level, where there is a cash machine that takes MasterCard, Cirrus and Visa cards. Before you ascend, check out the

Heyl's Corner Hamilton, Bermuda

Located by the Birdcage at the corner of Front and Queen Streets, Hamilton.

Here you'll find exquisite hand-embroideries from the Island of Madeira, possibly one of the largest selections to be found anywhere. Table dimensions are never a problem, as they welcome the opportunity to do specially commissioned work. Amongst their extensive range of linens are Double Damask from Ireland, Le Jacquard Francais and Souleiado from France and beautiful laces from Belgium.

Upstairs is the Souleiado Shop where you'll find these colourful cotton prints from Provence by the yard and in an exclusive range of accessories.

Here you'll also find a new collection of luxurious European Bedlinens.

Children are not forgotten either as they carry a delightful selection of hand-embroidered clothes from Madeira and hand-smocked dresses from Brazil.

The Irish Linen Shop

HEYL'S CORNER, 31 FRONT STREET, HAMILTON HM 11, BERMUDA TEL: (441) 295-4089   FAX: (441) 295-6552

Sportseller for sports clothing and footwear, and the Matchbox, a small kiosk that offers cigars, cigarettes, pipes and pipe tobacco. Adjacent to the Matchbox is the Harbourmaster, where leather bags, briefcases, wallets and other assorted leather goods tempt. Hang-it-All, immediately next door, has real and artificial plants for the plant lover, and Quality Dry Cleaners and Shirt Launderers is in this area. The adjacent Cotton Ginny dishes up hip fashions and accessories for larger women.

Upstairs you'll find Sound Stage for jazz, pop, country and western CDs, and Jeans Plus, where denim is the focus. Turn left at the top of the stairs to find Jazzy Boutique, which has fashions for the younger crowd. Bermuda Best Buys has typewriters, fax and dictation machines, word processors and other great merchandise. Hungry? Pop into Take Five, a great place with a sedate ambiance. The Accessory Box, another kiosk, has ties, hats and a few bags.

To the left at the top of the stairs is The Health Store — vitamin and mineral supplements, herbs and Bermuda honey might help you shop without dropping. Blades, a hair cutting salon, is next door, and through the glass doors you'll find a Federal Express office and Upper Deck, which specializes in sports cards and other sports collectibles. Casual footwear for children and adults is at Locomotion, and M. Keyes & Co. Ltd. can test your eyes and fit you with sunglasses and eyeglass frames. Women can get well-coiffured at Headway Hair Centre, and Caffe Latte espresso bar is a good place to pause and sip fine gourmet coffees. Cosmopolitan Liquors has, well, various liquors.

Washington Mall II

This area of the mall faces onto Church Street. There is a Häagen-Dazs to tempt and satisfy that craving for something sweet. Next door is the London Shop for men's clothing. Turn the corner around London Shop and stroll the walkway overlooking Washington Lane below; you'll find Mr. C's Boutique, a division of London Shop, and Accents & Country Crafts, an interesting little place where craft items from cute plaques to candles, unique little lampshades and quizzical little dolls are displayed. Nicholas Lusher Fine Art has a small selection of paintings, and Gorilla carries a selection of menswear geared more to the outdoorsy types. The Hosiery Hut pretty much speaks for itself: hose and leggings for women.

Washington Mall West

If you enter this section of the mall from Reid Street — yes, there's the Washington Mall entrance and the Washington Mall West entrance, and both connect at the cash machine and stairs — the Four Ways Pastry Shop is on your left, and opposite it is Sail On, offering an eclectic mix of items that defy any single category. Pass through the glass doors, and you'll find Secrets on the left for seductive lingerie, and another Cotton Ginny just across the way. The Source has sportswear, and Treats of Bermuda has candies, candies and more candies. All Wrapped Up offers greeting cards and wrapping paper for special occasions, the Colosseum sells belts and shoes for women and men, and The Edge has men's clothing.

Butterfield Place
Front St., Hamilton

Entered next to the Bank of Butterfield on Front Street, this set of shops features Voila, home of fine leather goods and accessories, including handcrafted Italian shoes for men. Just opposite is Louis Vuitton, displaying bags of the same name. Michael Swan Gallery (see our Arts chapter) features the airbrush art of its namesake, a Bermudian artist. The Hall of Names sits just across from Highlander, which focuses on Scottish cashmere and tartans. Adjacent are the offices of *Bermuda Magazine*.

The Emporium
Front St., Hamilton

Pass through the entrance to The Emporium, a group of shops next to Butterfield Place, and you'll find Bermuda Glassblowing Ltd. on the right, displaying a large, colorful and exquisite selection of the glassblowers' art. Alongside is Personalized Jewellery. To the left of the entrance is Tienda de Tabaco, which sells cigars and touts itself as a great place to enjoy them. Descend the low flight of steps next to the bronze statue of a nude former Miss Bermuda and Miss World, and directly ahead is The Gallery, where Haitian and local paintings, African masks and various moderately sized sculptures make for a collector's delight. To the right is Portobello for old stamps, coins and antiques. Next to Portobello is Eve's Garden, with tempting lingerie that would make modern Adam forget the apple. Kathy's Kaffee and Sushi Bar is at the back — it's a little hideaway in which to relax for a daytime or evening pick-me-up.

Photo: GIS

U.S. shoppers will be pleasantly surprised by the bargains they will find in Bermuda.

Other City of Hamilton Shops

Mailboxes Unlimited
48 Par-la-Ville Rd., Hamilton • 292-6563
Mechanics Bldg., Church St., Hamilton • 296-5656
Phase 1 Plaza, 8 South Rd., Smiths Parish • 236-5200
122 Middle Rd., Warwick Parish • 236-4267

With the main store here and branches in Smith's, Warwick and on Church Street, Mailboxes Unlimited is well-equipped to ship just about anything anywhere. They can handle all boxing, wrapping, airway bills, commercial invoicing and insurance. Photocopying is a cinch, and they sell boxes of all shapes and sizes along with bubble wrap, Styrofoam peanuts, brown paper and gift wrap.

Pegasus Prints and Map Shop
63 Pitts Bay Rd., Hamilton • 295-2900

Located in an old Bermuda home just across from the Hamilton Princess Hotel, this is an enchanting place where prints, maps and original Curtis botanical lithographs form an eclectic delight. Engravings from Perry shells and Denton fish help complete a fascinating mix.

The Bookmart
The Phoenix Centre, Reid St. • 295-1647

Containing Bermuda's largest selection of books, The Bookmart is accessed just off Reid Street via an escalator inside the Phoenix Centre. It is often overlooked by the visitor, but you should make the effort to drop by.

Stuart's
Reid St. • 295-5496

Major name-brand cameras (including Canon, Olympus, Minolta, Fuji, Nikon and

Pentax) along with televisions, tapes, film, tape recorders and other supplies make this Bermuda's leading center for photographic and electronic equipment.

Tolaram's
12 Reid St. • 295-4391

Family-owned, this store has a selection of designer accessories from sunglasses by Versace, Giorgio Armani and Christian Lacroix to jewelry by Ralph Lauren and Alan Faye Paris.

True Reflections
53 Reid St. • 295-9424

Right on the corner of Parliament and Reid streets, this shop has Bermuda's largest collection of books, puzzles and other items related to black Bermudian, African and Caribbean history. It celebrates ethnic culture and art. Jewelry from the Ivory Coast, Kente cloth accessories and African print shirts are also available.

Twice Told Tales
34 Parliament St. • 296-1995

This is a secondhand bookstore with a difference. Those who gather here can sit at one of a few tables for coffee and conversation. The atmosphere is relaxed, and you are invited to tarry a while and meet the locals.

The Scottish Wool Shop
Queen St. • 295-0967

Want to save up to 50 percent on U.S. prices for your memories of Scotland? Cashmere, lambswool and Shetland woolens are a bargain here. If you want to trace your ancestral Scottish clan, ask the staff about it; they may be able to help. Taylor's in St. George is an associated shop.

The Bermuda Book Store
Queen St. • 295-3698

This modest bookstore has a comprehensive selection of new books. Every so often they offer selected books at bargain prices.

H.S. & J.E. Crisson Ltd.
16 Queen St. • 295-2351
71 Front St. • 295-2351
55 Front St. • 295-2351
20 Reid St. • 295-2351
York & Kent Sts., Town of St. George • 297-0672
Water St., Town of St. George • 297-0107
Elbow Beach Hotel, 60 South Rd. • 236-9928
Marriott's Castle Harbour Resort, 2 Paynters Rd.• 293-2852
Sonesta Beach Hotel, 5 South Rd. and Sonesta Dr. • 238-0072
Southampton Princess Hotel, 101 South Rd. • 238-3904

To shop at Crisson is to indulge yourself in a friendly atmosphere where superior quality jewelry can be purchased at substantial savings over American prices. Begun by Herbert and Jack Crisson in 1921, the chain has grown to 10 shops islandwide. In addition to bracelets, brooches, necklaces and earrings, they are renowned for their quality watch selection, which features established names such as Rolex, Raymond Weil, Gucci, Seiko and Ebel at prices up to 30 percent below those in the United States. And don't overlook the special Bermudian jewelry designs. These make ideal mementos of your sojourn in Bermuda.

Cecile
15 Front St. • 295-1311
Southampton Princess Hotel, 101 South Rd. • 238-1434
Marriott's Castle Harbour, 2 Paynters Rd. • 293-2841

Fine designer clothing — brands such as Escada, Yves St. Laurent, La Perla and Louis Feraud are a few of the labels carried — is on display in what many locals consider Bermuda's leading ladies' boutique. Gottex swimwear is also available for those who take fashion to the beach.

INSIDERS' TIP

One of the best times of year to grab a bargain is after Christmas when Hamilton's leading stores usually slash prices on fine quality European clothing.

Astwood-Dickinson Co.
83 Front St. • 292-5805

Astwood-Dickinson has a reputation for providing jewelry and timepieces of exceptional quality. They have introduced a Bermuda Collection with unique Bermudian pieces — Cow Polly fish, Longtail and Sand Lantern, for example — created by their own staff. Having recently forged a partnership with Columbian Emeralds International, Astwood-Dickinson is poised to continue bringing in gems of superior quality. The watches and timepieces include established names — Tiffany, Patek Philippe, Cartier and others. As in other major shops in Bermuda, items here are available at substantial savings below to American prices. Branch stores are located at Walker Arcade on Reid Street in Hamilton and in H.A. & E Smith's in Hamilton.

The English Sports Shop
49 Front St. • 295-2672
Aston & Gunn, Queen and Reid Sts. • 295-4866
The Scottish Wool Shop, 7 Queen St. • 295-0967
The Outlet, Queen St. • 295-0084

Interested in trying out Bermuda shorts? Then pay a visit to this shop, where you'll find them in a myriad of colors. Have a ball combining shorts and polo shirts! There is also a lovely selection of sweaters for those chilly evenings at home; styles include Shetland, lambswool and the soft and luxurious Glenagle cashmere.

Trimingham's
Front St. • 295-1183
Somers Wharf, Town of St. George • 297-1726
Marriott's Castle Harbour Resort, 2 Paynters Rd. • 293-0792
Southampton Princess Hotel, 101 South Rd. • 296-1648
South Shore Rd., Paget Parish • 292-3423
Sonesta Beach Hotel, 5 South Rd. and Sonesta Dr. • 296-1647
Somerset Village • 296-1291

With entrances on both Front and Reid streets, the main location of Trimingham's is one of Bermuda's largest stores. Many consider it the local version of Macy's in New York City. Men's and women's clothing and acces

Whether you are shopping
for mementos of your stay in Bermuda,
cashmere sweaters, beautiful china and crystal,
perfume or cosmetics, Smith's has numerous
exclusive lines unavailable anywhere else on the
Island. The Difference is quality...at Smith's.

Smith's

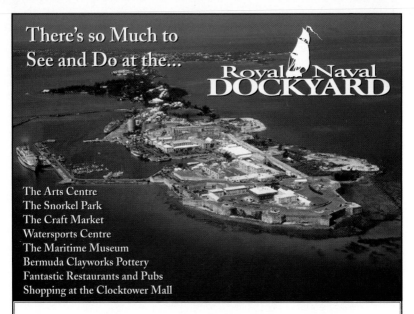

There's so Much to
See and Do at the...

Royal Naval DOCKYARD

The Arts Centre
The Snorkel Park
The Craft Market
Watersports Centre
The Maritime Museum
Bermuda Clayworks Pottery
Fantastic Restaurants and Pubs
Shopping at the Clocktower Mall

During the 1800's this immense naval fortress was built on the front lines of the British Empire to thwart the plans of the young United States of America to seize Bermuda. Referred to as the Gibralter of the West, the Royal Naval Dockyard's massive limestone walls now enclose a treasure trove of sights and activities that make the Western tip of Bermuda the favourite destination for both visitors and locals.

Always easily accessible by Bus, Taxi, Scooter or Ferry, the Royal Naval Dockyard is a great place to bring the entire family - and don't forget your camera! The historic ramparts offer spectacular views.

Visit the full service Watersports Centre and The Snorkel Park which offer a variety of personal maritime adventures and the Maritime Museum is a fascinating storehouse of over 300 years of Bermuda's seafaring tradition.

Works of a variety of local artists and craftspeople can be found at the Eastern end of the Dockyard which houses the Craftmarket, Arts Centre, and The Bermuda Clayworks Pottery, and a fantasmagoria of unique shops await you in the impressive Clocktower Mall.

There are plenty of opportunities for excellent eating and drinking throughout the Dockyard and there is always something going on, as a variety of cultural, sporting and entertainment events are regularly scheduled throughout the year. So make plans to venture West to the...

Royal Naval DOCKYARD

sories, furniture, jewelry, shoes, etc., are tastefully displayed. A family-owned business since 1842, Trimingham's claims to have Bermuda's largest collection of duty-free values, offering visitors up to 40 percent or more off U.S. prices on crystal, china and perfumes. You'll find Waterford, Portmeirion and Mikasa, plus fragrances from Estee Lauder to Christian Dior. There is a self-service restaurant, and elevator service is provided to the three floors. Trimingham's has several branch stores throughout the island.

H.A. & E Smith Ltd.
Front St. • 295-2288
York St., Town of St. George • 297-1734
Belmont Golf & Country Club, 97 Middle Rd. • 295-2288
Southampton Princess Hotel, 101 South Rd. • 238-0766
The Treasure Chest, Queen St. • 295-2288
Smith's Sampler, Royal Naval Dockyard • 234-2024

Simply called Smith's by locals, and with branch stores at York Street in St. George's, the Dockyard and the Belmont and Southampton Princess hotels (see our Resort Hotels chapter), this enterprise has been at the shopping vanguard since 1889. From English-tailored blazers to fine Italian silk ties and the traditional Bermuda shorts, Smith's is one of the island's largest clothing stores for men and women. Sitting right next to Trimingham's, it also carries fine leather handbags and lovely cashmere sweaters. There are hundreds of gift ideas, not the least of which is a Waterford crystal ship's decanter that is a reminder of Bermuda's nautical heritage. You can probably save as much as 30 percent on fine English bone china and crystal.

FYI

Unless otherwise noted, the area code for all phone numbers listed in this guide is 441.

Bluck's
Front St. • 295-5367
Town of St. George • 297-0476
Southampton Princess Hotel, 101 South Rd. • 238-0992

Regarded as crystal and china specialists, Blucks has branch stores at the Southampton Princess Hotel and in the Town of St. George. A number of their designs have been specially commissioned from European masters including Staffordshire, Herend, Spode and Caithness. The Bermuda theme is prominent in the original flower and bird designs. You'll find Staffordshire enamel boxes with the Bermuda longtail, a Bermuda Regiment ice bucket and Herend Bermuda flower plates, to name a few. Here you'll also find Royal Grafton bone china.

Walker Christopher Goldsmiths
9 Front St. • 295-1466

For some unique, unusual gold jewelry, this store fills the bill. The exquisite items will make you believe you've explored and found some ancient treasure chest. From South Sea pearls to a circa 2000 B.C. Babylonian cylinder seal carved from hematite, these folks have finds that enchant. Their items are one of a kind. The ancient coins turned into striking jewelry are superb.

E.R. Aubrey Jewellers
19 Front St. • 295-3826

Perhaps no other jewelry store can offer the kind of low prices that are synonymous with this shop. Diamonds, Colombian emeralds, sapphires and tanzanite are brought in bulk directly from the mines, and the jewelry is designed and manufactured by Aubrey's crafters. They create a complete range of jewelry including necklaces, bracelets, rings and bangles.

INSIDERS' TIP

When in St. George's, if you find you've run out of or forgotten bus tickets or lost your token, you can purchase tokens at St. George's Liquors, immediately next to the bus stop on York Street.

The Gem Cellar
Old Cellar Ln. • 292-3042

Reached from Front Street through Old Cellar Lane, almost directly opposite the area where horse-and-buggy drivers cater to visitors, this store's location was the turn-of-the-century site of one of many stables along Hamilton's Front Street. The Gem Cellar manufactures much of its own jewelry and has a selection of handmade Bermuda charms. These gemstone merchants and goldsmiths will also repair eyeglasses.

A.S. Cooper & Son Ltd.
59 Front St. • 295-3961
Reid St. • 295-3961
Somers Wharf, Town of St. George
• 297-0925
Southampton Princess Hotel, 101 South Rd. • 295-3961
Clocktower, Royal Naval Dockyard
• 234-4156
Elbow Beach Hotel, 60 South Rd.
• 236-5046

Marriott's Castle Harbour Resort, 2 Paynters Rd. • 293-8908
Sonesta Beach Hotel, 5 South Rd. and Sonesta Dr. • 238-8357

This store, which just completed its centenary celebration in 1997, has produced several mementos on English teapots, bone china mugs and other items. Designer diamond and gemstone jewelry is available along with silver and gold Bermuda charms. Fragrances from Cartier and Givenchy to Tommy Hilfiger and Calvin Klein are sold at duty-free prices. Known for its crystal and china, and a must-stop for those planning nuptials, Cooper & Son has the finest names, including Swarovski, Wedgwood, Lladro and Royal Doulton.

Artcetera
Burnaby Hill • 295-2787

Artcetera has a wide range of art products, and they also can help if you have something to e-mail or want to surf the Net. They also offer copy service, take orders for business cards and offer PC and Macintosh rentals on an hourly basis.

Christian Bookstore & Gift Centre
10 Burnaby St. • 292-3257

This book and gift store offers a large selection of religious-oriented books, T-shirts, puzzles, games, figurines and wall plaques. It's a delightful place for finding a devotional or inspirational gift for a loved one.

Heel, Sew Quik
34 Church St. • 295-1559

Need quick shoe repair due to all that walking? These folks will generally take care of the problem while you wait. They do clothing alterations, but that tends to take up to a couple of days.

Abyssian Imports
79 Court St. • 292-3208

African garments, particularly of the Ethiopian ilk, and incense, oils, silver and some leather bags are available at this store.

Dub City Records
46 Court St. • 292-6775

At this shop the specialty is reggae; you'll find it has the island's largest selection. There are also some track suits and T-shirts.

Southampton Parish

Rising Sun Shop
Middle Rd. • 238-2154

About a half-mile west of the Waterlot Inn, this treasure trove is filled to the rafters with diverse gift ideas and decorative pieces to suit just about any taste. Woodwork and crafts run the gamut from weather vanes to baskets and much else besides. This is one of the most interesting little places to stop on your journey.

Deja-Vu Flea Market
40 Middle Rd. • 238-8525

Looking for something different? Both the usual and the not so usual are packed into this shop, where secondhand items take on a new life. We have found everything from rare books on Bermuda to Tibetan rubbings and a complete dinner set used by the Carringtons on the television soap *Dynasty*. Rummage

around, and there's no telling what you may come up with.

Sandys Parish

This parish, comprised of Somerset, Boaz, Watford and Ireland Islands, is named after Sir Edward Sandys, a major shareholder in the Bermuda Company. The place name for Sandys (pronounced "sands") was Mangrove Bay, with the attached rhyming couplet, "All the Way to Mangrove Bay, There the Old Maids go to stay."

It was at Sandys Wreck Hill — a site of early fortifications — where it is said that in 1775, on the day before the infamous gunpowder theft at St. George's (see our History chapter), Bermudians on the ships that eventually carried the stolen powder to Gen. George Washington's troops came ashore, dismounted the 10 guns on Wreck Hill and rolled them into the sea. While such intrigue has found a place in the history books, this area is dubiously noted for the largest bank robbery in Bermuda's history — the culprit got away with more than a quarter-million dollars earlier this decade, and the caper has yet to be solved.

Dean's Bakery & Deli
**Manchester St., Somerset Village
• 234-2918**

This family-owned bakery is one of the hot stops for a lunch-hour sandwich or a pastry to thrill your sweet tooth. The muffins, scones, coffee rolls and apple and lemon turnovers are a delight.

Caesar's Pharmacy
**Manchester St., Somerset Village
• 234-0851**

One of the more recent additions to Somerset Village, the pharmacy dispenses not only prescription drugs, but also a few products (air purifiers, bedding, etc.) from the Asthma & Allergy Relief Centre on 61 Court Street in Hamilton.

Frith's Liquors
**Manchester St., Somerset Village
• 234-1740**

Staying in Somerset and needing a little

aqua vitae for a celebration? Pop into Frith's on Manchester Street or make arrangements for duty-free delivery to the airport.

Dockyard Specialty Retail Centre
Clocktower, Royal Navy Dockyard

Filled with Victorian charm, this former 19th-century Royal Naval building — running alongside the upper front are a line of flags from many nations — is eminently browsable. Some have likened it to a combination Quincy Market and London's Burlington Arcade. However, considerably smaller than either, it is delightfully Bermudian and has a myriad of inviting shops dealing with paintings, linens, perfumes, jewelry, books and clothing. There is also Beethoven's Restaurant and Bar (see our Restaurants chapter), which is very much like a European bistro.

Within these thick walls, which once throbbed to the "spit and polish" of navy personnel, are a score of shops. Enter the main door, turn left and wander to the end, beginning your amble at Carole Holding Print and Craft Shop, one of three shops owned and operated by watercolor artist Carole Holding. The others are at Town Square in St. George and at 81 Front Street in Hamilton. Her paintings of Bermuda are available as originals as well as prints. At her Clocktower shop, you also will discover beautiful varieties of seashells as well as cedar handmade dolls and Banana Dolls (see our Arts and Culture chapter); for the doll collector, these are a must. Right next door is a branch of Smith's, where cotton knit shirts and a range of perfumes are displayed. The Dockyard Humidor has premium cigars and specializes in Havanas. There are a wide range of choices, among them Cohiba, Montecristo, Romeo & Julieta, Partagas, Bolivar and Hoyo de Monterrey. They also carry humidors, lighters, cigar cases and cutters. A sister store is at Water Street in St. George's.

FYI

Unless otherwise noted, the area code for all phone numbers listed in this guide is 441.

Picturesque Bermuda, with its main store at 129 Front Street in Hamilton, is chock-full of photographic prints of Bermuda by photographer Roland Skinner, whose superb camera skills have captured Bermuda's famed beauty. Burrows Lightbourne is great for picking up a soft drink, cold beer or something stronger, and nearby Seaside Health Corner (not devoted to health, by the way) is a small outlet attached to Somerset Pharmacy and has toiletries, chocolates, books and some British jams and teas. Dockyard Linens has a modest collection of linens, including placemats and pot holders with a Bermuda theme.

Makin' Waves has gift items, and Uncommon Scents carries perfumes and colognes for men and women, from Spellbound to Michael Jordan. Dieters Fine Jewellers, just opposite, carries quality gemstones, gold jewelry and sterling silver. The lover of books may find an intriguing read at the Ship's Inn Book Gallery, where discovering a rare 19th-century book or a difficult-to-find first edition is not uncommon. Opposite is the Bermuda Railway Co. Ltd., which has a distinctive line of casual clothing. Trimingham's (see previous listing under the City of Hamilton) has mostly gift items including the Outerbridge's line of products — sherry peppers, barbecue sauces and Bloody Mary mix.

Turn left at Beethoven's Restaurant and Bar, pass the stands where you can pick up all manner of helpful information on almost every nook and cranny in Bermuda, and discover Nannini Häagen-Dazs. There you can sedate that compulsion for sweets with Perugina chocolate and Italian cookies. The Michael Swan Gallery has the artist's unique prints of various features of Bermuda architecture. At the Body Shop, the skin and hair care folks dote on using natural products, and the Gombey Trader has handcrafted Ber-

INSIDERS' TIP

Many shoppers feel the best time to visit Bermuda is during the winter months — you'll be able to save on a bunch of things, not the least of which being your accommodations.

mudian and Caribbean souvenirs, world-famous Blue Mountain coffee and the original handmade Gombey Rag Doll by Katee Kisk'adee. There is also A.S. Cooper's (see previous listing under the City of Hamilton) for a small selection of men's and women's clothing, Smuggler's Cove for gift items, Davison's for clothes to relax in and Calypso for casuals.

Our attractions, as you might suspect, have more to do with our environment, our history and our culture. Vast theme parks and fairgrounds you will not find here.

Attractions

If by definition an attraction must be attractive, then the whole of Bermuda is an attraction. The only arguably unattractive area is the BELCO site in Pembroke. And given that BELCO empowers us with electricity, we shouldn't complain about that.

Our attractions, as you might suspect, have more to do with our environment, our history and our culture. Vast theme parks and fairgrounds you will not find here. With the return of the American base lands (see our History chapter), those may come in the future, but for now our attractions are small rather than large, soothing rather than sensational. Here we list the places that have traditionally proved popular with our visitors. Many are free. When there's a charge, we'll tell you. For more fun things to fill up your free time, check our chapters on Parks, Recreations, Beaches, Kidstuff and Arts and Culture.

St. George's Parish

The Town of St. George

We must stress that our former capital is a major attraction in and of itself. Founded as a town in 1612 and as a corporation in 1797, St. George is our first and oldest town. Indeed, while Jamestown, Virginia, was the first English town to be founded in the New World, St. George's was the second. Jamestown being long since abandoned, St. George's is now the oldest English-speaking colonial town still in existence.

The corporation and people of St. George's are determined to protect and enhance its historic heritage. In 1995 they formed the St. George's Foundation, which initiated a town plan. Eventually, many of our streets will be paved (currently, most of them are tarmac), and street lighting, together with shop signs, will evoke the town's 17th- and 18th-century

past. The friendship that already exists between St. George's and Williamsburg, Virginia, the town that followed Jamestown, may well become cemented in an official twinship. Since 1996, St. George's has been the official twin of the ancient town of Lyme Regis, Dorset, U.K. That connection goes back to Sir George Somers, who was born there. With England, Bermuda and Virginia involved as apexes, the Bermuda Triangle may soon have far friendlier connotations altogether.

Take the time to explore the narrow, topsy-turvy town streets with evocative names such as Old Maid's Lane, Petticoat Lane and Featherbed Alley, and enjoy the traditionally Bermudian houses that are not obliged to compete with towering skyscrapers. St. George's is, of course, rich in history. Look through our History and Arts and Culture chapters for more information about museums and development. Be sure to check the local options in the Restaurants, Nightlife and Shopping chapters as well.

All right, the letter K does not come first in the alphabet, but King's Square is the town center and the natural starting point for a walking tour. It's also one of our favorite locations for outdoor celebrations, such as Emancipation Day and New Year's Eve, when we like to go down for music and fireworks. And throughout the year, it often resonates with the music of outdoor concerts (see our Annual Events and Festivals chapter).

As soon as you arrive in the square, you'll notice replicas of the stocks, pillories and whipping posts that were used as punishments. By Ordnance Island, you'll also see the ducking stool, used to dunk female gossips in the harbor. Most unfair, really, as it is a truth universally unacknowledged that men like to gossip as well. In the summer months particularly (actually, April through October), town crier Richard Olsen arrives most days dressed in 18th-century costume to announce re-enactment duckings. Some adults find these amusing, but be warned that younger kids may not. More sensitive perhaps to the barbarism of such practices, they often become frightened.

And now let us start with attractions in King's Square. After that, we will resume alphabetical order for the rest of the parish's attractions.

Visitors Service Bureau
King's Sq. • 297-1642

This is not an attraction in itself, but it is the key to the rest of St. George's attractions. Friendly staff will inform and advise you about excursions, tours, events, sightseeing, shopping and transportation. They will also sell you bus tickets. Check the blackboard for daily information about tours. April through October, the bureau opens from 9 AM to 1 PM and 1:30 to 4 PM Monday through Saturday. During the winter, the hours are generally 9 AM to 2 PM, but they are subject to change. Call directly to verify. As you come out of the Bureau you'll find Town Hall on your right.

Town Hall
5 King's Sq. • 297-1532

This municipal center houses on its ground floor what is traditionally known as the Mayor's Parlour. It is the meeting place of the town's Corporation, which is headed by the mayor, currently Mayor Lois Perinchief. You're welcome to check out the cedar furnishings and the pictures of previous mayors Mondays through Saturdays from 10 AM to 4 PM. (It closes for all public holidays.) External flights of stairs on both sides of the entrance take you to a movie theater where you can see a slide presentation on St. George's and its people. Admission is free. The theater is open Monday to Friday 10:30 AM to 2:30 PM. Tuesday, there's a presentation at 8:30 PM. December to April, the number of presentations is reduced. The theater also closes on all public holidays.

Deliverance
Ordnance Island • 297-1459

Stand in King's Square, and across the bridge you'll see a life-size replica of the original *Deliverance* that left Bermuda in 1610 to aid settlers in Virginia. For a small fee — adults and teens pay $3, children younger than 12, $1 — you can take a self-guided tour of the ship's interior. You'll see the small galley where the cook had to prepare food for 132 people. His equipment? One big pot. Explore the lower deck, where apparently 100 people were huddled together at all times during the voyage, and be thankful Atlantic transportation is infinitely more comfortable these days. Mannequins representing passengers and an audiotape describing the wreck of the *Sea Venture* help to evoke the cramped and dangerous conditions of 17th-century sea travel. The replica, by the way, is made of South American pine, teak and Bermuda cedar. However, the original was made out of the *Sea Venture's* wreckage, which was probably Irish oak.

The Statue of Sir George Somers
Ordnance Island

Just across from the *Deliverance* is a likeness of Sir George Somers, cast in bronze by Desmond Fountain. The admiral of the *Sea Venture* holds up his arms in a gesture of incredulous wonderment that he is finally about to make it to land. He stands on a plinth set in a circular pool of water.

The Bermuda National Trust Museum
The Globe Hotel, King's Square • 297-1423

Was this property once a hotel? Yes. During the mid-19th century the Globe Hotel was open for guests. However, its history goes back to 1699, when it was built as Governor's House specially for Samuel Day, a governor who turned out to have a disreputable character. He did not agree that the property belonged to Bermuda, to be used as a residence for future governors. When the next governor turned up to move in, he found that Day had secretly secured the title of the house.

Now a National Trust property, the museum houses exhibits featuring its own color-

FYI

Unless otherwise noted, the area code for all phone numbers listed in this guide is 441.

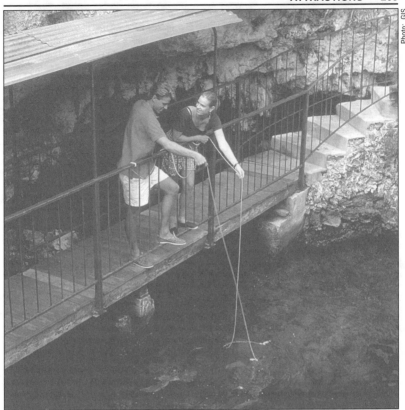

Photo: GIS

A couple drops their lines at the Devil's Hole.

ful history and the story of St. George's. Downstairs you'll find a model of the *Sea Venture* and a video room showing the National Trust's 13-minute film, *Bermuda: Centre of the Atlantic*. Upstairs you can check out the exhibit, "Rogues and Runners: Bermuda and the American Civil War." If you've read our History chapter, you know that many Bermudians made their fortunes by supplying arms to the Confederates. A Confederate agent actually set up office here and was responsible for overseeing the transportation of supplies from Europe through the Union blockade to the southern states in America. So you see, this museum has had a somewhat checkered past. Apart from holidays, it's open year round, Monday through Saturday, from 10 AM to 4 PM. Admission costs $4.

Carriage Museum
22 Water St. • 297-1367

This museum is right next door to the Carriage House Restaurant (see our Restaurants chapter). Before the days of cars, introduced here in 1946, we depended largely on horse and carriage or buggy for transportation. Each parish had a vehicle for carrying the dead. You'll see here the somber St. George's Hearse, a black wooden carriage with hanging curtains. Other, more cheerful vehicles include a wicker governess cart, ideal for carrying children, a ladies' phaeton, a barouche and a brougham. Admission is free; operating hours are 10 AM to 4 PM, Mondays through Fridays, year round. The museum closes on all public holidays.

St. Peter's Church
Duke of York St. • 297-8359

This is our oldest church; it also stands on the site of the oldest Anglican church in the western hemisphere. Situated on a hill, it has a long flight of brick steps. Walk up them, and you'll appreciate the simplicity of this stone building with its cedar door and shuttered windows. But you might like to imagine the original cedar and palmetto church, which was blown down by a gale in 1612. In 1619, Governor Butler built another church, where one year later Bermuda held its first General Assembly.

The present building was constructed in 1713, and a clock tower was added in 1814. Inside you'll find the font (possibly 15th-century) that was brought to Bermuda in the 1700s, and a three-decker cedar pulpit that dates back to the late 17th century. St. Peter's has two altars. The older one faces east, as is customary, and dates to 1612, when it was used in the original church. The other is freestanding and presently faces north. The cedar box pews and the gallery, where slaves once congregated, are visual reminders of the 18th-century social hierarchy. So is the royal box, reserved for the governor.

Other relics include a 1625 chalice, donated by the Bermuda Company (see our History chapter), and communion silver donated by King William III. Memorial tablets on the walls give historical information about local families and governors. Explore the church yard, and you'll find the slave burial ground as well as the graves of Sir Richard Sharples and his aide-de-camp, Hugh Sayers; they were assassinated in March 1973. You'll also find the "belfry tree," an old cedar that was there when members of that first General Assembly gathered together.

St. Peter's is open daily and for Sunday services. (See our Worship chapter for more information.)

Somers Gardens
Duke of York St.

Sir George Somers died in Bermuda in November 1610. His nephew, Matthew Somers, decided to take his body back to England. However, he had to be secretive about it since sailors were superstitious about corpses aboard ships. Apparently the body was embalmed and placed in a cedar chest that was shipped to Lyme Regis, U.K, but the heart and entrails were cut out. So it wasn't just his heart Sir George left in Bermuda. All his organs were buried at this site, which eventually became a public park in 1920. A marble tablet in this walled garden commemorates him. A brass tablet inside the church in Whitchurch Canonicorum, a village just outside Lyme, is England's memorial to Sir George.

St. David's Lighthouse
Lighthouse Hill, St. David's

People first saw the light in St. David's on November 3, 1879, when Bermuda's second and last lighthouse was officially opened. It's not as elegant as Gibb's Hill (see subsequent listing under Southampton Parish), being rather squat in comparison. But with its red and white paint job, it is cute and cheerful. Mondays and Wednesdays it's open from 9 AM to noon; Tuesdays it stays open until 2:30 PM. The rest of the week it's closed. The lighthouse is 55 feet from base to light and 285 feet above sea. Climb the 87 steps, and you'll reach the top for a great view of St. David's and St. George's. Admission is free. St. David's Lighthouse, by the way, was blown up in the movie *The Deep*. We were never worried. . . . The film crew had constructed a replica.

Gates Fort
Town Cut

To find this fort, head through St. George up Barrack Road and go to the end of the Cut Road. Since there's no formal entrance, you can visit any time you wish. The fort has two King George III guns on the gun platform and a guard house at the entrance. It's worth climbing to the top of the keep for a view of the Town Cut Channel and the boats and liners that glide through it. Admission is free.

VANIQA™
(eflornithine hydrochloride)
Cream, 13.9%

Rx Only

Net Wt 30g

VANIQA™
(eflornithine hydrochloride)
Cream, 13.9%

A2-P002C-11-00

Slavery Left an Ugly Mark, Even Here in Paradise

It's true we have no snakes in Bermuda. It's a fact that is gleefully pointed out by those who argue that our island is paradise. You won't find a rattler or a cobra on our shores. But figurative snakes are a different matter. We certainly have not escaped the evils of the world, however much we'd like to think so.

The greatest evil of Bermudian history was slavery, which grew out of the early 17th-century practice of importing black and Indian indentured servants to work on the island. According to the late Cyril Packwood, during the mid-1620s references to blacks and Indians changed from "indentured servants" to "life servitude" — in other words, their condition became slavery (see History). Go to the Bermuda Archives, and you will find chilling business documents and wills that almost casually refer to the buying, selling and bequesting of slaves.

For centuries those records, together with some accounts written by white historians, travel writers and letter writers, were the only written evidence of slavery. And while some of these writers might have deplored slavery and spoken against it, they mostly argued that, compared with plantation slaves elsewhere, Bermudian slaves were better off. Thus, there were virtually no books written on the subject that offered a slave's point of view.

One exception was *The History of Mary Prince, A West Indian Slave*, which was published in Britain in 1831. Mary Prince was actually Bermudian, having been born at Spittal Pond (or Brackish Pond, as she refers to it). She tells of the horrendous treatment she received in Bermuda, Turks Island and Antigua and of her eventual escape to London in 1831. However, few people had access to the book in Bermuda until 1993, when it was republished in paperback form. Copies of Mary Prince's story are available in our bookstores (see our Shopping chapter).

The thin veil concealing the reality of slavery in Bermuda was finally removed in 1975 by Cyril Packwood's *Chained on the Rock*, a book that strenuously argues the malignancy of slavery in Bermuda. Packwood's archival evidence clearly shows the treatment of slaves was just as cruel here as anywhere else.

We have slave stories in Bermuda, although the few that have been recorded are striking for what is omitted. Under the Spittal Pond listing in the archives, you'll find a reference to a slave called Jeffrey. All we know so far is that, helped by a young female slave, he hid in a cave for a month and was discovered. Who did he "belong" to? What relationship did he have with the girl? What happened to them afterwards? And when was this escape? We don't know. And we can only guess at his feelings throughout and after the escapade.

Other stories do include details, often disturbing. Yet again, so much is left out. Take the story of Sarah Bassett for in-

— continued on next page

Legend has it that a purple Bermudiana flower bloomed from Sarah Bassett's ashes.

stance. Older Bermudians sometimes refer to an extremely hot and sultry day as "a regular Sally Bassett day." Why? The answer's horrific. William Zuill records in *Bermuda Journey* (first published in 1946) that Sarah was found guilty of compelling her granddaughter to poison slave owners Thomas Forster and his wife with "Rat's Bane and Manchineel Root." As a result, in June 1730 she was publicly burnt at the Foot of the Lane or Crow Lane at the eastern end of Hamilton Harbour. The unusually high temperature that day, together with the fierce flames of the fire, gave rise to this old saying.

Who were the Forsters, and what happened to them? According to William Zuill, they "owned" Sarah as well as her granddaughter. They were still living, although ill at the time of the trial; their deaths were not recorded. Zuill also refers to the story in *The Story of Bermuda and Her People*, while Terry Tucker mentions Sarah Bassett in *Bermuda Today and Yesterday*. Both add that Sarah wanted a slave girl poisoned as well. Terry Tucker says the owners were actually called "Foster," not "Forster."

In *Chained on the Rock*, Cyril Packwood adds details that emphasize the horror of the incident. As he explains, from 1720 to 1730 slave conspiracies and poisoning plots against whites were common. Government reaction was to round up suspected poisoners and put them in jail in St. George's. Sarah Bassett, he argues, in fact "belonged" to Francis Dickinson, not the Fosters. He says that Sarah visited Beck, the granddaughter, who did "belong" to the Fosters. He confirms that she instructed Beck to administer the poisons to the Fosters, and that she wanted a slave girl called Nancy to be poisoned as well. What were Sarah's motives? Given that she had grandchildren, she was considered old and therefore without much "auction block value." According to Packwood's account, Sarah's actions were probably performed out of revenge for her own suffering.

He goes on to say that on June 2, 1730, she was indicted before the court in St. George's for poisoning several people. There were 10 witnesses for the king, including Mrs. Foster. (Mr. Foster and Nancy were too ill to attend.) When asked whether she was guilty or not guilty, Sarah answered, "Not guilty and for tryall put herself upon God and country." During the trial she was told that she could say what she liked, but court records show that "she made some slender denyall of the fact and said no more." The verdict as pronounced by the foreman was: "Guilty and we value her at one pound four shillings and six pence."

Three days later Sarah was brought back to hear the dreadful sentence: "It is the judgment and sentence of this court, that you Sarah Bassett the prisoner at the barr be return'd to the prison from whence you came and from thence you are to be conveyed to the place of execution where a pile of wood is to be made and provided, and you are there to be burnt with fire until your body be dead. And the Lord have mercy on your soul." Her response? "I never deserved it." Apparently she proclaimed that she was not guilty to the very end and was said to have cried out that God would prove her innocent. One legend has it that God did so — when her ashes were examined, a tiny purple iris appeared in full bloom. That iris is our endemic Bermudiana.

In *Bermuda Journey*, Zuill says: "It is curious that while so many punishments of bygone days should have been forgotten, the burning of Sally Bassett should have made such a deep impression that it became a Bermuda legend." But why is it so curious? While public executions were relatively common, burnings were not. Women accused of being witches during the 17th century were generally hanged. Horrendous as any execution is, a burning is particularly brutal.

And why was Sarah brought all the way from St. George's to Crow Lane to receive her punishment? Ordnance Island, minutes away from the jail, and Gibbet Islands in Smith's Parish were normally the sites of executions. Both Zuill and Packwood record

— continued on next page

that on her way to Crow Lane she was passed by many people, presumably in haste to get to the spectacle, and that she told them, "No use you hurrying, folks. There'll be no fun till I get there!" That she was made a public example, there's no doubt. Perhaps the site was chosen so that people from all over the island could reach it, and perhaps burning was chosen to dissuade others from poisoning.

But there are no easy answers to the other questions. When Sarah said, "I never deserved it," she was surely right. No human deserves to be a slave. But is that what she meant? Or did she mean that she did not poison the Fosters and Nancy? Was she sane or (as some people apparently argued) old and crazy? Insanity seems unlikely; her recorded words certainly reveal a shrewd understanding of the nastier side of human nature, as well as courage. And if she did want the Fosters poisoned, why implicate her granddaughter? Some of Sarah Bassett's descendents believe that Thomas Foster sexually abused his female slaves, including her granddaughter. And if Sarah was not a part of the Fosters' household, then it would be much easier for Beck to carry out the deed. But why poison a slave? Perhaps Nancy colluded with the Fosters or did nothing to help the other slaves. We can only speculate. We can also only guess what might have happened to Beck in the aftermath of the incident.

These days, younger Bermudians tend not to remark on hot weather with that grim old saying. Nevertheless the fate of Sarah Bassett should never be forgotten. It epitomizes the insidious effects of slavery, even on an island that many consider paradise.

Fort St. Catherine
15 Coot Pond • 297-1920

Visit this intact fort — originally built in 1614, with extensions added during the 18th and 19th centuries — for historic information, a splendid ocean view and a bit of supernatural excitement. Dioramas in the magazine highlight events in Bermudian history. Check out the swords, muskets and pistols on display, plus the 18-ton rifled muzzle-loaders on the gun floor. Never had the chance to see the British Crown Jewels in the Tower of London? Never mind; you'll find replicas in the keep here.

At the top of the tower, an audiovisual presentation shows how Bermuda fortified itself. Explore the cook house, and just off it you may well have a close encounter with George — he's a soldier and a resident ghost. An exorcism conducted in 1985 didn't work. From time to time he likes to do his bit for tourism by being friendly to visitors. Why not? We like to give him a ghost of a chance.

St Catherine's is open year round from 10:30 AM to 4:30 PM Monday through Sunday. Adults and teens pay $3; children younger than 12 get in for $1.

Hamilton Parish

The Bermuda Perfumery and Gardens
212 North Shore Rd., Bailey's Bay
• 293-0627, (800) 527-8213

Read our Flora and Fauna chapter and you'll know that Easter lilies were once an important part of our economy. We used to ship the bulbs to the United States. However, the flowers themselves were often thrown out. Colin Curtis, president and manager of the Bermuda Perfumery, told us that one day in 1929 his grandfather (William Blackburn Smith) watched thousands of these flowers being thrown into the sea. The waste was too much for him, so he hit on the idea of making perfume. A marine engineer, Smith designed and made the machinery necessary for the project. Visit, and you'll see that it's still in use.

Smith's daughter, Mrs. Madeline Scott, was an excellent floriculturist. She brought in a then-famous perfumer from France. Eventually their combined expertise led to the production of Easter Lily Perfume, which they manufactured in a small wooden building. Sixty-nine years later, Bermuda's one perfumery is still flourishing in a charming Bermudian farmhouse that's some 250 years old.

It's well worth a visit (admission is free) for several reasons: First, you'll get to see how perfume is made now and how it was made in the past. A guide will show you around the plant and explain *enfleurage*, the ancient method of extracting fragrance from flowers. Second, you can buy perfumes, colognes, and moisturizing lotions all made right here in Bermuda under the name of LiLi. Bermudiana, Easter lily, frangipani and passion flower perfumes are for sale in the gift shop in a variety of sizes. A quarter-ounce bottle of each costs $25. The latest fragrance, Paradis, is a blend of floral notes and costs $38 for a quarter-ounce or $29 for eau de toilette.

Lastly, once you've finished your tour, you can explore for free the nature trail set in 6 acres of lush garden and jungle land. Depending on the season, you'll see passion flower, thumbergia and night-blooming cereus vines, old garden roses and orchids of all types. In fact, all the flowers, trees and shrubs we mention in our Flora and Fauna chapter are growing in these beautiful gardens. Rest areas will let you sit and peacefully appreciate them. You may catch sight of Mr. Curtis checking out his latest hibiscis hybrid or his gingers imported from Hawaii and Tahiti. Whenever he travels, he always has an eye open for what exotic plants he can try planting here.

If you're stuck for a gift to take back home, the Calabash Gift Shop, on the property, has a variety of gifts from all over the world. From April 1 to October 31, the perfumery and gardens are open Monday through Saturday from 9:15 AM to 5 PM; Sundays it opens from 10 AM to 4 PM. The rest of the year it closes on Sundays and public holidays, but it is open Monday through Saturday from 9:15 AM to 4:30 PM.

Caves

Hamilton Parish is known for its limestone cave formations. In our Resort Hotels chapter we've already mentioned the Prospero and Cathedral caves found on the grounds of Grotto Bay Beach Hotel. Here we list tone more that is open to the public. Guides will escort you, mainly to ensure that you do not touch

the formations. In the past, visitors would break off pieces for souvenirs. However, the slow growth of these formations of stalagmites and stalactites (1 cubic inch every 100 years) depends on the remorseless dripping of water on stone. Negative drip means negative growth. Take pictures, by all means, but please don't touch. Perhaps you are confused between stalactites and stalagmites? Remember, stalactites *tumble* (that is, grow down from the cave's ceiling), while stalagmites *mount* (that is, grow up from the cave floor). When they meet and grow together, they are known simply as columns.

Crystal Caves
Wilkinson Ave. • 293-0640

These caves are not named after crystal substances; rather they are named for their subterranean pools of incredibly clear water. Look approximately 55 feet down through turquoise depths, and you'll see the bottom. The water comes in from Castle Harbour, so the depth fluctuates according to the tides.

Crystal Caves' known history goes back to 1907, when two boys inadvertently discovered the caves when playing cricket. They immediately took a lantern and a piece of rope to explore them. Since then, these stalagmite and stalactite formations have been open to the public. A guide will walk you along a pontoon bridge that crosses the pools. He or she will point out that the formations resemble the Manhattan skyline.

You can visit every day from 9:30 AM to 4:30 PM from April to October. Call directly for opening times between November and March. Adults pay $5; children 5 to 11 pay $2.50. Children 4 and younger can visit for free. You can buy a souvenir from the gift shop. Prices start at $5. Credit cards are not accepted for admission but are fine for gift buying.

Glass Blowing Studio and Show Room
16 Blue Hole Hill • 293-2234

OK, the Phoenicians started glass blowing in the 1st century BC. And the Venetians have been at it ever since the 15th century. Gail Cook, owner and manager here, brought glassblowing to Bermuda in 1986. We're so glad she did. For one thing, she and her staff

Fine flippered friends are among the attractions in Bermuda.

of glassblowers make uniquely Bermudian objets d'art. Plates, bowls, glasses and vases come in the vibrant blues and greens and pinks that are Bermuda's true colors. And exquisitely made longtails, bluebirds and angelfish will remind you of our fauna. For another, this ancient art is fascinating to watch. Visit the studio, and you'll see the glassblowers in action. They'll show you the base material — a raw glass powder of sand, soda, lime and silica. It looks gritty and a bit dirty, to tell you the truth. Yet by the end of the melting, coloring and blowing processes it becomes "such stuff as dreams are made on."

During the summer, the studio is open 9 AM to 5 PM Monday through Saturday and 10 AM to 5 PM on Sunday. September to December, it opens at 10 AM and closes at 4 PM. The glassblowers take a lunch break from noon to 1 PM, but the showroom remains open during this break. Prices range from $11.75 for a Ber-

muda tree frog, to $80 and higher for larger pieces.

Smiths Parish

Bermuda Aquarium, Museum & Zoo
North Shore Rd., Flatts • 293-2727

You're right, we listed the BAMZ in our Kidstuff chapter, but we urge adults to come here too. The aquarium has been a favorite attraction since its opening in 1928. If the weather happens to be unkind, then at least you'll have the chance to see the fish that live here. Tanks contain all kinds of marine life, including barracuda and a sinister moray eel that looks like a gigantic stuffed stocking. Less intimidating are green turtles, puffer, trigger and angelfish, wrasses and sergeant-majors. Tiny tanks show you tiny life, such as miniature crabs, bioluminescent corals and sea horses. Check out the North Rock exhibit — two giant tanks depicting the coral reef and its inhabitants. (See our Kidstuff chapter for more info.)

The Natural History Museum tells the story of Bermuda's environmental development; it also has an excellent exhibit on our whales and the part they played in our economy. In the outdoor zoo you'll find the Islands of Australasia Exhibit, complete with real wallabies, Australian bats, bearcats and three kangaroos. Look out for animals from other parts of the world: pink flamingos from the Caribbean and tortoises from the Galapagos. The BAMZ is open 9 AM to 4:30 PM, Mondays through Sundays, year round except for Christmas Day. Adults and teens pay $8, kids 5 to 12 pay $4, and children younger than 5 can visit for free. The Heritage Passport gives a 10 percent discount off these rates.

Devil's Hole Aquarium
Harrington Sound Rd. • 293-2072

Actually, there's nothing devilish about this natural aquarium. It offers a painless way of fishing — painless, that is, both for the fish and for you. A few seconds walk away from the admissions office takes you to a deep lake in a cavern where you can stand on a small bridge and "fish" with line and bait but no hooks. You'll see angelfish, snappers, moray eels and green parrotfish that are happy to take your bait and run. As Wendell Pond, owner and manager, puts it: "We may be skillful at one end of the line, but they're just as skillful on the other!" You'll also get to see Ninja, Stormy Eyes, Camouflage and Slow Poke. And who may they be? They are truly Bermudian green turtles. Born in captivity in 1988, they're still doing well.

Devil's Hole Aquarium was Bermuda's first tourist attraction. In the early 1800s, Mr. Pond explains, the roof of the cavern collapsed as a result of water rushing in from the South Shore, approximately 1.5 miles away. In 1834 Mr. Trott, owner at the time, decided to use it as a fish pond for the groupers he used to catch. Neighbors became curious and insisted on checking it out. Being a true entrepreneurial

Bermudian, Mr. Trott decided to charge an entrance fee.

These days that fee is $5 for adults and teens and $3 for children ages 5 to 12. Younger than 5, they pay 50¢. March 1 to November 30, Devil's Hole is open seven days a week from 9:30 AM to 4:30 PM. For winter times and days of operation, call Mr. Pond.

Paget Parish

Bermuda Botanical Gardens
Point Finger Rd. • 236-5291

Actually, these gardens can be accessed from the South Road and from Berry Hill Road, but we give the above address since you can easily reach it by bus. Yes, these 36 acres of gardens are a tourist attraction, but we love them too. We come here with our children for family picnics and parties. We come early in the morning for a jog or a walk. We come on our lunch hour for a break from stress. And once a year, we flock here for our annual Agricultural Exhibition (see our Annual Events and Festivals chapter).

Ever since 1898, when they were officially opened as "The Public Garden," they have been home to more than 1,000 varieties of plant life. You'll find all the flora we mention in our Flora and Fauna chapter and more, including exotic trees, shrubs and flowers that have been transported here during the last three centuries. Go down to the end of the park that faces the South Shore, and you'll find a wonderful banyan tree. This gigantic ficus tree came originally from Ceylon or India and is distinctive for its aerial roots that eventually reach the ground to form secondary trunks. Kids like to swing on the roots. Other exotic trees include an Indian rubber tree, an Indian laurel and an Australian banyan. Explore the gardens, and you'll come across a cacti and succulent collection, a plumeria collection (the trees here are more commonly known as frangipani), a palm garden and a rose garden. A small, walled garden for the blind specializes in fragrant flowers, herbs and shrubs.

Indoor collections include the Arrowroot

Factory and Fern Collection, the Exotic House (where you'll find a fantastic display of orchids and bromeliads) and the Cacti and Succulent House, where you'll find that cacti are not always prickly. Many of them produce amazing flowers.

Tuesdays, Wednesdays and Fridays, you can meet guides outside the Visitors' Service Centre at 10:30 AM. They will take you for an informative hour-long tour of the gardens. Tuesdays and Fridays, from noon until 2 PM, you can also take a guided tour of elegant, 18th-century Camden, the official residence of our premier. She doesn't live there, but she does hold receptions, parties and official functions when necessary. The Visitors' Service Centre is open daily from 10 AM to 4 PM year round, except on public holidays. Go there for information, of course, and also for light snacks. The gift section specializes in English botanical items plus books on gardening, flora and fauna and plant-related subjects. Prices range from $10 and $40. The gardens are open from sunrise to sunset.

Pembroke Parish

Hamilton

Cathedral of the Most Holy Trinity (Bermuda Cathedral)
Church St., Hamilton • 292-4033

Our cathedral is open daily from 8 AM to 5:45 PM. See the Worship chapter for information about its history and architecture.

Bermuda Underwater Exploration Institute
40 Crow Ln., Hamilton • 292-7219

In 1870, Jules Verne's imagination took readers 20,000 leagues under the sea. In 1997 this institute opened to let us explore at a more realistic 12,000 feet under the sea. Don't worry,

you won't get wet. You sit in a capsule and let video, motion, light and sounds take you on a seven-minute simulated dive. But there is far more to see — the dive is just part of a self-guided audio tour. As you enter the building, you'll see a giant map of Bermuda on the lobby floor and three steel chandeliers (modeled after oceanographic instruments) that give introductory information about the sea and Bermuda's marine heritage. You'll then follow a path that takes you to the exhibits.

With lots of multimedia and interaction involved, the exhibits open your eyes to the revelations of the ocean, the history of underwater exploration, marine life living at different depths and Bermuda's shipwrecks. Imaginative use of lighting, video and touch-screen televisions all make the tour interesting. So do examples of underwater craft such as the full-scale bathysphere (a spherical, cable-lowered diving compartment), first used by Beebe half a mile off Bermuda in 1934.

A room devoted to display of about 3,000 seashells is particularly worth seeing. Bermudian Jack Lightbourn very generously donated his magnificent collection to the Institute. Beautifully displayed, with special lighting emphasizing their delicate colors and sheen, these shells are a feast to the eyes. You'll see Bermuda shells that Lightbourn began collecting when he was just 11 years old. One tiny white shell with exquisite edging is actually named after him: the Murex Pternyotus Lightbourn. In addition, his collection includes a vast amount of foreign shells, many taken from the Pacific. Look out for the Australian trumpet that can hold up to three gallons of water.

The institute is open from 10 AM to 6 PM (last tickets are sold at 5 PM) Monday through Sunday, year round except for Christmas Day. Adults pay $9.75, children 7 to 16 pay $5, and seniors older than 65 pay $7.80. Children 6 and younger may visit for free. If you have a Heritage Passport, you get a 20 percent reduction on all rates. Your ticket is good for the

INSIDERS' TIP

Drive into Hamilton along Crow Lane and look for the historic Crow Lane Bakery. In 1790, that same building housed Mrs. Mary Wright's Coffee House. It also housed a room where merchants met to plan and create Bermuda's second town.

entire day. Given the detailed marine information you can find here, you'll definitely want to spend at the very least a couple of hours here. What's more, your ticket gives you access to the auditorium where you can watch movies on the ocean and marine conservation and exploration.

If you get hungry while exploring the museum, you can have a snack at the coffee bar, or you can visit La Coquille Restaurant for an excellent lunch, served between 11:30 AM and 2:45 PM. La Coquille is also open for dinner from 6:30 to 10:45 PM. (See our Restaurants chapter for further details.) Two gift shops may solve Christmas shopping problems: The Logo Shop sells T-shirts and other items with the institute's logo; the Ocean's Gift Shop specializes in Bermudian items that are unavailable elsewhere. Prices range from about 95¢ to $1,500 for a handmade reproduction of an old Bermuda dinghy. We emphasize that the institute is completely wheelchair-accessible and has bathrooms equipped for visitors in wheelchairs.

House of Assembly (Sessions House)
21 Parliament St., Hamilton • 292-7408

We may be a colony, but we certainly have our own parliament. In fact, ours is the oldest in the Commonwealth outside the U.K. And yes, we do retain the British emphasis on pomp and ceremony. You can visit the House Monday through Friday from 9 AM to 12:30 PM and from 2 to 5 PM, but parliamentary debates happen on Fridays from 10 AM, October through June. You're welcome to sit in the visitors gallery and experience debates between government leaders and the opposition. Do not be surprised to see one member wearing a full wig and flowing black robes. He is Mr. Speaker, and as arbitrator he has the unenviable task of maintaining order and

decorum. Notice we do not give a finishing time — debates have been known to continue until the early hours of the following morning. By the way, it would be *outré* to turn up in jeans. Smart casual dress is required.

Supreme Court (Sessions House)
21 Parliament St., Hamilton • 292-1350

The chief justice presides over the Supreme Court, together with a number of puisne judges, who try the more serious criminal cases. The court is downstairs in the Sessions House. "How can this be an attraction?" Well, our lawyers wear gowns and short wigs; our judges wear full wigs and red robes. What for? Wigs were first introduced in the 17th century, when Louis XIV of France wore one to hide his baldness. In England, they reached the height of fashion in the 18th century. Judges and lawyers continue to wear them because of tradition, and because, they argue, the costume encourages a more formal and respectful atmosphere in court. Visitors are welcome, although space is limited. The court is open for the same hours as the House of Assembly. Again, smart casual dress is required.

Visitors' Service Bureau
Front St., Hamilton • 295-1480

Here friendly staff will give you all kinds of information about Hamilton in particular and Bermuda in general. Bulletin boards will keep you posted about entertainment, festivals and events. You can buy transportation passes here and pick up a free Bermuda map and numerous brochures. April through October, the bureau is open 9 AM to 1 PM and 1:30 to 4 PM Monday through Saturday. During winter, the hours are generally 9 AM to 2 PM, but they are subject to change. Call directly to verify them.

INSIDERS' TIP

Although our single city shares the same name as one of our parishes, it was not named after the same person. Hamilton Parish, once called Bedford Tribe, was named after James Hamilton, second Marquis of Hamilton, England. The City of Hamilton was named after Henry Hamilton, governor of Bermuda from 1788 to 1794.

Fort Hamilton
Happy Valley Rd.

Built in the 1860s, this polygonal fort is well worth a visit for its view of the city and Hamilton Harbour. If forts interest you, then you'll appreciate the rare, 10-inch rifled muzzle-loader guns and emplacements for 60-pounder cannon on Moncrieff disappearing carriages. If you're into plants rather than military history, you'll enjoy the botanical gardens that have been planted in the dry moat. They contain a variety of tropical and subtropical ferns and plants.

Visit at noon on Mondays from November to March, and you might think you're in Scotland. The Bermuda Islands Pipe Band performs the Skirling Ceremony by the ramparts. You'll hear the haunting pipe music of Scotland and Ireland while you watch the Highland Dancers, who truly know what it is to have a fling. (See our Beaches and Parks chapters for information on other forts.)

Southampton Parish

Gibb's Hill Lighthouse
66 St. Anne's Rd. • 238-8069, 238-0524

In 1846 we had a May Day with a difference. That's when Gibb's Hill Lighthouse, the first one to go up in Bermuda, beamed out upon the island. Since then it's been one of our most familiar landmarks. Ships 40 miles away can see it, and pilots flying at 10,000 feet can pick up its flash 120 miles away. Tall (117 feet from base to light, to be exact), elegant and graceful, it's well worth a visit if only for the view at the top.

Pay $2.50, and you can climb the eight flights of stairs. The landings come in useful for rests (some of us need them) and for information about its construction. You'll learn that it's one of the few lighthouses in the world made of cast iron, and that its original light was a concentrated burner of four circular wicks. Count each step as you climb, and you should reach a total of 185. Once you reach the top, you can walk out onto a circular balcony enclosed by a railing. Warning: Do not look down, unless you are impervious to vertiginous drops. Instead, look across, and you'll see the South Shore, Hamilton Harbour and the Great Sound.

Once you hiked back down to the base again, for about $6 you can relax over a well-earned English cream tea in The Lighthouse Tearoom. Open 9 AM to 5 PM daily, the eatery offers breakfast and lunch as well. Sunday afternoons from 2 to 4:30 PM, Steve Crawford will serenade you with his classical guitar. Mementos of your visit are available at the Lighthouse Gift Shop, which sells collectors' light-

Photo: GIS

Somerset Bridge, which can raise its middle plank to allow the masts of sailboats to pass, is the smallest drawbridge in the world.

house teaspoons and ceramic lamps. However, the T-shirts ($19 each) may be more apposite. You can wear "I Made it to the Top" emblazoned across your chest.

Gibb's Hill Lighthouse itself is open seven days a week from 9 AM to 4:30 PM year round. That said, it does close on Christmas and sometimes during January for maintenance. Kids younger than 5 can visit for free. A word about Christmas: The lighthouse reminds us that Christmas is coming by its windows, which are studded with colored lights in season.

Sandys Parish

Royal Naval Dockyard

Like St. George's, the entity of Dockyard is an attraction in itself. In our History chapter, you learned that its fortifications began in 1809 as compensation for British ports lost in the American Revolution. Bermudian slaves and convicts transported from Britain slowly and painfully created this naval base out of limestone, which they quarried out of land at the entrance. Until 1951 it was, according to Ed Harris, author of *Bermuda's Forts*, an "imperial fortress." It has also been described as "the Gibraltar of the West." For many Bermudians, though, it was known as "Little England" and the venue where local apprentices learned trades, such as masonry and building.

These days you'll see our tugs in dock, but the days of the British Navy have passed. Many of the limestone warehouses and buildings remain but have been imaginatively converted into pubs, restaurants, shops and museums. We recommend that you visit by ferry (See our Getting Here, Around and Home chapter) — that way you'll enjoy seeing Ber-

muda from the water as well as the many attractions on hand here.

The most important museum here is the Maritime Museum, where you'll see the relics of our maritime heritage. Check our Arts and Culture chapter for details on the Maritime Museum, and for information about the Arts Centre, where exhibitions and workshops are held. For other attractions and businesses in the Dockyard area, check our Restaurants, Nightlife, Kidstuff and Watersports chapters.

Bermuda Craft Market at Dockyard
The Cooperage, 4 Freeport Rd. • 234-3208

We mention the Craft Market in this chapter because whether you are in the shopping mood or not, it's fun to visit. Here you'll find many of our crafts experts at work — the majority of items on sale are locally handmade. You'll find seashell candles, stained-glass ornaments and lamps, quilts, handpainted fabric designs and miniature cedar furniture. If you're into collecting Christmas tree ornaments, you're bound to find something Bermudian to hang on your tree, whether it's a tiny traditional cottage or a polished shell decorated with ribbon. Want to sample our loquat and surinam cherry preserves? They're on sale here for $2 to $5.75 a pot. If you're interested in Bermuda-related books, an excellent range is available. Prices of gifts range from about $5 to $2,000. The Craft Market is open daily from 10 AM to 6 PM, April to November. During the winter it closes at 5 PM. It's also open for all special occasions and holidays, except Christmas and Good Friday.

Bermuda Train Company Ltd.
No. 6 Valley Rd. • 236-5972

This is a brand-new train service offering a 20-minute loop from the Clock Tower in the Royal Naval Dockyard to the Cruise Terminal,

INSIDERS' TIP
Pick up a Heritage Passport from any Visitors Service Bureau. This booklet gives you discounts on admission for some of our attractions, including the Bermuda Aquarium, Museum & Zoo and the Bermuda Underwater Exploration Institute.

with an additional five stops along its route. Built especially for Bermuda, the 60-foot, scaled-down train — a replica of a Baldwin Locomotive — seats 44 passengers in its airy coaches. The unique shuttle service is available from 8:30 AM to 5 PM daily for $1 per person. On Mondays, Wednesdays and Fridays, starting at 11 AM, you can also participate in a fascinating train tour featuring the scenic and interesting attractions in the area. The one-hour tour and ride is $5 per person.

The Snorkel Park at Dockyard
Freeport Rd. • 234-1006

Staff here definitely feel that they offer relaxation, rather than a watersport. They offer marked snorkel trails and floating rest stations where you can view the fish and corals of our ocean fauna. Bring your own equipment, and you pay $5 per person for up to a day's snorkeling. Rent equipment, and you'll pay $10 an hour or $17 for the whole day. Lifeguards are on hand, and they'll be happy to tell you whether you've seen a wrasse or a butterfly fish. See our Flora and Fauna and Watersports chapters for information about underwater life. Next door to the Maritime Museum, this park is open from 10:30 AM to 6 PM Mondays through Fridays. Saturdays and Sundays it is open from 11 AM to 5 PM. During winter (November 1 to March 31) it's closed. After all, the fish like a vacation from being on show.

The days and nights in Bermuda are filled with an assortment of delightful children's activities that can be both entertaining and educational.

Kidstuff

"When the first baby laughed for the very first time, the laugh broke into a thousand pieces and they all went skipping about and that was the beginning of fairies."
—Sir James M. Barrie, *Peter Pan*

Welcome to Never-Never Land.

Bermuda is a not-so-far-away island wonderland filled with the gleeful laughter of joyful youngsters having fun in the sun. All you have to do is look into the eyes of our children and the young at heart living in Bermuda to realize it's the true-to-life island of make-believe Peter Pan spoke of to Wendy. Here, boys and girls continue to accept that fairy tales can come true, and life is a bowl of cherries ripe for the picking. The days and nights in Bermuda are filled with an assortment of delightful children's activities that can be both entertaining and educational.

What you will not find on our island are carnival-type rides and Disney-esque pomp and circumstance. But what you will find, we believe, might make you wonder why you ever went for that stuff. We have traditional kid-type fun (aquariums, minigolf, skating and splashy water attractions) and some things that are a bit more unusual (helicopter rides, ginger beer and frolicking with dolphins). We also have so many beaches, we've devoted an entire chapter to them (see our Beaches chapter).

So what are you waiting for, kids? Come away to our fairyland in the sea! Take hold of Tinkerbell's hand, and let's begin an ABC adventure to learn about all the magical things to do while vacationing in Bermuda. Oh, it's OK. You can bring along the parents for the journey. After all, they deserve a fun-filled vacation too.

In fact, Mom and Dad, if you want to arrange for a little time alone for a romantic dinner and stroll along Front Street, there are certified babysitting services at most of the major hotels and resorts across the island.

For details on Bermuda's child-care services see our Education and Child Care chapter. Also, take a look at the listings at the end of this chapter under Kid-Friendly Resorts. To locate two other treasure chests loaded with more fun and entertaining activities for the youngsters, X marks the spots in our Recreation and Attractions chapters. Happy digging.

Fun from A to Z

•A is for . . .

the assortment of adventures you'll find at the **Bermuda Aquarium, Museum & Zoo**, 293-2727, centrally located in Flatts Village, where there are activities for youngsters and their parents. Why not spend a day at the aquarium, learning about the island's environment and marine life as you visit fascinating exhibits?

One of the newest is the North Rock Exhibit, home to some of the treasured sea creatures that live in the crystalline waters around the most isolated outcropping of the Bermuda archipelago. Or travel down under to the recently constructed Islands of Australasia exhibit, which features the wildlife of Australia, New Guinea, Borneo and Malaysia.

There's also the Discovery Room — an activity center for children and their adult companions to use together. A popular venue for visitors to BAMZ, this room features various animals themes. Hands-on activities, colorful posters and wall displays, children's books, live animal specimens and CDI units (for Compact Disc Interactive . . . similar to CD-ROM) are provided to assist children in learning and understanding more about the world of nature.

There are also a host of summer programs for children at BAMZ, including the Aqua Camps Program, designed for school children up to Primary 7 (equivalent to grade 6). The camps are held in July and August with a focus on the aquarium, museum and zoo facilities, the island in general and the environment. Camp sessions are for one week, and visitors who become members of the Friends of the Bermuda Aquarium may attend. Cost is $100, and camps run from 9 AM to 3 PM daily. Preschoolers may attend camp for a half-day for $50 per week.

The Nature Encounter Program at BAMZ is held most weekends from September through July, usually early Saturday mornings. Here, groups of excited children between ages 5 and 12 meet at the facility to encounter nature during two-hour activity sessions. Kids can learn how animals move in different ways, have fun sorting animals into groups or be the first to spy a whale during a whale-watching trip.

• B is for . . .

the bountiful knowledge you'll gain when you visit the **Bermuda Biological Station for Research**, 297-1880, in Ferry Reach, St. George's. The Biological Station sponsors Coral Camp in the summer for students ages 11 through 14. Each of the five days of camp is divided between field observation (on land and in the water) and laboratory work, involving the use of microscopes and the recording of findings. Camp members will also be able to snorkel every day. The cost is $180, and interested parties can pre-register in March.

The station also, in conjunction with Cable & Wireless Bermuda, offers the Jason Project, but this is mainly geared to Bermudian children. Coordinated by the Jason Foundation for Education, the project aims to excite and motivate children to pursue careers in science and technology by letting them share in the thrills of scientific exploration and discovery. Since 1989 the Jason Project has provided an opportunity for children, teachers and parents to visit the Mediterranean Sea, Lake Ontario, the Galapagos Islands, Belize (to study the tropical rain forest), coral reefs and two sites along Mexico's Baja California peninsula and the Sea of Cortez.

FYI

Unless otherwise noted, the area code for all phone numbers listed in this guide is 441.

• C is for . . .

the captivating activities planned for the newest venture for the kids of Bermuda — the **Bermuda Children's Museum**, which is to be located in the Maritime Museum at the Royal Navy Dockyard. Working toward a goal of opening in early 1998, the Bermuda Children's Museum Society consists of volunteer parents, grandparents and supporters with the primary vision of establishing an interactive play and learning museum for children ages 2 through 12. Call 234-1433 for more information on the new kids' paradise.

A glimpse of what is to come is currently provided in the Children's Room, 234-1418, an activity center inside the Maritime Museum. This fun room provides a hands-on environment for kids to explore. (However, children must be accompanied by an adult.) The center's theme, "On Land and Sea," features a dress-up area with a naval motif for younger children. There are boats, cannons, a chest filled with a fantastic array of costumes, computers, quizzes and games in a variety of interactive areas.

Admission to the Children's Room is included in the ticket price for entrance to the Maritime Museum. Adult single tickets are $7.50, seniors are $6, children younger than 15 are $3, and children younger than 5 are free. Two parents can enter the museum with up to five children for a total of $15, and one parent and up to five kids can enjoy the fun for $9.

• D is for . . .

Bermuda's newest stars — six bottle-nosed dolphins that engage in deliriously funny antics at **Dolphin Quest Bermuda** at the Southampton Princess Hotel, 239-6957, in Hamilton.

On a 3-acre site at East Whale Bay, various interactive programs are available for children 5 and older, whereby they actually get to pet and swim with the dolphins. Prices start at $20, and space is limited. Reservations are accepted up to four days in advance. You can obtain special Dolphin Quest-Southampton

Princess Hotel packages by calling (800) 223-1818 (see our Resort Hotels chapter for more on the Southampton Princess).

•E is for . . .

equestrian. Whether you've ridden a horse before or just want to give it a try, there are several stables on the island that provide lessons, trail rides or just a trot around the riding pen for horse lovers.

Ask about the various stables at the social desk at your hotel. A local favorite, **Spiceland Riding Centre**, Middle Road, Warwick, 238-8212, offers trails rides for children 10 and older for $37.50 per hour. Pony rides are given all day on Saturday by appointment for children of any age. A 15-minute ride is $10. If you're staying on the East End of the island, try **Inwood Stables**, Radnor Road, Hamilton Parish, 293-4964. Inwood provides trail rides for children 5 and older for $35 per hour. Riding lessons and pony rides are $27 per half-hour. Note that appointments for pony rides must be scheduled 24 hours in advance.

More serious riders can contact the **Bermuda Equestrian Federation**, 295-4434. They'll be more than happy to acquaint you with the scheduled riding events that take place throughout the year. For more details on riding options, see our Recreations chapter.

•F is for . . .

the fun the kids are certain to have romping around in Bermuda's favorite family entertainment center — **Belly Busters**, 296-3333, a fantastic fun center conveniently located on Front Street in Hamilton.

This climate-controlled fun zone is a great get-out-of-the-heat place for kids to play and parents to relax. There are 8,000 square feet, making for a huge, imaginative play environment with a two-level climbing frame, a large variety of rides and games of fun and skill.

There is also a separate toddlers' area and private Birthday Room. Belly Busters' activities are especially geared to fit the developmental stages of kids from infants up to preteens, and all areas are handicapped-accessible.

Admission is $3.50 for children older than 2, free for those younger. Adults are free if accompanied by kids. Friday night is family night, with two children admitted for the price of one from 5 to 9 PM. Birthday parties are a neat option at Belly Busters. They run $12.50 per child on weekdays and $14.50 per child on weekends, and they include use of the entire facility, a party hostess, invitations, party hats, balloons, popcorn and punch. Parties accommodate eight to 26 children.

•G is for . . .

the gleaming beauty of the Gombey costume, explained at the **Gumba Trail and Outdoor Museum**, 293-7330, in the Royal Naval Dockyard in Sandys Parish. Due to the extremely hot climate of the later summer months, this seasonal walking exhibit runs every Wednesday from April through July — special tours may be arranged. Led by the Gumba (the tour leader), learn all about the traditions and culture of Bermuda with a focus on the customs, history and natural elements of our island. Hear the fascinating story of the tribal contributions of Pocahontas and the American Indians to Bermuda. Walking tours are held on Wednesdays from April through July at 11 AM and 12:30 PM. The hour-long walks are $5 per person and are cancelled on rainy days.

G can also be for golf, of the miniature variety. Visit **Golf Academy Driving Range** and **Adventure Mini-Golf Center**, 238-8800, on Industrial Park Road, Middle Road, Southampton. The 18-hole minigolf course is wonderful for kids, providing great entertainment and challenging play for the whole fam-

INSIDERS' TIP

Be careful of the undertow when swimming in the ocean. Lifeguards are on duty at several of the larger beach areas, and if you search diligently, you'll find coves that are ideal for the tiny tots.

ily. Adult admission is $7 per pre-sunset round, $8 once the sun goes down. Children younger than 10 (who must be supervised) and seniors are $6 per round. (See our Golf chapter for more information.)

•H is for . . .

one heckuva fun way for children ages 5 and older to get up close and personal with the bounty of Bermuda's sea life. It's called helmet diving. Before you enter the water on a long ladder at a fish-friendly location, an operator will place a helmet over your head until it reaches your shoulders. Take a deep breath and you'll discover that, yes, breathing is possible. The helmet is filled with air. Next, you'll descend the ladder until you reach the sea floor, about 10 feet under. (For more details, see our Watersports chapter.)

Try not to get too excited and jump up and down. That's rude to the fish. The two centers that offer helmet diving service are **Bermuda Bell Diving**, North Shore Road, Flatts, 292-4434, and **Greg Hartley's Undersea Adventure**, 1 Mangrove Bay Road, 234-2861. At the former location helmet diving costs $44 for adults and $33 for kids 12 and younger; at the latter it's $48 for adults and $36 for kids.

•I is for . . .

"I scream for ice cream" on a hot day spent in-line skating. An ice cream cone or sundae makes a yummy treat, especially if you've eaten all your vegetables at dinner. From the East End to the West End, Bermuda boasts some pretty tasty homemade ice cream, yogurts, sherbets and sorbets in many exotic flavors.

Many of our ice cream shops and parlors provide just the kind of retreat you need to make the perfect ending to a beautiful day. Some that Insiders frequent include **Bailey's Ice Cream Parlour**, Blue Hole Hill, Hamilton Parish, 293-8605. Bailey's becomes a household word when the temperatures get hot in Bermuda. It's certain to become one of your favorite spots, with its 20 flavors of homemade,

all-natural ice creams, sherbets, low-fat yogurts and fat-free sorbets. At **Double Dip Ice Cream Shop**, 119 Front Street, Hamilton, 292-3503, and **Double Dip Too**, 12 North Shore Road, Hamilton Parish, 292-5580, you're certain to find a tasty flavor made just to your liking. Be warmed you may have to stand to line with all the other ice cream lovers on the island. Visiting the West End? Stop by **Nannini Häagen-Dazs** for a refreshing sorbet or ice cream cone. They're at the Clock Tower, Dockyard, Sandys Parish, 234-2474.

Of course, I means in-line skating to lots of kids. If you would like additional information about in-line skating in Bermuda contact Allan Barker at the **Bermuda Inline Skating Association**, 295-8888. Also, see our Recreations chapter for more details on inline skating.

•J is for . . .

jammin' to the festive sounds at any one of Bermuda's many and varied outdoor concerts. Soca, reggae, rhythm and blues, classical, Big Band, pop and rock: You name it, we've got it. Bring a picnic and a blanket or chairs to enjoy live entertainment at Victoria Park, Bermuda Stadium, the No. One Shed, St. George's Square, Front Street or the Dockyard. Where there's plenty of space and good music, you're bound to have a good time. The Concert in the Park series at Victoria Park runs from April through September, with a different performer featured each month. (For more information, see our Annual Events and Festivals chapter.)

•K is for . . .

kids — the focus of **Kidfest**, Bermuda's only live theatrical production specifically designed for both parents and children. Having completed its fourth season in 1997, Kidfest is held in January and February, with three to four acts each season. Talented performers from across Canada and the United States bring to the island an array of delightful shows that are entertaining as well as educational. These magical performances are held at City Hall Theatre in

A family builds an elaborate sandcastle.

Hamilton. Shows are held on weekend nights, with tickets priced at $15. For more information, write the folks at Kidfest at P.O. Box DV 433, Devonshire, or call 236-1085.

• L is for . . .

leisurely laying back on the beach, reading a book borrowed from the **Bermuda Youth Library** and soaking up the rays as you listen to the surf and check out the longtails in flight.

Before visiting Bermuda, call to set the process in motion for obtaining a visitor's membership from the Bermuda Youth Library. The cost is $25 for the entire family. Each child will receive a borrower's card, and the $25 is refundable upon departure. To receive a card once you're in Bermuda, present your passport or other means of identification with your return airline ticket or ship pass. There is no limit to the number of books you may borrow. Contact the Youth Library, 74 Church Street, Hamilton, at 295-0487.

• M is for . . .

the merriment you'll experience when visiting the **Bermuda Maritime Museum**, 234-1218, at the Royal Naval Dockyard. Opened by Her Majesty the Queen in 1975, this complex, fortified keep is, at 6 acres, also Bermuda's largest fort. Visitors enter the museum over a wet moat by way of a drawbridge. The buildings, which were at one time filled with weapons and ammunition, are excellent displays of Bermuda's rich maritime history. There are intriguing exhibits of shipwreck archeology, including Spanish artifacts retrieved from our reefs and a fine collection of Bermuda boats in the Boat Loft.

The restored 1856 Dockyard Clock is on working display, and there are various new exhibits including the "Age of Discovery," celebrating the 500th anniversary of Columbus' discovery of the New World, and the Bermuda Monetary Authority Exhibit, which traces the history of Bermuda's currency from 1612. Plan to spend an entire day to see all the exhibits. The museum is open daily from 10 AM to 4 PM. Adult admission is $7.50, seniors are $6, children younger than 15 are $3, and kids younger than 5 are free. Two parents with up to five children are admitted for a total cost of $15, and one parent and up to five kids can all have fun for $9. With these group rates, additional family members cost $6 each.

• N is for . . .

no such thing as nothing to do in Bermuda. The Bermuda National Trust maintains the authentic properties of Bermuda. This includes homes, museums, nature reserves, a replica of the *Deliverance* in St. George's Square and several gift shops. No trip would be complete without a visit to the Globe Hotel the **Bermuda National Trust Museum** at the Globe Hotel, King's Square, St. George's, 297-1423. Open Monday through Saturday from 10 AM to 4 PM, the Globe Hotel was the office for the Confederate agent in Bermuda during the American Civil War. One of the newest exhibits "Rogues & Runners — Bermuda and the American Civil War" is filled with historical information. The video *Bermuda: Centre of the Atlantic* uses rare paintings and documents to tell the story of Bermuda and the forces that shaped her history.

Verdmont, located at Collector's Hill, Smiths Parish, 236-7369, is the most significant of the Trust's houses, showcases captivating period-planted gardens with impressive scenic ocean views. The 18th-century mansion house is most notable for the antique Bermuda cedar wood furniture and other period furnishing.

Admission is $3 per person for Verdmont and Tucker House and $4 for the Bermuda National Trust Museum at the Globe House. Combination tickets to all three are $5 for adults and $2 for students with ID. For additional details on various other properties, contact the Bermuda National Trust Headquarters at Waterville, an 18th-century house in Paget, between 9 AM and 5 PM Monday to Friday. The number is 236-8306.

• O is for . . .

the Onion Patches game card you can complete to receive a prize from the Bermuda National Trust. The game is a delightful treasure hunt to see if you can discover some of Bermuda's most cherished treasures involving our environmental and historic heritage. You can pick up your free kit, which contains the game board and some stickers, at Bermuda National Trust Headquarters at Waterville in Paget. Every time you spot one of the treasures, put a sticker in the matching box, writing when and where you saw it. Some of the locales are in attractions such as Verdmont, and when you take the Onion Patches game card, a child and adult are admitted free.

When you have completed filling in all the spaces on the card, take it to Trust headquarters at Waterville on Pomander Road in Paget, where they will make you a student member of the Bermuda National Trust, which is effective until age 16. You will also receive a small prize.

• P is for . . .

the plentiful, picturesque photographs or paintings you can create from the many scenic views you'll find while traveling about the island. No two scenes are alike, and you're certain to have your creativity stirred to conjure up some original artwork.

To take a look at the works of others, visit the **Bermuda National Gallery**, City Hall and Arts Centre, Church Street, hamilton, 295-9428; the **Bermuda Arts Society**, Bermuda Society and Arts Gallery City Hall, Hamilton, 292-3824; the **Masterworks Foundation**, 97 Front Street, Bermuda House Lane, HM12, 295-5580; **Windjammer Art Gallery**, 95 Front Street, Hamilton, 292-5878, and corner of Reid and King streets, Hamilton, 292-7861; and the **Bermuda Arts Centre**, Dockyard, 234-1801. To see Bermuda artists and touring exhibits from international countries, there are a host of private galleries throughout the island. (See our Arts and Culture chapter for details.)

• Q is for . . .

quenching the thirst you're sure to acquire, as summer temperatures soar as high as 95 degrees in the shade. Why not try one of our local favorites — **ginger beer**?

INSIDERS' TIP

The "exercise book kite," a pear-shaped kite made of brown paper textbook covers or brown paper bags and twigs of cane grass was an old-time favorite of Bermuda school children as far back as the early 1930s.

Kites Make For An Especially Good Friday

Oh, go fly a kite!

On Good Friday, everyone in Bermuda seems to be doing just that. All eyes are focused on the balmy, clear blue skies, and the entire island shuts down for a day devoted to festive gaiety. There's kite-flying, shooting allies (a game of marbles) and plenty of plain good eating, with lots of hot cross buns and codfish cakes.

Good Friday, or Kite Day, is one of the great traditions of Bermuda and has been celebrated in this unusual way for more than a century. However, if you ask any of our senior citizens how it all got started, you'll hear a different oral account from virtually every one you question.

Many stories relating to kite-flying on Good Friday have religious significance. One story tells how a Sunday school teacher, trying to explain the ascension of Christ to her students, illustrated the story by flying a kite on Easter Sunday. When the kite went soaring into the heavens she cut the string, and the kite rose higher until it disappeared into the blue.

Although the exact origin is unknown, kite-flying is believed to have started in the Orient or Greece thousands of years ago. Kites have been used in the practice of religion, science and, of course, children's games throughout the course of history. It was just a matter of time before kites made it to Bermuda, but little was written on the topic before the 1940s. The sport of kite-flying did not really take off here (pun intended) until after World War II. Perhaps it was the lack of television in the '50s that caused just about everyone on the island to become involved in the Good Friday ritual, either as a spectator or participant. And now the sport is on the rise again with just as many "birdie kites" filling the skies as those crafted by the numerous talented kite builders on the island.

— continued on next page

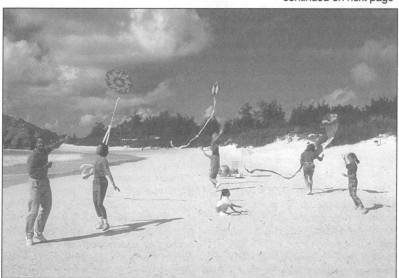

Photo: GIS

Flying kites has been a Good Friday tradition in Bermuda for decades.

Kite-flying is enjoyed by entire families, and there are many Bermudian households that produce kites for retail sale as well as personal pleasure. The original Bermuda Boxy Kite is one of the first kites many Bermudian children have the opportunity to make. Constructed from dead, dry fennel sticks, brown paper bags or (nowadays) plastic trash bags, it is simple to make — the connecting strings of the kite are generally just pushed through holes in the paper covering the kite sticks.

Kite Day is not just an occasion to view some of the colorful and vivid displays of kite mastery. You can also hear the various sounds produced by the kites' "hummers." One kite famous for this is the Somerset Kite, or the Buzzer, which makes the loudest high-pitched humming sound of any of the kite designs on the island. Another of our favorite kite designs is the Three-headed Roundie, known for its splendid patterns, shape and many hummers. It is definitely a beautiful sight to behold soaring against azure blue skies.

For Kite Day, most Bermudians tote their carefully crafted, cherished kites to Horseshoe Bay Beach in Southampton for the annual Bermuda Kite Festival. Thousands gather for a festive outing that begins with an early morning church and song service, followed by a kite competition, organized games and entertainment and a performance by the Gombeys. Started some 13 years ago, this popular Good Friday beach party brings together families, friends and visitors to cheer on the pitching of some pretty fantastic kites. Prizes are given for kites ranging from a maximum of 6 feet wide to the smallest kite at the minimum of 4 inches.

And the kite-flying can bring on a pretty hearty appetite. Between all the events, festival patrons enjoy fresh-baked, moist hot cross buns and fish cakes fried to golden-brown perfection. It's a delectable, tasty treat that has become a big part of Good Friday.

So the next time you come across a sole kite flyer on a windy spring day in your neighborhood park, stop and say hello. It just might be a Bermudian homesick for Good Friday.

This refreshing, nonalcoholic soft drink with a kick is actually made from ginger root concentrate. It's made by John Barrit and Sons, Ltd., 236-7171, and Metro Mineral Water in Devonshire, 236-6396, and it is available anywhere on the island where sodas are sold (including many vending machines). Counting calories? It's also available without sugar and goes great with most tasty local cuisine.

•R is for . . .

the rainbow after a warm summer rain. When you see one stretching across the sky in a multicolored ribbon arch, make a wish. Your pot of gold may be just at the rainbow's end.

After the rain, take the kids for a hike along **Bermuda's Railway Trail**. The trail follows the old railway line between Somerset and St.

George's, not including the 3-mile section that provided the basis for the major roads in and around the City of Hamilton. Anyone able is welcome to walk, run, hike or bike the trail — just pick it up and follow the signs. (For more on the Railway Trail, see our Attractions and Recreation chapters.)

•S if for . . .

snorkeling. See extraordinarily beautiful views of subtropical marine life in the calm, sheltered coves and inlets surrounding Bermuda. **Tobacco Bay** in St. George's Parish is a popular spot to snorkel for locals and visitors, offering a good look at lively tiger fish, parrotfish and an assortment of coral. At **Tobacco Bay Beach Pavilion**, 1 Coot Pond Road, St. George's, 297-2756, the nice staff will fit you with fins, mask and snorkel for $2.50 per half-hour.

• T is for . . .

the terrific tennis you'll play in the Bermuda. A favorite sport for Insiders, tennis courts are located across the island, with most of the major resorts and cottage colonies having their own private courts. Often, lessons are available for guests, including children who are 10 or older, at these properties. The **Bermuda Lawn Tennis Association**, 296-0834, offers tennis leagues, coaching, national team selection and more. More to our purposes, they provide great action for kids and families. The **Bermuda Tennis Foundation**, 296-2554, also contributes to the sponsorship of the game on the island and has programs for youngsters 10 and older.

• U is for . . .

uncovering fascinating new facts about the mysteries under the sea surrounding us at the new **Bermuda Underwater Exploration Institute**, East Broadway at the foot of the lane, Hamilton, 292-7219. (See Attractions) Check out an underwater wonderland where history and science meet state-of-the-art technology. At the Institute, you can explore the ocean depths, see shipwrecked treasures and weird creatures and even learn about marine environments at the same time.

• V is for . . .

viewing all there is to see from the **Gibb's Hill Lighthouse**, Lighthouse Road between South Shore and Middle roads, Southampton, 238-0524. Opened May 1, 1846, you can climb the 185 steps to one of the most spectacular views available of the entire island. And yes, the lighthouse is still in operation. Admission is $2.50, with children younger than 5 admitted free. (See our Attractions chapter for more information.)

• W is for . . .

walking — a favorite pastime of just about everyone who lives in or visits Bermuda. Join in **Nature Walks**, free outdoor excursions centered on specific nature themes, sponsored by the Department of Agriculture, Fisheries and Parks. Also, during spring break in February, the **Bermuda National Trust**, 236-6483, has a children's walk at the Spittle Pond Nature Reserve and a Palm Sunday walk. Mostly uphill, the Palm Sunday walk is recommended for children 8 years and older. (See our Recreations chapter for additional information about walking and our Flora, Fauna and Climate chapter for more on what you'll see.)

• X is for . . .

the Roman numeral 10. As in 10 extra ideas to consider while you're in Bermuda.

Don't forget to visit the underground crystal caves. See translucent formations of stalagmites at **Crystal Caves**, Wilkenson Avenue, Hamilton Parish, 293-0640. They're open every day from 9 AM to 4:40 PM (closed for lunch from 1 to 1:30 PM). Learn how glass is made at the **Bermuda Glass Blowing Factory**, 16 Blue Hole Hill, Hamilton Parish, 293-2234. Romp and play at the **Botanical Gardens** in Paget. Then pretend to set sail on Ordnance Island, across the bridge from St. George's Square, aboard the **Deliverance II**, a full-scale replica of the Bermuda-built pinnace that carried the survivors of the shipwrecked company of the Sea Venture, which washed ashore in Bermuda in 1609.

Then catch your breath and trek through **Fort St. Catherine** in St. George's. Peer at the fascinating fish and coral life in a glass-bottomed boat. Be awed by the **Bermuda Gombey Revue,** check out the **Historic Re-Enactment Ceremony** in St. George's Town Square and march to the "Beat of the Retreat" by the **Bermuda Regiment Band**.

INSIDERS' TIP

Entrance to the Bermuda National Gallery at City Hall in Hamilton is free for families on Saturdays, when the gallery is open from 10 AM to 4 PM. Don't forget to ask about the Treasure Hunt for Animals in Art.

Lastly, Christmas is a wonderful time to vacation in Bermuda. Join us for a festive **Yuletide party** in the historic homes of St. George's. The Bermuda National Trust sponsors this popular event. (You'll find additional information on other things to do in our Attractions and Festivals and Annual Events chapters.)

• Y is for . . .

the youth in you. The Bermuda Government's Ministry of Youth, Development, Sport and Recreation, 295-6292, annually produces a *Leisure Time Activities* handbook. Free to the public, this handy reference guide disappears quickly. It lists various performing arts, music and sports programs and is full of stuff to keep the kids occupied, including lists of summer camps. Be sure to get your copy no later than the beginning of March.

• Z is for . . .

zipping through the waves on a Jet Ski. This is fast becoming a popular watersport, but we advise extreme caution when kids are aboard — in fact, they have to be at least 12 to ride. To climb aboard a personal watercraft, contact **Wet and Wild**, Dockyard, 234-2426.

And Z is also for the z's the kids are going to be sounding out when at last they're fast asleep, plumb tuckered out from so much fun in the sun.

Kid-Friendly Resorts

Although many couples come to Bermuda to escape the patter of little feet and blaring sounds of video games, some of our leading resorts offer specially organized programs if you do decide to bring the kiddies along to our island paradise.

Most resorts and hotels offer special rates or plans to accommodate visitors with children. Many allow up to two children 16 years of age to stay free in the same room as their parents and to enjoy the same meal plan as their parents. The time of year when the kid-oriented plans are offered may vary. When planning your vacation, check with your travel agent on possibilities for accommodating the young ones. Here, we offer information on three of Bermuda's more kid-friendly resorts. Note that extensive information on each of these properties is at your disposal in the Resort Hotels chapter.

Sonesta Beach Hotel and Spa
5 South Rd. and Sonesta Dr. • 238-8122

So, you've brought along the novel you've been trying to read all year and booked a game of golf for later in the day. Don't worry.

Sonesta Beach Resort knows just what kids enjoy. The Just Us Kids program, from mid-June through the beginning of September for kids from ages 5 through 12, offers supervised activities in the morning or throughout the day.

Day excursions around the island are planned, with only a small fee charged to cover transportation and entrance fees. Lunch can be arranged and charged to the parents' room. Kids' breakfasts and dinners are free for guests that have bought a meal plan. Children's menus are convenient in all restaurants.

For smaller tots there is the Just Us Little Kids program on Monday, Wednesday and Friday from 1 to 4 PM. Activities for toddlers focus on arts and crafts, games, movies and "Computertots," a computer familiarization program for the tiny ones. Participating children must be potty trained.

Considering visiting during the Easter holiday? Sonesta Beach has an Easter Weekend program the kids won't soon forget. The Thursday before Good Friday there is a kite-making demonstration, and on Good Friday, kids will actually join in the tradition of kite-flying in Bermuda. There are kites for all children, and refreshments are served. On Saturday morning,

---

INSIDERS' TIP

Kite-flying is not allowed around the vicinity of the airport. This includes Kindley Field Park, Clearwater Beach, areas of the former base lands and the area along Ferry Reach. Kites can be a safety hazard to aircraft taking off or landing.

children are invited to gather on the Palm Court to decorate Easter eggs. Afterwards, prizes will be given out. Later that day, there's fun in the sun at the Boat Bay Beach, with activities including a sand sculpture contest. On Easter Sunday, the legendary Easter Bunny leads the children on an egg hunt. It's a wonderful time for everyone.

Southampton Princess
101 South Rd. • 238-8000

Camp Minor Manor at the Southampton Princess is geared specifically for children ages 5 through 16. Running from mid-June until the first of September, the activity program features Lenny's Loft game room from 8:30 to 11 AM, where children can participate in board or video games and play the jukebox or ping-pong. Children ages 2 to 4 may play in Lenny's Loft on Monday, Wednesday and Saturday from 9 AM to 2 PM. Infant and toddler sitting service is available at the resort at standard rates.

There is no charge for daytime activities (except lunch) conducted on premises. However, excursions away from the hotel require lunch and transportation fees. Should you need to have an escorted dinner for your children, this service is available at an extra charge in on-site restaurants only.

Additional on-property activities at the Southampton Princess include pool sports and beach fun and games; a special "Mocktail Hour" from 4 to 5 PM, with pizza, popcorn and soft drinks; sandcastle building, volleyball, badminton, tennis, table tennis and arts and crafts; movies on Tuesday and Friday evening, karaoke on Thursday, a teen mixer, a scavenger hunt and daily children's videos.

Grotto Bay Beach Hotel and Tennis Club
11 Blue Hole Hill • 293-8333, (800) 582-3190

The little ones will feel right at home when participating in Grotto Bay's summer children's program. Supervised by caring, qualified counselors, the Tree Frog Bunch is structured to help children enjoy Bermudian experiences.

For a minimal fee, children ages 4 and older can enjoy board games, swimming activities, treasure hunts, storytelling, beach fun, movie time, day excursions, fish feeding and more. Day activities are scheduled Monday through Saturday, starting at 9:45 AM and closing anywhere from 1:30 to 10 PM depending on the activities planned.

This children's program is not intended to be a babysitting service, although babysitting can be arranged through the resort's guest services desk for a fee. Rates range from $10.50 per hour for one child up to $13.50 per hour for four children. Add an additional 50¢ per hour for service provided after midnight.

PLATINUM PRINTS

For more than a century, collectors, museums and master photographers alike have valued one form of photographic print above all others. Just as platinum is the most coveted of precious metals, platinum prints are the ultimate expression of a photographer's art.

A BERMUDIAN OF RARE TALENT

Bermuda's own J. A. Mark Emmerson is one of only a handful of artists in the world who can currently claim mastery of this delicate art. Emmerson considers platinum printing, which he first learned in 1980, the ultimate expression of his life's work as a photographer. "I love the presence – the look of platinum prints," says Emmerson. "Their

archival quality is very important to me, but further than this, it is wonderfully satisfying to mix the chemicals, brush them on the chosen paper, and expose them, along with the negative, to the sun." Emmerson calls it "painting with light," and this painterly quality is one of the things that make platinum prints unique. Because of the hand-brushed emulsions and the other intricacies of the process, no two platinum prints are ever precisely the same.

THE INTRICACY OF PRINTING WITH PLATINUM

It often takes Emmerson an entire day to produce a single platinum print. He begins by hand mixing platinum compounds and light-sensitive solutions. The mixture is brushed onto art paper specially selected for its archival stability, as well as its colour, surface and sizing, and exposed, with the negative, to the sun. The exposed paper is then placed in a

developing solution, followed by a series of cleaning baths. The final result is an image of pure platinum, exquisite in depth and detail.

A RARE OPPORTUNITY

Because of the painstaking nature of the platinum printing process, and the excruciating selectivity Emmerson uses in choosing negatives appropriate for the platinum "look", there will never be huge numbers of his platinum prints flooding the market. This factor, along with the prints' artistry and archival stability, make them unusually sound investments.

Emmerson's platinum prints range in size from approximately 5" x 7" to 11" x 14". Subjects extend from plant studies to landscapes, as well as platinum prints of Bermuda scenes from the 1800's made from the original negatives in Mark's private collection.

For private appointment to view call (441)-292-6283/441-295-2626.

"In all photography there is nothing more beautiful, or more everlastingly permanent, or more completely satisfying to the cultivated eye, than the platinum print." The Photo-Miniature, May 1911

Arts and Culture

At first glance it might appear the art world here is so small that the entire picture could be set in a modest frame. But four of our artists have established reputations outside Bermuda, and their push for excellence and recognition serves as an inspiration to our other dancers, musicians and painters. Almost quietly, several of them are carving local niches as a springboard for jumping "the pond" — local vernacular for the surrounding ocean.

The rivalry within the Bermuda art community is strong, creating both an upside and downside. Competition is keen, but, says one dance school head, the student community is often deprived the kind of exchange that allows them to learn from each other. Art galleries and studios are generally owned and run by artists who use them to promote their own works.

Often the gallery or studio is a room or two in the artist's home. Each year most arts organizations have a major exhibition or performance, allowing established and new talent to showcase their creativity.

In this chapter we have organized local art and artists under the following categories: Music and Dance, Theater, Arts Centers and Museums, Galleries and Studios, Literary Arts and Arts Organizations. We'll bring you up to date with recent performances or exhibitions. It must be noted that several theater groups and organizations do not have a formal location, and telephone numbers may very often be a home or office number for a contact person. There may be some difficulty in getting through to someone who may be able to immediately provide information. But don't despair.

We suggest three places to call or check for current information related to events, exhibitions, plays and so forth. These are the Visitors Service Bureau, with offices in Hamilton (295-1480), St. George's (297-1642), Dockyard (234-3824) and Bermuda International Airport (293-0736); the hospitality desk or management staff at your hotel, cottage or apartment facility; and the *Royal Gazette*'s Bermuda Calendar, a listing of events, exhibitions, theatre productions and related happenings. Every Tuesday the calendar for the following week is published in the newspaper's Community section; on other days the information is broken down into a Today/Tomorrow format and published in the Today section.

Music and Dance

Bermuda Conservatory of Music
Colony Club, Trott Rd., Hamilton
• 296-5100

Formed by the 1997 merger of two leading music schools, the Bermuda Conservatory of Music is now the largest such school on the island. The union has brought together a 12-member faculty that offers instruction in piano and violin, with a few students studying organ, viola and guitar. Accredited by the Associated Board of the Royal School of Music of London, and the Royal Conservatory of Music of Toronto, the school offers its students access to further development in either the United Kingdom or North America.

Several programs are offered, with one directed at students as young as 9 months through a Mommy and Me program that owes much to the Suzuki method of immersion. This approach, developed by Japanese music educator Suzuki Shin'ichi, is based on his observations of young children's natural acquisition of language skills. Early musical training, without using written music, encourages parental participation. This approach has achieved tremendous popularity and success and has been adopted in many locales worldwide.

The school's Kindermusik program for ages 4 to 8 allows group experience to branch into individual preferences, as youngsters develop a leaning toward a favored instrument. However, the 800-strong student body is composed not only of youngsters, but also adults, a few of whom are at the so-called retirement age.

Bermuda Philharmonic Society
• 238-1108

This choral society and orchestra puts on four or more concerts each year, a couple of them open air shows and exchange concerts. New members are always welcomed. The contact person is Sue Blakely.

Gilbert and Sullivan Society
• 236-6872, 295-3218

Devoted to performing the works of Sir W.S. Gilbert and Sir Arthur Sullivan, those masters of the political and social satire, the society actually started life in 1972 as the Warwick Players before the name was changed. Sixty devotees comprise the current membership. Although Sullivan is perhaps best known for such works as *Onward Christian Soldiers* and *The Lost Chord*, Gilbert's lyrics were less religious or conservative, taking clever potshots at the legal system, the naval hierarchy, class warfare and general snobbery.

During the past 26 years G&S have performed a variety of musical shows, including the production of five Heritage concerts under the baton of local conductor Marjorie Pettit. Two of the musicals — *The Mikado* in 1992 and *A Little Night Music* in 1997 — were performed at the Bermuda Festival (see our Annual Events and Festivals chapter). In 1997, *Little Shop of Horrors*, originally an off-Broadway production set in an early 1960s New York

florist shop, was performed at the City Hall. In the 1998 Bermuda Festival, the society's choral program was enriched by operatic highlights from Saint-Saens and Verdi, and classical excerpts from Beethoven and Bach. Contact persons are Marjorie Stanton and Susan Bailey.

In Motion School of Dance
Chancery Ln., Hamilton • 292-7615

The Bermudian dance community received its most recent boost with the 1997 opening of In Motion School of Dance. The emphasis at In Motion is on providing a nurturing environment for young dancers to realize the fullest expression of their level of skill through both theory and practice. There is also a focus on guiding advanced students in understanding the business demands of actual production, from choreography to administration.

Elizabeth Pimental, the owner and director, is a member of the National Dance Company, has performed in the Premier's Concert, studied with the Alvin Ailey Dance Company and worked as a choreographer for the Miami Junior Orange Bowl. Contact her for further information.

Jackson School of Performing Arts
Arcade Bldg., Burnaby St., Hamilton
• 292-5815, 292-2927

Originally founded by Louise Jackson as a school of dance in 1953, Jackson School expanded in 1978 to include instruction in instruments, voice, gymnastics and theater. Student enrollment has grown from an inaugural 40 to more than 1,000. The gymnastics program, run as an after-school activity at several local schools, coaches kids from preschool age on up through higher grades, eventually leading to competitive levels.

The dance department, the backbone of the school, instructs in most disciplines, from ballet to modern dance, jazz and tap. Master classes tutored by guest teachers bring exposure to visiting professional dance companies. With an impressive list of performances, the school's students have strutted their stuff at the Columbus Celebration in New York with

FYI

Unless otherwise noted, the area code for all phone numbers listed in this guide is 441.

the National Dance Theatre of Bermuda, and in 1994 they danced before Queen Elizabeth and the Duke of Edinburgh during a royal visit.

Menuhin Foundation
• 295-2510

Founded in 1975 through the inspiration of virtuoso Lord Yehudi Menuhin — the American-born violinist who moved to London in 1959, was knighted in 1965 and became a British subject in 1985 — the Menuhin Foundation is a charity funded by private and corporate patrons and the Ministry of Community Affairs.

Following initial funding in 1976, the Heller, Barbican, Guild and New London quartets of young teachers visited Bermuda to perform and teach, inspiring through their talent and enthusiasm for music. As noted by Lord Menuhin, a quartet is the requisite nucleus of a performing string ensemble and provides the ideal teaching unit for imparting the art of string playing. With this as a guiding principle, he auditioned the London-based Heller Quartet before sending them to the Menuhin Foundation in Bermuda as its first teaching quartet.

Through the years since, the Menuhin Foundation Youth Orchestra (open to any string instrumentalist on the island between ages 12 and 21 at grade 4 and above) has performed at the Bermuda Festival. The foundation's teachers, as a quartet, caressed the strings at a private dinner held for Queen Elizabeth and Prince Philip at Government House, the governor's official residence. Notably, all teachers play in the Bermuda Philharmonic Orchestra.

Each January the foundation's annual student concert at the Anglican Cathedral features more than 250 participants. Frequent workshops involving the Youth Orchestra are organized by the foundation, one of the latest given by the English Chamber Orchestra. A desire to spread a love of string music to Bermuda's school children takes the foundation to most island primary schools, where free instruction in violin, viola and cello is delivered.

For additional information, contact Alison Johnstone at the number listed or write foundation Chairman John D. Campbell, Appleby, Spurling & Kemp, P.O. Box HM 1179, Hamilton.

National Dance Theatre of Bermuda
P.O. Box 1759, Hamilton HMHX • No phone

Leaping out of the hinterland in 1980, the National Dance Theatre of Bermuda (NDTB) has enjoyed success in Bermuda and abroad, most notably at the Quincentennial Celebrations in New York in 1992, the Carifesta in Trinidad that same year and the opening of the Gala Showcase of the International Association for Blacks in Dance Conference in Philadelphia in 1996, its second appearance at that event. The NDTB has built a nucleus of dancers trained in ballet, modern and jazz disciplines and now has a repertoire of more than 50 works. In 1997 it performed its first full-length classical ballet, *The Nutcracker,* with guest artists Elizabeth Dunn and Lorin Johnson, former members of the American Ballet Theater.

Theater

Bermuda Musical and Dramatic Society
Daylesford Theatre, 11 Washington St., Hamilton • 292-0848

Formed in 1944, this active theater society stages several major productions throughout the year. Very often it puts on workshops related to both acting and the technical aspects of theater. While most productions are held in its Daylesford Theatre, larger productions such as its Christmas pantomime are staged at the City Hall theater in Hamilton.

Theatre Express
• 236-3370

This professional repertory company performs between March and November at the St. George's Club in the Town of St. George, and at the Windsor Room in Marriott's Castle Harbour Hotel (see our Resort Hotels chapter). Performances are also staged at private clubs, and the company is available for conventions. For more information, contact Barbara Hooper at the number listed.

Arts Centers and Museums

St. George's Parish

St. George's Historical Society Museum
Duke of Kent St. • 297-0423

Collections of antiques, china, paintings, papers and documents related to Bermuda's history and development (and particularly that of St. George's) can be found in this storehouse of information.

Tucker House
Water St., Town of St. George • 297-0545

This 18th-century home, built around 1712, became the Tucker home in 1775, when Henry Tucker purchased it. For years the house, a legacy to generations of descendents, was at the center of 18th- and 19th-century political and social life. Of the family members who became notable abroad, one became a judge in Williamsburg, Virginia, and another a United States treasurer.

Tucker House, like Verdmont Museum (see subsequent listing), is run by the Bermuda National Trust. Architecturally, it is a good example of Bermuda's acquaintance with Colonial style. It is restored as faithfully as possible to the vanished era its furniture, china and silverware represent.

Displays include a tribute to Joseph Hayne Rainey, who fled to Bermuda with his wife, Susan, shortly after the outbreak of the American Civil War. He became a barber, operating out of Tucker House, and went on less than a decade later to be the first black man to be seated in the House of Representatives. A superb collection of 18th-century portraits and silver and an archaeological exhibit showcasing the findings from an extensive three-year basement excavation are also displayed. Together, they open windows to an intriguing time. The house is open Monday through Saturday from 10 AM to 4 PM. Admission is $3.

Smiths Parish

Verdmont Museum
Collectors Hill • 236-7369

Supposedly, many people have encountered a ghost in this 18th-century home. It is believed to have belonged to Capt. William Sayle, the leader of a band of Bermudian Puritans who fled to Eleuthera in the Bahamas in 1648. However, others believe that if a ghost does exist, it is virtually impossible that it is that of Sayle. The house and museum, with its collection of 18th- and 19th-century furniture arranged as though the home was still inhabited, is administered by the Bermuda National Trust. Verdmont is open Tuesday through Saturday from 10 AM to 4 PM.

Pembroke Parish

Bermuda Historical Society Museum
13 Queen St., Hamilton • 295-2487

This little museum is a treasure trove of old Bermuda-made silver and antique cedar furniture. The history of the island and its various eras leaps off the page and takes on substance through the furniture and other artifacts displayed here. It all forms a remarkable portrait of various aspects of what might be considered an old and genteel way of life.

Sandys Parish

Bermuda Arts Centre
Royal Naval Dockyard • 234-2809

Originals, prints and sculptures by a number of local artists grace the exhibition rooms of this fairly comprehensive center. Bermuda-made ceramics, jewelry and cedar work are also exhibited, along with a representative number of paintings.

Exhibitions showcasing various artists are held frequently through the year. These often have a particular medium, like the recent one showcasing fiber art. Artists revealed their skills in quilting, needlepoint and collage; there was a feast of entries that were either twisted, woven, stretched or sewn. Toward the end of 1997, "All That Jazz," designed to coincide with Jazzscape 1997 (see our Annual Events and Festivals chapter), featured works inspired by music. The juried mixed-media show, with top artists Robert Bassett and Jonah Jones, included bronze sculptures, oils and even images rendered in wire and papier-mâché.

Bermuda's Cedar Carvers

For centuries, from the very beginning of Bermuda's colonization, craftsmen have been shaping *juniperus bermudiana* (the Bermuda cedar) to use as furniture. Even now there are exquisite tables and chairs, staircases and banisters, doors and moldings that can be traced back to the 19th century, and in some instances, the 1700s.

What haven't come down through the centuries though, are artistic carvings, and it almost begs the question as to why not. Certainly the skill of the artisans could not have only been directed toward the functional. Surely there must have been a man or woman who took this most difficult of woods to work with and brought some artistic spirit to life. But there is nothing today to show that any such pieces have survived.

Close-up

However, as we approach the end of the century, cedar carvers have and are continuing to leave a mark on Bermuda's cultural pages.

Interpretations of subject matter range from realism to abstraction. Some of the carvings are architectonic in nature and are not dissimilar to some African carvings. This is actually not too unusual. In the world of sculpture, wood is principally associated with African art and certain sculptures of the medieval period. In this century Henry Moore, who was fascinated with Mexican and African art, manipulated the special character-istics, its vertical graining and organic nature.

Similarly, a handful of local carvers have learned to manipulate the tricky and eccentric grain of the Bermuda cedar, creating splendid works of art. Leading the world of the cedar carver is Chesley Trott, who has a studio at the Dockyard. His works are frequently imitated by young carvers.

But cedar is a curious wood. The oils that impart its distinctive aroma can present difficulties. If wood that is too young is used, as the oils dry out (and some parts will dry faster than others) there may be splitting. The solution is to leave the wood in log form until it is seasoned and dry, then place it in a shady area and simply leave it. Sometimes for three years; often for more.

"Cedar is a funny wood," says carver David Nisbett, a furniture craftsman with few peers who began carving cedar under the guidance of Trott. "You must work with the grain, and the grain can vary from piece to piece, and often within the same piece."

Aromatic and eccentric, beautifully grained, Bermuda cedar is scarce. "By the end of the century," says Roy Boyer, "most of the available wood will be green and unsuitable for carving."

Ecological disaster in the form of insects struck the cedar in the mid-1940s, wiping out 90 percent of forests within a decade. Today's stock is beset by timber thieves, who have been recognized as a huge problem by the Department of Agriculture and Fisheries. It all combines to make cedar extremely costly.

Ten to 12 years ago, cedar wood cost $13 to $15 per foot. Thirty years ago an entire tree cost between $30 and $40. Today, according to one carver, a prime log can cost as much as $5,000.

The impact both on antique as well as contemporary cedar furniture is incredible. Many a credit card has been embarrassed, as the finest local sculptures can be quite costly. Yet even though the prices of some works easily exceed $1,000, only a rare one or two carvers are making any kind of a living through their work. It often takes months to finish a particular piece. Hundreds of hours go into the initial shape of the creation, and for one carver, Garen Simmons, scores more hours are used to simply finish a

— continued on next page

piece. Garen's finishing involves using finer and finer grains of sandpaper until the wood is sanded down to the heart of its inner beauty. His patience and technique have led Garen to be engaged by other carvers to "finish" their works.

But Garen's most outstanding and original work is in his masks. These masks, though reminiscent of an African influence, are unique in style and appearance.

Several local carvers quietly labor away in backyard sheds, small, cramped garages or in backyards in the shade. They work to create artistic pieces that are rarely, if ever, seen by the general public.

The works of one such artist, whose realistic carvings of animals are so exquisite that his carving of a dog terrified a young nephew, are comparable to that of any woodcarver working anywhere. But this fellow prefers anonymity, and his carvings are not for sale at any price. His zoo of animals, all created to scale, occupy his living room.

The future of the local cedar woodcarver is unclear. Only a few carvers have managed to put aside supplies that will last them for many more years. Others are turning to using imported Virginia cedar.

Photo: Mid Ocean News

"Marriage" is one of Chesley Trott's most popular pieces.

Bermuda Maritime Museum
Royal Navy Dockyard • 234-1418

Housed in a 6-acre keep and officially opened by Queen Elizabeth II in 1975, the Maritime Museum is a testament to the once-powerful, 19th-century presence of the British Navy. The museum's exhibits are contained within six buildings with varying date stones (cornerstones, to you Americans) that indicate a span of construction between 1837 and 1852.

This is an exciting repository that vividly brings to life Bermuda's exciting and fascinating maritime past. Just within the main entrance, the Queen's Exhibition Hall has exhibits and information on navigation, whaling, pilots, steamships and the renowned Bermuda sloops. The 1849 Shell House, found on the north side of Keep Pond, reveals to visitors the Age of Discovery through the "Isle of Devils" exhibit. Other buildings, like the 1837 Shifting House, a three-gabled structure and the earliest of the ordinance buildings completed, have exhibits that are intriguing guideposts to local seafaring history. The Boatloft, with its "Pillars of the Bridge" exhibit, even covers the 50 years of U.S. forces in Bermuda.

The museum is supported by admissions and privately donated funds. It is open every day except Christmas from 10 AM to 5 PM.

Gumba Trail and Outdoor Museum
Cockburn Rd. • 293-7330

Life in Bermuda between the 16th and 18th centuries is explored at this museum. Particular emphasis is placed on the Gombey, whose masks are seen as a key to ancient traditions and a connection to the Native American ancestors of Bermudians. The signs, symbols and secrets of the Bermuda Gombey were decoded in a special 1997 exhibition entitled "Hieroglyphics." (For more on the Gombey tradition, see the Close-up in our Let's Explain Bermuda chapter.)

The easiest way to get to the museum is to go into the Dockyard and catch a bus or minibus in front of the Clocktower. Tell the driver you want to get off at the stop nearest the turnoff to the Gumba Trail, which is near the

T.S. Venture Sea Cadet building. The museum schedule is seasonal, so call ahead. Admission is $5 per person.

Galleries and Studios

St. George's Parish

Bridge House Gallery
Bridge House, Town of St. George
• 297-8211

This gallery of paintings and prints by a number of local artists is housed in Bridge House, a fine example of late-17th-century Colonial-style architecture. It is also home of the studio for artist Jill Amos Raine, noted for her watercolor scenes that seem to have captured every nook and cranny of St. George's. Original oils and watercolors by several other local artists — among them Diana Amos and Eric Amos, Otto Trott, Jo Linberg, Helen Daniel and Mary Tucker — are found here, as are prints by Molly Smith, Joan Forbes and Sharon Wilson.

Hamilton Parish

Clearview Art Gallery
151 North Shore Rd., Bailey's Bay
• 293-0484

With the work of artist Otto Trott as its core, this gallery, named after the guest house where Trott is resident artist, houses one of the island's largest collections of original oil paintings. Otto, a graduate of the Maryland Institute College of Art, explores several aspects of Bermudian life as well as the ubiquitous landscapes, seascapes and local flora.

Builders, an oil painting rendered on linen, shows workmen building a traditional Bermudian roof and captures the mood and skill of the mason's art. It was featured in the 1993 month-long Carib Art Exhibition, a traveling exhibit of contemporary works by artists of the Dutch, English, French and Spanish Caribbean that was organized by the National Commission for UNESCO of the Netherlands Antilles. Otto also exhibits in member shows put on by the Bermuda Society of Arts.

Pembroke Parish

Bermuda National Gallery
City Hall and Arts Centre, Church St., Hamilton • 295-9428

The beginning of the gallery can be traced back to 1982 and the foundation of the Bermuda Fine Arts Trust. After four years of little activity, the trust created a committee to oversee the short-term development of a proposed institution for major works of art. In 1991 the gallery appointed its first director, Laura Gorham.

Located on the second floor of City Hall in Hamilton, the gallery has five spaces, each with its own character. The main gallery has a well-proportioned open space that is ideal for abstract exhibitions. Among permanent collections are paintings donated by the late Hereward Watlington. This collection of 18 oils called "Restoration — Hereward T. Watlington Collection" covers the 15th to 19th centuries and consists of works by Reynolds, Gainsborough, Romney, Murillo and others.

The first international exhibit at the gallery was the 1993 exhibition, "Secrecy: African Art that Conceals and Reveals." Since then there have been several major art shows and exhibitions. Generally, a variety of concurrent shows are presented to the public that include works from the Bermuda Archives, the Bermuda National Trust and the Masterworks Bermudiana Collection, the centerpiece of which is a Winslow Homer watercolor.

Another permanent exhibition is "Celebration," a superb collection of 22 African art works ranging from masks to Senufo shrine figures that open a window onto the creativity and resilience of various African cultures. Many of these pieces were formerly on loan to the High Museum in Atlanta. Others were generously donated by an anonymous collector. Exhibitions have also included "Pop/Op Art of the 1960s and 1970s," and a selection of Georgia O'Keefe's Bermuda drawings painted on her island visits.

Toward the end of 1997, "Light, Air and Colour: American Impressionist Paintings from the Pennsylvania Academy of Fine Arts" featured 20 outstanding works by such artists as Daniel Garber, Birge Harrison and Cecilia Beaux. This exhibition was sponsored by

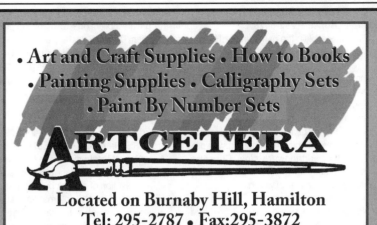

American International Ltd. to celebrate a half-century in Bermuda.

Heritage House Gallery
2 Front St., Hamilton • 295-2615

The venue for several exhibitions throughout the year, Heritage House has shown the works of many of Bermuda's leading artists at one time or another. In 1997 it held its 10th annual Christmas Small Picture Exhibition. Original oils, watercolors and prints are available for purchase, as are a number of varied antiques.

Masterworks Foundation
Bermuda House Ln., 97 Front St., Hamilton • 295-5580

From its inception, the Masterworks' "Bermudiana" collection invited the entire community to participate in what has become a fascinating experience that has brought the island a permanent collection of paintings by well-known artists. Works by Andrew Wyeth, Albert Gleizes, Jack Bush and Georgia O'Keefe indicate that American, French and Canadian artists are well-represented.

With Winslow Homer as the catalyst, the search for paintings (and the money to buy them) began seriously in 1987. A decade later, the list of painters whose palette and paints have shaped a historical and social pastiche of the island and its environment has grown. As perceived and interpreted by these visitors of the splendid brush stroke, images of West Indian immigrants, friendly societies, integration at fetes, landscapes and street scenes mix the expected with the unexpected. No medium has been ignored.

In spring 1997, Masterworks opened its artists-in-residence program at the Terrace in Dockyard. The vision is to recruit overseas artists and develop them to be ambassadors of Bermudian culture when they leave the island.

Exhibitions of paintings can be found at the Bermuda National Gallery, the Masterworks Gallery at 97 Front Street and the Colonial Insurance Company Gallery, which is in the foyer at Jardine House on Reid Street in Hamilton.

Michael Swan Galleries
Butterfield Place, Front St., Hamilton • 296-5650
Clocktower Mall, Dockyard • 234-3128

Michael Swan is an artist who uses pastels to capture Bermuda's houses in a unique way. A graduate of the Nova Scotia College of Art and Design, his medium is acrylic, his tool an airbrush. Michael's two galleries feature his works, which use stark shadows and contrasting colors playing off each other. His fascination with local architecture is obvious. Many of his originals hang in private collections, and he was one of four Bermudians whose paintings were exhibited in the Caribbean Art Exhibition in Bermuda in May 1995, then in Paris in October of the same year. He has also exhibited at the UNESCO International Art Exhibition.

Omax Ceramics Studio
Admiralty House • 292-8478

First, let's explain the name. In our History chapter, we spoke a bit about the term "onion," as it relates to Bermudians. Well, "Omax" means, quite simply, "Onions to the max." Get it?

Found in an elongated building close to one of the scenic trails leading to a sheltered cove with a small beach at Admiralty House, ceramic pieces at Omax are wheel-thrown from low-fire white earthenware clay. Christine Wellman's pieces are decorated with any of 10 different designs, all of which (colors included) have a connection to something typically Bermudian. In 1996 the parrotfish joined existing designs; the following year brought a Cuppa Soup bowl with handle. Other designs are the popular hibiscus, morning glory, combo, fish and the classic lizard.

The work is as functional as it is aesthetic. Practicality, merged with decoration, is a key feature of these creations by Christine. The decoration itself is done through a combination of sponging and handpainting techniques. Christine's background is actually in painting and print-making. She admits that she is not a traditional potter, and that the shapes of her creations do not always conform to the expected. Ceramics, she says, are her substitute canvas.

Regal Art Gallery
86 Reid St. E., Hamilton • 295-7441

Robert Bassett's paintings comprise the majority of the works featured at this gallery, which is owned and operated by him and his wife. Bassett's art offers a feast of brilliant, bold colors. Strongly influenced by the Bermuda gombey as well as the universal jazz tradition, the works are impressionistic interpretations of the black experience.

Highly successful, Robert has exhibited at a one-man show at Howard University in Washington, D.C., at the Museum of African American Art in Los Angeles, at the prestigious Montauk Club in New York and at a number of other galleries in the United States. Permanently represented by the Apex Foundation Gallery in New Orleans, he has participated in the 1996

New York Art Expo. His creations are also found in the private collections of many notables, among them Coretta Scott King and Sir Lyndon Pindling, former prime minister of the Bahamas. A deeply religious man, Robert gives credit for his creativity to "the greatest artist of all, God Himself."

Windjammer Gallery
King and Reid Sts., Hamilton • 292-7861
95 Front St., Hamilton • 292-5878

A number of local artists have their works exhibited here, making it home to a large selection of artwork by both Bermudian and international artists working in varied media. Among the several artists represented are Diana and Eric Amos, Bruce Stuart, Michael Swan (who also has his own galleries) and Maria Smith.

Paget Parish

Art House Gallery
80 South Shore Rd. • 236-6746

Joan Forbes, one of the island's most successful artists, is as well-known on Canada's Pacific coast as she is in Bermuda. Noted for watercolors that capture the diversity and serenity of the island, she has been featured in exhibitions in New York and Boston as well as the east coast of Canada.

While diversity marks her medium — she is comfortable with oils, acrylics, pastels or pen and ink — it is also present in her subject matter. Seascapes, landscapes, florals and portraits all display delightful color clarity and balance. Art House is filled with her original paintings, limited and open edition lithograph prints, and an array of her handmade craftwork. As a teacher, Joan is always happy to assist budding artists experiencing teething problems and firmly believes that everyone has artistic ability that can be brought to the surface with time and practice.

Mary Zuill Art Studio
10 Southlyn Ln. • 236-2439

"I've been painting since I could hold a brush," says 80-year-old watercolor artist, Mary

Bermuda's world-class National Gallery at City Hall houses an exemplary collection of old masters and also hosts exhibits from other selected museums worldwide.

Zuill, whose works have been purchased by visitors from a dozen countries including Switzerland, Germany, England, Scotland, Canada, Russia and the United States.

Yet despite her popularity, she does not enter exhibitions. Her landscapes and seascapes, along with gentle urban depictions (among them Hamilton, Flatts, Salt Kettle and Lower Ferry) have a warm simplicity, pastel-rendered in deft brush strokes. "I used to work in oils but find that medium too heavy," she admits, but emphasizes the permanence of her watercolors. In some paintings touches of black ink subtly highlight the trunks of palm trees, burnished cliffside rocks or sailboat masts. Her paintings occasionally reflect a simpler era; one has a homemaker on her porch talking with a door-to-door fisherman selling his catch from a wheelbarrow.

Working tranquil themes onto a big canvas appeals to this diminutive, spirited artist whose creations are surprisingly reasonable. A 24-by-18-inch painting can be bought for $300 to $400. And visitors who have photographed a favored Bermudian landscape and want a special painting reproduced from the photo will find this lady willing to consider doing it for them. She creates many of her works during December, January and February, when her home-based studio is closed. To get to it when it is open, turn onto Southlyn Lane, which lies opposite the entrance to Stonington Hotel. Follow the lane all the way to the top of the hill. A small sign indicates the way. The studio is open Tuesday to Friday from 10 AM to noon and from 2:30 to 5 PM.

Southampton Parish

Desmond Fountain
Sculpture Gallery
Southampton Princess Hotel, South Shore Rd. • 238-8840

Arguably one of the finest bronze sculptors in the world today, Desmond Fountain — whose life-size sculpture of Sir George Somers stands on Ordnance Island in St. George's — emphasizes that his sculptures are intended to seem natural and uncontrived. He has said his goal is that "anybody viewing the sculptures might subconsciously expect one to move at any moment."

Located in the mezzanine of the Southampton Princess (see our Resort Hotels chapter), the gallery houses an extensive number of his bronzes. Desmond's sculptures have been sold to buyers all over the world (prices run well into four and sometimes five figures), and his works can be seen in galleries in the United States, England and the Channel Islands.

Sharon Wilson Gallery
2 Turtle Pl. • 238-2583

Within an easy two-minute walk from Horseshoe Beach, this gallery has been owned and operated since 1976 by Sharon Wilson, a graduate of the Massachusetts College of Art. She is a pastel artist who has become a major part of the local art scene since the late '70s. She has been a veteran public school art teacher and is now a full-time artist and illustrator of children's books.

Sharon's pastels are remarkably sensitive portrayals of relationships within the local black community — a grandfather with his granddaughter, schoolgirls whispering secrets to each other, a mother plaiting her daughter's hair. Admitting that the interplay between people fascinates her, providing an endless supply of ideas, she sees herself as a storyteller. "Bermuda is a complex environment. Here it is easy to miss the feel of the people and their fears amid the backdrop of hibiscus and frangipani," she says. Stepping within this complexity, she speaks from it through pastels that are brilliant narratives of local life.

Her first book, *The Day Gogo Went To Vote*, is a celebration of South Africa's first democratic elections. It drew critical acclaim when it received the distinction of "Notable Book" from the Smithsonian Institute, American Library Association and International Reading Association. The *London Financial Times* also responded with plaudits for her work. In 1997 Simon & Schuster released *Freedom's Gifts*, a second book which received rave reviews from the *New York Times*. A third is expected.

Twin Art Studio
70 Middle Rd. • 238-8364

Self-taught artist Joan Thompson always loved to draw. Although she began in the banking industry, the burning desire to paint was too difficult to ignore. She resigned from the bank and began painting full time.

Although Joan mainly paints landscapes, with most of her scenes focusing on the Somerset and Dockyard areas, she is turning her talent (and it is an extraordinary one) toward capturing even more of the island's heritage and culture. Her media are oil, pen and ink and charcoal, but she has a fondness for the gouache technique, where watercolors are mixed with gum arabic to make them opaque.

Joan stays busy with commissions from customers in the United States, Canada, Australia and, of course, Bermuda. Her studio, easily accessed from Middle Road in Southampton, can't be missed. Just look for the sign with the cow in the field eating grass. "I feel that the cow looks so peaceful," she says.

Literary Arts

Bermuda Writers Collective
34 Long Ridge Pass, Devonshire DV01 • 292-3999

This is a mixed bag of multinational writers who meet periodically to share their work, mostly fiction in progress. No membership is required for participation in these readings, where incisive critiques are the usual format.

The collective has published the stories of members in three collections of short stories, *Palmetto Wine*, *The Vendor of Dreams* and *An Isle So Long Unknown*. The group meets intermittently throughout the year.

Arts Organizations

Bermuda Arts Council
• 236-9504

This council, whose members are appointed by government, was formed in 1969.

It receives an annual grant which is directed toward assisting individuals and art and cultural groups who apply for help. Over the years it has helped scores of Bermudians pursue various artistic endeavour in every possible cultural direction. As a registered charity, and despite the government grant, it can accept bequests and donations from the public. Chairman Charles Zuill is the contact person for this group.

Bermuda Society of Arts
City Hall, West Exhibition Room, Hamilton • 292-3824

In 1952, an informal and friendly get-together for resident artists was the setting for the formation for the Society of Artists in Bermuda. Among this group were Donald Kirkpatrick, Antoine Verpilleaux and Bermudian Charles Lloyd Tucker, who has been described as one of the few watercolorists who could capture the true blues and greens of Bermuda scenery. Four years later the original group became the Bermuda Society of Arts, a registered charity.

During the past 40-plus years, the society has grown into one of Bermuda's leading organizations directed to supporting art-oriented activities. Since 1987 it has blossomed to more than 600 members. The West Exhibition Room at City Hall in Hamilton is the venue for exhibits of members' works. Exhibits generally rotate every two to three weeks and feature new works. Each January the society's Annual Photographic Exhibition attracts entries from amateur photographers. During May, the Heritage Exhibition tells the story of some period or aspect of Bermuda's history through various visual media.

The West Exhibition Room is open daily, and there is always a current exhibit of members' works. Bronze or wood sculptures, portraits and paintings in oils or pastels or photographs focusing on a particular theme compose an ever-changing artistic landscape.

There are a number of annual arts events in Bermuda, from photographic exhibitions and competitions to classical concerts and jazz extravaganzas.

Annual Events and Festivals

Bermuda's calendar is filled to the brim with all kinds of sporting, arts and holiday events that draw hundreds or even thousands of spectators. Major holidays like Bermuda Day and Cup Match bring together diverse ethnic groups — visitors and locals among them — to rub shoulders and chat and let their hair down. And almost every parade brings out the Gombeys and majorettes who dance and twirl and strut their stuff through Hamilton. Islanders are serious about work, and just as serious about their fun.

Cultural pursuits are not shunted into the back seat but are at the forefront, beginning early in the year with the Bermuda Festival. There are a number of arts events, from photographic exhibitions and competitions to classical concerts and jazz extravaganzas.

The following selection of events and festivals is just a sampling (broken down by month) of what we have to offer here where the sun caresses the sea and together with the land forms a blissful union. Where possible, we have included prices, but bear in mind that prices may change. Unless we have indicated otherwise after describing each event, admission is free. We list the events (and note that in some cases venues may vary from year to year) roughly in chronological order and provide an address and phone number when possible.

We do suggest popping into the Bermuda Department of Tourism, located on ground level in Global House at 43 Church Street in Hamilton, 292-0023, and obtaining the latest booklets and pamphlets on various events scheduled throughout the year.

January

Bermuda Festival
Various locations, Hamilton • 292-8572, 295-1291

Having entered its 23rd year in 1998, this has become a major showcase for the performing arts, attracting international and local artists. The dazzling displays of orchestral music and jazz, theater and ballet begin around the middle of the month and run until the last week in February. The usual venues are City Hall and St. Paul's Centennial Hall, both in Hamilton, and St. John's Church, less than five minutes away (by moped or taxi) from Front Street.

Supported by volunteers, benefactors, sponsors and patrons, this festival is a prestigious one on the cultural landscape. Performers in 1997 included American jazz saxophonist Joshua Redman, called the "Crown Prince of Jazz" by *Downbeat* magazine; the Vienna Choir Boys; the English Chamber Orchestra; and Tafelmusic Baroque Orchestra. The National Dance Theatre of Bermuda presented *The Nutcracker*.

The program for '98 was equally exciting, with performances from the National Black Touring Circuit, which staged the modern comedy *Checkmates*, a play that explores the effect of the generation gap on two couples; the Royal Winnipeg Ballet, under the artistic direction of Andre Lewis; the American Boys Choir, which has sung at the Vatican, Westminster Abbey and the White House; and the Philadelphia Dance Company, or "Philadanco," as it is affectionately called. Comedy was not overlooked: Avner the Eccentric put on his mime, magic and clowning antics and thrilled Bermudian audiences the same way he has entertained crowds throughout the United States and as far afield as Tokyo and Tel Aviv.

If you want to attend any of the almost 50 shows put on by as many as 14 separate groups or individuals in 1999, take note of the phone numbers above. Tickets are $20, $25 or $30 for adults depending on the show; students pay $15. If ordering tickets from overseas, call for an order form, fill it out and return it with your check or credit card information at least 21 days before opening night. The mailing address is The Bermuda Festival Ltd., Suite 480, 48 Par-la-Ville Road, Hamilton HM 11, Bermuda.

A confirmation form will be mailed to you, but tickets will not be sent through the mail. Your tickets can be picked up at the festival box office near the Ferry Terminal in Hamilton after you arrive in Bermuda. Anyone with a hearing or other disability may request special seating, and organizers will attempt to facilitate specific needs.

Annual Photographic Exhibition
City Hall, Hamilton • 292-3824

Organized by the Bermuda Society of Arts and hung in the group's City Hall Gallery, this exhibition allows local amateur and professional photographers to showcase their best works. A number of the exhibitors are among the society's 700-strong membership (see our Arts and Culture chapter).

Entries span a number of classes, with cups given to each category's winner. Entrants can compete in as many classes as they wish. Among the various categories are Best in Show, Best Color photograph and Best Black and White photograph. Youngsters also get an opportunity to reveal their talents; the winner in this group skips happily away with the Best Junior Cup.

The Johnny Skinner Cup for photojournalism draws local magazine and newspaper photographers. Those who thrill to shooting fish and their environment through the lens, get a crack at the cup for the Best Underwater Photograph. This class is usually strongly repre-

sented, with all entries bringing a new respect for the beauty of Bermuda's sea world.

This popular exhibition opens windows on Bermuda's natural and urban landscape, providing intimate glimpses of a cosmopolitan society in the Atlantic. There is no admission fee.

PBA Southern Regional Bowling Tournament
Warwick Lanes, 47 Middle Rd., Warwick Parish • 236-5290

FYI

Unless otherwise noted, the area code for all phone numbers listed in this guide is 441.

A bevy of professionals descend on Bermuda each year for this late-January tournament that puts $20,000 up for grabs. Experienced overseas professionals and hungry local bowlers meet in stiff competition. "This is a hot, happening event," said Mike McCallum, president of the Bermuda Bowling Association, in an interview last year.

The aim is to firmly place Bermuda on the bowling map. One of the pros in last year's tournament was American Sam Zurich, who came into the competition with three national and 24 regional titles under his belt. One of the cuter aspects of the 1997 tournament was the celebrity competition. It pitted then-United Bermuda Party (UBP) Premier David Saul and Progressive Labour Party (PLP) leader Jennifer Smith (who are political adversaries), against UBP Sports Minister Tim Smith and PLP "shadow" Minister of Sports Nelson Bascome.

February

Bermuda Chess Festival
Sonesta Beach Hotel, 5 South Rd. and Sonesta Dr. • 238-2313

Organized by the Bermuda Chess Association, this invitational has attracted players from Iceland, Germany, England, Sweden, Brazil, Puerto Rico, Morocco, Slovenia, the United States and Canada. Several grand masters have squared off here, among them Nick deFirmian from America and Julian Hodgson from England.

Held early in February, the competition requires that players complete a minimum of 40 moves in the first two hours and 20 in the next hour. If there is no winner by that point, players have 30 minutes to finish the game. The 1997 competition, held in Southampton at Mermaid Beach Club's Jolly Lobster restaurant, attracted scores of chess devotees.

Bermuda Open Chess Tournament
Southampton Princess Hotel, 101 South Rd. • 232-0528

Following immediately on the heels of the Chess Festival, this event is held at the prestigious Southampton Princess Hotel. In fact, winners from the earlier event are encouraged to enter the Bermuda Open. Competitors range from beginners to grand masters, with the winner receiving $1,000 and an expense-paid return trip to Bermuda.

Annual Bermuda Rendezvous Bowling Tournament
Warwick Lanes, 47 Middle Rd., Warwick Parish • 236-5290, 236-4373

Open to all bowlers and sanctioned by the ABC and WIBC, the balls in this handicap tournament begin to thunder down the lanes around mid-February. Staged during four days at Warwick Lanes on Middle Road, this competition is sponsored by a number of local businesses, and there are many cash prizes. Bowlers' individual entry fee is $30.50; doubles team fee is $61.

March

Spring Break Arts and Sports Program
Various venues • (800) 223-6106

In the 1950s and '60s, Bermuda threw open its doors to college students who flew down to lark it up in the sun while enjoying a host of college weeks programs put on by tourism officials. The introduction of this Spring Break event in 1997 marks an attempt to revive college kids' interest in Bermuda, and it aims at more artistic and sports-oriented activities.

Photo: GIS

The Bermuda Pipe Band participates in a skirling ceremony.

The arts program offers university- or college-credit lectures and workshops conducted by some of Bermuda's leading artists. Various tours, among them visits to the National Gallery, the Bermuda Society of Arts Gallery and National Trust properties are part of the cultural initiative.

But this is still very much about having a great time on an island noted for its incomparable beaches and delightful waters. Free beach parties, boat cruises and complimentary lunches are hosted by the Department of Tourism. Transportation and nighttime activities are also covered under the Spring Break program. Among participants in 1997 were students from Atlanta Metropolitan College and the Rhode Island School of Design. In 1998, studies in marine biology and the culinary arts were added to the ongoing workshops in glass blowing, architecture and furniture making.

www.insiders.com

See this and many other **Insiders' Guide®** destinations online — in their entirety.

Visit us today!

But this is just half of the Spring Break experience. The other focuses on sports and runs concurrently with the arts offerings. Lacrosse, soccer, tennis and rugby are among the sports where participants can let themselves go. For detailed information about the Spring Break Arts and Sports Program, contact the Bermuda Department of Tourism at the listed number.

Bermuda Kite Festival
Horseshoe Bay

No one knows for certain exactly when or why Bermuda embraced kite-flying around the Easter season. The story goes that a Sunday School teacher used the flying of a kite to illustrate the way Christ ascended to the heavens. Once the kite was airborne at the full length of the string, the teacher is reputed to have cut the string, allowing the kite to be taken by the wind until it disappeared.

Whatever the original intent, kite-flying on Good Friday has become as much a part of the day as codfish cakes and playing marbles. So popular are kites around this time of year that a small, seasonal cottage industry has emerged, with several folks making scores of kites and selling them to shops and parents.

Good Friday at Horseshoe Bay in Southampton is a dazzling and exciting kick-a-ball-around, play-in-the-surf, listen-to-music, kite-flying festival. There are plenty of kites: colorful kites, small kites and big kites, such as the one entered in 1997 that secured the win for the Corporation of Hamilton in the "biggest kite" category. Almost two stories high (and proudly bearing the corporation's crest), it failed to rise to the heavens. "I'm not sure there's enough wind to get it up today," said one of the men who had taken three days to make, string and patch the 17-foot giant with blue and gold satin. More fortunate was a 10-year-old, whose 15-foot nylon parafoil kite took to the wind like a duck takes to water. And the smallest kite there? It could fit in the palm of your hand.

April

Peppercorn Ceremony
King's Square, Town of St. George
• 297-1532

Held on the Wednesday closest to April 23, this is a ceremony that, for all its color, pomp and pageantry, seems only to have real meaning to the governor and Freemasons of Lodge No. 200, a Scottish lodge established here in 1797. Of course, should you be on King's Square when the governor arrives in his landau (a four-wheeled, horse-pulled passenger carriage) wearing his ceremonial uniform, no doubt the pomp will fascinate you, even if the circumstance is somewhat obscure. .

The governor is greeted by local dignitaries and members of the St. George's Lodge. The Bermuda Regiment provides a guard of honor, and lodge members are turned out in full regalia for the handing over of the annual symbolic rent for their use of the State House . . . a single peppercorn (the dried berry of the pepper plant). Lodge No. 200 is the oldest Scottish lodge outside Scotland; after its members pay up, and when all the speeches are finished, the governor and his escort depart.

Photo: GIS

The annual Bermuda Day public holiday on May 24 celebrates the island's culture with a huge, junkanoo-type parade that winds its way through the streets of Hamilton.

Agricultural Exhibition
Bermuda Botanical Gardens, Point Finger Rd., City of Hamilton • 236-4201

"The thrill and excitement of those occasions is still remembered by those who saw them as children. Bourne's ice-cream stall, gay with streamers; barking, yelping dogs so fierce and determined to consume small boys should they succeed in breaking their chains; awesome cows, safely viewed from a narrow gallery between their stalls along which one hurried to the far end and escaped, miraculously unharmed; bandsmen, fascinating in their red coats, and a fine figure of a soldier standing on a box conducting the music with a long wand which he handled as easily as if it were a feather; cats, sad and uncomfortable in their cages and not a purr to be heard from any of them."

Thus was the agricultural exhibition as it was revived in the 1880s and described in *Bermuda Journey* by William Zuill. That late 19th-century exhibition of yelping dogs and sad-eyed cats took place near the western edge of the City of Hamilton. But an even earlier exhibition was staged in 1843 at Mount Langton, or Government House, the residence of the governor sited well north of the city limits. Then

called the Agricultural and Horticultural Exhibition, it was described in the *Bermuda Gazette* as "the first exhibition of the kind ever got up in Bermuda, the specimens of the various productions were as the fancy or interests of the cultivator dictated."

It has been said that at one of those exhibitions, a black woman who was refused the opportunity of selling her coconut cakes near the entrance, placed a curse of rain on the entire exhibition and all those that followed down through the years. Whether anyone has actually compiled and compared rainfall data for the period in question is not known, but on those occasions when it does rain at any time during the three-day exhibition, many Bermudians remember the "curse."

Today the exhibition, with its festive atmosphere, is akin to a county or state fair. And once inside the "Ag Show," you are transported to a marvelous world where the sound of the Bermuda Regiment Band meets that of the Somers Isles Jazz Band, and the smell of hot dogs and vegetables and horses and fruit and fish cakes intermingle with myriad other scents. And then there are the colors — ribbons and bows and pretty cake sculptures, and the eye is bathed in everything from a marzipan longtail to an eggplant cockroach.

This is a high point on Bermuda's equestrian calendar. More than 6,000 people make their way to the Botanical Gardens annually to watch riders guide their sweating mounts in show jumping displays, acrobats roll and leap and tumble, and majorettes smartly step and throw their batons spinning up into the sun, the return caught easily and smoothly.

It all kicks off toward the end of April and has been going strong now for more than 60 years. It is a reminder that, despite the precipitous decline in farmland over that period, farming and horticulture helped build Bermuda and have not completely surrendered to concrete and tarmac.

Buses are often rerouted to provide steady transportation to and from the main gate on Point Finger Road. It's only $5 to get you and a camera into the exhibition. (For more on the Bermuda Botanical Gardens, see our Attractions chapter.)

May

Heritage Month
Various locations • 292-9447

May is Bermuda Heritage Month and features a host of cultural and commemorative activities sponsored by the Department of Community and Cultural Affairs. For 1998, the theme is "diversity," and the focus is on the contributions made by the island's different ethnic groups through their cultural traditions and activities — visual and performing arts, music and food. Previous years have seen the spotlight trained on several historical as well as contemporary aspects of Bermuda, including an intimate look at Hamilton and its people, St. George's and Bermuda's environment. A display that illustrates the theme is set up at

the Bermuda Society of Arts Gallery at the Hamilton City Hall and runs throughout the month.

Conyers, Dill and Pearman Cycling Grand Prix
Various locations, ending in City of Hamilton • 295-6012

Named after the sponsoring law firm, this early May weekend cycling event, organized by the Bermuda Bicycle Association, is the biggest of its kind in Bermuda. Four days of competition culminate in a Sunday criterion through Hamilton. Top cyclists from England, Ireland, the United States and Bermuda go head to head. The Saturday before the criterion features a 75-mile road race preceded by a 10-mile time trial. More than 40 riders compete for total prize money of $10,000. Contact the BBA at the number listed for more information.

Annual End-to-End Charity Walk
Town of St. George to Royal Naval Dockyard • 299-8821

This scenic Railway Trail walk for charities (generally held the first Saturday of May) is one of the best ways to meet residents and see some of the most picturesque parts of the island. Beginning in King's Square in the Town of St. George and ending at the Dockyard, the 26-mile course can be daunting, even for those who walk quite a bit. Sore and blistered feet are common. Those who are wary of attempting the full distance can opt for a 15-mile alternate course that starts at Albuoy's Point in the City of Hamilton.

The walk, now in its 11th year, has during the past 10 years raised close to $1 million that has been distributed to 40 charities. More than 5,000 people have taken part, and donations have been collected from many corporate sponsors.

Youngsters can participate as well, and there is a mini-walk within the Dockyard for tod-

---

INSIDERS' TIP

From November through March, the Bermuda Department of Tourism offers a free evening lecture series on Bermuda. Scheduled topics for this year include Bermuda's Architecture, Culture and Traditions, Flora and Fauna, Marine Life, Fortifications, Art, Women in Bermuda's History and Bermuda's Prisoners of War.

dlers. For those braving either the end-to-end or middle-to-end, a pasta-loading banquet takes place the night before. Visitors can sign up at either King's Square or Albuoy's Point a half-hour before starting. In 1997 the minimum pledge for entry was $20; in other words, if your friends agreed to pay $5 each, you'd need four supporters. (For much more on the Railway Trail, see our Recreations chapter.)

Samuel L. Jackson Celebrity Golf Classic
Port Royal Golf Course, Middle Rd., Southampton Parish • 234-0974

This classic draws celebrities from the United States to the Port Royal Golf Course for an event that is more about raising money for two charities — the local Council Partners Charitable Trust and the Catalog for Giving in New York — than about competition. Between the two organizations, some 20 separate programs are funded. At the conclusion of last year's classic, $242,700 had been raised and split evenly between the two organizational recipients.

Jackson, an Academy Award nominee known for his role in *Pulp Fiction* and other movies, has been joined by nearly 40 celebs for the tournament that bears his name. Among the visiting duffers have been Joshua Morrow from the daytime soap, *The Young and the Restless*; Alonso Ribeiro of *Fresh Prince of Bel-Air* fame; and Anna Maria Horsford, one of the stars of TV's *Amen* and the *Wayans Bros.*

Golf at this classic is not taken that seriously, but the money that must be anted up by anyone wanting to play with the stars is: It costs $1,500 per day for the privilege. But it all goes to good causes. ACE Insurance Company Ltd., in association with Elbow Beach Hotel and Bank of Butterfield, is the presenting sponsor. Other corporate sponsors include the Bermuda Department of Tourism, Gosling Bros. Ltd. and Reebok.

The four-day early-May party is facilitated by 400 volunteers. Two other major events are the first night's black-tie opening gala, where cocktails, dinner and dancing to a couple of bands gets the classic off to a fun start, and a subsequent night of comedy. Tickets are $150 for the gala evening and $50 for the comedy night.

Bermuda International Film Festival
Various locations, Hamilton • 293-FILM

Launched in 1997 with a theme built around the concept of "Firsts," this festival attracted submissions from first-time directors, producers, screenwriters and actors. The opening gala, sponsored by the Bermuda Telephone Company, was at Fort Hamilton, a fortification built in the late 1800s to protect the city and harbor beyond. The fort's lovely garden oasis was the setting for invitees to relax with good food and fine music provided by a local band.

The 1997 festival — with three categories and, consequently, three prizes — was juried by American actress, author and producer Jane Alexander, *Mid-Ocean News* editor Tim Hodgson and Tom Shoebridge, president of Ottawa's Summer Institute of Film and Technology.

The 14 entries, many submitted with the help of the New Producers Alliance in London, Independent Feature Film Market in New York and the Toronto International Film Festival, comprised a cross-section of independently produced drama and documentary films. Entrants from a number of countries — among them the United States, Canada, Russia, India and the United Kingdom - participated. The wide-ranging subject matter was assessed for effective storyline and development, excellence in direction and the impact of those intangible, often human qualities that make a film work.

The two cinema venues were both in Hamilton — the Liberty Theatre on Union Street and the Little Theatre on Queen Street. The winning documentary was *Family Name*, a true-to-life mystery wrapped around family secrets. It followed director Macky Alston's search for descendants of slave owners and slaves from plantations once owned by his family. Honorable mention was awarded to a joint American-Russian production called *The Riddle*. Directed by Evan Brenner, it was about a 10-year-old Russian youth obsessed with his past.

The Audience Choice Award went to *Boston Kickout*, and Best Short Film was *Anna in the Sky*.

The closing gala, hosted by *Entertainment Weekly* magazine, was held at Ariel Sands Beach Club. The evening of music, barbecue, rustling palms and crashing surf capped a week of eclectic film enjoyment.

This event is held during the first week of May. A festival pass, at $100, provides a ticket to each film, including opening and closing films at the Liberty Theatre. Prices and some details are subject to change, but admission to individual films in this year's event should be in the $8 range. Film submission entry forms are available from the middle of September until January 31.

Bermuda Day Parade
City of Hamilton

First staged May 24, 1979, this has become Bermuda's biggest parade, an exuberant celebration and display of local culture and heritage. A cycling race, a 13.3-mile half-marathon from Somerset Village to the City of Hamilton (for Bermuda residents only) and Bermuda dinghy races in St. George's Harbour head up the list of sporting events during the day.

The parade itself gets under way in the afternoon after Bermuda's premier officially launches proceedings at Bernard's Park, which is within easy walking distance of Front Street. Thousands line Hamilton's streets, in some places three and four persons deep, as the various floats, dancers, marching bands, majorettes and Gombeys go past. As many as 50 groups have participated in the two-hour-plus parade, led by the Bermuda Regiment Band.

Many spectators stake out a favored spot, set up a chair, have a lunch basket at hand and just get comfortable. The decks of cruise ships overlooking Front Street are jammed with curious visitors who take in the color, music and jubilation of the carnival atmosphere. Bermuda's diverse culture is represented — among those participating are members of the Portuguese, Indian and Filipino communities. Special guests in 1997 included the Frederick Douglass High School Marching Band and Drill Team from Atlanta; it proved to be a big hit with the crowds.

With a number of prizes awarded for floats in various categories, the Best Parish Award in 1997 went to Warwick Parish Council for its "Bermuda Is Another World" entry.

Bermuda Open Karate Championships
Bermuda College, College Dr.
• 292-2157

Now in its 16th year, this is the oldest continuously run karate event in Bermuda. Open to both juniors and adults, the event averages drawing between 70 and 100 entrants. Participants at the May 24 championships have included competitors from England, the United States, Argentina, Germany and Canada. Judges are primarily instructors or senior-level

FYI

Unless otherwise noted, the area code for all phone numbers listed in this guide is 441.

INSIDERS' TIP

Visitors at participating hotels and guest houses can take advantage of an interesting November through March deal: On the day after the temperature falls below 68 degrees, admission is free for the Bermuda Aquarium, Fort St. Catherine and Bermuda National Trust properties. (See our Attractions chapter for more on these sites.)

This Cup Match Overflows With Bermudian Flavor

No other local event will give you a taste of Bermuda quite like this one. It is tradition seasoned with fun, daubed with color and molded like a cultural cassava pie. The biggest sporting event on the island (held the Thursday and Friday before the first Monday in August), it attracts up to 15,000 spectators. And why? Because this is *the* game of the year — a competition between St. George's Cricket Club and Somerset Cricket Club. It's East versus West. But this is not a field of dreams. This is hard ball. This is raw competition.

Die-hard cricket fans show up early, sporting their colors — dark and light blue for St. George's, red and dark blue for Somerset. They bring chairs, umbrellas and just about anything that will add to their comfort.

Fashions depend on the mood of the wearer, but you won't see jackets and ties. It is two consecutive days of revelry and socializing, and yet it is very much about cricket. The twain do meet, and link arms.

Cup Match has been played every year since 1902. Much has changed, however, since the early days. There was a time in 1916 when the match was almost cancelled because St. George's had difficulty in fielding a team. And in its struggling years, the match was not always a holiday, but this did not deter players or fans. They simply took time off from work and went to the game.

While the game is acknowledged as the crux around which the entire two days turn, the festival that surrounds the competition is also about food. Plenty of food. Curried mussels and mussel pies. Fish and chicken dinners. Peas and rice, codfish cakes and conch stew. Curried goat. Snowballs and soft drinks. Food stalls, as you will have by now imagined, abound. The area around the host club's field is ringed with them, music often emanating from within. So essential is the food that stall operators must apply for a plot to erect a temporary stall as early as January. Costs vary depending on size, but prices run up to $500 per day.

— continued on next page

Photo: GIS

The annual Cup Match is a social and athletic tradition. It is our Fourth of July and World Series, all in one.

During these two days (timed to coincide with Bermuda's Emancipation Day celebration), all roads lead to either Somerset or St. George's, the venue alternating each year. And getting there is a great deal easier than in the days of the train, when on one occasion in 1933 the train conductor, with a full load of passengers bound for St. George's and the match . . . fell off the train! The old Rattle and Shake plodded on without him. Rushing to a nearby house, the conductor managed to convey by telephone the urgency of the situation. A replacement driver was immediately sent from St. George's to Mullet Bay where a fortuitous incline slowed the train enough to allow him to jump aboard. Most passengers had no clue of how close they were to possible disaster.

But there was always fun upon arrival — the atmosphere, the intense but friendly rivalries between spectators. Today this rivalry is backdropped by jazz, soca and reggae music mingling with the buzz of the crowds, the crack of the ball against the bat, the cheers and clapping and the smells of food wafting on the hot and languid air. There are youngsters with tired and perplexed faces. And the intent eyes of gamblers who hope their luck will change. Yes, Dorothy, here there be gambling, and many folks show up for that very purpose. In this instance the wagering is on Crown and Anchor, a dice game often called the "Stock Market."

This is a game where the operator of the "table" (and it really is a wooden table that is divided into six clearly marked squares containing each of the four card suits — hearts, diamonds, spades and clubs — and a square each for, yep, a crown and an anchor) does his best to separate players from their dollars. He places three dice into a rigid, felt-covered "cup," shakes them, then turns the cup over onto the table but does not raise it. At that time bettors place their stakes down on the square or squares of their choice.

The operator then lifts the cup and reveals the dice. Each of the six faces of the dice has either a crown, anchor, heart, diamond, spade or club. Bettors are paid off dollar for dollar on any of the suits that come up matching the appropriate square on the table where they have placed their money. If all dice show the same, the bet is tripled, and for each time the crown or anchor shows when you have money placed on those square, your stake can be doubled or tripled. Of course, every player has a system, but at the end of the day it is a matter of luck, and very few operators lose money. As many as two dozen tables can be kept busy by gamblers and tens of thousands of dollars change hands over the two days.

So the Cup Match is also about winners — the winning cricket team and the gambler who beats the odds. It is about parents and children, and visitors who come the first time out of curiosity and return whenever they can. It is a game, and it is life. It is Bermuda in microcosm: a pastiche of sight and sound and scents wrapped up in two days of pure fun and enjoyment. There really is no other local festival quite like it.

---

students from the Bermuda Karate Institute, Zenji Ryu Bermuda and Bermuda Jujitsu Karate.

Spearheading the Bermuda Open Karate Championships is Skipper Ingham, the first person to establish and continue a martial arts school in Bermuda. Peter Urban, founder of American goju karate, has called him "Bermuda's Grand Patriarch of Karate." Together with his wife Kristina, Skipper has trained many students in goju karate during the 27 years since the Bermuda Karate Institute was founded. Among the most notable students is Gladwin "Roots" Phillips of Zenji Ryu Bermuda. He is the island's only international gold medalist in traditional karate sparring, winning his weight division in Buenos Aires in 1994.

Visiting judges for BOKC have included Chuck Merriman, former coach of the U.S. National karate team, and Joe Pina of Boston Tae Kwon Do. Sponsors are the Marketplace supermarket chain, Colonial Insurance, Darrell Travel and Phoenix Stores. Admission for spectators is $10 for adults and $5 for children younger than 12.

June

Queen's Birthday Parade
City of Hamilton • 292-2587, 238-1045, 295-0011

"At first I didn't know what was going on," said a visitor from Boston who was standing with more than 2,000 spectators amid last year's pageantry. What was going on was the Queen's Birthday Parade, held the third Monday in June as an official celebration of the birthday of England's Queen Elizabeth II (whose birthday is actually April 26).

This is one occasion when all the top political and civil service folks are in attendance. The premier, opposition party leader, chief fire officer, police commissioner and mayor of Hamilton (in top hat and chains of office) are all on hand. The governor, dressed in full ceremonial whites, plumed hat and blue sash, inspects the regiment troops. A *feu de joie* (a celebration involving the firing of rifles) 21-gun salute splits the air before the governor leads the crowd in three cheers for the queen.

"When you see something like this you know you're not in Boston," added the visitor. Indeed, old chap.

July

Atlantic International Junior Golf Championship
Various locations

This annual tournament is aimed at developing competition between junior golfers from countries bordering on or close to the Atlantic Ocean. Young golfers from Canada, America and the Bahamas normally attend, and the event tees off early in the month. A maximum of 175 golfers may enter the tournament, which is open to boys and girls in eight categories — from mini girls (12 and younger) and mini boys (aged 11 and 12), up to senior boys (aged 18 to 21).

Conceived in a spirit of goodwill and sportsmanship, the Atlantic International has during the past 21 years become a very popular event. The goodwill spirit is manifested islandwide, as visiting golfers get the opportunity to stay with local families, and several social activities contribute to their enjoyment of Bermudian hospitality.

Emancipation Commemoration
King's Square, Town of St. George
• 292-9447

On August 1, 1834, slavery was abolished in Bermuda. On that date nearly 5,000 slaves were freed. This historic event is commemorated toward the end of July in King's Square through dramatic readings, music and dance. Organized by the Ministry of Community and Cultural Affairs and the Corporation of St. George's, the evening event has had participants including the National Dance Theatre of Bermuda, the Mu-en Chorale and the Salvation Army Divisional Band. Various other groups and individuals also perform. Part of the commemoration is a visit to the burial ground for slaves and free blacks at St. Peter's Church on York Street.

September

Annual Sandcastle Competition
Horseshoe Bay, Southampton Parish
• 236-2930

This is an Institute of Bermuda Architects (IBA) event that takes place at Horseshoe Bay around the middle of the month. There are several categories — children (12 years and younger), teenagers ages 13 to 19, adults, families, organizations/companies and tourists. The entry fee for "Castles in the Sand" is $20 for the use of an 8-foot square plot. All proceeds go to the IBA Scholarship Fund. Entrants have four hours, beginning at noon, to erect their masterpieces. Judging is by an IBA council. Entry forms are available at the Planning Department, Government Administration Building, 30 Parliament Street, Hamilton. If inquiring about the event by phone, ask for Nicky Gurret.

October

Bermuda Jazzscape
Various venues in Hamilton, Town of St. George and Royal Naval Dockyard
• (888) 4ESCAPE

Jazz enthusiasts always bookmark a

couple of great events on their happenings calendar, and this one, just a couple of years old, is fast gaining popularity. For five days beginning early in October, international and local artists deliver what have been called by local writers "some of the most captivating jazz performances this side of the Atlantic."

Presented by *Travel and Leisure Magazine*, Jazzscape's past performers have included Nancy Wilson, whose vocal magic always captivates; David Sanborn, the veteran saxophonist and pop instrumentalist; and Arturo Sandoval, a premier trumpeter who crossed the pond to make great music under Bermuda's subtropical skies.

The festival kicks off with a giant jazz party along Front Street in Hamilton. While some details may change for 1998, last year the Sunset Swing at King's Square in St. George was a tribute to swing-era bands and had the old town rocking. The Warren Vache Quartet and local song stylist Gita Blakeney, among others, put on splendid performances.

An official Gala Opening Night Concert on the third night (reserved seats $55, general admission $45, with special VIP tickets available) featured performances by Wilson and by Sanborn's group. Ticket prices for the fourth day and evening, when the best of Bermudian cuisine, crafts and talent are presented, are the same as for the opening night concert.

Visiting aficionados will find shuttle buses to and from Dockyard, one of the three venues, available from all major hotels. For more information, you can also contact the Bermuda Department of Tourism.

November

Skippy Peanut Butter KICK
Pembroke Sunday School, Angle St.
• **292-2157**

Held November 1 at the Pembroke Sunday School, the Kids International Competition Karate (hence, KICK) event is solely sponsored by Skippy peanut butter through its local agent, Butterfield & Vallis. The event draws between 30 and 70 competitors, primarily from Bermuda but with a few from the United States. It is for karate students 17 years and younger.

Admission for spectators is $10 for adults and $5 for children younger than 12.

The Bermuda Tattoo
National Stadium, 50 Frog Ln.
• **238-1045, 292-0023**

For three nights in mid-November, the skies over Devonshire throb to the music of military bands . . . except when there is utter silence as drill squads are put through their paces. This tattoo (the name given to a performance by military bands) is the biggest event of its kind locally, and past performers, in addition to the Bermuda Regiment Band, have included the United States Marine Corps Band; the Celtic Cross Pipe & Drum Band; the Bermuda Regiment Silent Drill Team; the Lincoln & Welland Regiment Band from St. Catherine's, Ontario; the Bermuda Islands Pipe Band; and the Bermuda Regiment Attack Squad.

Tickets (prices, again, are subject to change) are $15 for adults and $5 for children and are available from the visitors service bureaus and Bermuda Regiment Headquarters in Warwick.

Annual Culture Shock
No. 1 Shed, Front St., Hamilton

Organized by Bermuda Tent Productions, this is the biggest reggae show in Bermuda, attracting between 4,000 and 5,000 people during its two-night run. Performed toward the end of the month, the event is two-tiered: There is Dancehall Night, its driving tempo and lyrics attracting a younger crowd, and Culture Night, which has a more adult following and music described as more rootsy.

Dancehall, originating in Jamaica, has become a major musical influence and has had an impact on many American rap artists and local reggae performers. The Bermuda event not only features top local reggae artists, but also top Jamaican singers. Past performers have included Judy Mowatt, Garnet Silk, Beres Hammond and Tony Rebel. Local acts include Bigga Dread, Ninja Cutty and Shorta Ranks, who has performed in New Jersey and The Reggae Lounge in Manhattan.

Advance tickets for both nights are $75. For individual nights, the advance price is $50, with tickets going for $60 at the door.

Jazz & Razzmatazz
The Princess, 76 Pitts Bay Rd., Hamilton
• 296-3429

Sponsored by the local chapter of Amnesty International as a late-November fund-raising event, this is the jazz extravaganza that brings together the largest number of local jazz performers in a concert that has become one of the most popular for local enthusiasts. In the hotel's Princess Rooms, more than 30 artists and groups annually take the stage before sellout audiences. Popular local performers at the event have included the Ralph Ebbin Trio, Gita Blakeney, Legacy and the James Richardson Trio. Proceeds aid the Amnesty organization, which has more than a half-million members worldwide and has been credited with saving the lives of 50,000 prisoners of conscience and other oppressed peoples. Tickets are $20.

CAFE LIDO & MICKEY'S BISTRO

The Sea Terrace, • *Elbow Beach Hotel* • *Paget.*

OPEN DAILY
Lunch: 11:45AM - 2:45PM • *Dinner:* 6:30PM - 10:30PM

Tel: (441) 236-9884
(441) 236-3535
(441) 236-7303

Tel: (441) 235-0698

La Coquille

RESTAURANT AND BAR AT THE
BERMUDA UNDERWATER EXPLORATION INSTITUTE

OPEN DAILY
Lunch: 12:00 NOON - 2:45 PM • *Dinner:* 6:30PM - 10:30PM

TEL: 292-6122

FAX: 292-8825

RESTAURANT AND SUSHI BAR

Restaurant
21 Front Street West
Hamilton HM 11, Bermuda
Tel: (441) 295-4207
Fax: (441) 295-8979

Hours
Monday through Saturday
Lunch: 11:30AM - 5:30PM
Dinner: 6:00PM - 10:00PM
Early Dinner Special:
Served before 7:30PM

Sushi Bar Hours
Sushi Bar:
11:00AM - 2:00PM/4:00PM - 10:30PM

LITTLE V VENICE

RESTAURANT
32 Bermudiana Road
Hamilton HM 11
Bermuda
Tel: (441) 295-3503
(441) 295-4362
Fax: (441) 295-8977

HOURS
Monday - Sunday
Lunch:
11:30AM - 2:15PM
Dinner:
6:00PM - 10:00PM

Our Early Dinner Special:
Served before 7:30PM

La Trattoria

RESTAURANT
22 Washington Lane
Hamilton HM 11
Bermuda
Tel: (441) 295-1877
(441) 292-7059
Fax: (441) 295-8974

HOURS

Lunch: 11:30AM - 3:30PM
Dinner
Summer: 5:30PM - 10:30PM
Winter: 5:30PM - 10:00PM

DAILY SELECTIONS OF
SPECIALS/EARLY BIRDS UNTIL 7:30PM

Intimate Dining at its Finest

Ascots
RESTAURANT

Bermuda's most elegant country manor, nestled in a tropical garden setting. Located in the heart of Hamilton.

We will custom cater any special event on location or on property. Weddings, business meetings, incentive groups.

Call For Reservations

24 Rosemont Avenue Tel: 295-9644

Weddings

So you've decided to get married. And you've decided you want a romantic but carefree wedding. It's at this point problems can occur. For starters, there's the sticky problem of relatives. We're not against relatives, rest assured, but we do realize that families of the bride and groom can have conflicting ideas on where and how the ceremony should be conducted. One family may be living in Washington, for example, while the other lives in Los Angeles. Meanwhile, the bride and groom are based in New England. How do you avoid pleasing one set of relatives at the expense of the other? The solution is easy: Come to Bermuda.

Traditionally, our island has always been *the* place to honeymoon; these days it's rapidly becoming a favorite location for the ceremony and reception as well. In 1996, out of the 1,602 marriages conducted here, 498 of them were overseas couples. The majority were from the Eastern Seaboard, but some came from as far away as Japan and Australia.

Of course people don't choose to marry here just out of tact or to escape a potential family war zone. They come because of our scenery and because of our romantic atmosphere. And they come because they know we approve of weddings. We're good at them. Besides, they feel that combining wedding with honeymoon will make for a more relaxing experience.

But, isn't it difficult to make all the arrangements from overseas? Isn't it nerve wracking? One bride from the United States told us, "I couldn't believe how *easy* it was. I scarcely had to do a thing." She, like many of our visitors and, indeed residents, used a wedding consultant to take charge of arrangements. These arrangements often include acquiring the license, arranging the ceremony and reception, advising on accommodation and coordinating the florists and the photographers. Consultants will also make hair and beauty appointments, and make transport arrangements to and from the ceremony location. Of course, you can arrange your own wedding without incurring a consultant's fee. But if practical details stress you, and if you're pushed for time, we strongly recommend that you do use their help, particularly if you have never been to Bermuda.

In this chapter, we'll talk about the legal requirements and about the ceremony and location choices available. We'll also list a sampling of well-established wedding consultants who are experienced in facilitating trouble-free weddings. And in our Close-up we'll tell you about our own wedding traditions, some of which you might like to adopt for a truly Bermudian celebration.

License to Thrill

Before you can marry in Bermuda, you have to fill out a Bermuda Government form or notice of your intended marriage and, together with a check for $187.50, send it to the Registry General (See Civil Ceremony heading below for address and telephone number). If you are younger than 21, you must send proof of parental consent. Where applicable, you should also send photocopies of divorce certificates.

Once the Registry General receives these papers, the registrar will put one announcement of your intended marriage in *The Royal*

Gazette and one other in the *Bermuda Sun*. Provided a Jane Eyre/Mr. Rochester situation doesn't happen (i.e., no one makes a valid objection), you will then receive your license. The procedure must be completed between 15 days and three months of your wedding date. The fee, by the way, includes your marriage certificate.

Where religious ceremonies are concerned, you also follow the above procedure. Wedding banns for overseas couples are not usually read unless some family members are living here and affiliated with a particular church.

A Civil Ceremony

The Registry General
Melbourne House, 30
Parliament St., Hamilton •
297-7709

If you want a civil ceremony, you'll tie the knot, so to speak, in the Marriage Room of the Registry General. Now some people are worried that registry office marriages are too impersonal and cold altogether. However, the Registrar, Mrs. Christopher, and the Assistant Registrar, Mr. Dowling, genuinely care about each marriage they conduct. They combine formality and warmth in such a way that the significance of the event comes through. They want you to feel that your wedding is a very special occasion. The room itself is beautifully decorated with an ocean view mural. Some couples like to add to the outdoor effect by having sand put on the floor. Staff are happy to comply and are unfazed by the sight of the bride and groom dressed in all their finery but in bare feet.

As soon as you acquire the license, you can make an appointment. Appointments can be any time between 10 AM and 3:45 PM Monday through Friday, and 10 AM to noon on Saturday. You will need two witnesses. They can be your relatives or friends, but staff will step in (except on Saturdays) if requested. The Registrar and the Assistant Registrar are not able to officiate at weddings outside or at any other location. There is no additional cost for the ceremony.

FYI

Unless otherwise noted, the area code for all phone numbers listed in this guide is 441.

Religious Ceremonies

Read our Worship chapter and you'll see that we have a diversity of religions and faiths. It is possible to have a religious wedding ceremony here if you come from overseas, but we must tell you that policies do differ from faith to faith. For example, although we have a Jewish community here, we do not have a resident rabbi. You are welcome to have a Jewish ceremony, provided your own rabbi is willing to come and conduct it. For a Muslim ceremony call Resident Imam-Ameer Shakir at either 293-9108 or 292-5986. He will be happy to help you. You can also have a Bahá'i wedding ceremony in Bermuda. A Bahá'i wedding officer will be happy to officiate either for an indoor or outdoor ceremony. Call 292-2723 for information about arrangements.

Where Christian weddings are concerned, policies vary from denomination to denomination. If you're Roman Catholic, a priest will marry you here only if you have Catholic family living and practicing their religion in Bermuda or if you once lived on the island and were a member of one of our Catholic churches. All Catholic wedding ceremonies must be held in a church. Clergy of some Protestant denominations do perform weddings for overseas visitors, and some are willing to officiate at outdoor weddings. We recommend, however, that you call the church of your choice and receive information on policy.

Wedding consultants, by the way, can suggest ministers who they know are willing to conduct marriage services. The cost of the ceremony itself can vary. An outdoor wedding can be anywhere between $150 to $250, while a church wedding can cost between $300 and $500. Again, check with the church of your choice for information about costs.

Ceremony Locations

You can marry in the Registry General (see above), in a church or in a hotel. However, outdoor weddings have become a very popular option here. As one bride put it, "I wanted my wedding to be natural and romantic at the same time. So I really wanted to be near the ocean." She got her wish. Her wedding was held on the cliff top overlooking the South Shore at Astwood Park (see the Beaches chapter).

If you, too, long for an outdoor wedding, we can offer a wonderful choice of location. As we've already told you, we approve of weddings, so you are welcome to marry in our public areas. You can marry, for example, on a public beach, and have a paddle afterwards, or in a beautiful park. You can even marry on the *Deliverance* in St. George's. Our forts also come in handy — some couples have married, for instance, on the top of Fort St. Catherine, also in St. George's. (Perhaps they sensed a battle ahead of them? Let's hope not.)

However, if privacy is important to you, and you don't want to be distracted by members of the public, you should consider having the ceremony in the grounds of a hotel. Some of our hotels have outdoor areas specially devoted to weddings. At this point, you might check out the Accommodations chapters for descriptions of their views and grounds. Check, too, our Attractions, Beaches and Parks chapters for more outdoor locations. Believe it or not, there are couples who want the ceremony on a boat. Look at the Water Sports and Yachting and Marinas chapters for boat charters.

Whatever venue you choose, you can make arrangements for seating, for champagne to celebrate the ceremony and for a focal point such as a moongate or a bridal arch to be set up. Go to a bridal consultant, and the staff will take care of these arrangements for you.

What about the winter? Outdoor weddings do happen in the winter. Remember our temperatures rarely fall lower than 68 degrees, and the sun doesn't usually desert us. Still, it's always a good idea to have a plan B in case the heavens decide to open. Marry at a hotel, for example, and you'll certainly be assured of an alternative indoor location.

What Happens After the Ceremony?

Sometimes the bride and groom hold a reception in the same outdoor location as the ceremony, but more commonly, after posing for photographs and relaxing with a glass of champagne, the party departs to a reception or a meal held at a hotel or a restaurant, or indeed on a boat. It's very difficult to generalize about receptions: They differ according to personal taste and to the size of the party. Some couples opt for a quiet meal either on their own or with family. Others have larger affairs altogether, and in the case of numerous guests — say more than a hundred — they may have buffet-style refreshments. Check our Restaurants chapter for menus. The Resort Hotels, Small Hotels and Cottage Colonies chapters will help too. Of course you can hire private caterers, but again this is probably easiest to do with the help of consultants. As for prices, again it's difficult to generalize. Once you know the kind of reception you would like and the number of guests, it's wise to call the hotel or restaurant direct to discuss prices.

Transportation

Car rentals are illegal in Bermuda, so for motorized transportation you will depend on taxis. If matching cars are important, you should book taxis in advance. Radio Cabs (see the Getting Around chapter) can provide uniform white Mitsubishi vans that comfortably take up to five people. They make sure that the cars are in tip-top condition and decorated with ribbons.

However, many couples like to follow the time-honored Bermudian tradition of a horse and buggy ride, usually from the church or the ceremony location to the reception. Typically, the driver will be formally dressed in navy blue Bermuda shorts, knee socks and a white hat. And his carriage will be decorated with flowers and ribbons. For romance there's nothing to beat this ride because, as we all know, love and marriage go together like a horse and. . . . Prices vary from about $180 to $400. Remember that you will be charged for the distance from the stable to the destination. It's wise, therefore, to choose a stable close to your ceremony location.

Accommodations

Read our Accommodation chapters and you'll see that we have a large range in terms of facilities and prices. If you want luxury then the Resort Hotels, Small Hotels and Cottage Colonies chapters will help you out. But if you're working with a tight budget, our Guest Houses and Housekeeping Cottages and Apartments chapters are the ones to check. One thing to consider is the distance between accommodation and ceremony location and between ceremony location and reception. The shorter the distance, the cheaper and more convenient the travel arrangements will be.

Of course, it's possible to hold the ceremony and reception in the hotel where you stay. If you use consultants, they will recommend that you make your own accommodation bookings, particularly if you are booking for a large group of guests. However, they will always give you advice on where to stay. Bear in mind that many of our hotels, even the most expensive ones, have wedding and/or honeymoon packages. These packages can offer special rates that can include the ceremony and reception as well as the accommodation. Call the hotel of your choice to see what packages they offer.

A Word About Showing Affection

"Let us be very strange and well bred: Let us be as strange as if we had been married a great while; and as well-bred as if we were not married at all." So said Mrs. Millamant in Congreve's *Way of the World*. Bermudians

---

INSIDERS' TIP

Don't be disappointed: To make all of the arrangements for your special day in Bermuda, book early. This is particularly true for Saturdays and Sundays. Whether you desire a traditional Bermudain wedding or something completely original, Bermuda is the ideal spot.

could well agree with her where being physically demonstrative about love is concerned. Holding hands is OK but we don't tend to passionately kiss or embrace in public, even if we have just got married. In private, of course, it's a different matter.

Bermudian writer Dale Butler has written a book called *A Hundred Best Places to Kiss, Smooch and Snuggle in Bermuda*. According to him, Horseshoe Bay in Southampton is the favorite (see our Beaches chapter), but he also cites more unusual ones such as an elevator in a local company. You can buy his book for $10 at any bookstore.

Wedding Consultants

A successful wedding is always the result of attention to detail. Details can include hair and nails beauty, flowers, music, photographs and videos as well as ceremony, reception and accommodation. Look in the yellow pages of our telephone directory, and you'll see that we have a wide selection of businesses offering services in those areas. While they would be happy for you to deal with them directly, we highly recommend that you choose a wedding consultant instead. OK, you'll pay them a consulting fee, but consider the number of telephone calls and the time you'll save. You'll also benefit from the consultants' expertise and knowledge of Bermuda's idiosyncratic ways.

So given that you're going to use a consultant, what's your first step? It may sound obvious, but picking the wedding date is crucial. If you're planning a fairly complex wedding, do that as soon in advance as possible to avoid disappointment. Remember that ministers, photographers and musicians can be very heavily booked, as indeed can the consultants themselves. Six months to a year's advance notice is the norm, although if you want marry almost on impulse, there may always be last minute cancellations.

So what will these consultants do for you? Let's start by explaining what they typically do *not* do. They don't usually take responsibility for the bride's dress. It's much safer and cheaper for the bride to bring her dress with her. However, it is possible to rent tuxedos here. As we've told you, they don't usually book accommodation either, but they will definitely describe and send pictures of hotels that might interest you (of course, this book does the best job of describing these properties that you'll find!). But they do everything else, including taking care of the marriage license and booking the person who will marry you.

Typically, they will start by discussing with you the level of formality you want, the number of guests and the kind of ceremony you require. They will be sensitive to budget and explain prices in relation to the size of your wedding. They will also arrange hair and beauty appointments (a hair do starts at about $25), and make sure that photographers are on hand to take pictures and /or videos.

What about bouquets and corsages? If you have flower arrangements in mind, you can send them pictures and they will coordinate with the florists. Prices for flowers vary, but a bridal bouquet starts at about $75 while bridesmaids' bouquets are usually about $50. They will also send you pictures of possible locations and of wedding enhancements such as cake, marriage arch or moongate (for outdoor ceremonies). If you want the famous horse and buggy ride, they'll book that too.

Music? Ah, "If music be the food of love, play on. . . ." They will arrange anything from recorded music to a live jazz or island music band, from an organist to a string quartet or a choir. On the day itself, they will be on hand to set up equipment (for an outdoor ceremony) and to make sure that everything goes smoothly. In addition to arranging receptions, they will also organize rehearsal dinners should you require them.

In the following listings we will include prices wedding consultants have quoted to us, but bear in mind all are subject to change. Credit cards for these agencies are fine.

Pembroke Parish

The Bridal Suite
Parkside Bldg., 3 Park Rd., Hamilton
• 292-2025

Allister and Carmen Simmons have owned and managed their bridal consultancy for the past nine years. In September 1997, one marriage they arranged was filmed and featured on a Learning Channel program called "The Wedding Story." That meant that close to 6 million viewers got to see a Bermuda wedding. The ceremony was held at Astwood Park, Paget, Mr. Simmons's favorite wedding location.

Judging from the number of happy bridal parties we see there most Saturdays, many people agree that the stunning views of the South Shore make it an ideal venue. Mr.

Tying the Knot in a Traditionally Bermudian Way

The first marriage recorded in Bermuda was on November 26, 1609, when Thomas Powell, Sir George Somers' cook, was married to Elizabeth Persons, the maidservant of Mistress Horton. No doubt they feasted on roast hog and cahow complemented by cedar berry wine.

Since that time weddings have become more complicated affairs altogether, and these days, Bermudian weddings can be showy affairs with a large number of guests. In fact, ironically, just as you may wish to marry here to avoid stress, many of us are tempted to marry off island to avoid the pressing problem of whom and whom not to invite. Hurt feelings on an island of this size are not a good idea.

But Mrs. Juliet Jackson, well-known on the island for her delicious and beautifully decorated celebration cakes (see Triple J's tip), laments the materialism of today's nuptial celebrations. Once upon a time, she says, weddings were primarily family occasions. There was no way receptions would be held in hotels; they would be held at the home of the bride's parents. Typically, the night before the wedding, the bride's and groom's mothers would take care of making the refreshments, usually, ham and egg sandwiches, and wedding cake, while the bride's and groom's fathers would take care of the liquor if it was served. Bridesmaids would serve the food and the groom's best man and friends would act as ushers. Usually, the brides wore long, white dresses with sweetheart necklines and veils while groom and the male members of the families wore black tuxedos.

— continued on next page

Photo: The Royal Gazette

Newlyweds depart in an old-fashioned carriage.

Honeymoons? Well, up until the early 1970s, Thursday afternoons were half holidays and the traditional time for weddings. Once married, the couple was expected to attend their church on the following Sunday and then have the families back for lunch at their new home. So honeymoons did not mean vacations away from Bermuda; they meant setting up house. Families would help out by contributing furniture and items, such as table linen, for the bride's "hope" chest. Often the gifts were handmade — a far cry from the bridal registries in shops that guests use today.

Yes, things have changed. But some traditions we still follow. Brides' dresses may have changed in fashion, but they do tend to be white. We've already told you about the horse and carriage ride custom. Some of our other traditions focus on the wedding cake. In some ways we believe that it is possible to have your cake and eat it too. In fact, we have two cakes: one for the bride and one for the groom. The bride's is traditionally a three-tier fruit cake, signifying the fruitfulness of the marriage, while the groom's is a single-tier pound cake, signifying prosperity. From a practical point of view, fruit keeps, you see. The top tier is carefully put away until the christening of the first child.

What about the cake decoration? Well, there are two traditions here. First, let's talk about the silver and gold custom. The bride's cake is first covered with marzipan and royal white icing. After that it's covered with silver. How do you get the silver to stick? Well, you paint small areas of the cake at a time with slightly beaten egg white, which makes a good adhesive for the three-inch squares of silver leaf that you then carefully place on the cake. Exactly the same procedure happens with the groom's cake, except his is covered with gold leaf. Silver represents innocence and purity while gold of course represents wealth and prosperity. As you might imagine, this procedure is very exacting and time consuming. It has to be carried out in a completely airless room; otherwise the leaves will turn into blobs.

On top of each cake is a cedar seedling placed in an appropriately sized vase. The bride's cedar should preferably have berries on it to symbolize fertility. On the day of the reception, the cakes, surrounded with ivy and/or fresh flowers, have a special table all to themselves. Once the cakes have been cut, the bride and groom plant the cedar seedlings. Bridal couples from overseas tend to have sprigs instead, since bringing

— continued on next page

seedlings back to their country could contravene laws concerning the importation of plants.

The gold and silver tradition, probably dating back to the 19th century, was originally practiced by wealthy white families. However, these days it's more widely adopted. And yet, some of us wonder why it is that the groom is not expected to be innocent and pure? Eventually, perhaps both cakes will have a mixture of silver and gold decoration, particularly since wives work these days and are just as responsible for their families' prosperity.

According to Mrs. Jackson, the second tradition also goes back to the 19th century. This one requires the bride's cake to be round and iced in white, with silver decorations added. These decorations are sometimes bay grape leaves sprayed with silver. The groom's cake, on the other hand should be square, two tiered and trimmed with blue and silver. Again the cakes are surrounded with flowers.

What other traditions? Well, when you're safely married, you'll be safer still if you walk through a moongate. We borrowed this idea from the Orient, perhaps at the end of the 19th century. Walk through this moon-shaped archway, make a wish and you should have happiness and prosperity for the rest of your life. Don't worry; moongates are not hard to find. Architectural examples are everywhere on the island — on streets, in gardens both private and public, inside hotels and on their grounds. The older moongates were made of Bermuda stone and often covered with vines. A famous one is in Par-la-Ville Park (see the Parks chapter), and another is next to the Bermuda Bakery on Pitts Bay Road, City of Hamilton. If a moongate is nowhere near your ceremony location or reception, worry not. Hotels or wedding consultants can usually rent for you portable wooden ones.

Another custom has to do with rice. Few people use confetti in Bermuda. Let's face it, it does cause unwanted litter. Traditionally, guests would sprinkle rice over the newlyweds, since rice also represents prosperity and fertility. These days we worry about the birds choking on it, so we tend to use birdseed instead.

So will you borrow some of our traditions, while perhaps including your own? If you do, you'll also be following the "something old, something new, something borrowed, something blue" tradition. The "blue," by the way, relates back to biblical days when that color, rather than white, represented purity. Whatever you choose to do, make sure that you let nothing to the marriage of true minds admit impediment.

Simmons can set up a portable moongate in the park. The diamond shape marked on the center of the arch represents, he says, the diamond in the engagement ring. Should the weather be indecent, you can have the ceremony at nearby St. Anne's Church, or at a hotel. But if a different outdoor location appeals, he is happy to arrange it.

If good photographs are a priority, he will advise you on the best times of the day and the evening for good light. In fact, the Bridal Suite has in-house photographers. Photograph prices start at $350 for 48 photos, plus album. For extra photos the rate comes down. Order 96, for example, and you'll pay $600. Videos also start at $350, and you can have a deluxe package that includes great scenes of Bermuda, as well as your celebration, for $700.

Out of the 498 overseas couples that married here in 1996, the Bridal Suite arranged 250 of them. "We make sure there's never a mistake," he told us. "We want every bride to be very happy — that's what's important." Consulting fees range from $475 to $700, depending on the number of guests. Both Mr. And Mrs. Simmons are members of Bermuda's Chamber of Commerce.

Wed in Paradise
Fort House, 9 Fort Hamilton, Hamilton • 295-1968

Janet Le-Page, co-partner and manager

of this consultancy, is certainly happy to tailor make your wedding according to your specifications. But she also offers six different packages whose prices include all itemized services and items as well as the costs of her own administrative services.

Let's take her Paradise Lakes package, for example, that enables you to marry on a boat. She will arrange marriage license, marriage certificate and minister, plus two witnesses if required. She'll arrange for a hair stylist to come to the bride on the day of the wedding and will organize the bridal bouquet and groom's boutonnières. She'll hire a motorized yacht and order champagne, soft drinks, hors d'oeuvres and a two-tiered wedding cake for bridal couple and four guests. How will she get you to Hamilton Dock? She'll get you to and from the dock in an open-topped car. And she'll arrange for a photographer to come as well. You'll exchange your vows while the yacht cruises gently around Paradise Lake, an area in the Great Sound known for its tranquillity and scenic beauty. How much? $2,225 for everything. Of course if you want extra guests there'll be additional charges.

This is the most expensive package. Others let you marry in St. Peter's Church (see the Worship and Attractions chapters), or under a moongate on a South Shore beach for between $1,625 to $1,744. Janet Le-Page is happy to arrange even more unusual ceremonies. You could, for example, marry on the seat of a bicycle made for two or at the bottom of the ocean floor. How would that be possible? You'd wear a helmet instead of a veil (see the Water Sports chapter). To be honest, no-one has (up to the time of publication) chosen that option.

Ms. Le-Page, by the way, is a member of the Association of Bridal Consultants in Connecticut.

The Wedding Salon Ltd.
51 Reid St., Hamilton • 292-5677

Owner and manager, Mrs. Barbara Whitecross, was originally from New England, but she has been in Bermuda for the last 17 years. "From the time I was very little, I always wanted to be a bridal consultant," she told us. December 1, 1984, she achieved her goal by setting up The Wedding Salon. Her aim is to "let the bride be in charge. She executes the orders, and I'll follow them through."

Her favorite locations? The Botanical Gardens and Gates Fort (see the Attractions chapter) are popular, as is Jobson's Cove. But of course the choice is yours. She coordinates the photographer, who charges $300 for the first hour and for the first roll of film. Thereafter they charge $100 an hour plus $75 for each roll of film. Depending on their length, videos range from $300 to $850.

In addition to coordinating services, Barbara Whitecross also has dresses for sale, ranging from $150 to $1,000, although these are mostly for locals. Overseas brides prefer to buy them abroad. But she does rent tuxedos for $80. She is a member of the Association of Bridal Consultants in Connecticut.

Devonshire Parish

Bermuda Weddings Associates
Rapose Cottage, 47 Watlington Rd. E.
• 236-7471

Shelly A. and Robin L. Hamill are co-owners of this consultancy. They started up in August 1994. Why? One reason was that they themselves had gotten married in Bermuda. "I didn't want other couples to make the mistakes we did," explained Shelly Hamill, the

---

INSIDERS' TIP

Call Triple J's Products at 238-2813 if you want the traditional silver and gold wedding cake. Mrs. Juliet Jackson makes and decorates all kinds of celebration cakes, but she specializes in creating ones for weddings. You don't happen to like fruit or pound cake? Then she will make and decorate whatever you like, whether it be rum, banana, strawberry mousse or carrot cake.

manager, who was originally from the United States. "For example, we decided on a DJ at 3:30 in the afternoon. A string quartet would have been much more appropriate."

She is willing to organize whatever wedding you require, but she specializes in large weddings. She does about 25 to 30 a year — no more — so she can really pay attention to detail and not do a rushed job. She's happy to arrange golf tournaments, fireworks, brunches, rehearsal dinners and parties as well as the usual wedding arrangements. She can even arrange for flags from the countries of the bridal party to be flown. One of her Bermuda weddings for a couple in New York was featured in the March 1998 edition of *Modern Bride*.

Her charges? She basically charges $100 an hour for her administrative charges with a starting fee of $500. In addition to arranging weddings, she also publishes an 80-page annual magazine called *Bermuda Weddings and Setting Up Home*. Call her if you would like a copy. Cost is $3.95 plus shipping. She is a member of the Association of Bridal Consultants in Connecticut, of the Bermuda Chamber of Commerce and of the Bermuda Credit Association.

Photographic and Video Services

Pembroke Parish

Memory Bank Video Services
Cedarparkade, Washington St., Hamilton • 236-3229, 295-3378

Dennis Sherlock established this business in 1981. Ever since he has created all sorts of videos for the VSB television station (see our Media chapter) including *The Curious Cook*. He is also very experienced at creating wed-

ding videos and offers a variety of packages that range from $350 to $1,000. For $350 he covers the ceremony (outdoors or indoors) and includes suitable graphics, together with panoramic shots of Bermuda at the beginning of the video. Dennis has plenty of music to choose from but is happy to let you provide the music of your choice. An additional video copy costs $20. Memory Bank often has bookings a year or even two in advance, but Dennis can sometimes cover spur-of-the-moment weddings, particularly if they occur on weekdays. You should note that credit cards are not accepted.

FYI

Unless otherwise noted, the area code for all phone numbers listed in this guide is 441.

Visual Impact Photography
63 King St., Hamilton • 295-4755

Ernest McCreight has run his own photography business since 1988. He's experienced at covering weddings and, as he puts it, goes "beyond the expected" to make sure your special day is elegantly portrayed and beautifully documented on film.

Ernest offers three packages. "The Bermuda Getaway" costs $250 for one hour's work and a minimum of 30 4-by-6-inch prints plus negatives. This is a popular option for couples on a budget. "The Bermuda Dream" costs $520, again for one hour and 30 4-by-6-inch prints with negatives, but this package also offers 24 5-by-7-inch enlargements, displayed in a beautiful leather-bound album from the Renaissance Collection. "The Bermuda Fantasy" package is $1,300. It offers two hours' photo coverage and a leather-bound album from the Mario Acerboni Collection containing 29 8-by-10-inch prints of your favorite pictures. Ernest uses Hasselblad photographic equipment that ensures enlargements of the highest quality. After the ceremony he takes "Lovestory Portraits" of the bride and groom against a backdrop of Bermuda's most breathtaking scenery. Additional hours of coverage are $80 each.

INSIDERS' TIP

Experienced makeup artists will come to your hotel on your wedding day. Ask your consultant for a recommendation.

Photo: GIS

A bride poses with a horse and buggy at St. Mark's Church.

Ernest has bookings a year in advance. However, last-minute coverage of weekday weddings can sometimes be arranged. It's important to book as far ahead as possible for weddings on Saturday or Sunday.

Some of our parks could best be described as our "green bits" or green open spaces where building is not allowed. Others are our conservation areas; they are examples of Bermuda's wildlife left in peace.

Parks and Conservation

So what are our parks like? Let's start by confessing that if you've got Yellowstone or Grand Canyon National Park in mind, forget it. Those, after all, are more vast than the whole of our island put together. Our parks are small. But we're proud of them because they are protected from the onslaught of concrete and glass that the 20th century has called "progress."

Our largest park area is actually the South Shore Park, the one that encompasses many of our South Shore beaches. It consists of 93 acres. Check our Beaches chapter for more information about it and about others that have beaches accessible to the public. And our smallest? Godet Rock is a tiny island in the Great Sound, consisting of 0.266 of an acre.

Some of our parks could best be described as our "green bits" or green open spaces where building is not allowed. Kindley Field Park in St. George's Parish, for example, is a grassy area edging Ferry Reach that is not particularly exciting. But it's important, nonetheless. We go there to watch speed boat racing or just to take a break from driving. We'd be horrified if someone were permitted to build on it.

Others are our conservation areas; they are examples of Bermuda's wildlife left in peace. Many of these parks are difficult to access because they have no trails. And some are deliberately restricted to visiting scientists or people who have a scholarly interest in the environment. Nonsuch Island, where cahows, skinks and other endemic wildlife still exist, is the best example (see our Area Overview chapter). Plans are afoot to make one of our conserved areas more accessible to the public. Paget Marsh on Lovers' Lane, Paget, will even-

tually have a boardwalk allowing visitors to explore the flora without damaging it.

But there are parks that do retain a wilderness effect while having pathways that make access easy. These, of course, we'll describe in our listings. Remember to think small while you're exploring them. Walk fast, and probably the longest time you'll take to get through them is at the most a half-hour.

So why not stroll instead? We recommend that you follow W. H. Davies' philosophy: "What is this life if full of care/We have no time to stand and stare?" There's certainly plenty to stare at: views of the ocean, Bermuda's lush foliage, birds, bees and butterflies. It's often a good idea to assume the eye level of a four-year-old. Look down, then, as well as up, and watch out for our wild flowers, our feathered grasses and for birds and lizards that scuttle in the bushes. Look out also for the riotous tumble of our hedges. Our Flora and Fauna chapter will help you with identifying some of our plants and animals.

Not all of our parks are "wild," however. Some, particularly the ones belonging to the Corporation of Hamilton, could better be described as gardens. If you're into manicured lawns, exotic flowers and trees, then these are the ones to wander through. And if you're into military history, you'll appreciate the parks that feature forts. (Check our Attractions chapter for more gardens and forts.)

How about recreational facilities? At present two have swings, slides and play equipment for kids. Warwick Long Bay in the South Shore Park we describe in our Beaches chapter. See the Mullet Bay listing below for our other. Pembroke Dump, once an area as unsightly as its name suggests, is currently being turned into a park and will eventually also have recreational equipment.

Bear in mind that only two of the parks we describe in this chapter allow you to drive through. Usually you leave your car or bike in the parking lot nearby and trust to Shank's pony. So here we go: Let time stroll.

St. George's Parish

Ferry Point Park
Ferry Rd., St. David's

Ferry Point Park consists of an island and a promontory. If a blend of history and varied landscape appeals, make it a priority to explore the maze of hidden pathways and the railway trail that take you to hidden bays, thicket and rocky open spaces. In the wooded areas you'll find Natal plum bushes. Their white flowers are very fragrant, and their red fruits, some people say, are delicious. Imagine sweetened milk, and you have some idea of the taste. Slopes of spiky asparagus fern will give a spring to your step. The effects of light and shadow on them create infinite varieties of green, thus, as Andrew Marvell put it, "Annihilating all that's made/ To a green thought in a green shade."

Enjoy, too, the Mexican peppers, the bamboo, the buttonwood and the fiddlewood trees. Follow the coastline, and you'll hear nothing but the call of birds and the lapping water. Sorry, we must correct that. Occasionally, you'll hear and see a jet from North America flying into the airport. Look out for white egrets that when observed from behind look like animated, elongated spoons bouncing along.

Once you reach Whalebone Bay, you may wonder why the sand on the bay looks darker and grittier than sand found on our other beaches. You'll remember that Bermuda sits on top of an inactive (we promise) volcano? This is the only beach on our island where you can see traces of volcanic rock mixed with the minuscule shells of the sand.

"What about the history," you might ask? Well, first of all, you'll find a cemetery with a large white marble cross commemorating Brit-

FYI

Unless otherwise noted, the area code for all phone numbers listed in this guide is 441.

ish soldiers who lost their lives in the 1864 yellow fever epidemic. Second, in the woodland you may well come across the remains of an old lime kiln. Lime was once essential for maintaining our white roof tops and for building construction. Third, cross the bridge to Ferry Island, and you'll find the old St. George's terminus for the ferry. Before 1871, when the Causeway opened, a horse-drawn ferry was the main means of transportation connecting the mainland with St. George's Island. Look across the water, and you'll see the remains of a later form of transportation: the old railway.

And last, you'll find forts here. On Ferry Island you'll see one called Ferry Island Fort, but of course. First built in the 1790s and rebuilt in the 1870s, it offered protection against the dreaded American enemy. On Ferry Point you'll find two more. Governor Sir Robert Robinson built Burnt Point Fort in 1688 to prevent illegal trading by Bermudian vessels as well as enemy ships invading. It's actually St. George's oldest fort. Martello Tower is a more recent one altogether, having been built in 1823. It's surrounded by an extremely deep ditch. We recommend that you cross the narrow bridge, enter the tower and climb the steps that lead to the top. Circular in shape, the tower offers circular views. Look west, and you'll have a clear view of Dockyard in Sandys Parish. Paradoxically, these views fill one with a feeling of spaciousness on the one hand and a realization of Bermuda's smallness on the other.

There's plenty of parking space at the entrance. Restrooms are there too.

Great Head Park
Battery Rd., St. David's

Explore this park, and you will find St. David's Battery on top of the cliffs of St. David's Head. It features two British breech loading guns that date back to the early 1900s and that are placed in batteries side by side. As Lance Furbert II points out in his leaflet "Forts of Bermuda in Bermuda's Parks," this battery "stands as a memorial to the men of the Bermuda Militia Artillery, the Bermuda Volunteer Engineers, the Bermuda Militia Infantry, and to all the Bermudian servicemen who served their country with honour at home and abroad." St. David's Battery, then, was manned during World War II.

In fact, the guns were never fired in anger, but they were fired to mark the death of King George V in 1936. William Zuill in his *Bermuda Journey* explains that Bermuda received the news of the king's death at night, and that Government House ordered the customary 21-gun salute to be fired immediately. Although there was plenty of ammunition, there were no blanks available. Because the officers thought there was no shipping in the area, they decided that the salute should take place anyway. Unfortunately a small gun boat, which had been waiting for daylight, was directly in the line of fire. It turned out to be a Bolivian boat manned by British sailors. The good news is that they weren't hit and happily celebrated the fact over scotch and sodas with the officers.

Great Head is well worth a visit for its views and wildlife. Be warned, though, that the trail can be steep in places and is therefore not ideal for people who have difficulty walking. The trails lead you through areas of open field and fairly dense thicket. On hot days, the archways created by overhanging spice trees and fiddlewood offer welcome shade and dappled light. Look out for palmetto, allspice and bay grape trees.

But lower your eyes, too, because small wild flowers, herbs and feathered grasses are plentiful. You may notice small green plants with bright red bracts; these are Joseph's coat or tiny poinsettia. Tiny lilac flowers on a slender stem are Jamaica vervain. Butterflies like this park and so do the birds. Listen carefully for bird song, including the cheerful call of the chick of the village.

Eventually, you will reach the top of the cliff. Rest for a view of the ocean, of St. David's Lighthouse and of the curving coastline. Then follow the cliff walk until you come to the battery. Great Head Park, by the way, has a small parking lot at its entrance and a portable toilet.

Littlehead Park
Cashew City Rd., St. David's

The entrance to this park overlooks pic-turesque Vaughan's Bay. Park in the small parking lot (a portable toilet is available) and follow the trail signs. For a few minutes you'll walk through woodland until you come to a cottage on your right and a yard. Don't worry; you're not trespassing. The land is definitely public. The small beach on your left is Gunner's Bay. Walk farther, and you'll see that the path hugs the coastline. That's why the land crabs like it, so watch out for their holes. Eventually you will come to Fort Popple where you'll have stunning views of the rocky coastline and, of course, of the fort.

"Why 'Popple?'" you might ask. It's named after Governor Popple who, fort passionate, built it in 1738. Once you've seen the fort, you can continue your walk until you come to the adjoining Great Head Park. See the listing above.

Mullet Bay Park
Mullet Bay Rd.

We list this one because it has recreational equipment for children. Located just outside the Town of St. George, it has swings, slides and climbing frames that should keep small children amused. While they release physical energy, you can sit on one of the benches and keep an eye on them.

Hamilton Parish

Blue Hole Park
Dolphin Dr., off Blue Hole Hill

This park is at the point where the Causeway meets Blue Hole Hill, opposite the Grotto Bay Beach Hotel and Tennis Club. Drive in, and you'll see a parking area on your right with restrooms. Follow the trail signs, and you'll find yourself in a thicket carpeted with elephant ears foliage that also climbs trees. Surinam cherry trees act as thick hedges, and sago palms (actually cycads, not true palms) abound.

A five-minute walk will take you to a pond at the end of an open grassy area on the right of the trail. Artificially created, the pond

INSIDERS' TIP

Dogs are welcome in Bermuda parks, but they must be on a leash.

fills what was once a garbage dump. On a hill there the Audubon Society has set up an observation hide complete with a bird blind. What's a bird blind? It's a small box with a slit that you can look through. That way you can see the birds, but they can't see you. Human faces can frighten them. The pond itself is often covered with algae, but look closely and you may notice herons. You'll certainly notice mangroves.

Continue following the trail and you'll come to a break in the hedge on your right — walk through it and you'll have a surprise. There before you is one of Hamilton Parish's numerous caves. Look down and across to see the deep blue of this cave's pool. Look up to admire the stalactites that resemble small rhinoceroses on a downward flight.

Go back to the trail and walk for a few minutes until you come to a clearing and a small cove overlooking Castle Harbour. Sit on a bench here and gaze at the mangroves, or check out more caves by the edge of the water. Then pick up the trail again to find a large wooden deck. Stand on it and you can view a sunken cave filled with water, again of the deepest blue. Below the surface barracuda silently skulk. You'll see still more mangroves surrounding the pool plus the feathery tendrils of Spanish Moss hanging from the trees. On clear days the trees and stalactites are perfectly mirrored in the pool. This park may be small, but there's magic to it.

Smiths Parish

Spittal Pond Nature Reserve
South Rd.

This reserve has two entrances: one at the eastern end of the property and one at the western end. Just for once, we want to reverse the spatial order we normally follow in this book and take you for a walk from west to east. As you drive through Smiths Parish with Hamilton behind you, you'll see on your left St. Mark's Church. The western entrance to Spittal Pond is just beyond it, on the opposite side of the road.

Drive in, and leave your bike or car in the parking lot. Most likely some feral or escaped chickens from the neighboring dairy farm will welcome you to the land of rural Bermuda. Go down some steps and follow the public footpath that slopes down into the woodland. Fiddle wood, Mexican pepper, cedars and allspice trees form a leafy tunnel. Interspersed with the trees are the vines of morning glory and elephant ears. Remember to look down as well as up, and look out for the wild flowers. Wire weed is common here. Actually, its name is most unfair to it; it has tiny apricot flowers that are delicate and pretty. If we have to discriminate between flower and weed, let's agree with Gerard Manley Hopkins: "Long live the weeds and the wilderness yet."

Come out of the tunnel and you'll see Spittal Pond on your left. The brackish pond with its surrounding marshland is a perfect sanctuary for herons, coots, ducks and geese. It's fenced, but as you continue along the footpath, you'll find plenty of areas where you can watch the birds without upsetting them. Look to your right, and you'll see the spectacular, craggy coastline of the South Shore.

Ahead of you is a gate leading to the sanctuary and to Spanish Rock. However, before you enter, check out on the right an extraordinary geological formation locally known as "Chequerboard." It consists of a flat floor of rock scored into distinct squares, surrounded by crags of varying heights that overlook the

www.insiders.com

See this and many other **Insiders' Guide**® destinations online — in their entirety.

Visit us today!

INSIDERS' TIP

Most of our parks have portable or porto cabin toilets. They're reasonably clean but unfortunately don't have running water. Bring bottles of water and paper towels, particularly if you have kids.

A quiet walk through one of our many parks gives new meaning to the word solitude.

ocean. To a geologist, the formation is interesting. For some years it was unclear as to whether the squared effect was artificial or natural. However, it is now agreed that the composition is indeed natural and that the lines or cracks happened as the marine limestone emerged from the sea. Ideally, you should visit Chequerboard in stormy weather. On any day the jagged effect of the rocks against sky and sea is dramatic but never more so than when the winds are high. Then the waves smash over the rocks, filling the squares with spray and pools of water. On calm, sunny days in spring and summer, it's a good vantage point for watching longtails swoop and soar.

Once through the gate, you have a short but steep climb up the cliff to Spanish Rock where you will find cast in bronze the initials of a sailor and the date, 1543. These initials were once thought to be "TFC" and were attributed to a Spanish explorer named Theodore Fernando Camelo. These days perhaps we

should call this area "Portuguese Rock" instead, since it's now believed that the inscriptions stand for Rex Portugaliae (King of Portugal) and for the Portuguese cross. No one is absolutely sure, but is seems likely that some shipwrecked survivor carved them while watching out for a sail from the cliff top.

Before you reach the bronze cast, notice a cavern on your right that is open to the sea. It's called Jeffrey's Hole. Why? Well, according to William Zuill in his *Bermuda Journey*, Jeffrey was a runaway slave who hid in this cave for a month. At first, his "master" thought that he had escaped by ship but eventually noticed that a 15-year-old female slave often disappeared at sunset with a package under her arm. He followed her and the next day found the cave with Jeffrey fast asleep inside. When did this happen? No one seems to know; the story is part of oral tradition.

Once you descend from Spanish Rock, you'll follow the path through more woodland.

You'll notice in this area particularly lots of dead casurinas and logs scattered throughout. Hurricane Emily in 1987 was mainly responsible for these, although subsequent storms have also left their effects. Why haven't we cleared them away? Well, dead trees also have their part to play in the ecological balance. Where there's natural decay, there's also compost, which will help to fertilize the soil.

Eventually, you'll come to an open area, with Spittal Pond still on your left and clumps of "Green Grow the Rushes O" on the edge of it. Take a moment to gaze at the pond and the bird life. A bright pink flamingo particularly likes this part of the reserve. Should it stretch its massive wings, you'll see that they're edged in dramatic black.

Cross the low wooden bridge across the water, and eventually you'll come to the eastern entrance that also has a car park. If you want to avoid returning by road, then turn left and left again. This time the pond will be on your left and you'll be following a pathway that runs parallel with the South Road. You'll pass a fallow field. Look out for clumps of wire weed and wild lantana (sage). Walk fast and the whole excursion should take about a half-hour. But there's so much to appreciate in this 34-acre reserve, you'd be wise to allow at least a couple of hours.

Devonshire Parish

The Arboretum
Montpellier Rd., off Middle Rd.

Before 1987, the Arboretum had more of an overgrown, heavily wooded effect. However, in the September of that year, Hurricane Emily hit and was particularly vicious in this park. Many of the trees were decimated. New trees and shrubs have been planted since, but today these 22-acres are more manicured park than conserved natural area. The grass is kept short, and the trees are carefully spaced. Ornamental and fan palms tend to grow in clusters, while ficus trees, poinciana and golden shower trees are also featured. Look out for Bermuda olivewood and black ebony trees, too.

As you enter the park (there's a small parking lot), you'll see ahead of you a small wooden gazebo where you can sit and agree with Jane Austen that, "To sit in the shade on a fine day, and look upon verdure, is the most perfect refreshment." Explore further, and you'll find a small ornamental bridge with pools beneath it. We won't tell you exactly where; it's more fun to discover it for yourself.

Although there's plenty of open space, no games or sports are allowed in the Arboretum. Horse riding's OK, though, providing you stick to the pathways.

Palm Grove Gardens
South Rd.

"A garden is a lovesome thing, God wot!" Come to Palm Grove Gardens, and you'll know it too. They are actually the property of Sir David Gibbons who kindly allows visitors Monday through Thursday from 9 AM to 5 PM. (There's no entrance charge.) During those hours, he also allows wedding ceremonies to be held here, provided no more than nine people are present.

You will find palms — about 22 different species, some of which are rare in Bermuda. The Fiji and the European fan palms, for example, are growing here. But so are the endemic Bermuda palmettos together with the more common, albeit aristocratic, Cuban royal, queen and princess palms. Notice that the trunks of the Jamaican coconuts curve out from the ground in contrast to those of the spindle palms that stand straight and tall.

We love this property for its bower of gloriously yellow allamanda and for its delightful garden ponds. You'll find two on the lower level of the grounds. One has a Fiji palm set in the center while another has small stone ornaments and an ornamental bridge. You'll also find on this level a moongate and a little house, both covered with trimmed dark green foliage. Inside the house is a wishing well house where you can drop a penny and make a wish. Walk through the moongate and you get good fortune for free. But your penny will go to charity.

Walk up the hill and you'll see the *pièce de résistance*: a pond with a grassy Bermuda map set in the middle of it. Most of the year water lilies and hyacinths add vibrant blues and pinks to the overall effect. Interested in birds? At the top of the hill there are parrots in an aviary.

Photo: GIS

Castle Harbour is the site of one of Bermuda's oldest forts.

If you're driving from Hamilton you'll see Ariel Sands on the right side of South Road. Palm Grove is the next turning on the same side. Drive in and park your bike on the side of the narrow road. No restrooms are available.

Pembroke Parish

Par-la-Ville Park
Queen St., City of Hamilton

Parlez-vous Français? In case you don't, we'll translate this park's name as "By the Town." It actually was by the town in 1814, but these days it could more accurately be called "Through the Town," since it runs across from Queen Street to Par-la-Ville Road.

Adjacent to the park on Queen Street is the Bermuda National Library and, next to that, the Perot Post Office, which incidentally does *not* belong to Ross Perot, as some American visitors assume. Here's the deal: In the early 19th century they were once the property of postmaster William Perot, famous for creating the first Bermudian postage stamp. We mention these buildings because Par-la-Ville Park was his back yard, so to speak. In fact, he infinitely preferred working in his garden to working at the post office. He tended his citrus groves and one year shipped as many as 40,000 boxes of oranges to Boston. But he also enjoyed planting the fruits, seeds and

tropical plants that his sons sent him from foreign lands. In 1847, his son Adolphus sent him a seedling from Demarara. That seedling is now the mammoth rubber tree you can see just outside the library. Unfortunately the citrus trees disappeared.

These days Par-la-Ville is a favorite place of relaxation for locals. From your point of view, it's therefore an ideal place to people watch as well as to appreciate the flowers, vines and shrubs in the gardens. Lunch times, you'll see the business crowd take a break from their offices. Then you'll notice that business attire for men, in the summer, anyway, is often jacket, tie, Bermuda shorts and knee socks. And after three o'clock, you'll see school children, manifestly relieved to have escaped the classroom, dressed in neat school uniforms and making dramatic entrances. Boys and girls sit on low walls and indulge in gossipy conversations about who's going out with whom.

Other resting spots are benches set under tamarind trees and a bower in the center of the gardens. But sometimes it seems as if Par-la-Ville is on the move. People bustle along the pathways in a hurry to get to work. However, there's always time for the Bermudian greetings ritual: "Good morning, how are you doin'?."

Enter the park from Par-la-Ville Road and you'll go through the vine-covered moongate that was built in the 1920s. See our Weddings chapter for information about moongates. Restrooms (with running water) are next to the Queen Street entrance.

Spanish Point Park
Spanish Point Rd.

Why is this point called Spanish? Because according to William Zuill's *Bermuda Journey*, the *Sea Venture* settlers found evidence here of an encampment, probably used by Spanish survivors of a shipwreck.

It's well worth a visit because of the picturesque islets and bays that surround the headland. It's also worth it for the views. Look west and you can clearly see the curve of Southampton and Sandys parishes and the Commissioner's House perched on a hill in Dockyard. Look east and you can see St. George's.

As you enter the park, you'll see Stovell Bay on your left. New, smart boats are moored here, contrasting with the wreck of the old Floating Dock *Bermuda* that in 1869 arrived in Bermuda in all its glory. It was the largest floating dock in the world and the first to be towed across the Atlantic. Now the poor thing is rusting away. But the birds like it. Herons, kingfishers and gulls like to perch on the hulk.

Mangroves, by the way, surround this bay. Go farther into the park, and you'll see Nelson's Bay where the water is very blue and very shallow. The beach is rocky and ideal for children who like to clamber in the rock pools. Benches under casurina trees overlook the water's expanse. Telephone, parking and restrooms are available at the entrance.

Victoria Park
Cedar Ave., City of Hamilton

This area did not always bear the illustrious name of Britain's monarch. Originally it was a playground for students of Mr. Deane's school nearby and so was called "Deane's Bottom." In the 1880s Hamilton Corporation turned it into a park and in 1889 added an elegant bandstand to commemorate Queen Victoria's Jubilee that had happened two years before. The band stand is still there, and we're all pleased about that.

Throughout the year, The Corporation and the Bank of N.T. Butterfield sponsor periodic outdoor concerts here. Usually each concert is dedicated to one type of music, such as jazz or rock 'n' roll or gospel. Weather allowing, a Christmas concert is also held, when the park rings out with carols and gospel music. The concerts usually start at about 6 PM and last for 2½ hours. When dark falls, in the winter months, the bandstand and the trees are lit with white lights, adding magical ambiance to the festivities. We love these concerts because they give us an opportunity to come together as a community and to enjoy top entertainment from our local musicians. Local band, Legacy, is very popular as is Shine Hayward, who plays a mean saxophone. Concerts are free. Check *The Royal Gazette* for notices of these concerts.

What can you see here during daylight? Victoria, as befits her namesake, has a more formal atmosphere than Par-la-Ville. A terrace leads down to a sunken garden where roses grow. A group of dwarf date palms stand together much like a family of kids posing awkwardly for a photograph. But there are tall palms, as well, and very royal they are too. Graceful mahogany trees add a touch of dark green to the landscape, while pink frangipani trees and plumbago bushes add pink, white and blue to the park's palette.

The tiny pink cottage at the edge of the park may make you think someone's living in it. Actually that's where the restrooms are, complete with sinks and running water. The main entrance to Victoria, by the way, is at the corner of Cedar Avenue and Victoria Street.

Sandys Parish

Hog Bay Park
Middle Rd.

The Bermuda Government officially opened this park in March 1997. However, many of us have enjoyed exploring its pathways for years. So what will you find at Hog Bay? We think you'll experience Bermuda here as it used to be before the introduction of motorized traffic and technology. Here you'll find rocky slopes, thicket, hedgerows and irregular-shaped arable fields where potatoes and other vegetables are grown. You'll also find the remains of a lime kiln and of a buttery that before the days of refrigeration was essential for storing perishables.

A number of different trails twist and turn around the fields, but if you keep southwest, eventually the ocean's expanse will appear magically before you. Climb the hill (known as Sugarloaf Hill), and you'll have magnificent views in all directions. Look west and across to the Lobster Flats and the outer reefs. You should be able to see the stakes and beacons marking the Hogfish Cut or channel. Look east and northeast for a view of the Great Sound, the City of Hamilton and Spanish Point. Beyond is the North Shore and St. George's.

After you've taken in the vistas, clamber down the rocks to the water where at low tide you can enjoy rock pools and perhaps a swim. Most days the water's like glass. Walk in the evening, and you'll have a magnificent view of the sunset over the water. Hog Bay is Bermuda's third-largest park, and indeed, the mixture of landscape it provides gives us the illusion that it's larger than the 38 acres it actually contains. It's also a Mecca for bird watchers. More than 120 species have been recorded here, including orchard orioles, olive-sided flycatchers, purple finches and rough-legged hawks.

As you drive on Middle Road towards Dockyard, you'll find it on the left, just past the Maximart Supermarket. If you reach Somerset Bridge, you'll know you've gone too far. A small parking lot and portable toilets are available.

Scaur Hill Fort and Park
Somerset Rd.

If you're heading out to Dockyard, you'll see a steep turning to Scaur Hill on your right, a few minutes after you've driven over Somerset Bridge (the smallest drawbridge over the Atlantic, by the way). You'll find a parking lot at the top and the fort to your right. This one was built by the British army in the 1860s, '70s and '80s to defend the Royal Naval Dockyard from possible American invasion. During the '80s, a deep ditch extending across Somerset Island was excavated and the fort was armed with 64-pounder guns on disappearing carriages.

In 1941, the enemy, of course, was not the United States at all. Indeed, the American 52nd Coast Artillery mounted two eight-inch railway guns here and, according to Lance Furbert II, nicknamed the fort "Cockroach Gulch." Let us not speculate why. Explore the top of the fort and you'll have wonderful views of the Great Sound. Look through the telescope (no charge) and you can see as far away as Fort St. Catherine and St. David's Lighthouse (see the Attractions chapters).

You'll also notice on the top of the fort a "Bermuda weather stone" that swings from a tripod and a notice with deep philosophical treatises. "If the stone's wet," it says, "it's raining. If it swings, it's windy." And so on. Believe it or not, some visitors actually read this notice and nod very wisely, especially when they get to the part: "When it jumps up and down there's an earthquake." Don't be one of them, will you? And bear in mind that if a blob of white appears on top of it, that does *not* mean it's snowing. It never snows in Bermuda. A bird is likely to be the culprit.

You can explore the moat, planted now with flowers and herbs, and walk down the ditch to the Great Sound. Park land to the east of the fort is manicured — the grass is always kept short. It's rich in cedars both young and old; and palmettos, fiddlewood, loquat and cherry trees abound. As you follow the pathway, the fort behind you, you'll see on your left a white stone construction that is a good example of one of our water catchments. And on your right, you'll see a turning off the pathway. Take it, and you'll find a bench where you can sit and muse on some of the Great Sound islands.

Continue along the pathway, and you come to an open field with a poinciana tree in the middle. Don't be surprised if you see a young child perching on one of its branches. Young children love that tree.

It's vital to remember when riding your rented cycle that we drive on the left side of the road, and at roundabouts we give way to the right.

Recreations

To everything there is a season, and a time to every purpose. . . . Holiday season surely means a time to play. Of course for one person play can mean passive relaxation, while for another it can mean a strenuous workout.

In this chapter we'll give you a potpourri of activities we've not mentioned elsewhere in our guide. We'll categorize the recreations, and within each category we'll follow our usual geographical procedure for listings: east to west, parish by parish. However, be warned that some of the recreations we mention are centered in one or two parishes only. We'll be as specific as possible about prices, though they are all subject to change. Because of our island's size it's possible to explore the whole country within a couple of days, so we'll also include in this chapter information about hiring transport.

Cycle Liveries

If you've checked out our Let's Explain Bermuda and Getting Here, Around and Home chapters, you will already know that car rentals are illegal here. Motorcycle liveries, however, are not; it's perfectly possible to explore the island without being dependent on the buses. Actually, motorbikes are very important, even for those of us who may own a car. On the whole, men go to work on the bike while women lay claim to the car. As for our teenagers, acquiring a motorcycle is almost an initiation rite. Come that magic 16th birthday, the lucky among them will hit the road in a trail of glory, much to their parents' apprehension.

You can always distinguish between a tourist and a local rider. For one thing, the rented cycles always have red-lettered license plates. For another, local riders often manage to be ingenious about carrying enormous amounts of paraphernalia while driving: bags of groceries, bags of laundry and sometimes

even the odd animal such as a dog or cat. At Christmas time you'll frequently see locals with Christmas trees precariously balanced over the bars. Please do not copy this behavior — unless you're very adroit it could lead to an accident. And for security reasons make sure your purse is zipped and not an easy target for snatchers. Bermuda is relatively crime-free, but we do have the occasional bag snatching. Also remember that in Bermuda it is mandatory to wear a helmet when riding on a motorcycle.

Normally, where driving is concerned, for many of our visitors right is right and left is wrong. Sorry, but in Bermuda left is definitely right (correct, that is). It's vital to remember that we drive on the left side of the road, and that at roundabouts we give way to the right. Actually when you hire a bike from one of our liveries, staff members will re-emphasize the rules of the road and make sure you are confident and stable on the bike. All the outlets we list have parking lots or training areas where you can practice before venturing out on our highways and byways. Staff will warn you not to drive too close to the curb and not to start your bike when facing a wall. They will also advise you not to try to walk your bike when the engine is running — bikes can have a nasty habit of running away from you.

All liveries will deliver bikes if you're staying near an area suitable for practicing. Pickup from your accommodation is always possible. What happens if your bike breaks down? Call the livery's number during operating hours, and the staff will arrange for a replacement to be delivered. If the breakdown happens at night, leave a message on the answering machine, then lock your bike securely and take a taxi. Frequently, liveries will reimburse taxi fares if a breakdown necessitates a cab ride.

Rates cover helmets, locks and third-party insurance. When we mention "daily rate," we mean the cost for 24 hours. Hire a bike at 10 AM, for example, and the daily rate lasts until 10 AM the following morning.

We give you a listing here of liveries that have locations other than in the hotels. Check out our various accommodations chapters for liveries operating at hotel sites; hotel staff will always be happy to make cycle arrangements for you. A few of these liveries also rent out pedal bikes. We strongly recommend you wear a helmets when riding a pedal bike, though they are not compulsory. The Railway Trail (see listing in this chapter) offers good places to pedal bike.

St. George's Parish

Dowling's Cycles
26 Duke of York St., Town of St. George • 297-1614

In addition to this livery, Mr. Dowling also has one at St. George's Club and at Grotto Bay Beach Hotel and Tennis Club. He rents out a variety of bikes including Dailum mopeds and SV Deluxe, Palio, Honda and Ascot scooters. Dowling's requires a refundable deposit of $20 plus a one-time payment of $15 for an insurance waiver. Rates are on a sliding scale: Hire a single-seat scooter, and you'll pay $38 (plus the insurance waiver and deposit) on the first day, and the rate will decrease day by day. By the sixth day your daily rate will be $12 from then on out. A double-seat scooter will cost $42 on the first day and from the sixth day will cost $14 a day.

St. George's Cycles
Water St., Town of St. George • 236-0839

For rates and information, check the Eve's Cycle's listing under Paget Parish.

Smiths Parish

Wheels Cycles (Devil's Hole) Ltd.
Harrington Sound • 293-1280

For rates and information, check the Pembroke Wheels listing.

Pembroke Parish

Oleander Cycles Ltd.
Gorham Rd., Hamilton • 295-0919

Oleander is open 8:30 AM to 5 PM every day, including public holidays. See the Paget listing for rates and more information.

Wheels Cycles (Astwood) Ltd.
117 Front St., Hamilton • 292-2245
Wheels Cycles (Hamilton) Ltd.
13 Dundonald St., Hamilton • 295-0112

Actually Wheels, the island's largest livery, has rental shops all over the island. Wheels has liveries in Marriott Castle Harbour and the Southampton Princess hotels (see our Resort Hotels chapter). This establishment uses Peugeot vehicles, so 90 percent of the bikes are scooters. In addition they have some Honda City Expresses and a few Dailum mopeds. Wheels requires payment by credit card — that way you don't have to pay a deposit. For any bike you hire, on the first day you pay a one-time repair waiver of $15. Rates work on a sliding system. For a single-seat scooter you'll pay $33 (plus the repair waiver) on the first day, with the rate decreasing day by day. By the sixth day your daily rate will be $9 thereafter. Want a bicycle made for two? The starting rate for double-seaters is $42 plus the waiver. On day seven and thereafter, the daily rate is down to $12. Call for special group rates.

> ## FYI
> Unless otherwise noted, the area code for all phone numbers listed in this guide is 441.

INSIDERS' TIP

Pick up the free *Bermuda Railway Trail Walking Guide* from your hotel or from the visitors service bureaus in St. George's or Hamilton. It has a map showing the different trail sections from Sandys to St. George's parishes and includes some railway history and descriptions of points of interest.

Wheels also rents mountain bikes for those who want a more energetic form of transportation. On day one you pay a one-time $10 repair waiver plus $10 rent. The daily rate is usually $10. However, rent the bike for more than two weeks, and Wheels will work out a special deal. These locations are open 8:30 AM to 5:30 PM every day, including public holidays.

Paget Parish

Eve Cycles Ltd.
114 Middle Rd. • 236-6247

Eve Cycles offers luxury double-seat Scarabeo scooters for hire. On day one, you pay a one-time third-party insurance rate of $15, plus $60. Rates decrease daily until the eighth day, when you pay a daily rate of $25 thereafter. Hire a Honda City Express (double-seat scooter), and the rates are cheaper. For the Honda, you'll pay $42 plus the $15 insurance on day one, then

the rates decrease until the eighth day when you pay a daily rate of $14 thereafter. A single-seat electric moped starts at $33 plus insurance and by the eighth day costs $10 every day thereafter. Use your credit card, and you pay no deposit. Otherwise a $20 refundable deposit is required. Eve Cycles is open 8 AM to 5:30 PM every day, including public holidays.

Oleander Cycles Ltd.
6 Valley Rd. • 236-5235

Oleander Cycles offers Address, Palio and Bunny scooters for hire. A refundable $20 deposit is required, plus a one-time repairs waiver payment of $15. For a single-seat scooter, on day one you pay $33; the rate decreases every day until the eighth day when you pay a rate of $12. For a double-seat scooter the daily rate starts at $42 and by the eighth day goes down to $15 a day. Credit cards are OK, and Oleander is open from 8:30 AM to 5:30 PM every day, including public holidays.

Southampton Parish

Oleander Cycles Ltd.
8 Middle Rd. • 234-0629

See the previous Paget listing for rates and information about motorcycles. This Oleander branch also offers pedal bikes for hire. Rates? $10 a day. The livery is open 8:30 AM to 5:30 PM every day, including public holidays.

Sandys Parish

Oleander Cycles Ltd.
Bldg. 18, Royal Naval Dockyard • 234-2764

Again, refer to the Paget listing for rates and information about motorcycle rental. This branch of Oleander Cycles is open 8:30 AM to 5:30 PM every day from April to October, including public holidays.

Bermuda's End-to-End Railway Trail

As you read in our History chapter, Bermuda did have an active railway from 1931 to 1946. In 1984 the government decided to designate the old railway lands as a path and bridle way to be used mainly for walkers and pedal cyclists. As a result, it's possible to follow the old train line from St. George's to Somerset, with the exception of the 3-mile section in and around the City of Hamilton that was replaced by roads.

Annual Charity Walk

The first Saturday of every May, the Bermuda End-to-End Committee organizes a pre-pledged island end-to-end charity walk, with funds going to four local charities. What do we mean by "pre-pledged"? Walkers ask friends and admirers of their fortitude to pay them money for taking part. In 1997 the minimum pledge for entry was $20 — if your friends agreed to pay $5 each, you'd need four supporters.

The walk starts at 8 AM in King's Square in the Town of St. George and ends in Royal Naval Dockyard in Sandys. How long does it take walk the island end to end? Depending on your pace, anywhere between six and eight hours. Light refreshments at stops along the route will keep you energized. Overseas visitors are absolutely welcome. Call Karon Wolffe at 299-8821 for information on the minimum pledge required and registration instruction. If a 26-mile walk intimidates you, then try the 15-mile alternative that starts at Albuoy's Point in the City of Hamilton at 11 AM and also ends at Dockyard. (For more information, see our Annual Events and Festivals chapter.)

Be a Trail Blazer

Of course, during the rest of the year you don't have to walk the whole Railway Trail. You can do as we often do: Drive to a small section, park your motorcycle and start your walk. Or alternatively, ride your pedal bike to and along the trail. You'll know you're on the right track, literally, when you notice brown "Railway Trail" signs. There are a few areas where riding a motorcycle on the trail is possible, but we don't advise it. Part of the Railway Trail's charm is the quiet. Motorized traffic blocks out the sounds of breezes, birds and insects. Besides, some of the pathways are so narrow that motorbikes could endanger those of us who want to stroll.

So what's the trail like? It offers a blend of Bermuda's scenery from ocean view to shady thicket; from arable fields to private gardens and properties; from open spaces to tunnels of greenery. The railway often hugged the shoreline and at various points crossed the ocean on trestle bridges. There were 33 bridges in all, 16 of which extended over water. Vestiges of those bridges can still be seen. If you notice concrete pillars emerging from the water, chances are they're old bridge supports. Pylons in Flat's Inlet in Smiths Parish are good examples.

If you're into flowers and birds, you'll see

many of the ones we mention in our Parks and Conservation and Flora and Fauna chapters. By the way, the trail is not completely continuous; it's often interrupted by main or tribe road. But the signs will show you how to pick up the trail again. Also, the trail often criss-crosses paths that lead to attractions, such as the Martello Tower in St. George's Parish or Fort Scaur in Sandys. Be sure to check our Attractions chapter for more on these.

A word about safety. On the whole Bermuda is relatively crime-free, but we're not perfect. We advise women not to walk alone, particularly after dark, and to make sure their purses are securely zipped.

Spas and Health and Fitness Centers

Worried that a holiday will relax you so much you'll wind up out of shape? Check out our Resort Hotels, Cottage Colonies and Small Hotels chapters, and you'll see that many lodging locations have exercise rooms for guests plus spa and beauty facilities. Here we'll give you a sampling of other health clubs that are used by locals but that also welcome visitors. Some offer exercise only, while others have massage and beauty facilities as well.

Pembroke Parish

The Athletic Club
Cedarparkade, Washington St., Hamilton • 295-6140

This facility offers full use of its gym, which is equipped with treadmills, stairmasters, free weights and other machines designed to bend you into shape. Locals pay a one-time fee of $175 plus $98 a month for use of facilities. If they want aerobic classes as well, they pay $108 a month. Overseas visitors are welcome. The cost is $17 a day for use of the gym plus $10 for an aerobics class. Facilities include whirlpools, saunas and a steam room. Feel like a massage? A one-hour session is $60; a half-hour costs $40. A personal physical assessment is $40. The Athletic Club is open 6 AM to 9 PM Monday to Friday, 8 AM to 8 PM on Saturdays and 8 AM to 2 PM Sundays.

Images Ltd.
Belvedere Bldg., 69 Pitts Bay Rd.
• 295-0615, 295-0616

Come to Images to enjoy a variety of hair and beauty treatments for very reasonable rates — reasonable for Bermuda, that is. A wash, haircut and blow dry costs $43, a manicure costs $17 and a pedicure is $25.50. Images is one of the few salons in Bermuda that offers Reiki treatments. In fact, beauty therapist Debbie is a Reiki master (doesn't sound PC, but that's what she is), and she uses this hands-on healing process to alleviate all sorts of aches and pains. For $50 she'll give you a five-to-10-minute consultation in which you'll explain where your painful areas are. Then it's time to lie down in a darkened room lit by candles, listen to music and meditate. Debbie will place her hands gently on the painful areas and energy points of your body. The heat generated by her hands relieves the pain. Often she incorporates Reiki into her massage, aromatherapy, reflexology and facial treatments as well.

Facials, by the way, are a particularly good value ($50 for an hour) since they involve massage of the hands and feet as well as the face, neck and shoulders. Debbie uses Jurlique cream and oil products for her face and body treatments. You bite your nails? Worry not. For $70 you can acquire a new set of acrylics. Tourists are welcome and spur-of-the-moment appointments are nearly always possible.

Magnum Power Force Gym
119 Front St., Hamilton • 292-7007

Believe it or not, owners and managers Ron and Karen really are called Magnum. Ron is Bermuda's only professional bodybuilder and wrestler. Locals pay a yearly membership of $700, or $340 for four months. Overseas visitors are welcome and pay $15 a day. If they come with a member, it's only $10. Certified trainers will help out with the cardio equipment, machines and weights. Magnum Power Force Gym is open 6 AM to 8:30 PM Monday to Friday and 9 AM to 3 PM on Saturdays and Sundays.

The Olympic Club
12 Dundonald St., Hamilton • 292-4095

This one is aptly named since it's said to

be home to Bermuda's major athletes. Partners and managers are Nick Jones and Scott Stallard, a well-known local photographer. In addition to a wide range of equipment, including weights, life cycles, wind racers and stairmasters, the club offers aerobics classes. The Olympic is the only center offering Spinning facilities and classes. Unfamiliar with Spinning? It involves riding a stationary bicycle that simulates all the challenges you could face in the outdoors, including uphill climbs and jumps. Coaches at the club offer instruction, and you might find it to be an invigorating cardiovascular workout. Twenty-four-hour notice is required for Spinning. Saunas and showers are available. Visitors pay $10 a day; locals pay an initial fee of $90, then can pay $35 a week or $75 a month. The Olympic Club doesn't take credit cards. It is open 6 AM to 9 PM Monday to Thursday, 6 AM to 8 PM Friday, 9 AM to 6 PM Saturday and 9 AM to noon on Sunday.

Total Fitness Center
24 Brunswick St., Hamilton • 295-0087

This center offers an aerobics program as well as a wide range of equipment, including stair-climbers, Cybex cycles, treadmills and free weights. Overseas visitors are welcome and pay $15 per day. The fee includes aerobics, towel service and use of the whirlpool. Aerobics classes run Monday through Friday at the following times: 7 to 8 AM, 12:15 to 1 PM, 5:30 to 6:30 PM and 6:30 to 7:30 PM. On Saturday a class is held from 9:30 to 11 AM. On Sunday? Even the super healthy-minded deserve a lie-in. An hour-long class starts at 10:30 AM. Visitors can get a personal fitness assessment for $80.

Total Fitness can pamper as well. They offer all sorts of body treatments, facials and massages, together with beauty treatments such as manicures, pedicures and waxing. Costs vary, of course. An hour's aromatherapy face and body massage costs $70, while a pedicure costs $30. Call to make an appoint-

ment. The facility is open from 6 AM to 9 PM Monday to Friday and 8 AM to 4 PM Saturday and Sunday.

Healthy fat-free food is on hand at the Prince Deli (open Monday to Friday from 8 AM to 4 PM). Salads, burgers and soups are available, together with sodas, juices and sports drinks. You should be able to lunch for under $10.

Horseback Riding

Ian Fleming once said: "A horse is dangerous at both ends and uncomfortable in the middle." It's a good thing he didn't live in Bermuda before 1946, when horses were a vital means of transportation. These days horse riding, of course, is recreational rather than necessary. Here we list two stables that offer guided trail rides. Visitors can rest assured that the horses are not nearly as dangerous as Fleming might have feared. In addition, we include a listing for a wonderful facility that offers riding for adults and children confined to wheelchairs or who have special needs.

Devonshire Parish

Lee Bow Riding Centre
Tribe Rd. No. 1 (Off Middle Rd.)
• 236-4181

Lee Bow offers private trail rides for up to four or five people at a time, in the mornings only. The ride lasts an hour and takes you to the Railway Trail along the North Shore. That means that you will enjoy at least a half-hour's riding without traffic and with views of the ocean. Either Tricia or Lisa will guide you. Cantering? That's at the guides' discretion and depends on your previous riding experience. If you're inexperienced, it's safer to stick to walking and trotting. A walk and trot ride costs $35 per person an hour; a canter trail costs $50 for up to two people. Note that Lee Bow does not accept credit cards. Starting times

---

INSIDERS' TIP

Kindley Playing Fields, once operated by the base in St. David's, are now open to the public. Areas are suitable for in-line skating and bicycling.

Photo: GIS

The scuba diving is world-class in Bermuda's sparkling waters.

for rides are from 8:30 to 10:30 AM. Book at least 24 hours in advance and arrive 20 minutes early for orientation. In the interests of safety, hats are mandatory.

Warwick Parish

Spicelands Riding Centre Ltd.
50 Middle Rd. • 238-8212

Spicelands is famous for its daily breakfast rides that take you along beach trails overlooking the South Shore beaches between Warwick Long Bay and Horsehoe Bay (see our Beaches chapter). The breakfast ride lasts 90 minutes and costs $50 per person. On your return you get a light continental breakfast. Starting time is 6:45 AM. A bit early for you? Well, early birds get to enjoy the coolest time of day, particularly in the summer months.

Monday through Friday the stable also offers one-hour rides, again on the South Shore, for $37.50 per person. Starting times are 10 and 11:30 AM and 3 PM. From May through September a ride is also offered from 6 to 7 PM. You should arrive at least a half-hour early so staff can instruct you. Children older than 10 are welcome, but those younger than 16 must be accompanied by an adult. Because tours involve as many as 16 horses, the rides are strictly walking only. Hats are available for everyone but mandatory only for riders younger than 18.

Bermuda Riding for the Disabled
WindReach Recreational Village, 5 Wind Reach Ln. (off Spice Hill) • 238-7433

Actually the telephone number above spells RIDE. This equestrian facility opened in December 1996, and we're so glad it did. It provides a permanent riding location for adults and children confined to wheelchairs or with other special needs. The stable has two paddocks where visitors can ride in a lesson format. Volunteers are on hand — sometimes as many as three per rider might be necessary. Bermuda residents have to have a certificate from a doctor saying that it's safe for them to ride. Overseas special-needs visitors are very welcome, if space permits. They should, however, have some prior riding experience. Call Moira Benbow, equestrian director, to discuss the requirements. There are just seven horses, so it's wise to book as soon as possible. Lessons take place Monday through Friday between 9:30 AM and 3 PM. On Saturday they're available from 9:30 AM to noon. Because WindReach is a registered charity, lessons are free. However, donations are always welcome. The facility is completely wheelchair-accessible. (See the subsequent WindReach listing in this chapter for information about other facilities in this village.)

FYI

Unless otherwise noted, the area code for all phone numbers listed in this guide is 441.

Other Recreational Sports

Read our Spectator Sports chapter, and you'll see that Bermuda residents can enjoy a wide variety of games people play. Read our Golf chapter, and you'll see that we have more golf courses per square mile than any other country in the world. Here we will talk about sports and/or facilities that we haven't mentioned elsewhere.

Before we start, though, a word about swimming. At present we do not have a public swimming pool where swimmers can come for recreational purposes. True, there's a public swimming pool on the grounds of Saltus Grammar School, Pembroke, but this is used by schools and clubs for competitive swimming. Chances are if you're staying in a hotel, your accommodation will have its own pool (see our accommodations chapters). How do locals manage without a public pool? Well, many have private swimming pools, and the rest of us are happy to dip in the sea. Check our Beaches chapter for ocean swimming choices.

What a Racquet

Badminton

The Bermuda Athletic Association Gymnasium
Woodlands Rd., Pembroke Parish • 236-7210

You can play badminton here year round on Tuesdays and Thursdays from 7:30 PM. Visitors are welcome and pay a $5 per evening fee. The number above belongs to Junior Durrant, president of the Badminton association. Call him for booking information. Shuttlecocks are provided, but only a limited number of racquets are available. There's no dress code, but you should wear rubber-soled shoes.

Squash

Bermuda Squash Racquets Association
Middle Rd., Devonshire Parish
• 292-6881

Visitors are welcome to play as guests at this club. Fees are $10 per person for 40 minutes on a court. The staff is available to assist from 11 AM to 2 PM and from 4 to 10 PM Monday through Friday. Call at least a week in advance to book a court. This club holds a number of tournaments throughout the year for players of every level of ability. In April or May, the club hosts the Bermuda Heinz Open, a Professional Squash Association-sanctioned world circuit tournament.

Tennis

Check our Spectator Sports chapter for information on tournaments and tennis events to take in. Many hotels and all of the cottage colonies have tennis courts (see our accommodations chapters), and here are two public tennis facilities that welcome overseas visitors. Note that proper dress for the game in Bermuda consists of tops and shorts (or dresses or skirts) specifically designed for tennis. The all-white rule is not so rigidly enforced as it was in the past.

Photo: GIS

Small but deep-water Hamilton Harbour is a destination for many cruise lines.

Kindley Tennis Courts
Clearwater Beach Rd., St. David's, St.
George's Parish • 293-5791

Originally these four courts belonged to the American military base. Now that the base has departed, residents and visitors can use the courts for $4 per person per hour (credit cards are not accepted). Call the above number for a court. You might want to combine a tennis game with a visit to Clearwater Beach (see our Beaches chapter). Changing rooms and showers are available. Tennis shoes and tennis dress code are mandatory. The courts are open from 1 PM to sunset Monday through Friday and 9 AM to sunset on Saturday and Sunday.

Tennis Stadium
2 Marsh Folly Rd., Pembroke Parish
• 292-0105

Book one of the eight courts by calling two days in advance. During daylight, you pay $8 per person per hour; after dark, it's $16 an hour (no credit cards, please). Changing rooms and showers are available. Tennis shoes and tennis dress code are mandatory. The stadium is open 8 AM to 10 PM Monday through Friday and 8 AM to sunset on weekends and holidays.

Spring Break Sports

Check out our Annual Events and Festivals chapter for information about the Department of Tourism's sports program for college students on holiday here during March.

Bored? Try Board Games

Pembroke Parish

Bermuda Chess Association
Chamber of Commerce, Front St.,
Hamilton • 238-2313

Visitors are welcome to play a game of chess here every Tuesday at 7:45 PM. Casual games are free; tournament play will cost you $5 per evening. In January or February, the Invitational Grand Master Tournament is held at Mermaid Beach. In addition, at the beginning of February, an international Swiss tournament is held at one of our major hotels. Regular grand master visitors are Julian Hodgson and Nick deFirmian.

Scrabble Club
Bermuda Public Services Association
Headquarters, Cedar Ave. • 238-3727

From January to May and September to November, you can play Scrabble at 8 PM on the last Saturday of each month. You need to be aware that British spelling is the official usage in Bermuda. We all know that Scrabble war can break out between American and British spellers, resulting in declarations of independence on both sides. In fact, in those situations Scrabble can more accurately be called "squabble." Mrs. Florenz Maxwell, president of the club, has resolved the problem diplomatically. Both spelling systems are allowed, and the *Official Scrabble Words* dictionary is always on hand. Visitors pay $3 per person per game. Call to confirm games.

Have a Ball Bowling

Warwick Parish

Warwick Lanes
47 Middle Rd. • 236-5290
Why not get bowled over by a night of inexpensive fun for the family? Warwick Lanes is home to the Bermuda Bowling Club. Membership for adults is $45 a year, and it allows cheaper games. However, non-members are welcome. Adults pay $3.50 per person per game; children pay $2.25. Proper bowling shoes are a must — rent them for $1.25 a pair. While waiting on your pins you can have a chicken sandwich or hamburger in the restaurant or enjoy a drink from the bar. Warwick Lanes is open 6 PM to midnight Mondays through Saturdays and 3 PM to midnight Sundays. Call to book games.

Bridging the Gap

Paget Parish

Bermuda Bridge Club
7 Pomander Rd. • 238-1332
Overseas visitors are welcome to play at this beautiful clubhouse. Open duplicate

games are played Mondays at 7:30 PM, Wednesdays at 9:30 AM and Fridays at 8 PM. Novice (0-20 and 20-90) master points games are held Wednesdays at 7 PM. And most afternoons, depending on demand, rubber bridge is played at 2 PM. Table fees are $8 a head. Visitors should call three or four days in advance to be sure of space. The clubhouse has a bar, and free coffee and tea are served.

You might like to know that the World Team Championship for the Bermuda Bowl, one of the most coveted prizes in international bridge, will be held in the year 2000 from January 8 to 22 at the Southampton Princess, Southampton Parish. Actually, this will be a 50th anniversary for the World Team of Four Bridge Championship, which was held in Bermuda in 1950. The silver jubilee was also held here in 1975.

Recreational Opportunities for the Physically Challenged

WindReach Recreational Village
5 Wind Reach Ln. (off Spice Hill)
• 238-2469
This village was founded by Alexander Mitchell and is the second project he has undertaken for people with disabilities. In 1989 he opened a farm in Ontario, Canada, to allow people of all ages and with all sorts of special challenges to enjoy the satisfaction of farming and working with animals. Since Mitchell himself has cerebral palsy, he knows firsthand the frustration of being excluded from activities that can, in fact, be possible. Often, he says, participation simply depends on self-confidence.

The village is at the time of writing in a developmental stage. It will have a two-story activity center with an elevator and rooms for meetings, educational events and craft activi-

INSIDERS' TIP

A sudden rain shower after a spell of dry weather can make roads very slippery. When coming to a halt on your motorcycle, be careful *not* to use right and left brakes simultaneously. That way you'll decrease your chances of skidding.

ties. It already has a petting zoo that is accessible to everyone. Meet the donkey, Eeyore, who's more stubborn than sulky; he's in no way been mistreated. Also meet Tilly and Annie, two miniature horses, and Magic, a very fetching gray-haired goat. Other animals include rabbits, rats (very small pretty rats, we promise, called Brie and Gouda) and a guinea pig.

A square-foot gardening project is under way, which will allow both children and adults in wheelchairs as well as others to grow vegetables, herbs and flowers. On the roof of the petting zoo is a meeting area with a bench for picnics. Want to see whales in April? A telescope with views of the South and North shores will make it possible. Sensory trails, all wheelchair-accessible, will introduce visitors to Bermuda's sounds and smells as well as sights. You'll be able to smell the aromatic fragrance of our spice trees, for example, or the perfume of Bermuda's cedar. Benches at strategic points ensure that people can rest or picnic.

In addition, WindReach has a fantastic play center with a sandbox, swings, slides, hammocks and a seesaw and trampoline. A water pump makes for fun but also for arm-muscle toning. The *pièce de resistance* is a tree house. Children in wheelchairs don't often get the opportunity to feel the sensation of being high up: This tree house is easily reached by wheelchair. Volunteers will be on hand to help.

A campsite allows visitors to have bonfires and singalongs. Eventually there will be "tebins" — a cross between a tent and a cabin — for overnight camping. All bathrooms, showers and telephones are easily accessible. There's no entrance fee, but since WindReach is a registered charity, donations, of course, are welcome. Overseas visitors with special needs are very welcome. Call Ann E. Lindroth, activity director, for information and to set a time to visit. See the previous listing in this chapter for the Bermuda Riding for the Disabled facility. It shares this location and works in partnership with WindReach, but the two establishments are autonomous.

Football (which Americans refer to as soccer) is considered the No. 1 sport in Bermuda. More than 2,000 Bermudians play the game weekly.

Spectator Sports

We may be a small country, but anyone with a mind to do so can certainly lead a sporting life. Check out the sports section of *The Royal Gazette*, and you'll see the range of sports Bermuda has to offer. You'll also see that we're not only interested in the international sports scene, but we also contribute to it. Bermudian soccer player Kyle Lightbourne, for instance, was the top goal scorer in 1997 for Walsall, a Second Division club in the U.K., and was subsequently transferred to Coventry Division, one of Britain's top 20 clubs.

The first Bermudian to play in a British league was Clive Best, who played for Westham (English Second Division) in the early '70s. Bermudian triple jumper Brian Wellman, a former world indoor gold medallist, copped a silver medal at the World Outdoor Championships in 1995. And sprinter Troy Douglas made the semifinals in the last three Olympics; he's the only Bermudian to ever turn that trick.

International events are sometimes hosted in Bermuda. In 1994, '95 and '96, the Mid Ocean Club (see our Golf chapter) hosted the Merrill Lynch Shoot-Out championship. In October 1997 the club welcomed the Gillette Championship Challenge, an event that brings in 24 of the world's top golfers — eight are chosen from the PGA tour, eight from the LPGA tour and eight from the Senior PGA tour. Also in 1997, the Southampton Princess resort hotel hosted the Davis Cup matches for American Zone III and IV.

Dr. Gerard Bean, trustee in charge of sports and special events for the National Sports Centre, has high hopes that more international events will be lured to Bermuda. Bean says by 1999 the Centre will have track and field facilities for a large range of sports, including cricket, soccer and hockey, and an Olympic-size swimming pool. Work on the facility is in progress.

In this chapter, we've chosen to document the spectator sports that we feel are the most popular. Having said that, we have, however, omitted sailing races that are very much part of our heritage. You'll find information about our yachting and fitted dinghy racing in the Yachting and Marinas chapter. Check our Annual Events and Festivals chapter for various golf tournaments. In some cases, we'll give a little of the history behind a sport, and, of course, we'll tell you what major events for each sport are held during the year. If we don't mention specific dates and months, it means they were not set in time for our publishing date. If there's an admission charge for watching, we'll note that as well. Be sure to check our Recreations chapter for information about sports we don't mention here.

Football

So what kind of football are we talking about? The kind that means players have to wear intergalactic headgear? No. In Bermuda, football definitely means soccer, the game where fancy footwork is essential and where, except for the goalkeeper, it's no hands allowed. Players do it for kicks.

Believe it or not, the first recorded game of football happened in England in the year 217 (in that time, however, the game consisted of about 300 players a side, and there were no rules). Approximately 17 centuries later, the British Army and Navy brought the game with them to Bermuda. In 1928 it became a fully organized sport and soon became very popular, with a variety of clubs being formed throughout the parishes.

Footnotes on Bermuda's Top Sport

David Sabir, general secretary of the Bermuda Football Association (BFA), says that football is without question the No. 1 sport on the island. He says more than 2,000 people play football weekly. Bermuda now has 22 clubs that are affiliated members of the BFA.

Do the clubs represent the parishes? Well, some of them include parish names in their titles. We have, for example, the Devonshire Colts (who, to complicate things further, do not play in Devonshire) and the Pembroke Hamilton Club. However, given that we have just nine parishes, you can see that each parish has more than one club. So, to give more examples, there's the Vasco de Gama Club in Pembroke and the Devonshire Recreation Club. Some teams are named after businesses who sponsor them; others take their titles from regional areas in Bermuda. There's the Robin Hood Team, Robin Hood being the name of a Pembroke pub, the Somerset Cricket Club (they play cricket and football) and the North Village Club. Schools are involved too — the Bermuda School Sports Federation is affiliated with the BFA.

There are several divisions: the First Senior Men's, the Alliance (with two subdivisions composed of reserve players for the First Senior Men's), the Second and the Commercial, which also has two subdivisions and is made up of veteran players. In addition, there's the Women's League and the Shell Youth League for players ages 8 through 21. There are at least five women's clubs such as the Rude Girls (of course they're not really rude) and the Dandy Stars.

Throughout the season, September to May, games are held every Saturday and Sunday at 12 venues across the island, such as White Hill in Somerset or St. John's Field in Pembroke. Cup games and finals tend to be held in the National Stadium at Prospect in Devonshire.

Admission for regular games is $3, and it's $5 for cup games. Cup matches to watch for are the Charity Cup, which kicks off the season at the beginning of September; the Martonmere Cup, named after former governor Lord Martonmere; and the Dudley Eve Trophy, which is fought for during the Christmas break from December 15 until New Year's Day. All the teams have a go in the FA Cup. Games and venues are always announced in *The Royal Gazette*.

Supporters can get emotional, Sabir explains. "Agony when there's defeat; celebration when there's victory." You don't, however, get the singing and the chanting that you'd hear in other countries. No betting either. What makes spectators support one club over another? Sometimes the support is simply territorial — the fans live close to the club. But often support is born from family ties with one particular club that might go back for generations.

What about the international scene? "We really want to push that," Sabir says. The BFA is a member of Concacaf (Confederation of North Central and Caribbean Football Association), and an affiliate of FIFA, the Federation of International Football Associations, since 1962. "These memberships put us in good stead for international games," Sabir says. Usually Bermudians play in about six international games a year with three held in Bermuda. For example, in 1996 the Kansas Wizards came to play here. The schedule for 1998 has not yet been arranged. If you're interested in attending any of these games the check the *Gazette* sports pages or call the BFA at 295-2199.

Sabir argues that football is important to the future of the island. "It acts a stress-release valve for people who are maybe out of work during the winter months. We also want it to promote family values. We want a drug-free environment with plenty of respect for the players, the spectators and for the game."

FYI

Unless otherwise noted, the area code for all phone numbers listed in this guide is 441.

Cricket

Cricket, of course, is a British and Commonwealth game *par excellence*. Keith Forbes, in *The Royal Gazette's* Bermuda Online, says it came to Bermuda via one Capt. J. Moresby in 1872. He introduced the game (before he became Captain-in-charge of the Royal Naval Dockyard) at a carnival held in Somerset, Sandys Parish, to celebrate "40 years since the unjust thralldom of slavery."

In 1902 three matches were held at the Royal Naval Field in Dockyard, once known as Moresby Plain. These were the forerunner games of our annual Cup Match — a two-day public holiday held on the Thursday and Friday before the last Monday in August. Officially, we celebrate Somers Day on Thursday (see "Shipwreck and Settlement" in our History chapter for more on Sir George Somers) and Emancipation Day on Friday. However, many Bermudians are more concerned about whether St. George's or Somerset's cricket team will win the cup.

Cup Match is well worth a visit to experience Bermudian tradition and culture. Supporters of each team go dressed in their new outfits (specially bought for the occasion), with the $10 entrance fee and extra cash on hand to spend on crown and anchor (a traditional betting game with dice). For more information, see the Cup Match Close-up in our Annual Events and Festivals chapter, which includes an explanation of how to play crown and anchor.

Stumped Over Cricket?

So you know all about Jiminy Cricket, but you haven't a clue about the game?

Cricket centers on two wickets — each made up of three wooden stumps topped with two crosspieces called bails. These wickets are placed 22 yards apart at opposite ends of a rectangular pitch (another name for the playing area) in the middle of a field. Two teams of 11 players take turns to bat and to field.

One batsman (OK, the term's not PC, but that's what the bat-wielder is called) stands at the far wicket facing the bowler (think "pitcher"). The batsman's partner stands at the opposite wicket. The bowler's aim is to knock off one or both bail. The batsman's aim is to prevent the bowler from doing so by hitting the ball as far as possible. If he fails, he's automatically out and another member of his team takes his place. If he succeeds and hits the ball far enough, he will attempt to gain a "run" by running in a straight line to the opposite wicket and exchanging places with his partner. If a fielder manages to catch the ball in midair, then the batsman is out.

During the two-day Cup Match event, this procedure can go on for hours. However, most matches are one-day events, with each team having one turn at bat. People who love cricket appreciate the leisurely pace of the game. British dramatist Tom Stoppard once said, "I don't think I can be expected to take seriously any game which takes less than three days to reach its conclusion."

If a batsman has "hit a six," it means he's scored six runs by hitting a ball over the field's boundaries without it touching the ground. (Runs, by the way, are not as hard to come by as they are in American baseball; a typical cricket score might include 200 runs in a one-day game.) If he's "bowled for a duck," he's out without scoring. And if he's stumped? Then the wicket-keeper (similar to a catcher in baseball) has knocked off a bail with the ball or his hand while holding a ball while he's out of the crease (the area immediately in front of the wicket) but not running. Clear as mud?

Cricketers can generally be recognized by their white peaked caps (some wear headgear), white open-necked shirts and white trousers. Cricket is the only sport in the world in

---

INSIDERS' TIP

St. John Ambulance Brigade attends crowd gatherings, including spectator sports, outdoor concerts and parades. Volunteers trained in first aid and as emergency medical technicians offer medical help to anyone in need at these events. A member of the Emergency Measures Organization, the brigade also provides ambulance and medical aid during disasters. If you're interested in learning first aid or CPR, call 236-7831. New volunteers are always welcome.

which both sides are dressed identically. Batsmen and wicket-keepers wear white leg pads and white gloves. The bats have separate handles attached to elongated, oblong wooden pieces that constitute the hitting areas. Why does one club here call itself the Willow Cuts? Because bats are traditionally made of willow wood. Decorum is the name of the game. What if a player loses his temper? It can't happen; that just isn't cricket.

Cricket divisions in Bermuda are known as "counties," and there are three of them: Eastern, Central and Western. The Eastern County has a 90-year tradition behind it and is affectionately known as the counties' granddaddy. Clubs such as Bailey's Bay, St. David's and Flatts play for their regional areas. The same holds true for the Western County clubs but less so for the more recently formed Central County that includes, for example, the Police Recreational Club.

Other cup matches include the Camel Cup in May and the Central County's Cup Final in June. Eastern and Western counties hold competitions in July and August. League cricket is played on fields all over the island, including the Wellington Oval in St. George's, the St. David's Oval, the Devonshire Recreation Club, Southampton Oval and White Hill in Sandys. For dates, times and venues of specific games check *The Royal Gazette* or phone the Bermuda Cricket Board of Control at 292-8958. Admission to weekly league matches is free; for cup finals and counties cricket (special matches held on various designated weekends), it's approximately $5.

Tennis

You might like to know that Bermuda feels responsible for introducing tennis to the United States. According to William Zuill in *Bermuda*

Journey, Bermudian merchant Thomas Middleton was first exposed to the game during a visit to England in 1871. He decided that this was an activity his wife would enjoy, so he brought tennis equipment back to Bermuda.

Whatever the reason (maybe she didn't enjoy it?), Thomas donated the equipment to Sir Brownlow Gray, who built the island's first private tennis court in the garden of his home, Clermont, in Paget. Mary, Gray's daughter, took advantage of the facility and eventually became Bermuda's first female tennis champion. Later, Mary Outerbridge, an American visitor from New York, played at Clermont and on returning to the States persuaded the Staten Island Cricket Club to create their own tennis court. Three years after Middleton's visit to England, tennis began in America.

Serving Up An International Mix

As Joseph Morley, administrator of the Bermuda Lawn Tennis Association (BLTA), explained, 1997 was a very good year for tennis in Bermuda.

For the first time ever, our country hosted the Davis Cup matches for American Zone III and IV (the Caribbean and Central American zones). Thirteen countries participated in this prestigious event, which was held at the Southampton Princess hotel in April. During the same month, the XL Bermuda Open Tennis Championship, an ATP Tour-sanctioned event, was held for the fourth consecutive year at the Coral Island Beach and Tennis Club in Paget (see the Horizons listing in our Cottage Colonies chapter for more information about Coral Beach). Will 1998 bring the same events to Bermuda? Definitely not the Davis Cup, but the XL will again take place.

INSIDERS' TIP

Spectator events are often held subject to weather. Last-minute cancellations are announced on local television and radio stations.

The XL Championship is an exciting event. Many of the games are held at night, which means locals can attend after they've finished work. No need to go home for dinner — hamburgers, chicken and salads are served under a marquee. Wine and beer are also served. And everyone enjoys the magic of Bermuda's balmy nights. As befits the traditional atmosphere of Coral Beach, male spectators usually wear jackets (actually, it's because many of them have come from the office)

The tournament, by the way, is for male players only. On the first Friday and Saturday of the event, spectators can attend qualifying rounds for free. Thirty-two players from all over the world participate in these rounds, out of whom four are picked to play in the tournament's main draw. Twenty-six players in the main draw are invited (based on the ATP ranking computer point system); two are "wild cards," usually players who have won international games some years ago but are not ranked highly at the time of the event; and the remaining four are the winners from the qualifying round. Australian Pat Rafter, winner of the 1997 U.S. Open and a Bermuda resident, has played in this tournament.

In 1997, tickets for main draw matches were $15 for day games, $20 for night matches and $25 for the final. (Rates for the 1998 XL are subject to change.) Spectators dress up for the final: Men wear suits; women don hats. About 2,000 spectators a day, many of whom come from abroad specially for the occasion, turn up for these games. Bermuda may be small, but it has the highest per capita attendance in the world for tennis. For more information, call Coral Beach at 236-2233.

The Local Scene

What about local tennis? Bermuda has eight BLTA affiliated tennis clubs, including Pomander Gate, Port Royal, The Reefs, All Bermuda Tennis and Coral Island Beach and Tennis. Players participate in Winter League tennis from October to March or April. Clubs host open tournaments throughout the year. For example, the Heineken Open is held at the end of May at the Tennis Stadium, 2 Marsh Folly Road, Pembroke, 292-7146. Top local players participate in this one. November is invitation tennis month, when overseas club players from countries such as the United States, Canada and England participate in games hosted by our clubs. Spectators are welcome, and admission is free.

In addition to the Winter League, the Commercial League, consisting of players from local businesses and companies, plays games from April until September. For dates, times and venues of specific games check *The Royal Gazette* or phone the BLTA at 296-0834.

Rugby

This game is named after Rugby School in England. One momentous day in 1823, a William Webb Ellis was playing soccer when he succumbed to an overwhelming urge to pick up the ball and run with it. That terrible infringement of soccer rules gave birth to a new game.

Interest in rugby spread to other countries. Feelings about it in America in the early days were mixed, however. The lack of precise rules, the ambiguities in the game and the complexity of the sport turned off U.S. players. In 1880 major rule changes were invoked, such as replacing the scrum with a line of scrimmage. But photographs of an apparently brutal game played between Swarthmore and Pennsylvania in 1905 drew the attention of President Theodore Roosevelt, who insisted on reform of the game to lower the level of brutality. He even threatened to use the big stick he wielded to abolish rugby by edict.

In 1906 the forward pass was introduced to the United States game. That meant that in the States, rugby died out for a while, replaced by American football. Since the 1960s, however, rugby has made a comeback across the pond.

INSIDERS' TIP

For summer events, be sure to wear a hat. The sun can beat down heavily.

Distant Cousins: Rugby and American Football

Rugby and football are similar, but there are major differences, particularly where equipment is concerned. Rugby players do not wear any padding or protection except for a mouthguard. The traditional uniform consists of a long-sleeved cotton shirt with a collar. Shorts are usually cotton and rise to about mid-thigh. Knee-length socks with turnover tops are worn along with boots similar to soccer cleats. Some forwards wear the optional scrum cap, which is made from leather or cloth and worn as protection for the ears.

The "pitch" is a grass field, but it nearly always features mud. (In fact, there should be a universal law compelling all rugby players to do their own laundry.) The goalposts are similar to those used in American football; they are shaped in the form of an H and stand on the goal lines at opposite ends of the field. The objective of the game is to score more points than the opposing team during the two 40-minute halves. A "try" is scored when a player places the ball in the opposition's goal area. A try is good for five points, with two additional points awarded for a successful place kick. A three-point "goal" can be scored via a free penalty kick or a drop kick. Play pauses for penalties and scores and when the ball goes out of bounds; the game is not stopped for injuries until the ball is out of play. Unlike American football, play does not stop with a tackle. How many players on each side? Try 15.

The Local Scene

This rugged sport's most important annual event is Bermuda's World Rugby Classic, which in 1998 will be held from November 8 to November 14 at the National Sports Club on Middle Road in Devonshire. The tournament is for former international players who have represented their countries, and players must be at least 33 years old. In the past, players participating have included Philippe Sella from France, Brendan Mullin from Ireland, South Africa's Danie Gerber and Mike Harrison from England. The tourney will mark its 10th anniversary in 1998, and teams are expected from New Zealand, South Africa, Argentina, Ireland, Scotland, Wales, the United States and Canada.

Will any of Bermuda's rugby players take part? Most probably, yes. In the past, they have been added to the French and Argentinean teams. In 1998, some will probably play on the English team as well. Daily admission will be $15, or you can pay $50 for a week pass. For $350, a silver pass will let you watch from a special tent and mingle with players, sponsors and special guests. A gold pass, costing $600, will give you the same privileges with the added advantage of free lunches and drinks. For more information, call John Kane, World Rugby Classic president, at 291-1517 or 236-9876,

The classic attracts about 2,500 visitors from overseas. It also involves five days of corporate hospitality. On the Friday before the final, an "Upfront Party" is held at Number One Shed, Front Street. There the teams perform (i.e., sing to extremely loud music). In addition, players participate in a golf tournament at the Riddell's Bay Golf Club in Warwick. No doubt they have to resist the urge to pick up the ball and run with it.

This event, whose sponsors include the Department of Tourism, XL Insurance, ACE Insurance, Heinz and APT (see our International Business chapter), has international television coverage through ESPN and BBC Rugby World.

If you fancy watching a local game, you can do so at the National Sports Club every Saturday and Sunday afternoon from October to April. Local teams are the Renegades, Teachers, Police and Mariners. Admission costs about $3.

INSIDERS' TIP

If during a cricket match you hear the bowler shout "Howzat!" you'll know that his bowl has succeeded in knocking down the batsman's wicket bail.

Running sports are a major pastime for locals and visitors alike.

Running

Bermudians love to run. You'll catch them at it first thing in the morning, last thing at night. Where? Everywhere. To quote Sir Winston Churchill, "on beaches, landing grounds, in fields, in streets and on the hills . . ." "Blood, toil, tears and sweat," might be apposite too. Sometimes you'll even see them out at lunchtime. To misquote Noel Coward: "Mad dogs and Bermudians run out in the midday sun."

Two key running events happen every year. The first is the Bank of Butterfield Bermuda International Race Weekend, held the third week of January. Where this set of races is concerned, "weekend" means three days, not two. The Bank of Butterfield Mile, held on Front Street and run by locals and top international runners, usually kicks off the occasion on Friday evening from 7:30 to 9:30 PM. On Saturday, there's the Bermuda International 10K and the Fitness Walk. Sunday, the Bermuda International Marathon (which negotiates the standard 26.2 miles) runs concurrently with a half-marathon.

Total prize money for the running weekend was $25,000 in 1996, with the male and female winners each pocketing $2,500. If you enter before December 17, the cost is $25 for the marathon and $15 for the half-marathon

or 10K. (For more information, see our Annual Events and Festivals chapter.)

The second big event for runners is the Bermuda Day Half-Marathon, which is run on May 24 and restricted to Bermuda residents only. It starts in Somerset in Sandys Parish at 9:30 AM and ends in Bernard Park, Pembroke. Whether they run or not, Bermudians love to watch this race. It's a happening that lets all cross-sections of our community come together. It's also the one event each year where a very sunny day is not a good thing — from the runners' points of view, anyway. Some spectators choose to watch at spots where they know the runners are going to be particularly challenged, so that we can offer encouragement. On Burnt House Hill (Warwick Parish), for example, you'll find spectators yelling, "Way to go!" Or when runners stagger up the hill sweating and writhing and look in serious danger of dropping out, you'll hear, "You can do it; you can do it." Runners who contort their faces in hideous grimaces are greeted with affectionate laughter.

Winners of this race (male and female) get $300 or $400 and trophies. However, many of those on hand are more interested in cheering on friends and relations who have no hope of winning. These competitors want the satisfaction of having completed the run and improved their personal-best times. It is a point of honor to wait for the last stragglers — they need the most encouragement of all. Many participants run for charity; some run while pushing children in push chairs; others wear crazy costumes. In the past, Bermudian Tom Butterfield, founder of Masterworks Foundation and Gallery, often ran in a tutu. Locals all agreed his legs were lovely. Call Richard Tucker, 292-4941, for more information. The entry fee is $10; late entries pay $25.

Cycling

Carlos DeSilva, president of the Bermuda Bicycle Association, says there is an active competitive cycling calendar here from February to the end of October. The Grand Prix, an international racing event sponsored by the law firm of Conyers, Dill and Pearman, takes place every May over a four-day period. In 1997 some 80 top professional riders from overseas participated, together with about 40 locals. A staged race, it consists of two circuit races in the City of Hamilton, a 10-mile time trial and a 75-mile lap race held at South Side, the former U.S. Naval Base in St. George's Parish. A total of $15,000 is divided among the top three veterans, top three women, top three men and top three juniors. However, DeSilva says the atmosphere is more friendly than competitive. (See our Annual Events and Festivals chapter for more information.)

The Heritage Day Classic, restricted to local cyclists only, is one of many Heritage Week activities. Starting around 8 or 8:30 AM, it precedes the Bermuda Day Half-Marathon on May 24. Cyclists ride from Sandys to Bernard Park in Pembroke Parish. Other races include the IBC Front Street Race, a local timed race held in Hamilton at the beginning of March, and the National Championships, which are held at the end of July at Clearwater, St. David's. At the end of the season, the Southampton Princess Hill Climb Championship in Southampton determines who can race up the hill in the fastest time. Spectators, of course, can watch

all races for free. For more information call the Bermuda Bicycle Association's DeSilva at 297-7968.

Triathlon

By now you no doubt know that we have keen cyclists and runners. Well, we also have keen swimmers. Put the three sports together and you get, of course, a triathlon.

David Morrison, former president of the Bermuda Triathlon Association, says the sport is popular and the attitude of participants is upbeat. "It's drug-free, and there's tremendous camaraderie among the athletes." Bermudian Jim Butterfield started triathlon events some 20 years ago. From the mid-'80s on, Bermuda has taken part in the International Triathlon Union World Circuit (ITU). And in September, Bermuda hosts the ITU World Cup Championship, where some of the world's best triathlon athletes compete in swimming, cycling and running races. Total prize money is generous — $100,000. For more information, call Neil De Ste. Croix, president of the Bermuda Triathlon Association, at 236-1884.

Another important two-day event is the Bank of Bermuda Triathlon, held either in August or September. The Individual Race takes place on the first day, usually with about 100 participants. These stalwart individuals swim 750 meters in Hamilton Harbour, get on their bikes for a 20-kilometer ride, then (as if that's not enough) proceed on a 5-kilometer run. The Team Race (about 100 to 150 teams of three participate) consists of a mile swim in the Harbour, a 15-mile bike ride and a 6-mile run. We're exhausted just writing about it. In 1997 American Karen Smyers, two-time winner of the World Cup Championship, came to Bermuda to support the Bank of Bermuda event, which attracts 400 to 500 participants and about 2,000 spectators. Both races start at 8 AM at Albuoy's Point, City of Hamilton. Call the Bank of Bermuda at 299-5483 for more information.

Other triathlon events include the National

Championships (dates depend on the dates for the World Championships), the National Duathlon and the National Sprint Championships, which are held in March.

We'd like to add that the Tri-Hedz Club offers a strong junior program. It paid off for 14-year-old Tyler Butterfield, Jim's son; he won the 14-year-old division of the American Championships held at Clairmont, Florida, in 1997.

Harness Racing and Horse Shows

Until cars were introduced to Bermuda in 1946, horses with carriages were among the chief means of getting around (along with the Bermuda Railway and the pedal bike). Today harness racing, revived in the early '90s, is a throwback to those days when horse-driving skills were important to daily living. It's also fun to watch.

Michael Cherry, president of the Bermuda Equestrian Federation, says the racing season starts in September and runs through March, with about 17 or 18 race meets during the year. In fact, harness racing is organized by the Bermuda Horse and Pony Driving Club, an affiliate of the Federation. The races usually take place on a Sunday afternoon at the National Equestrian Centre, on Vesey Street in Devonshire. Ponies harnessed to sulkies (small, two-wheeled frames with an unsprung seat) race against each other round a one-fifth-mile track. Prizes are bales of hay and feed; the atmosphere is more friendly than competitive. Spectators are welcome. Admission is about $4. For dates of races, call Michael DeCosta, president of the Bermuda Horse and Pony Driving Club, at 293-4964.

The Bermuda Equestrian Federation organizes horse shows that include jumping, dressage and equitation events. Other horse shows are held at local stables such as Hinson Hall in Smiths Parish and Spicelands in Warwick (see our Recreations chapter). For details of these shows, call the Equestrian Federation at 295-4434. In fall and spring, a horse-driving show is held at the Botanical Gardens in Paget (see our Attractions chapter).

Golf

Bermuda currently has more golf courses per square mile than any other country in the world. Check our Golf chapter for detailed description of our nine courses and for booking information. Here we'll give you a sampling of tournaments held on the island. All entry fees mentioned were accurate in 1997. If you need more information about these events, Tom Smith at the Bermuda Golf Association (238-1367) can likely help.

In addition to the Gillette Championship Challenge, mentioned in this chapter's introduction, the island also hosts the Bermuda International Open Golf Tournament for men. A four-day event, it's held in late October at Port Royal Golf Course and attracts many top players. Entry fees are $275 for professionals and $200 for amateurs. (The handicap limit is 6 for both professionals and amateurs.) In March the Bermuda Men's Amateur Championship is held at the Mid Ocean Club. This is a singles match-play event at scratch with a championship flight of 32 players and a handicap limit of 8. Entry fee is $225.

The Bermuda Ladies Amateur Championship is held in April at Riddells Bay Golf and Country Club. A four-day event, it is also a singles match-play event at scratch; the handicap limit is 24, the entry fee $200. The annual Belmont Invitational Tournament for Men is held at the Belmont Golf and Country Club. It's open to professionals and amateurs. For additional information about this event, call the tournament chairman at 236-6400.

For information about the popular Samuel L. Jackson Celebrity Golf Classic, see the May activities in our Annual Events and Festivals chapter.

Bermudians generally agree that the North Shore is different in scenery from the South. They often disagree, however, about which is more beautiful.

Beaches

Making Waves with Colors

Look at any travel article on Bermuda's ocean, and you will invariably find a reference to our "clear, sparkling turquoise waters."

What's the problem with that? Isn't it true? Put it this way: If Miles Davis had visited Bermuda for any length of time, he may well have played more than one kind of blue.

Yes, you will see that blue-green shade, but bear in mind that our part of the Atlantic Ocean is rarely just one color at any one time. The cloudscapes, the dark streaks of the reefs and the play of light and shadow make for a sea of contrasts. Sometimes the colors are as bright and dazzling as precious stones — sapphires and diamonds included. But let's not forget about the more subtle and muted shades either. In the half-light of early mornings, for example, the sea can have more the appearance of soft, gray silk that meets the horizon in a shroud of mist.

There's a geographical factor that we should consider as well. It's true that some of our beaches are on the eastern and western tips of Bermuda, and others (mostly private) are around the Great Sound and Harrington Sound. But many of our popular public beaches can be geographically divided into roughly two categories: those situated on the North Shore and those situated on the South Shore.

Bermudians generally agree that the North Shore is different in scenery from the South. However, they often disagree about which is more beautiful. It's a question of loyalty, you see. Bermudians who live on the North Shore will extol the "activeness" of their views. By that, they mean that you can more frequently watch the cruise ships gliding to the islands as well as more boating activity. They also believe the scenery is more truly

Bermudian and less touristy because there are fewer hotels but lots of Bermudian cottages. South Shore residents, meanwhile, will claim that a) more beaches are on the south side, b) more longtails live there, and c) the reef line is closer.

We will not take either side in this argument. But we will tell you that the ocean on the north side does often appear expansively more green than blue, whereas on the South Shore it's a darker blue, especially beyond the reef line — definitely more teal than turquoise. Moreover, the water temperature on the North Shore, during the summer months anyway, is warmer, while on the South Shore it's always refreshing, even on the hottest of days. Though it is true that there are fewer beaches on the North Shore, you should know that some locals, particularly older children, like to swim directly off the rocks there.

Bermuda on the Rocks

As you probably know by now, Bermuda is surrounded by reefs. That's why Andrew Marvell referred to the island (or islands) as a "watery maze." On the South Shore, reefs are easily visible and, in many cases, easily accessible. They are known as potboiler reefs or, more technically, "serpuline atoll" or "algal-vermetid" reefs that protrude from the water. What do we mean by accessible? Well, sometimes the potboilers are so close to the beach that at low tide you can actually wade out to them and enjoy the deep, natural rock pools (see Stonington Beach Hotel, Pompano Beach and Willowbank listings in our Small Hotels chapter). If they are not that close, at some beaches you can swim out to the reefs (again, more easily at low tide) and join the fish. (For more details on the marine life on the outer reefs, check the Diving and Snorkeling section in our Watersports chapter.)

If you're after surf, you won't find it on the North Shore, where the waves get short and snappy during windy weather. When the wind blows southerly, you'll get rollers on the South Shore beaches. Be careful of the reefs then because salt spray can camouflage them, and bear in mind that because of our reefs, the waves are never as high as they are in Hawaii, for example, or California.

To See a World in a Grain of Sand

Impatient for sand? Here we worry about another cliche in travel literature: "the shimmering pink sands of Bermuda." Let's be more prosaic. Our sands actually consist of trillions of tiny skeletons. Are they all pink? In his book, *Bermuda's Marine Life*, Dr. Wolfgang Sterrer explains why our beaches appear pink. It's "because the Red Foram, a tiny single-celled animal that grows in profusion on the underside of rocks, has a bright red skeleton. When the animal dies, the skeleton is eroded by the waves and gets mixed in with other such debris — broken clam and snail shells, sea urchin remains, pieces of coral — all of which are white. The Red Foram's remains give Bermuda's white sand its characteristic pink hue."

The name "foram," Dr. Sterrer explains, is short for foraminifer, which means "bearers of holes." Even so, our sand colors and textures do vary from beach to beach. Where they are particularly in the pink, we'll tell you.

Although our beaches are composed of shells, looking for larger ones on the shoreline is not particularly productive. It is possible to dive for shells, but we'd rather you refrain. See our Watersports chapter for details about protected species.

A Word on Land Crabs

Formally known as Red Land Crabs, these do generally prefer land. However, during the summer months the females have an overwhelming need to reproduce. They do this by making their way to the sea at least once a year, usually around midnight on the days following a full moon. Once they reach the sea, they shake themselves vigorously to release 100,000 larvae per female (yes, honestly!) into the shallows.

They then return to land, leaving their little ones to fend for themselves until they too reach land about a month later. Talk about family values. We mention this because a moonlight walk along the beach can mean a disconcerting meeting with these little creatures. In their haste to reach the water, they are not averse to pinching your toes.

Where to Go?

We have so many areas that can be described as beaches that we can't possibly report on them all. Actually, we can't visit them all either — about 80 percent of them are privately owned, either by individuals or by hotels. (See our Resort Hotels and Cottage Colonies chapters for more information on hotel-owned or controlled beaches.) True, it is legal to approach them by boat, provided you stay below the high-tide mark. But go above that mark, and you're definitely trespassing.

Our listings in this chapter will describe only the beaches that are available to the public. Some have lifeguards, changing facilities and beach cafes; most do not. We will specify when they do. If we do not mention one or more of these amenities, you may take it that they are not available. By the way, lifeguards here are fully qualified in swimming, advanced resuscitation and first-aid — indeed, they have to requalify every year. During the summer months they are on duty every day from 10 AM to 6 PM. No lifeguards are in service between November 1 and May 31.

A white flag posted means a lifeguard is on duty. A red flag means the currents are too dangerous for safe swimming. And a yellow one? That means you should be cautious and get advice on conditions from the lifeguard. If a beach has a reputation for riptides, we'll mention that too. As for parking, you may take it that unless we mention oth-

---

FYI

Unless otherwise noted, the area code for all phone numbers listed in this guide is 441.

erwise, there is plenty of space for cars and motorcycles. The two beaches listed in St. George's Parish can be reached by taking a minibus from the Town of St. George's (see our Getting Here, Around and Home chapter). All but two of the other beaches discussed are near bus routes.

We'll also tell you which beaches are suitable for small children, and which are particularly good for snorkeling. Be aware in Bermuda that there are absolutely no beaches where nude bathing is allowed. W. B. Yeats once wrote, "There's more enterprise in walking naked." Bermudians do not agree. Swimming and/or sunbathing nude or semi-nude is an indictable offense.

As usual, we will start in the east and move westward, parish by parish. However, to avoid confusion, in this chapter we will not use alphabetical order within the parishes. Instead, we will use a geographical order. You see, all the public beaches are part of Bermuda's national park network, and some can be right next door to each other (so to speak) in the same park. The chains of public beaches in Warwick and Southampton parishes, for example, are all part of the South Shore Park.

You'll find much more information about parks in our Parks and Conservation chapter. In this one, we will use the beaches' official names as headings and include the names of the parks in the address. If beach cafes and facilities are available, we will also include those phone numbers.

St. George's Parish

Clearwater Beach
Clearwater Beach Park, Mercury Rd., St. David's • 293-5092

Once the Americans returned the military base lands to Bermuda in 1995, Clearwater for the first time became acces-

sible to the public. It actually consists of two sandy beaches, both of which were artificially made for use by army personnel. They are now part of the Clearwater Beach Park that overlooks the Cooper's Island Nature Reserve.

The spaciousness of Clearwater makes it ideal for families, parties and functions. A large building left over from the base now houses Reid Clearwater Cafe, whose telephone number is listed above. You may buy the usual drinks, ice cream and hamburgers here, but you might also enjoy homemade mussel pies, fresh fish and other Bermudian specialties. You will definitely enjoy the friendliness of the staff.

Beach and swimming equipment are available for rent. Snorkeling gear costs $15 a day or $5 an hour. The rental prices we quote for the following are daily, rather than hourly, rates. Both beach mat and umbrella cost $5 each. A chair also costs $5; a lounger costs $16. Towels are $3 each, and an inflatable raft/mattress (they are known as "lilos" in Bermuda) is $16. You can also rent a huge barbecue, suitable for large parties — call Reid's for prices. It opens at 7 AM and closes at 9 PM. The building also contains changing rooms, showers and bathrooms, which you can use free of charge.

Lifeguards are on duty daily here from May 24 through October 31. They say the beach is, on the whole, safe though in the winter, some strong currents occur farther out to sea between small rocky islands. Dark patches in the water here signify turtle grass, a species of underwater grass that appeals to fish and particularly to green turtles. The lifeguards also recommend Turtle Bay, just around the corner, for snorkeling. If you're extremely lucky, you might just see a green turtle. In any case, you'll see turbots and parrotfish, hogfish and trigger fish. Should a small family picnic appeal, you will find the two cabanas containing hibachis useful.

INSIDERS' TIP

Should you get caught by a rip current on the South Shore, stay calm. Let the current carry you because it will soon weaken. Swim parallel to the shore, either left or right, and you will catch the waves or currents that will take you back to shore.

Tobacco Bay
Tobacco Bay Park, 1 Coot Pond Rd.
• 297-2756

The telephone number belongs to Kenneth Bascome, who owns and manages the Tobacco Bay Beach Pavilion right on the beach. He serves drinks and fast food, such as burgers and ice cream, at very reasonable prices. He also rents out equipment. Snorkeling gear, including mask, snorkel and fins, costs $8 an hour or $12 for two hours. Lounge chairs cost $2 an hour, and an umbrella is a flat rate of $5. That means you can sit under it all day if you want. Mr. Bascome would hate for you to get sunburned. Fancy a tube float? Three dollars an hour. Changing rooms and public conveniences are available for free. From November 30 to April 1, the cafe closes. Summer months, it operates 9 AM to 6.30 PM. (For more on the Tobacco Bay Beach Pavilion, see our Kidstuff chapter.)

Tobacco Bay, on the North Shore, is perfect for families and inexperienced swimmers. Small children can stay in more shallow depths or make sand castles on the small beach. The sand here is more yellow than pink, incidentally. Sound too dull? The rocks surrounding the bay make for interesting snorkeling. Snorkel around Snapper's Rock, for example, and you may well see a snapper. Four-eyed butterfly fish, blue angels and wrasse, including pudding wives, like Tobacco Bay. So do barracudas. Don't worry — they may look threatening with their sharp teeth, but they don't attack humans; they have a more sinister interest in the other fish for a lunch munch.

Talk to Mr. Bascome, and he will tell you that this sheltered bay was the locale for the 1775 "Gunpowder Steal." Local conspirators stole gunpowder from the British magazine, then loaded it into whale boats for transport to American ships. The plot caused explosions in more ways than one. Americans used the gunpowder in their Revolutionary War against the British. Given that Bermuda was (and is) a British colony, you can see why sparks flew here as well as in the United States (see our History chapter for more details).

www.insiders.com
See this and many other **Insiders' Guide®** destinations online — in their entirety.
Visit us today!

Hamilton Parish

Shelly Bay Beach
Shelly Bay Park, 55 North Shore Rd., Shelly Bay • 293-7208

The phone number we give here is for the Shelly Bay Beach House, where you may buy drinks, ice cream and fast food. Here, too, you will find bathrooms and changing rooms, but no showers are available. You can rent a locker for $1 an hour, snorkeling equipment costs $5 an hour, and umbrellas come at $1.50 an hour or $6 a day. Loungers and towels are $12 and $2.50 a day, respectively.

If you're feeling adventurous, either of two sailboats (Hobie Cats) are available for $40 for the first hour and $15 for each additional hour. A paddle boat can be fun too: Rent one at $25 for the first hour and $10 an hour thereafter. Remember that when you hire one of these boats, you must always keep within sight of the Beach House. In compliance with regulations, manager/owner Franz Egenolf is always on hand with his Jet Ski in case a rescue is necessary.

This North Shore beach and bay is absolutely perfect for children. The water is shallow (and yes, more often than not, it's blue-green), with no riptides to interfere with safe bathing.

INSIDERS' TIP

Some of our beaches are ideal for small children. However, a foot of water can be just as deadly as 6 feet. Never leave your children in the water unsupervised. Where toddlers are concerned, keep your eyes on them at all times. A lot can happen in 30 seconds. Remember, too, that babies and young children can sunburn easily. A sun hat is a must.

The sand on the beach and the sea floor is quite coarse. Pick up a handful, and you will find small white shells, many intact.

If your children get tired of sand and sea, they can try out the playground equipment in the park area. Swings, climbing frames and slides should keep them entertained. You might also like to check out the tidal pond, surrounded by mangroves and thickets. Here you may notice sora birds, warblers, herons and kingfishers.

Smiths Parish

John Smith's Bay
John Smith's Bay Park, South Rd.

This South Shore beach is an absolute favorite with locals. It's got sand — lots of it, with the pink bits included — and it's good for kids because they can easily keep in a shallow depth. More adventurous swimmers like to swim out to the reefs and meet with the fish. Snorkeling is certainly rewarding here. At the very least, you can introduce yourself to the parrotfish.

However, we must tell you that the water here is subject to riptides, although not as frequently as in some other South Shore beaches. (See the Warwick Long Bay listing below for a description of these currents.) It's just as well that lifeguards are on duty here during the summer. If the yellow flag is up, be sure to ask their advice on precautions.

There are public conveniences here but no other beach facilities. However, during the summer you can buy fast food and drinks from a mobile van restaurant. A pay phone is nearby and so is a bus stop. The grounds are shady, thanks to the Norfolk pine trees, cedars and the fronds of the palms. They are also ramped and completely accessible to guests in wheelchairs.

Pembroke Parish

Clarence Cove
Admiralty House Park, Spanish Point Rd., Spanish Point

Once you enter this park, follow the trail down the hillside until you reach the bottom. There you will find two magical little beaches tucked around a part of the North Shore, which is really more lagoon than cove. The swimming is so safe for children that during July and August holiday daytime camps are held here. The rest of the year it's fairly secluded.

Admiralty House, now a community center, was once what its name implies — a house for the British Royal Navy's admirals stationed here. In 1850 the Earl of Dundonald, commander-in-chief at the time, decided to excavate caves into the cliffs overlooking the sea. Or rather, he forced convicts to excavate them. Apparently the caves helped with the landing and storage of provisions. But in *Bermuda Journey*, William Zuill reckoned that the earl was satisfying his mole-like urge for tunneling and excavating.

According to Bermuda Online's Keith Forbes, "During World War II the property was

---

INSIDERS' TIP

Watch out for the purple and blue Portuguese men-of-war, especially in spring after stormy weather when they tend to be blown onto the beach. This jellyfish has a balloon float structure of about 8 inches and a mass of tentacles that can be anywhere between 20 and 60 inches in length. It's the tentacles we worry about: They can seriously sting you. If you do get stung, rinse the affected area with salt water, then soak it with vinegar, alcohol or after shave. Immerse the wound for at least 30 minutes in water as hot as is tolerable. Shave the area with a razor and shaving cream to remove cysts, and do not dry it off with a towel. Remember, you can get reinfected. If a sting causes you or a companion to go into shock, or if the pain continues to be almost unbearable, call the hospital at 236-2345.

at its busiest. It was crammed with the Royal Navy's intelligence staff. They encoded and decoded messages from convoys sailing between the United Kingdom and the USA, and from ships torpedoed at sea by German submarines and needing rescue services provided by the Royal Navy from Bermuda. They also sent signals directing attacking aircraft to proceed to where U boats were sighted." Dances for officers were often held in the ballroom. Before the days of motorized traffic, women in long dresses would somehow manage to arrange their skirts so that they could get there by pedal bike.

Paget Parish

Elbow Beach
**Elbow Beach Park, Tribe Rd. No. 4,
off South Rd.**

There are two sections to this magnificent stretch of South Shore beach. The eastern section is privately owned by the Elbow Beach Bermuda hotel and is accessed through the grounds (see our Resort Hotels chapter). The western one is open to the public; walk down to the end of the tribe road, and you'll see it immediately.

If you would like to benefit from the changing room, shower and bathroom facilities, you may do so by paying $5 to a cashier right on the beach. The fee gives you all-day beach privileges. If you fancy a chair or lounger and an umbrella, ask the beach attendant, who will bring them to you for a tip. Want lunch or dinner? You can have both at Cafe Lido and dinner at Mickey's, two restaurants that are like oases on the sands. At night, flood lights shine out on the waters.

We love the expanse of Elbow's sands and dunes; it allows us brisk walks or jogs for keep-fit routines. Actually, the fact that private Stonington Beach is on the one end and even-more-private Coral Beach on the other gives the illusion of even more length. And swimming is good, especially if you prefer swells to

calm. It can be as smooth as glass, mind you, but on windy days, this is probably where you'll get surf.

The reef is visible and reminds us of the bravery of one Bermudian, Antonio Marshall. In 1915 he sailed his whale boat to save nearly all the crew on board the British S.S. *Pollockshields* that had crashed on the reef in violent seas. The wreck is still there and is a favorite diving location (see our Watersports chapter).

Warwick Parish

Astwood Cove
Astwood Park, South Rd.

This park has open fields, thickets and cliff walks. It is a perfect spot for watching the longtails' aerial courtships and for appreciating the sweep of the South Shore coastline. Tables and benches make picnics comfortable. In fact, it's a favorite location for wedding receptions. The cove between and below the field and the cliff thicket is tiny and rocky. Rocks do make for good snorkeling, but they also make for cut feet. For small children or people who lack confidence in the water, it may not be a good choice. And the water can be rough.

Warwick Long Bay
South Shore Park, South Rd.

Yes, it's long. Very long and very spectacular. What's more, Warwick Long Bay has the advantage of being far less crowded than some of the other major South Shore beaches. Even in the peak season, you'll never find yourself just inches away from a perfect stranger.

The swimming here, however, may not be ideal for inexperienced swimmers or small children. At high tide particularly, you'll encounter a sudden shelf on the sea floor that can quickly take you out of your depth. Also, we must mention rip currents here. They occasionally can be created by depressions or hollows on the sea floor that run perpendicu-

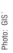

Beautiful Horseshoe Beach is one of Bermuda's most popular destinations.

lar to the beach. Shallow water from the breaking waves flows out through the hollows, setting up a current. Because there is no lifeguard service here, it is even more important that you observe the never-swim-alone rule. And if the red flag is up, do stay out of the water.

Even if you don't swim here, you will enjoy the cliff trails, cedars and bay grape trees. It's a good venue for birds too. March to September, look out for the longtails. Year round you'll see plenty of kiskadees (you'll certainly hear them even if you don't see them). On the beach itself, you may well see sanderling birds puttering along in twos and threes, together with ruddy turnstones that have small puffed-out chests. The sand? Yep. It's pink. And the water plays many an enigmatic variation on the blue and the green.

Kids can take advantage of the recently built playground in the park area. Lots of climbing and swinging equipment is there for them as well as a stationary train and a play house. Public conveniences are in the park area. If you're starving and thirsty, try the lunch wagon across the South Road opposite the beach for food and a snow cone.

Jobson's Cove
South Shore Park, South Rd.

OK, Warwick Long Bay is not ideal for kids, but Jobson's is. A tiny sheltered cove, it is surrounded by rocks. Very shallow steps are carved out of one of the rock-face backdrops. The water in most places is shallow and calm with a sandy bottom — perfect for kids who still depend on armbands to keep afloat. They can see, even without snorkeling equipment, parrotfish and sergeant-majors nudging around the rocks.

Our older local kids like to dive from the larger rocks into the few deep pools toward the back of the cove. We wish they wouldn't, though. A misplaced dive into shallow water can mean a serious accident; always go in feet-first. With that proviso, Jobson's is arguably the best beach on the South Shore for young families. It's a favorite setting for picnics.

Stonehole Bay
South Shore Park, South Rd.

Right next to Jobson's, this bay is a stunning combination of water, sand and rock. We all appreciate hearing the wind chimes of the Aeolian harp, right? Here we appreciate the swishing sound of salt spray against these dramatic Aeolian limestone rock formations. Swimming is generally safe although on windy days, the sea can be choppy. Public conveniences are available. Walk along the trail that leads westward, and you can try out another similar beach. A listing for it follows.

Chaplin's Bay
South Shore Park, South Rd.

If it matters to you in what parish you're sunbathing, then we must tell you that if you pick a spot toward the western end of this beach, you've reached Southampton. Swim at the eastern end, and you're still in Warwick. Tides come in; tides go out — the sea cares nothing about geographical divisions. Right next to Stonehole Bay, Chaplin's also has Aeolian limestone formations, and the same swimming conditions apply.

Chaplin's Bay is a favorite with locals. It offers more seclusion in the summer months. However, in January the red flag often goes up because it is then the venue for the Bermuda Regiment's shooting practice.

Southampton Parish

Horseshoe Bay
South Shore Park, 94 South Rd. • 238-2651

The telephone number we give here belongs to the Horseshoe Bay Beach House, which has a large outdoor terrace where you may consume your drinks and snacks (mostly fast foods and ice cream) under umbrellas. The Beach House also rents snorkeling and beach equipment. Daily per person rates are as follows: Towels cost $3, beach mats cost $2.75, snorkels and masks, rubber rings and lilos are $10 and noodles (no, not the edible kind — long, foam tubes for water frolic) go for $3. You pay a $20 deposit that is refunded if you bring back the equipment by 5 PM.

Showers, foot bath with taps, bathrooms and changing rooms are available to use free. Lockers cost $4.50 a day, and two pay phones are on hand. The Beach House opens at 9 AM and closes at about 5.30 PM. It closes altogether from November 1 through the end of March.

All that said, let us now describe what is probably the most photographed and definitely

the most popular beach in Bermuda. Be warned, in the summer months from about 10:30 AM it does get very crowded, particularly in the area by the Beach House. Litter could be a serious problem were it not for the fact that the sands are cleaned and raked every morning at about 8:30 AM.

You reach the beach by walking or driving down a fairly steep hill that leads off the South Road. (A signpost marks the road clearly.) You will notice a mass of oleander on your left. Look out particularly for the deep red blossoms that are less common in Bermuda than the pink and the white. Listen for warblers that enjoy the oleander thicket. Once you reach the sands, you'll see the curve of the beach that extends for about a quarter-mile. (Yes, it does resemble a horseshoe.) You'll also see that it is enclosed on each end by cliffs of more Aeolian limestone.

As for the sand, it's pink all right. It's also very fine, which is why the beach is a favorite for locals who love jogging or walking in the early morning or the evening. Pick up a handful of sand, and you'll find the red foram and also minuscule snail shells. As you sunbathe, on less-crowded days, you'll notice sanderlings and ruddy turnstones enjoying the beach as well.

Swimming? We wouldn't recommend it for arm-banded tots except on the calmest days. Even then, there's usually a swell that keeps the water temperature gloriously cool when the sun is blazing. But the sea floor is sandy and its gradient is gentle — if you're older but inexperienced, you can easily stay in your depth. On the other hand, you can swim out to the rocks on the western side and snorkel. Parrotfish and sergeant-majors are especially fond of Horseshoe. Here again, some of our locals like to dive from the rocks here. At low tide, this can be dangerous. If you love to dive, check the depth of the water first.

We must also tell you that occasionally those rip currents happen here (see Warwick Long Bay listing for a description of rip currents). We are thankful two lifeguard stands

INSIDERS' TIP

Unfortunately, some of our beaches do occasionally have patches of tar, washed up from ships. Use a paper towel soaked in baby oil to remove tar from your feet.

Photo: GIS

The shoreline of Bermuda keeps pockets of pink sand ready for discovery in private bays all along the South Shore.

are at this beach. Check the flags: If the red one is posted, give up that swim. At the western end of this beach, just in front of the cafe, walk up and then down a narrow cliff path, and you'll find the next beach, listed subsequently.

Port Royal Cove
South Shore Park, South Rd.

Most locals do not know the official title of this beach. It's commonly referred to as the Baby Beach. Many a parent has spent hours with toddlers here. Like Jobson's Cove, it's perfect for the very young. Slightly larger than Jobson's, with a larger expanse of sand, it can resemble a kindergarten in the peak season. Snorkelers like to explore the rocks, and children can easily see parrotfish even if they don't have a mask and snorkel. Again, older children like to dive from the larger rocks into the one small pool of deep water. And again, we wish they wouldn't. Jumping feet-first is far safer.

Church Bay
Church Bay Park, South Rd.

Now we come to the "religious" side of the South Shore. It could be that this one is so named because of St. Anne's Church on the other side of the road. It is the next beach after

The Reefs' private Christian Bay (see our Small Hotels chapter). Anyway, we must tell you that if you're a passionate snorkeler, this one's an absolute must. It's arguably the best beach on the South Shore for fish visiting. The potboilers of the reefs are very close to the shore, you see. Swim out to them, and you'll see parrotfish, blue and yellow grunts, wrasse, trunk, angel and four-eyed butterfly fish.

One rock particularly protrudes from the potboilers. Locals refer to it affectionately as Poodle Rock because from certain angles that's what it looks like. There's plenty of sand down to the water's edge. However, once you enter the water you'll immediately find that you are standing on flat rock. We mention this because the floor can occasionally be very slippery — wearing flippers might be a good idea. Once you leave the rock, you'll find yourself very quickly out of your depth. For this reason, it's not a good choice for inexperienced swimmers or small children. In addition, the water can be very rough.

On the eastern side, you'll notice limestone formations that resemble chimneys or pillars. If you're interested in military history, check out the ruined fort on top of the cliff down from the parking lot. The site has a 1612 marker. Picnic tables and public conveniences are available in the park area.

West Whale Bay
Whale Bay Park, Whale Bay Rd. (off Middle Rd.)

The name is appropriate since in April, if you're lucky, you just might see whales migrating north to their summer feeding grounds. During the late-18th and 19th centuries, Bermudian whalers set out in their whaling boats from this bay. They hoped for ambergris (an intestinal secretion of the whales that is used in perfume) and the other products, such as oil, that these massive mammals could provide.

Walk across a grassy field (with picnic tables and public conveniences), and you'll find this small beach tucked below a rocky cliff. There is pink sand, but at high tide the beach tends to disappear. It's a favorite with local families since the swimming is safe and the water inland is shallow enough for small children.

On top of the cliff, to the west of the parking lot, you'll find a battery. Originally a fort was built in the 1620s. Now it's more or less buried under the sand below a second one (built in 1876) that still exists. By the way, the view at West Whale Bay is toward the southwest. We mention this because its position means terrific sunsets over the ocean.

Sandys Parish

Black Bay
Lagoon Park, Malabar Rd.

Be warned: This one is not posted with signs. Once you cross Grey's Bridge on your way to Dockyard, you will see Lagoon Park on your right. On your left, immediately off the roadside, you will see grassy areas with benches. Stop here. There's no parking lot, but you should have no problem parking your motor bike on the grass. You will see the unruffled waters of Black Bay that are very rarely anything other than blue to green. About three tiny beaches come and go here with the tide. It's a perfect spot for picnicking and for children's swimming.

Mangrove Bay
Mangrove Bay Park, Mangrove Bay Rd.

This bay is a favorite for locals who like to fish and sail as well as swim. The mangroves, the boats in the water and the gentle curve of the shoreline give the bay a serene, picturesque quality. Swimming is safe. Look out for terns here, together with gulls and vagrant cormorants that come in the fall from North America. Christopher Isherwood, British playwright and novelist, once wrote: "The common cormorant (or shag)/Lays eggs inside a paper bag." A piece of nonsense, of course, except cormorants were really known as "shags" in the 19th century, and they do lay eggs inside a nest of seaweed. However, in Bermuda it doesn't nest at all. It just takes a break from the North American winter. What isn't nonsense is that Mangrove Bay was a favorite unloading anchorage for Bermudian smugglers in the 18th century.

No public conveniences are available at this site, but the Somerset Country Squire Inn is just minutes away as are the shops in Somerset Village.

Parson's Bay
Lagoon Park, Lagoon Rd.

Again, this one is not sign-posted, and it's not too close to a bus stop either. But it is the only bay with a beach on the side of Lagoon Road, just before the road name changes to Craddock Road. It's sheltered, with white coarse sand and shallow, calm water that's ideal for children. Families in small boats tend to stop here for a swimming break, while others prefer to set up canopies and picnic. Do not confuse this beach with the lagoon, however. The lagoon is almost completely enclosed in the middle of the park and is considered by some unsuitable for swimming, though in winter you might find herons and kingfishers there.

Somerset Long Bay
Somerset Long Bay Park, Daniel's Head Rd. (off Cambridge Rd.), Somerset Village

Enter the park, and you'll see a manicured grassy area much loved by locals for family cricket games and picnics. Public conveniences are available here. To your right, you'll see a nature reserve edged with bamboo, wild fennel and grasses that contains a pond that was resurrected from an old garbage fill in 1975. According to Eric Amos in his *A Guide to the Birds of Bermuda*, this reserve "is one of the most versatile birding spots in Bermuda." Resident coots and moorhens live in the pond while visiting birds often drop in. One year, a fork-tailed flycatcher from South America and a Siberian flycatcher from northeast Russia apparently came here for a Bermudian vacation. Do, then, look out for the birds.

All right, all right, you want the beach. Walk over the grass, the reserve to your right, and you're there. The long strip of coarse white sand is rarely very crowded, even in the summer months. The water is calm and very shallow. At low tide it is almost impossible for adults to swim out of their depth. It's perfect for children but not so interesting for the potential Olympic swimmer. Turtle grass is responsible for the dark patches in the water.

Take out a boat for a day. Tooling about in our sounds and harbors gives you an immediate sense of space and peace.

Watersports

For centuries, Bermudians could hardly view the sea as a source of leisure-time activity. A source of excitement, probably. Of challenge and danger, most certainly. From its earliest days as a settlement, Bermuda depended on the sea for food, travel and trade both legitimate and illegitimate (see our History chapter).

But as tourism began to surface toward the end of the 19th century, so did water-related fun. Visitors, mostly from America, would charter boats so they could enjoy our islands from an ocean perspective. Indeed, senior citizen Edward DeShields remembers one Capt. Joe Powell, who used to take Mark Twain out in his boat. The other literary celebrity that both Captain Joe and DeShields knew well was Eugene O'Neill, who lived on Harbour Road.

Today tourists can enjoy a large range of watersports. Even if you were not born a water baby, you should try at least once to see Bermuda from the water. Visitors sometimes ask, "Don't you ever get claustrophobic? Bermuda's so small." The simple answer to that is, "Yes." We do occasionally feel an overwhelming urge to get off island. . . . "Rock fever" is what we call it. The simple solution is to take out a boat for a day. Tool out into the sounds and harbors, and you immediately experience a sense of space and peace. Besides, seeing the island from the water lets you appreciate that Bermuda's beauty depends on a trinity of sky, sea and land.

In this chapter we'll introduce you to the variety of water activities you can enjoy here. The chapter is divided into sections so you can quickly find the water recreation that most appeals to you.

If it's fish you're after, then you must first decide what kind of relationship you want with these creatures. Do you want to gaze with wonder at the fish? Visit them in their own home, all the while being quiet, considerate and respectful? Then diving or snorkeling is for you. Where snorkeling is concerned, you can, of course, rent a small boat and go off on your own. See the Sailboat, Personal Watercraft and Motorboat Rentals section for information. However, for those who want some instruction on how to snorkel, together with information about our marine life, check out the Scuba Diving and Snorkeling and Motor Cruises sections. We tell you about our reefs, fish and shipwrecks. We also list the diving and snorkeling centers and tell you about prices, rules and regulations.

But you may want an unashamedly confrontational relationship with the fish. If you view them as potential lunch, then go to the Deep-sea and Reef Fishing section. There we discuss charters, catch policies and conservation regulations concerning protected species. So your dream is to catch a marlin? Many have done so here, so we'll talk about billfishing too.

Maybe you're more after water frolic. Again, check out the Sailboat, Personal Watercraft and Motorboat Rentals section, together with the Waterskiing and Parasailing section. For sailing yacht charters, turn to the Yachting and Marinas chapter.

A Word About Our Reef

By now, you likely know we have some 50 miles of barrier reef encircling our island. In fact, we have the most northerly coral building reefs known to exist in the northern hemisphere. We could never wish for a reef-free island, but we must admit our reefs were historically the curse of sailors attempting to reach our island. "Good grief, what a reef," they might have said while trying to negotiate through one of our channels.

Even today Bermuda is one of the most (if not the most) difficult area to enter safely by sea. It's not surprising, then, that there are more than 450 shipwrecks (that we know about) off our coastline. Our pragmatic streak has allowed us to put some of them to good use. Because many of these ships went down on shallow reefs, they can be viewed fairly easily by divers. The Department of Tourism, together with Bermuda dive operators, has instituted the Bermuda Shipwreck Certificate Programme. This program focuses on 12 of the wrecks, chosen for their historical interest, accessibility and photogenic qualities. Dive at one of these sites, and you will receive a Bermuda Shipwreck Certificate, printed on "parchment" paper. Each certificate names the shipwreck and gives a brief history of the ship and the circumstances of its sinking. See the Shipwreck heading in this chapter for descriptions of some of these wrecks.

FYI

Unless otherwise noted, the area code for all phone numbers listed in this guide is 441.

But divers, more interested in our marine life than the vestiges of past disasters, will appreciate the natural beauty of our reefs and the rich ecosystem they support. Eventually, mind you, reef life will form around wrecks. If you are interested in learning more about the living organisms in our ocean, we urge you to read *Bermuda's Marine Life*, written by marine biologist Dr. Wolfgang Sterrer. Curator of the Bermuda Natural History Museum and former director of the Bermuda Biological Station for Research, he is somewhat of a present-day Renaissance man. His interests extend to poetry, history, science and jazz (he plays in a traditional jazz band). The book entertainingly describes in short paragraphs 225 of the 5,000 species that live in our waters. Only Dr. Sterrer could compare the bulbous lips of the bluebone porgy with those of the Austrian Hapsburg family. We mention *Bermuda's Marine Life* because it is the main source of the information we give you about our underwater fauna.

So what is our reef like? Dr. Sterrer compares it with an inner city that is "relentlessly being torn down and rebuilt, simultaneously decaying and being rehabilitated." Constructed mainly of stony corals, it's also composed of a multitude of living organisms such as coralline algae, coral anemones, sponges and soft corals. Yet all the while, boring sponges, clams and barnacles are undermining its foundations.

When bits fall off in a hurricane, for example, new squatters arrive and set up house.

Dives close to the reefs reveal mysterious caverns, home to a myriad of living organisms. Actually, we were going to delineate between flora and fauna, but, as Dr. Sterrer points out, distinguishing between plant and animal in the underworld is often unbelievably difficult. A sea anemone is a flower, right? And a purple sea fan is a plant? Wrong. Both are animals. Does it matter? Yes, if you have the curiosity of a marine biologist. In the meantime, know that you will encounter corals (animals, too) of all shapes and sizes. There's hat coral and common brain coral and star coral. . . . We could go on for pages. You'll just have to come see for yourself.

Conservation Policies

"Is your reef healthy?" you might ask. Well, we have our fair share of worry about pollution, global warming and over-fishing. During the '80s there was excessive fishing, and certain species were seriously depleted. The large number of fish pots used by commercial fishermen certainly didn't help. Reef fish, particularly, got trapped in pots long after the fishermen had abandoned them. Numbers of grouper, red hind, rockfish and snapper all declined rapidly. People began to ask, "Where have all the fishes gone?"

Shellfish such as clams and conchs suffered too — not because of pots, but because of an islandwide addiction to clams casino (clams in a sauce topped with grilled bread crumbs and served in individual clam shells) and conch chowder. Harrington Sound, once the mecca of Bermuda's calico clams and conchs, was almost completely depleted. Not only did we miss the fish, but we also worried about the effects this decline would have on the health of our reef. That's the bad news.

The good news is that the government woke up to the problem. Since 1990, fish pots have been completely banned in inshore and outside waters within and beyond the reef. And certain species have come under protection. All corals, sea rods and sea fans, calico clams, conchs and numerous other shellfish are protected. There are specific conservation rules, regulations and amendments that are so complicated they need a book in themselves. But in effect, our policy is that we treat our coral reef as a marine park. Bear in mind, too, that if you stand on or touch coral, you kill it. When you visit the reef, follow this maxim and you won't upset your guide or instructor: Leave everything you see untouched. The only thing you can take is a picture. What about shell collecting? Consider this: About 500,000 visitors come to Bermuda each year. Suppose each visitor were to take one shell? Our answer, then, is "Please don't do it." Other fishing restrictions also apply — check the Deepsea and Reef Fishing and Charter Boats section for this information.

Scuba Diving and Snorkeling

At present there are six centers that specialize in diving and snorkeling. All dives are conducted by licensed scuba instructors. In addition, all the commercial dive operators we list are currently licensed by the Bermuda government and have their air tested annually. They operate daily, subject to weather conditions.

The diving season typically starts in mid-March and runs through November, although some operators operate year round. We'll tell you which ones do. What about visibility? During summer months on the northern and eastern reefs, you can see about 100 feet. Because the southern and western reefs are closer, visibility there is 80 feet. Water temperature July to September is in the mid-80s, so a one-eighth-inch wetsuit should suffice. The rest of the year, when water temperatures can fall to the low 70s, wear a ¼-inch wetsuit. When in doubt, follow the advice of your instructor, or err on the side of warmth.

Shipwrecks

You will find a list of divers' favorite wrecks in the Department of Tourism's *Where to Dive* leaflet, available in most hotels and guest accommodations. Here we describe just a few that are frequently visited by our dive center operators.

Let's start with the *Mary Celestia*, not to be confused with the *Marie Celeste* mentioned in this chapter's Bermuda Triangle Close-up. A high-speed side paddle-wheel steamer, *Mary* was a Confederate blockade runner. She sank in 1864 after a grim encounter with a reef close to the South Shore. Her paddle wheel stands upright in the water, and you can see her bow and anchor. The *Montana* was another paddle-wheeling steam Confederate runner, which also came to grief. She lies in 30 feet of water. Corals, both soft and hard, live on her.

Close to the *Montana* is the *Constellation*, a four-masted, American wooden-hulled schooner built in 1918. In 1943, on her way to Venezuela, she sank together with a cargo that included 700 cases of Scotch. You can see petrified sacks of cement as well as other salvage. The whisky? We're not sure. Perhaps there's a wee dram left. The *Constellation* was one of the wrecks featured in the book and the mid-'70s Nick Nolte movie *The Deep*.

Dive Centers

Our centers offer a variety of options — one-tank dives, two-tank dives or night dives. Generally, two-tank and night dives are for certified or experienced divers, but all offer scuba training sessions for novices. Special packages and certification programs are available. Call directly for details and prices.

Rates usually include tanks and weights, with other equipment available for rent. Prices are explained in the individual listings. Snorkeling rates are cheaper, of course, and include equipment and instruction. It's important to reserve in advance as soon as pos-

sible. People who delay making reservations until the last couple of days of their holiday tend to be disappointed. In the summer months the operators are heavily booked. You may reserve through your guest accommodation or by calling directly. In any case, call the center to explain your level of expertise. And now, here are our dive and snorkeling centers listed east to west, parish by parish.

Hamilton Parish

Blue Water Divers and Watersports
Marriott's Castle Harbour Resort, 2 Paynters Rd. • 293-2040

Blue Water Divers and Watersports actually has three operations: one at Marriott's Castle Harbour, one at Elbow Beach Bermuda and one at Robinson's Marina in Sandy's Parish. Michael Burke is managing director of Blue Water and chairperson for the Watersports Division of the Bermuda Chamber of Commerce. He's a skilled underwater photographer as well, having published *Wonders of the Sea*, a book containing many of his photographs.

You can pick up a diving and/or snorkeling trip here, or you can rent a variety of water toys, including Jet Skis and aqua bicycles. Please check the Blue Water listing under Sandy's Parish for diving and snorkeling rates and the Paget Parish listing for toy and kayak rental rates.

Scuba Look
Grotto Bay Beach Hotel and Tennis Club, 11 Blue Hole Hill • 293-8333, (800) 582-3190

Scuba Look is actually a division of Enterprise Submarine Ltd., which also owns Looking Glass Cruises (see our Nightlife chapter). But it's also the name of the 45-foot boat that

---

INSIDERS' TIP

Make your reservations for water activities, especially diving, snorkeling and fishing, at the beginning of your vacation. If you can make the arrangements before you arrive in Bermuda, all the better. That way you won't be disappointed, and you'll have more leeway where weather is concerned.

The Bermuda Triangle:
A Softer Stance on the Sinister Isosceles

Bermudians are often asked when they go abroad, "What about the Bermuda Triangle?"

Well, what about it? Does it make us worry about flying to Florida? Not a bit. Thousands of us go every year.

Before we get ahead of ourselves, let's explain exactly what we're talking about. According to the folks at the U.S. Coast Guard head-quarters, the Bermuda Triangle refers to "an imaginary area located off the southeastern United States. The apexes of the Triangle are generally accepted to be Bermuda, Miami, Florida, and San Juan, Puerto Rico."

This area has acquired a sinister reputation for peculiar goings on. Ships and planes, the argument goes, disappear in mysterious circumstances that can only be explained by the presence of supernatural or extraterrestrial forces. What we here on the island sometimes wonder is why Bermuda is particularly associated with it. After all, take Bermuda out of the triangle and you'd get the Florida Straight Line, right? Perhaps that doesn't sound quite as nefarious. And we really shouldn't be surprised. Centuries before the infamous triangle was heard of, Bermuda connoted danger, devils and wicked spirits (see our History chapter).

No doubt Vincent T. Gaddis knew this when in 1964 he coined the term "Bermuda Triangle" in *Argosy*, a short story magazine. The following year, in his book *Invisible Horizons*, Gaddis postulated a number of supernatural theories for ship and plane disappearances. In 1973 and '74, Adi-Kent Thomas Jeffrey and Charles Berlitz followed suit with their books, both called *The Bermuda Triangle*. Jeffrey speculated that the Triangle was responsible for the demise of the *Marie Celeste's* crew. The ship was found abandoned on the high seas in 1892, about 400 miles off its intended course from New York to Genoa, Italy. There was no sign of its crew of 10 and no hint as to what had happened to them.

What do we on the island think about this? Well, the lifeboat was missing, suggesting that the crew abandoned the *Marie Celeste* because they thought it couldn't weather the storm. But most importantly, the ship was found 2,000 miles east of the triangle — off Portugal, in fact. It seems that the Bermuda Triangle is able to stretch its limits at a writer's convenience. Some other disasters attributed to this storied geometric configuration follow:

• In 1945 five Navy Avenger bombers took off on a training flight from Fort Lauderdale, Florida, and were never seen again (except in Spielberg's *Close Encounters of the Third Kind*, where the pilots reappear from an alien spacecraft). The rescue plane dispatched to help them also disappeared without a trace.

• In January 1948, the British South American Airlines' plane *Star Tiger* vanished on a flight from the Azores to Bermuda.

• On December 2, 1954, the *Southern Districts* sailed from Port Sulfur with a cargo of (yes) sulfur bound for New England. Last seen on December 9, it failed to turn up anywhere.

Were these disasters caused by little people in spaceships or strange magnetic forces? Laurence D. Kushe didn't think so. In his *Bermuda Triangle - Solved*, published in 1975, he argued that all these events could be explained rationally. Dangerous cargo,

— continued on next page

The notion of the Bermuda Triangle doesn't deter countless sailors from trekking to the island.

possible human error and dodgy aircraft and seacraft were among the explanations. Let's see if we can apply one or all of these to the disasters we've cited.

Radio transmissions revealed that Charles Taylor, the leader of the Navy Avengers, realized that his compass had failed. Unable to get to get their bearings, it's possible that the pilots flew a reciprocal (180-degree) course out into the Atlantic. A brewing storm couldn't have helped either. In addition, it was said that Taylor was the only experienced pilot on the training mission — all the others were trainees. As for the rescue plane, it was a Martin Mariner aircraft, known as "the flying gas tank." It blew up 23 seconds after takeoff.

How about the *Star Tiger*? It was flying the longest commercial ocean crossing in the world at the time. The Avro Tudor aircraft suffered persistent mechanical problems. There were no weather ships along the route and no reliable weather information was available. A strong headwind, radio failure when the aircraft was 400 miles from Bermuda, and cloud cover that prevented celestial navigation all combined to doom the plane. Soon after this event, the Avro Tudor was withdrawn from commercial service.

The *Southern Districts* was a converted and much-patched World War II landing craft. Three crew members refused to sail on her because they felt that she was dodgy, even for coastal work. A similar ship, the *Southern Isles* had foundered in October. Shortly after *Southern Districts* disappeared, this type of ship was also withdrawn from service.

Now perhaps you can see why the Bermuda Triangle does not fill us with supernatural trepidation. We'll admit it's unusual in that it is one of two places on earth where a magnetic compass points to true north instead of to magnetic north. This alignment can make compasses go off the point. And we'll admit the Gulf Stream is important too. That vast ocean current makes its way across the Atlantic to northern Europe at what seems a stately 4 mph, but it can cause stormy seas. Hurricanes, unfortunately, like the triangle area too; they churn their way across the Atlantic from east to west.

But consider this: The Bermuda Triangle is part of one of the main water highways
— continued on next page

of the world. Thousands of ships and aircraft cross it every week, so occasional accidents are bound to happen, right? And given the vastness of the sea and its shelf, it's not surprising that some craft disappear without leaving debris.

One more thing: You might like to know that the Bermuda Monetary Authority (see our International Business chapter) issued one of the first triangular coins in the world. OK, its corners are softened a bit, but it's proof positive we're not against triangles out of principle.

will take you to dive on wrecks such as the *Rita Zovetto*, the *Cristobal Colon* and others that are seldom explored. A one-tank dive (check-in is at 8:15 AM or at 2 PM) costs $45, plus $35 for equipment rental (if necessary). A two-tank dive (check-in at 8:15 AM) costs $65, again with an additional $35 for equipment.

You've never been diving before? No problem. Check-in at 1:30 PM for instruction in a classroom and the pool, then go out for a dive where you will at all times be with a trained instructor. That costs $90, including equipment. PADI courses are also available. Call for more information. The Scuba Look staff is known for its friendliness.

If you don't fancy diving but want to snorkel instead, you'll go out on *Snorkel Look*, a fast, shallow boat that will cruise you through some of Bermuda's fishiest sites. A skipper will treat you to a lively and interesting historical narration on the East End of the island. Then the captain will anchor up in a couple of locations and let you float with the fish and maybe be touched by an angel. *Snorkel Look* departs at 10 AM and 2 PM daily. the cost is $35 for adults and teens and $18 for children 12 and younger. If you just want to go for a ride on one of the two boats, it costs $15.

The Scuba Look season begins March 16 and goes on to about the middle of November, weather permitting. Reserve as soon as possible by calling direct.

Pembroke Parish

Nautilus Instructor Development Centre
The Princess, 76 Pitts Bay Rd. • 295-9485, 238-2332

Nautilus has been given five stars by PADI. In 1995 it was featured in the PADI wreck diver video. The 40-foot dive boat leaves from two locations: the Princess's private dock and the Southampton Beach Club's dock (see our Resort Hotels chapter). Every morning certified divers can take two-tank dives with instructors at two of Bermuda's shipwrecks. Which ones? That's up to you. If you prefer a reef-only dive, mention it when you reserve.

Morning dives cost $75, tank and weights included. If you're leaving from The Princess, check in at 8 AM; you'll return at approximately 1 PM. From the Beach Club, check in at 8:30 AM; you'll return at 11:30 AM. Puzzled by the time discrepancies? It's because Hamilton is much farther away from the South Shore. If you leave from Southampton, you can get to the *Marie Celestia*, for example, in just four minutes. Afternoon one-tank dives are available for $55, tank and weights included. Departure time from Hamilton is 1 PM; return is 4:30 PM. From Southampton it's out at 2 PM, back at 3:30 PM. So you're not a certified diver? No problem. For $99 you can have one hour of training in a pool, then go out on the afternoon dive. If you'd rather float than sink, for $40 (which includes snorkeling equipment) you can join the afternoon divers. While they are plumbing the depths, you can snorkel above.

Equipment rentals for divers are as follows: Mask, fins and snorkel are $8, a regulator is $15 and BC (buoyancy compensator) and wetsuit are $10 each. Advance reservations are essential. Reserve by calling direct. Nautilus is open year round, though in December the Southampton Beach Club closes.

Paget Parish

Blue Water Divers and Watersports
Elbow Beach Bermuda, 60 South Rd. • 236-3535, (800) 223-7434

Read our Beaches chapter, and you'll see why Elbow Beach is so popular. Here, we'll just tell you that its stretch of sand and dune and its expanse of inviting ocean make watersports irresistible. Blue Water Divers and Watersports, located on the part of the beach owned by the resort hotel, is happy to supply you with a wide range of activities.

Into diving? If you're a novice, you can get diving instruction at the pool, where a one-hour lesson will cost $31. You also can take a certification course in the beach area; call to discuss rates, as they vary according to your needs and experience. Most exciting, you can go on a guided dive tour to the nearby reef, where you'll explore the wreck of the *Pollockshields*. Divers get to the reef in an underwater personal propulsion unit. Driving at about 2 to 4 knots, the guide will speed the divers (who use their hands and hang on to the vehicle) along the breakers and through the caves and tunnels for half the dive. Then the guide will anchor up at the wreck site for the latter part of the excursion. These battery-operated, electric underwater vehicles are entirely new to Bermuda. Only certified divers may take this trip, which costs $70 a person. Check Blue Water's listing under Sandys Parish for more information about diving facilities.

If snorkeling is more your idea of fun, you can rent equipment ($12 for two hours, $20 for eight hours) and check out the reef. For $34 per person, you can get instruction on snorkeling techniques and identifying flora and fauna, then take a guided snorkeling tour of the reef. Allowing for instruction, this program takes about two hours.

Feel like frolic? Elbow Beach can have that effect on you. For $19 an hour, try an aqua cycle (a water tricycle for two with giant wheels) and ride the waves. Kayaks, noodles, ball and paddle games and surfboards are available for rent. Call for prices.

Fantasea Diving
1 Darrell's Wharf • 236-6339

A PADI five-star dive center, Fantasea offers a number of options. Mornings, for $65, certified divers can take a 4½-hour trip to one of our reefs and one of our wrecks (most likely the *Xing Da* or the *Madiana*) and enjoy a two-tank dive. Daily departure is 8 AM from the wharf. You can take a three-hour afternoon trip for a single-tank dive. Favorite locations during the afternoon are the *Constellation*, arguably one of the best shallow-water dive sites in the world, and the close-by *Montana*. Daily departure is 1 PM.

So you can't dive but want to learn? Then the three-stage Discover Scuba program is for you. First, your instructor will give a brief orientation to the world of diving. Next, you will have your first underwater experience in a swimming pool or at the beach. Finally, you will join the afternoon divers for your first wreck and reef dive. The program costs $90 per person. Call direct for lesson times.

Experienced divers can take a dive at night for $60; call to arrange time and location. Rates for diving include tanks and weights. Other equipment (such as BC) is available for $9 per unit. A credit card number is required when you reserve. You can cancel without penalty if you do it by 5 PM the afternoon before your dive. You can buy a one-hour video record of your deep encounters for $55. An edited, cut version costs $250.

If a Jacques Cousteau experience does not appeal to you, try snorkeling instead. For $35, equipment included, you can float over the reefs while the divers view them from a lower perspective. Fantasea is open most of the year but does close for a couple of weeks in February or March. Incidentally, it has a concession at Sonesta Beach and Spa Hotel (see our Resort Hotels chapter). The telephone number at Sonesta is 238-8122.

Sandys Parish

Blue Water Divers and Watersports
Robinson's Marina, Somerset Bridge • 234-1034

Affiliated to PADI, NAUI and SSI, Blue Wa-

INSIDERS' TIP

If you're cruising in Hamilton Harbour and the Great Sound, ask your skipper to point out Buck's Island and a house there with a tower. The captain will most likely tell you Winslow Homer, original illustrator of *The Wizard of Oz*, lived there and referred to himself as king of the island.

ter Divers is Bermuda's oldest dive center. It caters to beginners and experienced divers. In the mornings, experienced divers can take a three-and-a-half-hour, two-tank dive for $70. They will explore one or two of the many wrecks that are just a 45-minute boat ride away from the marina. And, of course, they will explore the sea fans, huge finger corals and fish. Check-in at the marina at 8:15 AM for a 9 AM departure.

In the afternoons, certified divers, beginners and snorkelers get together for a two-and-a-half-hour trip that includes a one-tank dive out on the reef and a wreck. The cost for this dive and trip is $50. All rates quoted include tank, weights and belts. You can rent additional equipment, such as a wetsuit and regulator for between $6 and $9. Snorkelers can take the afternoon trip for $36, equipment included. Children 12 and younger can snorkel for $22. If you just want to go for the ride, you can do so for $14. Check in is at 12:45 PM for a 1:30 PM departure.

The uninitiated diver can take a three-hour resort lesson and dive for $91, equipment included. Videos of the trip cost $65. Certified divers can rent video cameras for $55 a trip. A credit card number is required when you reserve. You can cancel without penalty if you do so by 9 PM the evening before your dive. Call Blue Waters for information about group rates, special packages and certification programs. They are open year round.

Helmet Diving

So you'd love to see fish in their own backyard but you object to getting your face wet? Furthermore, you believe in standing on your own two feet? In short, you can't swim? Helmet diving is the answer.

This is how it works. Dressed in swimming gear, you go out in a boat to a location where there's a sandy ocean bottom but plenty of fish. With the boat moored, you gingerly descend halfway down a ladder to the water. An operator will place a helmet over your head until it reaches your shoulders. You will then somewhat resemble a medieval knight, but you'll be able to look through glass, which is more than he could. Take a deep breath and you'll discover that, yes, breathing is possible. The helmet is filled with air. It may feel a bit heavy, but worry not. Take another deep breath for courage and descend the ladder until you reach the sea floor, about 10 feet under.

Lo, and the helmet will feel lighter, and you and the fish will meet each other on your own terms. Children ages 5 and older can do it, and so can 80-year-olds. You can even keep your glasses on. Don't jump up and down though. That's rude to the fish. Here are the two centers offer helmet diving service.

Smiths Parish

Bermuda Bell Diving
North Shore Rd., Flatts • 292-4434

You can join *Caricha*, a recently refurbished 50-foot motor yacht in Flatts Inlet, just across the water from the Bermuda Aquarium. Owners Paul Pike and James Outerbridge will take you to a location just 'round the corner of Shelly Bay (see our Beaches chapter). On the way, they'll explain the procedure and calm any trepidation you may be feeling.

When they moor the boat, you'll follow the procedure outlined above. Ten to 12 feet under water, you'll soon be on pally terms with sergeant-majors and slippery dicks. You'll also discover that some of James's and Paul's personal underwater regulars are suffering from identity problems. Helen's OK — she swims like the angel she is right through a hoop. But Theodore's got a real identity crisis. *She* is a hogfish. James has named a recent newcomer Mortimer, but Paul doesn't approve. He wants Howard — the name goes so alliteratively with hogfish.

Daily departures are at 10 AM and 2 PM. The dive lasts approximately 25 minutes, but the whole trip is about three hours, depending on the number of people. No more than seven people dive at one time. While you're waiting your turn, you can watch on video as others dive; after you're through, you can watch yourself. The tape costs $25 if you want to keep it to show your grandchildren. When the water's cooler than 80 degrees, you'll borrow a wetsuit and warm up with complimentary hot chocolate. The fun costs $44 for an adult, $33 for a child younger than 12. Call for reservations, and be aware that excursions are subject to weather.

Sandys Parish

Greg Hartley's Undersea Adventure
1 Mangrove Bay Rd. • 234-2861

Climb aboard Greg's glass-bottomed boat, *Rainbow Runner,* at Watford Bridge dock in Somerset at 10 AM or 1:30 PM. (On Saturdays, only the 1:30 PM trip is offered) Come dressed in swimming gear and bring a towel. You'll take a 25-minute boat ride to a reef about a mile off the western end of Bermuda, with Greg briefing you all the while. Once there, you'll follow the procedure outlined above, find your feet (so to speak) and meet Greg's fishy friends on an underwater walk. Say hi to Oliver, the snapper who keeps everyone firmly under control. He has a right — he's been around for about seven years. If you're feeling really brave, you can also get on friendly terms with a moray eel.

The dive lasts approximately 25 minutes, and the whole trip is about three hours, depending on the number of people. No more than seven people dive at one time. You can have your picture taken for $6. On your return you receive a complimentary fruit juice or, in the winter, a hot chocolate. When the water is cooler than 80 degrees, you wear a wetsuit for free. A changing room and shower facilities are on board. While you're waiting your turn or for the others to finish, you can gaze at the fish through the boat's glass bottom. The cost for adults is $48; for children younger than 12, it's $36. Call Lynda Hartley for reservations, and be aware that excursions are subject to weather.

Snorkeling and Sightseeing Motor Cruises

St. George's Parish

Coral Sea Cruises
Ordnance Island, Town of St. George • 236-7637, 235-2424

OK, you'd love to see the fish, but you're aquaphobic. Even floating face down on top of the water just isn't for you. No problem. Take a trip with Beau Evans and Stephen McKey on their *Coral Sea* glass-bottomed boat. They'll zip you to the barrier reef that is just 15 minutes away from St. George's Harbour. Once there, you'll spend an hour watching the multicolored fish float under the glass while

Beau and Steve tell you all about life at the reef.

The trip costs $20 per person (half-price for kids younger than 12), and the ride out and back takes an hour and a half. On Mondays and Wednesdays, the *Coral Sea* leaves at 1 PM, on Thursdays it leaves at 11 AM and 2 PM, and on Saturdays it departs at 11:30 AM. Fancy a nature walk too? Then take the 2½-hour eco-cruise for extra sightseeing at Paget Island. There you can amble on the island and enjoy the flora and fauna. The fish and reef viewing is also included in the $30 rate. This trip departs on Mondays and Tuesdays at 10 AM (on Tuesdays, there's a second trip that starts at 1 PM), Wednesdays at 9 AM and Thursdays and Saturdays at 2:30 PM. On Fridays it leaves Dockyard (Sandys Parish) at 2:30 PM. Call to make reservations.

Devonshire Parish

Bermuda Barefoot Cruise Ltd.
8 Kent Ave. • 236-3498, 234-7609

Doug Shirley is skipper and owner of *Minnow*, a 32-foot custom-built picnic cruiser that has cover to chill out in the shade as well as plenty of space for sunbathing. You don't fancy cruising with strangers? Then charter Doug's boat, and he will take you anywhere you want (within reason, that is). Doug will take you snorkeling and sightseeing by water.

Ask any question, and he'll draw upon his huge amount of local information. He knows his fish (angels and parrots are his personal favorites), and he knows where to find them. We asked him where, but "off the West End" is all he would tell us. We can't blame Doug — he wants to make sure his secret spots stay secret. While we're talking about the West End, we should tell you the *Minnow* can cruise under Somerset Bridge, even when the tide is

very low. Want a picnic? Bring your own food, and Doug will make sure you stop at a great spot. His price, by the way, includes free sodas and rum swizzles. Beer and wine are available for $3.50 a drink. He also carries snorkeling equipment and all sorts of beach toys for children and the young at heart.

Doug's season runs from mid-April until December 31. People typically charter his boat for a minimum of four hours. That will cost you $410 for the first eight people and $15 for each additional person. You should book as soon as possible with your credit card. If you cancel within 48 hours of your scheduled trip, you'll be charged half price; cancel within 24 hours, and you'll pay the whole fare. Morning trips leave out at 9 AM. Doug will pick you up at Darrell's Wharf or any of the hotel docks. Call for arrangements.

Pembroke Parish

Bermuda Water Sports
1 Fairyland Ln. • 236-1500

Meet *Bottom Peeper*, a glass-bottomed boat with 150 square feet of viewing glass. For $25 you can take a two-hour sightseeing trip to the Sea Gardens off Somerset. Once you're there, you can view the reef and the wreck of the H.M.S. *Vixen* through the glass. Owner/skipper Colin Young will fill you in on reef life and the fate of the *Vixen,* and he'll feed the fish so you can watch them jump. Weather permitting, he might also take you to the wrecks of the *Montana* and the *Constellation*. A washroom and bar are available on board.

All trips on the *Bottom Peeper* depart from the Hamilton Ferry Terminal. This sightseeing trip starts at 10 AM every morning. For $40 per person you can make it a four-hour trip — it's the same destination, but you will snorkel as well. On your way to the reef, Colin will brief you on snorkeling techniques, and, together with his instructors, he will snorkel with you. On the way back, you can relax over complimentary rum swizzles, beers or soft drinks. This cruise starts at 1:15 PM. Halve all prices quoted for kids ages 6 to 12. Those 5 years and younger go for free.

On Tuesday, Wednesday and Friday, you can take a two-hour sightseeing cocktail cruise to the same destination. As you glide through Hamilton Harbour and the Great Sound, you should see sunset splendor. This trip costs $35 per person, all drinks included. You'll still view the fish, but you won't get to snorkel. Snorkeling and cocktails don't go together. Departure time is 5:30 PM.

Underwater disposable cameras are available for $20. Call Susan Young to make reservations and for information about lunch and dinner cruises and charter rates. Susan and Bruce operate from the beginning of April until the end of November.

Jessie James Cruises
Old Cellar Ln. (Walker Arcade), 47 Front St., Hamilton • 296-5801

Meet the friendly O'Connor family: There's husband and wife Jimmy and Jill, their son, Mark (cruise director), and husband and wife Ronnie and Dee. Next, meet their three boats: the *Rambler*, a 57-foot yacht; the *Consort*, a 48-foot motor cruiser, and their most recent acquisition, the *Looking Glass*, a 50-foot glass-bottomed motor cruiser.

During the summer season you can ride one of the boats for a four-hour "Snorkel Three Times" cruise that will take you to different locations. First you go to a beach with shallow water — novice snorkelers can learn the technique of breathing by mouth; experienced ones can snorkel around a small island. Next, you cruise out to the *Constellation* and *Montana* for a guided snorkeling tour. Finally, you will explore the corals and sea fans in a sea garden. Instructors are on hand to help and inform.

The cost is $45 per person, $25 per child ages 5 to 12, and Jesse James accepts no credit cards. Rates include all equipment, including snorkel vests and masks with individual prescription lenses if you need them. A full bar offering light snacks is on board. A changing room and shower facilities are also available. Departure points are Albuoy's Point, Hamilton, at 9:15 AM and 2:15 PM; Darrell's Wharf, Warwick, at 9:25 AM and 2:25 PM; and Belmont Wharf at 9:30 AM and 2:30 PM. The O'Connors also offer private charters. Call for details.

Paget Parish

Salt Kettle Yacht Charters
17 Salt Kettle Rd. • 236-4863

David Ashton is owner and skipper of two yachts. Here, we'll tell you about *Magic Carpet*, his 35-foot Flybridge motor cruiser. David will take you on private snorkel trips to Bermuda's coves and bays, where you can leisurely check out the sea urchins, parrotfish and other underwater life. If you need snorkeling instruction, he'll provide it along with stories about the island's past. Since there are more coral fish (such as puffers and porcupine fish) on the outer reef, David will take you there too. Exactly where you go depends on your choice and the weather.

Starting times are also up to you; call David to arrange them. *Magic Carpet* can carry up to 18 people, but the rates we quote are for up to eight people. Additional riders cost an extra $22 per person for day or evening trips. During the day the base rates are as follows: $350 for three hours, $420 for four hours, $600 for six hours and $720 for eight hours. Evening rates are $350 for two hours, $410 for three hours and $475 for four hours.

In addition, there is a four-hour Snorkeling Adventure trip for groups only (minimum, 10 persons). The $42 per-person rate includes a snorkeling session on the reefs and around

---

INSIDERS' TIP

The Bermuda Game Fishing Association is Bermuda's representative for the International Game Fishing Association. Call secretary Tom Smith at 238-0112 for extra information about our fishing.

some of the wrecks, plus a complimentary soda or rum swizzle on the way home. Departure is usually from the dock at Salt Kettle, though he does sometimes pick up tourists from Cambridge Beaches in Sandys. Call directly for reservations, departure details and information on his sailing yacht, *Bright Star.*

Sandys Parish

Pitman's Snorkelling
12 Westside Rd. • 234-0700

Mr. Pitman is known by some locals as "The Old Man of the Sea," but he likes to be called by his first name, Joffre. Joffre offers "comprehensive and sensitive" snorkeling instruction. This is particularly important for people who really want to experience the fish but can't swim. "Sometimes," he says, "I feel like a psychologist because I know how to get people over their fear of water."

From June through October, Joffre offers a daily four-hour tour in his 44-foot glass bottom boat, the *Fathom.* He usually makes for the Eastern Blue Cut, where for 1½ hours you can enjoy world-class snorkeling around underwater canyons with 60-foot drops. The trip is "aimed for the intellect," he says. On the way out and back, Joffre will share his extensive knowledge of the corals, the flora and

fauna, the *Lartington* shipwreck and Bermudian architecture and culture. You'll soon realize he has a passionate feel for what created the environment.

A changing facility is on board. Bring your own lunch, snacks and soft drinks. No alcohol, please. The cost is $45 per person, and credit cards are not accepted. Departure time depends on tides, visibility and weather conditions. Joffre flatly refuses to take people out if he knows there's little chance of seeing much. He strongly recommends that you call as soon as you arrive in Bermuda to make reservations. Departure location is usually Robinson's Marina, but discuss it with him when you reserve.

Sailboat, Personal Watercraft and Motorboat Rentals

Hamilton Parish

Blue Hole Water Sports
11 Blue Hole Hill, Bailey's Bay • 293-2915

Want to cruise around Grotto Bay, explore Castle Harbour and see St. George's from the

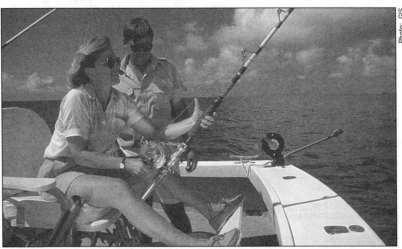

Anglers vacationing in Bermuda have broken many sportfishing records.

water? Blue Hole will rent you a 13-foot Boston whaler, equipped with anchor and bimini, along with life jackets and whistle. Remember that before the days of cars and mopeds, East Enders mostly traveled by boat, so you will be following in their footsteps or, rather, in their wake.

Rates are per boat, not per person. It costs $65 for two hours, $110 for four hours and $165 for eight hours. Prices include snorkeling gear and a cooler. If you want to feel like a true St. David's islander, rent light fishing tackle for $5 an hour or $15 for all day. After all, boating means fishing, right? Friendly staff will give you a briefing on the rules of the sea, and other craft are available. You can go on a Sun Cat for $35 an hour or hire a single kayak for $15 an hour (double kayaks are $20). Each additional hour costs $10. Take out a Sunfish for $25 for the first hour, $10 for each additional one. Windsurfing appeals to you? The rate's the same as for a Sunfish, and Blue Hole has a large range of equipment suitable for the most experienced as well as for beginners. Newcomers to surfing the wind can have a two-hour lesson for $60. If you're not renting a whaler, snorkeling gear costs $6 an hour or $18 for all day.

Southampton Parish

Pompano Beach Club Water Sports Centre
36 Pompano Beach Rd. • 234-0222

This hotel's watersports shop has many options for wet fun, and you don't have to be a guest to give it a go. We recommend a Sun Cat ($35 for one hour, $25 for a half-hour), which is like a motorized armchair for two. If you are tempted to go snorkeling, you can rent a mask and snorkel for $7 a day. (For much more information on Pompano's offerings, see the hotel's listing in our Small Hotels chapter.)

Sandys Parish

Mangrove Marina
Robinson's Marina, Somerset Bridge
• 234-0914

Rent one of Tony Roache's 14-foot Boston whalers, and the whole of the Great Sound, Hamilton Harbour, Ely's Harbour and the Sea Gardens off Daniel's Head will be yours to explore. You can sample the coves, the little islands and beaches, and snorkel to your heart's content. You can even zip over to Hamilton, tie up the boat and have lunch in town. Cruise under Somerset Bridge, and you're cruising under the smallest drawbridge over the Atlantic in the world.

These whalers are easy to operate and are equipped with an anchor, bimini and a map. They carry an extra jug of gas and life-saving equipment such as jackets, flares and a whistle. Friendly, experienced staff members with great senses of humor will brief you. In addition to telling you about the boat and rules of the sea, they'll also ask you not to go onto the North Shore or farther than Pompano Beach on the South Shore.

Rates are per boat, and credit cards are not accepted. Two hours will cost you $55, four hours are $85, and eight hours are $145. In addition, you'll pay for the gas you use, which averages between $10 and $15. The flat rate for snorkeling gear rental is $6, and it's $12 for light fishing tackle (including bait). A cooler can come in handy; it will cost you $4 to rent one. Boats can take up to four people, including children younger than 12. A 15-foot bow rider and a 15-foot whaler are also available. They can accommodate up to six adults. Rates are $10 an hour more than the ones previously quoted.

You'd rather paddle your own canoe? No problem. A single ocean kayak costs $15 for one hour, $25 for two hours and $40 for four hours. Add $5 an hour to those rates for a double canoe. The staff will give you instructions and,

---

INSIDERS' TIP

Barracuda are attracted to glittery stuff. Wear jewelry while diving or snorkeling, and they may come a bit too close for comfort. They want to inspect it, you see.

if you like, will take you on a banana boat ride. You'll sit in a "hydro sled" while they tow you around at whatever speed you like. For kids, that usually means the faster, the better.

Waterskiing and Parasailing

We have put these sports in a separate category so that you'll more easily find the few centers in Bermuda that offer them. Remember we mentioned in this chapter's introduction our trinity of sky, sea and land? Parasail and you'll experience it all in one ride! Bear in mind that times of sessions are subject to weather conditions. A beautiful sunny day without a breath of wind may make parasailing impossible. The operators will advise you about the possibilities or lack thereof when you make your reservation. For waterskiing wear swimming gear, but for parasailing wear ordinary comfortable clothes. You won't land in water.

St. George's Parish

**St. George's Parasail
Water Sports Ltd.**
Somers Wharf, Water St., Town of St. George • 297-1542
Jamal Harte will take you out in his boat a few feet from the wharf in St. George's Harbour. He will then make sure you're sitting safely in a harness attached to a parachute. A few minutes later you'll be up in the sky, literally higher than a kite. For eight minutes Jamal will cruise round the Harbour so that you can enjoy viewing our old town from on high. Don't worry that you'll end up in the water; you'll land on the boat. If you'd rather have company, you can take a tandem ride — two harnesses are attached to one parachute.

The cost for the fun is $50 per adult. Children ages 5 to 12 cost $35 per person. The center is open from 9 AM to 6 PM, and the boat leaves every half-hour. You should reserve about two to three hours in advance. In addition, Jamal offers banana boat and big tube rides) at $30 per adult for 15 minutes; kids pay $25 for the same length of time. St. George's Parasail is open from May 1 to October 30.

Hamilton Parish

Blue Hole Water Sports
11 Blue Hole Hill, Bailey's Bay • 293-2915
Michael Stevens (owner and manager) and Sean Correia will be happy to let you skim the waters of Grotto Bay or Castle Harbour on skis. In fact, they'll give you instruction in all types of waterski-type activities including wakeboarding, which they say is the fastest-growing sport on the island. One hour will cost you $95, 30 minutes is $60, and 15 minutes is $40. Waterskiing is available from April 1 to October 31. See the Sailboat, Personal Watercraft and Motorboat Rentals section in this chapter for other activities at Blue Hole.

Sandys Parish

Bermuda Waterski Centre
Robinson's Marina, Somerset Bridge • 234-3354
Kent Richardson is a champion waterskier and accomplished triathlon athlete. Yet he has lots of patience for beginners. He'll take you out into Ely's Harbour and teach you the intricacies of balance. The ultimate skiing experience, Kent says, is using one ski only, and he'll show you that too. One hour of fun will cost you $100, 30 minutes is $60, and 15 minutes is $30. The Waterski Centre operates from May 1 to the end of September. However, Kent will take tourists out during the winter months, subject to weather and demand.

INSIDERS' TIP

Spiny sea urchins are important to our ecosystem — they help clean the moss from our reefs. However, step on them and they don't like it. Their sharp spines will penetrate your skin and are difficult to remove. A general rule is: Don't put your foot in it.

Skyrider Bermuda Ltd.

Water Sports Center, Royal Naval Dockyard • 234-3019

Parasail here and you'll definitely ride the sky. But you'll go for a boat ride on the western end of Bermuda first. Then you'll sit in a chair made for two, take off and for eight minutes achieve a higher level of consciousness as you float above the island. You'll come back to earth on the boat. The cost is $80 per adult couple. Kids are welcome, provided they are accompanied by an adult. Younger than 13, they pay $32. If you just want the ride in the boat, it will cost you $32 as well. Try to reserve a day ahead. Skyrider operates from March to the end of November, weather permitting.

Deep-sea and Reef Fishing and Charter Boats

Come fish in Bermuda and you will take part in Bermuda traditions and much folklore. Many of our anglers, you see, were born with the sport in their blood. Their fathers (and sometimes their mothers) fished before them, and their grandfathers before that.

Louis S. Mowbray, former curator of the Bermuda Aquarium, once defined a fisherman as a "liar." We wouldn't dream of agreeing with him, preferring instead to define one as a "great story teller." You want an Insider's view of Bermuda's past and present? Talk to the men and women who fish. They will tell you tales that just don't appear on any brochure. Are they true? Who cares? As Nathaniel Hawthorne put it, "Nobody has any conscience about adding to the improbabilities of a marvelous tale."

Storytellers they may be, and you can take their tales with a grain of salt if you like. However, where the sea is concerned, they are the experts. Going to them (rather than a "friend of a friend") when getting the right information regarding our seas is crucial. That way you will be better assured of a rewarding and safe fishing experience.

Licenses, Safety, Conservation Rules and Regulations

So you want to go fishing. Your first question is probably going to be, "Do I need a fishing license?" The pleasantly simple answer is no. When you go out on a charter boat you are covered by the captain's license. Every charter boat we list is skippered by an experienced, licensed captain. Their boats are inspected and re-licensed yearly by the Bermuda government.

FYI

Unless otherwise noted, the area code for all phone numbers listed in this guide is 441.

All boats are equipped with lifesaving equipment (in accordance with U.S. Coast Guard lifesaving regulations), ship-to-shore telephones, toilet facilities and up-to-date fishing equipment, which includes fighting chairs, outriggers, all necessary tackle and bait. As we have already explained, we now have strict fishing regulations to protect our marine environment. You may not spear fish within 1 mile of any shore, you may not spear one while using an aqualung, and you may not use a spear gun at any time.

Our skippers will explain where they can and cannot fish, based on government regulations. For example, from May 1 to August 31 three ocean areas off the southwest, east and north shores of Bermuda are protected — they are breeding grounds for grouper. Captains will also explain size restrictions on catching fish. You can't, for instance, catch and keep a black rockfish that's less than 30 inches. The fish (and mammals) that can't be caught at all include whales, porpoises, dolphins, gag groupers (fine scale), Nassau groupers, red groupers, deer and green hamlets, mutton hamlets and tiger rockfish.

So what fish can you catch? Look to the next two sections.

Reef Fishing

Reef fishing, by the way, does not mean actually fishing on the reef. It means you won't go outside the reef line to where the continental shelf drops.

If sea sickness is likely to be a problem for you, then reef fishing may be a better option than deep-sea fishing. Inside the reef line the waters are usually more protected and less turbulent. Fish you are likely to catch include Bermuda chub, gray and yellow tail snappers, barracuda, porgies, hinds, amberjack, bonefish and assorted bottom fish. Light tackle is used.

Deep-sea Fishing

Captains on deep-sea trips will take you out about 10 miles offshore, depending on the weather and where they think there might be some good strikes. As soon as you go outside the reef line, you can feel the Atlantic swell — enjoyable for those of us with good sea legs.

So what fish to expect? Blackfin and yellowfin tuna, wahoo, shark, barracuda and dolphin. (Don't worry. We promise we're not referring to the Flipper sort of dolphin; we're just not that nasty. We mean dolphin as in mahi mahi or the dorado.) Marlin? Yep, we have those too — both blue marlin and white marlin.

Here we must mention the important matter of the tag-and-release policy. On the whole, you will be encouraged to release the fish that are not good to eat. Of course, if you bring in a fish that is likely to break a record of some sort, the skipper will probably be understanding about it. If you want a fish mounted, most captains can help you arrange it through agents here or abroad. (Ask about costs, since they depend on color and size of fish.) However, most mounted fish are artificial, their construction based on the estimated measurements of the fish you catch. Hence, it's often possible to keep the fish, so to speak, yet let it go. The government promotes the release policy by presenting certificates of release to anglers who have let fish go.

As for the fish that are good for eating, catch policies are at the captain's discretion. You should ask about them when you reserve your trip. Typically, the skipper will clean and prepare fillets that you can eat that night. Captains tend to avoid giving out enough fish to sell.

Rates and Reservations

The rates we quote in the individual listings are (on the whole) per boat, not per person. Where there are exceptions to this, we will explain in the individual listings. Generally, captains will take out groups of six who share the cost. They will take out fewer people if those guests agree to pay the whole charter price.

The rate includes all equipment, but it usually does not include drinks, food or a gratuity. (Gratuities are gratefully received but not mandatory.) Typically, guests bring their own lunch and drinks, although sometimes drinks are included in the rate. Often the captain prefers to negotiate times and prices with one person who represents the group. That way there's less confusion. Groups often come from conventions or are made up of people who are staying in the same hotel. You can reserve through your guest accommodation or one of the booking offices listed in this chapter, or, of course, you can call the captain direct. It's best to talk to him about arrangements anyway. Rates are subject to change.

In the summer months be sure to bring a decent hat and lots of suntan or sunblock lotion. That sea breeze may feel cool, but it won't stop you from burning in the sun. Wear comfortable clothing, including rubber-soled shoes with a good grip: You don't want to slip if you have to move quickly on the deck or bridge. Bring lunch and plenty of bottled water. Some captains allow alcohol, usually beer; remember that this can speed dehydration. If you're prone to sea sickness, alcohol's not a good idea.

And now to the listings, which are given in east-to-west geographical order, parish by parish. Note that we use the boat name in each header. A captain is known by his boat, right?

INSIDERS' TIP

Be careful of the Portuguese man-of-war jellyfish. Their tentacles can extend 50 meters, and they can badly sting you.

St. George's Parish

Barong
14 Jacob's Point Rd., St. David's
• 297-0715

This boat belongs to Capt. Peter Olander and his wife, Jeannie. The captain goes deep-sea fishing only. He usually departs from Ordnance Island, St. George's, or Marriott Castle Harbour at 6:30 AM. "The fish," Jeannie says, "bite early." A half-day costs $660 for up to five hours; that rate is for six people. Per person, the rate is $140. A full day for six people costs $840. No per-person rates are available for a whole day's fishing. All prices include free water, soda and beer. Catch policy? You'll get to keep enough to eat. A 24-hour cancellation policy applies; Capt. Olander will take your credit card number when you make reservations. Weather permitting, he fishes year round.

Pembroke Parish

Gringo
9 Old House Ln., Spanish Point • 295-3500

Capt. Joey Dawson's 35-foot Bruno carries the whole range of tackle for deep-sea fishing. For a half-day (four hours), he charges $600, and it's $750 for a full-day, eight-hour trip. He usually departs between 7 and 8 AM from the nearest dock to your accommodation. Sodas are included, but bring your own lunch.

Dawson concentrates on deep-sea fishing, aiming particularly for wahoo and tuna. Usually, he'll take you out to the Banks and the North Shore. Catch policy? He will always give guests what they can eat. As for marlin, the captain is a supporter of the tag-and-release policy. Dawson's season runs from April 1 to October 31. Credit cards are not accepted; you'll need to pay with cash or travelers' checks.

Eureka
11 Abri Ln., Spanish Point • 296-5414

The 65-foot Eureka is owned by Capt. Allen DeSilva (see subsequent listing for Mako 4) but skippered by Capt. David Soares. Soares takes the boat out deep-sea fishing from 8 AM to noon, Tuesday through Saturday. In the afternoons he goes reef fishing from 1 to 5 PM. On deep-sea trips, Soares goes outside the reef line by the North Channel in search of grouper, snapper, barracuda and shark. For reef fishing he stays closer to shore, where the water is calm and protected.

Rates are per person, rather than per boat. In both mornings and afternoons, adults and teens pay $60 a person; children younger than 12 pay $40 a person. On Sundays only you can have a full-day deep-sea trip from 7:30 AM to 4:30 PM for $100 a person. Passengers may keep the fish they catch. All departures leave from Albuoy's Point in Hamilton. Summer season runs from April 1 to October 31. However, depending on the weather, the Eureka will go out during November and March. Call for those rates.

Mako 4
11 Abri Ln. Spanish Point • 234-8626, 295-0835

Capt. Allen DeSilva will take you deep-sea fishing in his 53-foot Jim Smith sportsfishing boat, which he says is "the largest and fastest charter boat on the island." Yes, DeSilva will be sure to give you enough of the day's catch to eat, but when it comes to marlin, he favors the tag-and-release policy. By the way, a couple of years ago the captain broke a Bermuda record by bringing in a 1,352-pound blue marlin.

A half-day on the Mako 4 (7:30 AM to noon or 1 to 5 PM) costs $700. A full day (7:30 AM to 5 PM) costs $1,000. Sodas, beer and water are included in the price. DeSilva has a seven-day cancellation policy and requires a 30 percent advance deposit. The season runs from April 1 to October 31.

Princess
8 Tulo Ln., Spanish Point • 295-2370

Capt. David DeSilva, son of Capt. Allen DeSilva, has private charter or per-person rates for half- and full-day deep-sea fishing trips on the Princess. Most likely, David DeSilva will take you to the Argus or Challenger Banks in search of wahoo, tuna and blue and white marlin. He'll let you have enough of the day's catch to eat and will depart from any location you choose.

Half-day rates are $650 for a regular party of six, $110 per person. In the morning, the boat leaves at 7:30 or 8 AM (whichever you prefer) and returns at 11:30 AM; in the afternoon, you leave at 1 PM and return at 5 PM. Full-day rates are $875 for six people or $150 per person. Departure is at 7:30 or 8:30 AM, and you will return eight hours later. Sodas are included in all prices. DeSilva has a 48-hour cancellation policy and will need a credit-card number when you reserve. His season starts April 1 and runs through November 30.

Tango
8 Tulo Ln., Spanish Point • 295-2370

Capt. David DeSilva's speciality is reef fishing. With the *Tango*, he'll depart from anywhere you choose in Hamilton and take you to a reef line on his 42-foot custom-built boat. Where you go depends on where DeSilva thinks the fish are. He'll probably take you off the South Shore or to the northwestern side of the island. The pick of the catch goes to his guests. "That gives them incentive to catch fish," DeSilva says. His personal favorite fish is yellowtail snapper: "Fry it, stew it, boil it . . . it's always white and flaky."

DeSilva offers a full-day, eight-hour trip for $875; a half-day (four hours) will cost you $650. Departure times are mutually agreed upon. If possible, reserve with a credit card before you arrive in Bermuda. If you cancel within 24 hours of your scheduled trip, it'll cost you 50 percent of the rate.

Southampton Parish

Lady Gina
18 Coral Acres Dr. • 295-2370

Capt. Allan Virgil concentrates mostly on deep-sea fishing. *Lady Gina*, a 35-foot Bertram sportsfishing boat, therefore is equipped with Pan international rods, state-of-the-art reels and the latest trolling tackle. She's also air-conditioned. Departure location? It's at your convenience. If your group is staying at a hotel, Virgil will pick you up there or at the nearest dock.

As for catch policy, you will be allowed to take what you can eat that night. Where marlin are concerned, the captain encourages the tag-and-release policy whenever possible. However, if you want the catch of your life mounted, he'll be happy to arrange it for you. By the way, you might like to know that under Virgil's jurisdiction, a boy unexpectedly celebrated his 15th birthday in 1996 by bringing in a 792-pound blue marlin. A full day of fishing costs $875; a half-day is $650. Sodas are on sale at $1 each. Departure time is usually 8:30 AM, but it's open to negotiation.

Sandys Parish

Jamie C
5 Sound View Dr. • 234-3081

Capt. Sinclair Lambe and his 35-foot Main Coaster *Jamie C* will take you reef or deep-sea fishing. Robinson's Marina in Sandys is his preferred departure point. He'll pick you up in Hamilton, but he reminds you that it will deplete your fishing time. Lambe follows the tag-and-release policy for marlins.

Half-day deep-sea fishing trips are from 7 to 11 AM and costs $650. Half-day reef fishing jaunts are out from 12:30 to 5:30 PM and cost $550. There's no full-day reef fishing option, but for $850 you can deep-sea fish for eight hours (7 AM to 4 PM). Lambe enforces a 24-hour cancellation policy.

Bermuda has become a Cinderella with both slippers polished, annually luring more than 1,000 wave-dancing yachts to its harbors, inlets and bays.

Yachting & Marinas

Legend has it that after St. Brendan and 17 other seafaring monks hoisted sails over their currach (a boat made of tanned oxhide stretched over a wooden frame then slathered with fat to preserve the hide) and took a seven-year traipse around the Atlantic in the mid-6th century, they may have sailed into one of Bermuda's coves. To those who find an intriguing nugget of possibility in such a tale, St. Brendan and crew may then arguably be considered Bermuda's first visiting yachtsmen.

Almost 15 centuries later, the exploits of the Irish monk notwithstanding, Bermuda has become a Cinderella with both slippers polished, annually luring more than 1,000 wave-dancing yachts to its sheltered harbors, inlets and bays. Yet, every so often yacht skippers miss us completely and have to tack around and try again.

Although on a clear day Bermuda's low green hills can be seen 25 miles out, visibility can be slashed to less than 5 miles when the skies are gray, cloudy or hazy. On clear nights though, Gibb's Hill Lighthouse, erected between 1844 and 1846 and reputed to be one of the oldest iron lighthouses in the world, provides a clear beacon (500,000 candlepower) for craft up to 40 miles away. And speaking of beacons, North Rock Beacon, sited about 10 miles offshore on the island's most northerly reef, flashes a much dimmer light. Bermuda's other lighthouse, St. David's Lighthouse, is at the island's easternmost tip. Built of Bermuda stone, its white light of about 30,000 candlepower is visible from 23 miles and produced by a prism-reflected electric bulb of 1,500 watts. Emergency generators kick in if electricity fails.

As You Near Bermuda

When en route to the island, particularly if sailing June through November, keep alert for sudden tropical storms and hurricanes that can blow up from the southeast. Equally important, North Atlantic gales can strike with little warning between December and April, so maintain a keen eye on your barometer.

Bermuda Harbour Radio (which is also the Rescue Coordinating Centre) must be contacted on your approach and given an ETA. A continuous listening watch is kept on 2182 Khz USB (Upper Side Band) and on marine VHF Channel 16, which is the call and distress channel that should not be used unless contacting Harbour Radio or another vessel. Once initial vessel-to-vessel contact is made, move to a working frequency or indicated channel. Do not use the channel for general communication. Also, channels 10 and 12 are reserved for government tenders, tugs and branch pilots; they are not for casual boaters or yacht captains. Bermuda Harbour Radio and the Rescue Coordinating Centre can also help with matters related to customs, immigration, health and berthing.

Remember that St. George's is the port of entry for all visiting yachts, and all yacht captains and passengers must clear customs and immigration before traveling about the island (by land or sea). If you are in doubt about regulations or are unfamiliar with entering St. George's after dark, lie off until sunup. Once in St. George's Harbour, you'll find a 24-hour clearance facility located on Ordnance Island (near the *Deliverance* replica). And don't forget that illegal drugs (including marijuana), guns, plant and vegetable matter are forbidden. A valid passport is essential for all visiting yacht passengers who are not from the United States. U. S. citizens can use a photo I.D.

There are a few other things of which you must be aware. If you intend to visit for more than a week and live onboard your boat, health regulations must be complied with, and the Department of Marine and Ports, 295-6575, should be notified. And if Fido or Garfield is among shipboard companions, a general health certificate, issued by a licensed veterinarian no more than 10 days prior to arrival, is needed. Animals without relevant documents will be refused entry.

A word about bridge openings: The Swing Bridge, spanning the entrance between Ferry Reach and Castle Harbour, is opened on demand between 7:30 AM and 7 PM daily from April 1 to September 30, and from 7:30 AM to 5 PM daily from October 1 to March 31. If sailing from St. George's to Hamilton — a trip that can take up to two hours — going through the Swing Bridge can knock more than 30 minutes from your journey.

A publication that should prove extremely helpful is *The Bermuda Yachting Guide*, and we advise that you get your hands on one if you are interested in bringing your craft to the island. It is published by the Bermuda Maritime Museum Association, P.O. Box MA 273, Mangrove Bay MABX, Bermuda. The organization may be reached by phone at 234-1333. The North American distributor for the publication is Bluewater Books & Charts, 1481 S.E. 17th Street Causeway, Fort Lauderdale, FL 33316. The guide provides, among many other things, a list of places where proper charts can be purchased in the States. It is also a fine reference to the many anchorages in Bermuda and the easiest way to reach them.

FYI

Unless otherwise noted, the area code for all phone numbers listed in this guide is 441.

We have listed a couple of boatyards and marinas (and be advised that a marina in Bermuda is not quite the same as in the United States). Facilities vary, and berthing may not be available. Occasionally, free docking for a couple of days can be had in St. George, the old town priding itself on having catered to seafarers for almost four centuries.

And don't worry about that Bermuda Triangle business. We don't, and St. Brendan didn't.

Boatyards and Marinas

St. George's Parish

St. George's Boatyard Ltd.
25 Wellington Slip Rd., Town of St. George • 297-0877

Once inside St. George's Harbour, you'll find St. George's Boatyard to the west. It does a great deal of everything. A full-service facility that offers a do-it-yourself option, its services range from the hauling of up to 40 tons on a travel lift to carpentry, sandblasting, spray-painting and fiberglass repairs. There are showers and bathroom facilities, and 110- and 220-volt power supplies. At its Esso marine station, duty-free fuel is available to yachts in transit — maximum draft 7 feet at low tide. Other on-site services include welding and electrical and engine repair.

Captain Smokes Marina
Godet & Young, McCallans Wharf, 13 Wellington St., Town of St.George • 297-1940

The welcome mat is spread out here where a number of convenient services are on hand, among them fresh water supplies,

---

INSIDERS' TIP

If you want to get in a little fishing and are unfamiliar with the best spots, tune to Channel 06 when in local waters. This is the channel used by most Bermudian anglers, and you might pick up info on what fish are biting and where to drop your line.

110 and 220 electrical hookups and showers. The yachtsman or woman can transmit a fax, send or receive FedEx or UPS packages and make long distance telephone calls (phone cards are cheaper and available).

If your vessel or group of vessels can use the 500-gallon minimum, you may refuel from a duty-free Esso truck. Remember too that it is important to conserve fresh water; Bermuda, unlike other destinations, relies almost solely on rainwater for its potable supply.

Sandys Parish

Somerset Village

This area, so favored by Sir George Somers (see our History chapter) that it became known as "Somers' seate," is a rural village of small farms, quiet parks and nature reserves, open spaces, wind-beaten coastlines and several businesses including a couple of banks, restaurants, supermarkets, pharmacies and a family bakery. Composed of four islands — Watford, Boaz and Ireland Island North and South — it is best known for the Royal Naval Dockyard, where once-dilapidated 19th-century fortifications have been resurrected into major visitor attractions.

The Dockyard has two breakwater-protected basins of 4 to 5 fathoms. The north breakwater is a fine deep-water harbor. The Department of Marine and Ports uses a portion of the area known as the North Basin for maintaining its tenders, tugs and ferries. Its northwest corner has slipways for hauling craft with a draught up to 6 feet.

Dockyard Marina
9 Dockyard Ter., Royal Naval Dockyard, Ireland Island • 234-0300

This marina is within the confines of the century-old Dockyard breakwater, at the intersection of the North, South and Dundonald shipping channels. The deepwater port allows the marina to easily accommodate vessels alongside one of their convenient berths. Whether your stay is a couple of days or several months, water, dockside electricity, fuel, ice, newspapers and clubhouse facilities are available on a daily, weekly, monthly or yearly basis. Call ahead for price information.

West End Yachts Ltd.
Royal Naval Dockyard, Ireland Island • 234-1303

With old naval buildings forming a backdrop, this full-service boatyard has no problem providing a comprehensive range of services — long- and short-term storage, haulouts and launch, full rigging facilities, spraypainting and refinishing among them. With 7,000 square feet of workshops, the staff prides itself on being able to handle any repairs.

Yacht Clubs

The two we mention below have the "royal" designation. The granting of what is known as a "royal warrant" is an ancient tradition. In 1155, Henry II granted a royal charter to the Weaver's Company in Britain. Only a few more than 800 royal warrants remain outstanding. Most have been granted by the present Queen Elizabeth II, the others by the Queen Mother, the Duke of Edinburgh and the Prince of Wales. Only about two dozen warrant holders — among them the Royal Bermuda Yacht Club listed below — have held the distinction continuously since Queen Victoria's reign, which lasted from 1837 to 1901.

Royal Bermuda Yacht Club
Albuoy's Pt., Hamilton • 295-2214

Fifty years ago a local writer, in describing this club, noted that, "Neither fortune nor fame will necessarily qualify you for membership in the Royal Bermuda Yacht Club." The writer was right, this is a *very* private club.

Lying on Albuoy's Point in the city and commanding a fine view of Hamilton Harbour, the club was founded in 1844 when Samuel Triscott — who became a noted regatta organizer — and 29 others gathered under a calabash tree at Walsingham in Smiths Parish to form the Bermuda Yacht Club. It received its royal designation from Queen Victoria in 1845 and is one of the world's oldest yacht clubs, listed 12th in order of founding.

The RBYC has a breakwater-type dock with members' vessels inside and space available alongside the outer wall or stern-to; they have mooring buoys in a line parallel to the dock about 75 feet off. This is a popular place to dock since it is in the heart of Hamilton.

Berthing, available to non-members, is

stern-to, and maximum ship size is 80 feet. The cost without electricity is $1.50 per foot per night; with electricity, it's $1.75. Visiting yacht captains should tie up and enter the club to register so that an account can be opened in the boat's name. This will allow the crew to enjoy club services. The club does request that someone always remain onboard during the night for security reasons.

www.insiders.com

See this and many other **Insiders' Guide®** destinations online — in their entirety.

Visit us today!

Royal Hamilton Amateur Dinghy Club
Mangroville, Paget
• 236-2250, 236-8372

Dinghy racing, which became increasingly popular with sailing aficionados from the mid-1800s onward, was a motivating factor behind the formation of the Hamilton Amateur Dinghy Club (HADC) in the spring of 1882. Then, a small group of students from Charles E. Clay's school on Angle Street (what is now called "back of town") met above Gosling Brothers' Ltd., on Front Street in Hamilton. In a tiny room, they laid the groundwork for today's thriving club.

In 1883, following a visit to the island by Princess Louise, Marchioness of Lorne and the wife of Canada's governor general, the club applied to the princess for her patronage. The application was granted, and the club was able to append the title "royal." However, members received a shock in 1890, when Queen Victoria abrogated patronage by relatives and children (such as had been granted by Louise) and assumed sole authority for conferring the honor. The club's royal designation was rescinded. Not until 1953 did Queen Elizabeth II approve the reintroduction of royal to the club's name.

The RHADC sits on the rim of Red Hole, a bay at the eastern end of Hamilton Harbour. Its dock is large enough to provide space for visiting yachts. Although Red Hole is dotted

---

INSIDERS' TIP

When approaching Bermuda be aware that reefs can come up on you quickly; do not ignore your depth sounder. If faced with a serious but not life-threatening situation, use the urgent "Pan Pan" signal rather than the "Mayday" signal.

You Have to Be a Little Dingy to Climb Aboard This Bermudian Legend

The local dollar coin is stamped with its picture, it is part of the logo of the Royal Hamilton Amateur Dinghy Club, and it is one of the most eccentric little boats you will ever encounter. Not only will it threaten to dump you into the sea, odds are that if you sail it often enough, you will end up overboard.

Fourteen feet long with a 25- to 43-foot mast carrying between 300 and 1,400 square feet of sail, the Bermuda fitted dinghy occupies a sailing niche all its own. Racing them and winning is a challenge, and we're not just talking about having the swiftest craft. Victory may also

depend on how efficiently the bailer (one of six crew members) shovels water out of the boat as it spills in, and whether or not the skipper (as has happened) orders a couple of crew members over the side. Winning in these competitions will not be compromised by excess weight.

This is probably the only class that allows boats to finish with fewer crew members than they began with. One story tells of a winning boat rolling over and sinking after crossing the finishing line, putting the skipper into the harbor in which his crew had already been dumped.

These little rascals are susceptible to capsizing at the smallest wave, but dinghies have sunk during a race, been frantically raised, bailed, re-rigged and gone on to compete in later races that same day — and even winning! The boats offer a unique way of challenging wind, sea and competition.

The evolution of local dinghy races — the racing season is from May 24 to mid-September — can be traced to 1853 and the first one-masted open boat race in St. George's. The competitors raced small family boats (12-foot keels or less) generally used as transportation between St. David's and St. George's; there was no connecting bridge or road in those days.

These everyday transport boats were converted temporarily for racing. Often "fitted" with shifting ballast — a couple of sandbags or pieces of lead with rope through them — and built of Bermuda cedar, the fittings became more elaborate as dinghy races became increasingly popular within the sailing community.

As the Bermuda fitted dinghy evolved, one of its features became the iron fin, known to have been used in 1870 and possibly before; another feature was the introduction of temporary decking to reduce the amount of water shipped when racing. Hull lines improved, and once into the 20th century, various designs were explored. The Bermuda Maritime Museum at the Dockyard (see our Attractions chapter) has on display a fully rigged champion dinghy.

Photo: Panatel VDS Ltd

Sunday dinghy boat races are a sailor's dream and exciting to watch.

by local craft of every type, you may be able to secure a private mooring. Contact the club's dockmaster for information on services and costs. The RHADC, along with the RBYC and the St George's Boat Club, organizes a number of races throughout the year.

Yacht Racing

Bermuda has always been wedded to the sea, its love affair with sailing having spawned a racing calendar filled with competitions between all boat classes.

International racing spans more than a century here, with one of the earliest competitions held in 1849 when the American yacht *Brenda*, owned by George W. Collimore of Boston, was matched against the Bermudian-owned *Pearl* in the Great Sound. The *Pearl* won by 55 seconds.

Races organized by various clubs are held in the Great Sound almost every weekend, and specific class series are held throughout the year. These include tornados, dinghies, lasers, Etchells International one-designs and others. The Snipe Class is very active throughout the summer months.

The Bermuda Sailing Association is the governing body for yacht racing in Bermuda and is recognized by the Bermuda government and the International Yacht Racing Union (IYRU) based in London. The association's membership is comprised of the island's sailing clubs and individuals who participate in sailing activities.

Bermuda fitted dinghy racing is usually in full swing throughout June, July and August. These boats (see this chapter's Close-up) have been called bizarre. They are only 14 feet long but can cost more than $100,000 to build. Race venues are at Mangrove Bay, Hamilton Harbour and St. George's.

Newport-Bermuda Yacht Race

First held in 1906, when three boats competed for the Sir Thomas Lipton Cup (which was won by *Tamerlane*), this biennial race is often called the "Thrash to the Onion Patch." As one of the major events on the racing calendar, this high-powered competition attracts more than 100 participants. Several classes — yachts, sloops, cutters, ketches and yawls — are represented. The race begins in Newport, with craft leaving on the third Friday in June. Depending on weather conditions, the winner usually crosses the finish line just off St. David's Lighthouse late the following Tuesday or early on Wednesday.

Organizers — the Royal Bermuda Yacht Club, the New York Yacht Club and the Cruising Club of America — faced with dwindling interest, in 1990 changed the then-existing handicap system, replacing it with IMS (International Measurement System) rules. The event's reputation as a leading racing competition had been curtailed in 1970 with the introduction of the MHS handicap system that favored cruising-type yachts over the sleeker racing rigs. The IMS permits two racing divisions — cruising and spinnaker — with the spinnaker division competing for the St. David's Lighthouse Trophy. The introduction of the IMS rules revitalized the event, attracting a record 281 requests for entry. A total of 180 were selected.

Marion-Bermuda Cruising Yacht Race

This event is a more sedate affair compared to the Newport-Bermuda. First sailed in 1977 after getting the thumbs-up from Coles Diel, then-commodore of the RHADC, the four-to five-day race from Buzzard's Bay in Marion, Massachusetts, is held on alternate years to the Newport. This is an offshore event for cruising yacht skippers carrying an amateur crew, a limited number of sails and no spinnakers. Sponsored by the RHADC, the Beverly Yacht Club and the Blue Water Sailing Club, the Marion-Bermuda attracts more than 100 entries, with the finish line just off St. David's Lighthouse.

1997 Tornado Catamaran World Championship

In 1986 Bermuda hosted the 19th Tornado Catamaran World Championship. Just more than a decade later, the island accepted the International Tornado Association's invitation to host the 29th world championship, staged between November 9 and 15, 1997. It was the first time a venue had been used twice.

The fastest one-design boat in the world, the Tornado Catamaran (when not referred to as the Ferrari of the sailing world) is called a "bruiser" or "rocketship." Its popularity here is undeniable, with members of the Bermuda Tornado Association having competed in three Olympic championships and many world and regional competitions.

For the 29th world championship, the 71 teams from 21 different countries included the past five world champions and all the medal winners from the Atlanta Olympics. Held off the Dockyard in open water, the week-long, 10-race series was won by the Germans in a double-tiebreaker.

Yacht Charters

There are more than a dozen yachts from which to choose for that daytime or sunset cruise through Bermuda's placid waters. All are skippered by experienced, licensed captains. Weather permitting, most sail throughout the year, but a few only ply the waters between April and November. All yachts offer restroom facilities, and some have separate changing rooms.

Most charter yacht operations can be found in the phone book, and yacht and motor craft information can be found at the Bermuda Department of Tourism at Global House, 43 Church Street, Hamilton. In this section, we provide a couple of fine charter companies to get you started. More cruising options are listed in the Snorkeling and Sightseeing Motor Cruises section of our Watersports chapter.

Charter rates depend on the length of cruise (usually three to eight hours) and number of persons. Once you have decided on checking out a few, call ahead to get quotes; you'll find there is not a great deal of difference between operations. Most have ameni-

ties that include beer, wine and soft drinks, with food available on request. Reservations are required. Some of the charter yachts depart from a fixed location; others may be willing to make pickup arrangements that suit the client. Make certain you get all the pertinent details.

Sailing Charters

Allegro Charters
• 235-3481

Got a yen to cast off the landlubber life and see Bermuda from the sea? Allegro Charters and Captain Richard McGlynn operate two sailing vessels, *Allegro* and *Artemis*, each of which will take you into that relaxed and carefree nirvana you only dreamed about before Bermuda and its tranquil waters seduced.

A three-hour cruise on the *Allegro* will cost $35 per person; a six-hour cruise is $50 per person, with a maximum of eight people. Boats depart year round from Barr's Bay Park in Hamilton (near the Royal Bermuda Yacht Club), and overnight trips for couples can be arranged.

The *Artemis*, a 41 foot Robert Perry sloop, can take up to 20 people. A three-hour cruise costs $50 per person; a six-hour jaunt is $90 per person. You can also indulge yourself in an *Artemis* weekend escape, in which you will be pampered and catered to for two nights and three days. The charge is $650 per person, and it is all-inclusive.

Or you can choose from a flexible sailing schedule. For the *Allegro* it's $200 for a half-day and $350 for a full day; on the *Artemis*, you'll pay $400 per half-day and $600 for the full day. All charters include soda, bottled water and beer. Snorkel gear is also included if you wish to slip beneath the waters to enjoy the beauty of an undersea world you will be thrilled to experience.

INSIDERS' TIP

Clearances under local bridges are as follows: Swing Bridge in St. George's, 9 feet; Flatts Bridge in Hamilton Parish, 8 feet; Somerset Bridge, 11 feet 9 inches; Longbird Bridge (at the causeway), St. George's, 6 feet 6 inches; Watford Bridge in Sandys, 20 feet.

Yachts tied up at Royal Hamilton Amateur Dinghy Club after a race.

Sail Bermuda Yacht Charters
• **236-9613**

Departing from Albuoy's Point in Hamilton at 10 AM and 2 PM Monday through Sunday, *Alibi* Captain Bobby Zuill will take you on a "getaway half-day sail" — a relaxing, tranquil three-hour waltz through Hamilton Harbour, the islands of the Great Sound and toward the west end of the island. All you'll need will be a bathing suit and towel — and your camera, of course!

But it's not all just great sailing. A brief stop is made so you can swim in the enticing waters, and if you don't have your own, snorkeling gear is provided. A complimentary rum swizzle, Dark 'n' Stormy (if you haven't already learned, they're made with local black rum and ginger beer) or soda will quench your thirst, though you will be charged for additional beverages.

You will also have the option of choosing the Sunset Sail, which is a 90-minute "fantasy" sail that departs about an hour before sunset. Experience it. For further information and rates, call the captain.

Motor Charters

Pembroke Parish

Town & Country Yacht Charters
Three Market Ln. • 292-6050, 236-0127

For those who want the luxury of cruising in plush comfort and style, the *Lady Tamara* or *Lady Erica* should fulfill your fondest desires. Within these "Lady" boats you'll find wall-to-wall carpeting, excellent bar facilities and food. Fully air conditioned, the 100-foot *Lady Tamara* is superb for fashion shows, receptions, weddings and theme or post-conference parties. *Lady Erica*, though smaller at 60 feet, has all the luxuries of her larger sister, with comfort- able sofa seating and teak interior paneling. It is ideal for intimate VIP parties. For booking information and rates, contact Nigel Prescott.

BERMUDA'S
3 in 1 Golf
CALL 234-GOLF

PORT ROYAL
GOLF COURSE
Southampton

Office	234-0974
Fax	234-3562
Pro	234-0972
Fax	234-3630
Maintenance	234-1182
Tennis Court	238-9430
Restaurant	234-5037

ST. GEORGE'S
GOLF COURSE
Southampton

Office	297-8067
Fax	297-2273
Pro	297-8148
Maintenance	297-8370
Bar/Restaurant	297-2796

OCEAN VIEW GOLF COURSE
2 Barker's Hill, Devonshire

Office	295-9092
Fax	295-9097
Pro	295-9077
Fax	295-9078
Maintenance	236-6758
Bar/Restaurant	295-9069

Call 441-234-Golf to reserve your tee-off times at any of these three public golf courses before you arrive in Bermuda or while you are here.

If calling from outside Bermuda add area code 441 to the telephone numbers above.

Golf

William Wordsworth once described a game of golf as "a day spent in a round of strenuous idleness." Where Bermuda's golf courses are concerned, many golfers would argue that the word "idleness" just does not apply. "Strenuous," on the other hand, most certainly does.

At present, Bermuda has nine golf courses, all of which are scenic and all of which are tricky. Indeed, it's the very fact that they are scenic that presents special challenges to the most experienced of golfers. Proximity to the ocean means that water is frequently very much part of the play and can be a real hazard. A shot over a cliff and the sea, for example, calls for nerves of steel. In addition, where there's ocean, there's also wind. Sea breezes on the courses make for some interesting situations.

When is the best time of year to play golf in Bermuda? We recommend October to March since during those months, the courses are at their most lush. True, it might rain more, but remember that for golf courses, rain is almost always good news. It makes fairways even fairer. Furthermore, from November on, hotel rates tend to be reduced, and tee times are more readily available.

And there's the matter of tournaments. One week during October, January, February and March is given to tournaments that appeal to golfers of all ages and ability. You'll find specific information about tournaments in the Spectator Sports chapter. Be aware here, though, that visitors are welcome to spectate and even participate.

If you are visiting during the summer months, sunset golf (in the late afternoon until dark) might appeal to those who fear the heat or prefer to walk. While gas carts are mandatory during the day at some courses, you are typically allowed to hoof it in the evening. It also tends to be cheaper.

How do you reserve tee times? You can call the clubhouse directly, or, if you are staying

in a hotel, you can ask the staff there to make your bookings for you. Where the three public, government-owned courses are concerned, you can simply call the automated 295-6000 number to make reservations or cancellations and to receive information about course features.

In this chapter we alert you to the idiosyncrasies of Bermuda's golf courses. We will also, of course, tell you about fees and facilities. Should you go à la cart or not? We'll tell you that too. And in golf, as you know, if you ain't got that swing it *does* mean a thing. That's where the golf pros come in. Private lessons are available at nearly all courses, and we'll give you rates in the individual listings. First, we offer some information on how golf came to Bermuda, and why our golf courses are important to our environment.

History

As any Scot will tell you, golf is always identified as Scottish in origin. Did the Scots bring the game to Bermuda? It's possible, if Scots were officers here in the British Army. According to *The Royal Gazette*'s Bermuda Online service, golf started in Bermuda when "well-heeled British Army officers brought their golf clubs with them to while away the time during their assignments in Bermuda. They hacked away all over the place." In 1457, King James II of Scotland banned the game of golf in his country because he felt it interfered with time that should more properly be spent on archery practice. Presumably, governors of Bermuda were not so worried about their officers' marksmanship.

By 1905, there were apparently two golf courses here, neither of which is in existence today. But the story of golf in Bermuda officially started with the rise of tourism after World War I. Riddells Bay Golf and Country Club, Bermuda's oldest, opened in 1922. Meanwhile, the Furness Withy Shipping Line (See our History and Resorts chapters) developed two of our private courses: the Mid Ocean, which opened in 1922, and the Castle Harbour, which opened in 1931.

As tourism increased, so did the number of golf courses, which proved popular with locals and visitors alike. Today, there are three public and six private courses, but many hotels and cottage colonies can make arrangements for guests to play the private layouts since three open days are generally available for non-club members. At the moment, another private golf course has been promised to us. It will be situated on what was formerly the U.S. Naval Annex in Southampton Parish (now renamed Morgan's Point), and it will probably open in the summer of 1999. Designed by Jack Nicklaus, it will be an 18-hole, par 72 course, and rumor has it that the Golden Bear will model it after his favorite Pablo Beach golf course in California. Seven-thousand yards long, it will be Bermuda's first full championship course. It will also be the first completely irrigated course on the island. Plans are in the making for a luxurious clubhouse and a championship practice range.

For the Birdies

Today, Bermuda claims to have more acreage per square mile dedicated to golf than any other country. Whether this is true or not, it is definite that golf courses take up about 17 percent of our open space. Given that we have a total of just 21.6 square miles of land, our open spaces are obviously very important to us, and Bermuda is becoming more and more environmentally aware.

In the past, golf courses were not altogether friendly to the environment. For starters, they had a definite aversion to land crabs. What's wrong with land crabs? Well, besides having the curious habit of walking sideways, land crabs also like to make holes. Granted, holes are what a golf course is supposed to be about — nine are fine; 18 are even better — but the crabs were considerably more generous than that, pockmarking island courses. The result was that heavy pesticides were used to control them. The trouble with that solution was that the bird population suffered too.

In the mid-1970s, Dr. David Wingate, conservation officer at the Department of Agriculture, Fisheries and Parks, and president of the Bermuda Audubon Society, hit on the brilliant idea of bringing in some pairs of yellow-crowned night herons from the Tampa Bay Nature Reserve in Florida. He believed these birds had been prevalent in Bermuda at the time of the first settlers in 1609 and had suffered the same fate as the cahows (see our Flora and Fauna chapter). Yellow-crowned night herons live on shellfish, and Wingate nurtured them on small pieces of — yes, you guessed it — land crab, which they took to immediately. Today, these herons roam the mowed areas of Bermuda's golf courses and do golfers a favor. The herons thrive, the land crabs no longer have a holier-than-thou attitude, and pesticides are not as heavily used.

In the meantime, other birds also enjoy the golfing habitat. Bluebirds in particular are also happy at the courses (no cats are around to threaten them), and they help out by eating worms and caterpillars, cockroaches and crickets. Check each course for bluebird nesting boxes. Look out for that streak of blue, and remember there's more than one way to appreciate a birdie.

Bermuda Courses

And now for the listings, which, as usual, we will present east to west, parish by parish, subset by subset and thereafter in alphabetical order. A word about the parish designations: Mid Ocean and Castle Harbour golf courses are arguably in both St. George's and Hamilton parish. You see, golf knows no boundaries, and neither does Tucker's Town, that select area of land where both golf courses are definitely located. See our History chapter for more information about Tucker's Town. In the meantime, we have decided to be arbitrary about the parish issue.

St. George's Parish

The Mid Ocean Club
1 Mid Ocean Dr., Tucker's Town • 293-0330
Having hosted the Merrill Lynch Shoot-Out Series for two years, The Mid Ocean is defi-

> ## FYI
>
> Unless otherwise noted, the area code for all phone numbers listed in this guide is 441.

nitely Bermuda's most exclusive private golf club. The Furness and Withy Line wanted it that way right from the start. They bought land and beaches in Tucker's Town to lure the American rich and the famous who wanted luxurious seclusion. The owners financed this beautiful course as well as what was originally known as the Castle Harbour Hotel and the Castle Harbour Golf Club. Charles Blair McDonald, a titan of American golf, designed the course in 1922. Nine years later, Robert Trent Jones revised it. Many a famous politician has played here, including U.S. Presidents Dwight Eisenhower, John F. Kennedy, Richard Nixon, George Bush and Jimmy Carter. Golfing British prime ministers have included Winston Churchill, Harold MacMillan and Edward Heath. You might like to know that the legendary Babe Ruth also played here. At the fifth hole he managed to put two balls in the lake. Enough said. One can't be brilliant at everything.

Select though this club is, it is possible to enjoy a round here. Mondays, Wednesdays and Fridays are open days for non-club members. If you want to play on other days, introduction by a member is required, but many resort hotels and cottage colonies have club memberships. If you are a guest, they will be happy to make arrangements for you to play at Mid Ocean. (See our Resort Hotels and Cottage Colonies chapters for more information.)

So what is this illustrious par 71 course like? Comprising 6547 yards, it offers some extremely interesting water challenges. Four holes are near lakes and ponds, and the ocean comes into play as well. The signature hole is No. 5. Its dramatic, elevated tee forces you to drive your ball at least 200 yards over a lake before playing your second shot to a green that is well-protected by bunkers. There are surely lots of balls in that lake, likely including those two that Babe Ruth dropped. You'll be relieved to know that at the 9th hole, by Harrington Sound, a half way house offering cool drinks and snacks awaits you. No. 18 hugs the ocean and gives you great views. Mid Ocean can be tame on a nice day, but watch out for those ocean winds. On the opening hole, southwest winds can affect your play, and on the 17th hole in particular, wind plays a key role in your club selection.

Bear in mind that this is the only course in Bermuda where caddies still assist you. Carts are available, but walking the course is recommended. On average, the round takes about four hours and 15 minutes. Be sure to look out for the birds, as about 30 bluebirds have set up home at Mid Ocean. In addition, you may well see some great cranes, of the wading bird variety. And don't worry about summer brown out: Most tees and all of the greens are irrigated.

The clubhouse, pink and white and trimmed with cedar in true Bermudian style, looks down on the 18th green and is surrounded by the glorious South Shore. There you can enjoy a well-earned drink in one of two bars or dinner in the main dining room. You can munch on lunch too. Locker rooms and a well-stocked golf shop are available. In addition to the course, Mid Ocean has a driving range and two putting greens. Greens fees are $140, and carts are $40. Caddies work for $25 per bag, and, as we explained, are preferred. If you need lessons to cope with that tricky 5th hole, they cost $60 an hour. No half-hour lessons are available. By the way, Tuesday mornings from 7:30 to 11 AM are set aside for lady golfers.

St. George's Golf Club
1 Park Rd. • 297-8353

This 4043-yard, 18-hole course is Bermuda's newest. Designed by Robert Trent Jones as a par 62, it ranges along hillsides and overlooks the St. George's shoreline and Fort St. Catherine. Most of the holes are par 3s, with six par 4s just less than 400 yards on the shorter side of the course. Wind is an important factor in your game here and can demand careful club selection. Depending on the weather, on a couple of par 3s you might need anything from a 9-iron to a driver to reach the green. Watch out for the 14th hole. It's a dogleg next to Coot Pond, opposite Tobacco Bay. You have the

---

INSIDERS' TIP

Always wear correct golf attire. All shirts must have collars and sleeves. Shorts must, of course, be Bermuda length. Absolutely no bathing suits, jeans, gym shorts or cutoffs are allowed.

difficult choice between playing into the dogleg or going for the green. That's why it's more familiarly known as the "Oh no hole." Fairways are generally narrow and challenging.

Daily greens fees are $43. Play after 3 PM, and they're reduced to $21. Gas carts (mandatory on weekends and public holidays) cost $34, and pull carts are $7. A full set of clubs rents for $18; golf shoes for $6. You need lessons? No problem. Kim Swan will help you out at $40 for a half-hour. The clubhouse has a bar and restaurant where you can relax after your game, and there's a pro shop. Do not be misled by the word Club, by the way. Because the Bermuda government owns this course, no membership is necessary.

Hamilton Parish

Castle Harbour Golf Club
6 Paynters Rd. • 293-2040

Castle Harbour Golf Club's course dates back to 1927 when Charles Banks, close friend of Charles Blair McDonald, started to design it for the Furness Withy Line. Unfortunately, he died in 1929, two years before it was completed, so he never got to see the full glory of his work. Later, Robert Trent Jones added modifications. Gently undulating through the contours of hills, valleys and fields, this 6440-yard, par 71 course is renowned for its stunning panoramic views of the open Atlantic, Castle Harbour Bay and Harrington Sound. At the very first of the 18 holes, the dizzying blue view of sea and reefs could well distract you, so be careful. From there on, up-and-down fairways, together with unpredictable sea winds, make for interesting situations. So do blind holes. The finishing hole, a par 3, runs 234 yards along the harbor side to a well-targeted green that is protected by a large pond. Marriott's Castle Harbour Resort acts as a back drop. There, by the way, you can enjoy refreshments at The View bar and restaurant. The clubhouse has lockers and facilities. Castle Harbour was the venue for the 1984 American zone qualifying competition for the World Cup.

If you are a guest at Marriott's Castle Harbour Resort, greens fees are $100 a round. Otherwise, they are $110. Gas carts are mandatory here and cost $22 per person. Golf clubs are available for rent for $26, and golf shoes

are $8. Need professional help? A half-hour lesson costs $45. Double that fee for a full hour.

Devonshire Parish

Ocean View Golf Course
2 Barkers Hill • 295-9093

Originally a membership club, Ocean View is now a Bermuda government facility. In the 1990s, it has added a brand-new clubhouse (with a bar and restaurant), conference rooms, a well-stocked pro shop and lockers. It also has a driving range. As its name suggests, this course does overlook the ocean — the North Shore. A nine-hole, par 35 course that is just under 3000 yards, Ocean View is not as easy as it might look. Rolling hills make for challenges. The signature hole is No. 9, where a pond (very threatening indeed) is stuck in the middle of the fairway, 162 yards from the white tees. The course finishes with a blind, uphill dogleg. But when you get to the last green, you'll be rewarded with a stunning view of the ocean. You might even see a cruise ship glide by.

Greens fees are $32 for the whole day or $22 for nine holes. If sunset golf in the evening is for you, the fees go down to $16. Check for exact times. Gas carts (mandatory only on weekends and public holidays) cost $17 per person for 18 holes or $8.50 for nine. Pull carts cost $6. Club rentals are available for $20 per person; golf shoes for $6. Keith Pearman is on hand to offer playing lessons. His fee is $40 for a half-hour.

Paget Parish

Horizons and Cottages Golf Course
33 South Rd. • 236-0048

You may have already come across Horizons and Cottages in our Cottage Colonies chapter. If not, refer there for a detailed description of the property. Guests naturally get first preference, but this nine-hole mashie course is also open to members of the public. You might think a par 3 course of 1000 yards is nothing to be frightened of, but Golf Digest described it last year as "a thousand yards of pure poison."

Given that the longest hole, No. 4, is about 125 yards and the shortest are 75 yards (there

You'll never tee it up in a more beautiful setting.

are two or three of those), you can see why no carts are necessary. Not many golf clubs are necessary either. In fact, one Insider plays Horizons and Cottages with nothing more than a 5-iron. The 9th hole is the tightest and is the most picturesque point of the course. You hit back to the Main House and toward Garland's Cottage. Bluebirds, by the way, don't always think the grass is greener somewhere else. Six families have nested at just one green.

Guests pay $4 greens fees and have preferred tee times. Otherwise, the fees are $20 per person during the week and $25 per person during weekends and public holidays. It is generally not much trouble for a non-guest to play at Horizons. Junior players who aren't guests get to play for $10. No carts or shoes are available for rent, but you can rent clubs (three of them) for $2.50 a set.

Warwick Parish

Belmont Hotel and Golf Club
97 Middle Rd. • 236-6400

This 18-hole, par 70 course stretches more than 5700 yards and is very much part of the hotel grounds. (See our Resort Hotels chapter for a description of the hotel.) While guests receive preferential tee times, you can easily make arrangements to play here. The loca-

tion makes it an ideal choice for tourists — it can be reached by ferry on the harbor side or by bus on Middle Road.

Belmont's hilly course has very narrow fairways that run parallel to each other, and it also has small, narrow putting surfaces. Good tee shots and accuracy are, therefore, a must. What's unusual about this course is that Middle Road divides it. Your opening hole is on the harbor side, then you drive your cart through the tunnel that gets you across the road to the south side of the course. There you play holes 2 through 8. Then it's back to the hotel property for holes 9 through 18. The 11th hole is tricky, with the chance your second shot might go into, instead of over, a lake. The 17th is surely the signature hole, since it gives you a spectacular view of the Great Sound and Hamilton Harbour. After your game, you can relax in the snack bar and restaurant. A well-stocked pro shop is also on hand.

Belmont Hotel guests play free. However, they must pay for gas carts, which are mandatory at most times. For 18 holes, carts are $40; for nine, they cost $20. Other visitors pay $85 greens fees, and that price includes the cost of the cart. Pull carts (which may be used for sunset golf after 4 PM, when walking is allowed) cost $8 for 18 holes. Lessons are $40 a half-hour or $80 an hour. Club rental is $28 for a full set.

Riddells Bay Golf and Country Club
24 Riddles Bay Rd. • 238-1060, 238-3225

Described by Bermudian golfers as "a real gem" and "the course you must play," this is Bermuda's oldest course. It was born, so to speak, in 1922, but right now, in 1997, it is about to undergo a facelift. The clubhouse will be completely remodeled.

Meandering along Riddells Bay's peninsula, which measures just 600 yards at its widest, the 5668 yards of this par 70, 18-hole course offer scenic delights and plenty of challenges, including one pond and three ocean holes. As pro Darron Swan put it, "What we don't have in length we make up in beauty." So do take the time to appreciate the serenity of this setting, and notice the dark, mysterious roots of the mangroves that hug the water's edge. Winds from the sea are again an important factor, so that, ironically, shooting's no breeze. The 8th hole, a dogleg right, is the one to watch out for. If you're accurate, you shoot in to a green that's surrounded by water and a pond. If you're not, never mind: You've just added to the Great Sound's Grand Golf Ball Collection. From this hole you can see the benevolent gaze of Gibbs Hill Lighthouse — maybe it can cast light on the subject. Carts are not compulsory here. Play takes from three-and-a-half to four hours.

This is a private club, but tee times are set aside for tourists every weekday as follows: Monday and Wednesday, 8 AM to 2:30 PM; Tuesday, 9.30 AM to 2:30 PM; Thursday, 2 to 2:30 PM; and Friday from 10:30 AM to 2 PM. Weekdays, greens fees are $55 a person for up to 18 holes. Weekends and public holidays, it's $75. Club members play at a reduced rate. Gas carts are available at $40 each, and pull carts are $7. Shoes will cost you $5. Darron will be happy to give you an hour's lesson for $70 or a half-hour one for $40.

Southampton Parish

Port Royal Golf Course
Middle Rd. • 234-0974

Port Royal, a par 71 and one of Bermuda's three public 18-hole courses, has been described as the flagship of golf courses in Bermuda. Another of Robert Trent Jones' creations, its 6565 yards roll along the natural terrain of Southampton's cliffs overlooking the South Shore. It goes without saying, then, that you'll take in the greens of the water as well as those of the golf course. Elevated tees and holes with distinctive characteristics make Port Royal a challenging course to even the most experienced golfers.

The par 4 No. 1 is a 432-yard dogleg right with water in front of a heavily bunkered green. The par 3 16th is definitely the signature hole. Yes, it's beautiful, but it's also lethal. Depending on the weather, you'll use a pitching wedge or a 3-wood to shoot over cliff and ocean. Is there Spanish treasure sunk in the waters below? Possibly. But, depend on it, there's definitely a generous collection of golf balls from Port Royal. If you're in any danger of forgetting your experience at No. 16, you can buy a memento poster of the hole for just $2. And after you've survived the 16th, look out for the recently restored lake at the 17th. It's a great place to spot egrets. No. 18 is also interesting. It will literally uplift you (it's an uphill climb) all the way to the clubhouse, where you can collapse in the bar or restaurant for some much-needed sustenance. Play should take no more than four-and-a-half hours. By the way, Port Royal has "golf rangers" on hand to help you maintain proper pace of play. They recommend that players should take 15 minutes or less per hole.

Weekday greens fees are $65; weekends and public holidays, they are $70. Avoid weekends altogether if possible, as this course gets very busy. If you have no choice, book early for Saturday or Sunday to avoid disappointment. After 4 PM, you can play sunset golf for $21, and

---

INSIDERS' TIP

Please respect the pace of play. Always let the faster golfer through. And when completing a hole, leave the green as soon as possible. You can mark your scores or count your strokes when you're in your cart. In any case, do so when you're off the green.

boy will you see some glorious sunsets from this course. It's a west-end course, remember. Gas carts (mandatory only on weekends and public holidays) cost $34 per cart. Pull carts are $9; golf shoes are $10. You can rent clubs for $20. Need practice for that tricky 16th? Frankie Rabain offers lessons — call the clubhouse for details and rates. Port Royal's practice greens and driving range will also help you get up to par.

Southampton Princess Golf Course
101 South Rd. • 238-0446

This 18-hole, par 3 course surrounds the Southampton Princess hotel, which was once described by *Golfweek* as a "vast, beached pink cruise ship . . . sitting atop a bluff near the Gibbs Hill Lighthouse." For more information about this luxury liner of an accommodation, check the Resort Hotels chapter. In the meantime, know that this course is an ideal introduction to Bermuda's more challenging full-length courses.

Here, 2684 yards are neatly sculpted out of steep terrain, so any mountaineering skills you may have will prove helpful. The vertical drop on the first two holes is at least 200 feet, and the rise along the 178 yards of No. 4 makes for an uphill driving experience. Elevated tees, cunningly placed bunkers and a few water holes (three, to be exact) mean that you may need every club in your bag. Mountaineers may climb mountains "because they are there," but they also climb for the views. Get to the 16th hole that sits in a cup fringed with oleander, and you'll see the backdrop of Gibbs Hill Lighthouse and the blue of the ocean. Get to No. 18, and you can speed your way to the 19th: the clubhouse's fully licensed bar and restaurant. Play takes about two hours, leaving you plenty of time to enjoy Bermuda's other attractions. Incidentally, because of the hotel's irrigation system, the course always looks lush, even in the midst of summer.

For 18 holes, hotel guests pay $34 greens fees; other visitors pay $38. Gas carts are mandatory at most times and cost an additional $28. When available, pull carts cost $6 and so do golf shoes. Check out Bruce Sims for lessons at $70 an hour. Half-hour sessions are $35.

Golf Instruction

The Bermuda Golf Academy
10 Industrial Park Rd. • 238-8800

We have to get academic about this listing. We include it in this chapter because it offers a wonderful opportunity for adults and kids to practice and improve their game. Opened in 1996, The Bermuda Golf Academy features a 320-yard driving range with 40 practice bays. Don't worry if the rain pours down or the sun blazes too fiercely — 25 of them are covered. In addition, eight target greens are placed from 75 to 230 yards out, and a sand trap, located beside the range, allows you some out-of-bunker practice.

Floodlit at night, the facility will let you play until 10:30 PM. At present, after-dark golf is unavailable anywhere else in Bermuda. The facility opens at 8 AM. Need lessons as well as practice? Three professional golfers are on hand to help you out. If you're not photo-phobic, they'll even video your play. That way you can see yourself in action and receive professional analysis. Hour-long lessons are $55, and half-hour ones are $35. You can rent two clubs for $2. During the day, a basket of balls costs $4; after sunset, it costs $5. Children can get a basket for $3.50.

The driving range proved so popular that in 1997 the academy added an 18-hole minigolf course, suitable for the whole family. Featuring pagodas, waterfalls and brilliantly blue waterways, the course takes about 45 minutes to complete. How do you negotiate the 16th hole? You shoot a ball over a drawbridge. On weekdays adults older than 16 play for $7, and on weekends and public holidays it's $8. Children play any day of the week for $6. If they don't like miniature golf, send them to the jungle gym while you're doing your thing. When you're all through, you can relax over snacks and drinks at the licensed restaurant, appropriately named The Wedge and Divot. You'll find it in the clubhouse.

INSIDERS' TIP

Be kind to the course and always replace divots.

International Business

On weekdays, the City of Hamilton's streets are probably busiest between noon and 2 PM when many of us take a lunch break. Wander along Front and Reid streets or take a seat in Par-la-Ville Park off Queen Street (See our Parks and Conservation chapter), and you'll see lots of local women and men dressed in smart business attire. For many men, in the summer months anyway, that attire consists of Bermuda shorts with matching knee socks, jacket and tie. If you notice a dark gray suit, possibly pin-striped, trying to look cool in August, then you may be forgiven for thinking it's encasing a Brit on business here. On the other hand it might not be; the gray suit trend is catching on among Bermudians.

Come 2 PM, most of these people disappear into the offices that now characterize the city's landscape. "Wait a minute," you might object, "What about shops and restaurants? Might they not they work there?" The answer is yes, and they might work in one of our three banks, or in the public, or government, sector. But chances are that many of the people you see work in international companies. According to the Archer Report, released in 1997, international companies in 1996 directly employed at least 2,240 workers on the island, of whom 1,412 were Bermudian. Bermudians working in international companies comprise 5 percent of the total Bermudian work force of about 22,000 workers. (Including non-Bermudians, the total work force is about 33,000.)

So how many international companies are here? The report quotes a total of 9,246 at the end of 1996. However, we must explain that most are simultaneously here but not here. A most ingenious paradox? We'll explain. The 1996 Bermuda Government Employment Survey revealed that approximately 264 international businesses actually have offices in Bermuda. The rest are registered here but are not physically present, a common occurrence that we will explain. Even so, non-resident companies also greatly impact our economy. For example, in 1996 they contributed $91.8 million in professional and bank fees to the private sector and $27.5 million to the public sector. While we're talking money, we should tell you that during the same year international companies spent a total of $631 million in Bermuda. The companies with offices here contributed 78.7 percent of that total. Feeling dizzy with numbers? The important fact they reveal is that international business is Bermuda's main industry other than tourism. In fact, whereas tourism was once our main source of revenue, since 1992, the earnings from international companies have exceeded tourist intake. Let's take a break from figures for a while and talk about the companies themselves.

Read the business sections of our newspapers, and you'll almost certainly be introduced to the term "exempt companies." What they are exempt from is not, as many people think, corporate or income taxes. (Actually, there aren't any of either.) It's Bermuda laws that lead to the term. These companies are exempt from our laws that require limited companies in Bermuda to have at least 60 percent Bermudian ownership. And unlike local companies, they also are exempt from Exchange Control regulations and liability for stamp duties on the documents they execute.

However, exempt companies are not allowed to transact business in Bermuda; they are limited to using Bermuda only as a base for their business overseas. They are naturally restricted from dealings in arms or in other dubious activities. Often they are subsidiaries of companies (or of large groups of companies) based in countries such as the United States, Canada, the U.K. and Hong Kong.

So what kinds of business do these companies transact? Answer: They include private investment companies, trust companies, aviation and shipping and, most importantly, insurance companies. Some examples of firms with offices in Bermuda are Bacardi International Ltd., whose administrative (not manufacturing) headquarters are here; Esso and Shell, Transworld Oil, Arethusa (Offshore) Ltd. and American International Company Ltd. Most of our international companies are exempt, but not all. About 10 percent of them are what are known as permit companies. Like exempt companies, they're allowed non-Bermudian majority ownership but, in contrast, are also allowed to transact business in Bermuda. Sun Life Insurance of Canada is an example.

Why Bermuda?

So why are international companies, most of which are American-owned, attracted to Bermuda? According to Robert Stewart in his 1997 book *Bermuda: An Economy Which Works*, there are several reasons. These include the fact that Bermuda has political and social stability and enjoy a per capita gross national product of $27,500. The island has a reputation for being corruption-free and almost entirely scandal-free in our financial history. And our English common law system allows appeals from Bermuda courts to the

FYI

Unless otherwise noted, the area code for all phone numbers listed in this guide is 441.

Judicial British Committee of the Privy Council. (The Privy Council can be described as the commonwealth's supreme court. . . . International companies appreciate the objective decisions of this body.) A long-established and recognized legal system, then, together with our economic infrastructure of telecommunications, roads, airport and ports also attracts offshore companies. In addition, we have a professional infrastructure that includes accountants, lawyers, bankers, investment managers and insurance professionals.

But what makes Bermuda unique is the working partnership between government and the private sector. This partnership makes for a light but effective regulatory system that is particularly important to the insurance industry. Because this sector of our international business has grown dramatically since the mid-1980s, we'll discuss it in its own section, where we'll explain this public-private partnership more fully.

International companies looking to incorporate here have to be approved by the Bermuda Monetary Authority (BMA), which investigates shareholders and the people who want to do business on the island. Although the BMA is ultimately responsible to Bermuda's Ministry of Finance, it has increasingly seen a role as a buffer between the government and the private sector. It has its own building, Burnaby House, on Burnaby Street in the City of Hamilton. A physically separate identity is essential for ensuring that confidentiality and privacy concerning the legal, international flow of money can be credibly maintained.

The Bermuda Monetary Authority Act of 1969 led to the BMA becoming the sole authority to print, issue and redeem currency notes and to mint coins for use in Bermuda.

INSIDERS' TIP

If you're interested in volunteering for or contributing to one of our charities, visit the Centre on Philanthropy, at 7 Par-la-Ville Road in Hamilton. This center compiles a register of all Bermuda's charities. Staff will advise you on what organizations are available and which ones might best suit your interests and skills. A reference library is also available. Call 292-5320 for an appointment.

The BMA is also responsible for the following: supervising, regulating and inspecting banks and financial institutions; advising and assisting the government and public bodies on banking and other financial matters; fostering close relations between financial institutions themselves and between the financial institutions and the government; and, less important now than previously, managing exchange control and regulating transactions in foreign currency or gold on behalf of government.

If an international company is approved by the BMA, then it is registered. Exempt companies pay an annual fee to the government (the fee varies according to the activity of the company and the amount of share capital) and other government taxes such as the employer's payroll tax. The approval procedures, however, are a bit different for insurance companies.

The Importance of Insurance

OK, the motto on Bermuda's coat of arms means, "Whither the fates may carry us" (the original words are *Quo Fata Ferunt*), but believe us, in business matters we're just not that fatalistic. And we definitely believe in insurance. American International Group (AIG), our grandfather company, came to Bermuda in the 1940s, shortly after World War II. Many of the firm's international interests in China were being nationalized by the Communists, so Bermuda was an attractive location. Enter an animal known as captive insurance. In simple terms, a captive insurance company is one that is specifically formed to provide insurance coverage to its own shareholder. Effectively, it's a type of self-insurance that, according to Robert Stewart, "was developed (although not originated) by Fred Reiss, who established Bermuda's first captive management company, International Risk Management."

It was in the late '70s and through the mid-'80s that insurance and reinsurance companies started to proliferate. Elsewhere the insurance industry was suffering from a number of crises. Property, workers' compensation and liability insurance all became very expensive or completely unavailable in many parts of the world. In addition, the increasing number of natural and human-made catastrophes had serious financial impact on many companies. Those disasters included the Lockerbie bombing, Hurricanes Andrew and Hugo and the San Francisco earthquake. Later, insurance giant Lloyds of London in the U.K. came into disrepute when investors lost money or withdrew from the market. From 1988 to 1992, their losses were more than $12 billion.

As a consequence of these various events, many international industrial corporations started up offshore captive insurance subsidiaries and many of them chose Bermuda. In fact, we are now the capital of the captive insurance world, having more captive companies registered here than anywhere else on the globe. Since 1985, Bermuda has expanded beyond being purely a captive insurance domicile. Some companies such as ACE and XL have made the transition from being captive insurance companies to being publicly quoted companies. And other insurance and reinsurance companies not owned by the policy holders have also arrived. Examples include Mid Ocean Limited, Partner Re, and Centre Reinsurance Co. (Bermuda) Ltd., but there are many others. If the '70s and '80s were characterized by the growth of captive insurance, then the '90s can be characterized by the development of true open-market insurers. By the end of 1996, 114 of the 264 international companies physically present on the island were insurance related. And by the end of June 1997 a total of 1,477 insurance and reinsurance companies were registered in Bermuda.

Bermuda, as mentioned previously, is popular for its scandal-free reputation and low taxes, but most important of all is the fact that its regulatory system is less bureaucratic than those of other countries. In the U.S., for example, regulation can vary from state to state, and it tends to be more geared to the consumer. In contrast, as Robert Stewart puts it, "Regulation in Bermuda is geared towards business and the reputation and solvency of those who provide the insurance cover." This makes for more innovative underwriting. In addition, insurance companies in Bermuda are able to insure against punitive damages; that's not the case in many American states.

Insurance companies wanting to incorporate here have to deal with two different sets of regulations: one from the BMA (as happens with all international companies) and the other

from the Bermuda government's Registrar of Companies. The Registrar of Companies scrutinizes business plans or proposals. Where insurance companies are concerned, these two bodies interact closely.

Remember we discussed the working partnership between government and the private sector? The Ministry of Finance appoints advisory committees whose members are drawn from companies in the private sector. The Insurance Advisory Committee advises the Ministry of Finance on regulations, while the Insurance Admissions Committee advises the Registrar of Companies on insurance applications. Associations such as the Bermuda International Business Association (BIBA), the International Division of the Bermuda Chamber of Commerce (ICD), the Bermuda Insurance Managers Association (BIMA) and the Bermuda Independent Underwriting Association (there are many others) are important. Very often members on the advisory committees are also members of these associations. This partnership, allowing easy communication between government and the private sector, can work because the infrastructure managing our economy is so much smaller than those of the economic superpowers. And the partnership provides a flexible, efficient and uncomplicated environment for insurance companies.

If Bermuda benefits insurance companies, those companies also benefit Bermuda. Remember the mention of 2,420 employees in international companies? Well, 1,623 of them were working in insurance-related industries. And out of that $631 million international companies spent in Bermuda in 1996, $346.9 million was contributed by insurance-related companies.

Later on in this chapter we'll detail the benefits Bermuda reaps from international business, but here we must mention the contribu-

www.insiders.com

See this and many other **Insiders' Guide®** destinations online — in their entirety.

Visit us today!

INSIDERS' TIP

The Archer Report is a study prepared for the Ministry of Finance by Professor Brian Archer at the University of Surrey, England. It analyses the Bermuda economy and its export earnings.

Photo: GIS

Hamilton's majestic City Hall was designed by architect
Wil Onions to resemble an oversized Bermuda cottage.

tion insurance companies have made to professional education and training. The Bermuda Insurance Institute (BII), located in the Cedarpark Centre, 48 Cedar Avenue, City of Hamilton, is a professional education association representing and educating the local and international insurance industry. With 140 member companies, it provides a variety of courses and training services that lead to recognized qualifications for people employed in insurance-related fields. Qualifications include the CPCU, a qualification in property, casualty and underwriting, and an MBA in risk management.

We should also mention the Bermuda Foundation for Insurance Studies (BFIS), a multimillion-dollar plan started in 1996 that will further assist and educate Bermudians entering the insurance field. According to Keith Forbes of *The Royal Gazette's* Bermuda

Online, it aims to "develop, coordinate and oversee the availability, direction and funding of training and educational facilities specializing in insurance-related academic and professional designations." The program links the Bermuda College (See our Education and Child Care chapter) with New York's College of Insurance and the BII. Forbes also quotes the following information: "Since July 1996, the BFIS has received corporate and individual pledges worth $3.5 million over five years. In 1997 to date alone, $1.4 million in new pledges have been committed from ACE Insurance, Centre Re, Chubb Atlantic Indemnity Ltd., Global Capital Reinsurance Ltd., La Salle Re Ltd. and Johnson & Higgins (Bermuda) Ltd."

These pledges and donations show that Bermuda's international insurance companies are firmly committed to upgrading the training and qualifications our young people need to participate in the dynamic insurance industry.

Overall Benefits for Bermuda

We've already given you the numbers showing how many people these companies directly employ, but we should also consider the effect international business has on other sources of employment. Local management companies provide the international companies with banking, financial accounting and legal services. The banks, accounting and law firms also offer their services. Real estate companies benefit through office and home rentals, while local stores, telecommunications outfits and other service providers profit from additional business. More ancillary service employees such as maids, gardeners and interior designers are in demand as well. International companies also generate more visitors coming to Bermuda; they in turn generate more business for the airlines and hotels. Read our three chapters on hotels, and you'll see a growing trend toward catering to business travelers attending conferences.

While companies come here to make profits, they frequently want to give back to the community, and they do this in a myriad of ways. Companies outside the insurance world also support education. In 1995, for example, Corange Limited commemorated its 25th anniversary and commitment to life science research by donating $1 million to Bermuda College for its establishment of the Corange Science Centre. And in 1997 Orbis Investment Management pledged $500,000 to be used on education and youth development schemes. The ICD have donated at least $1 million in ICEA awards and scholarships for students to study some form of business. Fidelity Company, which donated more than $5 million to the Bermuda Underwater Exploration Institute (see our Attractions chapter), is just one of the many international companies that help to fund that institute, along with other establishments such as the Bermuda Biological Station.

In America there are about seven charities for every 10,000 people; in Bermuda there are

Photo: GIS

In the growing market of convention business, Bermuda is ideally suited, based on our proximity to the U.S. mainland and our modern telecommunications systems.

47.5 charities for the same number of people. Here again the international businesses help, not only in terms of financial donations, but also by offering free advisory services and instituting in-house programs whereby company employees commit to doing volunteer work for the community. Some companies, including XL and ACE, have set up their own charity foundations. And often company members will sit on boards of charity and scholarship committees to raise the standards of those organizations.

Many of the charities that benefit are health-related. Read our Healthcare chapter, and you'll see that P.A.L.S. (Patients Assistance League and Service) is an invaluable charity dedicated to enabling cancer patients to stay at home. Others are sports-related. Annual spectator events such as the World Rugby Classic (sponsored by XL Insurance, ACE Insurance, Heinz and APT) and the XL Bermuda Open Tennis Championship are supported by companies. Arts efforts benefit as well, with sponsorships being given to organizations such as the National Art Gallery (see our Arts and Culture chapter).

Other Impacts of International Business

Visitors just returning to Bermuda with memories of the City of Hamilton in the early 1970s may be in for a shock. Many of those

INSIDERS' TIP

The Risk Prediction Initiative (RPI) is an organization dedicated to encouraging collaboration between the international science and business communities. It's a research and educational program within the Atlantic Global Change Institute of the Bermuda Biological Station for Research. Many of our insurance and reinsurance companies are sponsors and participants. So far the program has offered workshops focused on issues such as weather prediction, and research on extending the records of the history of Atlantic hurricanes through paleoclimatolgy. For more information, call the Bermuda Biological Station at 297-1880.

old one- and two-story houses with verandas have been torn down and replaced with multi-story offices. Reid Street, Par-la-Ville Road and Bermudiania Road particularly have been transformed, to some people's consternation. There is a worry that the unique Bermudian flavor of the architecture has given way to blocks of offices that you could find in cities anywhere else in the world. Certainly the need for increased office space has meant that Hamilton has not retained the same quaint charm we enjoy in St. George's. (For more on architecture, see the Close-up in our Arts and Culture chapter.)

Visitors who once lived in Bermuda may also be shocked by the impact international business has had on rentals. Check our Real Estate chapter, and you'll see how expensive rents and property prices have become. In this respect, international business is a double-edged sword. Bermudian land and property owners, of course, benefit enormously. But we worry about those Bermudians who struggle, sometimes with two jobs, to pay for adequate housing for their families. Hopefully the lands and properties returned following the base closure will eventually help to alleviate the housing problem.

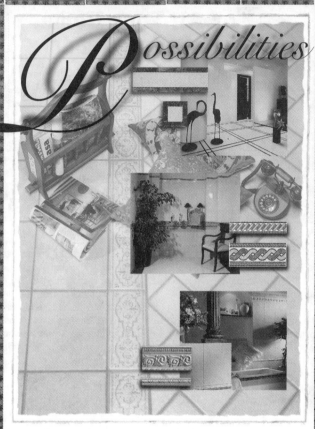

Possibilities

Soft & Sophisticated! Bright & Brash!
Fun & Fanciful! Warm & Welcoming!
Ceramic tiles for every taste and style!

Arnold's Tile Ltd.

One Mill Reach Lane, off Pitt's Bay Road, Pembroke
Telephone   441 - 296 - 3636

Real Estate

Where prices are concerned, we might be forgiven for thinking real estate in Bermuda is actually unreal — or perhaps surreal is more to the point. Given that we have only about 21 square miles of land that is densely populated, it's inevitable that buying property here is very expensive. In fact, some house names you may notice while exploring our island can be seen as wry reminders of the price we have to pay. "At Last," "Dream's End," "Last Penny" and the more smug "Sitting Pretty" are examples.

But if property is expensive for Bermudians, it's even more so for foreigners. Because of our limited land and number of houses, we have to restrict non-Bermudian property ownership and property speculation. Is it possible for non-Bermudians to buy property? Yes. In this chapter we'll tell you how and what non-residents may buy. We will explain the different rules and regulations that apply when buying a house as opposed to a condominium. But because most non-Bermudians residing here rent rather than purchase, we'll also focus on the rental market for long-term and holiday rentals. Prices and rents depend on location, so we'll mention the more exclusive neighborhoods as well.

It's more common than not that people wanting to buy or rent operate through a real estate agency. So we'll tell you what you can generally expect from agents and/or sales representatives. At the end of the chapter, we'll give a sampling of some agencies with details of their specializations.

Buying a House

OK, you're not Bermudian, and you want to buy a house here. The first thing any real estate representative will tell you is that your choice is restricted to houses that have a minimum Annual Rentable Value (ARV) of $43,800. Sounds reasonable? The bad news is that the ARV at present bears no true relation to the market price. In effect, your starting price to buy will be about $1.5 million. For that you can expect a substantial detached house of 4,000 to 5,000 square feet, probably with a pool on a half-acre or more of land. Your location will most likely be in one of the following exclusive areas: Tucker's Town; South Road, Paget or South Road, Southampton; Harbour Road, Paget; Knapton Hill, Smiths; or Fairy Lands and Point Shares, Pembroke. Some agents say that buying such a house right now for $1.5 million would be a steal. Market prices can be anywhere from $2 million to $5 million and occasionally have been known to hit $17 million.

Once you've chosen your house, you apply (through your real estate agent) to the Bermuda government for a license. You pay an application fee of $442, which is refunded if your application is successful. However, the license fee itself is 22 percent of the purchase price (doing the quick math, that's more than $300,000 for a $1.5 million home). It's a one-time fee, but if you sell the house to a non-Bermudian, then that buyer will have to pay it as well. And if you in turn buy another house, you pay another license fee.

You should also know that, as a non-Bermudian, you may own just one property at a time. Under exceptional circumstances you may have permission to acquire a second property, but that permission is conditional on selling the first one within 12 months. If you want to rent your house to a tenant, you must receive permission from the Minister of the Department of Immigration, who will rarely allow you to rent it out for longer than 12 months. Rent it to a non-Bermudian, and you pay a levy of 5 percent of the monthly rent.

You may be wondering how many non-Bermudians do buy houses in Bermuda. Well, at the moment the stock of houses available to them is about 292. Generally people who buy these properties do so because they want to retire here or because of tax laws in their own countries. The previous trend of buying holiday homes is apparently now on the decline. As you can see, buying a house in Bermuda is an extremely costly endeavor. A cheaper option is to buy a condominium.

Buying a Condominium

Condo living is a relatively recent phenomenon in Bermuda. When housing became a key issue during the '70s, the Bermuda government saw condos as a good way of meeting the housing demand without using too much land. And so the first condo complexes started to appear. Right now we have a variety all over Bermuda. Non-Bermudians can buy them, but again, they are restricted to condos in higher price brackets, with a minimum ARV of $15,300. In effect, the starting price is $350,000, but more luxurious units can go as high as $1 million. As with a house, you must apply for a license (the application fee is the same), which will cost you 15 percent of the purchase price.

The rule about acquiring a second property also applies. Condominiums available to non-Bermudians include Southdown Farm in Southampton; Mizzentops, Warwick; Inwood, Paget; St. James' Court, Flatts; and Grosvenor Apartments, Pembroke.

So what do you get for your money? Typically, you will have two to three bedrooms, a combined living/dining room area (sometimes, but not always, with fireplace), a well-equipped kitchen and two bathrooms. Of course, one advantage to condo living is that you don't have to constantly worry about external maintenance. In return for a monthly maintenance fee (the cost ranges from $300 to $500 a month), your water tank, roof and external walls are kept in good repair and the grounds are cared for by gardeners. Technically, grounds are communal, but sometimes tenants are allowed to create their own garden; if gardening is important to you, check the rules before buying. With the more expensive condos, you'll usually find additional communal amenities such as tennis courts and swimming pools. Policies regarding pets differ, but usually you're allowed cats, small pets such as birds and gerbils and, in some cases, dogs.

FYI

Unless otherwise noted, the area code for all phone numbers listed in this guide is 441.

Long-term Rentals

Most non-Bermudians who come here for employment rent rather than buy housing. Typically, they rent through real estate agencies that readily help them find suitable accommodations. There are no restrictions on what non-Bermudians can rent. However, there is currently a heavy demand for rental properties, and the result has been sky-high rental rates. Studio or one-bedroom apartments cost between $1,000 and $1,500 a month. Two-bedroom apartments or houses average between $1,800 and $2,500. Three-bedroom houses generally start at $3,500, but houses at that price are hard to find at the moment; you're more likely to find one at $4,000 to $5,000. Executive rentals — properties ideal for entertaining — are even higher, with a $7,000 monthly rent likely.

Location, of course, has a huge impact on rent. Take a three- or four-bedroom house in Tucker's Town, for example. Let's say it has two or three bathrooms, a living room, dining room and a den, along with a patio, swimming pool and a water view. What would that cost? Take a deep breath. We're talking $16,000 a month. Again, condominiums can be a more affordable option if you want that second bathroom and bedroom. Monthly rents start at $2,500 and go up to $4,500 and higher for the more luxurious ones in the central parishes.

When you agree to rent a property, you usually sign a one-year lease that gives you an option for renewal. However, three-year leases are sometimes available. You can break your lease (giving two to three months' notice) only if your work permit is pulled or you have to leave Bermuda. For an unfurnished property, the deposit is usually 50 percent of one month's rent. For a furnished one, you'll put one month's rent up front.

In addition to rent, you'll be responsible for costs of electricity, gas, telephone, cable television, utilities and pest control. You'll also be responsible for minor maintenance such as hinges, locks, fastenings and tap washers. Rent an accommodation for more than two years, and you should plan to repaint the interior. There may be additional costs, depending on the landlord. You could, for example, be required to pay part or all of the land tax on the property, and if you rent a condo, the owner could require you to pay part or all of the monthly maintenance fee as well.

Location

As we've already mentioned, some locations are exclusive. Tucker's Town, for example, is definitely the Land of Multimillionaires — particularly those who want ocean views, privacy and luxury. Point Shares and Fairylands are next on the exclusive list. If the most exclusive areas are not for you, you may

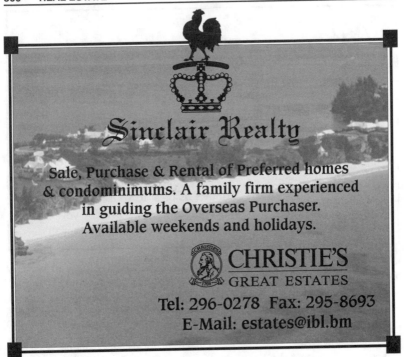
want to know the advantages of one parish over another.

Perhaps the first consideration is whether to commute or not. If you work in Hamilton, for example, how long do you want to drive? Live in St. George's, St. David's or Sandys, and you're 45 minutes to an hour away from work. Our rush-hour traffic picks up from 8 to 9:30 AM and 5 to 6:30 PM. If you're from a larger country (and let's face it, countries don't get much smaller than Bermuda), an hour commute might be no big thing. Yet strangely enough, the longer you stay in Bermuda, the farther apart distances seem. Sometimes a trip from Hamilton to St. George's (they are about 15 miles apart) can feel like a major excursion.

That fact makes the central parishes — Devonshire, Smiths and Paget — the most popular places to live. In turn, that means you may well find more reasonable rents on the eastern or western ends of the island. While we're on the subject of commuting, get this: Many people living in the eastern parishes would not dream of moving to the western ones. Why? Because of the sun. We're serious. Travel from the east,

www.insiders.com

See this and many other
Insiders' Guide® destinations
online — in their entirety.

Visit us today!

INSIDERS' TIP

Our high humidity causes our houses to be damp. Closet heaters help prevent mildew appearing on our clothes and shoes. Silica gel is also important for protecting wooden musical instruments, such as guitars and recorders.

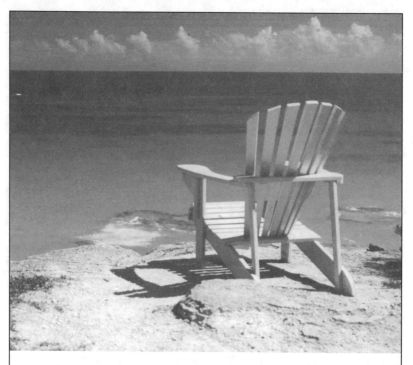

The finest in Bermuda real estate

THE PROPERTY GROUP, LTD.

represents the finest properties in every sector of
Bermuda's residential real estate market.

Just tell us what you are looking for. We will show
you, both directly and in co-operation with other
agencies, the best that Bermuda has to offer.

Let us guide you through the intricacies of Bermuda's
unique and fascinating property market. We invite
you to enjoy the special confidence that comes of
working with experts.

The Property Group
Ltd.

Tel: 441-292-6890 ● Fax: 441-292-6892
EMail: info@property-group.com
Sherwood, 65 Pitts Bay Road, Hamilton HM 08, Bermuda
P.O. Box 1312 HM FX, Bermuda ● www.property-group.com
Member, Multiple Listing Services (M.L.S.) Bermuda, Limited

and you don't get dazzled going to work or coming home from the city. Travel from the west and that "Busy old fool, unruly Sun" is in your eyes.

Those of us who live in Paget, Warwick or Southampton enjoy easy access to several grocery stores and to the South Shore beaches. We probably wouldn't move to St. George's or St. David's because of the noise of aircraft coming into the airport. On the other hand, those who do live on the eastern end would argue that since the base has gone, there's much less air traffic, and that after a while you don't even notice it. They have their own beaches as well. What about Somerset in Sandys Parish? Ah, that's God's country, innit?

Real Estate Agents

Strictly speaking, a real estate office in Bermuda has just one agent. Other personnel dealing directly with sales or rentals are technically "representatives," but they are often loosely referred to as agents. Nomenclature doesn't really matter, since they are required to be licensed in real estate. That means they have passed a tough exam covering mathematics and law, as they pertain to real estate, plus land tax and evaluations.

Why Go to an Agency?

Moving to a new country is always a challenge. You have to contend with different laws and practices and often with a whole new set of cultural attitudes. Bermuda's real estate agents know this, and they offer a range of services designed to help your move go smoothly. Throughout the complicated and lengthy procedure of buying or renting a home or condo here, agents can provide you with information about property evaluation, legal aspects and government requirements. They will also advise you on how to sign up for telephone service, electricity and/or gas and cable.

A few agents who deal in executive rentals share those high-end listings along with new information about suitable properties that are available. Deal with these agencies, and you often will be shown a property long before it is advertised in the papers. In fact, chances are the property will already be gone by the time it's advertised (yes, you read that correctly). Since there's heavy demand for executive rentals at the moment, you can see that it's wise

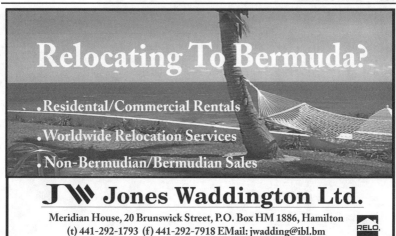

to use an agency. In our listings, we'll tell you which ones focus on upscale rentals and which ones focus on house sales.

Who is the agency working for? In America there are buyers' agents and sellers' agents and some who wear both hats. Disclosure regarding where an agent's commission comes from has been a big issue. Where sales are concerned in Bermuda, the agent charges the seller a commission, which is a set percentage of the purchase price. So agents here are working for the seller rather than the buyer. Where rentals are concerned, the property owner pays the agent either a finder's fee (consisting of half a month's rent for every year of the lease) or a management fee (10 percent of the rent). A management fee applies when the agent undertakes responsibility for the property regarding maintenance and tenants.

Real Estate Agency Listings

Pembroke Parish

Bermuda Realty Company Ltd.
LPG Building, 34 Bermudiana Rd., Hamilton • 296-2600

This company opened in 1994, but it re-sulted from a merger between the real estate operations of L.P. Gutteridge and the real estate operations of the Bank of Bermuda Ltd. Bermuda Home Limited is the parent company. At present it has 10 sales representatives, including the manager and five rental representatives. It offers full services, including sales to Bermudians and non-Bermudians, rentals and executive relocation, appraisals, evaluations and estate settlements.

C.R.E. Properties Ltd.
Washington Mall (upper level), Church St., Hamilton • 295-5487

You want to rent a cottage or house in Bermuda for a vacation? Beverly Sgobba, owner and president of C.R.E., will not only arrange it, but will also organize domestic help for you. Give her your credit card number, and she will (for no service charge) get you one week's groceries and, if you like, a rented bike. Utility services will be waiting for you when you arrive. If you need a fax machine or some other item, she rents it on your behalf from a rental agency.

Rent varies, but a two-bedroom beachfront cottage runs about $400 a night. You pay 20 to 25 percent of a week's stay as a deposit. Mrs. Sgobba will organize utility bills for you (renters get free electricity the first week but pay after that), deduct the amounts due from your deposit and send you

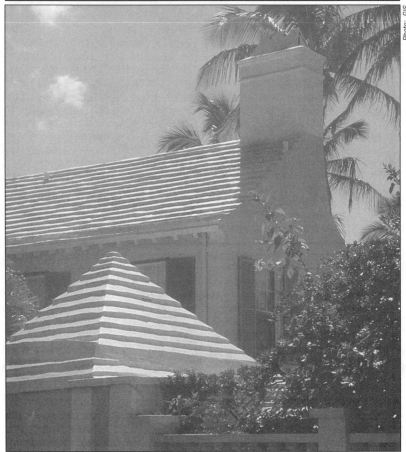

Photo: GIS

Bermuda's unique architecture and gardens fascinate visitors.

the remaining balance about six weeks after you return from vacation. Mrs. Sgobba also specializes in sales (to Bermudians and non-Bermudians) and long-term executive rentals. She serves on the executive committee of the Real Estate Division of the Bermuda Chamber of Commerce.

Dorchester Realty Ltd.
Chevron House, 11 Church St., Hamilton • 295-5252

Dorchester's history goes back to 1918. Not that it was called Dorchester in those days. The firm was originated by Meyer M. Malloy, possibly the first real estate agency on the island. Today Dorchester has five representatives and concentrates mostly on local sales. It has been particularly involved with the Boaz Island Development (condominiums available to local purchasers) and handles about 300 rentals.

Executive Relocation Ltd.
International Centre, 26 Bermudiana Rd., Hamilton • 232-0059

Iris Deveney-Doughty, assisted by her staff of two, specializes in helping executives and their families relocate to Bermuda. She can assist with buying a car, finding child care, booking a driving test and starting bank accounts. She takes charge of customs clearance and helps with pets coming into Bermuda and finding domestic help. Iris also makes sure the utilities are running and is always available to advise on schools, shopping and social organizations. She offers a relocation package that includes all these non-real estate services for a one-time payment. "There's no cut off time," she says. "I've helped executives move several times over to different houses in Bermuda."

Typically, companies pay for her relocation services. To protect their confidentiality, Iris prefers not to publish prices; call her directly for information on cost. In addition, she helps executives find housing for purchase or rent, but this is a separate activity from the relocation package. Her firm comes under the Hope Bowker Bermuda Real Estate umbrella (see subsequent listing).

Hope Bowker Bermuda Real Estate
International Centre, 26 Bermudiana Rd, Hamilton • 295-9191

Hope Bowker's real estate experience goes back to 1974. In 1981 she established her present firm, and in 1984 she chaired the executive committee of the Real Estate Division of the Bermuda Chamber of Commerce. She still serves on that committee. Hope specializes in sales and rentals to both overseas and local residents. She says her clients come from "across the board," but they certainly include those who want to rent or buy properties in the upscale range.

Kitson and Company Ltd.
Kitson Bldg., 5 Reid St., Hamilton
• 295-2525

Kitson's started in 1947, which means it's the oldest Bermuda real estate firm retaining its original name. Along with owner Kirk Kitson, there are seven agents who concentrate on selling and renting Bermuda's finer homes to overseas as well as local purchasers. Kitson also deals with short-term holiday rentals. Rents for these range from $360 a night to $1,000 a night for a luxurious house in Tucker's Town. In addition, this agency offers house management for property owners who do not want to rent

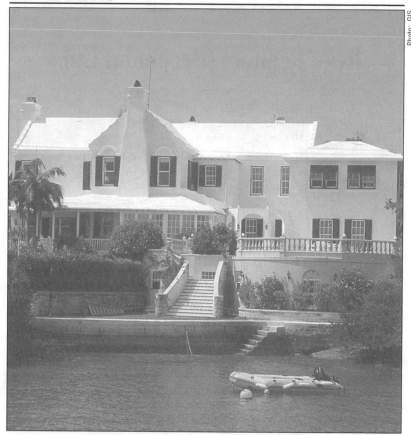

Bermuda's waterfront real estate is highly sought after
worldwide and the ultimate in prestige.

out their houses while away. For $200 a month, Kitson will check the properties, pay utility bills and even work out pension contributions and payroll for housekeeping staff still working while their employers are away.

Thomas B. Moss Real Estate Ltd.
Walker Arcade, Reid St., Hamilton
• 292-6294

Thomas Moss and his wife, Deanna, work together with two other representatives in this small company. They provide personal service for people requiring rented houses in the middle-of-the-road price range. (They tend not to deal with studios.) Established some 16 years ago, the company also deals with sales

for "the average middle class family" and offers property management services.

The Property Group
Sherwood, 66 Pitt's Bay Rd., Hamilton
• 292-6890

Cris Waldes-Dapena is president and owner of this company. She also serves as chair for the executive committee of the Bermuda Chamber of Commerce's Real Estate Division. Three rental experts and six full-time representatives work together as resident property specialists. In addition, Cris has two part-time representatives. The firm specializes in providing executive rentals in the highest price range and in selling houses in the middle to top price range.

Rego Ltd.
The Stables, Reid St. E. • 292-3921

Established in 1949, Rego has 13 representatives that specialize in selling more expensive properties to overseas purchasers. However, they do work with a more general market as well. Similarly, they specialize in the more upscale executive rentals but will help with the midrange ones. In addition, Rego handles property management.

John W. Swan Ltd.
26 Victoria St., Hamilton • 295-4255

With more than 30 years in business, this firm caters to a broad section of the market. Its six sales and three rentals representatives share the company motto: "Where service begins and satisfaction never ends." As well as sales and rentals, John W. Swan also offers appraisals and renovation services.

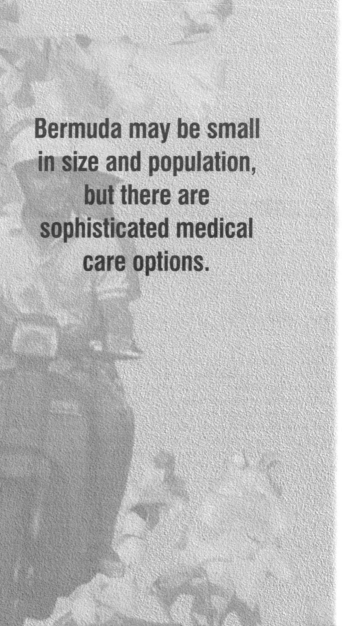

Bermuda may be small
in size and population,
but there are
sophisticated medical
care options.

Healthcare

Some people unfamiliar with Bermuda are under the illusion that we dress in grass skirts, that we live in huts and that our medical services are unutterably primitive. Well, we've yet to see anyone in a grass skirt, and our houses are hurricane proof, thank you very much. So what about our healthcare? We may be small in size and population, but we have sophisticated medical care. In this chapter we'll tell you about our hospitals, support groups and other health-related services. We'll also discuss hospital funding and medical insurance policies for residents and overseas visitors.

Hospitals

We have two hospitals in Bermuda, one dealing with general health, the other focusing on mental health. Both are maintained by the Bermuda Hospitals Board, a government-appointed entity headed by an executive director. Both hospitals are funded mostly from fees and from the Bermuda government's Employment Tax. This tax is payable partly by every local employee and partly by every employer throughout Bermuda. (See the Insurance section in this chapter for more information about health costs.) The Hospital Auxiliary, a volunteer organization, also contributes enormously to the hospitals' finances. Check their listing below for more information.

General Care Facilities

Paget Parish

King Edward VII Memorial Hospital
Point Finger Rd. • 236-2345

This is our one general hospital, and it has consistently received high ratings for quality of treatment and services from the Canadian Council on Health Services Accreditation. At present it has 324 beds in private, semi-private and public wards. It's well-equipped with modern facilities and technology that includes a dialysis unit (see subsequent information on this unit), a vein clinic and an up-to-date intensive-care unit. King Edward VII also offers diagnostic services such as a pathology laboratory, a hematology laboratory, ECG and EEG and diagnostic imaging such as X-rays, CAT scans and ultrasound. Therapeutic services available include dietary treatment, medical social work, occupational therapy and physiotherapy. The Bermuda branch of the Red Cross operates The Blood Donors' Centre within the hospital. (Call 236-5067 if you're interested in donating blood. Donors are always needed.)

What specialists do we have? King Edward has physicians and surgeons specializing in anesthesiology, diabetes, gerontology, internal medicine, obstetrics, gynecology, ophthalmology, orthopedics, pediatrics, pathology, psychiatry, radiology, surgery, urology and preventive medicine. Although cornea and ossicle transplants are conducted, no other transplants are available. Angioplasty and coronary bypass surgery is not possible here either. For surgery and treatments unavailable here, patients tend to be admitted to hospitals on the Eastern Seaboard of the United States or in Canada. King Edward VII has an excellent relationship with air ambulance companies in that area, so air ambulance transport is always possible in emergency situations.

The emergency department is, of course, staffed 24 hours a day and has a fast-track system for patients who have had minor traffic accidents. A separate doctor is on hand for dealing with "road rash" (the local term for those relatively minor, but painful, scrapes and bruises). In addition, emergency has a triage system by which a nurse assesses which patients need immediate attention. The hospital runs its own ambulance service and has six well-equipped ambulances staffed with trained emergency medical technicians. Visiting hours in the wards are from noon to 8 PM.

The Dialysis Unit

We are extremely fortunate to have a hemodialysis unit, and we are proud to tell you that no resident in need in Bermuda is denied dialysis. Situated opposite the King Edward VII Memorial Hospital entrance on Point Finger Road, the unit houses 20 artificial kidney machines. At present, the unit treats 60 people on an outpatient basis.

Before October 1978, when the unit first opened, Bermudians suffering from end-stage kidney failure often spent months on kidney machines in North America while awaiting transplant surgery. Since dialyzing can take four to five hours at a time, three times a week, they could not easily return to Bermuda. So you can see how important our dialysis unit is to us. And yes, it is possible for overseas visitors suffering from kidney failure to use the facility. Call the hospital to ask if space is available; demand can be high. Usually the winter season is not so heavily booked. Be aware the unit will not accept overseas patients who have Hepatitis B or are HIV-positive. (That restriction does not apply to residents, however.) Bermudians living abroad and wanting to return for a vacation are given priority. The cost is $643 a session, and you can pay with credit card or personal check.

Hospital Costs and Payments for Overseas Visitors

In general, you'll have to pay up front for medical costs incurred here, even if you're covered by a health insurance company in your own country. You can pay with personal checks, cash or credit cards. Eventually, you can submit receipts to your insurance company for reimbursement.

Bermuda's hospitals, however, will accept Blue Cross and Blue Shield insurance for people who may need inpatient services while visiting Bermuda. Inpatient daily rates for non-residents are now $973 for public ward accommodation, $1,162 for semi-private accommodation, $1,401 for private accommodation and $377 for the nursery. Patients can rent televisions and telephones. Outpatient costs and how they relate to insurance carriers are complex. Call the hospitals directly for more information and be aware that all costs are subject to change.

> **FYI**
>
> Unless otherwise noted, the area code for all phone numbers listed in this guide is 441.

The Hospital Auxiliary
King Edward VII Memorial Hospital, Point Finger Rd. • 236-2345, 236-2488

This organization was once known as the Women's Auxiliary. It started up in 1953, at a time when the government was not providing King Edward VII Memorial Hospital much money. A group of ladies got together to raise funds through activities, such as charity teas, fetes, white elephants and other events. Eventually, the women became known as Pink Ladies, because they wear pink uniforms. These days we have Pink Men as well; although they are willing to wear pink shirts, they prefer to be called Pink Panthers. So now you know.

Today the Hospital Auxiliary has 600 members and 200 active volunteers. Inactive members pay $30 a year dues; active ones pay $10. Active members save the hospital an estimated $1 million a year through volunteer work. They take charge of the front desk at the hospital's entrance, which means they an-

INSIDERS' TIP

As well as operating the Blood Donors' Centre at King Edward VII Memorial Hospital, the Bermuda Red Cross also has a hospital equipment rental service. Items include wheelchairs, walkers, commodes and crutches. Interested in first aid and CPR training? A nine-hour training course spread over three weeks costs $35, books included. Call 236-8253 for information.

swer visitor and telephone inquiries. They visit patients to bring a mobile library and hospitality cart and to take care of their flowers.

Perhaps most importantly, they operate the coffee shop and gift shop in the foyer. Open from 9:30 AM to 3:45 PM Monday through Friday and 9 AM to 1:30 PM Saturday, the coffee shop offers breakfast, lunch and afternoon snacks. It's quite a social center — people don't just eat there when they come to visit inpatients; they make a point of coming there especially for a meal. (There's no smoking, by the way, in the coffee shop.) The gift shop (same hours of operation as the coffee shop) has items that make for unusual presents, especially at Christmas, when it's famous for ornaments and Advent calendars.

The auxiliary also runs a thrift shop, affectionately known as the Barn, opposite St. Brendan's Hospital (see subsequent listing). People can drop off clothes, books and other items they no longer want anytime between 9 AM and noon Monday through Saturday. Volunteers sort and price the goods and put them on sale every Thursday and Saturday from 9 AM to noon. These combined operations generate $250,000 a year for King Edward VII Memorial Hospital. Should you come to Bermuda to live and find yourself with some spare time, the auxiliary is a great place to lend your services (active volunteers put in a minimum of 2½ hours a week). A junior contingent known as the Candy Stripers also offers volunteer help.

Yet another group within the Hospital Auxiliary is of particular interest to overseas visi-

www.insiders.com

See this and many other
Insiders' Guide® destinations
online — in their entirety.

Visit us today!

tors. The Overseas Family Health Service is dedicated to offering basic sympathy and support to visitors who become ill on vacation or whose relatives need medical help. Volunteers assist with shopping, finding accommodations near the hospital for relatives and obtaining access to telephones for calls abroad. The service also makes sure your baggage is secure.

Agape House
Point Finger Rd. • 293-2025

Just behind the King Edward VII Memorial Hospital, this very gracious 19th-century house is Bermuda's one hospice. Containing 12 beds and several communal areas such as dining and sitting areas, Agape House is dedicated to offering terminally ill patients unconditional care. The staff focuses on making patients physically, emotionally and spiritually comfortable for as long as there is life. They also offer outpatients day treatment such as infusions and transfusions. Trained nurses plus a resident doctor are funded by the King Edward VII Memorial Hospital board. Friends of Hospice is a charity that raises additional funds for Agape House. The charity also organizes volunteers who offer meal service, read and talk to patients and give general support. By the way, 24-hour visiting is available.

Montrose Substance Abuse Centre
16 Berry Hill Rd. • 236-2345

This outpatient center is next to King Edward VII Memorial Hospital and shares the same telephone number. Patients arrive at Montrose through referrals or self-referrals.

INSIDERS' TIP

So you're a breast-feeding mother on vacation, and your breast pump breaks down? Call the Nurses' Practice at 232-0264, and they will sell or rent you one. The practice is at 8 South Road, Smiths Parish, and Liz Bowden and Rita Stevens offer group and individual educational sessions on all aspects of pregnancy. In addition, they hold newborn baby clinics on Wednesdays and Friday mornings to discuss issues with new parents concerning allergies, baby development, nutrition and breast feeding. Overseas visitors are welcome.

Two nurses and two qualified substance abuse counselors offer three-week education programs to help beat substance addiction. Programs include films, together with individual and group counseling. Counselors give follow-up support for at least a year to each patient completing the program. Overseas visitors are welcome if they can stay for a three-week period.

Mental Health Facilities

Devonshire Parish

St. Brendan's Hospital
44 Devon Spring Rd. • 236-3770

St. Brendan's is accredited by the Canadian Council on Health Services Accreditation. It's a 162-bed psychiatric facility caring for acutely disturbed inpatients and outpatients. Programs include the In-Patient Psychiatric Programme, the Learning Disability Programme, Community Mental Health Services and the Montrose Substance Abuse Programme (see previous listing).

Outpatient services include 24-hour crisis intervention plus individual and group psychotherapy. The staff also works with community group homes and child and adolescent services. The hospital provides consulting and educational services to government and community agencies such as courts, prisons, nursing homes and the Health Department. The staff at St. Brendan's is happy to assist overseas visitors who need treatment or whose prescriptions need renewal. Visiting hours are noon to 8 PM.

Substance Abuse Support Groups

OK, holidays ought to be fun and restful, but as we all know, they can be stressful, particularly for people recovering from an addiction to alcohol or other substances. Since alcohol is highly visible and available in most of our supermarkets and hotels, we feel it's important to mention our support groups, where overseas visitors are warmly welcomed. In fact, they typically are overwhelmed by the friendliness and support they

INSIDERS' TIP

Need a physician, dentist or optometrist? If you're on vacation, hotel managers can often recommend doctors that are available. Otherwise, check the Yellow Pages in the Bermuda phone book for listings. We have no referral service in Bermuda.

receive from group members. Meetings here tend to be smaller than those abroad.

Our National Drug Commission distributes in our post offices and hotels a quarterly calendar of support group meetings held throughout the island. You can call the numbers below, and you will probably get a recorded message telling you the meeting venues and times for the week. Leave a telephone number, and a member will be sure to call you back. They are used to receiving calls from all over the world. Support group numbers are **Alcoholics Anonymous**, 236-8293; **Al-Anon**, 236-8606; **Narcotics Anonymous**, 293-0999.

Public Health Clinics

The Ministry of Health operates a number of day health clinics all over the island, primarily for women and children. The doctors, nurses and health personnel offer a variety of services including family planning, prenatal and antenatal care, inoculations, treatment and advice on sexually transmitted diseases, and dental clinics. In addition, should visitors or residents have cuts and bruises as a result of a minor traffic accident, clinic nurses can help them out.

Treatment is free. Though there's a charge for medications, it is at a much lower rate than usual. Antibiotics, for example, cost $5 a prescription. Baby clinics are for children up to 5 years old who need weight-monitoring, nutritional assistance, immunizations and treatment for common ailments. Overseas visitors are welcome to take their children should they become ill on holiday.

Here we list the clinics east to west, parish by parish. The Hamilton Health Centre is the only one open daily. If you call one of the others on a day it is closed, leave a message, and a nurse will get back to you.

St. George's Parish

St. George Health Centre
1 Old Military Rd., Town of St. George
• 297-8200

This clinic opens every Monday from 9 to 11:30 AM to deal with general health problems. Friday afternoons from 2 to 4 PM there is a baby clinic.

Smith's Parish

Smith's Parish Clinic
Middle Rd. • 295-4942

A baby clinic is open here every Tuesday afternoon from 2 to 4 PM.

Pembroke Parish

Hamilton Health Centre
67 Victoria St., Hamilton • 236-0224

Open daily from 8:30 AM to 12:30 PM and from 1:30 to 4:45 PM, Hamilton Health Centre offers all the services we mentioned in our introduction to this section. Thursday afternoons are known as "travel clinic." That's because patients can get all inoculations necessary for traveling abroad. The tetanus, diphtheria and polio inoculations are free. Others, depending on the type required, cost between $10 and $53. The clinic gives treatment to the indigent and will see any adult or child.

Warwick Parish

Warwick Health Centre
Middle Rd. • 236-0649

A baby clinic is open every Tuesday afternoon from 2 to 4 PM.

INSIDERS' TIP

P.A.L.S. (Patients Assistance League and Service) is a registered charity dedicated to enabling cancer patients to stay at home. Qualified nurses make home visits and help with dressings, medications and nutritional supplements. Overseas visitors suffering from cancer are welcome to call 292-3875 for help. The organization is centered at 1 Cedar Avenue, City of Hamilton, Pembroke Parish. Donations are greatly appreciated.

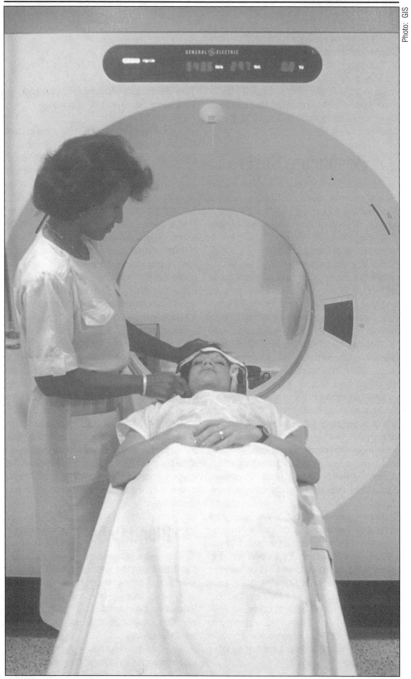

Photo: GIS

King Edward VII Memorial Hospital is a state-of-the-art facility.

Sandys Parish

Somerset Health Centre
55 Mangrove Bay Rd. • 234-0202

This public health clinic offers blood screening, family planning and healthcare for women every Tuesday morning from 9 to 11:30 AM. Friday afternoons from 2 to 4 PM, there's a baby clinic.

Healthcare Costs

Because Bermuda is a British dependent territory, overseas visitors sometimes assume that we have a national health plan. This is not true. All medical and dental practitioners, other than those working in the public health clinics, are in private practice.

So how do we pay for the care we receive? We have to confess that this insurance issue is very complex. There are, for example, no standard rates for health insurance because these are negotiated directly between employers and their insurers based on the number of employees in the workplace. Work in Bermuda, and your employer has partial legal responsibility for your health coverage and that of your non-working spouse and children. If you and your spouse are both working here, then either one employer or the other will provide the coverage for children. But be aware that health plans differ from workplace to workplace. Some may cover major medical, dentistry and optometry, as well as doctors' visits. You should discuss health plans carefully with your employer.

How much comes out of your salary for coverage? Again, this is difficult to answer. Generally the employer will pay half, and you will pay half. However, it's safe to say that between 8 and 10 percent of your salary is deducted to cover medical insurance, pension and government taxes. But note that your employer coverage does not cover any relative other than your non-working spouse or children. Should your parents come to visit, for example, any healthcare costs they incur are not covered.

Nursing

Pembroke Parish

The Bermuda Mobile Nurses Ltd.
12 Church St., Ste. 125, Hamilton
• 297-9696

Established in January 1998, this private service is owned and operated by Karen Barnshaw, Charmaine Bashir and April Vesey. All are highly trained intensive care nurses with six to 10 years of nursing experience in North America and the intensive care unit at King Edward VII Memorial Hospital here in Bermuda. Services include providing a medical escort on a commercial flight for people requiring hospital care abroad; home nursing care; accompanying tourists who have become ill in Bermuda back to their home country; accompanying tourists unable to travel alone to and from Bermuda; and being on call for participants in conventions. They will also provide nursing care for tourists in their accommodations.

Costs? Nursing care costs $30 an hour. Costs for escorting a patient abroad obviously depend on distance and length of flight. However, accompanying a patient to an Eastern Seaboard hospital would cost about $1,000, including airfare. All costs are subject to change. Direct payment is usually required, but receipts can be submitted to your insurance company. Credit cards are accepted. Call the pager number listed anytime, day or night, and one of the nurses will get back to you immediately.

Blood Laboratories

Quinton Butterfield owns and manages four labs for blood and urine testing. All the laboratories offer a range of chemistry, hematology, microbiology, urine and serology tests. Examples of tests include blood count, HIV, pregnancy, thyroid, cardiac enzyme and stomach ulcer testing.

Patients usually come with laboratory forms from their doctors. Overseas visitors are welcome, and forms from doctors abroad are honored. Four technicians are on hand to provide fast customer service. You'll get a pregnancy test result in 20 minutes. Others come back in 24 hours, though HIV test results take about a week because they are handled in batches.

Butterfield also provides profiles for many health and life insurance companies. Depending on the requirements, blood is either sent abroad for testing or is tested at the Bermuda laboratory. Single tests cost about $40. On average clients requiring a group of tests pay up to $250. Overseas clients pay directly and submit receipts to their insurance companies abroad.

Laboratory locations and operating hours follow. In St. George's Parish, East End Medical Laboratory, 1 Clarence Street, Town of St. George, 297-2502, is open Tuesday and Thursday from 8:30 to 11:30 AM. In Pembroke Parish, Central Diagnostics, 53 Union Street, Hamilton, 292-9940, is open 8:30 AM to 6 PM Monday through Thursday and 8:30 AM to 1:30 PM on Friday. Also in Hamilton, City Laboratory, 17 Parliament Street, 296-6313, is open 9 AM to 2 PM Monday through Thursday and 9 AM to noon on Friday. And in Sandys Parish, Sandys' Medical Lab, 32 Somerset Road, 234-3295, is open from 8:30 to 10:30 AM Monday, Wednesday and Friday.

Bermuda's emphasis on education has created a professional class that makes our country one of the best-educated per capita in the world.

Education and Child Care

Education

Among the many sights that intrigue first-time visitors to Bermuda are the thousands of school children in crisp uniforms. From the time a child enters primary school at the compulsory age of five until leaving secondary school at the minimum age of 16, uniforms are mandatory with each school identified by its own color skirt, jacket and tie.

The Ministry of Education governs our public school system, which includes one senior secondary school, five middle schools and 18 primary schools. The school year lasts nearly 10 months beginning in early September, with breaks at Easter, Christmas and during summer.

Bermuda's emphasis on education has created a professional class that makes our country one of the best-educated per capita in the world. According to the latest census, nearly 10 percent of Bermudians older than age 16 hold a post-secondary degree.

Some families still choose to send their children to boarding schools in America, Canada or the U.K., but there are almost 6,500 students in Bermuda's public and private schools. There high school graduates are prepared for further studies at the Bermuda College or institutions abroad. The United States, Canada and England are students' main choices for post-secondary study.

Public Schools

Bermuda approached the '90s cognizant that glaring deficiencies in the public school system could not be ignored. In 1988 educators, parents and business leaders came together to form an Education Planning Team mandated with examining where we were in terms of public education, where we had to go and the best way to get there. Far-reaching recommendations came out of frank and open discussions.

What emerged was the imperative of initiating a total restructuring of the existing education system. An active and more viable relationship between the community, schools and both the domestic and international business sectors was deemed critical.

Among the many points of concern at the time were an apparent lack of suitable preparation of students for the workplace, a higher dropout rate for boys and inadequate dissemination of the technical skills necessary for Bermudian students to compete in a rapidly advancing communications infrastructure.

The essence of the restructuring decision included the development of new curricula, the integration of students with special needs into regular classrooms and the putting in place of ongoing professional development for teachers. But the more contentious issue in the $124.5 million plan was the focus on the introduction of middle schools and senior secondary schools as key components of a revamped system.

A 1991 *Royal Gazette* poll revealed that while 72 percent of respondents supported restructuring, almost as many were against the establishment of a senior secondary school, believing that a school with 1,000 or more students would exacerbate problems such as drug use among school children.

One of the keys critical to the long-term success of revamping local education — an exercise that is not expected to be completed until 2002 — is the participation of the business community. Business involvement has emerged as a part of establishing what the Bermuda College's vice president of academic affairs has called "significant linkages" between educational institutions and the business sector. A key part of these linkages is the development of curricula that respond to the direct needs of business both now and in the next millennium.

An example of the relevance of this hand-in-hand approach is seen in the successful two-year insurance studies program begun in 1995 in direct response to insurance industry requests. Significantly, with Bermuda now established as a prominent international insurance center (see our International Business chapter), this program places graduating students squarely on the rung for entry and advancement in this specific sector. Similar cooperative programs involving tourism and other industries are being encouraged and explored.

The importance attached to the school/business relationship has resulted in some companies introducing an adopt-a-school program. Several major businesses have become active partners. Adoption programs have taken the form of work-shadowing, in which young students visit corporate offices to gain first-hand experience of the business environment. Whenever possible, corporate staff members visit classrooms. Other aspects include summer job programs. An ethic of excellence is encouraged.

The Ministry of Education also oversees a Business Education Partnership, designed to bring students together with key persons in an industry in which they show particular interest. A business Institute of Directors has introduced a Young Enterprise program that provides students with actual experience in establishing and managing companies.

Millions have been allocated for renovations to existing buildings, with $6.2 million spent in 1997. It is expected that more computers will be introduced into classrooms, and changed teaching methods will see staff organized into interdisciplinary teaching teams focusing on core subjects.

Middle Schools and Senior Secondary Schools

Introduced in 1997, the middle school changeover will be completed by 1998-99. The restructured Bermudian educational system will consist of six years of primary schooling (including kindergarten; kids typically begin school in Bermuda at age 5), three at middle school and four at the senior level.

While the middle school concept is not new to North America, it represents an entirely new direction for Bermuda. With visual arts, music, dance and theatre as additional subjects to enhance the core curriculum, and with business studies, technological education and computer-related instruction, students will be exposed to a wide range of subjects and activities not available under the former system.

This concept has required a different set of teaching approaches and skills. As a result, the Ministry of Education initiated a variety of workshops and training programs for teachers leading up to September 1997 when the five middle schools (former secondary schools that were revamped and renovated) welcomed students to a newly structured educational environment. The average class size in these schools is 24, but the pupil-teacher ratio (when all professional staff is included) hovers at roughly 13-to-1.

CedarBridge Academy (see this chapter's Close-up) is the island's first senior secondary school, with the Berkeley Institute expected to become the second in 1999. Both are structured to receive students from the middle schools and immerse them in a four-year program. Career guidance and other student support services are integral components.

Government's desire to answer questions and allay community fears regarding the overall educational direction resulted in the Minis-

FYI

Unless otherwise noted, the area code for all phone numbers listed in this guide is 441.

try of Education turning to two advertising agencies for their public relations expertise. The ad campaign centered on middle schools in 1997, with a series of newspaper advertisements and some radio exposure. Part of the motivation for this new approach was in response to an education audit by a team led by an Iowa State University professor. Among the findings was that communication to the public on the intentions, results and potential benefits of the restructuring had been inadequate.

Private Schools

Private schooling in Bermuda has always been regarded as superior to that of the public schools. When government announced plans to restructure the public system, some of the proposed changes resulted in an avalanche of applications to the island's six private schools, most of which are modeled on the British system. However, all offer the type of education that allows students to enter either North American or United Kingdom universities.

Unlike the BSSC (Bermuda Secondary School Certificate) exam taken by public school students, graduates at the private schools take the GCSE (General Certificate in Secondary Education), a British exam providing those who pass with a recognized qualification in the United States, Canada or the United Kingdom. The student then can choose to enter 11th or 12th grade at a U.S. preparatory school or take an associate degree at the Bermuda College. Note that the island's Roman Catholic and Seventh-Day Adventist schools operate on a U.S.-type grading system.

Although at one time most of private schools had a majority of white students on the rolls (and some were exclusively for whites), today that has changed. One or two schools have a fairly even racial ratio.

Pembroke Parish

Bermuda High School for Girls
27 Richmond Rd. • 295-6153

This is Bermuda's only all-girls school. Founded in 1894 by Mrs. Grosvenor Tucker and other prominent citizens, today it is a general academic school for grades 1 through 12. It is an affiliated member of the National Association of Independent Schools as well as a member of the European Council of International Schools. A student body of 634 (77 percent white, 23 percent black) enjoys an 8-acre campus, with the BHS modeled on Britain's prestigious Cheltenham Ladies' College.

Students here take the GCSE (General Certificate of Secondary Education) exams at age 16. These British exams provide students with a qualification accepted not only in the

U.K., but also in the United States and Canada. The student body is 71.5 percent Bermudian. Some 90 percent of graduates go on to university and college, with many attending Bermuda College.

Saltus Grammar School
St. John's Rd. • 292-6177

Founded in 1888 as a boys' grammar school, Saltus became coeducational in 1992. Today, with an enrollment approaching 1,000 students, it is considered the premier private school in Bermuda and has an international reputation. A member of the National Association of Independent Schools in North America, Saltus has within the past decade changed from an institution populated by white males to one that is reflective of the wider community. Current student enrollment is more than 35 percent female and 21 percent black. Seventy-four percent of students are Bermudian; 26 percent are from the international community.

The school's curriculum allows entry into both the European and American academic streams, with 95 percent of graduates entering universities in the United States, Canada and the U.K. Favored universities include Dartmouth in the U.K.; Yale, Brown and MIT in the United States; and McGill in Canada.

Mount Saint Agnes Academy
99 Dundonald St. W., Hamilton • 292-4134

This academy, now operated by the Hamilton Roman Catholic Diocese assisted by a board of governors, was founded in 1890 by the Sisters of St. Vincent De Paul (Halifax) who owned and operated the school until 1975.

An independent, fee-paying Roman Catholic school catering to students from kindergarten to grade 12, the student body is made up of 550 youngsters aged 5 to 18, most of whom are Bermudian. The remainder are children of non-Bermudian workers, mostly from America, Canada and Britain. Enrollment preference is given to Roman Catholics, but the school does accept students from other denominations. Non-Catholics comprise more than 25 percent of the student population.

Course work follows North American guidelines, and the school is accredited for the purposes of college entry after graduation. This facilitates ease of transfer between Bermuda and North America. Students from Britain find the curriculum at each grade level comparable to what they have experienced at home.

Warwick Parish

Montessori Academy
45 Middle Rd. • 236-9797

Located at Tivoli in Warwick in a magnificent hilltop property, the Bermuda's Montessori school was founded in September 1991, when the academy was opened. Although it began small, by September 1991 the academy opened its doors to 66 students ages 3 through 10. Today, with more than 125 students, there is an expectation that the school will include a middle school level in 1998.

Though relatively new to Bermuda, the Montessori method of education has been used successfully throughout the world since Dr. Maria Montessori opened her first school in Italy in 1907. The Montessori Academy encourages students to learn at their own pace in an environment that is less traditional and not so rigidly structured. Eight to 10 percent of the students have varying degrees of learning disorders, but the school's multisensory approach to teaching and learning brings out their potential. Students at Montessori take the California Achievement Tests, with results that often surpass those of children at other schools.

Warwick Academy
117 Middle Rd. • 236-1917

This school is not only the oldest in Bermuda — many believe it is the oldest in the New World, dating back to 1662 when it was established by the Bermuda Company. The academy joined the public school system in 1960 after almost 300 years as a private primary and secondary school. In 1990, how-

CedarBridge Academy Begins a New Era in Bermudian Education

On September 15, 1997, CedarBridge Academy in Devonshire Parish, the first of two planned public senior secondary schools, welcomed its first 1,200 students. Costing $60 million, it is Bermuda's latest and most modern educational institution.

As one of the key pieces in the island's restructuring program for its public school system, the thrust at CedarBridge is toward more project-based learning with a direct focus on skill acquisition. With curricula under continual development, it is expected that by 1999 — when the Berkeley Institute joins CedarBridge as the second senior secondary school — subjects at CedarBridge will be taught in 60-hour modules and at varying degrees of difficulty. At that time an additional year will be added to senior secondary schooling, making it a four-year process. Students' advancement will be at their own pace, with no promotion until they have mastered their current level of studies. By the year 2000, the BSSC (Bermuda Secondary School Certificate) will be replaced.

CedarBridge is the largest of the island's schools. Among its amenities are a state-of-the-art library, more than 260 computers (with plans to install more), a sick bay and electronic security. Wheelchair-accessible, the school is divided into three zones — central, north and south — with 32 main classrooms and tutorial rooms located in the south. Specialized subjects are taught in the northern zone where science labs, two music rooms, a design and technology area, fitness rooms and computer labs are housed. The gymnasium, cafeteria, business studies and trades classrooms are also in the northern zone. One of the school's finest features is the central zone's 640-seat Ruth Seaton James Auditorium, named in honor of a prominent local educator. It is Bermuda's largest and best-equipped auditorium.

While every emphasis is being placed on the maturation of students, staff development is currently at the top of the priority list. Out of $1 million set aside in 1997 to finance

— continued on next page

Photo: GIS

Cedar Bridge Academy represents a new era of education in Bermuda.

professional development throughout the entire public school system, $250,000 was earmarked specifically for CedarBridge and its 77-member teaching staff.

Initial responses from a survey conducted in 1991 showed that a majority of the community opposed the building of a "mega-school" in Prospect. When it was completed in 1997 and opened to accept registrations, an avalanche of applications poured in from students, several of them transferring from the private school system.

---

ever, it reverted to private status after being designated for conversion to a middle school as part of the government's restructuring program. The school's board believed it could better serve the community as a private school.

Student enrollment approaches 600, and final exams are for the GCSE. Eighty-five to 90 percent of graduates either enter the Bermuda College or go to universities or colleges in North America or the United Kingdom. Once an all-white private school, Warwick Academy today is 60 percent black, and the boy-girl ratio is 57 percent to 43 percent. The school's music program is considered one of the best on the island, and the musical potential of students is deliberately encouraged.

Southampton Parish

Bermuda Institute
Middle Rd. • 238-1566

Founded and run under the auspices of the Seventh-Day Adventist Church, the Bermuda Institute operates on the standard U.S. grading system. It offers a Christian-focused education aimed at not only bringing out students' best academic efforts, but also developing social, physical and spiritual qualities. It endeavors to integrate faith with learning.

With a student body of 508, the institute also has a special-needs program that involves a teacher working with students who may have some difficulty with academics. Bermuda Institute students who graduate after grade 12 with a high school diploma, transcripts and Scholastic Aptitude Test scores are able to move on either to Bermuda College or to schools overseas; 88 percent go on to universities or colleges in the United States, West Indies or the United Kingdom.

Higher Education

Bermuda College
1 College Dr. • 236-9000

Less than 2 miles from Hamilton, nestled in the heart of Paget, the Bermuda College has emerged as a school deserving consideration by students seeking higher education. This was not always so, and the struggle to gain acceptance as a quality school of advanced learning did not come quickly.

The college as it exists today is the result of an amalgamation of the Bermuda Technical Institute (established in 1956), the Bermuda Hotel and Catering College (established in 1965) and the Academic Sixth Form Center (established in 1967). The hotel and catering college began as a domestic science school in the 1930s. The technical institute was established to fill the void left by the closure of the Royal Naval Dockyard, which for many decades had provided young males with training in the trades. The Academic Sixth Form Center had been the springboard for high school graduates preparing to go abroad to university.

The Bermuda College Act of 1974 resulted in the college's establishment, and since its inception the institution has undergone a continuing physical, administrative and curriculum expansion. Including the more than $2 million spent to purchase the property on which its campus is located, more than $40 million has been spent on the school's development. Today Bermuda College serves an annual average of 500 full-time students. The college, governed by a 12-member board, has overcome a somewhat negative image held by the general public and students. Its academic, technical, hotel and business training is regarded as comparable to the level offered at North American institutions of equal size.

Although it does not have university status, Bermuda College's links with overseas universities and colleges allow graduates to transfer credits if they wish to enter a four-year degree program. Currently the college offers 10 associate degree programs and 15 certificate-level courses.

The continuing education arm of the college, as part of the Faculty of Continuing and Applied Studies, has formed viable links with a number of local organizations. Marketing its own brochure for each of the spring, summer and fall terms, this department serves an average of 1,500 adult students each year.

Bermuda Biological Station for Research
17 Biological Station Ln., Town of St. George • 297-1880

The BBSR is an independent, nonprofit research institution founded in 1903. Though located in Bermuda, it is incorporated in New York state.

The BBSR is engaged in numerous research and educational initiatives, among them the Risk Prediction Initiative, a program within the Atlantic Global Change Institute of BBSR. Its goal is to form a bridge between the international scientific and business communities.

The station's educational outreach programs are varied and dedicated to encouraging secondary and undergraduate students to pursue science careers. It sponsors a number of university-level courses, plus graduate and undergraduate internships. Grants supporting various scientific research projects are also available through BBSR.

While the initial reason for its establishment was to provide a base for overseas scientists engaged in research, a strong locally based research group is now in place. Resident programs cover four principal areas: marine biology and ecology, global geosciences, molecular biology and Bermuda environmental quality.

Those interested in examining published research papers on BBSR's work on Bermuda will find them in the station's E.L. Mark Library, which contains more than 20,000 volumes and 200 up-to-date scientific journals and abstracts covering the four key disciplines. Special publications and general books on Bermuda's

natural history and geography are also found at the library.

Among the current and popular activities supported and promoted at the BBSR is the JASON Project, founded in 1989 by Dr. Robert Ballard following his discovery of the wreck of the *Titanic*. Thousands of interested school children wrote and expressed such an interest in his discovery that Ballard and a team of associates developed the project. It aims at providing a vehicle for both teachers and students to take part in various global explorations through the use of advanced interactive telecommunications.

Since 1993 BBSR has acted as the Preliminary Interactive Network Site for Bermuda's school children and the general public when JASON explored two sites along Mexico's Baja California peninsula. Since then, JASON has visited Belize, Hawaii and Southern Florida. In 1998 the project will focus on Bermuda itself.

Continuing Education

Community Education Development Program
72 Middle Rd., Warwick Parish • 236-0829

This public education program was begun in 1980 to deliver a wide range of educational, recreational, social and cultural programs to various individuals, community organizations and groups.

With an initial enrollment of 428 students at the Warwick Community Education School, the program was extended three years later to St. George's Community School. That same year the Community Education Development Program (CEDP) became a permanent aspect of the educational landscape. Co-sponsored by the Ministry of Community and Cultural Affairs and the Ministry of Education, it is now affiliated with the International Community Education Association (ICEA), a non-governmental association for people working in local communities. Founded in 1974 in the United States, ICEA is a worldwide organization with members in more than 80 countries.

CEDP has grown tremendously since 1980, with an average of 108 courses offered during each of the spring, summer and fall terms. Several centers on the island make the

Photo: GIS

Bermuda's schoolchildren get a solid academic grounding in public and private schools.

program highly accessible, with certified, experienced instructors delivering training. Along with the Warwick location, other CDEP centers are at Sandys Community School (register at Sandys Middle School, 21 Scott's Hill Road, 234-1346) and St. George's Community School, 297-0007.

Low tuition has proven an incentive for participation. Tuition ranges from $40 to $100, with the majority of courses less than $60. Golden Agers (those 60 years and older) may register free if minimum requirements for enrollment have been met. (The exceptions are computer classes and those classes having an enrollment limit.) Be advised that materials do cost extra.

Academic, technical, computer and college preparatory courses are offered, plus others on do-it-yourself subjects, personal development, language, music, dance and fitness. At the end of each course participants are awarded a certificate of participation. The level of course work often serves as a bridge to more advanced education.

Although offered on a non-credit basis, these courses allow individuals of all ages to explore new fields, sharpen professional skills and enrich their personal lives through friendships and contacts made during the various semesters. Not only do Bermudians register for the course work, but non-Bermudians comprise 25 percent of those enrolled. The overall atmosphere stimulates cross-cultural friendships.

Since the inception of the CEDP, there have been more than 50,000 registrations. High enrollment has enabled costs be minimized. Seventy-five percent of participants are repeat students often taking two or more courses each semester. Many businesses sponsor employees to take accounting, management, supervisory or computer courses. Senior citizens and children have not been ignored. Scores of seniors take advantage of the opportunity to stay mentally and physically active as do numbers of children placed by parents in the Holiday Fun Camp Program, which is active over the Easter, midterm and Christmas holidays.

CEDP's goals for 1998 include developing additional community programs, among them the establishment of a central Community School Resource Center at the new CedarBridge Academy.

Adult Education School - CSC
16 Dundonald St., City of Hamilton
• 292-5809

The Adult Education School (AES), on the corner of Brunswick and Dundonald streets, was founded in 1958 by Mrs. Merle Swan Williams to offer persons 16 and over a second chance at obtaining an education. The focus was on equipping them to earn a GED.

Having faced and overcome various financial problems during the nearly four decades since, the school has emerged as a strong educational provider. Its young graduates often go on to earn placements in institutions overseas. By the end of 1997 the majority of the 100 students were between 16 and 20 years of age. But it is anticipated that this may change in the future, as the school's focus may return to the scholastic development of the mature student.

Government-aided, the school has full- and part-time teachers supported by volunteers. Classes are held during the day and evening. The school closes during the summer.

Child Care

Bermuda's child-care facilities are many, varied and of exceptionally high quality. Nursery school regulations formulated in 1984 do not recognize separations between nurseries, preschools and day-care centers. Both public and private preschools are geared toward preparing youngsters for the transition to the elementary school environment and its demands.

Government preschools focus on curricula aimed at merging play-time activities with learning, and social and emotional needs are considered equally important as physical development. Head Start, the now-familiar U.S. program that developed out of a need to provide help for disadvantaged children, has proven valuable in Bermuda's schools. With a government preschool in each parish, each school registers 4-year-olds from that parish every February for a September induction. Information on government preschools can be obtained by calling the Ministry of Education's Child and Family Services at 236-0224.

In general, however, curricula varies depending on whether the preschool is public or private. Many of the private schools are fundamentally traditional in their approach to

study, emphasizing the "three Rs." Some private schools place additional value on religious training, while others put less focus on teaching social skills.

A perusal of the number of child-care facilities in Bermuda — and this includes nurseries, day-care centers, preschools and after-school care — yields more than 40 establishments, with many of them offering a full range of programs and services including holiday camps, computer instruction and transportation services. New regulations related to child care are currently being developed. If legislated, these would become included in a Children's Act rather than in the Public Health Act, where they are at present.

Child Development Program
37 Tynes Bay House, Palmetto Rd., Devonshire Parish • 295-0746, 236-0224 ext. 205

Under the Ministry of Health, Social Services and Housing, this government program, directly administered by the Department of Child and Family Services, provides support for families with preschool children. Services are offered when children reach the age of 2, although a referral basis can lead to quicker access.

A major program feature is an assessment and evaluation aspect, applied to all children between 24 and 30 months of age. Staff members visit the home and, through various monitored tests with specific materials, evaluate how the child is developing and share their findings with the parents. Depending on the information gleaned from these tests, another assessment may be indicated, with one of four home visitation programs offered. These programs zero in on educational enrichment by encouraging verbal interaction between parent and child, behavior management that is positive for the child, the child's language development and the initiation of structured learning for those children shown to be lagging in developmental aspects.

Other features available to all parents include a parent library, parent discussion groups, a newsletter and developmental information booklets.

**Bermudians take
keeping current of both
local and world news
quite seriously.**

Media and Communications

Although we only find an occasional letter in a bottle washes ashore, Bermudians take keeping current of both local and world news quite seriously. A daily ritual for many Insiders includes enjoying a morning cup of java while quickly digesting the day's news in *The Royal Gazette*. The newspaper is then tucked away for a more passionate reading later in the evening, before we watch the day's events on one of the island's three local broadcast stations.

There is no documented evidence as to where our thirst for what appears to be a more than normal requirement of a "bit of the exposé" got started. However, it would only seem fair to say that it must have a lot to do with our being a mecca drawing businesses from around the world (see our International Business chapter).

The Featherbed Alley Print Shop — yes, on Featherbed Alley in the Town of St George — was the home of the first Bermuda newspaper: the *Bermuda Gazette,* printed in 1784. A must-see for curious visitors interested in learning more about the island's past, this print shop will allow you the opportunity to see how Insiders got their news before the days of e-mail. The Bermuda Library on Queen Street, just a couple of skips from Perot's Post Office in the City of Hamilton (the oldest post office on the island; read more about it in our Let's Explain Bermuda chapter), has a terrific reading lounge. A beautiful cedar stairwell leads up to the second floor of the building, where you'll find comfy sofas and chairs arranged in a casual setting. Newspapers from the United States, Britain, Canada and the Caribbean are available daily, though they may not be taken out of the library. The main library is open Monday to Friday from 9:30 AM to 6 PM and on Saturday from 9:30 AM to 5 PM.

By no means is Bermuda left in the dark when it comes to keeping informed of world events. The Bermuda Broadcasting Company, DeFontes Broadcasting stations and the Bermuda Cablevision Company provide a total of nearly 50 television channels. Programming includes family-oriented, educational and religious offerings, plus sports coverage and weather reports from across the United States and Canada. There's even a Portuguese channel from (you guessed it) Portugal. And you can tune into any of the island's eight radio stations for a wide selection of music and talk formats — the range of topics up for discussion might surprise you.

Newspapers

You can purchase the major American and Canadian daily newspapers at the larger hotels and in leading pharmacies on the afternoon of the publication date. Another delightful place where news is usually the topic of the

---

INSIDERS' TIP

Headed for a day in the great outdoors of Bermuda? Any transistor radio will receive Bermuda broadcasts. Both radio companies offer local and international programming 24 hours a day.

day is Twice Told Tales, 34 Parliament Street, Hamilton, 296-1995. This is one of the island's used bookstores, nestled directly across from the magistrate's court. Insiders regularly gather here to read, sip cappuccino and take part in lively debate, often centered on the day's current events.

Dailies

The Royal Gazette
2 Par-la-Ville Rd., Hamilton • 295-5881

Bermuda's only daily newspaper, *The Royal Gazette* was established in 1828. Historians say Donald McPhee Lee was recommended by his father, Robert Lee, a commissary general with the British military, as a solution to Bermuda's problem of not having a printer in the aftermath of the turbulent era of one Gov. Lumley. Delayed by a harrowing sea journey to Bermuda, Donald Lee did not publish the first two issues of *The Royal Gazette* (the day was saved by his brother, David Ross Lee, and the January 8 and January 15, 1828, issues were printed), but he arrived in time to print the third issue for January 22, 1828. Donald Lee published the paper without a break each week for the next 60 years, until the issue of January 30, 1882, just two weeks prior to his death.

The paper remained a weekly or biweekly publication until January 1, 1921, when it merged with *The Colonist* to become a daily newspaper — *The Royal Gazette and the Colonist Daily*. In 1946 the title was shortened to *The Royal Gazette*. For the better part of two decades, starting the next year, the *Gazette* also published a Sunday edition, but in 1963 that was discontinued. Today it is published six days a week.

The pulse of print media on the island, *The Royal Gazette* is an award-winning publication that reports local, international and business news daily. Letters to the editor are published and provide an excellent way for the community to comment on various social and political issues of the day. The newspaper is independent and not affiliated with any political party. Read religiously throughout the island, *The Royal Gazette* covers a tremendous span of subjects that are timely, informational, humorous and entertaining. In addition to its own editorial staff, the paper relies on wire services for up-to-the-minute information from around the world.

An average of 15,968 papers are printed daily and circulated islandwide. Papers are delivered door-to-door and sold at grocery and local parish stores, drugstores, eateries, gas stations and hotels. Subscriptions are available.

Weeklies

Mid-Ocean News
2 Par-la-Ville Rd., Hamilton • 295-5881

The first edition of the *Mid-Ocean* was published August 16, 1911. It was started by S.S. Toddings, who since 1869 had been the successful editor and owner of *The Colonist*. Published in Hamilton, it began as a four-page paper issued on Wednesday and Saturday.

Mid-Ocean News had various production schedules and incarnations from the early 1900s to the late '60s. It was a biweekly, then a tri-weekly, briefly a daily, then the government paper from 1951 to 1959. In 1968 it began publishing on Friday and continues to do so today.

The Mid-Ocean News Company was incorporated in 1947, and bought by The Bermuda Press (Holdings) Ltd. in 1962. While it is owned by the same company that publishes *The Royal Gazette*, *Mid-Ocean News* retains editorial independence and offers readers a different brand of local news than its sister organization. With sales of 13,000 to 14,000

FYI

Unless otherwise noted, the area code for all phone numbers listed in this guide is 441.

INSIDERS' TIP

Cable Channel 11, the "Bermuda Weather Station," offers a three-day forecast, updated several times throughout the day.

per week, the *Mid-Ocean News* covers events, sports and entertainment and offers reviews. The paper provides a weekly bulletin of the previous week's top local news stories and lists Bermuda nightlife and entertainment options.

The paper gives exclusive interviews with government dignitaries and notable figures in both the private and corporate sectors of the community. It is especially appreciated for its in-depth reporting and witty columnists, and it is an independent paper with no affiliation to any political party. It is also the only newspaper that regularly provides color photographs on the front page of each section. It is circulated on Fridays.

Bermuda Sun
41 Victoria St., Hamilton • 295-3902

Bermuda Sun first appeared at newsstands on May 11, 1964. The newspaper covers local events and issues and is generally thought of as less of an establishment newspaper than *The Royal Gazette* or *Mid-Ocean News*. However, it is not an "alternative weekly" but a mainstream newspaper with significant business and investment sections, a large section of local religious news and entertainment, sports and general and political news.

Bermuda Sun publishes legal advertising in Bermuda and has a contract to publish official government notices. However, it has no affiliation with any political party. The paper is published on Fridays, and weekly circulation is 12,500, entirely generated by street sales. A second, Wednesday edition is being considered for 1998. There is no home delivery, though overseas mail subscriptions are available.

Magazines

RG Magazine
2 Par-la-Ville Rd., Hamilton • 295-5881

RG Magazine, first published in January 1993 by Crown Communications, is a free publication usually circulated the last Thursday of every month as part of *The Royal Gazette*. *RG*

has carved a positive niche among the island's print media enterprises and has a favorable relationship with its readership. The most widely distributed magazine in Bermuda, the news- and lifestyles-based periodical focuses on topical issues, homes and gardens, food and travel and is filled with splendid full-color photographs. *RG* also provides a detailed calendar of events and has monthly columnists and book reviews.

The magazine is published by Crown Communications, a division of The Royal Gazette Ltd., which also publishes *The Bottom Line Magazine* (see subsequent listing) and a variety of special event, publicity and sports magazines for events such as the Gillette Tour Challenge Championship and the Samuel L. Jackson Golf Tournament. Crown's offices are in the same building as those of *The Royal Gazette* and *Mid-Ocean News* newspapers.

The Bottom Line Magazine
2 Par-la-Ville Rd., Hamilton • 295-5881

The Bottom Line first rolled off the presses in 1991. Now published quarterly, it is a general, in-depth business and economics magazine covering current news and information about the island and its largest and fastest-growing sectors — risk and insurance management and international business (see our International Business chapter). April's issue usually ties in with the annual RIMS (Risk and Insurance Management Society) Conference. An extra 2,500 issues are printed at that time, in addition to the 6,500 magazines normally published.

Bermudian Magazine
P.O. Box HM 283, Hamilton HM AX
• 295-0695

Bermudian Magazine is the island's oldest monthly publication, with the first edition issued on February 10, 1930. Since then, the editorial focus has centered on showcasing Bermuda's history, society, personalities, arts, architecture, homes and gardens and local lifestyles. Beautifully designed, it offers full-color features, essays, profiles and anecdotes. Published by the Bermudian Publishing Com-

INSIDERS' TIP

The Royal Gazette carries next-day stock reports.

pany, *Bermudian Magazine* is available at local newsstands for $4. Local subscriptions are $34, and overseas mailings are $40.

Bermudian Business
P.O. Box HM 283, Hamilton HM AX
• 295-0695

Bermudian Business, also published by Bermudian Publishing Company, is a quarterly magazine with a strong emphasis on the island's growing international business sector. It offers its readership in-depth features and analyses of the Bermuda insurance market, banking, investments, trusts, technology and financial services sectors. The annual Bermudian Business/ Deloitte and Touche Insurance Survey, published in the spring edition, has made it well-read both here and in overseas markets. At local newsstands, the magazine sells for $4.25. Subscriptions are $13 yearly in Bermuda, $30 a year in North America, $38 in the U.K. and Europe and $48 for all other regions.

This Week in Bermuda
P.O. Box HM 283, Hamilton HM AX
• 295-0695

This Week in Bermuda is a free publication that celebrated its 50th birthday in 1997. *This Week* provides visitors with updated weekly listings of cultural, family and sporting events as well as comprehensive information about the island's history, shopping, restaurants, nightlife, boating and watersports and public attractions. You can pick up *This Week*, published by Bermudian Publishing Company, at the Visitors Service Bureau in the Bermuda International Airport, at the Royal Naval Dockyard and in major hotels and guest houses throughout the island. Copies are also made available for conventions and groups and can be obtained by advance order.

Bermuda Magazine
5 Butterfield Pl., 67 Front St., Hamilton
• 292-7279

Described as the magazine that tells the world about Bermuda, *Bermuda Magazine* is a general interest magazine that covers the island's history, culture, art, society and any number of other subjects that help keep visitors in touch with their "home away from home." Subscribers here and abroad appreciate *Bermuda Magazine's* insights into the island's idiosyncrasies as well as its fresh, sometimes playful and irreverent approach to local issues. Published quarterly by Bermuda Marketing Ltd., *Bermuda Magazine* is available by subscription for $19.95 in the U.S. (where it's mailed from) and $27.95 elsewhere.

Radio

It may surprise you, but on our petite island there are eight radio stations. They are evenly distributed between each of our two broadcast companies.

ZFB 1230 AM
ZBM-2 1340 AM
ZBM 89.1 FM
Power 95 FM
P.O. Box HM 452, Hamilton HM BX
• 295-2828

The Bermuda Broadcasting Company operates two AM and two FM radio stations. ZBM-2 1340 AM broadcasts two talk format programs for mature listeners and airs international sporting events. ZFB 1230 AM offers religious programming and gospel music and three days per week airs the show "Sixty Something," designed to inform those in their golden years in Bermuda. The show runs from 10 AM to noon Monday, Tuesday and Thursday.

ZBM 89.1 FM plays easy listening music

---

www.insiders.com

See this and many other
Insiders' Guide® destinations
online — in their entirety.

Visit us today!

INSIDERS' TIP

The Sunday editions of the major newspapers from the United States and Canada are available at leading Bermuda drugstores by late Sunday afternoon.

The local media are out in force at most events.

for those who enjoy the mellow tunes. Power 95 FM, launched in 1992, rocks Bermuda with the latest music of today's generation. Diverse, it is current but reminiscent and, most importantly, downright funky.

VSB-1 1450 AM
VSB-2 1280 AM
VSB-3 1160 AM
VSB 106.1 FM (Mix 106)
94 Reid St., Hamilton • 295-1450

DeFontes Broadcasting Co. Ltd. presently operates three AM radio channels and one FM station. VSB-1 1450 AM plays country-western music 24 hours a day. VSB-2 1280 AM offers nondenominational religious programing. VSB-3 1160 AM features BBC World Service news and current event programing. VSB FM 106.1 is Bermuda's only station that plays an adult contemporary mix of tunes.

Television

Local Broadcast Stations

Bermuda Broadcasting Co. Ltd.
P.O. Box HM 452, Hamilton HM BX
• 295-2828

In 1997 Bermuda Broadcasting Company celebrated its 50th anniversary, and it continues to provide the island with two of its local commercial television stations. ZFB-TV Channel 7 (cable channel 2) is the Bermuda affiliate of the ABC network in the United States. ZBM-TV Channel 9 (cable channel 3) is the Bermuda affiliate of America's CBS network.

Bermuda Broadcasting Company also produces local programs including daily news broadcasts and a host of other shows such as *Un Deux Trois* (a children's language program)

INSIDERS' TIP

Every Friday, *Bermuda Sun* and *Mid-Ocean News* publish complete weekly cable TV guides. The *Mid-Ocean News* guide is inserted in the paper, but the *Bermuda Sun* listings must be purchased separately.

and *The Premier Talks to Bermuda's Young People*, a periodic talk show for teenagers that is hosted by the country's premier. The company also offered award-winning coverage of Bermuda's unprecedented 1994 run in the World Cup, delivering live satellite coverage as Bermuda competed in Canada, Jamaica, Haiti and El Salvador.

DeFontes Broadcasting (Television), Ltd.
94 Reid St., Hamilton • 295-1450

DeFontes Broadcasting began broadcasting in June 1991 from studios in the heart of Bermuda at Barkers Hill in Devonshire Parish. VSB-TV Channel 11 (cable channel 4) offers a mix of programing from Cable News Network, Channel America Network and NBC, of which it became an affiliate in October 1993.

VSB-TV has established itself as a leader in local programming by offering viewers an award-winning news broadcast with comprehensive weather and sports at 7 PM Monday through Friday, and in-depth late news coverage at midnight. Other programs include *Tourism in Focus*, produced by our Department of Tourism; the *Curious Cook*, a monthly cooking show; and *Inside Bermuda*, a talk show focusing on the events and personalities of Bermuda.

Cable Television

Bermuda Cablevision Ltd.
19 Laffan St., Hamilton • 292-5544

Bermuda Cablevision is the icing on the cake when it comes to TV on the island. The only cable subscription service available, it provides cable for about 13,000 homes and hotel properties in Bermuda. Through various packages, more than 40 channels are accessible 24 hours a day from the U.S., Canada, the U.K. and Portugal. This comes in handy, as local broadcast programming discontinues at the witching hour of midnight.

Closed-Circuit

The Bermuda Channel
5 Butterfield Pl., 67 Front St., Hamilton • 292-7279

The Bermuda Channel, an informational videotape service, is offered via closed-circuit TV to 70 percent of the island's major resorts and hotel rooms. Produced by Bermuda Marketing Ltd., this colorful, picturesque video is filled with information about Bermuda history, culture, sightseeing, sports, transportation, restaurants, shopping and much more. Updated annually, tapes can be purchased from Bermuda Marketing Ltd. for $24.95.

Internet Services

Logic Communications Ltd.
Richmond House, 12 Par-la-Ville Rd., Hamilton • 296-9600

Logic Communications, formerly Internet Bermuda Ltd., was Bermuda's first Internet service provider. With more than 4,000 dial-up and 1,500 corporate customers, Logic has experienced phenomenal acceptance among Bermuda's 60,000 residents. They began operations in January 1994. In 1995, Logic completed an agreement with Netscape Communications Corporation to become its master value-added reseller (VAR) for all of the Caribbean, establishing itself as a leading Internet provider. For dial-up customers, Logic offers more than just basic connectivity and e-mail. Personal web pages, help desk and several community websites are a few of their other services. The principal website address (http://www.logic.bm) is Logic's magazine-style site that offers information to tourists and locals alike. Current events are highlighted on the home page, where the local weather is updated three times daily.

Logic provides temporary dial-up accounts for the business traveler. In addition to dial-up connections, Logic offers a wide range

INSIDERS' TIP

Bermuda's first radio station went on the air on February 10, 1930. Thomas J. Wadson broadcast from his shop in Hamilton using the call letters TJW.

of corporate services that include dedicated-line connections to the Internet, website design and hosting, Internet/Intranet, security consultation and low-cost international faxing service.

North Rock Communications Ltd.
7 Washington Ln., P.O. Box HM 1661, Hamilton • 296-2700

Bermuda's Internet users now have a choice of Internet providers. In December 1997, North Rock Communications went online to become the island's second service provider. One surprise announcement, however, involved North Rock NetTV — a set-top device that allows users to surf the web, send e-mail and chat in newsgroups, all without owning a computer.

In conjunction with the global roaming network iPass, North Rock announced it will offer local-call Internet and e-mail access from more than 1,460 locations in more than 150 countries. Internet users can visit North Rock's website (http://www.northrock.bm) for more information.

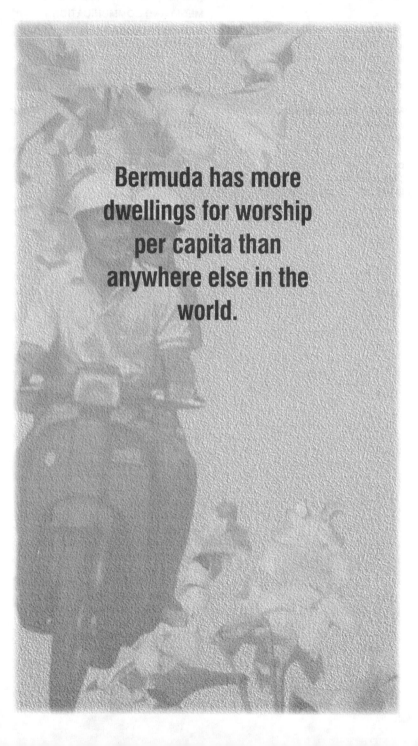

Bermuda has more dwellings for worship per capita than anywhere else in the world.

Worship

Bermuda is very much a churchgoing community. Perhaps it's the sheer beauty of our island, being isolated in the Atlantic Ocean or knowing as a matter of fact that we are sitting on top of a dormant volcano that brings godly reverence. Whatever the reason, with more than 100 separate places of worship representing more than 30 different faiths, we can safely say we are living in God's country. Like Mark Twain, who visited our shores on several occasions, we too (speaking for many Insiders anyway) enjoy living on a little piece of heaven right here on earth.

So it is not surprising that Bermuda has more dwellings for worship per capita than anywhere else in the world. If you're looking for a quiet place of solitude or a church to fit your particular style of worship, you are bound to find one to suit your liking. Traveling about, you will see a number of our churches add a distinguished presence to the landscape. From the traditional in architecture to the atypical, most churches are surrounded by beautifully manicured gardens, and many have adjacent cemeteries.

History

Bermuda is steeped in religious history. St. Peter's Church in St. George's is the oldest Anglican church in continuous use in the Western Hemisphere. The first building, made out of post and palmetto leaves, was in use by the end of 1612. By 1620 a permanent building had been assembled. The lines of the church can be traced in the unceilinged part of the church running from the font to the altar, and there are still certain areas of the original 1620 building that remain intact. In 1713, the church was reconstructed in stone with a vestry added to the north. Filled with Bermudian history and artifacts dating to the 1400s, St. Peters' should definitely be on your list of things to see. (Look for more details in our Attractions chapter.)

The Bermuda Cathedral, on Church Street in the City of Hamilton, was consecrated on May 11, 1911. The seat of the bishopric of Bermuda, this magnificently structured church stands on the original site of the Trinity Church, which was consecrated in 1855 and destroyed by fire in 1884. The arsonists were never caught. The Bermuda Cathedral measures 176 feet long and 88 feet wide across the transept. Seating as many as 1,000 people, it is often used as a venue for varied musical events. The church tower is 143 feet tall and open for tours throughout the year. It's an easy climb up 155 steps to see a spectacular view of Hamilton. Tickets can be purchased in the Cathedral Book Store.

Prior to the abolition of slavery on August 1, 1834, the Cobbs Hill Methodist Chapel — recorded to have been built by slaves "in the moonlight" — was consecrated November 17, 1827. Considered a black church, it led the way for many more churches with congregations composed predominately of black Bermudians. In May 1885, Bermuda's first AME (African Methodist Episcopal) Church, St. John's on Wilkerson Avenue in Bailey's Bay, was dedicated. More than a century later it has maintained its integral part in the AME's church community.

St. Paul's AME Lyceum Church on Court Street in the City of Hamilton also bears significant historical importance in the development of religious expression and culture for black Bermudians. In the church hall hang numerous historical photographs of bygone days — pictures of past pastors, church members, community personalities and the like — bearing witness to an era that will not easily be forgotten. Currently many important community functions are held in the church hall. Not too long ago, Susan Taylor, editor-in-chief of *Essence* magazine, spoke before a crowd at St. Paul's.

Worship in Bermuda chronicles family history too. Many Bermudian families are able to trace their history dating back decades or more through church records. It is not uncommon to find generations of one family belonging to a particular parish church for centuries. In many churches you'll find plaques, stained-glass windows, hymnals and other religious items given in memorial of deceased family members.

Bermudians are especially expressive musically during worship. Music is sacred part of most services, and many churches will have more than one choir singing during worship. Each year there is a concert in the Victoria Park showcasing local gospel choirs and singers from around the island. Various sacred music recitals are also sponsored by several churches during the year.

www.insiders.com
See this and many other
Insiders' Guide® destinations
online — in their entirety.
Visit us today!

A Melting Pot of Faiths

In this chapter, rather than give you individual listings of churches by parish, we thought it appropriate to give an overview of the denominations represented on the island. You may not have any idea how many faiths thrive here, but you will find the variety of worship options closely parallels the multiculturism of Bermuda.

A growing number of nationalities have added new spice to the melting pot of religious diversity here in our island home. Though the last census shows a large majority of our population still belongs to the Anglican or Roman Catholic churches, you will find that most religions are practiced. Some of these you might not expect to find on our remote island. We have Muslims, Rastafarians, Jehovah's Witnesses, members of the Ausar Auset Society, the Ethiopian Orthodox Church and practitioners of Baha'i and the Unity Foundation of Truth.

You will not find synagogues or a resident rabbi in Bermuda. However, the Jewish Community of Bermuda has lay leaders who conduct a Shabbat service on the first Friday of every month at the Unity Foundation of Truth on Reid Street. Torah study is on a Sunday, usually in the middle of the month, and is usually held at someone's home. For special holiday services, a visiting rabbi conducts worship. We have some East Indians that are Hindu, but you'll currently find no temples in Bermuda. Most of the Hindus living here maintain a temple for family worship in their homes.

The conventional mainstream churches on the island include the Anglican (Church of England), AME, Baptist, Roman Catholic, Methodist, Presbyterian, Lutheran, the Bermuda Division of the Salvation Army and the Seventh-Day Adventist. There are also a number of churches, perhaps with smaller congregations, that have established sound reputations within the community. They include the Brethren, Church of God, Church of Christ, Apostolic Faith, Church of God Prophecy, Christian Science, Church of the Nazarene, Church of Jesus Christ of Latter-day Saints, New Testament Church of God, United Holy Churches of Bermuda (Pentecostal), Worldwide Church of God and the Evangelical Church of Bermuda, which has served the community for more than 150 years.

A growing number of assemblies and ministries are represented as well. Some of these are the Pentecostal Assemblies of Canada (Maritime District), Pentecostal Assemblies of The West Indies, Revival Assembly of Bermuda, Living Epistle Ministries, Full Gospel Charismatic (Paget) Christian Assembly, Exousia Christian Fellowship, Touch Through Me Ministries, Hands of Love Ministry, and Cure Ministries — Christians United Reaching Everyone. Another sector of our population worships with Radnor Road Christian Fellow-

INSIDERS' TIP

A detailed listing of churches can be found in the Yellow Pages of the Bermuda telephone directory or by consulting the social desk at your hotel.

Photo: GIS

The Church of the Holy Trinity is in Hamilton.

ship or The Evangel Tabernacle (God's Deliverance Center). Both churches are nondenominational.

No matter how inclusive our listing may appear, there are certain to be those denominations and faiths that are not included in our listing. Still, we think you'll get the point: This is a country where freedom of religion is enjoyed and wholeheartedly embraced.

Practicing What They Preach

Throughout Bermuda's history, continuing to today, church congregations have been active in the community. Currently this can be observed in the crossover of ministers and pastors who are actively involved in the social and political arenas of our country. A reinforcing number of ministries have developed programs and services that make available emergency shelter facilities, free meals, medical screening and clothing giveaways to those in need.

Some churches also assist the Emergency Measures Organizations (EMO). This group was formed 20 years ago to bring together the services of government, the utilities and private agencies into one functioning body to assist the public with information before or after a storm or hurricane. In addition, there are several local radio and television ministries that provide scripture-based family and marriage consultation.

Several ministerial associations are available. There are pastoral alliances on the east and west ends of the island, and a new group is being formed for the central parishes — the Central Parishes Ministerial Fellowship. Historically, these associations have fostered fellowship, mutual understanding and support among ministers in Bermuda.

Whether you take a meditative stroll along the beach, attend Mass or visit a mosque, communing with a higher power can be a pleasant experience in a place as blessed as Bermuda. To further acquaint yourself with worship options on our island, you can find additional religious information and individual church listings in the weekend newspapers — Friday in the *Mid-Oceans News* and *The Bermuda Sun* and Saturday in the *Royal Gazette*.

Index of Advertisers

Index

Going Somewhere?

Insiders' Publishing Inc. presents 48 current and upcoming titles to popular destinations all over the country (including the titles below) — and we're planning on adding many more. To order a title, go to your local bookstore or call (800) 582-2665 and we'll direct you to one.

Adirondacks	Minneapolis/St. Paul, MN
Atlanta, GA	Mississippi
Bermuda	Myrtle Beach, SC
Boca Raton and the Palm Beaches, FL	Nashville, TN
Boulder, CO, and Rocky Mountain National Park	New Hampshire
Bradenton/Sarasota, FL	North Carolina's Central Coast and New Bern
Branson, MO, and the Ozark Mountains	North Carolina's Mountains
California's Wine Country	Outer Banks of North Carolina
Cape Cod, Nantucket and Martha's Vineyard, MA	The Pocono Mountains
Charleston, SC	Relocation
Cincinnati, OH	Richmond, VA
Civil War Sites in the Eastern Theater	Salt Lake City
Colorado's Mountains	Santa Fe
Denver, CO	Savannah
Florida Keys and Key West	Southwestern Utah
Florida's Great Northwest	Tampa/St. Petersburg, FL
Golf in the Carolinas	Tuscon
Indianapolis, IN	Virginia's Blue Ridge
The Lake Superior Region	Virginia's Chesapeake Bay
Las Vegas	Washington, D.C.
Lexington, KY	Wichita, KS
Louisville, KY	Williamsburg, VA
Madison, WI	Wilmington, NC
Maine's Mid-Coast	Yellowstone

Insiders' Publishing Inc. • P.O. Box 2057 • Manteo, NC 27954
Phone (919) 473-6100 • Fax (919) 473-5869 • INTERNET address: *http://www.insiders.com*